VINCENTE MINNELLI

CONTEMPORARY APPROACHES TO FILM AND TELEVISION SERIES

A complete listing of the books in this series can be found online at wsupress.wayne.edu

General Editor

Barry Keith Grant
Brock University

Advisory Editors

Patricia B. Erens
School of the Art Institute of Chicago

Lucy Fischer
University of Pittsburgh

Caren J. Deming
University of Arizona

Robert J. Burgoyne
Wayne State University

Tom Gunning
University of Chicago

Anna McCarthy
New York University

Peter X. Feng
University of Delaware

Lisa Parks
University of California–Santa Barbara

Vincente Minnelli

The Art of Entertainment

EDITED BY **JOE McELHANEY**

WAYNE STATE UNIVERSITY PRESS   DETROIT

Library of Congress Cataloging-in-Publication Data

Vincente Minnelli : the art of entertainment / edited by Joe McElhaney.

p. cm. — (Contemporary approaches to film and television series)

Includes bibliographical references and index.

ISBN 978-0-8143-3307-5 (pbk. : alk. paper)

1. Minnelli, Vincente—Criticism and interpretation. I. McElhaney, Joe, 1957–

PN1998.3.M56V56 2009

791.4302′33092—dc22

2008026320

∞

The paper used in this publication meets the minimum requirements of the American National Standard for Information Sciences—Permanence of Paper for Printed Library Materials, ANSI Z39.48-1984.

Designed by Chang Jae Lee

Typeset by Keystone

Composed in Minion

For Steve

Contents

Acknowledgments

This book has been a labor of love, the labor made so much easier by the help of many along the way. A special thanks to my editors at Wayne State University Press, Annie Martin and Barry Keith Grant, for their tremendous support of the project. From the moment of the book's inception, the enthusiasm of my contributors has made the process of assembling the book infinitely simpler than it might have been. I would especially like to thank Adrian Martin and Robin Wood for making it possible for me to successfully track down some otherwise elusive sources. My thanks to James Naremore for kindly loaning me the images for his *Cabin in the Sky* essay. I am also deeply grateful for the extreme generosity of the late Margaret Langley and of Vanessa Fox, respectively mother and sister of Andrew Britton, in allowing me to reprint "*Meet Me in St. Louis:* Smith; or, The Ambiguities," and to Maurice Glaymann for being equally generous in allowing me to reprint the two Serge Daney pieces here. A City University of New York research grant provided much-needed financial support. And finally, a very special thanks to Julie Kaplan.

Vincente Minnelli directing Deborah Kerr and John Kerr on the set of *Tea and Sympathy* (1956) (Courtesy Photofest).

VINCENTE MINNELLI

Introduction
Playing for Blood

JOE MCELHANEY

In *The Long, Long Trailer* (1954), newlyweds Tacy and Nicky Collini (Lucille Ball and Desi Arnaz) travel across the United States in a forty-foot long mobile home equipped with virtually every modern "convenience." At one point on their journey they visit Tacy's Aunt Anastasia in order for Nicky to meet Anastasia and the rest of the family. But Tacy also wants to pick up what she imagines will be a substantial check from her aunt as a wedding gift, money that she wants to put toward the purchase of a Deepfreeze. The family members greet Tacy and Nicky warmly and then express amazement at the enormity of the trailer, which Nicky must now back into their driveway. This action, however, leads to a string of disasters as Nicky loses control of the vehicle and runs over Anastasia's much-beloved rose bush, crushing and destroying it. "You ruined my rose with your lousy, stinkin' trailer!" she screams at Nicky and then bursts into tears. Tacy calms an equally hysterical Nicky and attempts to take charge of the trailer's parking. She orders everyone to cease barking out instructions to Nicky and instead guides the parking of the trailer herself, offering concise instructions and gestures to her husband. Everything proceeds smoothly until the trailer reaches the trellis that is attached to the house and overhangs the driveway, which is too low for the trailer's height. Nicky backs the trailer directly into this, causing the entire edifice to crash down. Tacy does not get her check from Aunt Anastasia, who sourly keeps the money to do repairs on the house. Tacy and Nicky slink away, getting what Nicky calls the "deep freeze" from the entire family.

This sequence stands as one of the most emblematic in the career of the film's director, Vincente Minnelli. *The Long, Long Trailer* is, like almost everything directed by Minnelli, an MGM film, attractively produced and well mounted, the kind of film in which people dine by candlelight even when they are eating in a trailer. It is also just as clearly a star vehicle for Ball and Arnaz, then the reigning queen and king of television through the sitcom *I Love Lucy*. *The Long, Long Trailer* is intended to showcase their comic talents, serving as a big screen and color extension of their television show. Like most of Minnelli's films for MGM, *The Long, Long Trailer* was a hit, pleasing fans of Ball and Arnaz while continuing to solidify Minnelli's reputation with his studio as someone capable of turning out polished, entertaining, and profitable films.

Between 1943, when he made his first film, *Cabin in the Sky,* and 1976, when he made his last, *A Matter of Time,* Vincente Minnelli was one of the most successful filmmakers in Hollywood. Although not as well known to the general public as Alfred Hitchcock, Cecil B. De Mille, or Otto Preminger (unlike them, he never produced his own films, nor were those films, in turn, ever sold on the basis of his name), he has long enjoyed a certain celebrity status. While that status is no doubt partly due to his first marriage to Judy Garland (whom he directed in five films) and to their daughter Liza Minnelli (whom he directed in his last film), Vincente Minnelli was nevertheless already being profiled and celebrated before his arrival in Hollywood. During his successful career on the New York stage in the 1930s, he garnered attention as an innovative director and designer of Broadway musicals as well as for his own personality, style of dress, and manner of living. This work on the New York musical stage brought him to the attention of Hollywood. To this day, his film musicals remain his most celebrated accomplishments, in spite of his great contributions to comedy and melodrama. He has been described as "the virtual father of the modern musical" for such innovative films as *Meet Me in St. Louis* (1944), *An American in Paris* (1951), *The Band Wagon* (1953), and *Gigi* (1958), the last of these winning him a Best Director Academy Award. In spite (and as we shall see partly because) of all this, Minnelli has been a figure of some controversy. Let us return to Aunt Anastasia's front lawn for a moment.

We are presented in *The Long, Long Trailer* with a very clean, ordered middle-class world, the kind Minnelli had already filmed so successfully in *Meet Me in St. Louis, Father of the Bride* (1950), and *Father's Little Dividend* (1951). In *The Long, Long Trailer* we have a newly married couple embarking on their wedding trip, stopping off at the home of a beloved relative in order to enjoy a brief family gathering. But this apparent harmony is quickly destroyed through a literal confrontation between two family dwellings: the home and the trailer. As the sequence unfolds it becomes clear that this confrontation is something more than an easily unavoidable accident or a momentary disruption within an otherwise harmonious family situation. "Film is like a battleground," Samuel Fuller, director of many war films and action thrillers, famously states in Jean-Luc Godard's *Pierrot le fou* (1965). "It's love. Hate. Action. Violence. Death. In one word, emotions." And in this sequence from *The Long, Long Trailer*, Aunt Anastasia's front lawn becomes another cinematic battleground, one of love, hate, action, violence, death, and emotions and, moreover, one in which a struggle for *control* is enacted. Control of what, though? And who is fighting whom here? The battle lines drawn in this sequence are not simply between the Collinis and their trailer, on one side, and Aunt Anastasia, her home, and the rest of her family on the other. Minnelli's methods are subtler—and more insidious—than this.

We know by this point in the film that Tacy has forced her husband into purchasing the long, long trailer. She has told him that she wants to be a good wife to him, cooking his meals and tending house as they travel for his job; and she feels that only this trailer will allow her to perform these duties in the manner she imagines for herself. (At no point does Nicky ever express a desire for Tacy to be this kind of wife.) However, the trailer brings nothing but misery to Nicky, precipitating one hysterical outburst after another from him as he fails to master the oversized vehicle. In spite of numerous setbacks and several accidents of her own with the trailer, Tacy remains utterly devoted to it, unable to give it up even though it seriously threatens the future of her new marriage. As for Aunt Anastasia, she appears to preside over her own domestic space more powerfully than her husband (who is a minor figure in the sequence), more powerfully than the rest of her family, and certainly more than her daughter, the spinsterish and almost catatonic "poor Grace." If her niece obsesses over a trailer above all else in the world, Anastasia demonstrates equal devotion to her rose bush. It is to this flower, we might infer, that she has given more loving attention over the years than she has to her own daughter, who becomes quite animated at the sight of the trailer flattening this rose to the ground and killing it. Both Tacy and Anastasia preside over their own particular worlds, both worlds ordered and shaped by their respective personalities and sensibilities; but these worlds are precariously held in place, capable of being destroyed at any moment, and perhaps for that reason guarded, fought, and obsessed over all that more vigilantly.

Two of Minnelli's most important critics, Jean Douchet and James Naremore, see *The Long, Long Trailer* in very different terms. For Naremore, the film is "essentially a cozy fantasy about married love";[1] Douchet, in contrast, has described it as "one of the most terrible satires of the American way of life."[2] How to reconcile such diametrically opposed readings? Naremore does not deny the film's satirical edge and argues that "with the exception of Frank Tashlin, no other Hollywood director of the fifties expressed such malicious delight in kitsch."[3] Nevertheless, for Naremore the film conforms to a pattern he detects as operating in all of Minnelli's comedies, in which the American dream is first deflated and then honored. Douchet, however, sees in *The Long, Long Trailer* something much more relentless in its drives, the film comprised of a steady accumulation of horrific and violent incidents in the lives of the young married couple as they haul this enormous trailer across the country.

Such discrepant readings are at the heart of some of the discourses surrounding Minnelli's work. Is Minnelli a director who made films that repeatedly challenged and subverted the ideology they were ostensibly intended to support? Or are such claims exaggerated, the social criticism or satire contained within a film such as *The Long, Long Trailer* perfectly in keeping with genre expectations and the cultural climate within which the film was produced and most likely not even noticed by spectators upon its original release? But such questions about the value of Minnelli's films extend beyond social and political interpretation. An even more persistent question about Minnelli has been whether he is to be taken seriously as a film artist at all. Is he not someone whose films are so dependent on the collaborative resources of Hollywood studios, on the intelligence of the scripts he was handed as a contract director, on the skill of his actors, and on the strength and richness of the genres within which he worked that he cannot be discussed as an auteur in the same manner that we discuss Hitchcock, John Ford, or Orson Welles, all of whom created films thought by many to be more formally innovative than anything by Minnelli? Is Minnelli little more than a skilled purveyor of "entertainments" rather than a cinematic artist of the first rank?

The essays collected in this book, while drawn from a wide range of sources across four decades, respond to these questions in a variety of different ways and employ a number of different methodologies. Not every essay here places Minnelli front and center in its approach. But each is designed to present a distinct perspective on the films. The essays are drawn primarily from French, British, and American writings, with the French and American essays constituting the majority (nine essays each). The strong French presence here is both deliberate and inevitable. While Minnelli was never the central figure to the immediate postwar French critics and filmmakers that Hitchcock, Fritz Lang, or Howard Hawks were, we may still speak of a "French Minnelli," in much the same way that Hitchcock, Lang, or Hawks were interpreted through the particular lens of postwar French discourses on the cinema. As we shall see, Douchet (who likewise wrote seminal texts on Hitchcock, Lang, and Hawks) is crucial to this history. But it also stretches beyond him, culminating with the three French essays with which this volume closes.

I want to make my own position here as editor very clear: I believe that Vincente Minnelli is one of the most important directors in American cinema. Consequently, the essays I have commissioned or chosen to include here have been designed to, in various ways, confirm this importance even if the approaches taken and the conclusions drawn often differ. The richness of Minnelli's work undoubtedly has some of its basis in the forms and structures of the genres out of which the films emerged. Also undoubtedly, Minnelli was very fortunate in having so many gifted collaborators, all of them making important contributions to the films. But having acknowledged this still does not take us far enough. I would argue that what we have in Minnelli's films is not simply a style, reducible to a handful of visual elements (a talent for interior decoration, an eye for color, a flair for camera movement), all of it held together by the power of certain genres and by the efficiency of the Hollywood studio system; rather, we find in Minnelli a vision, if not a philosophy, of (and for) cinema. And while this vision has definite historical, material, and cultural contours, it cannot be reduced to these contours either. As I hope this collection demonstrates, the films of Vincente Minnelli address fundamental issues in relation to the moving image and in relation to culture and to history. Moreover, Minnelli's intervention as a filmmaker within these individual works is crucial for understanding their production of meaning.

The essays here are arranged in a more or less chronological fashion, stretching from the early 1960s to the present day. While there is some interesting early criticism on Minnelli written in the 1940s and 1950s (principally James Agee's reviews in *Time* and *The Nation,* the writings of the English critics at *Sequence,* and the criticism of Guillermo Cabrera Infante in Cuba), the early 1960s mark the beginning of the first major attempts to fully come to grips with the entire body of work and to discuss Minnelli as a filmmaker in ways that extend beyond the purely intuitive and impressionistic. This period is covered in the first section of this book, "Minnelli in the 1960s: The Rise and Fall of an Auteur." The emergence of the *politique des auteurs* in France after World War II, with its reevaluation of American cinema and insistence upon the central role of the film director in forging a distinctive style in spite of the assembly line methods of Hollywood production, would be central in this evaluation (positive or negative) of Minnelli. Discussions of a filmmaker's approach to mise-en-scène was crucial to this *politique* since it was believed that through the ways a filmmaker staged action, handled movement, light, space, and gesture that an authorial voice emerged. Strongly influenced by the auteurist approach in France, Infante reviewed Minnelli's *Tea and Sympathy* (1956), identifying moments of "pure cinema" in the film's mise-en-scène, which proved to Infante "that the true poet is named Minnelli."[4] However, the writings of Douchet in the following decade would be the most fundamental in early assessments of Minnelli's work. Douchet was not the only French critic to write on Minnelli at this time. His colleague at *Cahiers du cinéma,* Jean Domarchi, was equally committed (together, they interviewed Minnelli for the magazine in 1962), and Domarchi was writing about (and interviewing) Minnelli before Douchet; at the other major French film magazine at the time, *Positif,* Jean-Paul Török and Jacques Quincey wrote an extended essay, "Vincente Minnelli ou le peintre de la vie rêvée," published a year after the first Douchet piece collected in this volume. There had been previous attempts at these magazines to deal with Minnelli. Jacques Doniol-Valcroze, for example, gave *The Bad and the Beautiful* (1952) a fairly lengthy review for *Cahiers* in 1953 as did Domarchi with *Lust for Life* (1956) in 1956; and Etienne Chaumeton wrote a general essay on Minnelli at *Positif* as early as 1954, while Marcel Ranchal and Ado Kyrou did early reviews for, respectively, *Brigadoon* (1954) and *Designing Woman* (1957). But the Douchet and Török/Quincey essays represented much more serious and sustained efforts.[5]

During the early 1960s, the auteurist critics at the English magazine *Movie* likewise showed an interest in Minnelli. The May 1962 issue published a chart ranking the tastes of the magazine's contributors in American and British directors. Minnelli was listed in the second category, "Brilliant," placing him in the company of such figures as Welles, Douglas Sirk, and Nicholas Ray. (The top category of "Great" consisted of only two directors, Hitchcock and Hawks.) Within the magazine itself during this period, however, the more extended essays concentrated largely on Minnelli's mise-en-scène while making few larger claims about the work. Mark Shivas argued that, unlike Lang, Ray, or Joseph Losey, "Minnelli's films do not express any consistent viewpoint." The style of an individual Minnelli film for Shivas arises primarily from the material the director is filming.[6] While *Movie* published two other important essays on Minnelli at this time, one by Paul Mayersberg on *Two Weeks in Another Town* (1962) and the other by Barry Boys on *The Courtship of Eddie's Father* (1963), the magazine never significantly challenged the widespread notion that Minnelli was to be understood primarily as a stylist rather than an auteur.

Consequently, it is Douchet's work that makes the greatest leap forward. In his first extended piece on the director, "The Red and the Green," Douchet has two major obstacles to face: his primarily skeptical colleagues at *Cahiers du cinéma* and the film on which he is writing, *The Four Horsemen of the Apocalypse* (1962), a critical and financial failure. For most of Douchet's colleagues, Minnelli was at best a gifted metteur en scène but not someone who could be considered an auteur on the level of a Hitchcock, a Lang, or a Jean Renoir. For many critics, at *Cahiers* and elsewhere, *Four Horsemen* only confirmed suspicions about Minnelli, the director here tackling historical and political material beyond what was felt to be his limited range. *The Four Horsemen of the Apocalypse* is one of Minnelli's most ambitious films, an adaptation of the Vicente Blasco Ibáñez novel and a remake of Rex Ingram's 1921 silent classic with Rudolph Valentino. The remake updates the historical setting from World War I to World War II, detailing a family of mixed Argentine, German, and French blood torn apart by divided allegiances due to the war. *Four Horsemen* is a film in which Minnelli's unhappiness over the screenplay and some of the film's casting led to a mise-en-scène that is so ornate it seems to be speaking a kind of stentorian visual language as a form of compensation. It is a film of allegorical imagery, elaborate montage sequences, detailed historical re-creations, and the use of documentary stock footage, anamorphically manipulated and color tinted. While for the film's many detractors Minnelli's style here essentially concealed a vacuum, Douchet proposed another reading.

Douchet undertakes a defense and explication of Minnelli as an auteur, arguing that *Four Horsemen* is at once a summation of Minnelli's work and his masterpiece, comparable to Hitchcock's *Vertigo* (1958) and Lang's *The Tiger of*

Eschnapur (1959). For spectators familiar with such stylized Minnelli films as *The Bad and the Beautiful* and *Gigi*, Douchet's argument that Minnelli is to be understood as a great realist might seem like an unconvincing provocation. But Douchet was not the first critic to raise the issue of realism in relation to Minnelli. In his review of *Meet Me in St. Louis*, Agee was already attuned to (and not entirely pleased with) the film's mix of artifice and realistic detail.[7] And in relation to *The Clock* (1945), Agee expressed a guarded admiration for the film's combination of "first-grade truth with second-grade fiction," while also drawing attention to Minnelli's handling of crowds as being so detailed that "you wonder whether some swarming, multitudinously human scenes were made in the actual city, with only a few of the actors aware of concealed cameras."[8] Douchet's emphasis on realism, though, emerges out of a postwar French critical and theoretical commitment largely influenced by André Bazin. Minnelli's films were of no real concern to Bazin, whose aesthetic of realism addressed itself more comfortably in relation to Roberto Rossellini, William Wyler, Welles, and Renoir. In one of his rare references to Minnelli, Bazin expressed his unhappiness that the release of Minnelli's film biography of Van Gogh, *Lust for Life*, meant that Bazin's beloved Renoir was unable to make his own film about the painter: "What was needed was a painter's son, and what we got was a director of filmed ballets!"[9] Nevertheless, even though Douchet's reading of Minnelli is descended from a certain Bazinian critical tradition, it manipulates that tradition to its own ends.

Douchet sees in Minnelli's cinema a "schizophrenic vision of the world," this schizophrenia the product of the clash between the poetic reverie Douchet regards as being fundamental to Minnelli and the "fear of reality" that Minnelli's work exhibits. This vision in turn affects the typical Minnelli protagonist, who is likewise affected by a dreamlike poetic reverie, a desire to withdraw from the harsh realities of the material world into a self-created realm of artifice. Such a self-created artificial world is based on a meticulous re-creation of details derived from an observation of the real but given a highly subjective and aestheticized reworking. If *The Four Horsemen of the Apocalypse* is Minnelli's most important film to Douchet it is because here Minnelli's world and its dreaming protagonists come up against a situation that pushes the implications of their desire to withdraw to its absolute limit. The violent clash of worlds and dreams is no longer expressed through a trailer destroying a rose bush but through war and the Nazi Occupation of Paris. In Douchet's reading, the Nazis project their own "collective and *uniform*" dream. This is "the maddest dream humanity has ever known," ravaging and destroying entire decors, culminating with the taking of Paris, a city likewise presented as another kind of "glittering" dream space. The film's protagonist, Julio, desiring neutrality above all else, must finally make a political decision at the end of the film, a betrayal of his Nazi officer cousin, leading to the film's apocalyptic final sequence in which both men are killed by RAF bombs as Julio makes an ironic toast to family.

In his review of Minnelli's next film, the equally controversial *Two Weeks in Another Town*, Douchet goes even further in what is perhaps the most eccentric piece of Minnelli criticism ever written. Building his review on Eric Rohmer's proposal that every great film (even if ostensibly a work of fiction) is a documentary, Douchet argues that *Two Weeks in Another Town* is fundamentally a documentary on four levels: a documentary on man and his social environment, on animals, on plant life, and on mineral life. What concerns Douchet here are questions of evolution and transformation tied to the "fundamental nature of cinema." *Two Weeks in Another Town* is in an especially interesting position in relation to these questions. The film is in many ways not only a continuation but also a reworking of *The Bad and the Beautiful,* one of Minnelli's most successful films, also starring Kirk Douglas and also set in the world of filmmaking. But *Two Weeks* is also clearly an attempt on Minnelli's part to create a type of European art film, influenced in particular by Federico Fellini's *La dolce vita* (1960), while still largely working within the formal parameters of his earlier melodramas.[10] Douchet does not note any of this, nor does he make mention of (and possibly did not know at the time) that the final cut of the film was taken out of Minnelli's hands, in itself a symptom of Minnelli's declining status within Hollywood. For Douchet, an artist is at the summit of his evolution when he "no longer condenses the various stages of evolution in time but lays them out *in space.*" *Two Weeks in Another Town* shows Minnelli's typical concern with the accurate reproduction of the details of a social world (here, that of the international coproduction filmmaking scene in Rome and of the Hollywood figures now working within it). But in this world, the characters assume animal-like characteristics and move within an allegorized human jungle. It is this kind of world from which the hero must ultimately detach himself if his process of evolution is to take place. Simultaneously, these Hollywood characters living in Rome also struggle to retain certain vegetative characteristics, "uprooted" from Hollywood while trying to (often parasitically) feed off of the new world into which they have been planted. Finally, the mineral world is represented by the decor with which Minnelli's films and his protagonists are so fixated.

Here, though, this decor, the falseness of the "insubstantial movie sets" of the film-within-the-film that Douglas is working on, serve as great barriers to evolution since the protagonists of the film are fully invested in this world of falseness and appearances.

It is not entirely clear how these four categories are *inherently* those of the documentary. They could just as easily be discussed in relation to traditions of realism and naturalism. Nevertheless, Douchet's insistence on this linkage is most likely a symptom of the direction at *Cahiers du cinéma* in the early 1960s, when the interpenetration of fiction and documentary (exemplified by the work of someone like Jean Rouch) was of enormous concern. In some ways, Douchet's essay is both linked with and the obverse of Fereydoun Hoveyda's "*Cinéma vérité*, or Fantastic Realism," written a year earlier for *Cahiers*. Hoveyda (writing primarily on Rouch and Edgar Morin's *Chronicle of a Summer*) attempts to explore the paradox of the type of documentary experiment Rouch and Morin are undertaking, resulting in what Hoveyda calls a "fantastic" rather than realist work. Douchet, in contrast, looks at a stylized Hollywood melodrama and sees in it a documentary. One of the values of Douchet's arguments about *Two Weeks* is how they open up possibilities for seeing Minnelli's work in relation to certain naturalist categories. If a "fear of reality" marks this cinema we also find in it a related fear of—and need to control—the natural world. In "The Red and the Green," Douchet refers to Minnelli's world as being like a "hothouse." Plants and animals grow and live in this studio-controlled world but in a somewhat overripe and sickly manner. We may be reminded here of Aunt Anastasia's rose bush, which does not grow "naturally" on her front lawn but has to be lovingly brought to life and shaped by its "creator" who must now watch it be destroyed by the savagery of her niece's mobile home.

For all of Douchet's brilliance, his readings of Minnelli do not appear to have had an immediate impact at *Cahiers* or to have significantly changed anyone's mind. As Douchet later told Pascal Bonitzer and Jean Narboni, only he and Domarchi were strong defenders of Minnelli's work at the magazine during this period.[11] In a roundtable discussion with a group of *Cahiers* critics three years after the publication of "The Red and the Green" (Douchet was not included in the discussion) the same clichés about Minnelli reappear. Jean-André Fieschi states that the real auteurs of Minnelli's films are its producers (notably Arthur Freed and John Houseman), and for Gérard Guégan "Minnelli's art derives its greatness from its subordination to American conventions."[12] By this point, auteurism had lost much of its polemical edge, and while work continued to be done at the magazine on the more recent films of favored auteurs, the terms of analysis had begun to change. The value of these auteurist works was increasingly being measured in relation to their self-referential status. The late works of Lang, Hitchcock, or Hawks were discussed as testament films, laying bare and making explicit the obsessions of their filmmakers.[13] For a variety of complex reasons, Minnelli's later films did not lead to widespread admiration within this context even though the films themselves were easily available to be interpreted in this manner, as Douchet's essays make apparent. The general perception that Minnelli was going into decline—something that the release of *Goodbye Charlie* in 1964 and *The Sandpiper* in 1965 (two very uneven but still interesting and important films) only confirmed—was no doubt part of this lack of interest in rereading his cinema.

I see two other obstacles to a more widespread appreciation of Minnelli's work in France at this time. One is that he was a notoriously difficult interview subject. Minnelli's struggles in clearly expressing himself through spoken language meant that he was never able to assume that necessary gurulike status with these critics and filmmakers as did more voluble and articulate directors such as Renoir, Hitchcock, or Rossellini.[14] This was also a problem in terms of his American and British reception, leading Charles Higham and Joel Greenberg to conclude that Minnelli's films are "elegant, glossy and decorative, but he has nothing to say, and the diffidence with which he discussed his films with us makes this fact entirely clear."[15] Minnelli's apparent shyness and his reticence in discussing the meaning of his work led many to assume that the ultimate source for coherence in the films resided elsewhere: genres, producers, screenplays.

The other problem in terms of Minnelli's French reception has more to do directly with the films themselves. Thomas Elsaesser has written that early French auteurism was a "control-freak theory," attracted to auteurs who expressed perfectionist impulses over their own films, preeminently rigorous formalists such as Hitchcock and Lang.[16] While I think that this is true to a certain extent, I would add here the importance among the early auteurists for a cinema that was at once rigorous *and* spontaneous, a cinema that, for all of its attention to form also expressed a fascination for when formalist control breaks down and gives birth to other kinds of revelations; hence the love of films that were formally expressive and innovative but (partly as a result of their attempts to give birth to new forms) awkward and uneven, films that alternated between convention and innovation, classicism and modernism, fiction and documentary. I am thinking here not only of the fascination with

Rossellini or Ray but also with (again) Hitchcock or Lang, whose work could also be read in these terms. Minnelli's cinema did not easily lend itself to this kind of critical method. Its visual style and texture, its formal shape and rhythms were more artificial and polished than the filmmakers who were making it into the *Cahiers* pantheon at the time, hence Douchet's need to claim Minnelli for realism and the documentary when all evidence seems to point to the contrary.

Bill Krohn's "Specters at the Feast: French Viewpoints on Minnelli's Comedies" offers an extremely useful summary of the variety of responses that Minnelli's films engendered within France from the 1950s through the early 1970s. An American critic strongly influenced by French critical method, Krohn is in an ideal position to explicate this history. Krohn's emphasis is, as the essay's subtitle indicates, on Minnelli's comic films, certainly the most neglected of the three genres with which Minnelli's name is most widely associated. While there is an ongoing uncertainty as to Minnelli's auteur status in these French writings that Krohn surveys, a number of these critics (including Rohmer and Luc Moullet) emphasize Minnelli's attention to the movements and gestures of his actors and how these so often evoke the world of dance. Such an emphasis emerges out of the postwar French concern with mise-en-scène. But it also suggests that genre in Minnelli is fluid rather than fixed, and that this fluidity emerges through Minnelli's concerns shaping seemingly diverse material into similar patterns. Krohn notes the strong links between the comic *Father of the Bride* and the musical *The Band Wagon,* both films centering on men caught up in theatrical productions (metaphorical in the case of *Father,* literal in the case of *The Band Wagon*) that induce nightmarish states. Krohn goes even further when he argues that the melodrama *The Cobweb* could, in fact, be seen as "the blackest of the domestic comedies."

I would add here that Minnelli's statement that comedy has no real value unless it is "played for blood"[17] implies an impulse on his part for creating seemingly placid, middle-class comic worlds in which violence (emotional and physical) continually erupts, calling into doubt the harmony and order to which these worlds are ostensibly devoted. In fact, it is difficult to think of any American filmmaker working at this time whose comic sensibility has quite the same bitter and sometimes violent undertone as does Minnelli's. The brilliant surfaces of Tashlin's world, by contrast, seem rather mild in that the chaos and comic violence in Tashlin is, from square one, a virtual given with little of the startling contrast Minnelli so often creates. The excitement Tootie experiences in the "wholesome" family musical *Meet Me in St. Louis* over a drunkard being shot ("His blood squirted out three feet!") also finds its way into the fashion magazine chic of *Designing Woman,* in which the spectators at a boxing match hold newspapers over their faces in order to avoid blood from the boxers being splashed onto them, a gruesome prospect that provokes Mirella (Lauren Bacall), the title character, to hysterically scream.

As Krohn indicates in his preface to the essay written for this collection, "Specters at the Feast" was written in 1978 for a brochure published in conjunction with a Minnelli retrospective in New York City. For roughly a decade prior to this, the literature on Minnelli continued to develop. In the United States in 1968, the leading American auteurist critic, Andrew Sarris, published *The American Cinema,* a volume of short essays on primarily Hollywood directors, with Sarris ranking them in various categories in terms of their ostensible value. As with the *Movie* chart published several years prior to this, Minnelli is placed in the second highest category, "The Far Side of Paradise." Unfortunately, Sarris followed convention in his Minnelli entry, referring to him as "more of a stylist than an auteur."[18] In 1973 Donald Knox published *The Magic Factory,* an oral history of the making of *An American in Paris.* Knox interviewed virtually every major surviving figure who worked on the film (including Minnelli), and the book is an indispensable document. However, in the book's preface Knox makes his thesis evident: "No single person made *An American in Paris;* it was a studio creation."[19] The book's foreword was written by Sarris who essentially followed Knox in his placement of Minnelli as auteur. For Sarris, if *An American in Paris* had an auteur it was George Gershwin, composer of the film's music—and dead for fourteen years before the cameras on the film even began to roll. The notion that Minnelli was not much more than a decorative metteur en scène of genre pieces had begun to harden into myth.

The following year Minnelli published his autobiography, *I Remember It Well.*[20] *That's Entertainment!,* a compilation of excerpts from MGM musicals, opened theatrically the same year with great success; and although many Minnelli clips were shown in *That's Entertainment!,* climaxing with the ballet from *An American in Paris,* shown in a hideously truncated version but declared by the film to be (via Frank Sinatra's commentary) the greatest musical number in the history of the genre, Minnelli's name was scarcely mentioned. (The film was dedicated to the producer of most of Minnelli's musicals, Arthur Freed.) In 1975 Hugh Fordin's *The World of Entertainment* was published; it is a production history of Freed's films, in which Minnelli's presence looms very large although, as with Knox's book, the emphasis is on collaboration, in this instance overseen and controlled by Freed. That same year Minnelli was an interview subject for Richard Schickel's television series *The Men Who Made the Movies*, along with Hitchcock, Hawks, Raoul Walsh, Frank Capra, George Cukor, William Wellman, and King Vidor. An interview book of the same title was published along with the series. During this time, Minnelli was struggling in the aftermath of the end of the traditional studio system and made only two films, *On a Clear Day You Can See Forever*, released in the summer of 1970 and not a great financial or critical success, and *A Matter of Time*, released six years later. The latter of these two films was the biggest disaster of Minnelli's career, the final cut taken out of his hands and with interpolated footage (including horrendous stock footage) shot by others intended to fill in the numerous gaps. Even in this bastardized form, though, and in spite of some awkward moments, it is an extraordinary work, long overdue for restoration. Reviewing the film at the time of its release, George Morris wrote that "if nothing else, *A Matter of Time* vindicates auteur criticism."[21] And indeed, the richness and complexity of the film is predicated less on its relationship to genre (to what genre or even set of genres does the film belong?) than to its status as a kind of "art film" embroidering upon various thematic, structural, and stylistic elements found across all of Minnelli's films. A year later Martin Scorsese's *New York, New York* opened and, with Liza Minnelli in the leading role, was partly an homage to Minnelli's MGM musicals. The same year, the first book-length study in English of Minnelli's musicals was published: Joseph Andrew Casper's detailed and descriptive *Vincente Minnelli and the Film Musical*. But the book did not make a significant impact at the time, and when the *Positif* critic Jean-Pierre Coursodon published his two-volume study of American directors in 1982 he began his entry on Minnelli by noting that the director's "reputation is currently at a low ebb."[22] Minnelli died in 1986 at the age of eighty-three.

Auteurism had, by this point, been challenged on a number of fronts. A fascination with the "death of the author" manifested itself strongly in academia during a period roughly coinciding with the significant expansion of film studies as a discipline. The study of cinema as a form of "higher education" was now drawn to other methodologies that challenged auteurism: structuralism and poststructuralism, semiotics, psychoanalysis, feminism, genre studies. Thomas Elsaesser's "Vincente Minnelli" and Jean-Loup Bourget's "Minnelli's American Nightmare" are transitional pieces in this regard. In both essays, genre assumes a central role, in marked contrast to Douchet's first essay, which notes essential differences in the Minnelli films in terms of genre but does not extensively explore these. While such a shift was no doubt indicative of an increased scholarly interest in genre, neither Bourget nor Elsaesser is willing to completely abandon the concept of the auteur. The two essays are transitional in other respects as well, both written in the late 1960s or early 1970s for essentially nonacademic publications, but produced by two critics then engaged in the early stages of a commitment to the discipline of film studies. Bourget's essay was not published until 1986, in *Positif,* just after Minnelli's death; and Elsaesser's did not receive its first wide publication until 1981, when it was reproduced in a BFI anthology on the musical, edited by Rick Altman. Both writers supplied new prefatory material for these later versions, in the case of Bourget primarily to sum up Minnelli's career in the immediate aftermath of the director's death. Elsaesser, on the other hand, attempted to distance himself from what he saw as some of the limitations of the auteurist approach evidenced in the earlier essay. He has supplied some additional refinements to that introductory section—as well to the main body of the piece—for this volume as well. Nevertheless, the 1970 version remains a formidable piece that needs no apologies.

For Bourget, Minnelli's work derives its force from its close ties to genre rather than from any auteurist transcendence of their conventions. Minnelli never seriously challenged those conventions, according to Bourget, but in-stead creatively worked within them. At the same time, Bourget writes that genre does not so much anchor the films as destabilize them. While one could argue that genres in Hollywood cinema are rarely pure, Minnelli's particular inflection of his genre material gives the films their distinctive quality. Bourget notes that within the films themselves there is often a strong opposition between two worlds, two realms; this, in turn, affects the dramatic and visual texture of the films so that an uncertainty about genre status may sometimes emerge. Echoing Sarris's detection of the "curiously depressing" tone to *An American in Paris* and *Gigi,*[23] Bourget adds that Minnelli's musicals often fail to supply the spectator with the kind of exhilaration and euphoria that au-diences traditionally expect from the genre. Bourget would be neither the first nor the last critic to note this undercurrent of melancholia to Minnelli's cinema, a melancholia present even when genre conventions appeared to suggest otherwise.

Elsaesser takes a somewhat different tack. Much of the early auteurist work on Minnelli emphasized the melodramas, possibly as a polemical response to the more widespread critical admiration for Minnelli's musicals. But Elsaesser shifts his concerns back to the musical, arguing that "all Minnelli's films aspire to the condition of the musical" and that the dramatic and comic films are musicals "turned inside out." Against the strong drive-oriented structure of Hollywood cinema and its mobilization of the forces of mise-en-scène to create a sense of absolute harmony between the drives of the characters and the "aesthetic gratification" of the spectacle that ensues as a result of this, Minnelli offers something more hesitant. The drives of Minnelli's characters are only superficially tied to the ideology of Hollywood in which "dynamism rationalizes or sublimates itself." Instead, Minnelli's characters primarily want to satisfy their own aesthetic needs, a satisfaction the outside world wishes to deny them. Reality here is not so much phenomenological as psychological and emotional. In the musicals, the protagonists are ultimately able to realize their desires; whereas in the comedies and melodramas the characters are "in conflict with a radically different order of realty," one that denies their desires from being achieved, all of this placed within a claustrophobic world of obsession and "mad frenzy." Because total satisfaction is achieved in the musicals and denied in the other genres, the musical becomes "a kind of ideal image of the medium itself" as well as "Minnelli's metaphor for the cinema as a whole." While this appears to slightly complicate the melancholic strain that Bourget and Sarris detect in the Minnelli musicals, Elsaesser nevertheless argues that it is not through "a 'naïve' assertion of will-power or happy-go-lucky bonhomie" that someone satisfies their desires but rather "a complex process of metamorphosis that transforms both the individual and his world." Elsaesser offers what is essentially an allegorical reading in which the films are at once about their own status as Minnelli films *and* statements about the nature of cinema in general, in which the protagonists are "metteurs en scène of the self." What is Tacy Collini, after all, as she guides her nervous husband to back the trailer up into her aunt's driveway, pushing everyone away and broadly gesturing to her husband, but another example of this type of metteur en scène?

―――――――

The broader contextualization of Minnelli's work in relation to genre and the mechanisms and structures of Hollywood cinema would continue to develop throughout the late 1970s and on into the next two decades. The musical would be treated to several important studies in the 1980s, most notably Alain Masson's *Comédie musicale* (1981), Jane Feuer's *The Hollywood Musical* (1982), and Rick Altman's *The American Film Musical* (1987) as well as Richard Dyer's "Entertainment and Utopia." While Minnelli's films figured largely in all of this literature, his status as an auteur was not a primary concern. Nevertheless, the larger investigations into genre during this period produced crucial insights into Minnelli's films, as we shall see through the second section of the book, "The 1970s and 1980s: Genre, Psychoanalysis, and Close Readings." Geoffrey Nowell-Smith's "Minnelli and Melodrama" from 1977 is one of the early examples of an attempt to map out some of the major elements of a mode or genre most often approached in an apologetic or derogatory manner in the past, Nowell-Smith doing so primarily within a Freudian and Marxist framework.[24] Melodrama as a dramatic and literary form emerges in the eighteenth century, coinciding with the emergence of the bourgeoisie, and speaks to the concerns and desires of this new audience. Melodrama presupposes an audience that is neither entirely dispossessed of power nor fully in control of it but instead occupies an economic, social, and political middle ground. Within melodrama, patriarchal family rights and the legitimacy of property and children are of central concern. Hollywood cinema inherits many of these concerns while also stressing the child's search for his or her sexual identity within "a symbolic law that the father incarnates." But melodrama traditionally takes on more than it can handle. Its drive toward the "happy ending" so often dictated by Hollywood conventions results in a symptomatic "excess" in the mise-en-scène (as well as in the music), similar to the Freudian concept of conversion hysteria. Minnelli's films, as the title of the essay indicates, are particularly symptomatic of this tendency. Like a number of critics before him, Nowell-Smith uses the term *realism* when writing on Minnelli, here in relation to the basic material of melodrama itself (in that melodrama must draw on clearly defined social worlds and types in order for bourgeois audience recognition to take place). But realism is incapable of fully accommodating the needs and anxieties being depicted within the films, leading to the recurrence within Minnelli of realist representation breaking down and building to the " 'hysterical' moment." Nowell-Smith will not be the last critic to use the word *hysteria* in describing Minnelli's films, and he notes the recurrence of such "excess" not only in the melodramas but also in the musicals, which "tend to be much more melodramatic than others from the same studio."

In spite of the enormous interest in melodrama in film studies beginning in the 1970s it was not Minnelli among auteurs who dominated the critical discourses but Douglas Sirk. Sirk's films, boldly iconographic and visually precise, were virtual diagrams of melodramatic form, ideal for the classroom and for written explication. Moreover, Sirk presented himself as a European intellectual, able to articulate a rich understanding of the history of melodrama

to interviewers. His adoption as a type of role model for Rainer Werner
Fassbinder, via Fassbinder's attempts to make commercial films that also criticized the values of the dominant culture, only solidified Sirk's reputation as the
ultimate auteur of 1950s Hollywood melodrama. While Minnelli's melodramas
became somewhat lost in the shuffle, some major work continued to be done
on the films, across all genres. Preeminent here is Andrew Britton's extended
analysis of *Meet Me in St. Louis:* "Smith; or, The Ambiguities," published
in 1978.

Within traditional genre studies, *Meet Me in St. Louis* has long enjoyed a
reputation as a film that ushers in a new type of integrated musical, one with no
ties to the world of European operetta. It is a film wholly American in subject
matter and style, and in which singing and dancing arises "naturally" out of the
narrative situations, performed by characters who are not professional entertainers.[25] Britton proposes a broader understanding of the film. Britton traces
the roots of the basic situations and conflicts of *Meet Me in St. Louis* across
various American traditions. The film's conventions "permit the containment
of conflict, but the particular process of containment exposes conflicts with
unusual clarity." As with other Minnelli critics, Britton notes the instability of
genre here, drawing particular attention to the film's fusion of the conventions
of the family musical with those of the horror film. What allows these genres
and traditions to coexist in *St. Louis* can largely be traced to the tension within
the film between male and female, adult and child, work and play, and in which
the bourgeois family and patriarchal institutions are the source of both stability
and repression. While critics such as Bourget and Sarris have intuitively felt that
the musical numbers in Minnelli's films often fail to provide the conventional
ecstatic release one traditionally expects from the genre, Britton offers a more
pointed analysis of this. He notes that women dominate virtually all of the
musical numbers in *St. Louis,* and the songs frequently play on various reversals
of gender conventions; but these numbers also emphasize the women as an
image, one the women ostensibly construct for other male figures but which
they also just as clearly construct for themselves and in which the literal
presence of the male is often unwelcome or disruptive to this narcissistic
pleasure. The songs, then, are defined by their elements of "containment and
overflow." The most disruptive character in the film is the youngest daughter,
Tootie, "the crux of the film, the register of its defining tensions." Throughout
the film, her attraction to violence and death is the source of much of the film's
humor, as she gives literal voice to and enacts the "sadism latent in the family
group." The Halloween sequence, in which Tootie dresses as a boy and in which

most of her friends are likewise dressed in costumes employing various elements of gender play or reversal, is pivotal. Here, Tootie's dream of being "the
most horrible" is realized when she throws flour in the face of the dreaded Mr.
Browkoff, the most feared man in the neighborhood, and symbolically kills
him. This action precipitates the children's bonfire and the burning of furniture as Tootie's supremacy is declared and the children reject socialization and
the Oedipus complex.

Such a reading may startle those accustomed to seeing *Meet Me in St. Louis* as
a wholesome family film, and it returns us to the type of question already raised
in relation to the two divergent readings of *The Long, Long Trailer* offered by
Douchet and Naremore: Minnelli films as cozy fantasy or as dark vision? Even
allowing for the often inherently contradictory nature of many cultural texts,
Minnelli's films, I would argue, have a special intensity in terms of the ways in
which these contradictions are laid out and given form. In relation to *Meet Me
in St. Louis,* Britton argues for the importance of taking into account "the
discrepancy between a dominant ideological project" and "the contradictory
implications set up by the realization of the project." Britton does not address
Minnelli as auteur at all here (although he has elsewhere made a claim for him
as "a radically subversive artist"[26]). But this issue of the "realization of the
project" points to the need for a more attentive accounting of Minnelli's
presence as auteur. One need only compare *Meet Me in St. Louis* with another
musical produced by Arthur Freed and made four years later, *Summer Holiday,*
directed by Rouben Mamoulian. The later film is clearly modeled on *Meet Me
in St. Louis:* it is another piece of small town Americana centering on a middle-
class family, with a similar investment in naturalistic musical performances and
with a number of sequences that evoke sequences from the Minnelli film,
including another gothic set piece, in this instance a journey for its teenage
male protagonist—visiting a saloon. The screenplay was co-written by the co-
screenwriter of *St. Louis* (Irving Brecher) and with the song's lyrics also written
by the lyricist of the earlier film (Ralph Blane). But there is not a trace of the
kind of ideological struggle and contradiction at work in *Summer Holiday* that
Britton so thoroughly uncovers in relation to *St. Louis.* In fact, *Summer Holiday,* while drawing on many of the same traditions at work in *St. Louis,* is an
inversion of the earlier film, focusing almost entirely on an adolescent male, and
unquestioningly affirming the values of the patriarchal bourgeois family that
Meet Me in St. Louis subjects to a very different investigation.

Dana Polan's "It Could Be Oedipus Rex: Denial and Difference in *The Band
Wagon;* or, The American Musical as American Gothic" argues for a "politics of

form" in relation to the Minnelli musical. In some ways a response to a strongly Oedipal reading of *The Band Wagon* by Dennis Giles, published in *Movie* in 1977, as well as a response to the preponderance of overdetermined psychoanalytic and Oedipal readings of films much in fashion in film studies in the 1970s, Polan makes a strong case for the rhetoric of spectacle. In such Minnelli musicals as *The Pirate* and *The Band Wagon,* an ideology of spectacle and show predominates and the films implicitly put their faith in "life as style and as art." For Polan, the musical is fundamentally a genre that is invested in the refusal to "grow up," to submit to the dreariness of family and any type of work that is not also a form of play. In this manner, it is a genre that refuses the Oedipus complex and "the repressive structures of all Father figures." *The Band Wagon* might initially appear to contradict Polan, especially as the film's oedipal nature is overtly signaled intertextually through the staging of *Oedipus Rex* that occurs early in the film. Polan resists the obviousness of these kinds of signposts and instead argues that the film's drives are not those of the adolescent male growing up but "of a middle-aged man becoming young again, becoming his past."[27] The oedipal scenario is ultimately resisted, overthrown, since it is "is built on contradictions it cannot wish away." Instead, the film becomes fantasmatic, remaking and remolding reality, both within the narrative content (the successful show-within-the-show at the end of the film) and by Minnelli's transformative and virtuosic mise-en-scène, which operates in a "gap between story and style."

Robin Wood's close reading of *Madame Bovary* (1949), while working loosely within some of the basic strategies of Britton and Polan, also draws upon other methodologies. Wood, one of the early critics of *Movie,* and a pioneering English-language critic on Hitchcock and Hawks, never wrote about Minnelli during the magazine's formative years. His 1986 essay "Minnelli's *Madame Bovary,*" though, more than makes up for lost time and is one of the finest single readings of a Minnelli film. While Flaubert's novel is one of the hallmarks of nineteenth-century literary realism—and against whatever claims of realism other commentators have made about Minnelli's cinema—the approach taken in the Minnelli adaptation is one that places the film much more strongly within a tradition of Hollywood melodrama, specifically the woman's film. The film's link with this tradition has frequently subjected Minnelli's treatment to critical scorn, as though the film were a betrayal of Flaubert's text. But Wood persuasively situates *Madame Bovary* within a post–World War II strain of melodramas centering on women in repressive small-town or family environments. Moreover, Wood also notes that the film should be understood as a star vehicle for its Emma, Jennifer Jones, and he draws links between *Madame Bovary* and such Jones vehicles as *Duel in the Sun* (King Vidor, 1946) and *Ruby Gentry* (King Vidor, 1952). *Madame Bovary* is, along with the neglected *Undercurrent* (1946), the only instance in Minnelli's work of a female-centered melodrama (unless we include *A Matter of Time,* although neither the overall tone nor visual style of Minnelli's final film is firmly within melodramatic traditions). More fully than any Minnelli critic before him, Wood emphasizes hysteria not simply as a symptom but as an underlying principle of the film, of Jones as star, and of Minnelli's work in general. This hysteria erupts most emblematically in the melodramatic set pieces throughout Minnelli, such as the violent fairground sequence near the end of *Some Came Running* (1958), the car rides in *The Bad and the Beautiful* and *Two Weeks in Another Town*, and, in *Madame Bovary,* the "neurotic waltz" sequence, culminating with the breaking of the windows. Unlike Nowell-Smith, Wood does not directly make use of Freudian models of hysteria but instead argues for a broader understanding of the term in which hysteria becomes "a valid reaction to certain social conditions" connected to the lack of autonomy in relation to money, power, and social position within a capitalist economy. As a "defining principle" of Minnelli's work, Wood notes that hysteria is not exclusive to the melodramas, also finding its way into the musicals, and he draws strong links, in particular, between *Madame Bovary* and *The Pirate* as complementary "hysterical texts." The kind of reading Wood offers in the second half of his essay represents a small part of the increased importance of close textual analysis ongoing in film studies (and largely French in origin) since the early 1970s. Many of these analyses were heavily structuralist and psychoanalytic in nature, most famously the *Cahiers du cinéma* "collective text" on John Ford's *Young Mr. Lincoln,* published in 1970. In 1976, Raymond Bellour, one of the major figures in the new concern with this type of analysis (particularly in relation to Hitchcock) published an exhaustive close reading of *Gigi* as an exemplary classical film in its formal logic. Through a close analysis of numerous motifs (including, most notably, Minnelli's use of mirrors and windows), Wood argues that hysteria in *Madame Bovary* is "embedded in the film's very structure, a structure of exceptional rigor and logic."

Finally, the essays from the 1980s culminate with a return to French criticism via two very brief pieces by the brilliant and influential Serge Daney, "*The Pirate* Isn't Just Decor" and "Minnelli Caught in His Web." Daney had been an editor of *Cahiers du cinéma* from 1973 to 1981 before leaving the magazine to write on cinema and television for the French daily *Libération*. Between 1988 and 1991, his column examined what happened to films when they were shown on television, and it was here that he wrote on two Minnelli films, *The Pirate* and *The Cobweb*. Within the context of Daney's essays, both of these Minnelli films are reduced to the dimension of a television screen. But for Daney such an apparent reduction does not diminish the interest of the films. Disputing the conventional wisdom that Minnelli's approach to the cinema is essentially decorative, he argues that what the sets in Minnelli's films have "lost in store-window impact" (by being shown on television), "they've gained in pure logic." Where Daney makes an original point here is in how he notes that Minnelli's approach to space is not only different from other filmmakers, it is also diametrically opposed to space in television, in which the decor is "something that is there before the actors" and where the actors must find ways to move about and interact without bumping into one another, a problem Minnelli's actors never face. The emergence of television coincides with the moment when American films "were losing their way," becoming increasingly scattered in their forms and intentions. Television simply reformatted and reduced these cinematic forms down to its own cramped spaces. It is not television that diminishes the decor of a Minnelli film but rather the decor of a Minnelli film that diminishes television. (It is significant in this regard that, unlike many of his colleagues, Minnelli never directed for television.) In the all-star *The Cobweb*, emerging near the end of the Old Hollywood, we find something close to a lost art in that "today no one would know how to democratically house so many characters in one film" and in which "doctors join with patients in the elegant therapy of a great ballet."

In 1989, the Museum of Modern Art (MoMA) held a complete retrospective of Minnelli's films and, in conjunction with Harper and Row, published Stephen Harvey's *Directed by Vincente Minnelli*, the first book-length study in English of Minnelli's entire body of work. Aimed primarily for the general reader and dismissive of some of the director's most important films, the book did little for Minnelli's critical reputation. That same year Robert Lang took a very different approach in *American Film Melodrama: Griffith, Vidor, Minnelli*, an academic text strongly influenced by psychoanalysis.

———————

During the 1990s, the discourses surrounding Minnelli's films inevitably began to reflect the increased interest in cultural studies, and along with this emerged a number of other related approaches emphasizing specific historical, material, and cultural contexts for the films. The increased importance of research, linked with an increased interest in historiography, becomes apparent in a number of these later Minnelli essays. For the first time, not only do Minnelli's various positions prior to becoming a filmmaker (department store window dresser, fashion photographer, theatrical set and costume designer) assume an importance in terms of assessing the films and the sensibility informing them, but also Minnelli's biography begins to enter into the writings. In particular, Minnelli's life and work now begin to be situated in relation to various discourses on modernity. As we shall see in the third section of the book, "The 1990s: Matters of History, Culture, and Sexuality," the question of modernity, or of the modern in general, will be applied to Minnelli's work in a number of different ways. For this book, Geoffrey Nowell-Smith's short essay "*The Band Wagon*" functions as an interesting transitional piece, especially when compared to his earlier "Minnelli and Melodrama." The psychoanalytic reading so central to "Minnelli and Melodrama" is no longer in evidence. Instead, Nowell-Smith focuses on the synthesis of high and popular culture at work in *The Band Wagon*. Such a synthesis, asserts Nowell-Smith, became central to Hollywood cinema as it attempted to achieve some measure of respectability. Implicitly, many of its films addressed the question of whether Hollywood constituted a distinct culture of its own, superior to traditional European cultural values. *The Band Wagon* is a particularly valuable film in this regard, a film that is "as a whole . . . quite extraordinarily rich in its representation of the intricacies of American cultural values." Nowell-Smith devotes some detailed descriptions of how the film repeatedly lays out its basic dialectic of popular and high culture, epitomized by the song "That's Entertainment," but which is also present to varying degrees in sequence after sequence. Nowell-Smith's emphasis on such a dialectic would soon be taken up by later scholars in relation to Minnelli's entire body of work.

In "The Adventures of Rafe Hunnicutt: The Bourgeois Family in *Home from the Hill*," (1960) originally published in *Movie* in 1990, Edward Gallafent, rather than addressing questions of the modern, examines the numerous ways in which Minnelli's film is part of a larger American cultural and literary tradition in its concern for the ritual of the hunt, the function of the family, and the passing on of patriarchal power. Gallafent sees such concerns as being fundamental to "some of the central tensions and contradictions" of American culture. While in some ways similar to Britton's essay on *Meet Me in St. Louis*, Gallafent's is much less concerned with the kind of psychoanalytic "uncovering" of a film that Britton performs and instead details the various methods by which *Home from the Hill* articulates the issues of what it means to be "a man," both within the world of the film and within the literary/cultural tradition from which the film so clearly emerges: Melville and Twain, Hawthorne and Faulkner. Here the film's treatment of space is central, both the domestic space of the Hunnicutt family home (so sharply divided along gender lines, with father, mother, and son each "marking" their own territory within the house) and the space of the hunt; in both instances, these spaces are at once literal and psychological. Douchet's naturalist reading of *Two Weeks in Another Town* is much less eccentric when placed alongside of the kinds of observations Gallafent makes about *Home from the Hill*. In *Home from the Hill,* not only does the hunt assume enormous symbolic importance (particularly in the wild boar hunt, another notable Minnelli "set piece"), but also throughout the film the equation of human and animal is insistent.

James Naremore's "Uptown Folk: Blackness and Entertainment in *Cabin in the Sky*" stands out among the Minnelli essays of the 1990s for several reasons. Whereas Gallafent places *Home from the Hill* against a broad American cultural and historical backdrop, Naremore's arguments are more strongly focused on one particular historical moment, the 1940s. Even though the film was Minnelli's debut as a director, *Cabin in the Sky* had never figured extensively in the literature on Minnelli. For one thing, the historical importance of *Meet Me in St. Louis* as an "integrated" musical had always overshadowed it. For another, the film's depiction of African Americans has (as Bourget notes) appeared to cause some later viewers discomfort, a discomfort that is, in my opinion, completely unjustified. Naremore traces the various ways in which *Cabin in the Sky* emerges out of four competing discourses on blackness prominent during the time in which the film was made: folkloric discourses on poor rural blacks in the American South; an NAACP-spearheaded attempt to combat what were perceived to be stereotypical depictions of African Americans in Hollywood films as comic and menial types; a discourse of "critical modernism" in which jazz and African-inspired dance are now regarded as being commodified by mass media and popular culture; and finally Africanism, in which blackness becomes associated with chicness, urbanity, and fashion, and linked with both the European avant-garde and the Broadway theater. In relation to Minnelli's intervention, it is the fourth of these that is the most relevant. Naremore notes how Minnelli's work on the Broadway stage was part of a general fascination with African and African American culture during that period, while his celebrity status at the time was one in which links were drawn in the press between Africanist aesthetics and Minnelli's visual sensibility. While *Cabin in the Sky* continues to cause critics and scholars some embarrassment today,[28] Naremore observes that Minnelli's urban sensibility has "tended to undermine the conservative implications of the material." The folkloric element of the film is for Minnelli more of a pretext than a source of profound investment, and the film itself "participates in the breakdown of the pastoral, the death of a certain kind of folkloric 'authenticity,' and the growing urbanization of black images in Hollywood."

Naremore's work on *Cabin in the Sky* later was incorporated into his book *The Films of Vincente Minnelli*, published in 1993. While only addressing five films in detail (*Cabin in the Sky, Meet Me in St. Louis, Father of the Bride, The Bad and the Beautiful,* and *Lust for Life*), this book represents the first extended attempt by an English-speaking film scholar to assess Minnelli's work within academic discourses on modernity. For Naremore, Minnelli represents a major example of a filmmaker caught up in the contradictions of the dandified male artist operating within industrialized capitalism, in which aestheticism and commodification go hand in hand. Throughout his career, from window dresser to stage designer to film director, Minnelli's work came to epitomize a certain cross breeding of "elite" and popular culture, bringing together such influences as surrealism, impressionism, postimpressionism, fauvism, and ballet and modern dance but designed in such a way as to appeal to a broad, popular audience. While Naremore's readings of the individual films are more cautious in their claims than those of most of the writers in this collection, his approach has opened up enormous possibilities for further contextualizing Minnelli's work from which scholars have (and no doubt will continue to have) enormously benefited.

Beth Genné's "Vincente Minnelli and the Film Ballet" and David A. Gerstner's "Queer Modernism: The Cinematic Aesthetic of Vincente Minnelli" discuss Minnelli in relation to his years prior to becoming a film director. Both writers, in particular, focus on the time Minnelli spent in New York as a designer and stage director. Genné's concern is with the ways in which Minnelli's use of dance in *Ziegfeld Follies, Yolanda and the Thief, The Pirate,* and *An American in Paris* become the most important instances of what she terms the "film ballet," a dance form with roots stretching back as far as the eighteenth-century *ballet d'action*. The crossbreeding of elite and popular culture so central to Naremore's arguments about Minnelli are indirectly confirmed by Genné's research on Minnelli's stage work, in particular his collaboration with George Balanchine on the stage production of *Ziegfeld Follies of 1936*. Here, Minnelli and Balanchine created what Minnelli later claimed was the first surrealist ballet on Broadway; while the show's dance-drama "Five A.M." became an "amalgam of jazz, modern, and ballet movement." Minnelli takes this "upscale" mixture of elite and popular musical and dance forms to Hollywood, where he continued to create surrealist-influenced dance sequences, ones often involving the dance enactment of a character's literal dream. Genné is attentive and insightful about Minnelli's visual sources and to his use of light and color. But she also offers detailed and useful analyses of Minnelli's moving camera in his filming of dance. Minnelli, more than any musical or dance artist who came to the cinema before him, uses the camera in a participatory manner. Unlike his great predecessor in the genre, Busby Berkeley, Minnelli's camera moves without obscuring the lines of the dancers or the choreographic design or the human scale of the dance, while fantastic effects are achieved within a more intimate and dramatically coherent framework. In reading Genné's vivid descriptions here, one is reminded of how little work has been done on Minnelli's use of the moving camera, in spite of his reputation as a master of the approach.

Gerstner's research is of a different order. Like Naremore, Gerstner discusses Minnelli within the modernist tradition of the dandy/aesthete/flaneur. But Gerstner's emphasis is on the "queer inflection" of such aesthetic movements and traditions, arguing that "Minnelli's creative atmosphere in New York was pressured within the conflicting historical discourses of American masculinity." Gerstner's essay foregrounds an element to Minnelli's life and work that had, in the past, largely been addressed covertly, if at all. Minnelli always publicly presented himself as a heterosexual. Nevertheless, the visual and dramatic sensibility at work in the films has suggested other possibilities, as has Minnelli's public demeanor: his feminine manner of speaking and moving, his flamboyant and colorful style of dress, and his elaborately decorated New York apartment and California homes, all of this *implying* a homosexual, regardless of whether this was the case or not.[29] Gerstner's project is not to "out" Minnelli the person, a very difficult task in any case as the historical details of Minnelli as a practicing homosexual are (as of this writing) inconclusive. Rather, Gerstner attempts to situate Minnelli's sensibility within a certain strain of queer modernist aesthetics that surrounded the director throughout the formative period of his career. Gerstner uses the early conflicts over set design between Minnelli and MGM's supervisory art director Cedric Gibbons as a foundation for his arguments about not only differing notions about modernist aesthetics in the work of Gibbons and Minnelli at MGM but also the larger relationship and tension between such aesthetics and masculinity. Minnelli's love of "effeminate" ornamentation and "excessive" detail in matters of design marks his sensibility as one that is available to be read as queer. Moreover, Minnelli's fascination with things African and African American was in itself part of a queer modernist aesthetic in the 1920s and 1930s, a fascination he shared with such major figures of the period as Carl Van Vechten and Florine Stettheimer, neither of whom Minnelli claims to have known but whom Gerstner nevertheless links with Minnelli through their tastes and cultural milieu.

What happens to Minnelli's sensibility when it arrives in Hollywood is another matter. While Minnelli's queer aestheticism may be grasped by a suitably responsive and informed viewer of such extravagantly designed 1940s musicals as *Ziegfeld Follies* and *The Pirate*,[30] and could also be extended (under very different circumstances) to such later films as *Gigi* and *On a Clear Day You Can See Forever,* this type of queerness is of minimal interest to a number of other major Minnellis: How, for example, is *Some Came Running* queer? One broader method for retaining this reading of Minnelli's work would be to address how sexual desire is expressed and given form in the films and of how the relationship between masculine and feminine behavior is articulated. Few Minnelli films invite this type of research as much as *Tea and Sympathy,* and here Gerstner supplies us with another important essay, "The Production and Display of the Closet: Making Minnelli's *Tea and Sympathy.*" *Tea and Sympathy* is one of Minnelli's most underrated films, long misunderstood due to its troubled production circumstances. In the Robert Anderson play on which the film is based (directed on Broadway in 1953 by Elia Kazan), a young man at a New England prep school named Tom is believed to be homosexual due to his feminine characteristics and interests. The stigmatization that occurs by his classmates as a result of this is clearly a type of homosexual panic and one that is most strongly expressed by the school's coach and Tom's housemaster, Bill Reynolds, himself clearly established in the play as a repressed homosexual. The coach's wife takes a liking to Tom and, in the play's final scene, seduces Tom as a way of proving to him that he is not gay.

But the play (like the film) allows itself to be read as one that deals with larger issues of "otherness," of scapegoating, and clearly analogous to (given the 1950s context) the McCarthy era, in which homosexuality and Communism (real or imagined in either instance) were often linked. Gerstner details much of the censorship and rewriting of the source material that took place during the film's production, noting that the film has suffered from a negative reputation among many gay film scholars who see the film as hopelessly compromised and evasive. As with some of the critical responses to *Cabin in the Sky* among scholars of African American cinema, gay film scholarship often persists in seeing *Tea and Sympathy* as a retrograde text.[31] Gerstner, though, argues that "Minnelli's use of an aestheticized mise-en-scène makes it possible to realize the anxiety-ridden intersections that exist between the discursive practices surrounding the making of the film (what to do about the homosexual and the transgressive woman) and the social conditions in which those discursive practices were situated (in what ways do the homosexual and the transgressive woman threaten American masculinity?)." Gerstner pays particular attention to Minnelli's use of the hyperbolized male body situated in an "aesthetically frenetic mise-en-scène," one that "visually heightens the cultural anxiety of masculinity in postwar America." I hope that future scholars will continue to address the film's mise-en-scène (one of the most complex in all of Minnelli's work) along the lines Gerstner establishes.

The example of both Minnelli the public individual and Minnelli the stage and film director presents us with an implied question: How feminine can a man be, and how much can his creative work partake of certain cultural traditions long associated with the homosexual, without him (necessarily) being a practicing homosexual? In this manner, the sensitive Tom, "accused" of homosexuality in *Tea and Sympathy,* may be seen as an indirect portrait of Minnelli who was likewise believed to be homosexual by many of his colleagues. Unlike the homosexuality of such directors as Dorothy Arzner, George Cukor, or James Whale, this belief was based less on concrete evidence of sexual activity (Minnelli married four times and had two children, although this by no means settles the matter) than on Minnelli's behavior, taste, and mannerisms. The character of Randy, the choreographer in *Designing Woman,* who Gregory Peck's sportswriter Mike likewise believes to be homosexual, responds to an overheard homophobic reference to him made by Mike by producing a snapshot of his children. But like Minnelli's biography, such evidence of heterosexual conduct only partially erases the sense of gayness being exuded. Indeed, it is the recurring *instability* throughout Minnelli's work of masculine and feminine, of homosexual and heterosexual as distinct categories that could be most useful for further research, particularly in terms of how they might help to elucidate the various tensions at work in the films and in the cultural and historical climate within which Minnelli was operating. Are these "terrible satires" on the American way of life, these "hysterical" texts that continually express a desire to retreat from the reality of the social world, the expression of a sensibility that is both attracted to but also horrified by the very prospect of "normality" in social and sexual relations? Minnelli's schizophrenic vision of the world and its attendant impulse to "play for blood" may have at least some of its basis in the anxiety produced by such irreconcilable gaps and contradictions.

———————

The final section of this book, "Minnelli Today: The Return of the Artist," is devoted almost entirely to new essays, either written for this book or published since 2004. Strikingly, in virtually every instance the concept of the auteur returns in these essays, albeit articulated in different ways and still often informed by the discourses influencing film studies since the 1970s. But Minnelli is a *defining* figure in relation to the arguments found in these later essays, and the impulse to marginalize him or to introduce him as an auteur in a defensive or apologetic manner ceases. The increased interest in film studies over approximately the last decade in relation to issues of performance and the theatrical, in relation to the film soundtrack, and in spoken language and the voice, has allowed for Minnelli's films to serve as particularly productive terrains for research. And so Minnelli the artist is on display here in these concluding essays, with no apologies offered by the writers. Moreover, the fundamental desire in Minnelli's films to not only express one's self in a solitary fashion but also to *perform,* to entertain, and to place one's body, gestures, and voice on display, informs a number of these final essays. In a new essay written for this volume, "Brushstrokes in CinemaScope: Minnelli's Action Painting in *Lust for Life,*" Scott Bukatman turns his attention to Minnelli's personal favorite of all of his films. But *Lust for Life*'s reputation has been checkered; it is a prestigious film (given its subject matter about a great artist, Vincent van Gogh) but is also frequently treated contemptuously by guardians of art history who regard the film (officially based on Irving Stone's romanticized novel) as a vulgar exercise trivializing Van Gogh's life and work. Rather than regard the film's melodramatic impulse as nothing more than a sign of its ties to Hollywood conventions, Bukatman more productively sees *Lust for Life* as engaging in a mythology of the artist strongly bound up with the 1950s. The film's emotional and visual intensity, while undoubtedly related to the film's status as a Hollywood melodrama, is one that Bukatman also links with a crucial historical moment preceding and surrounding the film's production: the fascination with American abstract expressionism, a movement crucial in the establishment of American art as a force with which to be reckoned during the postwar period. Citing the art critic Harold Rosenberg's argument that the abstract expressionists (epitomized by the Method actorish Jackson Pollock) were practicing a form of "action painting" in which the artwork became an event, a performance of grand gestures, Bukatman provocatively sees in *Lust for Life* a cinematic equivalent of such grand gestures. Minnelli's film wishes to capture the intense "physicality of the act of painting." As portrayed by Kirk Douglas, the version of Van Gogh the film offers is a kind of "American in Paris," a violent, inarticulate, childlike, and contradictory figure. Van Gogh is at once an "idler" and someone fanatically devoted to work, but work that is aestheticized, turned into spectacle and grand gestures.

My own essay "Medium-Shot Gestures: Vincente Minnelli and *Some Came Running*" is, as its title implies, devoted to less grandiose physical matters. This is the second of three essays in this book that performs a close analysis of a single Minnelli film. Rather than make large thematic, cultural, or formalist claims for Minnelli I have chosen instead to call attention to a typical instance of Minnelli's handling of a "minor" sequence, in this instance a brief early one from *Some Came Running,* with very little of his trademark visual fireworks. Without denying any of Minnelli's formal brilliance or ability to dazzle the spectator, I argue here for a certain subtlety of expression in terms of Minnelli's mise-en-scène. In particular, I focus on the role of gesture and on Minnelli's direction of actors, a largely neglected topic in the literature on this director. Refuting the cliché that Minnelli (in the words of Jacques Rivette) "neglects the actor" I call attention to the ingenious ways in which Minnelli frames his performers and stages his action in a sequence that might otherwise appear to possess little of his trademark visual flair. Minnelli practices, through its various subtleties and nuances, what has essentially become a lost art in the mise-en-scène of much of contemporary cinema.

In "Minnelli in Double System," Emmanuel Burdeau does a close analysis of the "She's Not Thinking of Me" sequence from another 1958 Minnelli film, *Gigi*. But whereas I concerned myself with the more localized elements of Minnelli's mise-en-scène, Burdeau addresses a larger concept. This brief, suggestive essay points to another kind of modernism in Minnelli's work, one tied not only to literature but also to cinema and its capacity for reproducing mechanisms of thought, through language (spoken or written) and through the image. The song being performed here is ideal for such explorations, as it largely assumes a type of monologue, first interior then exterior, in lyric form, as Louis Jourdan's Gaston goes to Maxim's with his mistress, played by Eva Gabor. As she waves at and flirts with unseen others across the room, we hear

Gaston's thoughts on the soundtrack as he recites the lyrics that are overtly about thought itself, his own (which he states clearly) and those of his mistress (which he imagines). Burdeau sees here an "exactly Proustian formula," one defined by "reverie or absence." In effect, *Gigi*, a film of sumptuous images, presents us with a "fracturing of cinema." Gaston's monologue is "a real-time critique, a reading of the image, and already the outline of an analysis." For Burdeau, the song is "the signature of a divided age of the visible, from which we still may not have completely emerged."

Whereas scholars such as Gerstner and Naremore have examined the influence of New York City modernism on Minnelli's work, Murray Pomerance uses this same urban space for a somewhat different aim. In "Style, Calculation, and Counterpoint in *The Clock*," written for this volume, Pomerance looks at Minnelli's first nonmusical film, set in New York, but shot entirely (aside from second-unit work) on MGM soundstages. Minnelli's facility with his mobile camera and the camera boom in *The Clock* has long been noted. But Pomerance moves beyond a formalist analysis to take in larger matters of spatial perception and knowledge. For Pomerance, *The Clock* treats New York as at once a precise geographical urban world (one with which Minnelli was well acquainted) and a space of myth, a method of looking at the world with which Minnelli was equally knowledgeable. In *The Clock*, New York becomes a type of playground for its protagonists, Alice and Joe, but one in which play is comprised of both aleatory and competitive games. This sets into motion a vision of New York in which its spaces are rational and ordered but also vertiginous and dreamlike. The latter impulse leads to an "often exaggerated, even intoxicated portrayal of places and citizens" with all of this "constituting a world of mask and trance." Pomerance does not, however, argue for the dominance of the latter over the former but instead argues that the film is equally attracted to both of these impulses, establishing "a counterpoint between style, desire, and feeling on the one hand and rational calculation, concern, and fear of chance on the other." One could, then, extend this argument about the film to a metaphoric reading of Minnelli's auteurist position within his entire body of work, perpetually torn between these two approaches, the modest studio craftsman of genre pieces and the deeply personal filmmaker attracted to chaos, excess, and bloodshed. As Pomerance accurately notes of *The Clock*, "The movie isn't an exercise in style; it is a statement about the importance of style."

In "The Immobile Journey of Helen Corbett," written for this volume, the Spanish critic and scholar Carlos Losilla examines another Minnelli film set in

New York City and made almost twenty years after *The Clock*, *The Courtship of Eddie's Father*. Treated condescendingly by Stephen Harvey, *The Courtship of Eddie's Father* is, in fact, one of Minnelli's finest works and, as much as the more obvious testament film *Two Weeks in Another Town*, a summation of Minnelli's cinema up through the early 1960s. The fluidity of genre in Minnelli is one that Losilla attributes to the director's status as a "postclassical" filmmaker, in which the "relationship to genres should necessarily end in terms of conflict, never harmony." *Courtship* is less a family comedy for Losilla than a late instance of a "comedy of remarriage" in which the conversation (so central to Stanley Cavell's arguments about romantic comedies of the 1930s and 1940s) gives way in Minnelli to arguments and heated debates, particularly in the scenes between Elizabeth (neighbor and best friend of the recently deceased Helen Corbett, mother of Eddie) and Tom (Eddie's father), which invariably end on a note of anger and bitterness. The child Eddie functions not as an obedient pupil but as a teacher to these bickering adults, particularly in the film's extraordinary final sequence, "one of the most *modern* from the '60s." Eddie is not precocious, however, and his presence is not entirely comic. Losilla links Minnelli with filmmakers such as Rossellini and François Truffaut in his concern with "the psychology of the infantile mind racked by pain." While Minnelli is for Losilla "the most classical of the postclassical directors" he is also "the most mannerist," obsessed with his own survival among the "ruins" of classical cinema. Minnelli's later films, like the later films of Sirk and Hitchcock, form a type of necrophilic cinema, dominated by ghosts and by relations between the dead and the living.

The complex relationship of Minnelli's films to classical cinema is also central to the Australian critic and scholar Adrian Martin's "The Impossible Musical," written for this volume. Here Martin tackles Minnelli's final musical, *On a Clear Day You Can See Forever*. If Minnelli's films had always existed in an uneasy relationship with the forms and ideologies of the classical Hollywood cinema from which they emerged, his films after 1960 are particularly striking instances of this uneasiness. For Martin, *Clear Day* is a "nervous" film, trying very hard to not be "old-fashioned." In the process, it becomes an "impossible" musical, full of "surface oddities" in its search for more modern modes of generic expression. The fluid, mobile frames and extended takes of Minnelli's earlier films make way here for a comparatively rapid cutting rate, an unusually heavy (for Minnelli) use of shot/reverse shot for dialogue scenes, and his signature cranes and tracking shots now either replaced by or coexisting with an insistent use of the zoom lens. At the center of the film is a narrative that has more in common with films about "unsynchronized" lovers who never seem to inhabit the same spaces of reality at the same time than it does with other musicals. Its male protagonist, Marc Chabot, is in love with a woman who is already dead, a previous incarnation of his current patient, Daisy Gamble. (In this manner, it is another instance of the necrophilic element of late Minnelli already isolated by Losilla.) *Clear Day* is a film in which its lovers never sing together. Its dominant musical form is the soliloquy (such a central form to *Gigi*, also written by Alan Jay Lerner) in which musical expression no longer (as it still continues to do in the transitional *Gigi*) circulates among couples or ensembles. Instead, the songs repeatedly enact "every manifestation of split and nonalignment between, and even within, the characters." The film is, by its very nature and structure, doomed to failure, to lack of fulfillment. Nevertheless, such a "failure" is also part of the film's fascination as it "lays out its problems while deliberately not resolving them." If a central element to Minnelli's cinema has always been "the difficulty of the central problem to be solved," then *Clear Day* represents a particularly striking late instance of this tendency.

This book closes with three essays that return us to the French. These essays were first published as part of a dossier on Minnelli in *Trafic* in 2005. The dossier appeared in the aftermath of an enormously successful retrospective of Minnelli's films at the Centre Pompidou in December of 2004 and January of 2005. (Burdeau refers to the series in passing in his essay.) *Positif* also published a dossier on Minnelli during this period, and Douchet spoke at the Pompidou (as did Bellour and Burdeau) and was interviewed by the French press in relation to the series. There had been other retrospectives of Minnelli's films in Paris in the preceding decades, but the Pompidou seemed to announce his reputation on an unprecedented scale, bringing about a significant revival of interest in his work. (The differences in the lackluster American response to Minnelli's films in the aftermath of the MoMA series and the more recent one at the Pompidou are striking in this regard.) The final essays in this book, while emerging out of a certain (largely French) tradition of looking at Minnelli also propose some new ways of examining the director's work.

In "*Ars gratia artis*: Notes on Minnelli's Poetics," the philosopher Jacques Rancière explores the relationship between art and entertainment, explicitly treated in *The Band Wagon* but a relationship that implicitly underlies Minnelli's entire body of work. Rancière does not state this here but his essay on Minnelli may be placed within his larger investigation into the notion of the "cinematic fable." Unlike the traditional fable, Aristotelian logic does not dominate the cinematic fable even if this fable still retains important links with the notion of a well-constructed tale. As Tom Conley has written in relation to Rancière, in the cinematic fable "the art of the *aftereffect*" is one that goes "against the grain of the prevailing narrative logic." Furthermore, these aftereffects "surge forth from the relation that the cinema gives itself to be, a relation with other arts but especially with stories and situations it inherits and recasts."[32] In this regard, Rancière does not argue for absolute distinctions between art and entertainment in Minnelli. On the contrary, we find here art's "absolute identification with entertainment," a world in which art, entertainment, and theatricality are always fundamentally tied to one another. Jeffrey Cordova is a negative figure in *The Band Wagon* not because he tries to combine art and entertainment but because he wants to make a *show* of it; whereas Minnelli's identification is with the "wandering players," those figures "who don't need to be told that Shakespeare was one of their own because they've always known it." Rancière is the second major French philosopher, following Gilles Deleuze, to write on Minnelli. In *Cinema 2: The Time-Image* (published in France in 1985) Deleuze addresses the "plurality of worlds" in Minnelli, in which dance is "not simply movement of the world, but passage from one world into another, entry into another world, breaking in and exploring."[33] For Deleuze, "musical comedy has never come as close to a mystery of memory, of dream and of time, as a point of indiscernibity of the real and the imaginary, as in Minnelli."[34] For Rancière, however, the opposition between dream and reality in Minnelli is "nothing other than the pleasure of the theater," dedicated as it is to "role changes, double meanings, and sudden reversals of fortune." Against those who see in Minnelli's protagonists a dreaming passivity, a world devoted to the mystery of memory, dream, and of time, Rancière argues that in these films it is "the ability to take matters in hand" that makes the difference.

The title of Raymond Bellour's "Panic" suggests a return to the notion of hysteria in Minnelli that so interested psychoanalytic critics in the 1970s and 1980s. But a psychoanalytic reading is not what Bellour produces. The panic being isolated here is one that is (like Rancière's "aftereffect") something that is "independent of the story," an aesthetic and emotional principle that both constructs and undermines Minnelli's entire body of work. For Bellour, panic is "the difference in the charges carried by two dreams suddenly rendered visible and more striking," a moment that passes "beyond all realism." Where can this panic be found? It can be found in "the body of an actress," such as the way that Deborah Kerr in *Tea and Sympathy* "transmits her feelings like a photographic emulsion," at times suggesting that her body would like to "break out of the limits of the frame." But it may also be found in the nervous and expressive treatment of light in *Undercurrent* and *The Bad and the Beautiful,* or in the strange, accelerating or receding camera movements of *Meet Me in St. Louis* and *Some Came Running.* Bellour vividly offers what is, in effect, a type of cinephilic reading of Minnelli, seizing moments outside of their immediate narrative function and instead fixating, in a highly subjective manner, on the physical or on the sensuous surface of things. Such a reading entails seeing the films as also being (and here we implicitly return to Douchet and the allegorical critical climate of the 1960s) about the fundamental nature of cinema itself. *Brigadoon,* strongly dominated by its own elements of panic and a "radical will to enchantment," becomes a work in which "the myth of cinema" is inscribed in the film as a whole; a film in which a community only comes alive once every hundred years in order to avoid being significantly affected by the upheavals of any century. We are in a world of "time without temporality," a world of "suspended time that is intrinsic to cinema."

For our final essay, we return to Emmanuel Burdeau. "Minnelli's Messages" proposes a number of different and provocative new ways for discussing Minnelli. First, Burdeau draws attention to the importance of the soundtrack in order to "indicate how hearing actually creates the image." Burdeau notes the importance of the voice in Minnelli, both "inside and outside of the shot," and the frequency with which Minnelli's films open with vocal situations, announcements, addresses. A Minnelli film is often one that is telephoned or marionetted, a world in which "listening is exposed in its pure state." As Minnelli's work develops, this act of listening becomes increasingly central until it almost completely dominates the structure of his last two films. But Burdeau also expands upon and rethinks the notion of the dream as articulated in the work of Douchet and Deleuze. For Burdeau, the Minnellian dream begins with the woman's stated desire to escape, a call the man answers. However, the dream does not so much close "like a trap" on the man once he enters the woman's dream as become (and here there is a link back with Losilla's essay) a type of dialogue between two dreaming individuals, an exchange. In fact, every Minnelli dream "must have two poles, female reverie and masculine hallucination."

Let us briefly return, then, to Tacy and Nicky Collini. What is Tacy's dream of her long, long trailer but literally a dream of escape, transformation, mobility? But is this dream also a dialogue between female reverie and masculine hallucination? If hallucination in this instance can be stretched to include

masculine hysteria or panic (since these are Nicky's dominant modes of behavior throughout the film), then yes. I would not, however, want to completely lose the concept (first articulated by Douchet) of at least the *desire* for
dominance on the part of one character, one dreamer over another in so many
of these films. The notion of the dream as a dialogue has enormous possibilities. But in closing, I also want to underline and reemphasize how often this
dialogue in Minnelli is a violent one, especially when it occurs between male
and female. "How is it that you cannot stand the sight of blood on anyone but
me?" asks Mike of his wife Mirella in *Designing Woman*. She cannot answer
the question. I hope that this collection will likewise lead to further questions
as well as to further analysis, debate, and dialogue on the films of Vincente
Minnelli . . . but no bloodshed.

Notes

1. James Naremore, *The Films of Vincente Minnelli* (New York: Cambridge University Press, 1993), 110.

2. Cited and translated by Bill Krohn in "Specters at the Feast: French Viewpoints
on Minnelli's Comedies," reprinted in this volume.

3. Naremore, *Films of Vincente Minnelli*, 110.

4. G. Cabrera Infante, *A Twentieth Century Job*, trans. Kenneth Hall and G. Cabrera
Infante (London: Faber and Faber, 1991), 115.

5. It should be noted that in Italy at this time, Adriano Aprá was also writing on
Minnelli and in terms not dissimilar to those of French critics. See this volume's
bibliography.

6. Mark Shivas, "Minnelli's Method," *Movie* 1 (June 1962): 17.

7. James Agee, *Agee on Film*, vol. 1 (New York: Perigee Books, 1958), 127.

8. Agee, *Agee on Film*, 1:358.

9. André Bazin, "On the *politique des auteurs*," trans. Peter Graham, in *Cahiers du
cinéma, the 1950s*, ed. Jim Hillier (Cambridge, MA: Harvard University Press, 1985), 249.

10. This relationship of *Two Weeks in Another Town* to European art cinema of the
1960s is the subject of a chapter in my book *The Death of Classical Cinema: Hitchcock,
Lang, Minnelli* (Albany: State University of New York Press, 2006), 141–200.

11. Jean Douchet, *L'art d'aimer* (Paris: Petite bibliothèque des Cahiers du cinéma,
2003), 11.

12. Jean-Louis Comolli et al., "Twenty Years On: A Discussion about American
Cinema and the politique des auteurs," in *Cahiers du cinéma, the 1960s*, ed. Jim Hillier
(Cambridge, MA: Harvard University Press, 1986), 201.

13. See Jim Hillier's discussion of this in *Cahiers du cinéma, the 1960s*, 15–17.

14. See Hillier's discussion of the importance of the director interview in *Cahiers du
cinéma, the 1950s*, 77.

15. Charles Higham and Joel Greenberg, *The Celluloid Muse: Hollywood Directors
Speak* (Chicago: Regnery, 1969), 13.

16. Thomas Elsaesser, "Too Big and Too Close: Alfred Hitchcock and Fritz Lang," *Hitchcock Annual* (2003–4): 15.

17. Richard Schickel, *The Men Who Made the Movies* (New York: Atheneum, 1975), 265.

18. Andrew Sarris, *The American Cinema: Directors and Directions, 1929–1968* (New York: E. P. Dutton, 1968), 102. Sarris's position on Minnelli has become more generous over the years. See, for example, his entry on the musical in *You Ain't Heard Nothin' Yet: The American Talking Film, History and Memory, 1927–1949* (New York: Oxford University Press, 1998), 54–58.

19. Donald Knox, *The Magic Factory: How MGM Made* An American in Paris (New York: Praeger, 1973), xvii.

20. In his autobiography, undoubtedly stinging after Knox's marginalizing of his work on *An American in Paris,* Minnelli writes: "Some erudite types point to *An American in Paris* as the perfect example of the studio-as-auteur theory. I disagree . . . Though I don't minimize anyone's contributions, one man was responsible for bringing it all together. That man was me." Vincente Minnelli, with Hector Arce, *I Remember It Well* (Garden City, NY: Doubleday, 1974), 228–29.

21. George Morris, "One Kind of Dream: George Morris on *A Matter of Time,*" *Film Comment* 12, no. 6 (1976): 21.

22. Jean-Pierre Coursodon, with Pierre Sauvage, *American Directors,* vol. 2 (New York: McGraw-Hill), 233.

23. Sarris, *American Cinema,* 101.

24. Nowell-Smith's essay should ideally be read in tandem with Elsaesser's classic text on 1950s Hollywood melodrama, "Tales of Sound and Fury," written in 1972. Elsaesser's essay raises a number of the same points, albeit in more extended form. See Thomas Elsaesser, "Tales of Sound and Fury," in *Movies and Methods,* vol. 2, ed. Bill Nichols (Berkeley: University of California Press, 1985), 165–94.

25. For an excellent analysis of the film in these terms, see Beth Genné's "Vincente Minnelli's Style in Microcosm: The Establishing Sequence of *Meet Me in St. Louis,*" *Art Journal* 43 (Fall 1983): 247–54.

26. Andrew Britton, *Katharine Hepburn: Star as Feminist* (New York: Continuum, 1995), 34.

27. I have argued elsewhere that this is an instance of how both *The Band Wagon* and *Two Weeks in Another Town* draw upon Freudian and Faustian master narratives. See McElhaney, *Death of Classical Cinema,* 183–85.

28. Far more critical appraisals of the film and of Naremore's approach may be found in Arthur Knight's *Disintegrating the Musical: Black Performance and American Musical Film* (Durham, NC: Duke University Press, 2002), especially pp. 147–58; and Adam Knee's "Doubling, Music, and Race in *Cabin in the Sky,*" in *Representing Jazz,* ed. Krin Gabbard (Durham, NC: Duke University Press, 1995), 193–204. See also Todd Boyd's commentary track on the *Cabin the Sky* DVD. Boyd cannot stop pointing out what he perceives to be the film's racial stereotyping. My own responses to these later readings of the film would be too complicated to address here.

29. At least two biographies of Judy Garland have claimed that Minnelli was homo-

sexual and that his marriage to Garland was little more than a pretext. (Where this claim leaves Minnelli's three subsequent marriages is unclear.)

30. Minnelli's queer sensibility is also the subject of a chapter in Matthew Tinkcom's *Working Like a Homosexual: Camp, Capital, Cinema* (Durham, NC: Duke University Press, 2002), in which Minnelli is situated alongside of the explicitly homosexual filmmakers Andy Warhol, Kenneth Anger, and John Waters. Tinkcom, while placing greater emphasis on camp as a type of modernist philosophy than Gerstner, follows Gerstner in his interpretation of the queer sensibility at work in Minnelli, especially in *Ziegfeld Follies, Yolanda and the Thief,* and *The Pirate.*

31. In a classic early text of gay film scholarship, Parker Tyler writes of *Tea and Sympathy:* "Besides being archaic, the film is a prodigiously silly fable, pulling the realities with which it deals dishonestly, systematically out of whack." Parker Tyler, *Screening the Sexes: Homosexuality in the Movies* (New York: Holt Rinehart and Winston, 1972), 249. For a contemporary (and largely negative) account of the film from a gay critic, see Richard Barrios, *Screened Out: Playing Gay in Hollywood from Edison to Stonewall* (New York: Routledge, 2005), 240–45.

32. Tom Conley, "A Fable of Film: Rancière's Anthony Mann," *SubStance* 33, no. 1 (2004): 92–93.

33. Gilles Deleuze, *Cinema 2: The Time-Image,* trans. Hugh Tomlinson and Robert Galeta (Minneapolis: University of Minnesota Press, 1991), 63.

34. Deleuze, *Cinema 2,* 64.

I

MINNELLI IN THE 1960S:
THE RISE AND FALL OF AN AUTEUR

The Red and the Green
The Four Horsemen of the Apocalypse

JEAN DOUCHET
TRANSLATED BY BILL KROHN

Far from clearing up the misunderstanding that hangs over the oeuvre of Vincente Minnelli, the release of *The Four Horsemen of the Apocalypse* will only worsen it. This is nothing to be shocked about—it would be shocking if the opposite had happened. *The Four Horsemen of the Apocalypse*, in fact, is this filmmaker's most important film to date, one that sums up the whole oeuvre by consciously recalling earlier films (*An American in Paris, Gigi, Some Came Running, Home from the Hill, Bells Are Ringing*). It sums up and surpasses what went before, as *Vertigo*, for example, does for Hitchcock, or *The Tiger of Eschnapur* for Fritz Lang. To understand this film, then, is to penetrate the whole oeuvre of a filmmaker wrongly considered to be a minor one whose talent is confined to comedies and musicals.

First of all, the only elements Minnelli has kept from the novel by Vicente Blasco Ibáñez, previously filmed by Rex Ingram, are those that will feed his own reverie, a uniquely poetic reverie that produces a purely fantastic film—taking "fantastic" to mean, of course, an intimate comprehension of things and events, the only true realism that is possible.

Those who are not prepared to follow the internal evolution of this reverie —and they are legion, even if, in the best cases, they do appreciate the decorative and pictorial qualities of the marvelous spectacle they are being offered— will criticize the filmmaker, who collaborated closely on the adaptation and dialogue, for the liberties he has taken with the novel, if only by transposing it to the last war. By the same token, they will reproach, in the name of an art of verisimilitude, the implausibilities—or what seem to them to be implausibilities—in the re-creation of the Resistance and of Paris under the Occupation. What must be understood is that Minnelli has in fact sought to paint a very truthful portrait of the period—but it is a truth seen from within. *The Four Horsemen* is the opposite of reportage. It is a meditation on the dreams that impel men to act.

Which explains why the scenes from newsreels (Nazi meetings, aerial squadrons, bombardments, etc.) are shattered, anamorphosed, vividly colored—in short, dismembered like cubist Picassos. Visible reality is willfully denied. Documents are no longer used as documents, but as instruments of unreality and fantasy. Only their internal, poetic significance interests Minnelli. Moreover, the period re-creation that he undertakes is shaped by a parti pris. He deliberately ignores the material hardships of the Occupation—the problem of provisions is barely touched on (Uncle Mark, a German general, offers Julio a car and gasoline; Marguerite comes home with a sack of food)—and he never even bothers to show a line of people waiting in front of a store. Yet when he paints certain historical scenes with scrupulous care (Notre Dame protected by sandbags, the race to take shelter during an air-raid alert, the blackout, the exodus of 1940, Nazi troops marching down the Champs-Élysées, the famous image of the crying Frenchman who was, we know, the symbol for America of defeated France, students being rounded up, scenes of resistance and prison, etc.), it's because they correspond to his inner reverie.

That reverie proceeds from a schizophrenic vision of the world. (Having decided to film the life of a painter, the great colorist of filmmakers headed straight for Van Gogh.) Which is to say that it is fed by a passionate quest for a dream impelled by fear of reality—for the artist, seeking a refuge to protect himself from the world is an absolute necessity. Shut up in himself, he observes reality all the better through the slits in his ivory tower. Withdrawn within his universe, detached from other people, *neutral,* he watches and notes with exactitude and in the smallest detail the agitation of the world he perceives without participating in it. In this sense, and only in this sense, is Minnelli a great realist.

But this attitude, by turns satiric, fantastic, or dramatic, betrays a suffering born from the sharp, heightened consciousness of total solitude experienced to the fullest, and the deep disturbance this provokes. To defeat these inner demons and find his balance, the artist has to bring the violent, intimate conflict of dream and reality into his work. He has to leave his refuge and confront his enemy, reality, in order to negate it. Through his art, Minnelli intends to transform the world into his dream. He refuses the world as it is, but invents another decor for it, an ideal shell of splendor and beauty.

In that decor, he imagines characters whose lives unfold with a clarity and precision of line that are all the sharper because of the almost Martian distance he occupies with respect to them, thanks to his own schizophrenic tendencies. But he imagines them as different from what they are. Cut off from others, he is obliged to re-create them from without, as he re-creates the world, by minutely copying what he observes. All the meticulous care expended in refining the many infinitesimal touches that characterize Minnelli's oeuvre and way of working makes him one of the most faithful painters, one of the most impartial critics of man and contemporary society.

But it also betrays the inner laceration of the artist who cannot capture the true nature of the beings moving under his gaze because he is obliged to project his own sentiments and inner drama onto them. Which is why he always puts them in a situation that evokes his own conflict. Each Minnelli character pursues, in effect, an inner dream: For the characters, that dream—a futile one in the comedies, a wondrous one in the musicals, an intense one in the melodramas—is essential. It is more than their raison d'être —it is their very existence.

Hence the need each character feels to give flesh to his dream. Each wishes to surround himself with a decor that bears the mark of what he is, of what he loves, of what he desires, of his deepest aspirations. That decor becomes his domain and his refuge from reality. But what value can a shelter have that has been constructed from the materials of the enemy? To do that is to put himself at the enemy's mercy, to feel the permanent anguish of the dream's fragility, and therefore of life's fragility. Unless he protects the decor from time and space by letting his dream swallow him up, giving himself entirely to its enchanted domain (*Brigadoon*), or allows the world to invade the decor and watches impotently while it is being laid waste (*Father of the Bride*), the Minnelli character tends, by his actions, to preserve his decor and his dream from reality—a futile act, in any event, as the melodramas prove, where reality triumphs and makes dreams and decors collapse. As the comedies also prove, where only an ironic ending leaves the characters, at least provisionally, in possession of the decor. And as the musicals prove, where the marvelous realizes dreams and delivers the characters from reality. Is the refusal to act, absolute neutrality like Julio's (Glenn Ford) in *The Four Horsemen*, a solution? Certainly not. "I suppose no one is helped by being deceived, and yet how comforting it is for a while!" says Marguerite (Ingrid Thulin) to Julio in the park of Versailles, a political decor conceived by a king to protect himself from reality, which reality one day invaded, destroying both king and decor.

What Minnelliesque face does this terrible reality wear? How does this snake, as Madariaga, the Old One (Lee J. Cobb) calls it, present itself, "which nothing can keep from slipping into a garden,"[1] like Julio's car, gliding through the Norman countryside, breaking through the best guarded barriers to sow destruction and death in the home of his cousin Heinrich (Karl Boehm)? In the simplest and most pernicious way imaginable: as a dream. *Reality is the dream of others, but it is also one's own dream.* (When it comes to describing the evolution of this inner reverie, *The Long, Long Trailer* is the exemplary Minnelli film.) How could it be otherwise? Each man wishes to fulfill his being and make his dream a reality. He therefore projects it into the world, remakes his environment in his own image and materializes all that in an appropriate decor. But when the dream assumes a *body*, it finds itself for this very reason subjected to contingency. That body can be destroyed by other bodies. (In Minnelli, we see decors ravage other decors, like the trailer devastating the garden and home of Lucille Ball and Desi Arnaz's family, or the unhappy encounter of the worlds of boxing and haute couture in *Designing Woman*, etc.). It can even be reduced and demoted, literally, to being *just* a body.

This is how the portrayal of the Occupation of Paris in *The Four Horsemen* must be understood. Paris is first seen as a decorative element, scintillating with light and color, vibrating with joyous laughter: Julio's drive down the Champs-Élysées, views of the Place de la Concorde. The Nazis take the same route when they arrive in Paris. But in the first sequence Julio belongs to the decor—he is its soul. In the second, a naked body is being violated. Paris becomes the frame for the birth of an ideal love, realizing the intimate dream of Julio, which Minnelli considers the greatest of all dreams, since it is the perfect communion of two beings, two dreams. That dream, because it is profound and true, will be able to retract and hide in Julio's apartment, sheltered from the first decor, Paris; but it won't escape from the reality that has invaded Paris, taking possession of that first decor, eating away at the dream, beginning the slow, inevitable process of disintegration and death.

Because the Nazi dream, collective and *uniform,* elaborated in meetings held in Hitler's scarlet lair, unfurls over Europe, destroying town after town, decor after decor. Now we can understand why the stock-shots have been deformed—their supposed objectivity documents a reality that originates, in fact, in the maddest dream humanity has ever known. And why the newsreel scenes Minnelli reenacts always show people whose decor is in danger, carrying pieces of furniture and familiar objects away with them—in an absurd ballet that leads nowhere and seems to go in circles, since no refuge is possible when the entire decor of a country has collapsed—and finally watching, stupefied or with a steady gaze like Marguerite, the taking of Paris. This also explains why the first shot of those reenacted scenes is a view of Notre Dame, the city's heart and supreme refuge, the poetic equivalent, on the level of a city, of Julio's apartment—Notre Dame protected by sandbags, a shelter that is in need of shelter from reality unleashed. And finally, it explains Minnelli's refusal to evoke the material problems of the period. In his films, man does not live by bread alone. He is nourished by dreams, and devoured by them.

The Nazi dream takes hold of Paris like a decor emptied of the dream that conceived it, a body that it can do with as it wishes, just as general von Kleist, commandant of Paris, and therefore of the decor, intends to possess Parisian women, elements of the decor, without their permission ("When I want a woman, I make no demand that she want me," he says, showing his epaulet: "My charm resides here.") He sets his cap for Marguerite, who is dancing with Julio because she hoped, by coming to this soiree, to relive the happiness of their first meeting, of the era before the war, when Paris was a jewel case for their intimacy. But that's impossible now. The Nazi dream has strewn the decor of her dream with the decor of its uniforms. The meaning of Paris has changed. The city of true love has become the city of vile love (which corresponds to a historic truth: In their insane dream Hitler and his thugs, had they won, would have made France, and principally Paris, a brothel for their elite troops). At the same time Marguerite has become just an object of desire. This whole scene, one of the most terrifying in the film, repays on close analysis: how all these Parisians, attached to their old way of life, watch one another in fear of being dispossessed of it; how Julio, who is "the commandant of a somewhat larger region" than the general, confronts reality for the first time; how and why Heinrich saves him. All the later scenes of Nazi receptions, or the shot where Julio, going to join the Resistance, passes a bunch of soldiers tormenting some girls under the steady gaze of two children, accentuate this degradation of a decor that is produced by a moral degradation, culminating in a scene of orgy and prostitution that sickens the hero. The camera leaves Julio's gaze and, moving up to his brow, like a petition to heaven, dissolves to the news of the death of Chi-Chi (Yvette Mimieux), a little modern Antigone who refuses to sacrifice the soul of her dream and becomes a symbol of the Resistance.[2]

The Resistance is seen, in effect, in *The Four Horsemen*, as the urgent necessity of saving the decor. More precisely, as the absolute need to liberate a decor that has been invaded by another decor: the Nazi uniforms. A liberation that is destined to fail, for in this film Minnelli describes his anguish at being confronted by a reality that is always present, always menacing, which surrounds and suffocates him as surely as the Germans closing in on the rebellious students, or inversely, the Parisians encircling the Nazi officer's burning car after the assassination. The fight against reality that no one can avoid is a war of attrition that is lost in advance, leading inevitably to death. As soon as one cannot seek refuge in one's dream, being obliged to fight against assaults from the outside either to impose it or preserve it, an implacable process has begun: Defeating or resisting reality secretes new realities that must, in turn, be combated. Thus, in the very place where they have taken refuge, we see Resistance fighters endlessly making German uniforms. Action leads to action, then to the dream of that action, a dream that creates new realities to nourish its desire for action.

In its inexorable race, life itself engenders the Four Horsemen of the Apocalypse, whose names are Conquest, War, Pestilence, and Death. In Minnelli's vision, living means conquering the world to shape it in the image of one's dream by means of a decor. This necessarily means taking from others, through theft or destruction, the very nature of their own dream; it also means waging constant war against the conquering reality of others' dreams, which encircle and threaten our own. Julio, who has conquered Marguerite and taken her from the decor of her husband, can boast of his "neutrality." But it will be impossible for him not to confront, in his turn, the world, and learn about reality and its violence. This external process of destruction is followed by an internal process of self-destruction. The fundamental need Minnelli's characters feel to make their dream real leads inevitably to its degradation and something like its pestilence. Little by little, each one loses the intensity that gave birth to his dream, forgets its quality and satisfies himself by enjoying just its decor, ends up preferring the body to the soul, and, killing the spirit, sows gangrene. In this refuge that each constructs with the stones of his dreams to protect himself, he finds himself trapped and finally entombed. The dream closes back up on itself and carries the one who conceived it to his death. That is the terrible revelation suddenly experienced by Madariaga, the Old One, who has given life and who now realizes that all life is a dream that wages war with other dreams and ultimately destroys itself.

It's enough to open one's eyes to this admirable spectacle to see how Minnelli has "realized" his reverie on Life. Since decors are the materialization of dreams, they should live the life of dreams and come to life as dreams do. This becomes the dynamic role of color: red, gold, green. In these colors, dreamed for their affective and symbolic value (red corresponding to conquest and war, green to degradation and death, the brilliant gold of Madariaga's great scene contrasted with the gold leaf of the decors where the two uncles live, etc.), we watch the slow, inevitable destruction of a decor.

TRANSLATOR'S NOTES

1. In the English dialogue: "Where is the garden where the snake has not come?"

2. Douchet's description does not completely correspond with the sequence he is describing as it appears in the film. During two parts of the sequence Ford's eyes are superimposed over a montage of the gala, intercut in the second part with explosions. Out of the explosions come the Four Horsemen, and the scene dissolves to Lukas's office, where Boyer announces that Chi-Chi has been sent to a labor camp—not that she is dead. Her death is not announced until the end of the sequence. The movement of the camera during the gala sequence (although this is mostly an effect of montage) is pulling back and up, until the last shots of the crowd are from a very high angle—maybe that's what he intended to describe.

I checked the text against the version that was published in the *Cahiers,* and there's no difference. Perhaps it was misprinted there and never corrected, or perhaps Jean just misremembered.

Additional translator's note: In the "Conseil des dix" for March of 1962 and, apart from Henri Agel and Jean-Louis Bory, who gave it three, Douchet, who gave it four, was the film's only fan. Political critics Louis Marcorelles and Georges Sadoul gave it one star; Eric Rohmer, two; and Jacques Rivette, a black ball: "Initule de se deranger."

Two Weeks in Another Town

JEAN DOUCHET
TRANSLATED BY BILL KROHN

Since it is the subject of *Two Weeks in Another Town,* let's talk about cinema. "Every great film," wrote Eric Rohmer, "is a documentary." He meant that a film only draws its force from the truth of its description of characters and milieu—that it should inform us perfectly about the functioning of the latter to teach us everything about the former. Minnelli's last film meets that requirement—it faithfully portrays the fauna of Hollywood, uprooted from its natural setting and obliged to obey the hard laws of economic evolution by trying to maintain its way of living, feeling and dreaming in a very different setting ("in another town") and trying to make the films from which it cannot—hence its pain and alienation—detach itself. *Two Weeks* bears witness to a very contemporary phenomenon of American cinema (cf. our last issue),[1] and criticizes it.

But there is more. The term *documentary* immediately evokes films that objectively record the processes of life: the inorganic life of minerals; the organic life of vegetables, animals, and men; and also the mechanical "life" of machines, made by men. The idea of transformation is important, then: the passage from state A to state B—in a word, evolution. The idea of evolution seems to correspond to the fundamental nature of cinema (much better than the idea of movement, which is too vague, not specific to cinema—for instance, dance—and the cause of numerous aberrations: "pure" cinema, montage cinema). For however we envision cinema, it can have but one object: life. To capture it at its source, reveal its tremors, trace its course, seize it at the moment it expires—that is the unique and noble mission of the documentary. It requires respect, humility, and intimate, almost loving understanding of the thing being looked at. It condemns all speculation on the part of the looker— tampering with the film and the camera, blocking the screen—who denies the Other, the better to affirm himself at that Other's expense. The fact remains, then, that documentary and cinema are one.

Where does this leave us? With this observation: A great film, even if it comes from the realm of pure fiction, cannot dispense with the documentary aspect inherent in the art of cinema. Inherent, because the documentary solidity (verified by various sciences) of works like *The Odyssey,* the Bible, the romances of the Round Table, or even *The Thousand and One Nights* and *Don Quixote*—I am deliberately citing only works with mythical heroes and stories —is the best guarantee of their universal popularity, and therefore of their truth, if universality can be considered the best criterion of aesthetic value. But who doesn't see that there is a difference? Literature describes reality by transposing it to re-create it, obliging the artist to invent metaphor (for example, "Celluloid and Marble" by Eric Rohmer). Whereas cinema records the reality offered to its gaze; it constrains the artist to submit completely to the thing and its development. All that is required of him is to find, intuitively and immediately, the sap that has formed the bark. The miracle of cinema is that the camera films this mysterious current, this inner movement that produces the outward appearance of the thing, its bark.

A consequence of this: Filming man objectively implies that the filmmaker must at the same time show all the evolutionary stages leading to man. Every great film is all the more a documentary because it is all possible documentaries at once. *Two Weeks* proves this. First, it is a documentary about man. Both his life in society (reflecting that of a particular group, accurately portrayed in its particularities), and the life of the social machine, its functioning, its mechanics, and the oeuvre that it constrains man, who is in conflict with it, to produce by his labor.

But it is also an animal documentary, because *everything,* in man's *physical* behavior (and this kind of documentary can only be concerned with physical behavior) derives from the animal. (So much so that we know of no great film that can't be transposed into the animal kingdom.) Look at *Two Weeks:* from the old, fallen lion, Edward G. Robinson, and the furious lioness, his wife, to the supple beauty of the panther who loves to claw (Cyd Charisse), all the inhabitants of this jungle struggle to hold onto their piece of power, their territory. The characters' looks, attitudes, gestures, their prowling and leaping, are animal reactions. The fact that the idea of territory turns out to be illusory and fanciful has to do with the superior side of man. This is his drama. Man, represented by the hero, has to learn to accept his evolution (and evolution in general), and therefore detach himself from all previous stages, in particular the animal stage, which is closest to him, characterized by the will to conquest and possession.

The documentary could also be transposed into the vegetable kingdom. The phenomena of plant life also find their correspondences in human life (beyond what we call "vegetative" life) in the realm of feeling—which, in Minnelli's films, depends on the milieu it is fed by. Just see how all these uprooted Hollywood characters try to remain rooted in the realm of cinema.

Finally, it is scarcely necessary to show, given the importance of the decor as a projection of the characters, how the documentary will also deal with the mineral side of man, lead or gold, steel or rotted wood. The fact that the characters of *Two Weeks* prefer their insubstantial movie sets, made of painted canvas and papier-mâché, to the sumptuously baroque stone of the Eternal City (Minnelli shows baroque forms as the last stage of the stone's evolution: its *explosion,* the very image of the violent inner movement that agitates the characters), is sufficient evidence of their weakness, seemingly masked by their cruelty. The only world they trust is an imaginary one with no foundations.

At the summit of an artist's evolution he no longer condenses the various stages of evolution in time but lays them out *in space*. The four realms are now side by side, and man evolves (*Tabu, Hatari! The River*), or learns to evolve (*The Tiger of Eschnapur, Sansho the Bailiff, Home from the Hill*) harmoniously, finally assuming that superiority that was so difficult for him at the beginning. Now evolution becomes a temporal problem. The past rears its head in the present, a present that is burying itself in the past. (This is the case with *Two Weeks.*) A future where man is or is not liberated from his shackles, permitting him to flower, depends on that struggle. The conflict in the script at the level of the individual affects the destiny of mankind. If the hero has to free himself from everything that keeps him from fulfilling himself, society too must denounce a rigid mentality that hinders its progress, and the species must finally detach itself from the prior species from which it evolved. Thus Kirk Douglas, when he exorcises his past, denounces a society (the one that makes cinematic products and the one that consumes them) attached to an outdated conception of man and art, offering in this way, through his "sacrifice," an opening for humanity.

Clearly this temporal problem of evolution, embodied in the form of a developmental curve and a journey, always runs headlong into fixity. The fascination of this fixity has to be vanquished. Kirk Douglas, by reintroducing movement in the mise-en-scène of the film he takes over in midproduction (a baroque movement like that of Rome, which he is the only one to have penetrated), hasn't solved his own problem. That is only a palliative. He has to travel back within himself to the source of the fixity that obsesses him (of which his wife is less the object than the pretext, the point of fixation); he has to rediscover his real aspiration: the refusal to live, death. He reaches that point when his wife, after playing "bar girl" to ensnare him, abandons him at the drug party. Now nothing can free him from his past and the temptation of immobility but a mad car ride, an excessive movement, the flux of life ensnaring the pernicious dream in turn and destroying it. Master of movement, he finishes his journey from Hollywood to Hollywood and lays the groundwork for his future and the future of others (the young actor), which is ours as well.

It's not astonishing, then, that this documentary cinema (the only one we love), after all these torments, sings the praises of madness. That is man's task today: to tear himself away from the attainments of the individual, of society, of the species itself in order to confront a future that provokes anxiety only because it contains (perhaps) the most astonishing promises for man's evolution. Every great film is a documentary on the courage and grandeur of madness, of human wisdom.

TRANSLATOR'S NOTE

1. Douchet is referring to *Cahiers du cinéma* 152, the American Cinema issue put out in January of 1964. This article must have sat in the drawer for a while. (I don't find any reference to the film in the Conseils des Dix, an odd omission.) The summing up of Douchet's "decor" theory appears in his Minnelli entry for the Dictionary in #152. Here he takes a new tack, which seems to be a reply to the two star rating Rohmer gave *Four Horsemen* two years earlier—Rohmer is quoted twice as the source of the aesthetic in the name of which Douchet is defending *Two Weeks*.

Specters at the Feast:
French Viewpoints on Minnelli's Comedies

BILL KROHN

WHEN HE CROSSED THE BRIDGE . . . ; OR,
HOW I CAME TO WRITE "SPECTERS AT THE FEAST"

In 1977 Jackie Raynal, who owned and managed two repertory cinemas in Manhattan with her husband Sid Geffen, invited her old friend Serge Daney, who was then editor-in-chief of *Cahiers du cinéma*, to hold a Semaine des Cahiers at the Bleecker Street Theatre in Greenwich Village. Not long before, I had noticed that whoever was programming the Bleecker was showing interesting double bills—for instance, *Nathalie Granger* and *Sherlock Jr.*—and asked a friend who knew people to arrange an introduction.

The three of us hit it off, and Sid and Jackie asked me to put together a little booklet to be handed out at screenings during the Semaine explaining what had become of the *Cahiers* after 1968. Except for quotes lifted from *Cahiers* reviews of the films being shown, the contents of that booklet are all available online at Steve Erickson's Serge Daney Web site (http://home.earthlink .net/ steevee/), and the interview I did with Serge for it—twenty written questions, to which he supplied written answers—was eventually used as the introduction to the POL edition of his collected writings from the *Cahiers* period. Serge and I also became friends, and he asked me to be the American correspondent for *Cahiers*.

At the time I was supposed to be finishing my doctorate in English literature at the CUNY Graduate Center, and in my naïveté (Film Studies had not become the going concern it is today), I thought that such a publication might make me appear unserious in academic circles, where I was already viewed as something of a "creative risk." So I used a pen name I had devised for my first critical pieces on Raoul Walsh and Terence Fisher in *Rear Window,* a mimeographed publication put out by Roger McNiven and Howard Mandelbaum, who had changed the name after selling the original one, *The Thousand Eyes,* to Sid and Jackie for a magazine they planned to publish in support of programming at their theaters. T. Leo French—for T. Leo Moore, the last great mayor my hometown, Electra, Texas, ever had, and "French," obviously, because I loved France—was shortened to T. L. French for the *Cahiers* booklet, which was "Thousand Eyes Number 2."

"The Thousand Eyes Number 1" had consisted of quotes lifted from various critics writing about Ingmar Bergman (a method Sid favored for keeping down costs on the magazine), who had been the subject of a prior retrospective at the Bleecker and its sister theater the Carnegie Hall. "The Thousand Eyes Number 3" was *The Films of Vincente Minnelli,* in support of a retrospective at the two theaters on January 7 to March 9, 1978. Edited by Penny Yates, the manager of the Carnegie, it contained a filmography annotated with lifted quotes and three original essays by Joel E. Siegel ("The Musicals"), George Morris ("The Melodramas"), and me ("The Comedies"). I never met my coauthors, but Penny helped me with my research by screening *The Courtship of Eddie's Father* for me in her office at the Carnegie Hall.

My approach was pretty offbeat. Seizing the opportunity to read everything written about Minnelli in French—in back issues of the *Cahiers* at the Lincoln Center Library, and in a French Minnelli book that contained (are you listening, Sid?) lifted quotes from magazines like *Arts*—I discovered an evolving theory of Minnelli's cinema in French that I managed to squeeze into my critical survey of the comedies. When I handed the piece in, a little nervously, I described it to Jackie as "an epic of the human spirit," a lofty phrase that spoke to the fact that the theory was the creation, not of one author, but of several, although Jean Douchet had eventually emerged as the Hegel of the enterprise, as well as the successor to André Bazin as the intellectual father of the next generation of *Cahiers* critics, including Serge Daney.

It was interesting to revisit the Douchet essays while I was translating them for this book. Looking them up in my *Cahiers* collection, I noticed that Douchet's very strange review of *Two Weeks in Another Town* appeared long after the film opened, which made me curious to know what internal debates had preceded publication of the piece. (*Two Weeks* never figured, for some reason, in the famous "Conseil des dix," which laid out the range of French opinion, *Cahiers* and non-*Cahiers*, on all new films in French release.) Certainly the fact that the arch-Bazinian Eric Rohmer was then editing the magazine goes a long way toward explaining why, after laying the foundations for criticism of Minnelli as a maker of dreams about dreams, Douchet pulled off a world-class dialectical reversal with a Bazinian defense of *Two Weeks* as a documentary.

In 1978 I merely found this puzzling, but the fascinating coherence of the larger history unfolding before my eyes set me dreaming about doing a whole book of which "Specters at the Feast" would be one chapter, tracing the history of several major Hollywood auteurs in the pages of French film journals, which I proposed to call *Doing the Existential-Semiotic Trans-Atlantic Celluloid Tango*.

I don't know if I ever actually proposed that project to anyone, but I chose an untranslatable English title because I knew that kind of history would be most useful to American critics and theorists who were interested to know where some of their ideas come from. The editors of the first BFI volume of *Cahiers* translations did something like that by including a section of Nick Ray reviews, which can be complemented by reading Bernard Eisenschitz's biography of Ray, where he comments film by film on the evolution of the director's reputation in France.

I attempted something along the lines of "Specters" again when I wrote my introduction to a book published by the Locarno Festival in 1997 where current American filmmakers talked about unappreciated American masterpieces. To shed light on an interview with Jim McBride about *In Harm's Way*, I indulged my curiosity by reviewing the history of Preminger criticism in the *Cahiers* and shoehorned what I learned into the introduction, but the French translator, appalled by my lighthearted tone, refused to translate it, and the book appeared without an introduction.

Finally, in 1998 I was asked to select production documents at the Margaret Herrick Library relating to the making of *North by Northwest* for a supplement to the *Cahiers* on the occasion of the film's reissue. With the pleasure principle again in the driver's seat, I proposed doing an article instead, planning to read everything in French on that one film and work it in somehow, but instead I found that the documents were telling me their own story, one that was every bit as interesting as the epic voyage Vincente Minnelli's Parisian doppelgänger had made through the minds of a few brilliant critics in the 1950s and 1960s. The article became one chapter of a book—my first in English under my real name—and the theory it expounded, for better or worse, was my own.

Specters at the Feast:
French Viewpoints on Minnelli's Comedies

All of Vincente Minnelli's comedies are hilarious, except *I Dood It,* a project that he took on in midstream, and *The Courtship of Eddie's Father,* which transcends its genre. This would be a good track record for anyone, but for a director who is also a master of romance and melodrama, and who has for some reason acquired the reputation of being "more of a stylist than an *auteur,*"[1] it is an almost Shakespearean accomplishment. Minnelli has had strange luck with critics. Discovered belatedly in France and promoted by the *Cahiers du cinéma* into a cult figure in the 1950s, he has suffered ever since from critical backlash to their early, impassioned defense of him as a practitioner of pure cinema. It was a defender who wrote, in 1957, that *Lust for Life* marked the culmination of Minnelli's project of creating "a pictorial cinema," adding that "in this sense, and in this sense only, Minnelli is an *auteur* of films" (68).[2] This made it all too easy for future Stalinist Louis Marcorelles to refer to him condescendingly, a year later, as "the Beau Brummel of the camera" (86), and the image seems to have stuck in a lot of people's minds. Other directors—John Ford, for example—have gotten away with flashy early periods and late periods during which they were permitted to exercise their "mature styles" on material so stale that it makes *The Sandpiper* look like *Moby Dick,* but it was Minnelli's fate always to be identified with the garish excesses of his early films (like *Ziegfeld Follies,* which the reviewer for *Le Figaro* called "a music-hall for Zulus,"[3] and to be described in the 1960s, by the magazine that had championed his most daring experiments, as "a nice guy" who "doesn't have a lot to say" (172).

Much of this has to do with his early career as a set designer and with the shock of discovery people felt here and elsewhere when *An American in Paris* was released in 1951. The first impact seems to have obscured for some observers the very identity of the man who made the picture. In his article for the *Cahiers,* Frédéric Laclos described the rain-swept drama of opening night at Cannes and replied to local critics who were disturbed by the aesthetic implications of re-creating Paris on a Hollywood soundstage: "Dislocating the reality of stone and water in favor of essentially poetic values and structures corresponds exactly to what all artists do, be they painters, writers or musicians." Clearly someone had been doing the work of an *auteur de cinéma*, using film the way a poet uses language, but Laclos assumed that "the someone" was Gene Kelly. Minnelli's name is mentioned nowhere in the article.

The comedies supplied some of the early impetus for repairing the omission. French audiences did not get to see *The Clock*, which had called Minnelli to James Agee's attention in the 1940s, until 1964. Consequently, it was the release of *Father of the Bride* and *Father's Little Dividend* on the tail of *An American in Paris* that gave Minnelli's defenders their first solid evidence of what he could do without the inspiration of Gene Kelly's dancing feet. In a review of *Designing Woman*, Eric Rohmer wrote:

> Vincente Minnelli belongs to the category of filmmakers whose best interests dictate confining their talents within the limits of a very narrow specialty. This turns out to be vaster, however, than the very particular genre of the "show" to which, after the failure of more ambitious works like *Madame Bovary* and *Lust for Life*, we had wished to confine him. *The Long, Long Trailer* and *Father of the Bride* had already put us on the right track, but after *Designing Woman* no further possibility of doubt. The auteur of *An American in Paris* is not only an excellent director of musical comedies, but an excellent director of comedies, period.[4]

This measured tribute to his versatility only confirmed what Minnelli had been at some pains to explain to Jean Domarchi and Charles Bitsch when they interviewed him in 1957: that his aim as a director had always been to find the appropriate style for each new film (74). This attitude, and the respect it implies for subject matter, is already apparent when we contrast the splendors of the romances to the spare, foursquare virtues of the comedies, where "plastic and poetic enchantment," as Jean Wagner noted in a review of *The Reluctant Debutante* (99), is put aside in favor of "a comic efficacy which is never below the finest successes of the genre." Yet Minnelli's aestheticism is still in evidence, particularly in the later comedies. Rohmer's description of *Designing Woman* correctly implies that Minnelli had treated the genre developed by Hawks, McCarey, Capra, Cukor, and Stevens (his favorite comedy director) as an objet d'art. "The performances of Gregory Peck, Lauren Bacall and Dolores Gray have the same acrobatic quality as Gene Kelly's dancing. *Le gag* rebounds from each of their reactions—irreproachably realistic—as on a trampoline, only to tumble back superbly, a few seconds later, as into the most reassuring of nets." The film, in fact, is a "latent ballet," a description Wagner would apply, with good reason, to *The Reluctant Debutante:* "The characters glide and soar, talk too much or not at all, separate, come together and bustle about in activities as vain as they are futile. Until the moment when the ballet becomes actual: in the very midst of a dance, Kay Kendall and Rex Harrison throw themselves into a genuine, dizzying ballet." Wagner considered this film to be a minor work—"the best English comedy of the year"—but there would always be extremists for whom overt aestheticism was all that mattered about Minnelli. In an earlier note on the same film (93), Luc Moullet had praised the "admirably inhuman, mechanized playing of Kendall-Harrison and Angela Lansbury," concluding that in spite of (because of?) the "remarkable imbecility" of the plot—trying to marry off Sandra Dee, with John Saxon glowering in the role of a disguised count—*The Reluctant Debutante* was in fact "Minnelli's masterpiece." As Rohmer knew quite well, these flourishes with the genre merely exploited a principle of aestheticism inherent in all American comedy: "The miracle—an almost daily miracle—of American comedy is to achieve as subtle a depiction of a coarse milieu as some dramatist or novelist might formerly have done of a society a thousand times more refined, without departing for a second from the most absolute naturalness." "Faire marivauder 'l'homme des classes moyennes'" (this untranslatable phrase contains more than a touch of self-description) is by definition an exercise of style, and Minnelli goes at it in just that spirit, creating a world of comic stock-types— demonic lawyers, snooty caterers, tyrannical nurses, thugs, snobs, deformed teenagers, hot-headed workmen, and obnoxious friends—with physiognomies as distinct and firmly drawn as the guests at Da Vinci's *Last Supper*. When Desi Arnaz staggers into the trailer park office at the beginning of *The Long, Long Trailer,* the man he finds to tell his story to is not just any stranger, but the archetype of the Understanding Stranger, with a fatherly face wrinkled from years of warm smiles, puffing contentedly on a pipe: "Tell me about it, son." "Well you see, it all started when we bought this trailer . . ."

But even the most polished comedy has to be about something, and Minnelli's comedies are distinctive and consistent in their thematic preoccupations. *The Long, Long Trailer* is consistent with the pattern for what Serge Daney calls the "domestic comedies" (283), which recount the frustrations of a man (Spencer Tracy, Desi Arnaz, or that "ordinary man," Rex Harrison) ensnared in a costly, embarrassing hassle that escalates into a nightmare, like the Bergmanesque wedding-dream in *Father of the Bride*. The plots of these films—some of which are based on real-life nightmares—allow for lots of the kind of mild social satire that the French are always quick to interpret as a virulent indictment of "the American way of life." More important are the opportunities for engaging portrayals of obsessive personalities. Still on *The Reluctant Debutante* Wagner notes that: "A typically Minnellian trait is the automobile obsession of one of the characters, or Kay Kendall's marital obsession, or Rex Harrison's alcoholic obsession. As in any comedy—but Minnelli, if we are to believe his confidences, seems to be particularly haunted by this theme—the whole action reposes on a misunderstanding between two or more people." Satirical intentions are most in evidence in the *Father* pictures, where Spencer Tracy's voice-over solidly anchors the universe of comic grotesques in a single point of view. In *Designing Woman* this device is discarded in favor of a polyphonic soundtrack that lets each character's obsession have its say, prompting Domarchi (79) to concede that Minnelli's presumed satiric rage at this world of "futile beings," umbilically joined to their respective milieus, is tempered by a larger-minded version of Howard Hawks's famous ethic of professionalism: "What one does is less important, after all, than the way one does it. Our ballet teacher is worthy of respect, because he is a real ballet teacher. Mike is a real reporter, competent and courageous, and Marilla is a real dress designer, dominated by the problems of her métier. All are no doubt the consenting victims of their milieus but are professionally above reproach. . . . It is this discrete apology for the 'work well done' that moves me." But here we have touched on a major theme, for Domarchi would not be the last *Cahiers* critic to see Minnelli's obsessed characters as artists, and to interpret the comedies as aesthetic manifestoes.

Nothing could seem more improbable on the face of it, but what is really happening, after all, in these "domestic comedies"? A man is driven by his muse (his wife?) to squander all his substance on a dream: a gigantic yellow trailer that plays music when you open the door, a Roman orgy of dinner parties and debutante balls, a "blessed event," or a wedding that turns into "a big theatrical production, a big flashy show that we can't afford." Viewed in this light, Spencer Tracy's ordeal is not different in kind from the damnation of Fred Astaire in *The Band Wagon*. The midwestern banker, ravaged by the expense of his daughter's wedding, and the song-and-dance man who almost gets blown off his feet by a minefield of overcharged smoke bombs are both living out versions of what Minnelli's most inspired critic, Jean Douchet, would call "the problem of the artist . . . confronted by the work of art which absorbs him, but which also menaces him in his very existence as soon as he has created it." Conversely, on the same high level of abstraction, it could be argued that a quirky melodrama like *The Cobweb*, with "its perverse extended family of inmates and doctors," and Richard Widmark slugging it out with a whole trio of hysterical women over who is going to do the drapes for the common room, is really the blackest of the domestic comedies.

The basic premises for this kind of "form-meaning" approach to Minnelli were laid out by Jacques Joly in his article on *Home from the Hill* (121), where he spends most of his time talking about the furnishings in Robert Mitchum's den:

> Minnelli is often reproached for his cult of form. . . . Nevertheless, the beauty of his films owes nothing to technique and everything to his sense of man. . . . What is *mise-en-scène* if not, precisely, the confrontation of a character and a set? It is therefore by *mise-en-scène*, and by *mise-en-scène* alone, that Minnelli shows himself to be a great humanist, because it reveals this fundamental truth: that each man is his own *metteur-en-scène*, and that every human gesture has meaning only as a function of a decor, an atmosphere.

A few months later Minnelli fanned the flames when he imprudently expounded to Domarchi and Douchet a theory of milieu and character, explaining that he had wanted the low-life characters in *Some Came Running* to look as if they were living "inside a juke-box" (128): "You can't separate the character from his milieu, isolate him arbitrarily by close-ups. His milieu, his way of life, the chairs where he sits, the room he lives in, all that is part of his personality. It's this man's history. It's how people see him—why shouldn't we see him the same way?" A word to the wise is sufficient, and in a lengthy exegesis of *The Four Horsemen of the Apocalypse* (129), Douchet started turning Minnelli's remarks into a system: "Each Minnelli character pursues, in effect, an inner dream. . . . Each one wishes to surround himself with a set which bears the mark of what he is, what he loves, what he desires. . . . But when the dream assumes a body, it finds itself for this very reason subjected to contingency." Beneath the suave surface of these films, he became convinced, there lurked "a universe of venomous or carnivorous plants," where "everything devours or is devoured": "In this hostile climate, a sickly, nervous hypersensitivity colors everything that touches or surrounds it, and materializes its dreams in a set (physical and human), hoping by this definition of its territory to preserve itself. A vain hope: in this closed, hot-house world, one cannot grow and expand except by feeding on other people's dreams, and immediately being subject to the attacks of their reality." Since reality, in a Minnelli film, is always somebody else's dream, the conflict between dream and reality finally comes down to a conflict between two dreams, two sets: as in *The Four*

Horsemen of the Apocalypse, where prewar Paris is a set invaded by another set, and "the Nazi dream, a collective and uniform dream, unfurls over Europe, destroying town after town, set after set." Or as in *Designing Woman,* which Rohmer had already described as a story of incompatibility "not between two spouses, but between their respective friends and milieus."

Given all this, it is not surprising that Douchet would consider the *Ben-Hur* of situation comedies, *The Long, Long Trailer* to be "the exemplary Minnelli film." In an article for *Objectif* he detailed the process by which the "internal reverie" embodied in the monstrous trailer conquers the world, and then turns on the dreamers themselves:

> So our heroes realize their dreams of conjugal felicity by buying a mobile "home," an immense trailer painted an aggressive yellow. How this itinerant touch of yellow clashes with the decor of the landscape; how the external world penetrates this home and ravages everything (the marriage scene, then the camping scene); how this "dream décor" then ravages and destroys other people's decors (the indescribable scene where the trailer destroys the house and garden of "poor cousin Grace"); and finally how the trailer, weighed down by rocks—the will literally to appropriate the world—gathered as a souvenir of the "wonderful trip" by Lucille Ball, becomes at the top of a mountain a menace which threatens to crush the couple: this is, succinctly summarized, the story of this film, one of the most terrible satires of the American way of life.[5]

At the end, when Desi has told his story and it is the other man's turn to speak, we discover that he owns a trailer, too.

Had Douchet wished, he might have added a biographical level to his reading by arguing that the film is the personal nightmare of a director girding up his loins, in 1954, to do battle with CinemaScope. But Douchet's dream had long since swallowed up Minnelli's. When *Two Weeks in Another Town* opened in 1962, he saw a cosmological "documentary" about the evolution of an artist, containing within it the whole history of human society, and of evolution in the animal, vegetable, and mineral kingdoms as well.

But by now the battles had been won; when *Goodbye Charlie* slithered into Paris theaters, it found a receptive audience. Michel Cournot wrote a rave review in the *Nouvel Observateur* devoting several pages to an analysis of the film's first three sequences and concluding: "*Goodbye Charlie* is not, it seems, a 'great' Minnelli. Bah, a little Minnelli is already so many things . . ."[6] A few weeks later, in a note tucked away at the back of the magazine, the *Cahiers* panned *Goodbye Charlie*. The hatchet was entrusted to Jacques Bontemps, who simply asserted that the film was "poorly acted" and "badly directed," referring darkly to "a paranoiac cult of more or less phantom personalities" that had made it fashionable to see in "this anodyne comedy" a terrifying statement about Death.

The magazine was in the process of reappraising its own *politique des auteurs* and Minnelli, who had become a kind of symbol of the omnipotence of mise-en-scène, was an inevitable target. In a note on *The Sandpiper* (171), Jean-Louis Comolli explained:

> Minnelli's films are the putting into play of an all-powerful set, living with a life of its own as a milieu englobing all things and being and signifying them par excellence, etc. Interdependence: the characters are part of this Protean décor, the dramas are its difficult actualizations, the dream-films its extreme resolutions, etc. But this relationship, strict and total as it is, implies reciprocity; if not, there would be no cinema, but only an effort at mise-en-scène. If everything comes down to the set, the corollary of a set rooted in everything and founding its necessity there is no less essential.

In short, if the script or the actors are bad, "everything crumbles, and the set becomes just painted paper again, a foil for the silliness of the puppets whom it was supposed to metamorphose." Having "deconstructed" itself, Minnelli's oeuvre was now ready for the final indignity, which came in 1971: a structuralist-Freudian reading of *On a Clear Day You Can See Forever* by Pierre Baudry (229), who suggests that this uneven reprise of the great theme of lovers separated by time is really "a tale of counter-transference, the story of a psychoanalyst 'trapped' by the delirium of one of his clients." But after what Minnelli had done to the theme in *Goodbye Charlie*, which is about Tony Curtis struggling not to fall in love with his best friend after he has "come back" as Debbie Reynolds, no interpretation could really be called reductive.

Fortunately, because of a typically spooky Minnelli time warp, *Goodbye Charlie* was not the last of the comedies to appear in France. *The Courtship of Eddie's Father*, made in 1963, was not seen in Paris until 1966. It is about a widower, played by Glenn Ford, who is pursued by three women (each, of course, with her own distinctive "décor"). There were a lot of grisly sex farces using this three-women formula in the early 1960s; what made this one special was a remarkable performance by Ron Howard as the widowed man's son, who helps him make up his mind. Brash, tiny and *weird*, looking like America's answer to Jean-Pierre Léaud, Howard communicated his energy to the other players, and Minnelli exacted from Glenn Ford and Shirley Jones the performances of their lives. The result was one of his loveliest and most personal films; had it been released a few years earlier it would have been treated as royally as Hawks's *Man's Favorite Sport?* an abstract and less endearing work the *Cahiers* found "exemplary" in 1964. But in 1966, after the successive shocks of *Goodbye Charlie* and *The Sandpiper,* there were no bouquets left to throw. "The esthetic conceptions exposed in *The Courtship of Eddie's Father,*" wrote Michel Mardore (176), "justify our former infatuation and our violent disavowal of the recent productions. Today we see the worm and the apple inseparably."

Mardore interprets the film as a dangerously absolute apology for artifice, in its trashiest forms. When Eddie warns, for example, that in the comic books "skinny eyes and a big bust mean a bad lady," skinny-eyed Dina Merrill turns out to be a bitch on wheels. Later he will reveal to his father "the nature of love, by picking as his girlfriend a dreadful little girl, whom he knows to be dreadful. He imposes his choice with imperial dignity, and obliges his father to define and assume a personal attitude." And in the legendary goldfish scene he shows him how to mourn; unable to cry for his dead mother because of an implicit pact of manly stoicism, Eddie freaks out when one of his pet goldfish dies, and Glenn Ford freaks out, too: "A fish is a fish, a mother's his mother! You don't shed the same tears for both!" "Does that mean," asks Shirley Jones, "that you shouldn't cry at the movies?" That night Eddie catches his father watching a love scene from *Mogambo,* on the verge of tears. So much for realism. Or as Jerry Van Dyke explains to Stella Stevens, the only way to go is to "fake it." These aesthetic conceptions are, of course, Minnelli's own: "Here is a man who throws a challenge at us: 'Between the four walls of my soundstage I can paint you anything, including the whole of America.' And in his way, within the system he has created for himself, he makes good his word." Having demonstrated the aggressive didacticism of the film, Mardore ends with a paradoxical tribute to Minnelli's "barbarism" and "bad taste": "Minnelli's implicit bad taste is not a fault. It even tends to be a virtue in an art that will always be the last to take harmony and pastel tints for a criterion of quality. Let us love in Minnelli his aggressiveness, rather than the *douceurs* of the man of the world. To the extent that *Eddie's Father* is like an aggressive manifesto, it interests us. From the maximum of arbitrariness, the *meneur du jeu* tries to obtain a maximum of emotions. Sometimes he succeeds, sometimes he fails, but the effort inspires a certain respect." Such hard-won lucidity should not be taken lightly, particularly when it helps us understand a difficult film. Eddie may be a didactic character, but he doesn't spell things out. Like his creator, he prefers to speak in parables, jokes, and images, as he leads his father through the maze of symbolic displacements Freud called "the mourning work" and Proust "the intermittences of the heart." Parables, jokes, and images: when Eddie writes his happy ending, he seals a marriage between two people, and two sets, which must be made in heaven, because from the beginning Glenn Ford's apartment and Shirley Jones's apartment—two units of mass-produced "good taste" in the same luxury high-rise—have been impossible to tell apart. But the film is scarcely, as Mardore would have it, a "cruel" satire of the American way of life. In a "Letter from the U.S.A." (160), written in 1963, after seeing it in its American release, Jean-Louis Noames noted with characteristic precision that "if the problems posed by Minnelli's cinema have sometimes been those of America, their resolution has always been affected a little outside of her, before or after"—in the innocent past of *Meet Me in St. Louis* or the uncertain future of *Two Weeks in Another Town*. "With *The Courtship of Eddie's Father*," he concludes, "it is far from America that the solution is situated, between a man and himself, his image and his shadow. With innocence recovered, life also returns, the most beautiful music of all."

NOTES

1. Andrew Sarris, *The American Cinema: Directors and Directions, 1929–1968* (New York: E. P. Dutton, 1968), 101.

2. References to the *Cahiers* will be indicated by giving the numbers of the issue cited in parentheses.

3. References to other French sources are taken from Marion Vidal's *Vincente Minnelli* (Paris: Seghers, 1973).

4. Eric Rohmer, *ARTS* (November 1957).

5. Jean Douchet, *Objectif* (February–March 1964).

6. Michel Cournot, *Nouvel Observateur*, March 25, 1965.

Minnelli's American Nightmare

JEAN-LOUP BOURGET
TRANSLATED BY JEAN-PIERRE COURSODON

The death of a writer cannot fail to change our reading; it is indeed that death which, as it interrupts his writing, turns a given number of books into an *oeuvre*.
PHILIPPE ROGER, *Roland Barthes, roman*

In July 1986 Vincente Minnelli died in Los Angeles at age eighty-three. His long career, which coincided with the apex of the MGM-Freed musical comedy style, then with the revival of the flamboyant melodrama, had produced a beguiling body of work. Its qualities were acknowledged, twenty or twenty-five years ago, thanks to the enthusiasm and remarkable analyses by such French critics, writing for both *Positif* and *Cahiers du cinéma,* as Jean Domarchi, Jean Douchet, Dominique Rabourdin, and Jean-Paul Török. Ironically, alas, this critical recognition came at a time when Minnelli's creative activity was on the wane. *Say It with Music,* a musical biography of Irving Berlin that the director and producer Arthur Freed had been contemplating for a long time, never came to fruition, and Minnelli would only make two more films, *On a Clear Day You Can See Forever* and *A Matter of Time.*

Minnelli worked in only three genres—the musical, straight comedy, and melodramas, with about the same number of films in each: thirteen musicals, from *Cabin in the Sky* (1943), his first "solo" film, to *On a Clear Day* (1970); eleven dramas or melodramas, from *Undercurrent* (1946) to *The Sandpiper*

(1965); and ten comedies, from *The Clock* (1945) to *A Matter of Time* (1976), his last film. A similarly general overview indicates that the majority of his musicals deal with dreams and most of his dramas with reality, while the comedies fall into either category: some have a fairy-tale quality (*The Clock;* the "Mademoiselle" episode in *Story of Three Loves,* 1953; *The Courtship of Eddie's Father,* 1963; *A Matter of Time,* which has been described as "a Cinderella tale"); the others are rather nightmarish, although realistic (*Father of the Bride,* 1950; *The Long, Long Trailer,* 1954; *Goodbye Charlie,* 1964).

One may add that the musicals tend to be examples of "art" according to Hollywood conventions (the glorification of show business in *Ziegfeld Follies,* 1946, *The Pirate,* 1948, *The Band Wagon,* 1953; the surrealistic sets of *Yolanda and the Thief,* 1945) while the heroes in the dramas are often "artists": the writers in *Madame Bovary* (1949), *Tea and Sympathy* (1956), *Some Came Running* (1958), the filmmakers in *The Bad and the Beautiful* (1952) and *Two Weeks in Another Town* (1962), the painters in *The Cobweb* (1955), *Lust for Life* (1956), *The Four Horsemen of the Apocalypse* (1962), and *The Sandpiper.*

This overview of the functions of genres in Minnelli's work, however, is helpful only as far as it goes, since the notions of "dream" and "reality" remain general and vague and may be more characteristic of the genres than of the director. Thus the following claim by François Truchaud in his Minnelli book seems most adventurous: "There is a perfect correspondence between the world of musical comedy and Minnelli's world. This correspondence has resulted in a long-standing confusion: what looked like the conventions of the musical (dances, the theme of the dream, non-realistic colors) was actually the expression of his universe."[1] It seems more reasonable to argue that the genre conventions (which are quite real and not just apparent) did not prevent Minnelli from expressing his "universe," while their falling apart caused him to remain all but silent after 1965. His post-MGM efforts are unconvincing: *Goodbye Charlie* (Twentieth Century-Fox) is a failure aside from its admirable precredit sequence; *On a Clear Day* (Paramount) is only half successful; *A Matter of Time* (American International) found (most unfairly) no supporters at all. As justly noted by sociologist I. C. Jarvie, the decline of the musical was mainly due to the decline of the studio system and the vanishing of the specialized personnel the studios employed.[2] Unlike such directors as Stanley Donen or Blake Edwards, Minnelli didn't seem able to give his career a new orientation. Therefore, rather than coinciding exactly with the expression of the Minnellian universe, as Truchaud claimed, the conventions were what made such a universe possible. And since it is quite as true that Minnelli's films are unlike those of other directors, one must make a careful distinction be-tween genre conventions and the director's personal contribution.

SOME CAME RUNNING: THE TRIUMPH OF ANTITHESIS

Consider, for example, *Some Came Running*. This admirable film is predi-cated on a series of clichés and stereotypes that are not essentially different from those found in, say, the unbearable and ludicrous *Peyton Place* (1957, in which Arthur Kennedy also appears). To mention a few: the stereotypical small town, Parkman, Indiana, whose citizens hide their dissatisfactions and shameful desires (e.g., Arthur Kennedy's attempt to seduce his secretary) behind a facade of respectability. There is the stereotypical lady teacher played by Martha Hyer, and, even more stereotypically, the Shirley MacLaine charac-ter, a variation on the traditional prostitute-with-a-heart-of-gold. This mate-rial (from the James Jones novel) is far from being at all original or distin-guished. Moreover, the fact that the film features two of the three major members of the Sinatra "clan"—Sinatra himself and Dean Martin—might give us pause (one recalls the harmless mediocrity of *Robin and the Seven Hoods*, the 1963 Gordon Douglas movie inspired by the friendship of the Rat Pack members) and suggest that the viewer will be treated to such conventions of the clan's films as drinking bouts and poker playing (which indeed she/he is). Upon reflection, however (and after seeing the film), one realizes that its aesthetic principle is precisely the systematic confrontation of those various conventions. Jim Kitses once quite rightly remarked to this writer that *Some Came Running* flouts the Aristotelian rules of drama, since the Shirley Mac-Laine character, who seems to come out of a musical, should never meet Martha Hyer's; one must go further and realize that everything in *Some Came Running* is based on the glaring impossibility of such encounters.

Indeed, *Some Came Running* is based on a radical, melodramatic opposi-tion between two realms: the daytime world of Parkman, Indiana, respectful of social proprieties, a world of business (Frank Hirsh), family (the Hirshes, the Frenches), school (Gwen French), friendly but stiff cocktail parties, opposed to the nighttime world of Bama Dillert, the professional gambler (whose gambling activities are opposed to Frank Hirsh's commercial occupa-tion), of Ginny Moorhead, a semiprostitute, of her boyfriend Raymond etc. . . . The latter is a world of bars, drinking bouts, brawls, and neon lights. Minnelli described it in the following terms: "*Some Came Running* was about a small town, a cheap part of town. It's involved with bars and gambling places, cheap restaurants and neon signs: the whole thing is more or less like the inside of a jukebox. In a way that is the color scheme of that film because it belongs there with the characters—rather cheap gamblers, and a girl like the one played by Shirley MacLaine. The whole color sense is realistic actually, but it has a sense of fantasy because it's selected that way."[3] Dave Hirsh (Frank Sinatra), a writer, oscillates between the two realms: he derives his inspiration from the lower depths but his readership is upper middle class. On Parkman's side are his childhood, his family roots (although he has become estranged from them), and the temptation of respectability offered by Gwen French (Martha Hyer). On the opposite side: the seduction of alcohol and easy money, Ginny's pathetic but touching attachment to him. Each realm is dealt with in its own different style (photography, music, actors' performance); *Some Came Running* actually describes the invading of the bourgeois world by the artist and his shady friends.

It is therefore true, in a sense, that Martha Hyer and Shirley MacLaine do not belong in the same film; just as Arthur Kennedy on the one hand and Dean Martin on the other do not either. Far from downgrading the oppositions (which are based on a different series of stereotypes and conventions) Minnelli enhances them. The director's role, then, in this case is both to visually under-score each stereotype and to multiply such figures of style as the antithesis. The decor in which each character lives provides a good example of this visual materialization of clichés. When Dave Hirsh first arrives in his hotel room he immediately arranges his decor, characterized by a taste for literature and a taste for drink: books by Faulkner, Steinbeck, Thomas Wolfe, and F. Scott Fitzgerald are set side by side with a bottle of bourbon. Thus Dave is introduced to us as writer/drunk, a first antithetical couple. The decor at the French family's home is both bourgeois and intellectual: even the kitchen has shelves filled with books, and such paintings (or at least reproductions) as a Canaletto and Cézanne's *The Red Vest* can be observed on the walls: it all connotes security, beauty, and peacefulness. Bama Dillert's place, in contrast, boasts the kitschiest of objects, a lamp whose shade is an exotic dancer's grass skirt swaying to the rhythm of her hips—the object simultaneously connotes bad taste, low social status, but also a lack of sociocultural prejudices. As for Shirley MacLaine's character, it is overdetermined through a multiplicity of stylistic markings: makeup, accent, vocabulary, as well as the red flower in her hair, her bunny-rabbit-shaped purse, and the garish orange-colored souvenir pillow she asks Dave to get for her, which bears the openly sentimental word "sweetheart."

Conflicts pit Dave against his brother Frank; Dave against Gwen (except for his attempt at harmonization when he pulls out the hairpins holding Gwen's prim bun—the scene is filmed in a half-light that visually symbolizes a possible conciliation, since it is equally distanced from the realms of day and night. It is a freed woman, no longer trying to repress her sensuality, who is suddenly revealed to the spectator and to Dave); and Gwen against Ginny (again, Minnelli goes all the way and doesn't hesitate to bring together the two women fighting over Dave; he films their encounter in classical shot/reverse shot fashion, placing them before a background that emphasizes the unseemliness of the situation, as Martha Hyer is seen against the "natural" background of the window while MacLaine is shot in front of a classroom blackboard). The French's lifestyle and Dave's own cannot be reconciled, and the coming together of Dave and Ginny is soon threatened, as in the famous carnival sequence, a violent coda punctuated by garish colors—blood-red, purple—and music to match: a red light bathes Raymond, Ginny's shady, self-appointed protector, who is fiercely jealous of Dave and drinks alcohol straight from a bottle before throwing it away empty.

Stylistically and thematically, moreover, the climax of *Some Came Running* echoes other melodramas as well as other—nondramatic—Minnelli films. The shot of a drunken man about to kill his rival can be found in Douglas Sirk's contemporary *Written on the Wind* (Robert Stack coming home before the beginning of the flashback), while the carnival sequence recalls such other outbursts of color as the ballet in *An American in Paris;* stylistically, the sequence has often been compared to Minnelli's musical comedies. It is like a dramatic version of the Mickey Spillane spoof in *The Band Wagon*'s "Girl Hunt" ballet (traces of it will reappear in *Bells Are Ringing,* 1960); and that the red light that bathes Raymond is the same that surrounded Gene Kelly's head when he claimed to be the ferocious Macoco in *The Pirate*'s "Pirate Ballet." Minnellian melodrama clearly sits at the crossing of two axes: a Minnelli style (which also owes a lot to MGM) and 1950s wide-screen, Technicolor melodrama (e.g., the films of Nicholas Ray, Elia Kazan . . .).

MIXINGS AND SHIFTINGS

What appears more specifically Minnellian is the frequent relying upon stylistic shifts that reflect antagonistic relations within the films, but also reflect the unstable status of movie genres. Genres in Minnelli's work are never pure; they always seem to yearn for the status of some other genre. Thus *Cabin in the Sky,* the first film he directed alone, belongs to a genre, and even to a subgenre, the musical featuring naïve blacks (that is, blacks as whites naïvely saw them around the turn of the century), which is as conventional as can be, and whose conventions today seem unacceptable to many viewers. One of the oddities of *Cabin in the Sky* is the brutal shifting from dream to nightmare toward the end of the film: we are at the Paradise dancing bar (actually a den of iniquity) when a tornado suddenly causes the roof to collapse and two people are killed. Georgia Brown (Lena Horne), the sophisticated femme fatale with a dazzling smile who foreshadows the type embodied by Cyd Charisse in *Two Weeks in Another Town* (and who wears a flower in her hair like Ginny Moorhead) becomes hysterical. Although everything soon goes back to normal, what took place was an arbitrary intrusion of melodrama one may rightfully find surprising in a genre film. The same holds true for *Meet Me in St. Louis,* another film from the realm of dreams, or more accurately of nostalgia for a past that obviously never existed. For a brief moment the film becomes a nightmare, at least for one of its characters (young Margaret O'Brien) in the ghostly, witch-haunted Halloween sequence; and, as in *Cabin in the Sky,* there is no distanciation at all; the spectators must share the little girl's fear and imagine themselves for a while in a horror movie. (Minnelli conjures up a similar atmosphere in the little boy's visit to the witch in "Mademoiselle.") The shift from dream to nightmare reoccurs briefly in *Brigadoon:* the frantic chase through the forest as the village is threatened with extinction because of the desertion of one of its denizens. The atmosphere very exactly foreshadows *Home from the Hill* with its use of hunting as a metaphor for virility.

The convention in *Bells Are Ringing* derives from fairy tales (Judy Holliday claims to be named Melisand, thus anticipating Melinda, Barbra Streisand's character in *On a Clear Day*), fairy tales that are supposed to transform the lives of average Americans. *Bells Are Ringing,* however, doesn't oppose reality and fantasy, which go hand in hand in the film. Judy Holliday was well known for always playing down-to-earth characters, and several sequences rely on the *populisme,* the unanimism that characterized *The Clock* (in which the actual central character is the City of New York) and which is supposed to be so foreign to Minnelli's sophistication. As she waits for Dean Martin, Judy Holliday cheerfully greets passersby, walks by a movie theater that plays *Gigi,* and through example prompts Dean Martin to start singing among the crowd. The scene is filmed in a high-angle shot that stresses the unanimous sharing of happiness on the smiling faces of the New Yorkers. Later, however, an awkward situation opposes "Melisand Scott's" plebeian simplicity to the name-dropping sophistication of show business people at a party where everyone mentions the first name of some Broadway or Hollywood celebrity while Judy Holliday can only come up with Rin Tin Tin! The interest of this sequence doesn't lie in its hypocritical satire of Hollywood but in the fact that Minnelli's sympathies are ambivalent: at that specific moment, the film proves unable to work either as a satire of Hollywood or a satire of Judy Holliday; as a result it becomes dramatic. The Holliday character is awkwardly out of place in the midst of the group she finds herself with, her presence there no less incongruous than Shirley MacLaine's in the classroom. One has the same feeling with *Gigi*, in which the society of the belle epoque is examined more critically than nostalgically (unlike in *Meet Me in St. Louis*): as it describes the shift from naturalness to sophistication, the film constantly seems on the verge of rebelling, of becoming more of a bitter dramatic comedy than a musical.

It is true that some of these devices are commonplace in musicals (the conflict between naturalness and artifice is also found in George Cukor's *My Fair Lady*); with Minnelli, however, the conflict is present in the very style of the film and not only in the dramatic structure. Moreover, Minnelli's musicals are far from always producing the kind of exhilaration audiences experience in other musicals, and their conclusions don't always affirm the triumphant reconciliation of nature and artifice that is the rule of the genre.

One should also note the changes in tone between *Brigadoon*'s contemporary sequences and the rest of the film, or the stylistic break between *Goodbye Charlie*'s dramatic, bumpy precredit sequence and the rest of the film, which seems most conventional. Among dramas there is James Mason's cameo as Flaubert in the introduction and conclusion of *Madame Bovary*, and *Four Horsemen*'s fantastic prologue as the horsemen ride against a stormy sky. While a shift in tone like the one in *Goodbye Charlie* may seem extreme, it is by no means unique, as similar internal breaks were already present in, for instance, *Father of the Bride*, on the face of it one of Minnelli's least personal films, but for this very reason one of the most revealing. *Father of the Bride* is a very carefully fashioned movie, with a wealth of small touches that are tender or amusing, or both, but whose general effect is nearly unbearable for a modern viewer. Somehow, as early as 1950, Minnelli was making a picture that summed up all the horror of the coming decade in a vision of stifling upper-middle-class family life. In retrospect it seems strange that Minnelli, whose married life must have been quite stormy, was actually the auteur of this film in which the yet unrealized, dazzling outbursts of the melodramas are foretold. *Father of the Bride* lacks the nostalgic distancing that made *Meet Me in St. Louis* so unique— the dreariness of the present terribly dulls the vision. Still a few indications do remain at the beginning and end—too flimsy to rescue the film from artistic failure and justify its distasteful ideology, but enough to throw a light on the rich intertextual relationships within the Minnellian oeuvre.

FATHER OF THE BRIDE: A NIGHTMARE-COMEDY

The film opens with a long tracking shot on the aftermath of the wedding feast—a cluttered table with leftover food, a littered floor, displaced pieces of furniture—in other words, an atmosphere of desolation. The balance of the movie is in the form of a flashback whose ostensibly happy, even mawkish tone is belied by Stanley Banks's introductory statement, directly addressed to the audience: "I would like to say a few words about weddings. I've just been through one—not mine, my daughter's. Someday in the far future I may be able to remember it with tender indulgence, but not now. I always used to think marriage was a simple affair. Boy and girl meet, they fall in love, get married, they have babies, eventually the babies grow up, meet other babies, they fall in love and get married and so on and on and on. Looked at this way it is not only simple it's just plain monotonous. I was wrong. I figured without the wedding." In 1950 most moviegoers and critics probably felt that the father's disgruntled attitude was a case of comic, somewhat unseemly exaggeration—for them, what to Stanley Banks had been a nightmare was just a delightful family comedy. A modern viewer, however, shares Banks's uneasy feeling, which a distance of quite a few years has only made more acute. Jean-Paul Török and Jacques Quincey have aptly called Minnelli "the Painter of dream life," but this admirable phrase should sometimes be complemented by its counterpart: "the painter of life's nightmare." From 1942 to 1953 (or thereabout) Minnelli was able to paint dream life only in musicals, his so-called comedies often being nightmares; later (1954–62), when he had a chance to direct melodramas, he introduced the dreamlike elements of the musical genre into them.

Structuring a traditional familial comedy in the form of a flashback is quite unusual; yet Minnelli does it in both *Father of the Bride* and *The Long, Long Trailer,* giving us another example of genre movies that aspire to the status of a different genre. And perhaps also of an auteur (semiconsciously) aspiring to a different, higher status within the Hollywood system. The device consisting of making a film's main action into a flashback framed by a present-time opening and closing could be termed *fateful* and was common (especially during the 1940s) in films noirs, thrillers, and mysteries: a movie that opens with a murder—a classical introduction in such *noirs* as Billy Wilder's *Double Indemnity,* Michael Curtiz's *Mildred Pierce,* or John Farrow's *The Big Clock*—thereby instills a notion of predestination in the viewer's mind, since she/he knows "ahead of time" that the hero is condemned. It is therefore quite surprising to find such fateful openings in comedies like *Father of the Bride* (offering the spectacle of a disaster area and Tracy's dire description of his experience) and *The Long, Long Trailer* (a marriage in the process of breaking up). Minnelli gave these two films a dramatic structure associated with thrillers and dramas, a good example of a form conflicting with the work's explicit content (Cukor uses a similar device in *The Marrying Kind*).

A confirmation of this view is given later in *Father of the Bride* when Spencer Tracy has an actual nightmare—which is, with the opening, one of the film's few outstanding scenes. He dreams that, as he walks his daughter (Elizabeth Taylor) down the aisle, the floor becomes soft beneath his feet and threatens to engulf him; his legs buckle and he collapses, surrounded by the sneering faces of the guests—"family and friends"—looking like so many hellish apparitions. His clothes are reduced to shreds, he loses his jacket, is left wearing nothing but a tattered shirt, and wakes up screaming. In a sense this nightmare is more real than the appearances of the comedy, since it very literally strips naked the fundamental hostility of this middle-class society with church, friends, and relatives bunching together to deprive Tracy of his comfort, his individuality, and even the respectability of his clothes. It is interesting to compare this sequence with the "real" wedding ceremony that takes place the next day. The Elizabeth Taylor character is (as she remains throughout the film) frightening in the way she espouses the conformity of her time, evident in the regal manner with which she walks down the aisle on her father's arm. One is made to feel the power of bourgeois dynasties, the children's ability to become stereotypes of their parents. From then on the film does become nightmarish, although less explicitly so, which will allow it to come full circle and end up where it started. A "small reception" is scheduled to take place . . . for two hundred and fifty people, as this middle-class family turns out to be incapable of choosing between class (the number of guests) and middle, or mediocre (the reception will take place at home, as though it *were* intimate). The Banks's house is systematically torn apart by the caterer whose ambition is to facilitate the circulation of air and guests: the furniture is moved about, a marquee is put up in the garden, and so forth. Of course the expected flow—a symbol of the harmonious blending of social classes—will not happen, the temperature under the marquee will be "halfway between a Turkish bath and a greenhouse." While the telephone keeps ringing off the hook the house becomes a battleground fought over by decorators and florists with conflicting ambitions. Tracy won't even be able to see his daughter during the reception and will be treated like an intruder in his own house. Worrying that there might not be enough champagne a scornful hired help tells him: " OK, OK, mister, don't worry, you'll get yours." The conventional happy ending only takes over—in extremis—when Taylor, after she's made her exit, calls her father on the phone to say goodbye.

Party sequences are considered Minnelli's personal mark, like Fritz Lang's hand or Hitchcock's cameos: there is one in each of his films. In *Father of the Bride,* the most interesting (maybe even the only interesting) sequences are "the master's signature." This must be more than a mere coincidence: a sign of the director's false relationship to the material he has been assigned. An earlier sequence already followed the implacable logic of a rising nightmare: at a more modest party given to announce Taylor's engagement, Tracy has prepared martinis for his guests, but they don't care for them and request old-fashioneds and other cocktails instead. He has to spend the entire evening bartending, unable to leave his tiny kitchen even for one moment. Worst of all, when all the guests have gone (except one who has passed out drunk) Tracy's wife asks him: "Where on earth have you been?"

Two Melodramatic Self-Portraits

Such movies as *Father of the Bride, The Long, Long Trailer,* or *Goodbye Charlie* are not films that have "escaped from their maker" (as is sometimes said of the occasional great film signed by a thoroughly run-of-the-mill director), but on the contrary are instances of an auteur escaping (or attempting to escape) from his own film. At the same time, it might very well be that Minnelli was the type of director who could only give his best within the frame of a system—that is, both within the highly hierarchical structure of a studio and within the limits of a body of stylistic and thematic conventions, or even of a code of (self-) censorship. An illustration of such a phenomenon may be found, on an almost anecdotal level, in the relationship between the two Minnelli films dealing with Hollywood's (changing) point of view on Hollywood, *The Bad and the Beautiful* and *Two Weeks in Another Town.* The former is structured as a series of flashbacks describing the relationships that existed between film producer Jonathan Shields (Kirk Douglas) and his collaborators, a director (Barry Sullivan), an actress (Lana Turner), and a novelist-turned-screenwriter (Dick Powell). The film's lesson seems to be that Shields enabled all of them to reach the height of their art, although he cruelly wounded them on a personal level. In this Minnelli film produced by John Houseman, the film producer, rather than the somewhat nondescript director, is presented as the actual artist. As a matter of fact, the question is theoretically and historically complex. It is clear that the Shields character is largely inspired by David O. Selznick; Minnelli has confirmed it.[4] But in order to know it one only has to look at the *text* of the film and the splendid railing of the Shields estate, a quotation of the opening shot of all Selznick productions. Selznick was an exceptional character among Hollywood producers; his conception of production included the function of director. Still, *The Bad and the Beautiful* was made at a time when studio and producer left a strong stylistic and ideological imprint on their films; indeed, in Minnelli's film the continuity of the studio is emphasized by the immovable presence of Walter Pidgeon.

Ten years later, as the industry was abuzz with talks about "runaway production" (numerous "Hollywood" films being shot, for financial reasons, in Spain, Italy, and other foreign countries), the team of *The Bad and the Beautiful* went to Rome to make a kind of self-portrait of the runaway situation: *Two Weeks in Another Town*. The team included Minnelli, producer John Houseman, screenwriter Charles Schnee, and actor Kirk Douglas. In the fiction, however, the status of these individuals in relation to one another has changed. Kirk Douglas, who played Shields in *The Bad and the Beautiful*, becomes in *Two Weeks in Another Town* what he is "in reality," a movie actor; moreover, the film director (Edward G. Robinson's Maurice Kruger) rather than the producer is now in the limelight. As an added complication, references are made in *Two Weeks* to an earlier film, starring Kirk Douglas and directed by Robinson, which is supposed to be a masterpiece characteristic of their early manner and of a mastery they seem to have lost; the film is none other than *The Bad and the Beautiful*. The paradox may then be stated as follows: the 1962 director claims as his masterpiece a 1952 movie that insists that a film's auteur is the producer; or, put another way: Minnelli claims as his masterpiece a film by John Houseman. Actually, in our eyes there is no doubt that the auteur of those films is Minnelli; neither is there any doubt that they couldn't have existed without MGM, John Houseman, and the Hollywood tradition they both refer to and to which the latter film clings in hope that it isn't completely dead. The very motto of the director in *Two Weeks*, "The real Kruger sound," echoes the studio's (historical) motto: "The Real MGM Sound." At a time when the *politique des auteurs* triumphed, it didn't seem excessive to credit the director for the films' technical perfection.

The Bad and the Beautiful and *Two Weeks* actually provide an exceptional instance of literal intertextuality, as the latter film includes the screening of two scenes from the former—especially the one in which Kirk Douglas talks Lana Turner into conquering her inferiority complex and her fears of becoming an actress. The scene thus becomes more richly meaningful; the point is no longer just the fact that the "model" of the Lana Turner character was Diana Barrymore; the viewer's attention is directed—naturally enough—to the formal qualities of the sequence, and particularly to the actors' melodramatic emoting, which Kruger considers the apex of his own style: heightened acting of two performers often associated with melodrama (Kirk Douglas more implicitly than Lana Turner; still, see his parts in Richard Quine's *Strangers When We Meet* and Elia Kazan's *The Arrangement*), emphasized by the use of close-ups and expressionist lighting. One might point out other, less literal relationships between *Two Weeks* and *The Bad and the Beautiful*, notably those two dramatic climaxes: Lana Turner's and Kirk Douglas' s respective wild automobile drives. The meaning of such sequences can only be understood in relation to the (rhetorical) conventions of Hollywood literature: they are visual metaphors expressing the character's helplessness, and often his or her denial of the truth about him/herself. Frequently an accident puts an end to such a ride, working as *révélateur* of the truth.

In *The Bad and the Beautiful* the Lana Turner character is distraught because she has caught Shields, who claimed to love her, with another woman; she gets in her car and drives away, speeding madly in a scene that, according to Minnelli, was "choreographed": "We had to have the car revolving around the camera, and we explained the action to her much as you might explain choreographed movements to a dancer."[5] The ending in the rain will be imitated in another Lana Turner film, Michael Gordon's *Portrait in Black* (1960). In *Two Weeks*, Jack Andrus (Kirk Douglas) bears a scar from a car accident that symbolizes the failure of his marriage to Carlotta (Cyd Charisse); this time around the wild drive is deliberately used by Andrus to elucidate the cause of that accident: was he drunk, or trying to kill himself? He decides to experiment by getting inebriated then launching his car into an infernal race (in the company of a terrified Carlotta) from which he emerges unscathed—which proves to him that the accident was not as accidental as it appeared. This is a baroque/expressionistic variation on the familiar theme of the character coldly seeking to solve a problem by crashing his/her car into a tree (Bette Davis in Alfred E. Green's *Dangerous* or John Garfield in Michael Curtiz's *Four Daughters*).

Two Weeks, set in Rome, stands at the intersection of two axes: the director's concerns and the ambitions of the producer who clearly wished to beat Fellini at his own game;[6] as a "Fellinian" film, *Two Weeks* is certainly a failure, but as a "Minnellian" film it definitely is not. Thank God *Two Weeks*, unlike *La dolce vita*, is not a boring epic on boredom; the Trevi Fountain is used in a metaphorical sequence, the editing of which reflects the fountain's baroque style while providing an "objective correlative" of Andrus's feelings; moreover, that fountain follows the ones on the Place de la Concorde in the opening of *An American in Paris*, seen again in *Gigi* (the song "Gigi" that, through the artifice of editing, brings together in one single dream space the Gardens of the Observatoire, the Fontaine des Quatre Parties du Monde, and the Alexander III Bridge). Thus *Two Weeks*, a melodrama, also aspires to the condition of the musical comedy insofar as it tends toward a formalist style. The Roman nightclub sequences are filmed with expressionist, hellish lighting like the ones in *Some Came Running* or Sirk's *Imitation of Life*. Critics who easily accept such stylistic figures in a musical have proved more reluctant when they are grafted onto melodramas. Thus Henri Agel admitted: "Should I confess . . . that it took me a long time to understand Minnelli's non-choreographic side? The shock came one day from the extraordinary *Home from the Hill* . . . a great, daring film . . . for the frenzy with which a filmmaker, both delirious and magnificently in command of his means of expression, throws himself into the most intense confrontations and the most violently colored orgies."[7] Such reluctance has deep roots: a naïve distrust of formal insincerity, a refusal to accept a film as both highly artificial spectacle and a source of emotion—in other words, as melodrama.

Another Sirkian device, rarely noted yet frequent in Minnelli's films, is the use of mirror reflections whose function is to participate in the formalization of the film while coloring its significance: mirrors question the characters' commonplace reality while enhancing their symbolic role. Such mirrors are everywhere in *Two Weeks* as in *Some Came Running;* in the latter, Dave Hirsh's reflection in a mirror is often seen before he enters the frame—an "objective correlative" of Dave's duality, his oscillating between Gwen and Ginny, Parkman and bohemia, and so on. Minnelli, referring to *Madame Bovary*, remarked: "Throughout the picture I kept using mirrors, the mirror in the farm showing her always trying to glamorize herself, dreaming of something she wasn't; in the seminary, where she read the French romantic novels of the time; and then in the ballroom, when she glances into the glass and sees herself surrounded by men in the one perfect image that fulfils her romantic hopes. And then you see her in a dingy hotel room with her lover, and a cracked mirror displays her ruin; it is a recurring image that nobody noticed."[8]

TEA AND SYMPATHY: PICTORIAL NOSTALGIA

Some Minnelli films may aspire to the condition of musical comedy but without comparable violence. Such is the case of Tea and Sympathy, a most remarkable film, often ignored by critics who only saw in it a controversial subject matter watered down by the transition from stage to screen. As in the Robert Anderson play, the hero (John Kerr) is a student with an intense artistic sensibility who is accused of being homosexual, but the film version eschews the implication that, conversely, the virility of Deborah Kerr's husband is only the mask of a latent homosexuality. Minnelli's film, however, in no way intends to tackle the problem polemically: who is homosexual? It describes the conflict in terms of (apparent) reality and (deep) desire. The husband exhibits all the outward signs of virility, but they are only pretence. While not necessarily a homosexual, he is nevertheless unable to live with his wife and becomes a wreck when she leaves him. A similar problem affects John Kerr's father, whose own virility on the one hand is little more than an addiction to lewdness. John Kerr's virility, on the other hand, is never exhibited. Instead, it proves itself through his love for Deborah Kerr, a love she ultimately returns. The solution to the conflict involves numerous melodramatic archetypes: the wife sees the student as a sort of reincarnation of her first husband, killed at war (see Robert Mulligan's Summer of '42), the song John Kerr plays at the beginning, "Plaisir d'amour," is the veritable anthem of melodrama (see Henry King's Seventh Heaven). The lovers are united in the natural environment of an autumnal forest, therefore (a subtle pictorial harmony) reddish like Deborah Kerr's hair. Masculinity and femininity are seen not as antagonistic (as implied in all theories of virility) but as complementary, since both are, in Minnelli's eyes, artistic: to the pink of the flowers Deborah Kerr has planted in her garden John Kerr brings the complementary blue touch of forget-me-nots.

The solution of the conflict, however, belongs to the realm of dream, since the film is a flashback, the receptacle of a paradise lost. Tea and Sympathy is thus extremely close to Brigadoon, in its pictorial tone, the nostalgic sweetness of the emotions it stirs up, and the opposition it establishes (less explicitly than Brigadoon because of the difference in genre) between the artist's desire or dream (deep reality) and the "real" that is mere appearance. (Such is the fundamental idealism of Hollywood melodrama, but also, in a sense, its pessimism. The same thematics can be found, with important individual variations, in Frank Borzage's films as well as Douglas Sirk's.) An ultimate example of drama aspiring to the status of the musical, *Tea and Sympathy* even includes an actual sequence of choreography, the astonishing "music room" scene in which John Kerr and his clumsy friend imitate each other's walk.

Minnelli's work, then, admirably illustrates the tensions perpetually imposed upon Hollywood's genre system, and which explains why that system is a fluid one. It also illustrates the paradox of an auteur who could only express himself within the genre system while simultaneously tending to question it. Aware of the limits of the Hollywood production system, Minnelli ceaselessly tried to break away from it through the brilliant emphasizing of the arbitrariness of a given genre by bringing into it elements belonging to another genre. One might argue, then, that in his work even the thematic and stylistic "inconsistencies" are disposed according to a consistent order. Granted, he did not truly reach beyond the limits of the system; he explored them from the inside, as evidenced by his failure to make personal works outside the confines of MGM. But he has shown that the auteur can bend genre conventions for personal expression without breaking them. He doesn't challenge the validity of the thematics of melodramas, or of the rhetoric of the musical, but he combines the two elements in an original fashion. As his career developed, he first made musical comedies that aspired to the status of (melo)dramatic films, then, increasingly, melodramas featuring the return of the repressed— the musical's color and dance.

NOTES

1. François Truchaud, *Vincente Minnelli* (Paris: Éditions Universitaires, 1966), 24.

2. I. C. Jarvie, *Towards a Sociology of the Cinema* (London: Routledge and Kegan Paul, 1970), 175.

3. Ernesto Serebrinsky and Oscar Garaycochea, "Minnelli Interviewed in Argentina," *Movie* 10 (June 1963): 24.

4. Charles Higham and Joel Greenberg, *The Celluloid Muse* (New York: New American Library, 1972), 204.

5. Ibid.

6. In a television interview (Toronto, December 1972) John Houseman stated that the film was "a mistake anyway" and "not good enough after Fellini."

7. Henri Agel, *Romance américaine* (Paris: Éditions du Cerf, 1963), 69–70.

8. Higham and Greenberg, *Celluloid Muse*, 204.

Vincente Minnelli

THOMAS ELSAESSER

When this article was published early in 1970 in the *Brighton Film Review*, the house journal of the film society of the University of Sussex, auteur studies had already become quite unfashionable. And among the genres, the reputation of the musical (after the mid-1960s box-office and critical failure of big-budget productions such as *Hello, Dolly!*) was probably at its lowest point ever. Although I was addressing myself to students who bought and read the magazine mainly for its biweekly listings rather than for the lengthy articles we smuggled in at the back, I felt sufficiently involved in the gathering momentum in Britain around questions of auteur versus genre, structural versus thematic criticism, ideological versus textual analysis to want the *Brighton Film Review* to contribute to these debates. The convenient provincialism of a seaside university gave us the cover to argue, for instance, in favor of our *cinéphile* obsessions, while nonetheless keeping a watchful eye on what *Screen* and other film magazines were doing. Although committed readers of *Movie* and the yellow issues of *Cahiers du cinéma,* we put less emphasis on auteurist themes and gave more attention to *style*. We tried to be informative and broadminded enough not to scare off our readers, but we nonetheless hoped that our expository manner carried a polemical edge that London would take note of (it did).

The essay on Minnelli, occasioned by a small retrospective we had been organizing, wanted to push author studies a little further in the direction of genre (claiming that all of the director's films were musicals at heart, with the melodramas a form of musical turned inside out), while opening up the rigid boundaries drawn around genre in the studies on the western or the gangster film, published by the British Film Institute. I therefore related the concept of the musical to some more general notion of a "drive- or goal-oriented" structure that I claimed was underpinning all Hollywood filmmaking of the time. The individual genres and their historical mutations could then be understood as partial aspects of a totality whose overall constellation was centered elsewhere. Perhaps the argument ended up being somewhat circular: I see Minnelli as an auteur because his practice of the musical/melodrama genre allowed one to study the dynamic structures to which much of ("classical") Hollywood style conforms. At the same time, his aesthetic exemplified these principles by the way his films transgressed or exceeded them. I am quite sure that at the time I failed to see just how close such a set of equations came to undermining the dominant opposition "auteur versus the system" on which a good deal of the polemics of the auteur theory depended.

After positing this "drive-oriented" structure, the article does not pursue this point, except to explain its presence in terms of the exigencies of audience identification, rather than as a critique of American society of the time, or as a reflection of ideological conflict. In this (as in other articles written at that time) I wanted to explore the idea that Hollywood's global strategy had always been aimed at binding its audiences on a psychic-affective level: in other words, *realism* (the representation of a reality) was not the main issue, but the embodiment of affective intensities and emotional energies were. In Minnelli, the continuities and breaks, in short, the modulations of the drive and its obstacles, define both the narrative and the visual rhetoric (the mise-en-scène) of a given film. They also create the illusion of unity that constitutes the *style* specific to not just this director's work (I also wrote about Douglas Sirk, Nicholas Ray, and Sam Fuller in this vein). What seemed to make Minnelli exemplary, and for me put him on a par with Jean Renoir and Fritz Lang, was that in his films the act of seeing, the constraints and power relations it gave rise to, appeared so uncannily foregrounded that the action always tended to become a metaphor of the more fundamental relation between spectator and mise-en-scène, audience and (invisible, because ubiquitous) director. Fortuitously, but perhaps fittingly, my article ends with a brief analysis of *Two Weeks in Another Town,* which Paul Mayersberg in *Movie* had already called a "testament film." There the director (visible, but split between two protagonists) loses control over his creation, evidently also a comment on the changes that were taking place in Hollywood filmmaking during the 1960s: the very same changes that made the auteur and mise-en-scène criticism (whose unspoken third term had always been the studio system, its implied "other") historically obsolete as a determining force, and by the same token, available as a theoretical construct.

What remains is to ask why critics should have invested, and still invest, so much energy in the auteur theory, given that it had always been perverse, deliberately flying in the face of what we know about mass media, popular culture, and their history. Auteurism's victories always had to be snatched from the jaws of common sense. In Eisenstein's *October* there is a scene where a Bolshevik soldier, after penetrating to the czar and czarina's bedrooms, turns everything upside down and finally slits the eiderdown with his fixed bayonet: in vain he is looking for the source of misery that forced him to revolt. None of the banal objects before his eyes can satisfy the desire for a glimpse at origins, in a scene as "primal" as any Freudian critic could wish. A similarly frustrated voyeurism is documented from those who in 1789 stormed the Bastille, and it was undoubtedly what moved the sansculottes to tearing up Marie Antoinette's bed linen during the occupation of the Tuileries. Such may be the auteurist's rage and desire, except that he is after the source of his pleasures rather than his miseries. In the history of the American cinema, apparently so completely dedicated to the impersonality of *histoire,* a dimension of *discours* had always been intermittently visible. Whether the trouble in the system, or the icing on the cake, it was the fate or privilege of the auteur critic to attribute this "extra" or "excess" to the director. And this probably for good reason: film studies in the 1970s and beyond appeared to have settled the vexing question of why films give us pleasure, by deciding that in the cinema the spectator enters into a dialogue with his or her own split self and alienated subjectivity, be it Marxian or Lacanian. Insofar as auteur criticism perhaps never sufficiently acknowledged the narcissism of the *cinéphile,* it stood exposed by its fanatical identification with the narcissism of the filmmaker. But for those who talk to themselves most intensely through the intermediary of an (imaginary) "other" or a (external) "supplement," there will remain the need, however rhetorically displaced or nostalgically recalled, to reinvent the author, if only, as Roland Barthes has remarked, because his disappearance would imply, finally, also that of the critic and reader. The auteur is the fiction, the necessary fiction one might add, become flesh and body in the director, for the name of a pleasure that seems to have no substitute in the sobered-up deconstructions of the authorless voice of ideology.

VINCENTE MINNELLI

Minnelli's critical reputation has known a certain amount of fluctuation. Admired (or dismissed) in America as a "pure stylist" who, in Andrew Sarris's phrase "believes more in beauty than in art," his work reached a zenith of critical devotion during the late 1950s and early 60s in France, with extensive studies in *Cahiers du cinéma,* especially in the articles by Jean Douchet and Jean Domarchi, who saw in him a cinematic visionary obsessed with beauty and harmony and an artist who could give substance to the world of dreams.

In England *Movie* took up his defense, from the first number onward. But strangely enough, the contributors concentrated almost exclusively on Minnelli's dramatic films of the early 1960s (a memorable article by Paul Mayersberg on *Two Weeks in Another Town* comes to mind), and gave rather cursory treatment to the musicals, while the later films, such as *Goodbye Charlie* (1964) and *The Sandpiper* (1965) were passed over. With this, Minnelli joined the legion of American directors whose work was supposed to have suffered decline, if not total eclipse in the Hollywood of the middle and late 1960s.

The following remarks are a first attempt to disentangle a few essential characteristics from a singularly rich and varied body of work and to trace some of the dominating lines of force in his style. Above all, I am concerned with the fundamental unity of Minnelli's vision. At the risk of displeasing the genre critics and antagonizing those who share the view that thematic analysis generally exhausts itself in what has (rather summarily) been referred to as "schoolboy profundities," I would like to look at some of Minnelli's constant themes and furthermore conduct some kind of special pleading for Minnelli as a moralist, even though this will mean flying in the face of the "stylist" school—both of the Sarris variety and *Movie,* who claim for Minnelli as for Cukor that he never writes his own scripts, and therefore never uses other people's material for the propagation of his own views, that he confines himself to the interpretation, the mise-en-scène of the ideas of others, and that, consequently, his work is best regarded as lacking in consistent themes and rather excels on a supreme level of visual competence.

I think this is a fundamental misunderstanding. True, there are super-ficially two "Minnellis"—one the virtual father of the modern musical, and the other the director of dramatic comedies and domestic dramas. Other critics—even sympathetic ones—would probably claim a different Minnelli for almost every film—the loving "pointillist" of American period pieces or of "Gay Paree" (*Meet Me in St. Louis, Gigi, An American in Paris*), the catalyst for Gene Kelly and Fred Astaire musicals (*Ziegfeld Follies, Yolanda and the Thief, The Pirate, The Band Wagon, Brigadoon*), the ingenious vulgarizer of painters' lives (*Lust for Life*) and best-selling novels (*The Four Horsemen of the Apocalypse*), the handyman who puts together a star vehicle for an ambitious producer (*The Reluctant Debutante*), and lastly perhaps the "difficult" direc-tor of such problem pieces as *Some Came Running, Home from the Hill*, and of Hollywood self-portraits—*The Bad and the Beautiful* and *Two Weeks in An-other Town*.

Altogether, Minnelli has directed some thirty-two films, not counting the episodes and sketches contributed to other people's films. It might seem diffi-cult to find a personal vision in as vast an oeuvre as his, not to mention the fact that all films (except one) have been made in the MGM studios, under the supervision of a few, themselves very gifted and articulate, producers like John Houseman (four films) and Arthur Freed (twelve). But surely anyone who is reasonably familiar with his films will see in Minnelli more than the glorifica-tion of the metteur en scène, the stylish craftsman of the cinema, the dandy of sophistication. I for one am convinced that Minnelli is one of the purest "hedgehogs" working in the cinema—an artist who knows one big thing, and never tires to explore its implications. In Walter Pater's famous phrase, all romantic art aspires to the status of music. My contention is that all Minnelli's films aspire to the condition of the musical. In this resides their fundamental unity. However, in order to substantiate this point, I shall insert a few remarks to explain what I mean by *musical*.

The classic Hollywood cinema is, as everybody knows, *the* commercial cinema par excellence—out merely to entertain. Usually this is taken to be a fundamental drawback, at worst utterly precluding its products from the realms of serious art, at best, presenting the filmmaker with formidable odds against which he has to test his worth, as artist *and* entrepreneur. I shall try to show how deeply Minnelli's conception of his art, indeed his "philosophy" of life, is formed by the conflict between the necessity of circumstance and the vital need to assert—not so much one's self, but rather one's conception of meaning, one's vision of things. It furnishes his great theme: the artist's strug-gle to appropriate external reality as the elements of his own world, in a bid for absolute creative freedom. When I say artist, I hasten to add that this includes almost all of Minnelli's protagonists. (Insofar as they all feel within them a world, an idea, a dream that seeks articulation and material embodiment.)

Yet there is another side to the "commercial cinema" syndrome, which is rarely ever given its full due. (At least in England: in France, the *Positif* and *Midi-Minuit* critics have always paid tribute to the commercial cinema qua commercial cinema.) I am referring to the fact that perhaps the enormous appeal of the best Hollywood cinema, the fundamental reason why audience identification and immediate emotional participation are at all possible, lies in Hollywood's rigorous application of the pleasure principle—understood almost in its Freudian sense as the structure that governs the articulation of psychic and emotional energy. It seems to me that a vast number of films "work" because they are built around a psychic law and not an intellectual one, and thus achieve a measure of coherence that is very difficult to analyze (as it must be extremely difficult for a filmmaker to control and adhere to), and yet constitutes nevertheless an absolutely essential part of the way the cinema functions—being indeed close to music in this respect.

For a superficial confirmation of this fact, namely that there is a central energy at the heart of the Hollywood film that seeks to live itself out as completely as possible, one could point to the way in which—superimposed on an infinite variety of subject matters—the prevalent plot mechanisms of two major genres of the American cinema (the western and the gangster film) invariably conform to the same basic pattern. There is always a central dynamic drive—the pursuit, the quest, the trek, the boundless desire to arrive, to get to the top, to get rich, to make it—always the same graph of maximum energetic investment.

For the spectator, this means maximum emotional involvement, which depends upon, and is enhanced by, his maximum aesthetic satisfaction—or rather, by the skillful manipulation of his desire for as total a sense of satisfaction as possible. Intellectual insight and emotional awareness are transmitted in the best American cinema exclusively as a drive for *gratification,* which the audience shares with the characters. The more a film director is aware of this interrelation of morality and aesthetics in the cinema, the more his mise-en-scène will be concerned with the purposeful ordering of visual elements, to achieve a kind of plenitude and density, which inevitably, and rightly, goes at the expense of ideas. In other words, there seems to exist, particularly in the American cinema, an intimate relationship between the psychological drives of the characters (i.e., the motives beneath the motives that make them act), the moral progression they accomplish, and the aesthetic gratification afforded to the audience by the spectacle; and these are held together by some profound mechanism, identical in both audience and characters—be they criminals, detectives, gunfighters, shop assistants, songwriters, or millionaires.

Perhaps one of the most interesting consequences of this fact is that this, if true, would entail a thoroughly different concept of cinematic realism, which would have nothing to do with either literary realism or the realism of pictorial art. For what seems to me essential to all of Minnelli's films is the fact that his characters are only superficially concerned with a quest, a desire to get somewhere in life, that is, with any of the forms by which this dynamism rationalizes or sublimates itself. What we have instead, just beneath the surface of the plots, is the working of energy itself, as the ever-changing, fascinating movement of a basic impulse in its encounter with, or victory over, a given reality. The characters' existence is justified by the incessant struggle in which they engage for total fulfillment, for total gratification of their aesthetic needs, their desire for beauty and harmony, their demand for an identity of their lives with the reality of their dreams. Minnelli's films are structured so as to give the greatest possible scope to the expansive nature of a certain vitality (call it "will," or libido)—in short, to the confrontation of an inner, dynamic, reality and an outward, static one. Minnelli's typical protagonists are all, in a manner of speaking, highly sophisticated and cunning daydreamers, and the mise-en-scène follows them as they go through life confusing—for good or ill—what is part of their imagination and what is real, and trying to obliterate the difference between what is freedom and what is necessity.

What, in this context, characterizes the Minnelli musical is the total and magic victory of the impulse, the vision, over any reality whatsoever. The characters in his musicals transform the world into a reflection of their selves, into a pure expression of their joys and sorrows, of their inner harmony or conflicting states of mind. When Gene Kelly begins to dance, or plays with the first words of a song, say in *Brigadoon,* the world melts away and reality becomes a stage, on which he and Cyd Charisse live out their very dream. Or when Louis Jourdan, in utter confusion about his feelings, rushes to the Jardin du Luxembourg to sing the title number of *Gigi,* Minnelli leads him into a wholly mysterious, wholly subjective landscape of the imagination, pregnant with the symbols of his newly discovered love for the one-time schoolgirl. Such confrontations with their innermost worlds always give the characters a kind of spontaneous certainty from which, ultimately, they derive their energy.

The Minnelli musical thus transforms the movements of what one is tempted to call, for lack of a better word, the *soul* of the characters into shape, color, gesture, and rhythm. It is precisely when joy or sorrow, bewilderment or enthusiasm, that is, when emotional intensity, becomes too strong to bear that a Gene Kelly or a Judy Garland has to dance and sing in order to give free play to the emotions that possess them. And it is hardly exaggerated to compare what Minnelli did for the musical with Mozart's transformation of the comic opera. One only needs to hold a Busby Berkeley musical—with its formally brilliant but dramatically empty song-and-dance routines and elaborate visual compositions—against even an early and comparatively minor Minnelli effort, say, the "Limehouse Blues" sequence from *Ziegfeld Follies,* to see how the musical with Minnelli has been given an authentic spiritual dimension, created by a combination of movement, lighting, color, decor, gesture, and music that is unique to the cinema.

Thus defined, the world of the musical becomes a kind of ideal image of the medium itself, the infinitely variable material substance on which the very structure of desire and the imagination can imprint itself, freed from all physical necessity. The quickly changing decor, the transitions in the lighting and the colors of a scene, the freedom of composition, the shift from psychological realism to pure fantasy, from drama to surreal farce, the culmination of an action in a song, the change of movement into rhythmic dance—all this constitutes the very essence of the musical. In other words, it is the exaltation of the artifice as the vehicle of an authentic psychic and emotional reality. Minnelli's musicals introduce us into a liberated universe, where the total freedom of expression (of the character's creative impulse) serves to give body and meaning to the artist's vitality in the director, both being united by their roles as metteurs en scène of the self.

The paradox of the musical—namely that a highly artificial, technically and artistically controlled decor and machinery can be the manifestation of spontaneous, intimate movements, or the visualization of submerged, hardly conscious aspirations—becomes not only Minnelli's metaphor for the cinema as a whole, but more specifically, it also makes up his central moral concern: how does the individual come to realize himself, reach his identity, create his personal universe, fulfill his life in a world of chaos and confusion, riddled with social conventions, bogus with self-importance, claustrophobic and constricting, trivial and above all artificial, full of treacherous appearance, and yet impenetrable in its false solidity, its obstacles, its sheer physical inertia and weight?—epitomized in the sticky, rubbery substance Spencer Tracy has to wade through, as he is trying to reach the altar, in the nightmare sequence of *Father of the Bride.* Minnelli's answer, surprisingly enough for this supposedly obedient servant of other people's ideas, is a plea for chaos, where his characters embrace flux and movement, because it is closest to the imagination. Minnelli's motto might well be that "better no order at all than a false order."

And here we have the crux of the matter: the Minnelli musical celebrates the fulfillment of desire and identity, whose tragic absence so many of his dramatic films portray. Looked at like this, the dramas and dramatic comedies are *musicals turned inside out,* for the latter affirm all those values and urges the former visualize as being in conflict with a radically different order of reality. In his nonmusical films—from *The Clock* to *Home from the Hill,* from *The Cobweb* to *Two Weeks in Another Town*—tragedy is present as a particular kind of unfreedom, as the constraint of an emotional or artistic temperament in a world that becomes claustrophobic, where reality suddenly reveals itself as mere decor, unbearably false and oppressive. That is when the dream changes into nightmare, when desire becomes obsession, and the creative will turns into mad frenzy.

It is in this absence of that freedom that the musical realizes and expresses through dance and song, through rhythm and movement, by indicating that peculiar fluidity of reality and dream that alone seems to offer the possibility of human relationships and of a harmonious existence—it is in the absence of this that Kirk Douglas or Judy Garland, Robert Mitchum or Glenn Ford and Ronny Howard (*The Courtship of Eddie's Father*) suffer anguish and despair, neurosis and isolation, spiritual and physical enclosure, if not death. And it is precisely the possibility, the promise of a return to chaos, to movement, that saves Judy Holliday (*Bells Are Ringing*), Gregory Peck and Lauren Bacall (*Designing Woman*), Rex Harrison and Kay Kendall (*The Reluctant Debutante*) in the dramatic comedies from becoming hopelessly trapped in their own worlds.

Minnelli's films invariably focus on the discrepancy between an inner vision, often confused and uncertain of itself, and an outer world that appears as hostile because it is presented as a physical space littered with obstacles. Life forces upon the characters a barely tolerable sense of rupture, and the Minnelli universe has its psychological raison d'être in a very definite and pervasive alienation. But instead of lamenting this modern condition, almost all his films concentrate on portraying the energies of the imagination released in the individual during this process of (social?) decomposition. Too often this has been seen merely as a total abandon to the faculty of make believe, of the beautiful appearance through which Minnelli is supposed to celebrate Hollywood escapism.

This view, even if applied only to the musicals, is an untenable simplification. Minnelli's concern is always with the possibilities of a human creativeness asserting itself in and through a world that is so obviously imperfect. True, imperfections are taken for granted, they are global, because Minnelli is dealing not with a given reality but with the psychological and emotional predicament it produces. Two types of heroes come to symbolize this situation: the artist and the neurotic, two ways of dealing with the actual that are obviously not unrelated. That he sees them as intimately connected states of being constitutes the coherence of his moral vision and the unity of his themes.

Whereas the "neurotic" dilemma is either treated comically (*The Long, Long Trailer,* the dream becoming a nightmare, or *Goodbye Charlie,* in which the reincarnated hero involuntarily undergoes a sex change) or tragically (*Home from the Hill, The Four Horsemen of the Apocalypse*), art and neurosis form the explicit subject of *The Bad and the Beautiful, Lust for Life, Two Weeks in Another Town.* Even in the musicals, where the triumph of the creative temperament seems assured, it is not by a "naïve" assertion of willpower or happy-go-lucky bonhomie, but through a complex process of metamorphosis that transforms both the individual and his world. The inner vision is essentially flawed, and so long as the protagonist cuts himself off from life, his dream is static, a passive nostalgia or worse, a self-limiting delusion. As a consequence, the external world seems to him nothing but oppressive, false and alien—an attitude that none of Minnelli's films vindicate as an adequate response, though they often make it their starting point.

Three of Minnelli's greatest musicals, *The Pirate, Brigadoon,* and *The Band Wagon,* open with such typical situations of the "self-in-exile." In *The Pirate,* Judy Garland, about to be married to a fat, wealthy businessman, sighs over her fate and looks romantically into the distance while dreaming of Macoco, the legendary Caribbean pirate, coming to take her away. In *Brigadoon,* a disenchanted Gene Kelly, playing an American tourist, stalks about in Scotland, having lost his way in the wilderness of the Highlands. And in *The Band Wagon,* Fred Astaire in the role of a once-famous star gets off the train in New York to discover that the big party at the station is cheering some other celebrity.

Although these may seem archetypal situations of the genre, they recur in all of Minnelli's films, whether musical or not. *The Courtship of Eddie's Father* is a particularly striking example, with father and son feeling completely lost in their own home (a family situation common to at least a dozen Minnelli films). And the implications are finally made explicit in *Two Weeks in Another Town,* where the hero is first seen in a mental hospital. In other words,

Minnelli starts from a characteristic disorientation about the relation of self and world, from which originates the impulse toward action. Whatever his protagonists do becomes therefore automatically identified with a desire to realize themselves by transcending an indifferent or restrictive environment.

This makes the Minnelli character live in the tension of a necessary isolation and an inevitable drive toward domination. It is as such a central theme of the American cinema. But whereas one easily assumes this to be in Minnelli's earlier films an exclusively aesthetic concern—a need for beauty, for living out a romantic fantasy—the moral dimension is never obscured. And if the very early films do emphasize the final articulation of a harmony, the later ones turn to the ambiguous conditions of the creative will, whether in the form of a self-destructive obsession (*Lust for Life*), a manic manipulation of others (*The Bad and the Beautiful*), or a tenacious determination (*Home from the Hill*).

In some of the earlier films, for example, Minnelli's attitude can be seen to alternate between optimism about the individual's potential to make the world conform to his dreams and an equally acute sense of the tyranny over others implicit in its realization. But this is never blown up to the dimensions of ponderous moralizing; on the contrary, it is always contained in the insignificant story, the unprepossessing event. In *Meet Me in St. Louis*, for example, near tragedy ensues when the father of the household decides to move his big family to New York, and thus to uproot them from their small self-contained world. It is the typical Minnelli dilemma of the will of the individual opposed to the always-fragile fabric of human harmony. The father's announcement of his intention falls on the family like a bolt out of the blue, and their world is visibly coming to a halt. In tears, the family scatters to various parts of the home, leaving the mother and father alone. The mother begins to play a song on the piano as the father sings, and the sound of their harmonizing gradually brings the rest of the family out of hiding. As the family gathers near the father and mother, Minnelli's editing conveys the precise feeling of a rhythm recommencing, and the characters "circulate" once more through the house as if their blood had begun to flow again, with gestures and movements that approximate a graceful dance. By contrast, in *Father of the Bride*, the same situation is inverted, and Spencer Tracy, as the father, is progressively more exiled from his own home because of the banal and conventional ideas and preconceptions his wife and daughter are trying to foist on him.

The clearest expression of a corresponding optimism is in *The Clock*. It is the story of a GI on a twenty-four-hour leave and a girl from the country who happen to meet in a railway station. In this film, full of the most unpromising stereotype material, Minnelli magnificently communicates the elements of his vision. For example, the obligatory stroll through Central Park becomes the pivot where the real New York in all its oppressive strangeness transforms itself into an integral part of the couple's experience of themselves. As they listen to the bewildering noise of the city, the sounds merge into a kind of music, and through its rhythm, the couple find each other—the city literally brings them together. This is important, because the film is built on the tension between the fatality of the clock, the diffuse chaos of the city, and the will of the lovers. Against a world circumscribed by time and ruled by chance (their initial encounter, the various accidental separations, the careless indifference that surrounds them), Minnelli sets the determination of the couple to realize a common happiness. Insignificant though they are in the human sea, their naïve trust in love at first sight appears as heroic because it is supported by a belief in the human will and its power to transcend the given. Judy Garland and Robert Walker here exemplify the Minnelli "philosophy" par excellence: the freedom of the individual, his creative potential, consists in perceiving order and design in chaos, whose meaning is revealed when it becomes dance. The film opens with a crane shot into the crowd at Pennsylvania Station, showing the aimless movement. It ends with the camera craning out from the station, and as Judy Garland is seen walking away, even the crowd has a regular flow and a definite rhythm.

Although the polarity between two worlds, or worldviews, is Minnelli's central structural device, the meaning of the themes is defined by the nature of the energy the characters bring to bear on the world as they find it. The spectrum is wide, with innumerable shades and variations. Whether it is the genteel joie de vivre of *Meet Me in St. Louis,* the instinctive stubbornness of Eddie in *The Courtship of Eddie's Father,* the dream of a luxury trailer (*The Long, Long Trailer*), or the fantasy life of a switchboard girl (*Bells Are Ringing*) —common to all of them is the sense that without this energy the world would always disintegrate into mere chaos.

As with many Hollywood directors, the basic purpose of Minnelli's handling of visual elements is to encourage audience identification. But no other director has such a keen and differentiated eye for the mesmerizing qualities of a setting, a particular decor. Not inappropriately, Jean Domarchi once compared Minnelli to Hitchcock, saying their conception of the cinema is "alchemistic"; the elements of Minnelli's mise-en-scène are indeed geared toward producing an overall impression of unreality, engrossing the spectator by a sense of timing and a fluidity of movement that exaggerates the natural relativity of time and space in the cinema to a point where the visual spectacle becomes a kind of hallucination.

This means that the mechanism of identification (or projection) normally understood rather crudely as referring only to the audience's empathy with the protagonist is amplified to include the setting, which no longer functions as an objective point of correlation but becomes absorbed into the action as the natural extension of the protagonist's being. The characterization of the Minnelli hero therefore reduces itself to the barest outlines of a specific individuality. His role is to indicate a sequence of psychological situations of general significance, and not to illustrate the ramifications of a unique case. What matters is not his character (i.e., his moral principles, his credibility as a rational and sentient human being) but his personality (i.e., the set of attitudes and physical responses he displays in given situations).

Where it is a question of substantiating or explaining a human relationship in terms of psychological motivation, Minnelli therefore invariably presents the conflict as a clash of settings, an imbalance of stylistic elements, such as a contrast of movements or a disharmony of colors or objects. The bright yellow trailer in the landscape of *The Long, Long Trailer*, for example, jars so painfully that it suffices to undermine the couple's pretensions to a free and natural life. At other times the violence of a gesture is set off against an otherwise smooth or harmonious visual surface, and when Barry Sullivan in one of the opening scenes of *The Bad and the Beautiful* slams down the telephone, an incongruous but highly dramatic contrast is created in opposition to the dreamlike setting in which an actress is being filmed by the camera crew. Minnelli constantly reduces his stories to their moments of visual intensity, where he can project the dramatic conflicts into the setting. Where other directors use the cinematic space to clarify the intellectual complexities of their plots (Otto Preminger, Lang), Minnelli relates distance (or lack of distance) to varying degrees of subjective intensity. Thus, an important function of the mise-en-scène is to interiorize the rapport that exists between spectator and action by reproducing a similar tension of identification and projection within the film itself—achieved very often by a typical Minnelli camera movement that consists of an unobtrusive, but very fluid, traveling forward, interrupted by an almost imperceptible craning away usually held as a general shot until the fade-out. This makes the Minnelli hero emerge in many ways as the creator *and* spectator of his own life, realizing himself most fully in a world he can transcend by using it as the decor of his own mise-en-scène. Conversely, the moment of rupture—doubt, despair, nightmare—is equally dramatized in the interrelation of hero and environment, and the world of objects becomes either solid and immobile or bristles with a recalcitrant life of its own.

In these cases, it is the gesture, sometimes aggressive, more often hesitant, that is extended into the alien territory that defines the protagonist's sense of personal identity, and the most subtle changes in his state of mind are relayed through his position and behavior as his body responds to the setting. Barry Boys in an article on *The Courtship of Eddie's Father* has given a fine analysis of the opening of the film, with Eddie precariously poised in the once-familiar kitchen, which through the death of his mother has become a hostile world.

This means that there is an obvious analogy between the approach of his characters to their predicament and the cinematic medium. Thus the mechanism of projection and identification are reflected in Minnelli's films as the two phases of a character's development: projection of his vision upon an environment, identification (or breakdown of an identification) with a decor, a created world.

In the musicals, where the characteristics of Minnelli's cinema are most transparent, one can see a kind of recurrent pattern of situations, which forms the archetypal Minnelli structure (what differentiates his nonmusical films is mainly that though these situations are present, they are not necessarily in this order): (1) The moment of isolation (the individual vision as imprisonment), (2) the tentative communication (the vision materializes as decor), (3) the rupture (the decor appears as mere appearance and delusion), (4) the world as chaos, (5) the world as spectacle/the spectacle as world.

In a sense, this pattern represents a kind of catharsis of vision, to which corresponds the clarification of emotions through the purging of their opposites: what emerges from the contradictory impulses of solitude and euphoria, frustration, despair, and delirious monomania is a measure of self-fulfillment, often merely implicit—where all emotional extremes feed into the creation of "the show," and where the energy is finally disciplined in the movement of the dance. The classic example of this is *The Pirate*. Judy Garland (Manuela), dreaming of the pirate, sees Macoco materialize in Gene Kelly, only to discover that he is an impostor—a discovery that creates emotional chaos for her (she loves him all the same) and actual chaos on the island (there is a price on his head). Manuela, finally renouncing her romantic fantasies, joins Kelly's humble theatrical troupe, and the film ends with an ironic number, significantly titled "Be a Clown."

Likewise, in *Brigadoon*, Gene Kelly's desire for another world materializes in the legendary village of Brigadoon where he meets the girl of his life, only to discover that the whole village and its inhabitants will have to disappear again for another hundred years. But Brigadoon is also being threatened by one of the inhabitants who wants to escape from the magic spell and live a "real" life. The villagers hunt him down and he is finally killed. Kelly returns to New York, but the mad chaos in the fashionable bar makes him long so much for the enchanted world of Brigadoon that he returns to Scotland, and miraculously, Brigadoon appears once more, conjured up by his faith. In marrying Fiona, his dream girl, Kelly accepts the "unreality" of Brigadoon and is prepared to live for only a day every hundred years—metaphor for the artist living only through his art, whatever the cost to "real life."

In *The Band Wagon,* too, the pattern is in evidence. Here it is particularly the different stages of Astaire's reimmersion into the world of show business, the different and often disastrous shows, that liberate the character from his egocentric projection, and by a series of debunking maneuvers and parodies (e.g., the staging of *Oedipus Rex*), Minnelli establishes the idea of the spectacle as the measure of things. This is summed up in the theme song "That's Entertainment": "everything that happens in life / can happen in a show . . . anything, anything can go / —The world is a stage / the stage is a world / of entertainment."

The notion of the artist as actor, however, not only relates the hero in a complex way to his environment, it also allows Minnelli to pursue the theme of artistic creativity into its most banal guises, where a common human denominator—the role-playing of all social life—serves to illuminate what is after all normally considered a privileged state of being. An essentially artistic temperament is revealed in all those who—from switchboard girl to Hollywood tycoon—want to act upon a given reality, change it, transform the material of their lives through the energy of an idea, an obsession, or merely the tentative groping to live up to the boldness of their imagination. But this theme of an energy in search of a material form hardly ever communicates itself in Minnelli as achievement. On the contrary, it is radically relativized as process—a permanent becoming—and rhythm, gesture and color are the properly cinematic signs of a spontaneous and contagious vitality, embodied in the musical as in no other genre.

Thus, despite the obvious difference between Judy Holliday's blunt vivaciousness in *Bells Are Ringing* and Leslie Caron's spiritual and graceful sensibility in *Gigi,* both films share the common drive for a liberation that inevitably leads to the spectacle, and both films are, in this sense, concerned with the ethics of the mise-en-scène—in one film understood as the (benevolent) influence on other people's lives, in the other as the assumption of a role in a formalized and stylized society. In *Bells Are Ringing*, Judy Holliday wants to play the good fairy to the clients of a telephone answering service, but at first she creates merely confusion, chaos, and mischief. But although her role-playing makes her seem unreal to herself, her clients eventually bind together—to produce a theater play. In an important aspect, however, her predicament highlights one of the inspirations of Minnelli's art. Through Judy Holliday's escapades we see a dichotomy between the richness of the American imagination and the restrictive force of a conventional morality. Significantly, the police handcuff her for her flight of fancy, ironic symbol of society's attitude to the creative artist.

If *Bells Are Ringing* concerns the responsibility of the metteur en scène, *Gigi* is an example of the apprenticeship of the mise-en-scène. Gigi has to learn how not to be natural, how to calculate her movements and judge the meaning of each gesture. She has to learn the conscious use of appearance as a way of retaining a personal spontaneity and freedom through the language of social grace. In *Gigi* it is difficult to know how to take this aesthetic education—the color symbolism tells the story of a degradation, with Gigi's red and green becoming gradually a merely fashionable mauve and pink. Yet the process seems inevitable, and Minnelli obviously prefers a conscious grace to a false innocence. In this sense, *Gigi* more than any other film is about the commercial cinema. And by subjecting his inspiration to the rigors of the system, Minnelli seems to praise the chains that tie the Hollywood artist so often to the banal story, the vulgar sentiment, the platitudinous cliché. However, unlike other aesthetic moralists such as Max Ophuls or Renoir with whom he has much in common, Minnelli has an entirely American reliance on an unbroken stream of vitality and energy. But as with them, what defines value for him is the *conception* of the world, not its material basis. In this sense, even the most "unreal" of his melodramas or musical comedies acknowledges a level of existence, a dimension of the actual that many a European director studiously ignores, and which Hollywood itself seems to have lost under the impact of TV-style instant realism. Who is then to say whether Minnelli's aestheticism is pernicious mystification or not, rather the realism of the truly cinematic artist?

But Minnelli has dramatized the dilemma of filmmaking explicitly in his two films *The Bad and the Beautiful* and *Two Weeks in Another Town*. In both films seemingly fundamental moral distinctions between art and life are seen to become more and more ambiguous, as the laws and conditions of filmmaking impose themselves on an already inauthentic model of life. The film to be, the artifact, assumes the dimensions of an inexorable necessity, exposing the moral flaws and human weaknesses of those involved in its creation—a banal point perhaps, had not Minnelli balanced this indictment of Hollywood in *The Bad and the Beautiful* by the dramatization of a grandiose, all-devouring obsession of an artist who spares neither himself nor others in order to remain true to his inspiration. Through the character of producer Jonathan Shields—cynical, cunning, and demonic, who sacrifices everything in order to make films—Minnelli explores the nature of his own commitment to the cinema. Shields, by destroying their private lives, liberates the creative potential of his director, scriptwriter, and leading lady, who had all been imprisoned by their petty worries and emotional fixations. *The Bad and the Beautiful* shows the visionary as the most ruthless realist, dominating a world with an energy so radical that it can only come from the intimate knowledge of its degradation.

Art as the destruction of "ordinary" life—this is the central ambiguity at the heart of Minnelli's vision. And in *Lust for Life,* the film about Vincent van Gogh, he pays homage to a greater artist, yet at the same time sharpens his own theme to its paroxysm. The Nietzschean intensity of Van Gogh's vision produces paintings of life as no human eye has ever seen them, but it is also a demonic urge that dissolves and severs all human bonds and finally destroys Van Gogh. In the film, the two sides are linked symbolically. As his isolation grows, the yellow colors of a superhuman light invade the canvas. But here Minnelli confronts a dilemma that transcends the framework of Hollywood, namely that of the morality of art. What are the values it creates, whom does it serve, and to what ends?

If these questions receive an ambivalent answer in Minnelli's films, where the artist finally redeems and justifies his trespass on "life," it is partly because for Minnelli the artist is not privileged in either status or sensibility. All those who are capable of experiencing existence by its intensity ("Why must life be always measured by its duration?"—Deborah Kerr's complaint in *Tea and Sympathy* is symptomatic) and have the courage of their inspiration are artists in Minnelli's films, whether creative in an accepted sense or not.

It is when dealing with the "real" artist, as in *Lust for Life,* that the question of the value of ordinary life becomes problematic, and in *Two Weeks in Another Town* the demonic element in the Shields–Van Gogh personality is portrayed as unambiguously neurotic and incapable of dealing with his life. Through Jack Andrus (all three characters, significantly, are played by the same actor—Kirk Douglas) Minnelli insists above all on the human price to be paid for the artist's venture. In this film, the "art" is shown to be inept, and the society is simply decadent. The assertive energy that in the early films mediated the rupture is explicitly and nostalgically evoked by Minnelli quoting his own *The Bad and the Beautiful*. A feeling of guilt and failure, by contrast, always makes reality seem apocalyptic. In *Two Weeks* it is the spectacle in its corrupt form (one director taking over from another, everyone working behind one another's back) that comes to dominate, and the central protagonist, instead of being the force that precariously balances two mutually complementary orders of reality, is a schizophrenic, just released from a mental hospital. Although the film in the end appears to suggest the possibility of a new start, this is both a return and an escape, and the outcome is finally left open. What weighs, however, more heavily is the "death" of the director in the film—Minnelli's alter ego, but also his counterself—whose once-creative vision has turned into a morbid and self-destructive introspection, to which he finally succumbs.

II

THE 1970S AND 1980S: GENRE, PSYCHOANALYSIS, AND CLOSE READINGS

Minnelli and Melodrama

GEOFFREY NOWELL-SMITH

What this paper claims is that the genre or form that has come to be known as melodrama arises from the conjunction of a formal history proper (development of tragedy, realism, etc.); a set of social determinations, which have to do with the rise of the bourgeoisie; and a set of psychic determinations, which take shape around the family. The psychic and social determinations are connected because the family whose conflicts the melodrama enacts is also the bourgeois family, but a complexity is added to the problem by the fact that the melodrama is also a particular form of artistic representation. As artistic representation it is also (in Marxist terms) ideology and (in Freudian terms) "secondary revision," but it cannot be simply reduced to either. As artistic representation it does not "reflect" or "describe" social and psychic determinations. Rather, it *signifies* them. This act of signifying has two aspects: on the one hand it produces a narrated or represented content, the life of people in society; and on the other hand it narrates and represents to and from a particular standpoint or series of standpoints, "subject positions." Now it might be thought that the former aspect, concerning the content, is a question for social (historical-materialist) analysis, and the latter, concerning the form, a matter for psychology or psychoanalysis. What I shall claim is that this is not the case and that the positions of the narrating are also social positions, while what is narrated is also psychical. The "subject positions" implied by the melodrama are those of bourgeois art in a bourgeois epoch, while the "represented object" is that of the oedipal drama.

MELODRAMA AND TRAGEDY

Melodrama originally meant, literally, drama + melos (music), and this eighteenth-century sense survives in the Italian *melodramma*—grand opera. In its early form melodrama was akin to pastoral and was differentiated from tragedy in that the story usually had a happy ending. Not much of the original meaning has survived into later—Victorian and modern—usages of the term, but the differentiation from tragedy has become, if anything, more marked. The principal differences are two, both of them the result of developments in art forms generally that began in the eighteenth century and were consolidated later. The first of these concerns modes of address and the second the representation of the hero(ine). At the time it should be noted that in many other respects the melodrama is the inheritor of many tragic concerns, albeit transposed to a new situation.

MELODRAMA AS BOURGEOIS FORM

One feature of tragic and epic forms up to (roughly) the eighteenth century is that they characteristically deal with kings and princes, while being written by, and for the most part addressed to, members of a less exalted social stratum. (The authors, even Homer, are, broadly speaking, "intellectuals," while the audience is conceived of, however inaccurately, as "the people.") With the advent of the novel (cf. Antoine Furetière's *Le roman bourgeois*) and the "bourgeois tragedy" of the eighteenth century, the situation changes. Author, audience, and subject matter are put on a place of equality. As Raymond Williams has noted, the appeal is directly to "Our equals, your equals."[1] Mystified though it may be, the address is from one bourgeois to another bourgeois, and the subject matter is the life of the bourgeoisie. This movement of equalization generally goes under the name of (or is conflated with) realism, but it also characterizes forms that in other respects are not conspicuous for their realism, such as the melodrama.

Insofar as melodrama, like realism, supposes a world of equals, a democracy within the bourgeois strata (alias bourgeois democracy), it also supposes a world without the exercise of social power. The address is to an audience that does not think of itself as possessed of power (but neither as radically dispossessed, disinherited, oppressed), and the world of the subject matter is likewise one in which only middling power relations are present. The characters are neither the rulers nor the ruled, but occupy a middle ground, exercising local power or suffering local powerlessness, within the family or the small town. The locus of power is the family and individual private property, the two being connected through inheritance. In this world of circumscribed horizons (which corresponds very closely to Marx's definition of "petty bourgeois ideology") patriarchal right is of central importance. The son has to become like his father in order to take over his property and his place within the community (or, in variant structures, a woman is widowed and therefore inherits, but the question posed is which man she can pass the property on to by remarriage; or, again, the father is evil and the son must grow up different from him in order to be able to redistribute the property at the moment of inheritance, etc., etc.). Notably, the question of law or legitimacy, so central to tragedy, is turned inward from "Has this man a right to rule (over us)?" to "Has this man a right to rule a family (like ours)?" This inward turning motivates a more directly psychological reading of situations, particularly in the Hollywood melodrama of the 1950s.

ACTION AND PASSION

Aristotle defined *history* as "what Alcibiades did and suffered."[2] Doing and suffering, action and passion are co-present in classical tragedy, and indeed in most art forms up to the romantic period. There is then a split, producing a demarcation of forms between those in which there is an active hero, inured or immune to suffering, and those in which there is a hero, or more often a heroine, whose role is to suffer. Broadly speaking, in the American movie the active hero becomes protagonist of the western, the passive or impotent hero or heroine becomes protagonist of what has come to be known as melodrama. The contrast active/passive is, inevitably, traversed by another contrast, that between masculine and feminine. Essentially the world of the western is one of activity/masculinity, in which women cannot figure except as receptacles (or occasionally as surrogate males). The melodrama is more complex. It often features women as protagonists, and where the central figure is a man there is regularly an impairment of his "masculinity"—at least in contrast to the mythic potency of the hero of the western. It cannot operate in the simple terms of a fantasy affirmation of the masculine and disavowal of the feminine, but the way it recasts the equation to allow more space for its women characters and for the representations of passion undergone throws up problems of its own. Insofar as activity remains equated with masculinity and passivity with femininity, the destiny of the characters, whether male or female, is unrealizable; he or she can only live out the impairment ("castration") imposed by the law. In their struggle for the achievement of social and sexual demands, men may sometimes win through, women never. But this fact about the plot structure is not just an element of realism, it reflects an imbalance already present in the conceptual and symbolic structure. "Masculinity," although rarely attainable, is at least known as an ideal. "Femininity," within the terms of the argument, is not only unknown but also unknowable. Since sexuality and social efficacy are recognizable only in a "masculine" form, the contradictions facing the women characters are posed in more acutely problematic form from the outset. For both women and men, however, suffering and impotence, besides being the data of middle-class life, are seen as forms of a failure to be male—a failure from which patriarchy allows no respite.

THE GENERATION GAME

To describe as patriarchy the law that decrees suffering and impairment (if only as motors for dramatic action) and decrees them unequally for men and for women, is also to raise the problem of generations. The castration that is at issue in the melodrama (and according to some writers in all narrative forms) is not an ahistorical, atemporal structure. On the contrary, it is permanently renewed within each generation. The perpetuation of symbolic sexual division only takes place insofar as it is the father who perpetuates it.

It is not just the place of the man relative to the woman but also that of the parent (male) relative to the children, which is crucial here. Melodrama enacts, often with uncanny literalness, the "family romance" described by Freud —that is to say the imaginary scenario played out by children in relation to their paternity, the asking and answering of the question: whose child am I (or would I like to be)? In addition to the problems of adults, particularly women, in relation to their sexuality, the Hollywood melodrama is also fundamentally concerned with the child's problems of growing into a sexual identity within the family, under the aegis of a symbolic law father incarnates. What is at stake (also for social-ideological reasons) is the survival of the family unit and the possibility for individuals of acquiring an identity that is also a place within the system, a place in which they can both be "themselves" and "at home," in which they can simultaneously enter, without contradiction, the symbolic order and bourgeois society. It is a condition of the drama that the attainment of such a place is not easy and does not happen without sacrifice, but it is very rare for it to be seen as radically impossible. The problems posed are always to some extent resolved. Only in Max Ophuls's *Letter from an Unknown Woman*, where Lisa dies after the death of her (fatherless) child, are all the problems laid out in all their poignancy, and none of them resolved.

HYSTERIA AND EXCESS

The tendency of melodramas to culminate in a happy ending is not unopposed. The happy ending is often impossible, and, what is more, the audience knows it is impossible. Furthermore, a "happy ending" that takes the form of an acceptance of castration is achieved only at the cost of repression. The laying out of the problems "realistically" always allows for the generating of an excess that cannot be accommodated. The more the plots press toward a resolution the harder it is to accommodate the excess. What is characteristic of the melodrama, both in its original sense and in the modern one, is the way the excess is siphoned off. The undischarged emotion that cannot be accommodated within the action, subordinated as it is to the demands of family/lineage/inheritance, is traditionally expressed in the music and, in the case of film, in certain elements of the mise-en-scène. That is to say, music and mise-en-scène do not just heighten the emotionality of an element of the action; to some extent they also substitute for it. The mechanism here is strikingly similar to that of the psychopathology of hysteria. In hysteria (and specifically in what Freud has designated as "conversion hysteria") the energy attached to an idea that has been repressed returns converted into a bodily symptom. The "return of the repressed" takes place, not in conscious discourse, but displaced onto the body of the patient. In the melodrama, where there is always material that cannot be expressed in discourse or in the actions of the characters furthering the designs of the plot, a conversion can take place into the body of the text. This is particularly the case with Minnelli. It is not just that the characters are often prone to hysteria, but that the film itself somatizes its own unaccommodated excess, which thus appears displaced or in the wrong place. This is the case both in the musicals (*The Pirate, Meet Me in St Louis,* etc.), which tend to be much more melodramatic than others from the same studio and where the music and dancing are the principal vehicles for the siphoning of the excess but where there may still be explosions of a material that is repressed rather than expressed; and in the dramas proper, where the extreme situations represented turn up material that cannot be represented within the convention of the plot and mise-en-scène.

It should be stressed that the basic conventions of the melodrama are those of realism: what is represented consists of supposedly real events, seen either "objectively" or as the summation of various discrete individual points of view. Often the "hysterical" moment of the text can be identified as the point at which the realist representative convention breaks down. Thus in the scene in *The Cobweb* where the lake is being dragged for Stevie's body there is no certainty either as to what is being represented (is the woman Stuart is talking to Meg or is it Karen?) or as to whose point of view, if anybody's, is being represented. The breakdown of the stable convention of representation allows such questions to be temporarily suspended in favor of what is, at one level, simple narrative confusion but on another level can be seen as an enactment of a fantasy that involves all the characters the plot has drawn together. At the level of this collective fantasy, Stevie is Stuart's and Meg's "child" and therefore the child Stuart could have had by Meg, did he not already have children by Karen (from whom he is estranged). The possibility of Stevie being dead brings this submerged fantasy to the surface but not directly into the articulation of the plot. Realist representation cannot accommodate the fantasy, just as bourgeois society cannot accommodate its realization.

PROVISIONAL CONCLUSION

Melodrama can thus be seen as a contradictory nexus in which certain determinations (social, psychical, artistic) are brought together but in which the problem of the articulation of these determinations is not successfully resolved. The importance of melodrama (at least in the versions of it that are due to Ophuls, Minnelli, Sirk) lies precisely in its ideological failure. Because it cannot accommodate its problems, either in a real present or in an ideal future, but lays them open in their shameless contradictoriness, it opens a space that most Hollywood forms have studiously closed off.

NOTES

1. Raymond Williams, "A Lecture on 'Realism,'" *Screen* 18, no. 1 (1977).
2. Aristotle, *Poetics,* chapter 9.

Meet Me in St. Louis
Smith; or, The Ambiguities

ANDREW BRITTON

In *Capitalism, the Family, and Personal Life,* Eli Zaretsky writes: "The family," to the Victorian bourgeoisie, was a "tent . . . pitch'd in a world not right." "This is the true nature of home," wrote John Ruskin; "it is the place of peace; the shelter, not only from all injury, but from all terror, doubt, and division. . . . So far as the anxieties of the outer life penetrate into it . . . it ceases to be a home; it is then only a part of the outer world which you have roofed over and lighted fire in." It stood in opposition to the terrible anonymous world of commerce and industry: "a world alien, not your world . . . without father, without child, without brother." The Victorian family was distinguished by its spiritual aspect: it is remote, ethereal and unreal—"a sacred place, a vestal temple." As in the Middle Ages, so now with the bourgeoisie, the domain of the spirit had once again "separated off from the realm of production."

Meet Me in St. Louis is set in a precise geographical location at a precise historical moment—1903/4, the turn of the century—yet the temporal specificity is, instantly, mythic. Simply to plot a course within those historical/topographical coordinates is already to proceed across a landscape that has been colonized by mythology, and from which history has been expelled. St. Louis is as much "south" as one can be while remaining "north," and in a film in which the supreme disruption is figured as a move to New York, one set of the ambiguous connotations relating to "south" is powerfully evoked—the connotations of elegance, refinement, culture, "organic community," that Mark Twain, in his denunciation of the myth, associates with the European tradition of aristocratic, chivalric romance of which Sir Walter Scott is the supreme, and most pernicious, exponent. (The myth is, then, dualistic, contradictory—alongside the ethos that produces *Gone with the Wind*, the stress on the contaminating rottenness of southern Europeanism—Edgar Allan Poe, *Uncle Tom's Cabin*, *Pudd'nhead Wilson*, William Faulkner. One notes in this context the extraordinary ambiguity of the attitude to the south in, say, John Ford.) Simultaneously, "1903/4" calls up the myth of "Edwardianism"— the last halcyon days of the nineteenth century before the twentieth begins in 1914, to which Edward Elgar, writing in 1917, pays significant tribute: "Everything good and nice and clean and fresh and sweet is far away never to return."

Meet Me in St. Louis (1944) is roughly contemporary with *The Magnificent Ambersons* (1942) and *Shadow of a Doubt* (1943); and while, in all three films, the myth is placed, its invocation, in the context of the family (the romance of the family, as opposed to what Freud means by "the family romance"—the oedipal relation with which the films also concern themselves), testifies, in various ways, to its potency. Orson Welles's response to the "magnificence of the Ambersons" is as systematically ambivalent as Minnelli's to the Smiths, and in Hitchcock's film (on the script of which the Thornton Wilder of *Our Town* collaborated). Uncle Charlie, the "monster" whose psychosis is directly attributed to the American family, tells his niece, as three generations gather round the family dinner table (children, parents, grandparents in the photo), "Everyone was sweet and pretty then—not like now." Anne Newton, in the same film, not only reads *Ivanhoe* but also aspires, like southern ladies "in books," to gather orchids with white gloves.

The difficulty inside the sense of nostalgia (less apparent in the Hitchcock, which lacks that sensuous response to the object of criticism so characteristic of the Welles and the Minnelli) can be defined by offering, as a third term, Henry James. *Washington Square*, set in the 1830s, written in 1880, is as trenchant an analysis of bourgeois patriarchy and its associated oppression of women as any the realist novel has produced. Yet the book's marvelous tension depends not only on the ambivalent response to Dr. Sloper (both monster and angelic intelligence, both the figure of repressive social law and supremely refined [self-]consciousness), but also on a topographical ambivalence. The revulsion from the urbanization of New York ("the long shrill city"; "the murmur of trade had become a mighty uproar") is only half concealed by irony at Dr. Sloper's expense, and has, as its corollary, the sensuous, inward evocation of the very culture the novel condemns ("This portion of New York appears to many persons the most delectable") for which, at one point, the narrator actually apologizes ("My excuse for this topographical parenthesis . . ."). What is "tension" in *Washington Square* becomes, increasingly, vacillation. The culture, after all, determined James's repression of his homosexuality; and that repression (inseparably, the refusal to follow through the logic of the social analysis) produces, finally, the impotent male protagonists who have never "had their lives" so characteristic of the late period (*The Beast in the Jungle, The Ambassadors*). The subtext of the latter novel is, indeed, the novel about gayness that James is incapable of writing. The ambiguities of nostalgia emerge very strikingly, in *Meet Me in St. Louis,* in the singing of "Have Yourself a Merry Little Christmas," in which Esther attempts to console Tootie (and herself) by escaping from the present through creating the future (New York) as the past ("Happy golden days of yore"). The project is doubly, and disturbingly, inflected by giving the song, as context, Tootie's desire to dig up her "dead" dolls from her graveyard and take them with her to her new home.

The New York/St. Louis antinomy is an opposition between oppressive, dehumanized urbanization ("cooped up in a tenement") and the "organic community" between "the city" and a city that nevertheless *isn't* a city. "It just doesn't seem very big out here where we live." The New York of *Meet Me in St. Louis* is not the "wonderful town" of *On the Town* (and is the use of "town" there, rather than "city," significant?), but the metropolis of the antiurban tradition discussed by Morton and Lucia White (*The Intellectual versus the City*). The Whites suggest that the crux of hatred of the city is the hatred of "commerce, industry, and massive immigration" (consider the importance of Mr. Smith's being a businessman, and the film's repression, from its ethos of "southness," of the blacks), and that therefore antiurbanism did not emerge, as far as the American city was concerned, until the nineteenth century. They quote Crèvecoeur, who distinguishes between the "simple and cordial friendliness they [visitors] are to expect in [the] cities of this continent" and the "accumulated and crowded" cities of Europe. "They are but the confined theater of cupidity; they exhibit nothing but the action and reaction of a variety of passions that, being confined within narrower channels, impel one another with the greatest vigor." The "bad" city, while it suggests compactedness, antifreedom, the negative of American space, commerce ("cupidity"), also evokes, in this description, a sense of violent, seething, untrammeled, implicitly erotic energies—the city as repository of libido, so central to the film noir. Typically, Crèvecoeur admires, in contemporary New York, both the "enlightenment" social values (hospitality, a contained cosmopolitanism) and that sense, crucial, also, in Ben Franklin, that America is the place where universal engagement in commerce does not entail destructive competitiveness and is consonant with perfect social stability. Noncompetitive free enterprise not only "binds the whole together for general purposes" but also contains sexuality—"Industry and constant employment are great preservatives of the morals and virtue of a nation" (*Poor Richard's Almanac*). To the extent that it draws on Crèvecoeur's preindustrial American city and makes use of conventions for the presentation of sexuality arrived at by a process of sublimation, *Meet Me in St. Louis* and the genre to which it belongs (small town domestic musical/comedy) suggest a sort of modified pastoral convention.

"1903/4" becomes in fact, the point at which "city" can still mean "community"; and one can compare the film, in this respect, to *It's a Wonderful Life* (1946). In Capra's film the myth of community depends for its efficacy on the freezing of the development of capitalism at a certain point—the point before which capitalism's defining characteristic—the desire to produce an economic surplus—has become evident. Hence the film's central structural opposition between George Bailey (James Stewart) and Mr. Potter (Lionel Barrymore), between the accumulation of capital and the constant diffusion of capital back into the community ("Your money's in Joe's house"), translated into useful, socially beneficial objects, between, that is, "the capitalist" (bad) and the circulation of capital without capitalists, no one at any point making a profit at anyone else's expense. On this level, the film's repeated crises, which finally reduce Bailey to attempt suicide, are essential to its project, in that without them Bailey would be seen to be becoming Mr. Potter. One can relate this to Zaretsky's remarks to the effect that at the moment of the supreme development of bourgeois capitalism the family, its basic unit, is imaged as a refuge from it by saying that Capra's film moves toward locating the family within an essentially decapitalized capitalism, and that *Meet Me in St. Louis,* while on one level roundly denying the family's immunity, operates on another as if the denial were not taking place (it can be read, that is, as if it weren't).

One can approach an analysis of the ambiguity through decor, an iconography at which point *It's a Wonderful Life* again provides a point of reference. The imagery of the last five minutes of the film, after George's "salvation"—snow laden streets, trees festooned with fairy lights, decorations, presents, warmth, hospitality, "hearth and home"—relates directly to the iconography of a certain kind of Christmas card, still extant, frequently with a Regency/Victorian/Edwardian setting; the image, for example, of a coach traveling across a snowy landscape toward the lighted windows of a house just visible in the distance, or of passengers disembarking in the snow before a glowing doorway. Whatever has been done thematically—and It's a Wonderful Life has been profoundly subversive—the iconography has its own potency based on a prospective sense of "being at home inside"—the anticipation of warmth, security, sociality, apartness from "outside." Consider the way in which, in the first scene of I Walked with a Zombie (1943), Betsy's self-confidence, her (illusory) sense of self-coherence, is associated with the spatial confidence of the inside/outside opposition by the device of framing her and her interlocutor against windows beyond which snow is falling—the film being concerned thereafter simultaneously with the breakdown of self-coherence and the dissolution/transgression of boundaries.

The credits of Meet Me in St. Louis are set within rococo gilt frames, with cameo insets of flowers in vases; and the film's temporal advances (associated with transitions in nature—the passage of the seasons) are marked by dissolves from a samplerlike image to its "reality." The picture, literally, "comes to life"; and the first instance of this (the movement from the credits to the narrative) as well as subsequent ones, reinforces the sense of entering the picture through camera movement—through the smooth, elaborate crane-cum-tracking shot that carries us forward into the fiction by accompanying the movements suddenly revealed within it—the horse-drawn wagon heading up the street and then the figure of a boy riding a bicycle toward a large house. The concept of "the frame" will be crucial in the film; and here the entry to the picture that comes to life is the entry to a defined, mythological space, a space of confidence, a conventionalized world bounded, ordered, delimited by a frame, appropriate expectations for which have already been sufficiently defined by the credits sequence. Frame and convention (generic and representational) make the spectacle world cohere, the coherence completed by that self-projection into the frame that the film encourages. Like the Christmas cards, the opening shots set up the anticipation of "at homeness," which becomes, immediately, inseparable from the notion of the family in that the film invites very strongly an identificatory regression not to childhood as it was, but to a cultural myth of "childhood-in-the-family-as-it-ought-to-have-been-and-might-possibly-be." The film is the product of a society in which the myth, the need for the idea of the family, is so intensely powerful that it can depend on functioning as a petite madeleine for individuals whose particular experience may not correspond at any point to the image of the family being offered.

Frame and convention (generic and representational) make the spectacle world cohere.

This is the point perhaps, to suggest certain qualifying elements that feed into the film from other sources. If Hollywood affirms the family massively, one must give equal emphasis to the complementary impulse to reject it, both being rooted in the sense of home as "vestal temple," the sacred domain of woman as the embodiment of civilized social values. The most obvious form of the rejection produces that ongoing tradition of flight from home/community/woman from Henry David Thoreau to *On the Road* and *Cross of Iron*, frequently accompanied by a paradoxical, despairing nostalgia for what has been lost ("You can't go home again"). Equally important is what one might call the "alternative small town tradition," the first major instance of which is Herman Melville's *Pierre* and which proceeds through Twain (*Pudd'nhead Wilson, The Man That Corrupted Hadleyburg*) to Sinclair Lewis (*Babbitt, Main Street*) and Sherwood Anderson (*Winesburg, Ohio*). It is also significantly developed by James (consider the concept of "Woollet, Massachusetts" in *The Ambassadors*).

In the context of *Meet Me in St. Louis*, certain characteristic elements need to be stressed:

1. On the first page of *Pierre,* Melville makes the connection between the myth of the small town, a debased pastoral convention reinforced by the antiurbanism of Wordsworthian romanticism, and the sublimation of sexual-

ity. The innocence of this Arcadia ("brindled kine") consists in the ignorance of the energies that will later disrupt it.

2. Those energies are embodied, in the pastoral, by Comus; and the link between sexuality, the devil, and the darker nature of the forest emphasized in Milton's poem is reiterated, in the New World, in the paradigm libido/wilderness/Devil/Indian, the forces that surround and threaten the community. In *Pierre* as in *The Scarlet Letter* they emerge inside the community as female sexuality. Both novels, indeed, suggest versions of *Comus* with the sexes reversed, Pierre and Dimmesdale in the role of "the lady" (who now succumbs to temptation) and the sexuality of both Hester and Isabel associated with "the blackness of darkness" and vast savage natural forces (thunder and lightning, the forest). But the attitude to sexuality and to "the fall" is correspondingly more ambiguous; and the tendency to affirm the energies embodied in the women and their liberation of the men as human consciousness is offset by the chaos they unleash and the emasculation they threaten to induce. There is a direct line of descent from Isabel and Hester and her daughter Pearl ("a demon offspring") to the small town "vamp" (Gloria Grahame, say, in *It's a Wonderful Life*, or supremely, Bette Davis in *Beyond the Forest*), Tootie in *Meet Me in St. Louis*, and the devil children of the diabolist cycle, Regan and Carrie. It is a line that, as *Pierre* makes clear, has to be associated with the hubris of Melville's heroes: Ahab's vow "in nominee diaboli" has been inherited, in the modern horror movie, by the female child.

3. The characteristic form of the possessed child's rebellion is a repetition of the crime of Satan—the overthrow of the father (or, as in *Carrie*, the phallic mother), the figure of the Law. Pierre's last gesture on leaving his ancestral home is to destroy his father's portrait ("Henceforth, cast-out Pierre hath no paternity and no past"); Tootie kills Mr. Brockhoff; Regan becomes the Devil, kills her potential step-father, and, finally, both representatives of the Holy Church. In all three cases the Law of the Father continues to reassert itself, and the child is vanquished.

4. *Pierre* is built on the theme of the oedipal romance, and its enforcement within the idealized nuclear family. Pierre, impelled by love of Isabel, breaks out of his incestuous involvement with his mother only to discover that Isabel is his sister; and in the final chapter beholds in the portrait of Beatrice Cenci the icon of "the two most horrible crimes . . . possible to civilized humanity—incest and parricide." Once more the apparent innocence of the female child ("so sweetly and seraphically blonde a being") assumes the burden of guilt, but now as the emphasis on "blonde" conveys, the stigma passes from the dark

lady to the likeness of Lucy, the archetypal "sweetheart" of the opening chapters, and from her to Pierre, who is guilty in her image. The indissoluble themes of parent-murder and oedipal confusion that continue to inform the Gothic (*Psycho,* the devil child films) are also paired in *Meet Me in St. Louis* in which the Halloween sequence has its significance in the rejection of Father and Oedipus complex, the two determinants of the all-American romance.

5. The sense that the domesticated small town male is castrated is an obsessive cultural preoccupation and surfaces in numerous movies (*Shadow of a Doubt, Meet Me in St. Louis, It's a Wonderful Life, The Searchers, Kings Row,* etc.). The castration may be the punishment for rebellion against the Father (Ahab's lost leg; Pierre's vision of Enceladus, and his final cry of "Pierre is neuter now!"; Regan's appropriation of the phallus and her recastration by the two priests in *The Exorcist*). Alternatively, and far more frequently, the man is castrated by women (the small town is a matriarchy and the phallus is stolen by a monstrous wife/mother; Mrs. Glendinning in *Pierre;* the narrator's wife in Melville's outrageous short story, *I and My Chimney;* Mrs. Newsome in *The Ambassadors;* the inhabitants of the boarding school in *The Beguiled;* etc.). The man is unmanned by the contagion of domesticity, and is left either absurdly embattled ("I and my chimney will never surrender") or hopelessly lost and ineffectual (Strether) or pernicious (Babbitt). If Tootie relates to the first type of Satanic hubris, then John and Mr. Smith relate clearly to the second.

The richness of this material is clearly inseparable from its profound contradictions. To take only the question of female sexuality: while the energies embodied in Hester, Isabel, Regan, the film noir vamp, Davis in *Beyond the Forest,* Jennifer Jones in *Duel in the Sun* are supremely fascinating (and thus, at some unconscious level, espoused) precisely because they are subversive of patriarchal order, as soon as that order has been subverted and the satisfactions of anarchy indulged, order must be instantly reasserted if only by the punishment of the agent. The rationale of the contradiction emerges most clearly in the extremist of cases. Thus, while Isabelle frees Pierre from castration by his mother and releases the impulse that rejects the patriarchal law, it is only, as his sister, to trap him in incest and castration once more. Tootie and Regan kill the Father, but the very act entails the dissolution of the Oedipus complex, and must be canceled out. The breakdown precipitated by female sexuality is to be desired, in that the institution it undermines is felt as repressive, but the cost is always too high, in that it is always seen, quite correctly, to involve a threat to possession of the phallus. Time and again woman plunges order into anarchy, but the terms of the new order are always so horrific that the old is reinstated. *The Exorcist* is an almost diagrammatic illustration of the process, and represents as such a partial return to sources—a new inflection of the meeting of the small town and the Gothic, Satan and female sexuality in *Pierre* and *The Scarlet Letter*. It transpires that the small town, the outpost of a civilization created and consecrated in the name of woman, has actually taken the serpent to its bosom. Satan has not been expelled to the wilderness at all. The guardian of the "vestal temple" herself contains the forces that continually threaten to destroy it. Hence the crucial significance of those films in which the link is made between the Lady and the Indian.

The link between the family film and the horror film (touched on by Robin Wood in *Personal Views*) emerges very concisely in that extraordinary moment in *Meet Me in St. Louis* when, on Halloween night, the Smith house turns into the Bates house from *Psycho*. The space of confidence opened up in the first shot of the narrative is strangely lost as a forward tracking shot takes us this time toward a Gothic mansion at night, scarred by the shadow of a dead tree, the orange light of the windows no longer connoting a safe "inside" but assimilated by a dissolve to a shot of lurid skull masks and candles burning inside scooped-out pumpkins. The continuity between the two aspects of the house is carried out in the decor—in the heavy clutter of Victoriana, objets d'art, drapery, and its tone of slightly suffocating luxuriousness. Pairs of white candles transform mantelpieces into altars (the "vestal temple"), while the bad connotations of "southness" return in busts and figurines of Moors. *Psycho* makes the undertones explicit with its pastoral/allegorical icon of female nudity, its stuffed birds, its cast of clasped hands, its beckoning baroque statue presiding at the foot of the staircase.

The sublimation of female sexuality (the attempt to "block the hole" in Stephen Heath's phrase) call never rid itself of the perpetual danger that the hole will reassert its presence. Regression to home and mother—to home as mother—contains the possibility of refinding the mother's body, of ending up "inside" with a vengeance (the Bates predicament). Indeed, consider that cycle of films, contemporaneous with the 1940s domestic musical/comedy and the film noir about dead or missing women who remain as portraits, as potent forces immanent in the decor. The cycle is initiated by *Rebecca* (1940), which sets up also the recurrent Hitchcock image-complex of appalling mansion, impotent male, and castrating mother (Rebecca reborn in Mrs. Danvers), which proceeds through *Notorious* and *Under Capricorn* to *Psycho*. The structure is, of course, not simply Hitchcock's but an element of the American Gothic on which Poe worked countless variations.

Meet Me in St. Louis is one site of intersection of various complex strands. Its conventions permit the containment of conflict, but the particular process of containment exposes conflicts with unusual clarity.

If "St. Louis" suggests a myth of the organic community in a lost Golden Age, then the idea of "the fair" is the furthest reach of the myth—"It must look like a fairy land." The last moments of the film—the camera tracking into a huge close-up of Esther's face on her rapt, repeated murmur of "Right here where we live"—convey an achieved union of the "normal"/everyday and the miraculous. They put forward, implicitly, for the spectator's consent, the proposition that "your home town too is miraculous if you only stop to look at it." (*It's a Wonderful Life* offers a similar conclusion while extending it through the allegorical mode to induce a sense of cosmic confidence in an anthropomorphized universe.) The proposition draws on a strangely secularized variant informed by the "entertainment-as-Utopia" syndrome (see Richard Dyer's essay in *Movie* 24) of a familiar assertion of the Puritan ethic—the divine is immanent in the mundane—which lends itself to a multitude of possible inflections (from Herbert's "the daily round, the common task" to Hopkins's "inscape").

With the exception of the choruses and Judy Garland's solos, the songs in *Meet Me in St. Louis* are characterized by a process of "naturalization"; it is stressed that various characters can't sing "well" (professionally) or aren't used to singing (Agnes, Grandpa, Tootie). The device finds its most beautiful expression in the singing of "You and I," where Mrs. Smith's lowering of the key to accommodate her husband's voice and her quiet, unobtrusive anticipation of the key line ("Through the years . . ."), magnificently convey that reaffirmation of monogamy and family unity through the guidance of woman that culminates in the transformation of solo into duet while, around the singers, the family returns, silent and unobserved. The naturalization both foregrounds the aspect of "performance" and partially covers it: the characters are singing because they want to, not because they are singers.

One can relate this to the way in which the songs are not marked off and isolated as "numbers," but erupt out of the narrative, unless the sense of "tableau" or "performance" is justified diegetically, as, for instance, in "Skip to My Lou" or, most conspicuously, the "Cakewalk," which is explicitly a performance for an audience in the narrative, and which places the proscenium arch within the frame. Thus the first statement of "Meet Me in St. Louis" develops through Lon's humming it sporadically in the course of conversation, Agnes taking it up "naturally" as she goes upstairs, her passing it on to Grandpa, and, finally, its transference to Esther as she arrives in a buggy with her friends—each shift of voice, as it introduces an individual binding him/her into the family, an emphasis reinforced by the movement of each individual into or toward the house. Thus Esther's appearance recapitulates the arrival of Lon in the first shot and reinforces the notion of "binding in" by formal symmetry. Subsequently, both elements (naturalization, community through song) are amplified in Mr. Smith's remark that everyone is singing "that song," St. Louis becoming a grand extension of the family. The fluid continuity between musical and nonmusical elements is carried also in the mise-en-scène, in that characteristic flow of movement that both asserts spatial continuity and, as in Ophuls, a self-conscious delight in physical grace, in the "musicalization" of the camera (consider, for example, the scene in which John and Esther extinguish the lights, with its complex counterpoint between (a) Esther's deliberate fabrication of "romantic" atmosphere; (b) the acknowledgement of, respect for, and embodiment of the romantic sensibility implicit in the elaborate crane shot in which the scene is realized; and (c) the deflation of both artifice and romanticism that proceeds from John's insuperable stolidity). The "binding in" is extended to the audience by way of that forward craning movement toward the "inside" initiated by the first shot and repeated as a structural principle thereafter in, for instance, the two dance scenes.

But the first song sequence already introduces conflicting elements, which cluster around the pointed opposition between work and leisure. As Agnes enters the kitchen she remarks to her mother: "You should have taken a swim with us." To which Mrs. Smith replies: "With all I have to do?" All the singers in the first number—Lon, Agnes, Grandpa, Esther—are nonworkers, and their "freedom" is set against the domestic labor of Katie and Mrs. Smith and the business of making ketchup, which everyone wants to taste different. At once, a tension is set up (and stated, here, in a light key) between the celebration of the leisure and release from responsibility that is shown to be expressive of, and to produce, unity (Lon, Agnes, Grandpa, Esther, St. Louis, all united across space and time in the singing of the song), and work within and for the family, which precipitates conflict (the ketchup). Two parallel and mutually opposed lines of suggestion have been established: the wonderful is everyday versus the wonderful is opposed to the everyday, in the second case the singing becoming instantly anarchic in its implications. One might compare the use of "the fair" here with that of the myth of Vienna in *Shadow of a Doubt*. It is at the moment that she is released from work by her daughter at the beginning of the second dinner sequence that Mrs. Newton, primping her hair in front of the mirror, begins to hum the "Merry Widow Waltz," immersing herself in the ethos of "romantic dream," the sexual connotations of which have already been sufficiently established.

The first song is also remarkable for that assimilation of Grandpa to the female children, which reasserts itself in the scene in which Mr. Smith announces the family's departure for New York, and which, while it underlines the work theme (the young and old can be "irresponsible" because they are dependents), also feminizes him and places him on a more fundamental level with the women against the man of the house. (This too is ambiguous in that Mrs. Smith's "What about Katie, Grandpa and the chickens?" gives him and the female servant the status of nonhuman property.) Indeed, "Meet Me in St. Louis" systematically links all the children and Grandpa with the emphasis on the female children (Lon's contribution is minimal): Agnes and Esther in the first statement, Esther and Rose in the second, with, via the dissolve to the duet from Tootie's "Wasn't I lucky to be born in my favorite city?" the implicit collaboration of the youngest daughter. It is the father who, in disrupting the song, violates the unity ("For heaven's sake stop that screeching!"), and through him the theme of the oppressiveness of the work undertaken in the name of the family at once becomes explicit.

There are nine song sequences in the film. Of these all but one ("Skip to My Lou") are initiated by women, and with the same exception, individual male characters feature significantly in only two—Grandpa in the first statement of "Meet Me in St. Louis," Mr. Smith in "You and I." Apart from one line in "Skip to My Lou" ("Lost my partner"), the "hero" does not sing at all. The preeminence of women musically—which coincides of course with the narrative premise—is complex in its implications; and it becomes necessary at this point to consider Judy Garland's solos and their relation to the film as a whole:

1. Woman as predator. The number is preceded by Rose's provocative walk up the porch steps in an attempt to attract John's attention, and then by Rose and Esther strolling out and posing themselves nonchalantly on the balcony for the same purpose. Both strategies are conspicuously unsuccessful.

2. The reversal of the convention that dictates that sexual aggression is the prerogative of the male is contained within and defined by the convention that prescribes marriage as the destiny of the female. Esther and Katie have just been discussing Rose's "problem" ("The brutal fact is she isn't getting any younger") and throughout the film the concept of "marriage at all costs" is repeatedly foregrounded.

3. Inseparably from 1. and 2., woman as image: both Rose and Esther attempt to draw the attention of the male by creating themselves in and as conventionalized images of "femininity." Songs and nonmusical narrative

alike emphasize Esther in a frame: the frame of the proscenium arch in the Cakewalk and, in "The Boy Next Door," "Merry Little Christmas" and the "Bannister Song" the frame of the portrait, the icon. Indeed, the "Bannister Song" makes the imagery explicit by uniting the connotations of theater and of picture. The number is preceded by the extinguishing of the lamps, the prelude during which Esther's "performance," however unappreciated, is in preparation (the perfume she "saves for special occasions"), and which subtly suggests the lowering of the house lights around the "stage" that the staircase will finally provide. Esther leaves John gazing up at her from the foot of the staircase and, at his prompting ("How does it go?"), takes up the poem into song and herself into poetic image ("He watches the picture smiling"). Elsewhere, the concept of the picture frame is echoed by the frames of window and mirror and reinforced in, for instance, the scenes in which Esther prepares for the two dances, where the adoption of an artificial and oppressive "femininity" is associated with the donning of costume ("I feel elegant but I can't breathe").

Once again, the image of the frame works in terms both of the narrative and of the relation of spectator to film. "The Boy Next Door" is a courtship display for the absent male spectator in the diegesis (John), and also a performance on set for the absent spectator who will be provided by the screening of the film in a cinema. Just as Esther stages herself in the window frame, longing for John's attention, so Judy Garland, the star, performs a musical number for the contemplation of the spectator. And, like a spectator, John is passive. He does not sing—he watches.

The terms in which the Esther/John relationship is initiated are structurally crucial. It is emphasized that Esther does not know John, and that her imagination has transformed him into an ideal figure: "My only regret is that we've never met / Though I dream of him all the while." John is introduced, from the girls' perspective, standing on the lawn in front of his house dressed in white, the whiteness suggesting not simply an immaculate ideal, but also a tabula rasa, an emptiness onto which emotions can be projected. Thus if Esther's desire at this point is expressed in re-creating herself and in projecting herself as an image, then the object of desire is perceived in similar terms. Posed in profile with his pipe, John is instantly an icon of "normal," clean-cut manhood, the guardian of hearth and home, the complex tone of the scene—and of a great deal of the film—consisting in the fact that while the conventions of desire are made ironically explicit (desire is shown to be determined by convention), we are nevertheless invited to feel a degree of sympathetic involvement with characters who are uncritically governed by them.

In his account of the female Oedipus complex that, satisfactorily resolved, initiates "normal" womanhood and locates the female child "correctly" within the institutions that precede her, Freud suggests that the girl's desire is transferred from the father to the man who, as husband, will replace the father. Glossing this in *Psychoanalysis and Feminism*, Juliet Mitchell remarks that "there is an obvious link between the security of Oedipal father love and the happy hearth and home of later years." By marrying the boy next door, who appears at once in the image of the father, the girl reproduces the family structure and in the same action, reproduces society. Similarly, the girl relinquishes her hostility to her mother (consider Esther's concern to echo Mrs. Smith's judgment in the ketchup controversy), and identifies with her in relation to the father. This structure remains beneath the open hostility to Mr. Smith in the second half of the film in that the proposed move to New York directly threatens the smooth reproduction of the same social/familial order through the marriage of the two eldest daughters. The female rebellion against the real father (Mr. Smith) operates in the interests of the law of Father (the institutions of patriarchy) and is explicitly concerned to perpetuate the status quo. Similarly, of course, acquiescence in the move north would operate in the same interests. By concentrating on the social construction of desire within the family, the film succeeds in setting up a dramatic context in which the constraints on the female characters to reproduce the patriarchal order become apparent, all the more strikingly because of the apparent impotence of the given father figure.

Mitchell continues, quoting Freud, that it is through her identification with her mother that the girl "acquires her attractiveness to a man, whose Oedipus attachment to his mother it kindles into passion." At the beginning of *Meet Me in St. Louis* John is living alone with his mother (his father, presumably, dead), and during the extinguishing of the lights sequence, his only response to Esther's perfume is the remark that it reminds him of his grandmother. At the end of the second dance sequence, the Esther/John relationship is ratified in an image that condenses, with perfect simplicity, the logic of the "family romance." Esther, having been duly punished for her conspiracy against Lucille by dancing with each of the "perfect horrors" she has originally selected as Lucille's partners, is finally rescued from the last of them by her grandfather who cuts in, in the name of an "oriental" custom that fixes the status of woman as that of an item of property ("When a stranger admires one of your possessions, it's common courtesy to offer it to him"). Esther responds with relief and gratitude ("You're the first human being I've danced with all evening"), and the grandfather tells her how proud he is of her acceptance of the penalty he has imposed. The camera cranes up and we see the grandfather guiding Esther as they dance, toward and behind a huge decorated Christmas tree at the far end of the room. When Esther emerges on the other side, she is dancing with John, and the waltz the orchestra is playing becomes "Auld Lang Syne." The moment is beautifully exact: as the old year becomes the New Year, John takes the place of the father/grandfather and loves Esther in the image of the mother/grandmother, the connotations of ritual reenactment and repetition underlined by music, imagery (Christmas—the annual festival of the "holy family"), and movement (the unbroken circle).

But the film is significantly more complex than this in ways that have, perhaps, already been implied and which are bound up with John's status as "the ideal." One needs to account for the fact that while, on one level, the Esther/John relationship is offered as a paradigm of the "American romance" (girl meets and marries boy next door), John scarcely exists in the film as anything more than a token and is played and presented with an innocuousness that markedly sets off, by contrast, the intense vitality projected by Judy Garland. One needs to account, that is, for the discrepancy between a dominant ideological project that is clearly there in the film, which will be read as being there, and which is given in the narrative data, and the contradictory implications set up by the realization of the project.

The point here is the extraordinary way in which John becomes effectively superfluous to the four of Esther's songs supposedly inspired by him, the songs being transmuted into a form of communion between Esther and her own desire. In only one of the four (the "Bannister Song") is John directly physically present, and not only is it sung by Esther, the "smiling picture" of the lyric, in praise of her own beauty ("The loveliest face in town"), but also, during the singing, she scarcely looks at John at all, her gaze remaining fixed on some distant space off-camera while John continues to gaze at her, entranced. (The device is repeated in "Merry Little Christmas," in which Esther is clearly addressing herself rather than John, whose absence, as Esther's pretext, is signaled before the song begins by the lowering of a window blind, or Tootie for whom the advice delivered in the song is conspicuously ineffective.) Similarly, "The Boy Next Door" culminates in Esther's poses before the mirror in the hallway and her rapt solitary dance; and the first meeting with John is preceded by further intense self-scrutiny in a mirror framed by blue material similar in shade to that of her dress. Downstairs we discover that John is also dressed in blue, and Esther is continually associated with the color throughout the first half of the film.

Esther's creation of herself as a picture comes to appear less as a method of attracting John than as a way of allowing an image of herself to emerge for herself. John functions as an alibi that allows her to dramatize her own desire on a private stage for her own eyes. Hence the immediate appearance, in "The Boy Next Door," of the image of the mirror, and Esther's performance before it; the "ideal," the "overestimated object" of romantic love that, according to Freud, is always informed by the primary narcissism in which the child "was its own ideal," recedes or becomes the catalyst of those moments in which desire erupts for itself. Consider "The Trolley Song." Esther begins singing in the moment at which she sees John racing after the trolley and catching it at the last minute. This is also the moment at which she turns her back on him to look inside the tram, and the entire song is delivered in the midst of a circle of admiring women who form her background and chorus, gazing in at her as their center. On the line "His hand holding mine," Esther clasps her own hands together, and both her singing and the impulse that informed it are cut short abruptly when Esther becomes aware of John's presence next to her. They seat themselves immediately on opposite sides of the trolley platform and Minnelli dissolves directly to the Halloween sequence. Thus while "The Trolley Song" is ostensibly precipitated by John's arrival and is dedicated to him as the "ideal" ("He was quite the handsomest of men"), the actual staging of the number physically excludes the male; and the one moment in which a man intrudes into the performance, by raising his hat to Esther, provokes her withdrawal, shaking her head emphatically.

It is useful at this point to recall Jacques Lacan's definition of desire: "Desire is irreducible to need because it is not in principle a relation to a real object which is independent of the subject, but a relation to the phantasy. It is irreducible to demand in so far as it seeks to impose itself without taking language or the unconscious of the other into account, and requires to be recognised absolutely by him." Thus one can point to two aspects of "The Boy Next Door." Esther's desire relates to the fantasy of John ("We've never met"), an emphasis underlined by the dialogue before the song ("I want it to be something strange and wonderful"). Simultaneously, the dance before the window captures exactly "the desire to have one's desire recognized" that the scene has already established as a ruling motive.

The songs in *Meet Me in St. Louis* mark repeatedly a point of tension between containment and overflow. They continually override their authority while only being conceivable within its terms. They suggest moments of license and bear as such all the hallmarks of the defining restrictions. Thus the celebration of female desire in "The Trolley Song" is dramatically contingent on John, but does not survive his physical presence. Similarly, "Skip to My Lou," the communal youth dance, while it takes place within (is contained by) the Smith household, clearly functions in part as a rebellion against ideological constrictions—a rejection of hearth and home ("I'll fly away to a neighboring state") and of prohibitive morality ("I don't care what my friends say"). Indeed, the end of the song is marked by one of the girls falling over onto the floor, the incident suggesting very simply the shock of "reentry," the abrupt transition between two worlds. More significantly, the very concept of "St. Louis" itself is redefined in this context. From the first scene of the film the dream of the "fair" is the alibi for the release of those energies that are defined in opposition to work. Yet the extraordinary bleakness and flatness of tone of the final scene (to which Robin Wood has drawn attention) is a sufficient testimony to the failure of correspondence between the energies and the ideal in the name of which they have been allowed to emerge. It becomes clear, indeed, that in taking the "fair" as ideal, the energies have been devoted to their own entrapment. The fair is the repressive, quotidian reality etherealized, and the final scene is dominated by imagery of sublimation. The exhibition itself is merely glimpsed, across a stretch of water, as a display of brightly shimmering lights and has been built, we are told, on a drained bog. John, briefly alone with Esther, tells her, "I liked it better when it was a swamp and there was just the two of us," before they are summoned to rejoin the family, two nuns shrouded in black appearing spectrally in the background. The connotations could scarcely be more explicit: sexual energies, the life of the body, associated directly in John's remark with the swamp, are to be purified by assimilation to the small-town-as-Celestial-City, and the summoning of the couple to join the family group is presided over by figures suggestive equally of the Holy Church and death. Real relations and conditions of existence are sublimated in imaginary ones: the fair, twinkling beyond the mirror line marked by the river (and the final track in on Esther's face suggests strongly that the fair is the outward projection of an internal image), becomes exactly, in Lacan's phrase, "the presence of an absence of reality." It is crucial here that Tootie, though subjected anew, like Esther and John, to the prohibitions of the renewed, reaffirmed, idealized family (she is asked not to eat too much, "you'll spoil your dinner"), proceeds at once to undo the sublimation in her account of her dream (which is to be set against Esther's "I never dreamed anything could be so beautiful"): "I dreamt a big wave came up and flooded the whole city and when the water went back it was all muddy and horrible and full of dead bodies!" The apocalyptic vision, so central to the American Gothic from Poe to Roger Corman and *The Exorcist,* suggests not simply a wish (it emerges in a dream) or a portent (The Fall of the House of Smith), but also the perception of a reality, of that face of St. Louis concealed by the fair. In a previous scene Mr. Smith has declared, "We'll stay here till we rot!" Tootie knows that they are rotten already. It is, perhaps, significant that she shows scarcely any interest in the fair throughout the film.

This sublimation theme has already been firmly established in the treatment of money: Mr. Smith's attempt to repress the energies that find expression in music is balanced by the attempt of the female members of the family to repress the economic reality in which the family is bound up, and which dictates Mr. Smith's decision to move to New York. To Rose's "I hate, loathe, despise, and abominate money!" Mr. Smith replies at once, "You also spend it"; and the exchange neatly inflects the film's central opposition in economic terms—St. Louis in apotheosis as "the fair" versus St. Louis as economic unit. Thus the final scene, as it sublimates sexuality into marriage and family, represses money elsewhere (into "New York," into the swamp), and forgets the problems of the continuing economic viability of the family Mr. Smith has brought forward ("I've got to worry about where the money's coming from"). The three occasions on which the family is reassembled after the divisive split attendant on Mr. Smith's announcement all depend consciously on the repression of those problems. "You and I," while it reconvenes the family group, affirms not the family but the couple (the family does not join in and is not mentioned in the lyric), and affirms it too in isolation from society in "metaphysical" terms of the triumph over time and adversity ("You and I together, forever"). The immediate problem—which is, precisely, the family as a locus of conflicting interests—at a moment of economic crisis is completely avoided. Subsequently, Mr. Smith's change of heart after Tootie's destruction of the snow people is presented unequivocally as a piece of stoical window dressing, the violence of which comes over equally as bitter resentment of the family that has forced it on him, the suppression of his own desires and aspirations, and an attempt to make himself believe that it is, after all, his own decision. Indeed, the "happy ending" is achieved by two displays of "male dominance" that are shown to be victories in campaigns of attrition mounted by the women; the forthright proposal of Rose's suitor ("I don't want to hear any arguments") is at once qualified by Esther's remark: "He's just putty in your hands." The women have won, and the palm of victory is their own entrapment with their castrated men, inside patriarchal institutions.

This brings us to Tootie—the crux of the film, the register of its defining tensions. If Mr. and Mrs. Smith suggest the couple achieved as basic unit of the family, each with their "sphere" (home and business), and Rose and Esther are characterized by the desperate struggle to insert themselves in the same structure and perpetuate it ("We can't be too particular"), then Agnes and Tootie, the youngest sisters, embody and express a potential anarchy, a possible subversion of the structure. The film is quite clear-sighted about the kind of possibility; there is not a hint of sentimentality, nor any pretence that the return of repressed energies in Tootie are uncontaminated by repression. Consider, for example, her obsession with death (Twain's Emmeline Grangerford in *Huckleberry Finn* affords a useful parallel in contrast), which is used as an overtly neurotic inflection of capitalist possessiveness; she hoards dead matter ("I'm taking all my dolls—the dead ones too. I'm taking everything!"), and part of the impulse behind the destruction of the snow people is the determination that no one else should have them if she can't. Similarly, the dolls suggest a morbid surrogate family in regard to which her inferior status in the Smith house is replaced by the power of life and death ("I expect she won't live through the night").

This last represents, perhaps, the correct emphasis. The power of life and death is the power of the Father; and Tootie's usurpation of the Father's function is the extreme instance of that pattern of reversal of which she is the focus, whereby the ostensible values of the Smith household are inverted and their underlying logic revealed. Thus, for example, in the present case, the obsession with death and physical cruelty comes across both as a distorted recognition of the body, the physical nature the family ethos represses, and as a magnification of sadism latent in the family group in any case, and surfacing in such jocular exchanges as that between Agnes and Katie about the fate of Agnes's cat ("I'll stab you to death in your sleep and then I'll tie you to two wild horses till you're pulled apart!"). It is a measure of the film's intelligence that Agnes and Tootie can be seen both as profoundly subversive of an order based on repression and as themselves already caught up in the network of repressiveness. Both elements frequently emerge simultaneously; Agnes and Tootie's undisguised giggling amusement at Esther's romantic daydream after her reconciliation with John serves equally as an implicit comment on the boy-meets-girl romantic love the family so easily recuperates and as a type of the oppressive, prying inquisitiveness on which Rose immediately comments ("It's very difficult for a person to have any private life in this family").

Three scenes repay particular attention:

1. The first dance sequence might itself be compared with that extraordinary, because emblematic, moment in *The Exorcist* in which Regan, having been packed off to bed, intrudes on her mother's party while the adults are gathered round the piano singing "Home, Sweet Home" to the accompaniment of a priest, and pisses on the carpet. Agnes and Tootie, likewise sent off the bed, likewise intrude and are compared by John, who sees them first, to vermin ("There are mice in the house"). The grownups adopt at once the familiar tone of maudlin patronage ("She's such a sweet little thing"), and Esther attempts to appease Tootie's desire to join in by suggesting that she sing an "appropriate" nursery song—that is, to perform as a child. Tootie refuses vehemently ("You know I hate those songs!"), and proceeds, in the face of some opposition, to sing a forbidden ballad ("I was drunk last night, dear mother"), with the word *drunk* censored. The moment is remarkable and of considerable complexity. Tootie's appearance immediately follows the singing of "Skip to My Lou," in which the group's resentments and rebelliousness have been contained in the allowable license of "party high spirits." Tootie violates the license both of the party and of her own role as female child (she should be in bed, should be a sweet little thing), and does so by mimicking not simply intoxication, but also sexual reversal—the presumed singer of the ballad is male. Again, the outrageousness is contained: the song promises future sobriety in return for mother's forgiveness, the forbidden word is not pronounced, and the entire incident is promptly "covered" by the performance of "The Cakewalk" in which marriage and settlement is reaffirmed ("Two live as one, One live as two, Under the bamboo tree"), as is woman's place within it ("I want to change your name"). It is important here that Tootie's ballad is the only unaccompanied musical number in the film, and that "The Cakewalk," by emphasizing the conventions of "performance" to a marked extent, restores, formally as well as ideologically, a sense of the proprieties. But there is a residual tension, analogous to that underlying "The Trolley Song." The voice presumed by the lyric, as by the drunkard song, is male but the lyric is performed by two sisters. As in the other case, while the song affirms the centrality of the male, the performance excludes him, "The Cakewalk" finding a further nuance in giving a song in praise of exogamy ("I want to change your name") to two female members of one family. The ironic play of connotations and contradictions is central to the film's concerns.

2. The Halloween sequence. As I have tried to suggest, *Meet Me in St. Louis* implies a tension between the supremacy of patriarchal institutions and the impotence of particular men. The tension is beautifully expressed by the

moment when, while the women of the household are gathered around the dining table waiting for Mr. Smith to come downstairs, a crash is heard from above as he trips over one of Tootie's roller skates. Raising her eyes, Katie mutters dryly: "The Lord and Master!" The phrase is not simply ironic, since Mr. Smith's decision, in the ensuing sequence, to vet all incoming telephone calls is a sufficient demonstration of his real power, and the incident also prepares the idea, to be developed later, that he is as much encumbered by his family as the family by him. All these connotations meet in the prevailing suggestion that the power structure of the patriarchal family is totally insufficient to the exigencies of the reality; and while to the extent that they are devoted to circumventing Mr. Smith, the women's actions proclaim that the power structure need not be taken seriously but merely lived with, they serve to reinforce the structure to the extent that they are supremely preoccupied with the necessity of marriage. It is appropriate then that Mr. Smith should fall on Tootie's skates, since in the Halloween sequence it is not an individual, but the very function of the Father that, through Tootie, comes under attack.

The sequence takes the principle of reversal to its extreme and logical conclusion. The conventions of the domestic musical comedy become the conventions of the horror movie. With the exception of the film's opening sequence shot and the trolley sequence (the latter largely involving, in any case, the use of back projection), the Halloween sequence is the first to take place out of doors, and is structured by the motif of boundary transgression so fundamental to the horror genre: Tootie moves outward from the space of confidence, the known and established world (for spectator as much as character) through a transitional zone, to that "other space" where her self-imposed task must be executed. The visit to the voodoo ceremony in *I Walked with a Zombie* and Lila's exploration of the Bates house in *Psycho* offer suggestive parallels in that in all three cases the other space exists explicitly in an inverted mirror relation to the known space, and that each sequence moves toward the discovery, by the female protagonist, of a monstrously potent parent figure beyond the last forbidden door. The pattern and its psychoanalytical implications are generic "givens," and the relation to the descent myth (and thus to structures that overflow the genre—see for instance, Vladimir Propp's analysis of Russian fairy tales) is equally clear: in this case, Tootie has undertaken a mission that, if fulfilled, will entail a reward (acceptance by the other children).

The mission here is parricide and the spirit of Halloween, as the film depicts it, is a massive, concerted rebellion against the symbolic Father—the Father as Law, as totem figure, as the embodiment of power and prohibition.

Tootie en route to "kill" Mr. Braukoff on Halloween night.

Thus Mr. Smith, the castrated small town father, becomes Mr. Brockhoff and is endowed, in Tootie's imagination, with all the ideas of absolute power and dark, forbidden energy the "real" father so conspicuously lacks—sexual potency and control of women ("He was beating his wife with a red hot poker"); indulgence in alcohol (remember Tootie's identification with a drunkard in her ballad); and abominable rites ("He burns cats at midnight in his furnace"). It is of the essence, then, that Tootie's crime is not literal murder but a handful of flour in the face: she is not killing an individual but desecrating a totem.

Most significantly, given the film's concerns, the rebellion consists in the rejection of the Oedipus complex: all the boys are in drag, and most of the girls too, including Agnes and Tootie. Momentarily, and fantastically, the basic principle of socialization in patriarchal culture is triumphantly overthrown, gender roles disintegrate, and, as household furniture is heaped joyously onto a blazing bonfire around which the children dance like demons or "savages," Tootie, the female child, is unanimously declared, in place of Mr. Brockhoff "the most horrible of all." It is this triumph of the child that distinguishes the Halloween sequence from say, *Zombie, Psycho, The Exorcist, Carrie,* and indeed the end of *Meet Me in St. Louis,* in which the repressive energies embodied in the parent figure are indomitable and enforce either "tragedy" or the bluff of the happy ending; either "things could not have been different" or "things do not need to be different." If the small town myth is, as I have suggested, the heir of the pastoral convention, both serving to provide extremely formalized models of ideal communities in which sexuality is rigidly contained, then the appropriate analogy for Tootie and the children is Comus and his "rout."

The contagion of anarchy spreads immediately into the world of order. Agnes and Tootie nearly succeed in derailing a tram by placing a dress stuffed to resemble a body across the tracks, and Rose's outraged protest that everyone might have been killed produces from Agnes the sublimely amoral reply: "Oh Rose! You're so stuck up!" Disaster is averted by the intervention, appropriately, of John in the interests of the paternal order, but Tootie's lie (she pretends that John has not rescued her, but beaten her up) immediately precipitates the repetition by Esther in the "normal" world of the crime committed by Tootie in the underworld—Esther avenges her sister by beating up John on his own front porch. The misunderstanding is subsequently cleared up and "natural" relations reinstated, but the raison d'être of the entire sequence is the reenactment of breakdown in the Esther/John relationship with the accompanying inversion of purely conventional gender characteristics (the repeated phrase "you've got a mighty strong grip for a boy" / "for a girl"), and the willing assumption by John of a posture of masochistically passive submission ("If you're not busy tomorrow night, could you beat me up again?"). Indeed, the token of reconciliation becomes John's deliberate adoption in his request to Esther to help him turn out the lights, of the role of timid "femininity" that she has previously exploited ("I'm afraid of mice"). The release of chaos reveals nothing if not that the proprieties are quite arbitrary, perilously fragile, and contradictory: the roles John and Esther are culturally required to adopt effectively invert the actual characteristics of the relationship.

3. The "killing" of the snow people. While the sequence, which again takes place at night and out of doors, repeats the murder of Mr. Brockhoff, this time in the context of the Smith family itself, the particular inflection is significantly different and profoundly ambiguous. On one level Tootie's impulse is conservative: she dreads the prospective disruption of the status quo and, in particular, the absence of the Father (Esther discovers her sitting up so as not to miss Father Christmas: "I've been waiting such a long time! . . . How will he find us next year?"). On a second level, the attack on the snow people is an

attack on the Father, the intensity of which is exacerbated rather than assuaged by Esther's assurances that "some day soon we all will be together," since it is the united family that ensures Tootie's repression. The sequence ends with Tootie and Esther in tears, at the very moment that Esther's stoical insistence that "we can be happy anywhere as long as we're together" breaks down. The suggestion that it is "being together" that perpetuates the misery is very strong, and it is maintained as an undercurrent to the end.

It Could Be Oedipus Rex
Denial and Difference in *The Band Wagon;* or, The American Musical as American Gothic

DANA POLAN

Written at the beginning of the 1980s, this essay had as its immediate critical context the sheer importance that French Freudianism had assumed in contemporary cinema studies. My intent was to take Vincente Minnelli's flashy musicals as examples of an American popular art that didn't fit the French Freudian interpretive model and that nonetheless still were salient cases of cultural production that spoke trenchantly in the ideological terms of their time. While I find it less pressing to engage in specific theoretical disquisitions around psychoanalysis, I think the larger point stands—that popular culture's ideological work often occurs less at the level of narrative "meaning" and more in the visual show and spectacle of that culture as evident, engaging formal play.

THE AMERICAN MUSICAL AS AMERICAN GOTHIC

Early in the film *The Band Wagon,* the fallen hero Tony Hunter (Fred Astaire) disembarks from the train that has brought him to New York and proceeds to

Tony Hunter (Fred Astaire) sings "By Myself" in *The Band Wagon* (1953).

his rendezvous with the playwrights Les and Lily Marton. In a scene shot to emphasize cool browns and grays, Hunter advances along the train platform and sings what amounts at this narrative point to his credo, "I'll go my way by myself, all alone in a crowd." Later, he will reprise the song at the film's end, just before the woman of the story, Gaby (Cyd Charisse), attests to her devotion to him and confirms that he no longer will be alone.

As Tony walks from left to right, the camera following him in a tracking shot, a magazine rack appears in frame from the right, almost as if propelled into his path. Suddenly, and for a brief moment, the grayness and brownness give way to a riot of hot colors in the bright covers of the magazines on the stand. Formally, the moment acts like a burst of vitality in a field of quiet. Tony picks up a book, looks it over, puts it down and continues on, leaving the magazine rack and its show of color behind.

What does such a moment mean? Or, to ask a more fundamental question, does it *mean*? There is a sense in which the burst of color virtually takes off from the story—takes off from any contribution to narrative flow. It is a moment in which the musical performs its own generic identity, self-reflexively demonstrating how this musical about musicals is fundamentally a spectacle, an act(ivity) of showing forth of form for the sake of showing off form. As such, this minor scene is only one example in an array of examples where style becomes subject, where subject turns into style, where story developments exist only as an alibi to enable new spectacles to come into view. What we have in the force of such spectacle is an explicit demonstration of art's use of its conventions not so much for their meaning but for their ability to become a good show, a self-evident form that makes manifest its own aesthetic nature. Such a conversion of subject into spectacle, or demonstration of the gap between story and style, runs through *The Band Wagon*. It is there in the scene where people in three different rooms watch theater producer/director Jeffrey Cordova (Jack Buchanan) describe his modern-day version of *Faust* to prospective backers. Each room is painted a different lurid color, and an insistent editing that jumps from room to room to room creates a montage based on the collision of colors. Again, the distinctiveness of the colors, the emphasis on their sheer differences of tonality from one another, has no contribution to make to the narrative as such; we are once more turned into witnesses to the virtuosity of a spectacle that has little or no narrative sense.

The concern with spectacle culminates most explicitly in the long section of the film devoted to showing scenes from the successful Tony Hunter production of the play "The Band Wagon." The proscenium arch and the frame lines of the film merge as this "backstage musical" film finally delivers its payoff and presents its show to us. (Only twice—before and after the "Girl Hunt" ballet—do we see images of a viewing audience. The film maintains little of the pretense that we are actually seeing the stage production within its narrative world.) This is the final "sense" of the film, its raison d'être; everything has led to this point where the story stops and pure show takes over. Even though the Martons' early description of their play presented it as a "light, intimate show" about a struggling writer, the musical numbers that we now see seem to have little or no connection to such a plot. Instead, what finally unifies these song-and-dances is the simple fact that they are all song-and-dances. The "Band Wagon" show within the film *The Band Wagon* is the final triumph of spectacle and, as such, it serves to unify subject and style since the play that Hunter finally succeeds in putting on becomes identical to the film that Vincente Minnelli and crew put on for us (this unity is signaled obviously by the fact that the film and the play within the film have the same title). Hunter's accomplishment is MGM's accomplishment and is ultimately the accomplishment of spectacle as sense of the musical and as the "real" meaning of show.

To understand the ideological project of such a film, then, it is necessary to deal with this nature of style—to investigate the politics of form and the work it performs. Under the influence of methodologies borrowed from literary study (such as narratology), the conjuncture of semiotics and ideological criticism has all too often tended to look at a politics of *narrative logic* and thereby isolate from the film the values of character and their story functions. Where Stephen Heath, for instance, asserts that the classic Hollywood film involves a narrativization of space in which each new cut, each new revealed space, becomes caught up in a logic of story and subject, we need to realize that in that case the critic's emphasis on *narrative* meaning is itself part of the process of narrativization.[1]

In this sense, the emphasis in 1970s and 1980s psychoanalytic film criticism on the oedipal trajectory as the fundamental mechanism of classical cinema's "family romance" is itself a process of narrativization. The oedipal story becomes both a component of the films and an a priori tool by which critics tautologically find that story at work everywhere. For instance, Raymond Bellour declares that "film gradually leads to a final solution which allows the more or less conflicting terms posed at the beginning to be resolved, and which in the majority of cases, takes the form of a marriage. I've gradually come to think that this pattern organizes—indeed, constitutes—the classic American cinema as a whole."[2] At certain moments, Bellour's model loosens—specifically, in moments when he acknowledges the influence of Roland Barthes's sense of the pleasure of the text as a pleasure in excess of the codes of story[3]—but the model quickly contains the moments of euphoric excess, and Bellour's debt to Claude Lévi-Strauss's understanding of communication as a social code whose ultimate meaning is the exchange of women takes over. In his analysis of *North by Northwest,* for example, Bellour acknowledges Hitchcock's irony, his humor, indeed his play with the codes of storytelling, but rather than seeing the use of such comic distance as a source of potential conflict between narrative and tone, Bellour reads play as held within the functions of the oedipal trajectory and as contributing to the male protagonist's accession to the Law of the Father. As Bellour puts it, "that Hitchcock, here, gives in to seduction, to the ironic prestige of the improbable (*invraisemblable*) in order to tighten all the more the logic of the quotidian, I only see in this a redoubling of the abstraction where there is more avowed more deliberately . . . the rule of the Hitchcockian fable."[4] Irony becomes rule; the improbable becomes the logical and the inevitable.

What such oedipal criticism finally leads to is a taming of the force of contradiction: the classical Hollywood film (and already the idea that there is such a singular entity is part of the taming) becomes the site of an eternal return of the same. Play becomes a mere bribe by which texts inscribe viewers into the narrative and so enable a particular process of subjection. For Stephen Heath, for example, "the power of such an apparatus [that of the cinema's encoding of looks to engage point of view and identification] is in the play it both proposes and controls: a certain mobility is given but followed out—relayed—as the possibility of a constant hold on the spectator, as the bind of a coherence of vision."[5] The oedipal trajectory becomes one of the mechanisms of this binding—a process by which both character and (male) spectator accede to a truth that, fictively, imaginarily, closes up the gaps of cinema's essential differences (for example, the differences of shot to shot variation). Play, contradiction, difference, become no more than a "lack" that the movement of narrative fills in.

The theory of the oedipal trajectory becomes a domesticating practice, both literally and metaphorically, in which the excessive becomes the systemic, in which men, for example, are read as mothers' sons and, then, finally, as wives' husbands. But if narrative engages in this domesticating, so does psychoanalytic narrative criticism that domesticates Hollywood films and uses the details of textual analysis not so much to show the complexities of films but, instead, to insist precisely on the absence, or rather the recuperation, of complexity and on the insistent determination of a structure—the oedipal narrative—over the text's unfolding. What we finally end up with is only a more refined version of manipulation theory in which the cultural work of the dominant order is seen ultimately to reproduce, without space for contradiction, the structures of capitalism by providing an ideologically necessary inscription of human subjects into those structures by means of the airtight logic of the cinematic apparatus. Thus, for instance, Raymond Bellour ties oedipalization historically to property relations and the concept of individuality forged by the French Revolution. To follow the path of Oedipus is to grow up into an adult of the dominant order—domesticated, married, fictively complete, and ready to assume one's necessary place within the social structure.[6]

And yet, what a number of critics who question this psychoanalytical model have found in their own work on the Hollywood film is the contradiction of the oedipal trajectory by any number of processes that put to the lie any simple equation of narrative and domestication. For example, analysis of contradictions in the musical and the melodrama has found them to be particularly open areas of investigation. Thus, Robin Wood finds Minnelli's *Meet Me in St. Louis* to be a Gothic musical in which the drive toward family and toward growth into family roles, finds itself countered by another force, an opposing style, which borrows its iconography from the horror film: where a domesticating criticism might understand *Meet Me in St. Louis* as a celebratory film in which the girls move beyond obedience to the father in order to become wives committed to stand-in father figures, Wood suggests that the film "can more convincingly be read as a relentless study of the psychopathology of the Family."[7] Similarly, the melodrama represents a troubling of the Family Romance, a refusal of characters to follow a domestic trajectory. The melodrama is not simply the journey into manhood, but a play on the very logic of heroism, of growth into maturity. Thus, for instance, Geoffrey Nowell-Smith suggests that, "in the American movie the active hero becomes protagonist of the Western, the passive or impotent hero or heroine becomes protagonist of what has come to be known as melodrama.... [The melodrama] often features women as protagonists, and where the central figure is a man there is regularly an impairment of his masculinity.... [The melodrama] cannot operate in the simple terms of the fantasy affirmation of the masculine and disavowal of the feminine."[8] While Nowell-Smith's either/or that puts the western into the position of "simple fantasy" ignores how the western might also itself be a site of contradictory impulses, his discussion does pinpoint how one other genre (melodrama) adopts an ex-centric position in relation to the model of the oedipal trajectory. This is not yet to make a claim about any potential subversive power of the musical or the melodrama but merely to suggest that one must search for the force of these genres, whatever that force may be politically, in a realm other than that of simple domestication, a simple binding.

The melodrama and the musical exceed the oedipal model in part through the force of style. What at first seems merely expressive or symbolic in the melodrama—for example, the jukebox garishness of the town in *Some Came Running* as a sign of inner turmoil—is finally not so much expression as enactment; here again, content becomes form. Nowell-Smith's comparison of melodrama to Freud's notion of conversion-hysteria suggests this: "The laying out of the problems 'realistically' always allows for the generating of an excess that cannot be accommodated.... The undischarged emotion that cannot be accommodated within the action, subordinated as it is to the demands of family/lineage/inheritance, is traditionally expressed in the music and, in the case of film, in certain elements of the mise-en-scène. That is to say, music and mise-en-scène do not just heighten the emotionality of an element of the action; to some extent they also substitute for it" (this volume, p. 103).

In Minnelli musicals, there is also conversion of narrative events into spectacle events, similar to that in the melodramas. Where the plot may begin with a woman's entrance into domesticity—as in *The Pirate* where Manuela is betrothed to the bourgeois mayor of the town—form soon takes off and becomes a force running counter to domestication. In *The Pirate*, Serafin the clown's prowess with spectacle is a repetition of the film's own mastery of spectacle in which gliding cameras, radiant Technicolor, the texture of songs, all have the force of an argument for a style and way of life, for life as style and as art. To be sure, *The Pirate* ends with a man and a woman in each other's arms, as if domesticity has won out, but significantly, they come together less as lovers than as performers, as clowns. Dressed in costume and looking out at us, their stage the frame of the film, they exhort us to "Be a clown, be a clown," to somehow partake of spectacle. This exhortation is no less ideological than the force of domesticity, but it works in another direction to acknowledge the claims of a pleasure principle against a performance principle. The musical substitutes the sociality of *Homo ludens* for that of *Homo faber*.

The Pirate displays, and literally is, a contagion of spectacle within a world ostensibly geared to rationality.[9] On the diegetic level, *The Pirate* is about spectacle; the aristocratic Manuela is drawn into a world that she had once disdained—the world of vaudeville, of the stage, and, by extension, of enter- tainment in general. But more significantly, *The Pirate* represents spectacle at the very level of its mise-en-scène. From its opening image showing us the picture book of Mack the Black, as Manuela turns the pages, only her hands visible as we hear her read, to the last shot of the film (Manuela in clown costume and in the embrace of a man as she looks straight out at the camera), *The Pirate* enacts the increasing spectaclization of the world. The stage becomes a central locus for the film as its characters find it necessary literally to *stage* events in order to reveal their meanings. For example, at the film's climax, when Manuela pretends to be hypnotized in order to trap Don Pedro, she leaves the audience in attendance at Serafin's hanging, and goes up to a stage that just happens to be there. Only on stage are her actions significant enough to make Don Pedro reveal the truth (that he is Macoco the Pirate) that he has so well hidden under the veneer of bourgeois respectability. And the film can have Don Pedro reveal that truth only by having him step up on the stage too. He must be caught in the world of acting to and for someone else. To go further (as the film does), he isn't simply captured; rather, he is entrapped through the use of vaudeville props such as juggling pins, hoops, and such that beat him down and literally surround him. Spectacle becomes an all-pervading, inescapable force. As a narrative, *The Pirate* seems to be about meaningful change, but its diegetic progress is already predetermined by its initial commitment to a myth of spectacle that controls the kind of development it can enact. "Narrative" here becomes a predictable unfolding of a basic premise that, in the case of *The Pirate,* is that of the fundamental rightness of spectacle as a mediation of/for all differences.

One scene in *The Pirate* is virtually symptomatic in its desire to banish all meanings other than spectacle from its field of attention. This is the moment early in the film when Manuela sees the ocean, the ocean that she has long dreamed of. It is also the moment that Serafin first sees her. Here the two sides of the film's central thematic structure—the woman's desire and discourse versus the man's—collide. But the film has already tipped the balance. From the start of the film, Manuela's desire is already a desire for an unreality; the ocean is for her a sign of fantasy, a sign of the male world of adventure that she has read about in books and wants to enter. In the ocean scene, then, what has already been determined is now overdetermined (in Freud's sense of a radical condensation of meanings that can often at first have seemed contradictory). Two shots here demonstrate and enact the whole aesthetic project of spectacle. The buildup to these two shots is as follows: Manuela walks toward the sea, the camera tracking before her. Suddenly, her face illumines with rapture. She has evidently seen the ocean. But there is as of yet no corresponding shot of the ocean to complete her look. Instead, at the precise moment that the rapture bursts out on her face, Serafin pops into the frame as if by magic, as if somehow called forth as the object of Manuela's desire (even though she doesn't yet know that). Manuela proceeds onward out of frame, unaware of Serafin, but she has already lost the game. The film henceforth acts as her unconscious, redirecting her desires to what the film defines as their true goal. Now the real question of the film—the question it has always been asking as it assumes its place within the ideological project of Hollywood cinema: how will the two main characters get together?—pushes aside its decoy question: how will Manuela get her pirate dream? We then get two shots in which all the contradictions of film spectacle can be read—two intercut shots of an ocean—each shot about a second long, and separated by a medium distance shot of Manuela seeing. In the first of the two shots of Manuela seeing, she is alone: she and the ocean form a veritable couple through the rhetoric of the shot/reaction shot pattern. But in the cut back to Manuela after the cutaway to the ocean, Serafin has entered the frame to stand beside her, and Manuela's gaze reluctantly shifts from the ocean, her ocean, to this man who has entered her space. Manuela's story has become Manuela's and Serafin's. The two shots of the ocean are the only two shots of the film not filmed on a set. Only here, for two seconds out of almost two hours, does any world, any other scene, try to insist its way into the action. And, symptomatically, the shots have no force, nothing to make them real. The ocean that opens up to worlds beyond the frame of the story disappears as the film moves inland to the studio-set town in which Manuela lives. *The Pirate* is then in some way the enactment of the loss of a woman's desire under the influence of the world of spectacle for which cinema, the film *The Pirate* itself, is a metonymic representation. The narrative of the film is always a narrative inside spectacle; the film cannot outrun the fact that it is shown.

The musical number, as Jane Feuer argues, is primarily a folk art form, calling for involvement in the aura of spectacle in an age dominated by the utilitarian loss of aura.[10] Consequently, and I mean this in no way as a negative remark, the musical is an infantile art form, concentrating on, reveling in, and enacting the desire to refuse to become adult, the desire of/for performers to refuse to turn into mommies and daddies, to refuse to punch into the time-clock work of calculation and reason. If the oedipal trajectory insists on the need to go beyond primary attachments, to cast off infantilism for the sake of "respectability," the musical is a world that refuses this trajectory (even when its story doesn't). There is something profoundly American about the American musical; its spectacle is the populist assertion of the beauty and strength and vitality of everyday people against the repressive structures of all father figures.

Indeed, the two explicit references in *The Band Wagon* to America signal this. The first occurs in the song, "That's Entertainment," where one line suddenly proclaims, "Hip hooray, the American way." This is producer/director Jeffrey Cordova's America, a place of power lorded over by father figures. Against this, Tony Hunter will herald a different sense of America. Rejecting Cordova's call for him to become "Tony Hunter, 1953," Tony says, "I declare my independence—Tony Hunter, 1776." The heroes of American cinema are always declaring their independence, killing all fathers to move into a "free" world where everyone is always young.[11]

At the same time, there is something fundamentally socially perverse about this desire to not grow up, to remain in the world of spectacle. In *Love and Death in the American Novel*, Leslie Fiedler discusses Gothic literature as a perverse literature in terms that apply also to the musical.[12] For Fiedler, Gothic literature ties together suffering artist and suffering hero through their common inability to support, and accede to, the sentimentality, the bourgeois domestic rites, of the romantic novel. Against any possibility of union in marriage, the Gothic hero recoils into positions of suffering (an inward retreat) or lusting (an outward attack), a menacing assertion of power that tries to take what it cannot bear to ask for.

In *The Band Wagon*, Tony Hunter also refuses sentiment and romance. His power, as with the theatricality of the Gothic hero, lies in his ability to show off himself, to convince through the sheer bravura of performance. The structure of *The Band Wagon* may not share the fantasmatics of the oedipal trajectory that imagines manhood to be a growth into social responsibility. But it is no less fantasmatic in its emphasis on a trajectory of spectacle, on its faith in spectacle as a contagious force that draws everyone into its power. Tony Hunter argues early in the film that he is no more than "Mrs. Hunter's little boy, Tony," and the fantasy of the film is to show how much little boys can accomplish.

Pre-oedipal or anti-oedipal, the fantasy of *The Band Wagon* is nonetheless one involved in sexual politics. Its desire is to show the potency of little boys, to suggest that the show and play they engage in are powerful masculine forces. Part of the ideological function of the American musical is to put the lie to certain stereotypes of sexual difference and suggest that art, more specifically the art of dance, is not the exclusive realm of a female principle. The dancing of Astaire or Kelly is an attempt to suggest that men can devote their time to dance and still be men. In *The Band Wagon*, this masculine conquest of the world of dance receives a specific representation in the conflict of ballet and soft shoe: ballet is not only the art of refinement—a high art—but also an art stereotypically belonging to women. Tony Hunter finds the ballet form repressive—and the film emphasizes this repressiveness in a shot that shows Hunter awkwardly emoting while balletic dancers sweep past him. The ballet form would require Tony to change and give up who he really is. (Encouraging Tony to be in the modern version of Faust, Jeffrey Cordova exhorts Hunter to grow up, to become "better than you ever were.") To realize his true fantasy, Tony must reject the balletic world and stay the child he has always been. Gabrielle Gerard (Cyd Charisse) is initially the symbol of all that Tony fears, but by putting on a show, his show, Tony captures Gerard, tames her difference.

Rosalind Coward provides a succinct definition of the oedipal trajectory as a narrative of renunciation: "For the boy, the Oedipus complex is a constant and *growing* factor. He is sensually bound up with the mother and his active phallic sexuality leads to fantasies of sexual intercourse or 'marriage' with the mother. Only the threat of castration brought by rivalry against the child's sensual involvement with the mother, coinciding with the child's realization of anatomical difference, forces the child to renounce the mother. It is castration which is structural of desire."[13] In *The Band Wagon*, Tony renounces renunciation (literally, since much of the film chronicles how he has made a wrong turn by accepting to act in Jeffrey's play of "stature") in order to learn and return to the fundamental lesson of the infantile fantasy: that it is best to be what you've always been—a little kid.

Dennis Giles, in an article that sets out to oedipalize *The Band Wagon*, argues that the film chronicles a boy's successful growth into the responsibilities of adulthood.[14] Tony starts in infantile dread: "He [Tony] fears leaving the comforts of the original unity and, once out of the womb state, seeks to return to the former existence in which he lay immobile. The Astaire of *The Band Wagon* dreads the other world of the show and the new identity it promises" (16). But as Giles reads the film, Tony soon gains the help of a maestro—a figure Giles compares to Vladimir Propp's notion of the donor and to Dante's Virgil—in the form of Gabrielle Gerard. The maestro is a guide who leads the terrified hero to a place of peacefulness. In Giles's description of the film's narrative, "At this crisis [of child faced with the Otherness of experience], the Astaire character is taken in hand by Cyd Charisse as the ballet star, Gaby" (15). Thus, for Giles, Tony's declaration that he is a little boy is something he learns to renounce by growing up and beyond it, by learning that the world out there is nothing to be afraid of.

But when he quotes this declaration, Giles doesn't give it in full: "I am Mrs. Hunter's little boy, Tony—*song-and-dance man.*" The last part matters for it links childhood with the job of performer. To be Mrs. Hunter's little boy is to be a song-and-dance man; it is to have the best of two possible worlds. When Tony tries to play a modern-day Faust with the aid of Gabrielle, he does emerge into the world of adulthood and Otherness as Giles suggests, but ultimately, he discovers the self-alienation, the denials that run through that world, and he rejects this growth, this call to ostensible stature and maturity as a betrayal of his original identity. He leaves the false show, inappropriate to his needs, and puts on the show the Martons had originally written for him—the show that he initially recognized as perfect for him.

Interestingly, Giles's oedipal argument contains counterarguments that make the case for Tony's rejection of any call to adulthood. Giles pictures the security of maternal warmth and of childhood as a stasis that Tony seeks to return to. Noting that Gaby's final declaration ("The show's a hit. . . . As far as I'm concerned, it's going to run forever") presents the notion of a "permanent show" as a solution to all problems, Giles goes on to argue that "the permanent show is indeed a cure for the previous drama—its conflict, its agon(y) since the showing arrests the flow of time. . . . The show bears a resemblance to the state before birth, echoing its timelessness, its ultimate unity of lover and beloved" (14). This indeed is the sense of the film—the show as a solution to drama. But the point then is not that of an adolescent growing up but of a middle-aged man becoming young again, becoming his past.

If there is a development in Tony's character, it is a development in reverse. He changes from the aged Tony Hunter, has-been, into the graceful Fred Astaire whose every dance movement belies the passage of time. We watch Tony become not the artiste everyone wants him to be, but the song-and-dance man he once was. From the grayness and bleak despair of the opening to the ending in which Tony proves his energy, the film enacts the triumph of spectacle as the art of vitality, of life.

The opening of the film presents Tony in a fallen state, and his quest for artistic stature can only lead him to fall further. In the very opening images, Tony is absent from the film, and therefore, he literally has no power, no chance to make a spectacle of himself. The first scene shows an unsuccessful auction of his hat and cane, his show trademarks. The next scene shows Tony hidden as two men lament his fall and contrast his failure to the success of Ava Gardner. At this point, Tony can appear only as an advertising image in a magazine one of the men is looking at; this is a powerless Tony, reduced to the role of spokesperson in/for someone else's spectacle. When Tony finally does appear, it is only to acknowledge and second the laments of the two men. Coming off the train, he meets Ava Gardner playing Ava Gardner. The meeting confirms Tony's fall, not only because, on a narrative level, the reporters he thought had come to see him have actually come to greet Gardner, but also because it imagistically concretizes the contrast between Gardner and Hunter that the two men in the train established. Gardner stands out here because we are in the presence of the actress herself; we are in the grip of the cameo as privileged moment. Gardner is Gardner, not just a role, while Tony is as of yet an incomplete Fred Astaire. He must do what we expect Fred Astaire to do to redeem himself, to grow into his character: he must dance and sing.

The song that follows—"By Myself"—is a subdued one and is only partially satisfying of our demand that Fred Astaire do what we have come to the movies for: to see him perform. Even that gaudy magazine rack upstages him. It is not until the next number that Hunter lets go, becomes Fred Astaire, becomes the spectacle that we have gone to the movies to see. This dance occurs at the height of Hunter's immersion in the Otherness of social experience. Friendless and in the midst of Times Square, he looks at the gaudy arcades, hot-dog stands, amusement centers that were once the locations of Broadway in his youth, and he gives evidence of his sense of alienation in this world of quotidian strangeness. His reaction is to aestheticize this world, to take over its spectacle by a conquering spectacle of his own. (Significantly, his reaction is doubled by the music, by the film itself, which moves from the motivated hurdy-gurdy sound of the arcade to the melody that Astaire will sing.) When he trips over the shoe shiner, Astaire/Hunter's spectacle-power is concretized. Not only does he gain an audience but he also meets someone he can impute his anxieties to, project them onto. He sings about his problems in the second person, making the solutions to his dilemma an imperative for his listener ("when *you* feel as low as the bottom of a well and can't get out of the mood, do something to pick *yourself* up and change *your* attitude"). By projecting his fears onto another person, Hunter gains in strength and power. While the shoe shiner enters into the dance, first as dancing shoe shiner but then finally as dancing equal, Hunter ultimately asserts his difference, his special and superior qualities, insofar as his last dance motion—paying the shiner—restores to the spectacle an economic relation of boss and worker. The scene establishes Hunter's power, his capability, which is linked to his identity as song-and-dance man. As Fred Astaire, he is a successful show.

The scene dissolves immediately to a poster that heralds Jeffrey Cordova's production (at every level of control) of "Oedipus Rex." The dissolve signals a central conflict of the film. We move from a spectacle that Tony has taken possession of (gaudy Times Square, which became the arena for his performance) to one controlled by others. Tony, who had initially not recognized the name Cordova, will come all too quickly to learn who Cordova is. Literally, Cordova is the symbol of the oedipal trajectory, the force of that which Tony must agree and accede to if he is to mature. Cordova is the powerful Father (he calls Tony and the Martons "kids" even though Tony, no doubt, is his age). Cordova is the Law who demands that Tony renounce rivalry and immaturity and grow up castrated into a position of respectability. Jeffrey is omnipotence; for the Martons, for example, he is the guy who "can do anything" or who exerts, in Lily's words, a "hypnotic control." He possesses a kind of magic as his assistant, Hal, learns when Jeffrey performs the impossible and signs Gabrielle Gerard for the female lead of his play ("Next time," Hal tells a newspaper's drama desk, "If I tell you Mr. Cordova is casting Tallulah as little Eva, believe me"). Jeff's power also involves a claim to the control of spectacle. Where Tony establishes himself in the "Shine on Your Shoes" number as a performer, a doer, an actor literally, Jeff turns him into a spectator or an ineffectual participant in the spectacle of others (for example, he sends Tony to watch Gabrielle Gerard perform her ballet, a sight that will fill Tony with dread and doubt).

DENIAL AND DIFFERENCE IN *THE BAND WAGON* 143

Most significant in this respect is Jeff's manipulation of Tony in the "That's Entertainment" number. Jeff sits Tony down in an armchair and performs to him. The song reduces contradictions into aesthetic form and serves as a kind of contagion in its sweeping discussion of the plots that are entertaining. This contagion catches up with Tony who joins in with the admission that "it could be Oedipus Rex"—that is, that the Otherness of Jeffrey's production is ultimately not foreign to the world of entertainment. With this admission, Tony enters into an oedipal world, a world in which he will be blocked from the realization of his desires by a stronger figure. Jeff becomes the creator of Tony's reality (Jeff announces to his cast that the theater they are rehearsing in will become "our sun, our moon, our stars") and of Tony's language (Jeff changes Tony's lines, tells Tony how to act).

Jeffrey functions as an all-powerful force who becomes the very source of Tony's world. More than that, Jeffrey becomes the virtual creator of all the characters who henceforth appear in the film and who, as Jeffrey's surrogates summoned up by him, extend his power, his destruction of Tony's aura. For example, Paul Byrd (James Mitchell), the choreographer Jeff hires for the show so that he can also sign Paul's girlfriend, Gaby, is an echo of Jeffrey, a conspirator in the attempt to contain Tony, to capture him up in the structures of respectability. Paul first seems to be on the side of youth—the world of spectacle as good show, good, clean fun—and when he first hears that Jeffrey plans to do a musical, he is disdainful. But when he learns that the story is to be a modern-day version of Faust, his interest emerges. In the film's symbolic structure, Paul—like Jeffrey—is a sign of high culture, of the denials of both American populism and the American success story of individualism.

The first part of *The Band Wagon* divides, then, into two parts for Tony: a "before meeting Jeffrey Cordova" and an "after meeting Cordova." The poster of "Oedipus Rex" signals the division, and until Tony makes his declaration of independence, everything takes place under Jeffrey's control. Yet not quite everything. Outside of any narrative contribution, certain moments, certain scenes act as a kind of return of the repressed to show the contradictions of Jeffrey's project. After Jeffrey's initial talk to his cast, the film goes into a long sequence of moments of rehearsal. The sequence, shot according to a montage common for this moment in backstage musicals, once again shows the triumph of spectacle over story as dance and anecdotal joke imagery (for example, the technician's attempts to produce a cloud of smoke) preempt any sense that what we are seeing is just a rehearsal of a modern "Faust." The montage, frenetic in its cutting, but also representing moments of hustle and bustle in the rehearsals, imparts a vitality to the film that Jeff's project is lacking. One joke in the montage, trivial though it may ultimately be, crystallizes this. Les Marton asks Paul to audition a buxom, sultry blonde who, in response, dances in a virtually burlesque fashion, as Les watches in delight. Paul, ever the high artist, rejects her and picks, in the film's stereotypes, a less showy, more artistic woman. Even in this throwaway scene, the two worldviews of the film collide: Paul's, with its devotion to utility and reason (the right woman for the right part) and to "serious" art; and Lester's (like Tony's), with its playfulness, its deferment of reality for the sake of pleasure.

Part of the danger to Tony of Jeffrey's power is that it is virtually unbridled. It creates effects of repression far beyond Jeff's original intentions. Jeffrey's overwrought version of *The Band Wagon* is the central figure of this, but it also shows up in the way in which Tony comes to find Jeffrey's threat projected onto other characters and intensified in the process. Paul, for example, is a stiffer version of Jeffrey; he may be young but we never see him doing the vaudeville routines that Jeff performs to attract Tony into the Faust production. (This is one reason why the film keeps Jeffrey, after Tony takes over, but gets rid of Paul. Paul is unbendingly conventional, restrictive and restricted; Jeffrey, in contrast, finally shows humility and becomes part of Tony's show.)

Central to this projection of Jeffrey's power is the figure of Gabrielle Gerard. She is virtually called into being by Jeffrey's needs, summoned by of an enumeration that has the force of genesis. "We need somebody with fire, charm, grace, beauty, and Gabrielle Gerard," is the way Jeffrey puts it; Gabriel is not woman for herself, but woman for others, alienated through the language of the Father, literally defined and brought into being by that language.

While film theory's analysis of the male look in film has tended to understand that look as a source of male control, a fetishistic fixing of the woman in place, Tony's look at Gabrielle is one that fixes *him,* a look that calls his strength into question. In a shot/reaction shot sequence that alternates Tony looking with Gabrielle performing, Tony first declares that "she's fabulous, a sensation—the loveliest thing I've ever seen" and then wonders "she's a little tall, isn't she?" This first minor doubt grows into a major anxiety even though the Martons do their best to allay Tony's fears. For Tony, Gabrielle is threat in all its purity, all its estranging intensity. She is estranging in that she is Jeffrey's creation and Paul's possession; she is outside Tony's influence, attracted to his spectacle only when she is distant from it (she admits that she's seen his films but at museum retrospectives). That Tony has no hold over Gaby shows forth in her second appearance in the film, which has a privileged status since Tony is not present in the scene. We learn what Tony cannot know at that point—that Gaby is ruled by Paul, that she is part of a nexus of possession. (Paul, as he says, knows "this girl," knows how to make her operate. For example, early in the scene Paul ends an argument by telling Gaby "your nose is shiny," an observation that sends her off to the powder room. Paul knows Gaby well enough to control her through her stereotypical female vanity.)

In his initial encounters with Gabrielle, Tony will learn the way of the world all too quickly; Gabrielle's references to his real age cut him, emasculate him. A metonymic expansion of Jeffrey's original and originary power, Gabrielle is a threat insofar as she is the pure Other, the different, the not-for-Tony. But she is also the threat of "woman," of sexuality (she is not an innocent but has a boyfriend), and of adulthood.

In the American Gothic, as Leslie Fiedler suggests, the initial solution for the male faced with the threat of the feminine is retreat, a recoil from the woman, from women, into an asocial relationship that is a scandal to social respectability: "the typical male protagonist of our fiction has been a man on the run, harried into the forest and out to sea, down the river or into combat—anywhere to avoid 'civilization,' which is to say, the confrontation of a man and a woman which leads to the fall to sex, marriage, and responsibility" (26). But the flip side of recoil is attack, the covering up of fear through self-deceiving swagger (it seems not accidental that some of the last pages of *Love and Death in the American Novel* deal with tough-guy writers like Dashiell Hammett, Raymond Chandler, and Mickey Spillane as a new wave of the Gothic). In much film noir, for example, the woman's danger is intensified by film style (the shadow-filled mise-en-scène; the twists of a plot made chaotic by the machinations of a woman's treachery), all the better to justify the hero's (and the film's) disposal of her. Again this is part of the infantile perversity of a genre opposing the impositions of "respectable" adult sexuality. Against accession to the law of the Father, the film noirs engage in a fantasmatic restructuring of options open to the male.

Tony's option, the film's option, is precisely that of swagger, of swagger as spectacle, of dance as demonstration. Tony rebels, walks off stage, and the film rebels, shifting from the stage world that had dominated the previous minutes of the film to now show us spaces other than the enclosed reality that Jeffrey had built for his cast. We are now in the presence of a new structuring of reality. Following Jean Laplanche's and Jean-Baptiste Pontalis's definition of the Freudian phantasm as an "imaginary scenario in which the subject is present and which figures, in a fashion more or less deformed by defensive processes, the accomplishments of a desire and, ultimately, an unconscious desire,"[15] I would argue that *The Band Wagon* is here explicitly a phantasm. The film functions precisely as a figuration of desire. It shows a fantasmatic understanding of social reality as something that you can simply walk out on, and of work—after all, Tony is Jeffrey's employee—as something that you can just leave when its demands become too great. More than that, it ultimately figures reality as something that one can remake, that finally *needs* a strong hero to remold it; the film finally casts the phantasm's subject, Tony, into the role of savior who restores order to a chaotic world. *The Band Wagon* shows the reality that had scared Tony, the reality that Jeff had promised to control, falling apart, breaking at the seams. The oedipal drive becomes a farce; it is built on contradictions it cannot wish away. It must give way. The power of a Father like Jeffrey is ultimately self-defeating because it is ultimately self-creating, self-delegating in its power; as omnipotence, it has no higher reality it can derive its energy, its legitimation, from. An ex nihilo power, the force of Oedipus, as Freud admitted in *Moses and Monotheism*, is an arbitrary force: as Freud concedes, "in the case of the victory of patriarchy, we cannot point to the authority which lays down the standard which is to be regarded as higher. It cannot in this case be the father since he is only elevated into being the authority by the advance itself."

The Band Wagon shows Jeff's world literally cracking apart around him. The center does not hold. While early scenes had emphasized Jeff's prowess as a director (the guy who could do anything), we now witness his complete failure, and significantly, we witness this failure after Tony's outburst and declaration of independence. All the early rehearsal scenes had shown Jeff in full directorial control; now he shows himself to be incompetent in his every action as if in reaction to Tony's assertion of power. With the overdetermination that Freud found central to the mise-en-scène of the phantasm, *The Band Wagon* shows Jeff's production to be a failure not just because it is a modern-day production of *Faust*, which would have been a sufficient charge against it, but also because it is a *bad* modern-day production of Faust. Not merely are its sets overblown; they fall apart, break down. Nothing earlier in the film had suggested that Jeff could fail to produce his play, but just simply that he shouldn't produce it. But now, a fantasmatic structure necessitates that Jeffrey fail in every possible way, that everything conspire to call Tony into play and make him the figure that comes to the rescue by reasserting the proper form of spectacle.

If Gaby is a metonym for all that is wrong in the world of the Other, then she must become the stake, the pivot, in the restructuring of reality by the filmic fantasy. When Tony storms off the stage and thereby begins the humbling of the Father, Gaby comes to Tony's apartment to apologize. While she is doing so at Paul's command, her action goes beyond what Paul requires of her, and she is suddenly freed from the repressive structure that had held her to Paul's and Jeffrey's world. She changes camps in one of those conversion scenes so important in the Hollywood spectacle—a conversion without reason, without motivation, a conversion that is abrupt but intense. What might seem the limitation of the Hollywood film in its elision of the forces that drive people to act; what might seem the aesthetic deficiency of an art devoted at all costs to having boy get girl, no matter by what contrivance even when the girl can't stand the boy—all this is actually the talent of a certain kind of cinema: its power not to represent "reality" but to engage in a fantasmatic and ideological redefinition of "reality" that is coherent and insistently optimistic about its transformative powers.

In Tony's apartment, Gaby is, in one moment, the secure woman of high art and poise, noticing Tony's paintings and knowing immediately that one is an early Degas, and then, in the next moment, she is all insecurity, crying her heart out, confessing that all along she has been nervous and afraid. As with the shoe shiner, Gaby here allows Tony to lose his anxiety by seeing it in, and projecting it onto, others. As her crying becomes more and more hysterical, Tony becomes more and more controlling, tossing off one-liners at Gaby's expense ("I would say that you're more plain than ugly"). For no reason but the fantasmatic needs of Tony and of the film, Gaby has retreated from her strong position as woman of power to a position of stereotypical weakness: woman as crybaby, woman as emotional, woman in need of a man to help her out (looking for something to wipe her eyes, Gaby fumbles with a scarf tied to her bag, but Tony gallantly sweeps out a handkerchief). Against Dennis Giles's argument that Gaby is the maestro leading Tony on to a new identity, Tony now becomes the maestro pulling Gaby away from the inferior world of classical ballet to a world Tony has always known, the world that is ultimately right for Gaby too (and for Cyd Charisse too whose best dancing occurs when she breaks from the classical ballet mode). Her first number in Tony's "Band Wagon" production signals the changes in Gaby and in the world of spectacle that Tony has made her join. Against Jeff's declaration that his theater would be the cast's "sun," Gaby's song now heralds "a new sun in a new sky." Popular spectacle is rebirth, an infusion of new life (the costuming amplifies this as Gaby's radiant gold outfit virtually explodes onto the screen and suggests her new energy).

Film scholars have long noted the centrality of artist-figures in Minnelli's oeuvre. The true artist, as the Minnelli film often pictures him, is a figure of bursting talent, sheer virtuosity, who simply has to look inside himself to discover artistic power. As a phantasm, this notion of the artist takes on the qualities of magic. Against those figures the films associate with a brute and vulgar reality, the artist creates his own reality, finds that reality is pliant when one approaches it fantasmatically. Where much of *The Band Wagon*, for instance, details the arduousness of Jeff's rehearsals, all Tony has to do is announce his desire to put on the real "Band Wagon" play and, after one quick shot of a train rushing to a town on the play's tour, the show suddenly is on. All sense of work is banished; the play simply bursts into being. The camera sweeps in and we are inside spectacle. Quotidian necessity has vanished.

If there's a populism in *The Band Wagon*—in its sense of people discovering a community in spectacle against the stuffy world of stature and pomp—this image of the artist as remaker of the world also establishes the film as the triumph of individualism (significantly, when Tony comes into power, he refers to his cast as "kids," just as Jeffrey had done; he is now the shepherd of the flock). "Dancing in the Dark," the dance number where Tony and Gaby truly dance together for the first time, concretizes this individualism, this sense of the artist as virtuoso, and signals its elitism. (This is a central contradiction in art working under the sign of the American dream: it affirms the powers of the people, the need to be just one of the boys, but also calls for Horatio Algers who become celebrities by standing above the world. It is not for nothing that in *Rio Bravo* Chance [John Wayne] doesn't join in the communal singsong: to be an American folk hero is to be of the people but also above the people.) Tony initiates this process of individualism with a speech to Gaby that celebrates the need to throw off the bonds of authority, to realize that power lies in "you and me": "No one consulted us. We're the only ones that matter in this whole thing, not those geniuses out there telling us what to do." The possibility of their own spectacle thus called up, Gaby and Tony head off for the park in a carriage, and their journey becomes a discovery of a world that Jeff's art had closed off to them. They notice the stars, nature, the passers-by ("Do you know what those are on those benches? People . . . happy people"). The mythology here is that of a passage from the artificiality of culture to the innocent reality of Nature. (Significantly, though, the scenes in the park are all shot in the studio. As in *An American in Paris*, which pretends to show a real Paris but ends with the title "The End. Completely filmed in Hollywood, USA," what *The Band Wagon* celebrates is the conversion of culture and nature alike by Hollywood spectacle, a reality of unreality, a form that claims to be beyond the merely cultural or the merely natural.)

Disembarking from the carriage, Gaby and Tony stroll through the park and come upon dancers on a dance floor. All the conventions of narrative lead us to expect that Gaby and Tony will join the dance and make their spectacle there. But, significantly, they pass through the crowd of dancers and it is not until they are alone that they begin to dance. The world of performance and spectacle rejects the elitist pretensions of high art, but it also rejects the coming of the masses, the threat of the crowd as gray anonymity. (Performances in Minnelli films tend to avoid large cast numbers. Eschewing the multiplicity of bodies in the dances of a Busby Berkeley, the Minnelli number emphasizes the way talent stands out, as figure from ground.)

In regard to this imaging of the triumph of individualist artistry, it seems to me not accidental that the supreme spectacle of the film, its big finale, is a tough-guy detective story. The fictional detective is precisely a kind of artist, specifically a storyteller who comes upon an incomprehensible reality and imprints a plot upon it. For example, for Dashiell Hammett, the Continental Op is literally a maker of fictions as he arbitrarily tries out a way of framing the world and then steps back to observe his social canvas (*Red Harvest*). *The Band Wagon*'s "Girl Hunt" sequence borrows from this detective tradition and shows Astaire/Hunter as Rod Riley, a man who, like all detectives, converts ignorance into knowledge through force and the forceful insistence of masculine identity. Riley is an ultimate shaper of reality, putting everything into its categorical place: the guilty and the innocent, the dead and the alive, the blonde and the brunette. In contrast to the urban anomie that Tony Hunter had evidenced in the beginning of the film as he made his way through Time Square, the "Girl Hunt" sequence shows a Hunter who is safe in the city because this is a city of his own creation, a city within a play within a film.

The "Girl Hunt" sequence shows film technique asserting its virtuosity (to such an extent that we see angles and camera movements that make no sense for what is supposedly a stage production). This aestheticization of reality is the project of spectacle, and Tony's power is a doubling of the power of the film itself. Tony, by becoming director of a play, and of a woman, gets the chance to prove himself by the conversion of resistant matter into aesthetic form. If Tony develops in the film, his development is only a realization of a quality he had all along. A throwaway line in the beginning of the film suggested Tony's initial power and stands as a marker to indicate how far his power will grow. One of the two men on the train that brought Tony to town describes Tony's early captivating influence on the man's wife ("He nearly broke up our home"). Tony's influence is a virile one, but initially it was a virility of distance, the virility of a star who exerted power over audiences by remote control. When Gaby comes into the film with her choreographer/boyfriend, Tony can realize his home-breaking talents at close range. It is important that Paul be a choreographer; for Tony, to take over direction of a play is also to take over direction of a woman. Where Tony and the Martons had joked in an early scene about his prowess, acknowledging it but seeing it as only a game, an act (when Lily says, "Hey, mister, can I have your autograph?" Tony gallantly but playfully sweeps her up in his arms), Tony's interaction with Gaby—the way she fantasmatically converts to his cause—allows him control and impact a directness of power that early scenes had only hinted at.

But direct and powerful though this intervention may be, it is no less aesthetic, an interposing of roles of theatricality between self and the world. The woman is possessed less by male *sexuality* than by male "spectacularity." Revealingly, this film, in a genre often dismissed as mushy sentimentality, about two people—a man and a woman—coming together, never shows a scene of strong love between these two characters. (Gaby and Tony do kiss at the very end, but the kiss is sandwiched between two moments of aestheticization: namely, Gaby's final speech and the end number.) Instead of romance, we get a mediation of romantic interaction through a constant posing and playing in which characters seem to be implying something but never getting around to explicitly saying it. For better or for worse, the effective representation of heterosexual relationships seems to pose a difficulty for Hollywood art as American art. We are endlessly in the world of domestic melodrama where sexuality is symbolically stunted, or in the world of the musical where people don't so much talk to each other as couch their interactions in the form of song and dance—that is, a distanced form in which any reality of the self is submerged by a kind of presentation, a show, of the *surfaces* of the self. The seemingly great romances of Hollywood cinema often actually show romance displaced—into sham, into game (for example, the double entendres of *The Big Sleep* where the characters talk about sex in terms of a horse race and never get down to business); into the guise of toughness or cleverness or cool; into role playing (for instance, the lead characters of *To Have and Have Not* are always Steve and Slim to each other even though these are not their real names).

Tony Hunter does get a privileged scene in which he tells Les how much he's in love with this girl (and the phrasing "this girl," identical to the way Paul referred to Gaby, suggests the distance, the reification, in the heart of love; Gaby is still a token, a placeholder). But the scene's power is that of a confessional, a private moment whose force does not extend into the public sphere. When Gaby and Tony are together, they do not love, they aestheticize. "Dancing in the Dark" shows them coming together in agreement for the first time, but it is an agreement to be a spectacle, to wordlessly show off the talent of the body in performance.

Two scenes, which are intercut with the spectacle of Tony's "Band Wagon" production, show Tony and Gaby together, but again, love can only remain unspoken, the banished subtext that characters try to pronounce but finally remain silent about. The first scene shows Tony addressing Gabriel on the train as they return to New York for the premiere of "The Band Wagon." This scene, just before Tony tells Lester about his love for Gaby, shows Tony displacing the admission of love into a game. With obvious theatricality, he turns the interaction into a little skit: "Say, who's the pretty girl? This couldn't be the mousy little Miss Gerard. Why, you've been with the firm for years. . . . Say, you're beautiful!" When he knocks over Gaby's writing pad and realizes that she's writing to Paul, a reality stronger than Tony's little game seems to assert itself, and Tony recoils by sending Gaby off. "You must be tired," Tony tells her and, like Paul's "Your nose is shiny," an observation takes on the force of a command. Gaby absents herself.

When Gaby and Tony next meet, their encounter takes place in the doorway to the theater as they prepare for the opening night of "The Band Wagon." The scene is an intimate one—only the third time that Gaby and Tony have been alone in the film—but the intimacy is a forced one in which love is undeclared, a structuring absence, the one thing that cannot be mentioned.

> *Tony:* I just want to say that no matter what happens tonight, it's been . . .
>   [His voice trails off]
> *Gaby:* I know, Tony. It's been that for me, too.
> *Tony:* I've been wanting to ask you something . . . What I wanted to ask . . .
>   Perhaps I better not.
> *Gaby:* I wish you wouldn't.

Likewise, Gaby's end-of-film declaration is a culmination, a symbolic condensation, in which sexuality is displaced by spectacle. Tony emerges from his dressing room to find the whole cast assembled to throw a party for him. Gaby steps forward and concretizes their relationship in a speech that turns love

The final shot from *The Band Wagon*.

into a "permanent show." As she speaks, the camera cuts closer and closer to her face, giving her speech all the power of a final consecration:

> The show's a hit but no matter what happened, we feel it was wonderful knowing you, working with you. Maybe some of us didn't see eye to eye with you at the beginning. Maybe we thought we wouldn't work out together but we have [cut to a closer shot]. Yes, there were obstacles between us but we've kissed them goodbye. We've come to love you, Tony. We belong together. The show's going to run a long time; as far as I'm concerned, it's going to run forever.

Life turned into long-running show, reality turned into aesthetic production, love turned into spectacle—this is the final phantasm of *The Band Wagon*. Tony and Gaby do kiss for a moment but then, "May we say something?" ask Jeffrey and the Martons, and we are launched into a finale of "That's Entertainment." Oedipus has been left behind with a world of responsibility, a world where people face the social Other. As Dennis Giles notes, "the show not only abolishes distance but time" (14). The permanent show is the show of spectacle as imaginary form, recoiling from the everyday world to insist end-lessly on the transcendental qualities of art as infantile fixation, as the final controller of sexuality and human relationship.

NOTES

1. Stephen Heath, "Narrative Space," *Screen* 17, no. 3 (1976): 68–112.

2. Raymond Bellour, "Alternation, Segmentation, Hypnosis: An Interview with Raymond Bellour by Janet Bergstrom," *Camera Obscura* 3–4 (1979): 71–103, at 88.

3. For a moment of hesitation in Bellour, see ibid., 75: "Does the use of binary oppositions bring about an unjustified reduction of the reality of the object in favor of its structure and its meaning, at the expense of its multiple phenomenality."

4. Raymond Bellour, "Le blocage symbolique," *Communications* 23 (1975): 235.

5. Stephen Heath, "The Question Oshima," in *Ophuls,* ed. Paul Willemen (London: British Film Institute, 1978), 76.

6. Raymond Bellour, "Un jour, la castration," *L'Arc* 71 (1978): 9–23.

7. Robin Wood, "The American Family Comedy: From *Meet Me in St. Louis* to *The Texas Chainsaw Massacre,*" *Wide Angle* 3, no. 2 (1979): 9.

8. Geoffrey Nowell-Smith, "Minnelli and Melodrama," *Screen* 18, no. 2 (Summer 1977): 115–16.

9. The following paragraphs on *The Pirate* incorporate material from my essay, "Above All Else to Make You See: Cinema and the Ideology of Spectacle," in *Postmodernism and Politics,* ed. Jonathan Arac (Minneapolis: University of Minnesota Press, 1986), 55–69.

10. Jane Feuer, "Hollywood Musicals: Mass Art as Folk Art," *Jump Cut* 23 (October 1980): 23–25.

11. For the classic study of myths of independence, rebirth, and youth in American culture, see R. W. B. Lewis, *The American Adam: Innocence, Tragedy, and Tradition in the Nineteenth Century* (Chicago: University of Chicago Press, 1955).

12. Leslie Fiedler, *Love and Death in the American Novel,* rev. ed. (New York: Dell Publishing, 1966).

13. Rosalind Coward, "On the Universality of the Oedipus Complex: Debates on Sexual Divisions on Psychoanalysis and Anthropology," *Critique of Anthropology* 15, no. 4 (1980): 11.

14. Dennis Giles, "Show-Making," *Movie* 24 (Spring 1977): 14–25. Further references in text.

15. See the entry on "Fantasme" in their *Vocabulaire de la psychanalyse* (Paris: Presses Universitaires de France, 1967).

Minnelli's *Madame Bovary*

ROBIN WOOD

If Minnelli was among the most neglected and misrecognized of the major Hollywood directors, *Madame Bovary* is perhaps the most neglected and misrecognized of his major works. Even Stephen Harvey, a critic with a long-standing commitment to Minnelli's films, in an obituary in *Film Comment* (October 1986) explicitly dedicated to the setting right of misconceptions, comes up with this extraordinary pronouncement: "Minnelli indicted Emma as an overweening provincial doomed never to find the beauty she sought—primarily because she had such ghastly taste." The remark (itself in "such ghastly taste" for anyone open to the film's emotional impact) seems to tell us more about Harvey (or the milieu within which he operates) than about Minnelli. Whatever else, his *Madame Bovary* is not the work of a trivializing snob: as Emma dies of arsenic poisoning we are not invited to reflect that she got what she deserved for not possessing a more sophisticated view of interior decoration.

The only attempt in English that I know of to examine and assess the film in any detail is the chapter devoted to it in George Bluestone's *Novels into Film,* which, as one of the most grotesquely misguided and misconceived pieces of writing ever perpetrated by an evidently serious and intelligent critic, provides a useful starting point. Bluestone's entire assault on Minnelli's film collapses in ruins as soon as its underlying assumption is spelled out—which he very considerately does for us: "In brief, the implication is that the filmmaker who would tell Emma's story must find visual equivalents for Flaubert's language. . . ." In fact, it is not really accurate to say that Bluestone examines the film in detail; its detail remains inaccessible to him, because he totally ignores all the major factors that create it. He discusses the film in only one context, that of Flaubert's novel, a completely ahistorical approach that removes it cleanly from the actual context (national, social, industrial, temporal) within which it was produced. Bluestone's conception of the possible range of relationships between film and source is hopelessly narrow; to inform us that Minnelli (who has at least been widely recognized, to the point of cliché, as one of the American cinema's most fully formed and masterly stylists) "must" find visual equivalents for Flaubert's language strikes one as a singular piece of effrontery.

To return the film from Bluestone's ahistorical vacuum to its material context, I want to discuss it in relation to four major determining factors, all of which he ignores, but on the complex interaction of which its richness of signification depends: auteur, star, and period of production.

1. Auteur. Bluestone does manage (twice) to refer to "Vincent [*sic*] Minnelli" as the director of the film, but he offers no account of Minnelli as an artist and shows no awareness of any of his other films. It would be more profitable to discuss *Madame Bovary* in relation to *The Pirate* (made the year before), with which it has a great deal in common thematically and stylistically, than in relation to Flaubert.

2. Star. Bluestone does not find it necessary even to mention that Emma is played by Jennifer Jones, despite the fact that on one level *Madame Bovary* is quite plainly a star "vehicle," with Jones's image/screen persona contributing significantly to its tone and meaning. It would be more profitable to discuss it in relation to *Duel in the Sun* and *Ruby Gentry* than in relation to Flaubert.

3. Genre and Period. Bluestone also neglects to acknowledge (let alone discuss) the genre to which Minnelli's film (for all its prestigious literary derivation) patently belongs, and of which it is among the supreme examples: the Hollywood melodrama, and more specifically its subdivision the "woman's picture." Furthermore, the film belongs to a particular (and particularly

important) phase of the genre's evolution: the period following the end of World War II. It would be more profitable to discuss it in relation to *All That Heaven Allows, The Reckless Moment,* and *Beyond the Forest* than in relation to Flaubert.

Bluestone might object that he never proposed to discuss any of these issues: his professed concern is purely with the ways in which novels have been adapted. This scarcely exempts him, I think, from the responsibility of passing judgment on a film whose nature he never even attempts to define. In any case his underlying premise is, to say the least, dubious. An attempt to "translate" a great author's creativity into another medium almost invariably kills it; the only sound criterion is the degree to which the filmmaker has been able to make the material his own, the medium for his *own* creativity (which may be, and in the case of Minnelli/Flaubert is, quite antipathetic to that of the writer).

Bluestone's indignant starting point for the proliferation of his objections is the film's foregrounding of Flaubert/James Mason in its prologue and epilogue (and throughout, in Mason's offscreen narration), his point being that Flaubert regarded authorial invisibility as a supreme value in the creation of fiction. What Bluestone misses is the immediate practical function of the framework: not to defend the novel against charges of immorality in 1856, but to safeguard the film against censorship in 1949 (its very production had been threatened by the Hays Office). However, by far the most important difference between novel and film lies in the author's (and reader's) relationship to the central figure: Flaubert's celebrated detachment (described more brutally by D. H. Lawrence: "He stood off from life as from a leprosy") is replaced by Minnelli's passionate commitment to and identification with his (and Jennifer Jones's) Emma Bovary; the Flaubertian assumption of clinical objectivity (which in practice becomes often indistinguishable from contempt) gives way to an all-pervasive, precariously controlled hysteria.

It is the principle of hysteria that draws together here, in a magnificent unity, Minnelli, Jones, and the woman-centered melodrama. Susan Morrison wrote about "the hysterical text" in *CineAction!* no. 6, in relation to *New York, New York* and *Written on the Wind;* I want to argue that *Madame Bovary* is one of Hollywood's supreme expressions of that phenomenon. First, perhaps, it is necessary to defend hysteria as a valid reaction to certain social conditions ("Don't be so hysterical" is always understood as a reprimand, and "hysterical" movies are generally condemned as such by reviewers anxious to establish their own superior poise). Popularly it has always been, and in general still is, associated with women, as a particularly "feminine" disorder, and, while Morrison (following Freud) correctly points out that women do not have a monopoly on it, its popular attribution to women within patriarchal cultures is not without relevance. Broadly speaking, hysteria (I use the term more in its wider, popular sense than in the strict psychoanalytic one, though the two are obviously connected) can be seen as a response to the frustration of the desire for power—the power, at least, to make one's own decisions, control one's destiny, achieve a measure of personal autonomy, all of which under a capitalist economy will be inevitably involved with power over money, and under a patriarchal economy with power over sexuality: the twin mainsprings of the woman's melodrama.

The tendency to hysteria, then, is logically inherent in the basic materials of the genre. It may of course be treated or inflected very differently by different filmmakers: Otto Preminger's *Angel Face,* for example, might stand as the great extreme exemplar of the rigorously nonhysterical presentation of the ultimate in hysterical subject matter (compare Preminger's devastatingly poker-faced treatment of the final catastrophe, filmed in "objective" long shot, with the climactic car rides of *The Bad and the Beautiful* and *Two Weeks in Another Town*). Hysteria is a major component of both Minnelli's directorial personality and Jones's screen persona. Indeed, in the case of Jones it is the one consistent factor that connects the disparate roles she has played, the opposite poles of the image (innocence/sensuality), from Saint Bernadette to Pearl (*Duel in the Sun*) and Ruby Gentry. (Even her ingenue in *Since You Went Away* is remembered primarily for the big hysterical scene that follows the revelation that Robert Walker has been killed in action.) The suppressed "religious" hysteria of her Bernadette is easily (given the psychoanalytic reading of religious ecstasy as sublimated eroticism) transformed into the directly erotic hysteria of Pearl, Emma, and Ruby.

Hysteria is also a central defining principle of Minnelli's work, linking the melodrama and the musicals (too often treated as distinct expressions of his artistic personality). I should make clear that I am not subscribing here to any romantic notion of art as direct and unmediated self-expression—that is, Minnelli was feeling pretty hysterical one day so he shot the ball scene from *Madame Bovary.* Neither, however, do I subscribe to current absurd notions of the artist's nonexistence: the opposition developed within contemporary film theory between "personal expression" and the deployment of signifiers, as mutually exclusive models of how works of art come into being, seems to me stupid and pernicious. Minnelli understood hysteria, emotionally and intellectually, as a response to feelings of powerlessness and entrapment, and he was able to dramatize it (without ever abandoning artistic/intellectual control) in many of his finest films. That is why he is able so often to identify with hysterical female protagonists: Judy Garland in *The Pirate*, Shirley Mac-Laine in *Some Came Running*, Jennifer Jones in *Madame Bovary*. One manifestation of this hysteria was noted long ago in *Cahiers du cinéma*, I think by Jean Domarchi, who identified "the destruction of decor" as a recurrent motif in Minnelli's films, cutting across all the genres in which he worked. One thinks of Tootie's assault, in *Meet Me in St. Louis*, on the snow people (a family group, the incident immediately answered by Mr. Smith's decision to restore and reinforce family unity by staying in St. Louis "until we rot"); the systematic destruction of the mobile home in *The Long, Long Trailer*; Manuela's attack, in *The Pirate*, on Serafin, necessitating the destruction of Don Pedro's parlor; the climactic smashing of the windows at the height of the ball scene in *Madame Bovary;* the demolition of the drapes in *The Cobweb*. In all these cases the decor that is destroyed embodies an ideological (rather than merely physical) entrapment or constraint. The perfect example is that from *The Pirate:* Manuela's hysteria is a reaction against both the false macho posturings of Serafin (insofar as the objects are flung at *him*) and the possibility of entrapment in a bourgeois marriage (as the decor actually belongs to Don Pedro, Manuela's prospective husband).

Three addenda: 1. I do not want to suggest that the expression of hysteria in Minnelli is restricted to "the destruction of decor," which is merely a convenient, if potentially reductive, formula. There are also, for instance, the wild car rides of *The Bad and the Beautiful* and *Two Weeks in Another Town*, the frenzied climaxes of *Some Came Running* and *Home from the Hill*, and various musical numbers (so different from their counterparts in the MGM Kelly/Donen musicals of the same period): Astaire's surrealist dream in *Yolanda and the Thief*, Garland's fantasy of power and castration in *The Pirate* (where she is identified with both the mule and her "ideal ego" Serafin), Oscar Levant's power-and-pianism fantasy in *An American in Paris*. 2. As certain of these examples already indicate, neither do I wish to suggest that hysteria in Minnelli is restricted to female characters: see, for instance, Kirk Douglas in all his Minnelli movies but especially *Lust for Life*, Robert Taylor in *Undercurrent*, George Hamilton in *Home from the Hill*. 3. Nonetheless, the final and ultimate expression of hysteria in Minnelli's work takes female form: Ingrid Bergman in *A Matter of Time*, Minnelli's last and perhaps most intensely personal film, whose mutilation is among the great Hollywood tragedies. (In this age of restorations, is no one interested in reconstructing Minnelli's original version before it is too late?)

Madame Bovary and *The Pirate* belong together as companion pieces, complementary "hysterical texts" within radically different genres, their differences determined by generic potentialities—in each case potentialities Minnelli drives to their extremes. Both films are centered on a young woman motivated by unrealistic and unfulfillable romantic aspirations (Manuela's yearning to be carried off by a storybook pirate closely corresponds to Emma's self-identification with the heroines of romantic literature). In both cases the romantic aspirations are viewed ambivalently: on the one hand they are seen as misguided, incapable of realization, and potentially self-destructive; on the other they represent the only escape available within the heroine's environment from its economic and ideological constrictions—especially, the suffocation, for the woman, of a traditional bourgeois marriage. Further, both films dramatize the frustrated woman's tendency to seek identity (in herself or vicariously) with the male position, its power and freedom: hence Manuela's identification, in the "pirate" fantasy, with her vision of Mack the Black as ideal ego; and Emma, denied any recognition as autonomous being within her own life, longs for a son who, as male, will inherit the power and freedom she lacks. Richard Lippe, in an article on *A Matter of Time* in *CineAction!* emphasized the importance within Minnelli's work generally of notions of creativity and performance, as valid and realizable means of self-fulfillment, of transcending social/ideological entrapment; Emma's tragedy is that her essentially creative aspirations can find no form worthy of them, within her social environment but also within the generic environment. Hence the diametrically opposed progress of the two films. The musical genre can enable *The Pirate*'s "utopian" happy ending: Serafin and Manuela are able to cast off (respectively) macho presumption and romantic fantasy; the climactic number ("Be a Clown") is a celebration both of the collapse of gender difference in androgyny and of the creativity that makes such a resolution possible by allowing the couple to move outside the social norms, as performers. Within the melodrama, the "happy ending" can seldom be more than what Sirk called an "emergency exit," more or less derisory as a proposed resolution of the conflicts (*Under Capricorn* provides one of the rare significant exceptions). In *Madame Bovary* Minnelli (and here we may acknowledge a little help from Flaubert, the alibi of "great literature" facilitating the avoidance of emergency exits) drove the implications of the genre to their logical conclusion in Emma's final act of tragic desperation.

The traditional account of the evolution of the melodrama in the late 1940s connects it to the situation of women after the Second World War: during the war they had been encouraged to come out of the home and take the place of the absent men in the work force, discovering for the first time a measure of autonomy, earning money in their own right, no longer dependent upon the weekly generosity of their husbands; they also began to discover the potentialities of women's solidarity. When the war ended and the surviving men returned, the ideological pressure was reversed and every effort was made to convince them that their correct place, and the one they had really always wanted (it was, after all, the "natural" one), was back in the home as housewives and mothers. The films can be read as in part a response to the resulting tensions, so long as we bear in mind that there is no clear break in the genre's thematic, merely an exacerbation of problems that were always there and which the melodrama had consistently addressed. What needs firmly to be refuted is the simpleminded notion that the films are part of a propagandistic patriarchal-capitalist conspiracy, solely conceived to teach female spectators that if they don't behave and accept their traditional role they will be ruthlessly punished. It is certainly crucial that the films were made primarily for a female audience (one might again contrast Flaubert's novel, the reader of which is clearly constructed, in his position of superiority, as male), but it seems extremely doubtful that women used to be so stupid as to pay their pocket money to sit through film after film in order masochistically, stoically, or complacently to identify with the heroine's punishment at the end; or that filmmakers like Minnelli, Ophuls, and Vidor were so stupid as to think they were so stupid. In order to reach their intended audience, it was necessary for the films to dramatize the existing societal tensions as intelligently and forcefully as possible. It is further obvious that the great female stars functioned as identification figures, and they all, in a wide variety of ways, embodied types of transgressiveness. The films show that punishment for transgression is inevitable *within the existing social conditions;* but, by the time the punishment is reached, the social conditions have been effectively discredited, so that the punishment is registered as unjust, excessive or monstrous. My eldest sister, herself a strong and assertive woman who spent most of the Second World War (in England) in the women's branch of the armed services, identified totally with Bette Davis throughout (and prior to) this period, never missing a Davis film. It is clear to me that what she identified with was Davis's strength and habitual transgressiveness, even (perhaps especially) in films like *The*

Letter where the character was explicitly designated "wicked"; the punishment was a minor, if inevitable, annoyance. Similarly, we cannot even begin to appreciate *Madame Bovary* unless we accept and share Minnelli's identification with Jennifer Jones. From a conventional moral standpoint Emma's behavior is selfish and immoral (the conventional moral standpoint being by definition patriarchal); from *any* moral standpoint it is harmful to others and ultimately self-destructive. But the basis of identification is the principle of hysteria—the instinctive response to powerlessness and the stifling of creativity—that gives rise to and accounts for that behavior. Emma cannot be blamed for breaking the rules of patriarchal capitalist society: she had no say in the making of them. It is striking that only one character in the film is permitted a speech morally denouncing Emma: the felicitously named Monsieur L'Heureux, the hypocrite moneylender, the film's ultimate monster and spokesperson for capitalism, who denounces Emma from the illustrious position of a man "in the business of making money—a recognized, honorable profession."

The principle of hysteria is embedded in the film's very structure, a structure of exceptional rigor and logic. Its midpoint and conclusion marked by Emma's two suicide attempts, it is built consistently on her efforts to realize her romantic aspirations in concrete forms, every attempt followed by a corresponding frustration, every frustration motivating in its turn a new attempt at self-realization, producing a "weave" of aspiration/frustration that develops inexorably, accumulating ever-increasing intensity, toward the two "suicidal" climaxes. The pattern is precise and consistent enough to be charted:

Aspiration	Frustration
Romantic Fantasies	Farmhouse
S_1	
Charles M_1	"Not exciting"
Wedding	"Vulgarity" H_1
Yonville	Drab house
Interior decoration	Start of credit notes M_2
Salon M_3	Marquis's laughter H_2
Desire for son	Birth of daughter
(who will have the power Emma lacks)	
Invitation M_4	
Ball M_5	Charles's drunkenness H_3

A1: Léon seduction	Madame Dupuis's intervention H4
Hippolyte's foot	Charles's failure to perform the Operation H5
A2: consummation H6	Charles on the stairs, child's Alienation M6
A2: elopement (i)	L'Heureux—Rodolphe's name Required H7
elopement (ii) S2	Rodolphe's betrayal H8
Suicide 1	
Opera in Rouen	The aging tenor H9
A1: Assignation S3	Squalid room H10 M7
A1: consummation H11	Maid's hostility, child's rejection, Bills
(To L'Heureux for money)	(power of attorney)
A1: resumption (gondola bed)	Tacky decor
Léon: papers	Employer's rejection HL1
A1: continuation	L'Heureux spying H12
To Guillaumin (money) S4	Attempted assault H13
To Léon (money) (A1 concluded)	Léon a clerk HL2 Home M8
To Rodolphe (money) (A2 concluded)	Rodolphe's rejection H14
Suicide 2	

Key:
S: Strom, H: Humiliation, HL: Humiliation of Léon, M: Mirror, A: Adultery

It remains to suggest something of the film's richness of connotation. Rather than attempt an exhaustive analysis, I shall isolate a series of recurring motifs, some (but not all) of which are notated above on the chart; some are specific to the film, and others belong more generally to the genre but are developed and orchestrated by Minnelli with particular system and intelligence.

1. Storms: clearly a staple of the "hysterical text," externalizing the characters' inner tumult (compare the leaves blowing into the house at the beginning

and end of *Written on the Wind,* or the storms that, in Hitchcock's great melodrama, mark both the initiation of Marnie's trauma and her eventual recall). In *Madame Bovary* Minnelli uses storms to connect Emma's two suicide attempts, and to link both to her first meeting with Charles—her initial illusion of escape that leads to the subsequent entrapments of which her life consists.

2. Emma's dresses. The motif is established from the outset in the incongruously extravagant dress in which Emma presents herself to Charles in her father's farmhouse kitchen. Emma's dresses—always *too much,* too grandiose, often simply too large for their environment, emphasizing the way the decor hems her in—become the expression of her frustrated creativity, epitomizing not only her drive to construct herself as glamorous object, as work of art, but also her desire to burst the bounds of her social context.

3. Birds. Emma's ball dress is decorated with birds in flight, which appear to have just taken wing. The romantic aspiration this expresses is answered in one of the scenes of ultimate humiliation, the visit to Monsieur Guillaumin to recover the credit notes, Guillaumin attempting to profit from Emma's economic subjugation by assaulting her: his parlor is full of caged birds.

4. Italy as romantic escape. Emma and Rodolphe are to elope to Italy; it is Rodolphe's betrayal that precipitates the first suicide attempt. The implicit aspiration is answered in the reality of Emma's affair with Léon Dupuis: in the pretentious and tacky hotel room in which they keep their assignation, the bed is in the shape of a gondola.

5. Money. The woman's lack of autonomous access to economic power haunts the melodrama, often peripherally, though in some of the finest examples (*Caught, The Reckless Moment, Beyond the Forest*) it becomes a central issue. Introduced near the beginning of *Madame Bovary* (interior decoration/start of credit notes—see chart), it is taken up in Monsieur L'Heureux's insistence that a man's name guarantee payment for the accoutrements of Emma's elopement with Rodolphe. In the second half of the film the motif virtually takes over. The culminations of Emma's two adulterous relationships are not the romantic fulfillment to which she aspired but the woman's desperate plea for financial help from a man who is either unable (Léon) or unwilling (Rodolphe) to respond positively. Emma is finally destroyed by men's control of the economy and women's enforced ignorance of its workings.

6. Mirrors. Mirror imagery recurs throughout the Hollywood melodrama and films related to it (see, for example, Hitchcock's use of mirrors at particularly "loaded" moments of *Under Capricorn* and *The Wrong Man,* signify-

ing respectively the construction and destruction of illusory images of wholeness). Yet, Sirk apart (and he only in *Written on the Wind* and *Imitation of Life*), no one has used mirror images as complexly and systematically, as a structuring procedure rather than as decoration, as Minnelli in *Madame Bovary*. I have not attempted in the chart to annotate all the recurrences of mirror imagery, preferring to draw attention to the eight occasions where it achieves clear structural significance. Also, it must not be reduced to a single "symbolic" meaning: the connotations shift and change in relation to the progress of the narrative, moving from Emma's vanity through her construction of an illusory image of romantic fulfillment, to the destruction of that image and the culminating revelation of the reality to which Emma has descended. Here I single out five of the eight instances: (i) Emma in the farmhouse in her enormous dress is shown as an image in a mirror, like a painting, the work of art she inspires to become. (ii) It is the purchase of a mirror—with a very ornate frame, in which Emma can develop her ideal image of herself—that initiates the process of credit notes that gradually becomes decisive to Emma's downfall: as child-woman in a world where men are the adults, she is still too completely under the sway of the pleasure-principle to take heed of the material realities that will destroy her. (iii) Central to Emma's development is her vision of herself at the ball, in her dress with the birds in flight, reflected in another ornate mirror, surrounded by a number of admiring young men, grouped and posed as in a painting: the illusory perfection of her ideal self-image. It is swiftly followed by the ominous building hysteria of the dance, Emma's fainting spell, the smashing of windows. (iv) Waiting for her assignation with Léon in the squalid hotel in Rouen, Emma, wearing the same dress (now absurdly incongruous within the constricting decor) momentarily recaptures that ideal image; but the hotel mirror is cracked and tarnished, the fantasy cannot be sustained. (v) Finally, just before her last visit to Rodolphe to beg for money, Emma sees herself as she has become, pallid, drawn, haggard, and tries desperately and unsuccessfully to re-create herself by applying makeup.

7. Windows. Mirror and window imagery are often associated within the melodrama (again, *Madame Bovary* apart, this is most thoroughly systematized in the films of Sirk, notably *Written on the Wind*). The imagery of windows carries its own inherent ambiguity (entrapment/escape) and can therefore be inflected in quite different ways in the work of different filmmakers: for example, a recurrent motif in Renoir's work is the opening of windows, in Ophuls's their closing, a detail that is very suggestive in relation to

Emma (Jennifer Jones) in the ball sequence from *Madame Bovary* (1949).

the overall thematic of both directors. *Madame Bovary* explores the possible connotations very complexly. Again, I shall isolate a few key instances rather than attempt an exhaustive account. (i) Emma surveying and caustically cataloguing from her upstairs window the monotonous daily routine of Yonville: she looks out from the entrapment of her home to see nothing but the entrapment of the small town. (ii) The smashing of the windows at the ball. The ball scene is at once one of Minnelli's finest musical "numbers" and a supreme enactment of the "hysterical text." Indeed, although the smashing of the windows is diegetically motivated (Emma begins to faint, and needs fresh air), it is more cogently *demanded* by the emotional progress of the sequence, its brilliantly orchestrated escalation into hysteria. The guiding idea is once again the collision between the pleasure principle and the reality principle: Emma's rising ecstasy is systematically intercut with Charles's increasing drunkenness, the sequence culminating in Emma's humiliation when he invades the dance floor to claim her. But the source of the hysteria lies in Emma's misrecognition of illusion (the "ideal" mirror image) for a sustainable reality: her clinging onto the sense of an illusory romantic fulfillment becomes increasingly more desperate, the dream becoming increasingly nightmarish, precipitating the "destruction of decor," a decor whose longed-for luxury and extravagance is but another entrapment. (iii) Emma/Léon. Richard Lippe pointed out to me that the smashing of the windows at the ball is echoed in Léon's smashing his fist through a windowpane in the Rouen hotel. The connection confirms the parallel the film develops between Emma and Léon, her romantic illusions about herself echoed in his fantasy that he is a partner in the law firm in which he is in fact a mere clerk, her humiliation as a woman echoed in his as an employee, both deprived of power and self-respect, both victims of "the system."

Finally, the two suicides (attempted and successful, midpoint and end of the film) are linked by window imagery, worked out very precisely in terms of opposition and parallel. When Emma attempts to throw herself from the window after Rodolphe's betrayal, the camera views the action from outside, static; Emma's death scene is framed by two shots looking out from the bedroom window over Yonville, the second (the acknowledgement of the moment of death) a tracking shot moving from a medium close-up of Charles (looking, as usual, vaguely troubled by his chronic inability imaginatively to comprehend the woman he loves) to the open window and then forward, to exclude the room and frame the town beneath the nocturnal sky. The camera movement outward toward freedom (the only such movement in the film) can be read as evoking the birds-in-flight on Emma's ball dress, the shot becoming from this viewpoint Minnelli's final celebration of her spirit at the moment of her final defeat. But there is nothing sentimental about this, the celebration being qualified by an equally strong irony. The use of the window and the view of the town also evokes Emma's commentary on small-town routine and tedium; what the camera movement reveals is not the open sky but Yonville, the imprisoning and creativity-stifling environment in which other Emmas may be struggling to find expression and fulfillment amid conditions that render both unrealizable. The shot's function is as much structural as expressive: it draws together the threads of the film in a single camera gesture.

The Pirate Isn't Just Decor

S ERGE D ANEY

T RANSLATED BY B ILL K ROHN

Here comes the question: Does a Minnelli film gain or lose on television? A perfectly legitimate question (although after a while it begins to feel a bit like niggardly calculation), but let's begin with another one. Since this is Minnelli, who is famous for his sense of decor, the question is: How is your place decorated? Next to what knickknacks, what wallpaper, what lighting (halogen or indirect), what real or fake library, what coffee table, what designer lamp or old-fashioned lampshade does your television set officiate? In other words: In what kind of setting (1988) is the little image of the great *Pirate* (1948) lodged, with the signature luxury of its MGM sets that dazzled when their reds glowed, unrivaled, within the huge images being projected in a darkened theater?

And here comes the answer: What difference does it make, since *The Pirate* and its sets hold up splendidly? Because what they've lost in store-window impact they've gained in pure logic. Because, quite simply, this is not a "decorative" film. That's the decisive point. For if there is a type of film that loses its aura by being deported to the small screen, it's the decorative film, one that risks being less accomplished in matters of decor than the "interior" where it is seen. That confrontation, while unconscious, can be quite cruel.

Contrary to what one might think (or retrospectively hallucinate), when *The Pirate* was made, American musical comedy didn't seek to expand space or open transversed lines of flight within the image. It was satisfied with the square screen. If Serafin–Gene Kelly wants to conquer anything, it's the vertical space of the flies, the crow's nest, or the gallows that threaten him. Dreams and bodies soar, spin around one another, approach without touching, and accumulate without promiscuity, never cramped for space in a frame they have not yet begun to contest. The dream is a flight that never leaves home, one that transports its decor on the back of its images wherever it goes.[1]

Minnelli's characters always lie and never stop dreaming. A dream is the only truth because it is a decor, and one can fight in and for a decor. One might even say that it's the only concrete thing in the world, much more so than words. Manuela is ready to "sacrifice" herself to save the decor of the little Caribbean town of Calvados [*sic*] and adapt it to her dream. But more than that is required: One must inhabit a decor, animate it with one's dances and trances, bring it to life. The decor is, in the most moral sense imaginable, a "value," and like any value it is always to be conquered and never really won.

Which is why a Minnelli decor is different from that of other filmmakers. Transplanted to television, it makes it cruelly apparent what a television decor is: something that is there before the actors, something that the actors have been wedged into, where they will attempt anything but dance steps. Television, which lives in fear of someone bumping into something, empties its stages and simplifies its movements. Whereas cinema, which for a long time had no fear of overpopulated stages and images, knew how to make Judy Garland and Gene Kelly move without ever bumping into each other.

When that does happen it's a sign that they're losing their footing, and that their power to dream has been diminished. It's at the moment when Serafin, unmasked, is speechless before Manuela, who is beside herself, that, very discretely, he bumps into a humble chair. Kelly's talent is knowing how to do this elegantly. It lasts a second and is very beautiful.

—October 15, 1988

NOTES

1. "A dream . . . that carries its decor on the soles of its shoes . . ." Cf. "A traveler carries his native land on the soles of his shoes."—French proverb.

Minnelli Caught in His Web

SERGE DANEY

TRANSLATED BY BILL KROHN

"It's me," says a voice.

"Me who?"

"Me, *The Cobweb* (1955)."

"Another Minnelli?"

"Look at me. I'm very beautiful; I'm very psychological."

"And you have a fabulous cast, I know."

"What you don't know is that James Dean was supposed to play the role of the young neurotic."

"Oh yes, I know. Dean was too expensive, so John Kerr got the part. Minnelli tells all that in his autobiography, page 285." I was being rather curt.

In fact, I had several reasons to be irritated. My "auteurist" side told me that this Minnelli was yet another meditation on decor, since it describes how a "modern" psychiatric clinic—patients and doctors alike—descends into a collective nervous breakdown brought on by the need to change the *curtains* in the clinic's library! *The Cobweb*, obviously, is very "Minnellian." At the same time, I had not forgotten that my mission was not to prove that an auteur is faithful to himself but to evaluate how films come across on the small screen, *one by one*. Basically, I was afraid that the great Minnellis of the 1950s, with their washed-out Eastmancolor, cut-down CinemaScope, and psychological themes, would not come across as well as the pure musical comedies of the previous period.

"Obviously, you prefer *The Pirate*," sighed the film, which had divined my thoughts.

"It's not that," I lied. "It's just that television is often hard on 50s films."

"I see—you want to humiliate me."

"Not at all," I said, giving in.

So I saw *The Cobweb* again and admired again the way Widmark, Grahame, Bacall, Gish, Boyer, Kerr, Strasberg, and Levant shared the space-time continuum of the film. Today no one would know how to democratically house so many characters in one film, each with his own problem, and speaking fluent Freud—especially the patients. The optimism of Minnelli, Houseman (a great producer), and Gibson (the screenwriter) is strange—their conviction that psychoanalysis is the best method, modern and humane, and that it can definitely cure as long as doctors join with patients in the elegant therapy of a great ballet. Isn't self-government[1] the goal Dr. Widmark is pursuing for his patients?

But a ballet of symptoms is no longer a musical comedy. A dance or a song has a beginning and an end. They *resolve* something—dialogue never does. *The Pirate* fitted into the square Technicolor screen; *The Cobweb* no longer fits into the space of the studio or the running time of a "normal" film. The cobweb knows that it is tattered, in danger of being simplified and patched up with spit, bailing wire, and fervent prayers. Just from the way Minnelli confines his actors in extremis to a common space, one can tell that the crisis of the studio system[2] will not be long in coming.

Which is why the curtains in the library are so important. They are like coming attractions for the New Hollywood's new look, which will be fatal to Minnelli. There is Gish, a penny-pinching skinflint, who wants them made out of rep or chintz. There is Grahame, the boss's neglected wife, who wants them made out of muslin. And there is Bacall, who is closer to the patients and wants them to make the curtains themselves. In the film the last solution will win out. In reality, it will be the second. Muslin curtains are horrible—like Grahame, they anticipate *Dallas*.

If the decor is ugly—ugly enough to make strong men flee—it's because it is no longer a refuge. A man of taste, Minnelli flees ugliness. Panicked flights at the end of *Home from the Hill* and particularly *Some Came Running*. Flight of the deranged young painter (John Kerr) at the end of *The Cobweb*. Flight of Minnelli and his crew to a river being dragged on a rainy night—outside the studio that can no longer hold them, "far from home."[3]

The film touches us, but not the way it did before. Perhaps because we know all too well what happened next. Television appeared in the United States at the moment when films were losing their way: too many characters, too many ideas, too many directions and, above all, too many boring parts. Television reformatted those riches, adopted a dime-store version of Freud, plugged the lines of flight that we can see so well in Minnelli because he is still resisting them and only gives in to them after an argument.

So much so that when we see *The Cobweb* on the small screen, it's as if television, after rummaging through its drawers, is exhibiting the sick swarming that preceded it, which it was obliged to put in order.

—October 22, 1988

Translator's Notes
1. In English in the text.
2. "Studio system": in English in the text.
3. In English in the text.

III

THE 1990S: MATTERS OF HISTORY, CULTURE, AND SEXUALITY

The Band Wagon

Geoffrey Nowell-Smith

Between about 1920 and 1960, the cinema, and American cinema in particular, was, along with the radio, the main vehicle of cultural experience for the majority of the population in the industrialized world. Cinema and radio rocketed into this position of prominence within twenty years or so of being invented—cinema by 1920, radio by about 1925; they have now lost this position to television (which is on the one hand a form of radio with illustrations, and on the other hand a way of showing movies, rather small, in the home).

The high point of film going was reached in the United States and Great Britain just after the Second World War, in France, Germany, and Italy a little later. It actually peaked in Britain in 1946, with 1.6 billion admissions. That number of admissions in a country of 50 million people meant about thirty visits to the cinema per person (man, woman, or child) per year; it meant that about half of the population probably went to the cinema at least once a week. (Figures for continental Europe are on the whole lower.) In most countries, except under special conditions such as war, the majority of main feature films watched were American. In America itself, of course, the overwhelming majority of films watched were (and remain) American.

The Hollywood movie is often referred to as escapist. This is true to the extent that the viewer was invited to escape into a world that contained strong elements of wish fulfillment. But the wishes that were imaginatively fulfilled through identification with characters in a movie were not trivial. They had to do with the achievement of the ideals of American society. Hollywood films throughout the classic period can often be read as parables of the resolution of conflicts facing individuals as asocial subjects, as citizens, or as members of a social or ethnic group. As such, they provided a cultural-imaginative framework for everyday existence, both for Americans and for the rest of us growing up within the American sphere of influence.

This is all, by now, received wisdom. What is less often recognized is that the Hollywood movie not only performed this role but also could be quite self-conscious about the fact of having it and the way it performed it. Very early in its history, in fact, the Hollywood movie, as well as producing representations of things outside itself—cowboys, and gangsters, and vamps, and girls and boys next door—begins to produce self-representations and, with this, various discourses to do with the nature of the culture diffused by the cinema and its legitimacy. Hollywood films about Hollywood include some about the process of filming and film projection, such as Buster Keaton's *Sherlock Jr.* (1924) and *The Cameraman* (1928), but they also include a number that address themes such as the moral panic generated by reports of profligacy, corruption, decadence, and vice in Hollywood itself. *Show People* (King Vidor, 1928) and *The Bad and the Beautiful* (Vincente Minnelli, 1952) are probably the classics of the genre, but it dates back at least to *A Girl's Folly* (Maurice Tourneur, 1917). With the development of this reflexivity also comes the asking of the question: what is the relationship of the movies (and in particular the movie you are watching now) to other cultural and artistic forms?

There is an inner logic in most art forms that leads to self-questioning and self-reflexivity, but whether this logic will be activated depends on external factors. In the case of the cinema, the most important factor was a very strong drive for respectability. The cinema started downmarket; it could undercut other forms of fairground and arcade entertainment. But it wanted to go upmarket, to attract affluent audiences, and the people in the business had, I think, a genuine desire—not snobbish, not mercenary—for culture. But as the cinema pushed up against the frontiers of the bourgeois cultural world—the world of the classic novel, the drama, the opera, the symphony concert—so it was forced to call its own forms into question—its derivation from melodrama and the dime novel, its use of Tin Pan Alley and jazz. What was the status of the cinema's synthesis of high-cultural and popular-cultural elements? Did it actually constitute a distinct culture, separate from and potentially antagonistic to traditional high culture? Was it inferior, equal, or even superior to traditional culture? Was it the new American culture, replacing the traditional culture of Old Europe? If so, could it claim the political virtues of modern democratic America against the class-ridden feudal character of Europe? Is the longing for the new culture, the one represented by the movies and popular music, an emblem of American citizenship? At which point, of course, we connect with the other set of problems raised by the Hollywood movie, and referred to earlier, their contribution to the construction of individual identities in the American context.

This cultural dialectic finds wonderfully condensed expression in a Warner Brothers cartoon from 1936 called *I Love to Sing-a*, directed by Tex Avery. This takes place somewhere in America. Professor Fritz Owl is identified as a professional musician and a first-generation immigrant, speaking English with a thick *Mittel-Europäische* accent. He would appear, from his name, to be German, though probably not Jewish, in spite of the traditional connection of Jews and music in Hollywood films (*Humoresque*, 1920; *The Jazz Singer*, 1927). At the beginning of the film Mrs. Owl has just given birth to a clutch of four eggs. When tapped, the first owl sings an excerpt from a Verdi aria, prompting the father to compare his son to Caruso; the second plays the violin, prompting the father to compare him to Fritz Kreisler; and the third plays the flute, prompting a comparison to Mendelssohn. But when the fourth egg is tapped, this owl bursts into an energetic version of "I Love to Sing-a" from the Al Jolson film *The Singing Kid*, also released by Warner Brothers in 1936. This baby Owl can't sing conventional music, but he can sing what in the jargon of the time is referred to as jazz. As the film goes on, the parents attempt to teach their son classical music but the youngster rebels, prompting his father to throw him out of the house, much to the mother's distress. The son, now calling himself "Owl Jolson," winds up on a radio amateur show. His distraught parents and siblings hear his voice over the radio and rush to the station for a reunion. Hearing his son's voice in this public arena causes the father to do an about-face as he now encourages his son to continue with his jazz singing. This jazz, furthermore, is what the people want; and it is by singing jazz that Little Owl can make the transition from the world of the family to that of society at large, which is also in his case the transition from European to American culture, and of course the surmounting of the oedipal crisis. Little Owl is then reconciled to his family, who henceforth are all integrated into American society together in the white ethnic melting pot. The film ends with the entire family singing and dancing together to "I Love to Sing-a."

With this example in mind, I now turn to Vincente Minnelli's classic MGM musical, *The Band Wagon* (1953), where a similar theme is explored, but, needless to say, with considerably more sophistication. It is, for a start a full-length film, with more space for intricacies of plot development. It is also an MGM film, and MGM was at the time the most upscale of the major studios, with a heavy investment in cultural values. Not only did it come from MGM but also from the unit at the studio headed by Arthur Freed that also produced the Stanley Donen–Gene Kelly musicals such as *On the Town* (1949) and *Singin' in the Rain* (1952), in which the dialectic of high and popular culture certainly puts in an appearance, if only a passing one. But above all the director and mastermind of the film was Minnelli, probably the most culturally sophisticated of all Hollywood filmmakers since Ernst Lubitsch.

The Band Wagon is now available on DVD, as the Hollywood studios discover the residual value in their golden past. But when I first saw it in the 1970s (on a 16 mm print from Films Incorporated) it was a rare pleasure, and the film was then best remembered for containing the song "That's Entertainment!" that gave the title to the MGM compilation film of 1974 in which the history of the MGM musical was shown as an unremitting series of jolly, popular, entertaining numbers. As we shall see, the truth, as far as *The Band Wagon*, and indeed the song, is concerned, is sadly distorted by this association. Jolly number "That's Entertainment!" may be, but in the way it is placed in the film makes it more than that, while the film as a whole is quite extraordinarily rich in its representation of the intricacies of American cultural values.

The film starts with actor/dancer Tony Hunter, a character played by Fred Astaire and partly modeled on him, returning to New York from Hollywood, where his career is all washed up, in the hope of restarting a career in the theater. When he arrives at the station, the press is there, but they haven't come for him but for Ava Gardner, who happens to be traveling on the same train. Tony is greeted by his friends Lily and Lester Marton (Nanette Fabray and Oscar Levant), who have written a show for him to perform in, to be directed by fashionable actor-producer Jeffrey Cordova (Jack Buchanan). Tony professes never to have heard of Cordova. He is also disconcerted by the way New York has changed, by the way the theater district around 42nd Street and Times Square has gone downscale and famous theaters that used to cater, as he remembers it, to the "carriage trade" have been turned into penny arcades (he'd have been even more put out if he'd visited it forty years later). But he decides to face the changed reality, and when Lily and Lester leave him he goes into the arcade, which is not at all shabby and is brightly lit in saturated colors. Tony, the film implies, was just being grouchy and middle-aged in deploring it, and in any case he soon cheers up. He has his shoes shined by a large black man (Leroy Daniels), who joins him in an impromptu dance number. Thoroughly revived, Tony succeeds in activating a mysterious box in the middle of the arcade that bursts open and starts playing a Sousa-type march while American and other national flags shoot forth in all directions.

After this energizing encounter with American (but also cosmopolitan and multiethnic) popular culture, Tony sets out for the theater when he rejoins Lily and Lester in time to see Jeff Cordova come off stage at the end of his own adaptation of *Oedipus Rex*. The performance (what we see of it) is all stage effects and dirgelike incantations. It is clearly high culture, but of a singularly empty kind. As for Cordova himself (Jack Buchanan at his self-parodying best), he has an upper-class manner but is also quite vulgar. The contrast with the world of the penny arcade is stark, and definitely to the advantage of the latter. It is hard to see what a couple of old troupers of the musical stage and screen such as Lily and Lester would want to have to do with Cordova, even if he does have a great (though, it is heavily hinted, inflated) reputation.

Nevertheless, Lily and Lester present their plan to Cordova, and we get another culture reversal. So, far from Cordova moving across to direct a musical, he will move the musical across to his world. He declares that the story is a modern Faust; he rewrites it on the spot, all the while protesting that there is no fundamental difference between high culture and popular culture, and between "the magic rhythms of the Bill Shakespeare's immortal verse and the magic rhythms of Bill Robinson's immortal feet." It is, he says, "all entertainment." (Bill Robinson was a leading black entertainer of the 1920s and 30s who became accepted by white audiences only fairly late in his career, thanks in part to the tribute paid to his talent by Fred Astaire in 1936 in George Stevens's *Swing Time*.)

Tony is skeptical but is won over by Jeff's bluster, and Jeff then leads the little quartet in a rendition of the song-and-dance number "That's Entertainment!" (I say song-and-dance number, but while all four of them sing, Oscar Levant manages to be out of frame whenever there is any remotely stylish dancing to be done.) The song will return at the end, in a different context, as a kind of apotheosis and with Jeff no longer as leader. In its first appearance, however, it is very much his song, and the lines about *Oedipus Rex* (the parricide if not the incest) and *Hamlet* ("The ghost and the prince meet / and everyone ends in mincemeat") have a strong contextual appositeness, whereas others such as "Hip, hooray, the American way" have less immediate resonance, at least for the time being. The marriage of high and popular culture has been formally announced—although, like all marriages in musicals, there will be many a plot twist before it can be allowed to proceed.

Having talked Tony into his conception of a show that will not only be entertainment but "relevant" and "modern," Jeff now sets out to secure the services of a classical ballerina, Gabrielle Gerard (Cyd Charisse), to play opposite him. To do this he needs the cooperation of her boyfriend/agent/choreographer Paul Byrd (James Mitchell). Paul is a cold fish and a suitable foil for Jeff's deviousness, but he too is won over by the promise of being allowed to choreograph his protégée. It is agreed that Tony and Gaby will meet each other after a performance of a ballet in which she is starring.

The audience is then treated to the spectacle of Cyd Charisse performing some classical ballet, which she does competently but, as Tony waspishly observes, she is rather tall for a ballerina. Neither party turns out to be eager to consummate the proposed meeting, and when they do find themselves in the same space, on a staircase, Tony seems mostly anxious about being paired with a woman who is taller than he. Their conversation is edgy and tentative and when Gaby refers to having seen Tony's movies "at the Museum" (i.e., MoMA [Museum of Modern Art]) Tony explodes, claiming she is putting him in the same category as the dinosaurs. The clash of cultures is paired with a clash of generations, in which, intriguingly, the representative of classical culture is the youthful one, in contrast to the aging popular hoofer who is seen as halfway ready for embalming as a museum piece.

The tune of "That's Entertainment!" now returns, almost as a leitmotif, setting the tone for the film as a whole. The rehearsal, however, is chaotic, with Tony unable to cope with some of the balletic movements and contradictory advice being given on all sides. Tony decides he has had enough and, after a petulant, even childish, outburst—"I am not Nijinsky, I am not Marlon Brando," (just then performing Mark Antony in Joseph L. Mankiewicz's film of *Julius Caesar*) "I'm Mrs. Hunter's little boy, Tony, song-and-dance man"— he makes a "Declaration of Independence" and storms off stage.

Alone in his hotel room, he continues his fit, throwing papers around and smashing records. Gaby comes upstairs to make things up. Again, the encounter starts with a misunderstanding. She looks at the paintings on his wall and remarks that she has never seen such splendid prints in a hotel. He responds that they are not the hotel's but his, and are originals. If they were, they would be worth millions, since there is a Modigliani, a Van Gogh, a Toulouse Lautrec, a Renoir (I think), something that looks like a Paul Klee, a Degas, and a number of other impressionist and early modern paintings. It is the Degas that attracts her attention and gives her a chance to show that, at least in terms of art appreciation, they are on the same wavelength. But it is only when she breaks down and starts to cry that he softens and decides that she is not one of his persecutors but a fellow victim.

The scene is also interesting because, as well as establishing a shared culture, it introduces the idea of Nature. Gaby's reconciliation gift is a bouquet of flowers, and a flower painting is prominent on Tony's wall. Gaby and Tony then go out, but instead of getting into a yellow taxi to go to a cocktail lounge, they take a horse-drawn cab to Central Park. As they go they comment on the presence of grass, trees, and open sky. They then walk through the park, passing a bandstand where there are numerous dancing couples. Rather than joining the couples, Gaby and Tony walk through them. Then, in the presence of Nature—or, rather, a studio set implausibly representing Nature—they move spontaneously into a natural dance routine, very different from the stiff balletic movements forced on them in the play. This slide from walking to dancing was an MGM specialty, pioneered by Gene Kelly rather than Astaire, but here Astaire does it beautifully and Charisse matches him. The walk picks up, their bodies begin to sway slightly, their feet cross in front of them, and before we know it they are dancing.

The show, called "The Band Wagon," is now ready to go on the road. Except that it isn't. The production team is still arguing and the production itself is collapsing under the weight of its scenery: "More scenery in this show than in Yellowstone National Park," says a stagehand. However, it opens on time and the backers promise a champagne reception at the hotel after the show. In the event, the show predictably flops and the party is a nonevent. Nobody turns up and the smartly dressed French waiters are left standing in an empty room.

Not only are there no guests at the party; the cast doesn't show up either. Instead they retire to a hotel room and drown their sorrows with a crate of beer. Lester and Lily join them and Lester hammers out a few chords on the piano. Tony recognizes them—not surprisingly, since they are the introduction to a song that older spectators will recall as one that Fred Astaire has sung before, in a 1931 musical revue also called *The Band Wagon:* a German-style drinking song called "I Love Louisa." Tony leads, and the rest of the cast members join in.

The contrast between the smart reception downstairs and the impromptu get-together in the room adds a new dimension to the cultural contrasts set up by the film. The reception, with its champagne, formal dress, and French-speaking waiters, is both class and nationally coded. France is labeled as the source not only of the expensive paintings in Tony's hotel room but also of the accoutrements of upper-class life. The get-together, with bottles of beer and folks in casual check shirts, by contrast, is Germanic. The opposition European sophistication versus American spontaneity is doubled and overdetermined by one between specifically French refinement and a German *Gemütlichkeit* that belongs on the American side to the extent that German immigrants can be seen (along with Poles, Irish, Italians, etc.) as part of popular America, whereas the French are not so seen. This division has a historical rationale in that the French did not on the whole form part of "the poor, the huddled masses" who immigrated to the USA from the middle of the nineteenth century onward, but it is perhaps more relevant to note that in other Minnelli/MGM films, such as *An American in Paris* (1951) and *Lust for Life* (1956), France is clearly identified with high culture, and in *Gigi* (1958) with refined (if decadent) upper-class manners as well.

The cast members decide that even if "The Band Wagon" as modern Faust is a disaster, the show must go on, with a different content even if under the same name. So it is again rewritten, in much simpler form. The spirit of the troupe is generous enough to allow a chastened Jeff back into the fold, and he soon buckles down to the discipline of working democratically with and under a team of old troupers. The new show sets out on tour, in preparation for New York, and it is a real hodgepodge of neo-Vaudeville elements. There is a night-clubby, girl-with-group-of-muscular-guys number. There is a white-tie-and-tails routine, in which Jack Buchanan has to stand up to Fred Astaire and holds his own. There is the comedy song "Triplets." And there is a country number, called "Louisiana Hayride," which is so corny as to make *Oklahoma!* look positively sophisticated. Narrative is suspended. Only the slightest of story lines seems to connect the numbers that will form the new show, and the only visible separation/connection between them in the film is provided by shots of express trains carrying the cast from New Haven to Philadelphia, to Boston, to Washington, to Baltimore, and finally toward New York. By implication the show is being put together as they go along and will only be ready, with the final number choreographed, when they are ready for Broadway. As for the money, it is suggested that Tony might pawn a Degas to keep it running until the profits roll in. Meanwhile, Paul has left the show. There is talk of asking him to choreograph the final number, but it comes to nothing. Tony and Gaby are drawing, or being drawn, closer together. The final, spectacular number showcasing the stars' talents is now revealed. It is called "Girl Hunt," and is a "modern" dance, with a popular urban iconography, a sort of stylized film noir, which contrasts on the one hand with Cordova-culture—the endless reworking of European myth, from Oedipus to Faust—but also on the other hand with the hayseed ruralism of "Louisiana Hayride." "Girl Hunt," in this context, functions as a negation of the negation, a demonstration that American culture can challenge European on its own ground and not just on the level of the affirmation of a retarded populism. It is not actually a great dance number, either by Minnelli's standards or by those of Donen and Kelly (*Singin' in the Rain* has a better noir-ish number, also with Cyd Charisse). But it does have a rich iconography, an affection for the sort of pulp fiction (and films) it parodies, and, as one would expect, a clever score that mixes orchestral music, big-band jazz, and hints of jazz modernism. After the cheesy (if tongue-in-cheek) Americana of "Louisiana Hayride," this is Art with a capital *A*.

"Girl Hunt," it should also be noted, although supposedly part of the stage show, is strictly a film number, with editing and mise-en-scène of a kind only possible in film. As such it is yet another example of the way the show being put on by the cast is wrapped into the movie. "The Band Wagon" on stage is at one level the subject matter of the film *The Band Wagon,* but at another level it is barely distinguishable from the film that envelops it.

The show ends with Gaby's declaration of love for Tony, disguised as an affirmation of group solidarity among the cast, and with a reprise of "That's Entertainment!" now sung by a quintet including Gaby and then by a chorus, celebrating the victory of the values represented by the show "The Band Wagon," but also, of course, the movie itself. The words have changed. Instead of the threatening references to *Oedipus Rex* and *Hamlet* the audience is now promised pure romance and a happy ending. "No death, like you get in Macbeth / no ordeal like the end of Camille," they sing rhapsodically. "The world is a stage / the stage is a world of entertainment."

This is a moment of total closure, locking the company together, locking Gaby and Tony, and bonding the audience with the cast in never-never land. Shakespeare's simile of all the world being a stage—that is, *like* a stage—here becomes a declaration of identity: the world *is* a stage, the stage *is* a world, the essence of that world is that it is entertainment. Fortunately, this hideous epiphany is not all that the film *The Band Wagon* has to offer, whether to spectators at the time or later. For it has been preceded by something richer, subtler, more challenging—a dialectic of culture as seen from the studios of Metro-Goldwyn-Mayer, in Culver City, California, USA.

This dialectic, as I have tried to show, is more than an affirmation. It is a working through of an argument, and although the conclusion is in a sense preordained the issue is an important one. The reason why the conclusion could not be other than it is, is that the cultural values being affirmed are those of MGM, and an MGM movie could hardly be expected to affirm other ones. But a trivial and foregone conclusion does not make the issue not worth debating. For in the course of laying claim to its own status as art form, the musical *The Band Wagon* has deployed a panoply of arguments about high and popular culture, about its nature as American art, and about what it is to be American. Many of the subtleties of this panoply of argument will have passed audiences by, particularly in Europe. But the broad drift is clear enough, then and now alike.

This essay was originally a lecture delivered at the Association of Art Historians conference in London in 1989, where it was illustrated by numerous film clips. It has been prosed out and revised (with help from Joe McElhaney) for publication in this volume.

The Adventures of Rafe Hunnicutt
The Bourgeois Family in *Home from the Hill*

Edward Gallafent

On its initial release, Vincente Minnelli's 1960 melodrama *Home from the Hill* was variously described by mainstream reviewers as having "a certain low-Faulknerian likeability" and being a "long, rambling tale . . . aimless, tedious, and in conspicuously doubtful taste." Such descriptions both relate it to matters that, elsewhere in American culture, could be recognized as "serious," and denigrate it in terms ironically comparable with the treatment of Faulkner thirty years earlier.

My purpose here is to take such connections "seriously." The matters to which the film addresses itself—the significance of the hunt, the nature and purpose of the family, the transmission of patriarchal power—are continually recycled in American culture because they recall some of the central tensions and contradictions of that culture. To take up such matters need not necessarily be a matter of intention; this is not an essay on Vincente Minnelli but a consideration of how the film, consciously or not, meets the challenge of the energies inherent in its material.

The film deals with the relationships of a Southern landowner, Captain Wade Hunnicut (Robert Mitchum) with his two sons, the elder, illegitimate

Rafe (George Peppard) and the younger, legitimate Theron (George Hamilton). Broadly, it operates by dramatizing two conflicts, the struggle for Theron between his father and his mother Hannah (Eleanor Parker), and the shifting of the commitment of Theron's sweetheart Libby Halstead (Luana Patten) from Theron to Rafe.

The film opens by locating its title in a quote from Robert Louis Stevenson in which an American commonplace is signaled: "Here he lies where he longed to be; Home is the sailor, home from the sea, And the hunter home from the hill." The world invoked is of "home," of the family and the bourgeois order. Home is being opposed to space, to the threat to identity posed most famously by the immensity of the sea—the American classic here is Herman Melville's *Moby-Dick*. What makes home so desirable is the myth of stability, centered on family, property, and stable family relations and therefore primarily concerned with stable definitions of sexuality. And the relief in these lines, the sense that a felt longing is at last satisfied, turns on the return of the man to the home.

In other words, we might say that these lines are playing with the hoped-for identity, in terms of definitions of male sexuality, between what it means to be a "man" (a hunter, a sailor) and a "family man." For if the world of the home operates on a relatively narrow definition of what it means to be male (most importantly a father within the terms of the bourgeois patriarchal order), its crucial instability is its apparent failure to supply from within itself any terms in which this kind of maleness can be learned. Typically, it is necessary for the boy to become a "man" somewhere else, away from the family and away from the house—on the river, in the woods, on the battlefield. Only then can the hunter come home, if—and here is the tension and anxiety that has affected so much American art—he still wants to. "I can't stand it," says Huck Finn when, after his journey down the Mississippi, the prospect of "civilization" rears its head again: "I been there before." I want to look at *Home from the Hill* as an inflection of this problem, the anxiety in American culture that the necessary acquisition of "maleness" may render the world of home and family untenable. Any given instance of this pattern is also firmly related to its historical moment: just as Mark Twain's treatment of Huck is a comment on the America of the 1880s, so Minnelli's melodrama is looking at the America of Eisenhower and the years following the end of the Korean War.

Perhaps the main way in which this is felt is in the film's treatment of the possibilities open to figures of different generations, in terms not only of Minnelli's analysis of the characters but also of their own hopes and ambitions. The opening chapters of Twain's novel focus on what a father is against what a son might possibly become, both through individual psychology (Pap's resentment that Huck might become "better" than his father) and through historical possibilities (Twain's nostalgia for the lost Mississippi—and lost America—of the pre–Civil War period). In an analogous way, *Home from the Hill* is looking at the difference between a generation associated with active wartime service and the sons and daughters brought up in peacetime.

This is the point of establishing, at the beginning of the film, Wade Hunnicut as Captain Hunnicut; it is being implied that he is a veteran, presumably of World War II. We see a man whose relation to the home is uneasy enough, a leading citizen of the town who is also its leading adulterer and who has been sexually estranged from his wife for many years. But he is also a man whose ambitions for his son are very different and constitute, in the first half of the film, a specific project. In allowing Hannah complete control of Theron's upbringing, he has, as he sees it, rooted his son firmly in the home. Now, with his father in charge, Theron's induction into manhood will not be on the battlefield but in the woods, where the right kind of experience will return him to the house as a successful hunter, a man who can preserve the bourgeois order whose threatened breakdown is felt in Hannah and Wade's sexless marriage. This is the project that seems on the brink of realization in the central party sequence, where Wade can say to Hannah, "You and me, together we made a first rate person," and command her reluctant assent: "I suppose we've been good for something." Furthermore, if the contradiction between "home" and the world of the hunter can be dissolved for Theron, Wade believes that this triumph will redeem his marriage to Hannah. She will unlock her bedroom door, his adulteries will cease, and the image of the successful family, which adequately expresses and contains the sexual energy of its members, will be restored.

This fantasy, central to the film's meaning, is complementary to Wade's adulteries. One aspect of the psychology of the hunter is that the activities of the chase (and Wade's adulteries are firmly identified with "hunting") are felt as separate from the world of home and family. Against the awareness of the potential disruptiveness of the hunt (the death or eclipse of the patriarch) is posed the sentimental assumption that what has been left behind must incarnate order (successful patriarchy). A clear instance is that moment toward the end of *Moby-Dick* when Ahab and Starbuck, facing the final confrontation with the whale, are momentarily complicit in an idealized fantasy of their families that centers, of course, around their role as fathers. Nantucket is conveniently distant—neither man will live to negotiate the return from the fantasy to the realization of what the home contains. But such a return is very much the structure of the opening of *Home from the Hill*, a series of scenes that move Wade from hunt to home:

1. The hunt conceived as space, both literal (the opening shot of the sky and the ducks) and psychological (the all-male group of hunters).

2. The denial that the hunter is in any way implicated in the home. When a cuckolded husband shoots Wade, the emphasis is strongly on the unexpectedness of the violence and the lack of any connection between Wade and his assailant. His first words to the cuckold are, "I don't believe I know you," and when the cause of the shooting becomes clear, Wade's response is to deflect the image of the restrictive home onto someone else—home is "where you ought to be," he tells the husband. This leaves him to assert his freedom as a (sexual) hunter; he tells the doctor, "It's my right to cross any man's fences when I'm hunting."

3. The awareness of family. In part, this is signaled by the arrival of Wade in the town to see the doctor with whom a story must be agreed upon in order to explain the wound to the community. As a guarantee of his confidentiality, the doctor offers the family: "I'm a friend of your wife." An important role here is played by Rafe, who (not for the last time) acts as the agent of Wade's return to the home. On the journey, Wade, after commenting that he is in "no hurry to get home," tries again to insist on women as the happy unindividualized objects of his desire: "I can't even remember which one she was." Rafe's reply, "He's only got one woman, he has no trouble keeping them straight," points up a paradox that reflects as much on Wade's marriage as it does on the cuckold's. Within the exclusivities of the family, "no trouble keeping them straight," refers only to the identities of the wives and not to their behavior.

4. The nature of home. The concluding part of this movement from outside to inside ought to be a movement from the public world to the private one, into the most private space of all, as Wade moves through the house to the bedroom. But the force of the scene is that the most private space of all fails to be private. Hannah's sexual rejection of Wade is figured here in the insistent concentration on open doors, part of a sustained thread of imagery in the film. The first shot of Hannah, taken through an open doorway, and her first line, with its overtones of seduction—"You need some help, Wade?"— offer a version of the unhappy home radically different from Wade's. Hannah's response to Wade's refusal to make their sexual relations exclusive is not a matter of retreating further into the exclusivity of the locked room but of

Eleanor Parker and Robert Mitchum in *Home from the Hill* (1960).

leaving her sexuality standing, as it were, in the open. In this scene Wade first raises the image of the successful family, arguing that his adulteries are the product of Hannah's rejection and would cease if she ceased to reject him. But Hannah knows, as she makes clear later in the party scene, that such exclusivity is a fantasy. To accept Wade would simply make her the most beautiful "of them all." The crucial point is not her rejection of him sexually so much as her rejection of any participation in the terms of his fantasy, whether of the unhappy home (the wife locking out her husband) or of the happy home (husband and wife locking out the world).

The scenes in which Wade embarks on his project of taking Theron away from Hannah and making a man of him display a structural feature that is also important elsewhere in the film: the parallels between particular scenes and sets of scenes. The meaning of the snipe-hunting sequence depends in part on its relation to the earlier duck hunt. Similarly, the scene in the house with Theron and Wade must be read against the earlier scene with Hannah and Wade.

The point connecting the snipe-hunting scene with the earlier hunt is that in both cases we see Wade with a figure of the younger generation whose lack of success in the hunt signals failure, as Wade sees it, in sexuality. His reply to the cuckold's threat that he won't miss next time is a deliberate sexual gibe, "You ain't got one more shot in you, boy," and connects directly with his distress on finding Theron by the lake. He has been duped by Wade's cronies into the "snipe hunt" and is shown as a figure of fun, the phallic gun replaced by the bag and whistle. In both cases, a failure of maleness in the hunt is connected with a failure in the family—the husband who misses his target has an adulterous wife, the boy made into a jackass is no son to his father.

Minnelli cuts to the scene in which Wade looks around Theron's bedroom. Thomas Elsaesser has written that a repeated configuration in Minnelli's films is that of "father and son feeling completely lost in their own home."[1] Here the device establishing this alienation refers us back to the scene between Wade and Hannah through the similar failure to enclose the space, marked again by the emphasis on open doors. Theron is presented as a child whose anxiety about his position in the family is expressed in his creation of a "private" world that is innately fragile and fails to be an unambiguously personal space within the home. An analogous case in Minnelli's work is Tootie's (Margaret O'Brien's) family of snow people in the Smith garden in Meet Me in St. Louis.

Perhaps the only figures who can successfully create private enclosed space do so not as an assertion of the family but as a rejection of it. Leaving the door of Theron's room open, with the comment that he will show him how a man lives, Wade takes Theron into his study—the scene begins with an explicit shot of his closing its substantial double doors. Again Meet Me in St. Louis provides an analogous moment; Mr. Smith (Leon Ames) effectively thwarts the wishes of his entire family by coming in from work and insisting on shutting himself into the bathroom. The right of the father is conceived as the right to space unviolated by the rest of the family.

The character of Wade's study, the only part of the home in which he is not lost, is clearly marked. Its basic quality is its turgidness, the sense that it is overstuffed and dead, that its decoration, with its ranks of guns and bright red chairs, is a substitute for the sexuality that is repressed in the rest of the house. But most crucially, it is a turgid version of the American pioneer cabin, with its collection of hunting gear, its inappropriately enormous stone fireplace, and the three hunting dogs on the hearthrug. As such, it is an entirely proper setting in which to teach Theron to be a "man" in the sense of rejecting the family. Wade's characterization of the successful patriarch turns on his not needing the usual signs of connection with family or a wider society, not because such a connection is absent but because it is based on a power structure that is felt to be unassailable. Wade characterizes himself as a man who need carry no identification (everybody knows who he is), no cash (everybody will give him credit), no keys (nobody dare steal from him), and no watch (everybody waits for him and he for nobody). Why such a figure should be alienated from the family is not perhaps entirely obvious until we recognize the origin of this list: a configuration normally associated with the world of the hunt has been relocated as an assertion of patriarchy. The image of the man without the usual props of urban life is found elsewhere in American texts that argue that in order to know the natural world most fully it is necessary to leave such things behind and become as the Indian was. Ike McCaslin in Faulkner's *Go Down, Moses* (1942) is only allowed his first sight of the great bear, Old Ben, when he has relinquished not only his gun but also the watch and compass with which he is "still tainted." If the relinquishment of civilization is the condition, loss of family is the consequence; inflections of this vary from the virginity of James Fenimore Cooper's Natty Bumppo to the flashes of sexual nausea in Ike McCaslin (who dies a childless widower). So, far from underpinning Wade's sanguine assumption that the hunt is about the acquisition of maleness that can be reimported without effort into the home, his list evokes the hunt in an ominous way. This instability becomes more evident later—here it is registered mainly in the set, for, as Wade tells Theron that "what every man hunts out there is himself," the camera pans across the crowded paraphernalia of the room.

The most explicit moment of the scene is Wade's attempt to "test" Theron's use of the carbine by having him discharge it in the room. I think that the point can only be to terrorize Hannah, a fact that Theron registers in his astonished "You going to have me shoot this gun off in the house?" Wade's reply deliberately ignores the question of "home": "It's a big fireplace, Theron, don't you think you can hit it?" What Wade wants (and gets) is a tacit pact between the men to violate the hearth. The close-ups of Wade and Theron, followed by the shot of Hannah on the far side of the closed study doors, now establish that the male group disrupted at the very beginning of the narrative is reasserted in a more specific form, the first hint of the rejection of the mother.

In a less complex narrative, it might be possible to go on to plot Theron's acquisition of "maleness" in a simple, linear way. We see him learning to shoot with Rafe's assistance, and his introduction to the woods. This is followed by the assertion of his adult maleness in the dinner table scene, which begins with Wade telling him to shave before he comes to his "mother's table" in future and ends with the displacement of Hannah by the group of tenant farmers and the assignment of the boar hunt to Theron. It concludes in the successful boar hunt, the presentation of the trophy to Theron, and the beginning of the courtship of Libby. To describe it like this is, I think, to see it very much as Wade sees it when he talks to Hannah about his pride in Theron during the party scene that concludes the hunt. But on closer examination of this structure, a pattern emerges within: the suggestion that this initiation has been a positive one is undermined by the relation of the series of scenes centered on Theron and Wade to the parallel series centered on Theron and Rafe. The two scenes in which Wade asserts Theron's maleness within, or rather against, the home (the shot in the hearth/Hannah's dinner table) are respectively followed by sequences offering strikingly different inflections of Theron's skill with a gun (shooting bottles at Rafe's cabin/the hunt for the wild boar), followed by two conversations (Rafe and Theron discussing girls/Wade and Theron discussing fear). It is worth comparing these scenes a little more closely.

The scene outside Rafe's cabin stands in clear contrast to the violence of the shot into the hearth that preceded it. There are obvious movements here from night to day and from the enclosure of the study to the space of Rafe's yard. Something closer to a genuine pioneer cabin appears in Rafe's shack, with its verandah and rocker—only the dog is a literal link with Wade's study. The moment at which Theron shoots out the bottom of the bottle of beer Rafe is drinking neatly signals the opposite inflection of the question of Theron's marksmanship from the earlier shot. A moment of tension and disturbing complicity between the father and son gives way to a moment of trust and delight as Theron exults in his skill and Rafe responds, not with terror that he might have been hit, but with gentle irony. The scene dismisses any aspect of competition between the two—it is simply arguing that they enjoy being with each other.

The hunt for the boar is exactly the opposite. From the first, Theron wants to be alone, and resents Wade's insistence that Rafe should go with him. At least in Theron's mind, this sequence is about competition—despite Rafe's assurance that he has no desire to steal the honor of the kill, Theron leaves him asleep so that he alone will confront the beast. While the successful hunt can be said to confirm Theron's maleness and align him firmly with Wade, it does so in terms that are located outside the society and the family, and which are arguably negative. For example, at the end of the hunt, it emerges that Theron has disobeyed his father's instructions and not climbed a tree for safety after his close-range shot at the boar. Wade discovers this with approval, commenting that he too never climbed the tree—their mutual male pride seems to turn on the refusal of even this one gesture of self-preservation, freezing male identity in the figure of the solitary hunter and the one shot that *has* to count. In the comparable moment in the earlier sequence, Rafe and Theron have climbed a tree—they are sitting in the branches trying to attract deer by rattling antlers. Here the hunt is seen as a shared business, ruefully comical (they are both soaking wet), but offering them an intimacy that enables Theron to admit, in his confidences about girls, the extent of his sexual insecurity. The boar hunt is placed between this moment and the next scene in which we see that insecurity, as Theron and Rafe sit in the car outside Libby's house. Thus Theron's courtship of Libby follows not the intimacy of hunting with Rafe but the isolation of hunting the beast.

Again, these distinctions are following established patterns in American culture. Contact with the world of nature has always been capable both of a negative inflection when seen as the experience of an isolated individual and of a positive inflection when shared and offered as the medium of transmission of human contact. In *Moby-Dick,* Ahab's mania is linked with the figure of Pip, the child who is cast accidentally adrift and goes insane in the immensity of the ocean. Juxtaposed with this by Melville is Ishmael's famous description of the squeezing of the whale's sperm, the exploration of nature as the context of love: "let us all squeeze ourselves into each other." Equally, in *The Adventures of Huckleberry Finn,* the idyllic times enjoyed by Huck and Jim on the raft have their opposite in the vertigo that overcomes Huck when isolated from his companion by the fog. The trick that he plays on Jim when they are reunited (claiming that their separation has been a dream) clearly relates to Huck's anxiety about his awakening to the sight of the "monstrous big river."

It is a commonplace that the myth expressed in the positive inflection here is not only one of human contact but also more specifically of racial harmony. A particular case of this is when the racially "other" figure takes on the role of the father, transmitting the skill of the hunt but, because of his "inferior" position, doing so outside the terms of white patriarchy. In *Go Down, Moses,* Ike's mentor is the appropriately named Sam Fathers, who is both Negro and Indian in origin. The moment in which he "dipped his hands in the hot smoking blood and wiped them back and forth across the boy's face" is exactly echoed in the story Rafe tells of himself and Chauncey and his own first hunt. Wade's treatment of Theron stresses only the son's similarity to the father in terms of knowledge and behavior, rather than any initiation into a hitherto secret world.

The attenuation of the importance of such transactions can be felt in Rafe's tone as he hands Theron the boar's tail: "Here's a trophy for you, sonny—you can wear it behind your ear." What was a vital rite has become an awkwardly crude symbolic act, and what we see here is less an initiation into nature than an induction into patriarchy, using the natural world only as a medium in which patriarchal power can be displayed. The effect of Wade's whole project is to assert patriarchy precisely in the term outlined in the first scene in his study: the family conceived as a power structure the patriarch must dominate.

The subsequent scenes of Theron's courtship of Libby operate within these terms. The opening line of this sequence, Rafe's plea to Theron, "Go ring the doorbell, will you please," introduces the point; Rafe knows that the appropriate place for Theron to meet Libby is inside the Halstead home, submitting to the context of her family (specifically, her father). His failure to do this is followed by his insistence that Rafe speak for him, which suggests their intimacy but is also faintly ominous, carrying with it a hint of instability, as the character finds himself in a position for which he is not directly responsible. A comparable configuration is found in *The Bad and the Beautiful*, where Rosemary Bartlow (Gloria Grahame) feeds lines to her husband (Dick Powell) in his telephone conversation with Jonathan Shields (Kirk Douglas) in Hollywood and initiates a chain of events that leads to her infidelity and death.

On the evening of the party, Theron's failure to get past Halstead's front door obviously follows from his earlier failure to meet Libby in the context of her family. As Albert Halstead (Everett Sloane) slams the front door in Theron's face, we should recollect the earlier treatment of space; we are in the world where the family is defined through the locked door. As Theron walks away, there is the sound of a locomotive whistle in the distance—opposed to the exclusivities of the family is the emptiness of space.

That an understanding of the home as a cluster of private and public spaces is not just Wade's or Albert Halstead's but also now Theron's is demonstrated in the scene in which Libby goes to the Hunnicut home. Having been shut out from the Halstead house, Theron now shuts himself and Libby in. We see him taking her up to the attic and closing the door; the study and stairway doors are left open. Not only does this underline the retreat from the family (like Wade's study, it is another "private" space in the house) but also the set itself, with its jumbled props of family life, is expressive of Theron's own confusion about the family. Libby's sense of herself and her life, expressed in one of the number of lists that punctuate the film, that she will "get married, have lots of children, can peaches, get fat" has no equivalent in Theron. All he has is his desire, and Libby herself is a little nervous at this, staring out of the window and trying to divert Theron into the recognized ritual of courtship. She attempts to locate their first meetings firmly in the social world, announcing that she often goes to the library at a particular time of day. From here, the movement can be, she hopes, toward the family—her public introduction to the Hunnicut home, the formal proposal, the white wedding.

But Minnelli cuts, not to the library but to the woods, to the couple's picnic, which will end in the sexual act in which Libby's baby is conceived. The setting here is one of the more positive notes in the relationship, representing an escape on Theron's part from the fantasy of the locked door. Here, as in the earlier scene with Rafe, he is again free to express his sexual insecurity, and Libby can express active sexual desire—the virginal white of her previous two scenes here gives way to her scarlet dress, while Theron now wears white. This symbolism has its famous antecedents. The allusion to the central symbolic color in Hawthorne's *The Scarlet Letter* underlines the fact that, like Hester Prynne and Arthur Dimmesdale, Theron and Libby in the woods are refugees from the social order, and that making love gives them no new context but simply invites punishment by the old one. They are both rejecting the containment of sexual activity within marriage and rejecting the assumption that sexual prowess is the privilege of the patriarch; the derisive "boy" of Wade's initial insult to the cuckolded husband receives a new inflection when Theron says "I wish I weren't such a kid," and Libby replies as she pulls him down to her, "Never mind."

After they have made love, Theron returns to the Hunnicut home in the early hours of the morning. Such a return from a realm in which more radical expression is possible can be a moment of Gothic excess, as the strain of adjusting to the repressions of town and family prove almost too much. (Dimmesdale's fantasies, as he walks back into Boston after meeting Hester in the woods for the last time, are a case in point.) Certainly the scene here has some Gothic elements (the time of night, Hannah's appearance and acting style) and is the setting in which she recounts to Theron the secret of the family: the fact that Rafe is Wade's son. Her apparent intention is to present Wade as a monster and to "win back" Theron with the revelation that Wade has compromised the patriarchal line (Theron is not the oldest son). But the story is fatally relevant to the image of the family that Theron has inherited from Wade; its monster is not the father but the mother, not Wade but the creature that Hannah finds in the house making a "sound like a cat meowing," Rafe's mother.

Hannah's story is one variant of a myth about the disruption and reassertion of order within the family that might be characterized as follows: a woman enters a house assuming that she incarnates the order of "home" only to discover that the building is already inhabited by a monstrous female presence. Among the many variations of this are *Jane Eyre, Rebecca, I Walked with a Zombie*, and *Psycho*—Andrew Britton has pointed out its relevance to Minnelli in his account of *Meet Me in St Louis*.[2] Where it deals with the restoration of order, the myth obviously has to do with the defeat of the "monstrous" by the "good" woman, and Hannah, at least consciously, sees it in such terms: the assertion of the good (socially legitimate, bourgeois) line over the corrupt one (illegitimate, lower in class terms). Theron takes it as a story not about class but only about sexuality, about the vulnerability of the hunter at the moment he submits himself to the home and the threat of castration from the female within it. As a result, Hannah is seen but implicated in rather than defeating the monstrous presence.

All this becomes clearer in the next scene, in which Theron confronts Wade. His appeal to his father to recognize Rafe is based on an idea of the male pride that ought to be shared by the three of them: "If you were any kind of a man you'd be proud of him." In the climactic exchange that follows, Wade's answer combines a disgust at female sexuality with a stress on the socially degraded nature of the woman: "His mother was a tramp, a sand hill tacky having her child by the edge of a ditch." His rejection of Rafe is finally a defense of the bourgeois order. Theron's response is not to defend, but further to insult the mother, his "rejection" of the father taking the form of disgust at the animality of his woman: "She must have been some pig to crawl in bed with you." While Theron and Wade are superficially in total antagonism here, their rejection of the mother makes them complicit in a way that relates to the earlier scene of the shot in the hearth. The point is made in part by Minnelli's presentation of them in a two-shot, facing each other in more or less identical postures, and in part by Wade's otherwise odd failure to take up the insult. His gesture with his hands here, suggesting that he is content to leave it there, is almost as if he recognizes that this response is not altogether unsatisfactory to him. The closing shot of the sequence again parallels the earlier incident; it is of Hannah staggering on the stairs as she hears the exchange between the two men.

The same point is a central feature of Theron's remaining scenes in the film, in all of which his apparent rejection of the father is contradicted by other elements. His surrender of his keys and money to Rafe, for example, in the next scene, is explicitly to make restitution. But implicitly it is a repeat of the earlier rite of the hunter/patriarch. Theron is acting out his role as inheritor of the patriarchal line, just as his father had outlined it to him. It is also glanced at in the opening of the scene in which he finally breaks with Libby. She begins by acknowledging, "You look older," and he replies ambiguously, "I've been all right."

The rejection of Libby further aligns Theron and Wade in that Minnelli juxtaposes it with Wade's humiliation of Albert Halstead. Both scenes are prompted by the discovery that Libby is pregnant, and Theron's rejection of marriage is no great distance from Wade's presentation of a social order in which marriage is another form of commercial exchange: "You've been in business long enough not to try to sell me any damaged goods." But perhaps the strongest link between the two scenes is in the exercise of the power of patriarchy. Theron's sexual insecurity has entirely disappeared, and he is clearly conscious of his power to dispose of Libby as he likes. Wade's treatment of Albert Halstead in the next scene is only an even more explicit version of the same kind of power.

That this power is one of the main concerns toward the end of the film can be shown by pausing for a moment over a detail of plot. Why does Albert Halstead, on overhearing the men outside the church after the baptism of Libby's baby, shoot Wade? He knows that the "accusation" against Wade is untrue, as the earlier interview scene has shown, and anyway the baby now has a "father." He does so because the myth of Wade's sexual prowess—the men are idly speculating on how many bastards he has fathered—is the final stroke of Albert's sexual humiliation, the product not just of Wade's behavior but also of the sexual politics of the whole society (the sense of this moment as a public occasion is crucial). It is brilliantly suggested by his encounter with one of Wade's tenants at the gate of the Hunnicut mansion after the interview; the moment is entirely continuous with Wade's gibe to the cuckolded husband at the beginning of the film. It is because Wade invites violence in terms not local to any one individual that Minnelli does not show Albert in the scene in which Wade is killed. The death appears as the impersonal result of his position, continuous with his opening line in the film: "Who the hell did this to me?" By killing Wade, Albert reasserts his masculinity (the gas station attendant mistakes the driver of the speeding car, thinking Albert is Wade). Finally, Theron kills Albert with one shot, fired from the hip—the complete identification of gun with phallus.

It is a moment that signals the final eclipse of Wade's project. The killing of men in wartime, which was supplemented by the killing of the boar, has given way to the killing of a man. Theron is not even "Captain" Hunnicut, and this violence cannot be reintegrated into society; there is no attempt to suggest that Theron's departure here is anything other than a defeat. But another factor must be invoked. In order to understand it fully we must understand that its emotional center is the embrace between Theron and Rafe, and cannot be read outside an exploration of Rafe's function in the film.

An obvious and important antecedent to the figures of Theron and Rafe can be found in Tom Sawyer and Huck Finn. In Twain's novels, they are not actually brothers (though they pretend to be toward the end of *The Adventures of Huckleberry Finn*), but we view them in some important respects in the terms in which we see Theron and Rafe. Theron and Tom are both figures whose place in the bourgeois order starts by being apparently unassailable, but through them we see that order criticized. As in *Home from the Hill,* violence is crucial in Twain's work to the expression of that criticism. Tom's childish fantasies of mayhem culminate in the bullet that strikes him in the calf during the "adventure" he has engineered, and this violence again has a firm relation to the family, from the beginning of the book (a condition of joining Tom's gang of "robbers" is having a family to be killed in the event of disloyalty) to the end (the game of helping Jim to escape is offered as a way of tormenting the Phelps family). The most explicit and apocalyptic expression of this, the Shepherdson/Grangerford feud, includes the murder of Buck Grangerford, a figure comparable to Tom. But this episode is tucked away in the middle of the narrative. Unlike Minnelli, Twain concludes with the continuing assimilation of the violence into the middle-class order. At the end, the bullet that struck Tom has become one of the symbols of his authority: "his bullet round his neck on a watch guard for a watch."

The figure of Huck Finn is an obvious antecedent of Rafe. The crucial parallel is that neither Huck nor Rafe is entirely outside the order of which Tom and Theron are the "natural" inheritors. In both cases, their status is not that of outcasts but rather as having been very exactly "placed" by society as dependents who cannot be allowed to partake directly of the power of patriarchy. When Huck at the opening of the novel is taken away from his father and put with the women, the intention is not to turn him into Tom Sawyer but to give him a relationship to the society that prevents real privation while blocking access to power. His wistful fascination with the novel's procession of adult white males marks a muted awareness that power is concentrated in their hands, and that it is in relationship to one of them that he might learn to manipulate it. The kinds of father figures extend from the fascists (Sherburn, Grangerford) to the imbecile, castrated Uncle Silas; it is not surprising that the figures to whom Huck is most attracted and partly resembles are the con men, the duke and the king, who represent a subversion of the terms of the patriarchal power exercised by the others, manipulating it through role, disguise, and deceit. Minnelli's interest in the figure of the con man is most obvious in Gene Kelly's role as Serafin in *The Pirate*. An unrealized Minnelli project in the early 1950s was a version of Twain's novel that placed central emphasis on the King and the Duke (Kelly and Danny Kaye).

The moment at which this aspect of the Huck figure surfaces most clearly in Rafe is in his first scene with Libby. The function of role here is to offer a way out of the constraints that generally operate in the first encounter of boy and girl. The problem, as Minnelli seems to have felt it, is that the encounter may be repressively trapped inside the terms of home and family (girl meets boy-next-door) and drained of energy exactly to the extent that it fails to disrupt them—as with Esther (Judy Garland) and John (Tom Drake) in *Meet Me in St. Louis*. Alternatively, the encounter that takes place outside (in the city or the wilderness) suffers the opposite problem, that of establishing some contact with the society without losing its energy (the problem that faces Judy Garland and Robert Walker in *The Clock*). Insofar as Rafe approaches Libby here not as the suitor but as the suitor's spokesman, the problem of their relation to a context that would raise questions of money and social class can be evaded. Libby can respond to Rafe sexually without feeling threatened, and Rafe can feel attracted to her without risking the rejection by her family. Indeed, the attraction depends in part on their mutual relief at being free for a moment from those constraints.

Paradoxically, the other point stressed in the scene is that they could make a success of living together in this society. In this respect, Libby and Rafe are the exact opposite of Libby and Theron, for whom a belief in "love" is juxtaposed with a series of settings that express an inability to realize a coherent domestic context for the emotion. Here the opposite assumptions (they are not in love, they will not get married) are coupled with an equally consistent stress on a series of contexts that emphasize a substantially domestic world in which they might share tasks. Plotted together, the two "romances" look like this:

1. Rafe's encounter with Libby takes place as she is washing the car, which she continues to do as they talk. The activity suggests simple control of the literal domestic world. Libby is dressed in working clothes—an open-necked blouse and rolled-up jeans.

2. In the next two scenes with Theron, which I have already discussed, the keynotes are entrapment in the house and Libby's presentation of herself as a virgin. In the first, she runs up the Halstead stairs in a frothy white party dress, and in the Hunnicut attic she is wearing simple white clothes.

3. Theron's and Libby's picnic in the woods is the only scene in which we see Libby with both men, and the sequence begins not with the lovers but with a shot of Rafe walking toward them, with a hoe balanced across his shoulders. Partly the point is about class—the world of work opposed to the leisure generated by the Hunnicut fortune—and this relates to the conversation that follows Theron's cocky suggestion that Rafe should get himself a girlfriend. Rafe offers in response one of the film's lists: he sleeps with his boots on, drinks beer in the morning, and has a skunk for a house pet. But the items here point straight toward a domestic setting of a kind for Rafe, a sort of easy order very different from the jumble and alienation of the Hunnicut attic. Libby is recognizing this when she replies to Rafe's list with one of her own, an account of marriage that is only slightly ironic: doing the dishes, paying life insurance, taking the kids to the dentist, mowing the lawn. This echoes elements of her earlier list in the attic scene, to which Theron had no answer. Even at the moment when Libby seems most firmly linked with Theron, the evocation of a possible domestic world is still something shared with Rafe.

4. Setting Theron's final rejection of Libby in the Halstead car is important. The connections are with the previous scenes acted out in Wade's truck. Both the reluctant return home after the first shooting incident and Theron's asking Rafe outside the Halstead home to drive round the block again use being inside the truck as an expression of uneasiness about the domestic context.

5. The scene in the supermarket, like the car-washing scene, involves tasks that could have figured in one of Libby's lists about family life. Libby's appearance also clearly recalls the earlier scene. Then Rafe's role as spokesman for Theron had insulated them from the threatening social world, but now the stress is all on the fragility of social position and the ability of the bourgeois world to destroy those who have threatened its order (the scene immediately follows Albert Halstead's humiliation by Wade). The anxiety with which Libby arranges her hair while Rafe parks the shopping trolleys and his concern that she should not be seen crying in public mark their awareness of this vulnerability, which is very much the context for Rafe's offer of marriage. It will save Libby and her child, who will otherwise be outside patriarchy, from "running around loose" in the world.

However, this does not successfully resolve the contradictions of the family. Marrying Libby is in part a redemption of the past (Libby and her baby are analogous to Rafe's mother and himself) and in part a reintegration of Rafe into the bourgeois order (he and Libby take over the Halstead home). But it is bought at a cost; Rafe knows that Libby would have married Theron, that certainly for the Halsteads and possibly for Libby the sense of gratitude is mixed with resentment. The point is perfectly articulated in the scene immediately after the wedding, where the uneasiness of the whole party culminates in Albert struggling irritably with the broken screen door. Rafe's offer to fix it is a delicately ironic inflection of the stress on his control of the domestic world. (Obviously, this moment also relates to the wider symbolic use of doors in the film, annotating Albert's failure to sustain the order implied by the closed door, and Rafe's qualified reassertion of that order.)

The tensions are also evident in the bedroom scene. Rafe's line: ("I haven't been in a room this nice since I went to the hospital to have my appendix taken out") is a wry comment on his newly acquired social position and a deflection of the private and erotic connotations of the room. The bedroom represents an impasse for Rafe and Libby just as much as it did for Wade and Hannah at the beginning of the film. In both cases, the couples are together not for the sake of each other but for the sake of the child, and the difficulty is in reestablishing between them a successful sexual relationship that also upholds the bourgeois order. It is entirely appropriate, then, that Libby and Rafe are brought together through the melodramatic device of her nightmare. The desire for Rafe that has been repressed ever since their first encounter can now be expressed (they are married) but must emerge in such a way as to give support to patriarchy. Thus the nightmare can't be admitted to be an expression of Libby's repressed sexual desires; rather, it is seen as a manifestation of an anarchic force, from which she needs Rafe's "protection" in the form of his conjugal presence.

If we take it that the image of the sexual union of Rafe and Libby is still set about by references to what has been excluded (Libby's nightmare, the figure of Theron looking up at the bedroom from the street), can any redefinition of the family be seen as going on here? Rafe has been described by Laura Mulvey as a figure who "re-establishes the family and 'feminine' values."[3] Presumably what are thought of as "feminine" values are moments such as the scene in his cabin in which he covers the sleeping Theron with a blanket and his first response to Libby's nightmare: "I'm going to tuck you in." But to see this only in terms of gender and family role is to dislocate it from its context, the establishment of Rafe through his attitude to nature and the hunt that can be defined by looking at an area in which attitudes to nature and to family intersect: the interest in animals, both wild and domestic.

This is one of the film's carefully structured ways of expressing the difference between Wade and his immediate family, and Rafe. For Wade, domestic animals are emblematic of absolute power (they come to heel at the snap of his fingers) and can be sacrificed with equanimity (his comment to Theron about the boar killing all three dogs). Animals that will not come to heel are used as images of violent disgust (Hannah compares Rafe's mother to a cat, Theron likens her to a pig). For Wade, Hannah, and Theron any identification with an animal is anathema—Hannah's boast to Wade is that Theron won't come to heel like a dog.

Contrast this with the opening moment of the film. As the would-be assassin aims, Rafe and the dog simultaneously sense the movement. From this moment, Rafe is identified with the animal world, rather than set up over it. This is expressed in several ways. One of these, as I have already discussed, involved the implications of Rafe's account of his first hunt. There is also the row between Wade and Theron over Rafe; Theron points out to his slightly baffled father that his treatment of Rafe is like his treatment of the dogs. The exchange is important because it leads directly to the scene where Theron, fleeing the Hunnicut home, arrives at Rafe's cabin. Immediately when he enters, Rafe tells him to shut the door. He has been bathing a puppy and is holding the wet creature in his arms. In the ensuing conversation, Rafe reveals that as a child he was tethered to a post to keep him away from the Hunnicut home. When Theron falls asleep, Rafe covers him with a blanket and the puppy lies on the bed beside him.

What is offered here is a different possibility for the meaning of the domestic. The Hunnicut and Halstead homes are attempts to contain sexual activity, the closed door excluding the threatening male figure. Rafe's door is a protection against nature, his cabin a place of light and warmth as opposed to the dark and cold outside that would kill the puppy. The set confirms this, with prominence given to the fire and to the striking table lamp. Rafe's concern with literal, physical warmth is repeated several times in the rest of the film and is always linked with the image of home and the identification of man with animal. In the supermarket scene, Rafe describes himself as "storing up nuts for the winter." In the final scene between the brothers, his first action is to put his jacket around Theron's shoulders and say, "It's getting dark, cold, let's go on home." His other line is: "You're just a colt"; after they have embraced he tucks the jacket back.

This last scene perhaps poses the limits of Rafe's position. Here a sense of home that is not sexually repressive can still momentarily be evoked. In the scene with Libby, though, Rafe's tucking her up is presented as taking place firmly within the context of the reestablished order and in no sense overturns it; the film never denies the coherence of the repressive apparatus. Rafe is shown as a man with a profound relation to nature and sense of his kinship with the animal world, but this cannot be simply imported into the home and is associated, in a way that can be traced back firmly through Faulkner's Ike McCaslin to Cooper's Natty Bumppo, with a degree of spiritual isolation. In part, this has to do with his sense of having a past not accessible to people like Theron and Libby. In the cabin when Theron begins, "I know all about you," Rafe replies, "All about me—I don't think you do." What Theron is claiming as the whole truth about Rafe (his newly discovered relationship to patriarchal power) is countered with the picture of Rafe with Chauncey and with his mother, both figures for whom the keynote of Rafe's public response is reserved diffidence. The crucial scene here (cut from the print released in the United Kingdom) occurs just before the scene in the woods with Libby and Theron; it shows Rafe visiting the unmarked grave of his mother and encountering Hannah. In their conversation, he can express to a woman something of the emptiness he feels at his isolation from the power structures of the society—he says to her that it would have been better if he and his mother had never been born. No moment in *Home from the Hill* is more resonantly American than this encounter of victims. The scene obviously has a close relationship to the final meeting of Hannah and Rafe at Wade's grave, which at first has something of the same mood. Hannah's attempt to assert the coherence of Rafe's family through a conventional hallowing of the child ("Is he *very* beautiful?") is answered in a way that is a reminder of the fractures in this structure: "He looks like his daddy." Rafe's cautious, gentle irony extends to the gravestone, a "nice, handsome marker." This is his mood until he reads the inscription, discovering that Hannah has acknowledged the paternity that Wade denied: "Father of Raphael and Theron." There is apparently no doubt that Rafe welcomes this final reintegration into patriarchy. Hannah seems to be claiming that the inscription only acknowledges what was always true: "He had two fine sons." Rafe, however, makes his awareness of his rebirth specific: "Not till today he didn't." As Huck says at one point about the Phelps family: "It was like being born again, I was so glad to find out who I was." The last gesture is to reintegrate Hannah into the family; the film closes with Rafe telling her how Libby and he are "green" with the baby and taking her "home."

Two points remain: the name being on a gravestone, and Hannah's response to Rafe's astonishment as he reads it: "Don't you think I'm capable of a human gesture for once in my life?" The final reestablishment of Rafe within the order of the society takes place via monumental masonry. The sense of definite

Hannah acknowledges Rafe's (George Peppard) paternity on her husband's gravestone in the final shot of *Home from the Hill*.

acknowledgment goes along with the suggestion that Rafe (now Raphael) is trapped by the relationships inscribed in the fixity of the stone. A comparable moment is at the end of Cooper's *The Pioneers* when the young hero and heroine include the name of Nathaniel Bumppo on the grave of Major Effingham. It is an invitation to accept their social order that is seductive (Natty follows the letters with "deep interest") but has to be rejected: the scene opens with Natty literally lying on the grave that bears his name, but by its end he has, like Huck, left civilization behind.

As for Hannah's comment, it may be a claim to generosity now, but at the same time it is clearly a confession of past guilt. Perhaps this is the grimmest note of all; to be allowed back into the home, she has to pay, and the admission of her guilt is the price.

NOTES

1. Thomas Elsaesser, "Vincente Minnelli," *Brighton Film Review* 18 (February 1970). Reprinted in this volume.

2. Andrew Britton, "*Meet Me in St. Louis:* Smith; or, The Ambiguities," *Australian Journal of Screen Theory* 3 (1977). Reprinted in this volume.

3. Laura Mulvey, "Douglas Sirk and Melodrama," *Australian Journal of Film Theory* 3 (1977): 27.

Uptown Folk
Blackness and Entertainment in *Cabin in the Sky*

JAMES NAREMORE

Between 1927 and 1954, the major Hollywood studios produced only six feature films that took place in an all-black milieu: *Hallelujah!* (MGM, 1929),
Hearts in Dixie (Fox, 1929), *The Green Pastures* (Warner Brothers, 1936), *Cabin
in the Sky* (MGM, 1943), *Stormy Weather* (Twentieth Century-Fox, 1943), and
Carmen Jones (Twentieth Century-Fox, 1954).[1] The period in question was the
heyday of classic cinema, bounded at one end by the introduction of sound
and at the other by a shift toward a decentered, "package unit" mode of
production;[2] more importantly, 1954 was also the year when the Supreme
Court ordered public schools desegregated, paving the way for a civil rights
movement that would have a lasting effect on all the media. Until then, any
studio film purporting to deal exclusively with black experience was truly
exceptional and controversial. The six films just listed are therefore among the
most unusual products of American show business. No proper history of the
movies should ignore them, and they deserve far more critical analysis than
they have received.[3] Viewed from a late twentieth-century perspective, one of

the most interesting of the "all Negro" productions was MGM's *Cabin in the Sky*, starring Ethel Waters, Eddie Anderson, Lena Horne, and a host of well-known black performers. This film warrants special attention—not only be-cause of its considerable entertainment value, but also because it appeared at a crucial juncture in the series, when African Americans were increasing their demands for better treatment from the movie industry, when black musical performers were receiving a degree of celebrity they had not enjoyed before, and when the federal government was engaged in a semiofficial drive to encourage more pictures with black casts. Although *Cabin* was manufactured in Hollywood's most conservative studio, it was designed to appeal to a variety of audiences, binding them together in the name of wartime solidarity; in certain ways, it can be described as a liberal or historically transitional work, and it tells us important things about the complex, sometimes troubled rela-tions between ethnicity and modernity.

Of course, in general terms, *Cabin* was no different from the other five studio-produced films about blacks. They were all products of a segregated society; they were all written, produced, and directed by whites; and they were all musicals or melodramatic narratives that made extensive use of song and dance, thus reinforcing the white culture's perception of African Americans as a fun-loving, "rhythmic" people. As a group, the six films also depended upon a vivid binary opposition between city and country that structured both classic Hollywood and many aspects of the culture at large.[4] The social tensions and ideological contradictions expressed by this opposition were always crucial to any art or entertainment that involved blackness; notice, for example, how the country/city polarity functioned in early uses of *jazz*, a term that had been ap-propriated by white songwriters from Tin Pan Alley and turned into an ambig-uous, highly flexible signifier. Was jazz a primitive music, a people's music, or an entertainment music? All three possibilities were suggested by critics, and the term seemed to oscillate between diametrically opposed meanings. On the one hand, jazz was associated with flappers, skyscrapers, and the entire panoply of twentieth-century modernity; on the other hand, because it originated with African Americans who migrated to the northern cities, it connoted agrarian or precapitalist social relations, and it could be linked to a pastoral myth. Thus Kern and Hammerstein's *Show Boat* (1927) and Gershwin's *Porgy and Bess* (1935)—two celebrated "modern" stage musicals—were grounded in folkloric treatments of blacks. Even Warner Brothers' *The Jazz Singer* (1927) evoked both the city and the country. Throughout most of the film, jazz represents a force of modernization that disrupts a conservative Jewish household; but when the protagonist enters show business, he reasserts old-fashioned values by donning blackface and singing "Mammy."

The same contrasts can be observed everywhere in *Cabin in the Sky*, which uses black-influenced popular music to tell a story about a rural community threatened by a world of gamblers and nightclubs. But as I hope to show, *Cabin* creates a different effect from earlier pictures of its type. Whatever its artistic merits (and these are far from negligible), its treatment of the country/city theme is ironic or insincere, signaling an important change in mainstream cinema's negotiation of racial issues. Even though the film is never free of reactionary sentiments, it is in some ways an entirely modern work, generating what Richard Dyer has described as a "utopian" feeling of energy, abundance, intensity, transparency, and community—a vision of "something we want deeply that our day-to-day lives don't provide" (177).[5] Dyer qualifies his observation when he lists *Cabin* among a group of musicals that are "bought off by the nostalgia or primitivism which provides them with a point of departure" (188); nevertheless, I would argue that *Cabin*'s nostalgia is on one level quite superficial, and that its primitivism is transformed (for white audiences at least) into a paradoxical sophistication. Ultimately, the film participates in a kind of capitalist progress, contributing to the breakdown of a pastoral, the death of a bogus authenticity, and the growing urbanization of black images in Hollywood. In fact, there is an important sense in which *Cabin* was "saved" or "made progressive" by the very forces of mass-cultural aestheticism and commodification that leftist critics usually condemn.

To fully appreciate such ironies, we should first examine *Cabin*'s historical context, bearing in mind Mikhail Bahktin's observation that all art operates in a "dialogically agitated and tension-filled environment."[6] For obvious reasons, the environment surrounding this particular film was especially agitated, and it requires careful scrutiny. I shall therefore propose that *Cabin* was situated uneasily among at least four conflicting discourses about blackness and entertainment in America during World War II.[7] The four discourses were composed of a variety of texts, including speeches, newspaper items, critical and theoretical writings, and artistic representations; for the most part they were generated outside Hollywood, and they tended to cut across the usual political divisions between right and left, affecting both the production and the reception of the film. By examining each in turn, we can begin to recover *Cabin*'s historical specificity, showing how several artists at MGM responded to the racial dialogue of their day. In the process, we can begin to make informed judgments about the film's cultural politics.

I

Cabin was shaped first of all by a vestigial tradition of "folkloric" narratives having to do with poor blacks in rural southern communities. I hasten to emphasize that nothing in the film was generated by an indigenous, agrarian culture, and that folklore itself is a suspiciously modern phenomenon, born of late eighteenth-century attempts to distinguish between the learned and the popular. We should remember, however, that the discourse on the folk can have different uses. For the most part, the childlike mammies and pappies who once populated our songs, stories, and movies were figments of a reactionary white imagination—embodiments of what Peter Burke describes as everything "natural, simple, instinctive, irrational, and rooted in the local soil."[8] But another kind of folklore has been important to the historical consciousness of African Americans, and during the 1930s folkloric images of black people were frequently used by the WPA and the Popular Front on behalf of a progressive social agenda. The entire artistic culture of the Depression was in fact somewhat "folksy" in tone, ranging from public murals to Leadbelly recordings, from the American Communist Party's folk-song movement to John Steinbeck's *The Grapes of Wrath,* and from off-Broadway theatrical productions like *Mule Bone* to Pulitzer Prize hits like *The Green Pastures.*

Cabin in the Sky has an ancestry in this mostly liberal, 1930s-style folkloricism. The film was based on a 1940 Broadway musical by Lynn Root, concerning an impoverished Georgia laborer named "little Joe" who is wounded by gunfire during a dice game. Joe's devout wife, Petunia, prays for his recovery, and black emissaries of God and the Devil are sent to earth to do battle for his soul. Joe is given a short reprieve so that he can mend his ways, but the Devil complicates matters—first by allowing Joe to win the Irish sweepstakes, and then by sending a temptress to lure him away from home. In the end, Petunia's faith wins out, and she and Joe ascend into heaven. Root's quasi-allegorical plot was rendered in the form of a colorful, mainstream spectacular, but many of the black performers, including such figures as Rex Ingram and Katherine Dunham, were associated in the public mind with a kind of folkloric art; indeed, the show's lyricist, John Latouche, had worked with the WPA and had written a famous Depression-era cantata titled "Ballad for Americans." Not surprisingly, when MGM purchased the property, it conceived the forthcoming film as a substitute for *Porgy and Bess* (which was unavailable for purchase), and it hired Marc Connelly, the author of *The Green Pastures,* to work on the screenplay.[9]

By the time *Cabin* went into production, however, African Americans had enlisted to fight in a war against fascism, and a second discourse about race was emerging, foreshadowing the civil rights movement of the next decade. Immediately before the war, Walter White, the executive secretary of the NAACP, had met with a group of Hollywood executives and stars—including Walter Wanger, David Selznick, Darryl Zanuck, and James Cagney—to discuss "the limitation of the Negro to comic or menial roles."[10] Then in 1942, the NAACP held its national convention in Los Angeles, where White called for an end to racial stereotyping and greater participation by black workers in Hollywood craft unions. Later that same year, at the invitation of Wendell Willkie, White made a similar speech to the East Coast Committee on Public Relations of the Motion Picture Producers Association, which promised him it would "effect as rapid a change as possible in the treatment of Negroes in moving pictures."[11]

Not coincidentally, *Casablanca* and *In This Our Life* were released by Warner Brothers in 1942, and several of the subsequent wartime pictures, including *Sahara* (1943) and *Bataan* (1943) showed urban blacks pitted against Nazi or Japanese antagonists. Equally important, the Office of War Information financed a handful of documentaries about black participation in combat, among them Carleton Moss and Stuart Heisler's *The Negro Soldier*. During the same period, black musical performers, some of them bearing flamboyantly aristocratic names, were featured in movies about contemporary show business: Count Basie, Duke Ellington, and Nat King Cole worked at Republic Pictures in 1942–43, as did Louis Armstrong and Dorothy Dandridge; and in 1943, Fox produced *Stormy Weather*, starring Lena Horne and a virtual pantheon of jazz entertainers. Meanwhile, as Thomas Cripps has pointed out, the sentimental depictions of plantation life in Julien Duvivier's *Tales of Manhattan* (1942) and Walt Disney's *Song of the South* (1946) were denounced by black organizations—this despite the fact that both films "might have been lauded for efforts in social progress" only a few years earlier.[12] When *Cabin in the Sky* and *Stormy Weather* went into production, the *New York Times* reported that both pictures had been given the explicit encouragement of the Roosevelt administration:

Two major studios, Metro-Goldwyn Mayer and Twentieth Century-Fox, in producing pictures with all-Negro casts, are following the desires of Washington in making such films at this time. Decisions to produce the pictures, it is stated, followed official expression that the Administration felt that its program for increased employment of Negro citizens in certain heretofore restricted fields of industry would be helped by a general distribution of important pictures in which Negroes played a major part.[13]

But even though Hollywood and Washington seemed to be collaborating in an effort to employ minorities, many black leaders were dismayed by the idea of MGM's musical about rural colored folk. *Cabin* had never been the sort of picture to appeal to most white southerners, but it also threatened to offend its more liberal audience in the predominantly urban centers where Lowe's, Inc. owned theaters. One sign of the trouble the film might encounter was a letter from Hall Johnson, the conductor of a black choral group hired to perform in *Cabin,* to associate producer Albert Lewis. Johnson (who had also worked on the 1935 adaptation of *The Green Pastures*) warned that, "Negroes have never forgiven the slanderous misrepresentations of [Connelly's play], and when after five successful years on the stage it was finally made into a picture, they did not hesitate to express their opinion."[14]

Almost concurrently, an influential group of white intellectuals was voicing a quite different complaint, growing out of what might be termed the discourse of critical modernism. Some participants in this third discursive activity believed in an indigenous folk culture that could be captured on film, but they argued that the black folk and jazz music in particular had been commodified, controlled, and transformed by the media and the WPA; as a result, important local differences were being erased, and America was moving ineluctably toward a one-dimensional society. A locus classicus of such reasoning was James Agee's "Pseudo-Folk," published in *The Partisan Review* in 1944, less than a year after *Cabin in the Sky* was released. Agee was especially disturbed by the "decadence" of swing music, and he worried that the latest fashion in pop tunes would have a bad influence "among Negroes, . . . our richest contemporary source of folk art, and our best people en bloc."[15] To his ear, swing was a corruption of true jazz, which had been produced "where the deep country and the town have first fertilized each other."[16] As examples of the fake, mass-cultural populism that was destroying jazz and overtaking America like a "galloping cancer,"[17] he cited the declining quality of Louis Armstrong's most recent work; the sleek, big-band arrangements of Duke Ellington; the "pseudo-savage, pseudo-'cultured' dancing"[18] of Katherine Dunham and her troupe; and Paul Robeson's performances of John Latouche's "inconceivably snobbish, esthetically execrable 'Ballad for Americans.'"[19] Although he never mentioned *Cabin in the Sky,* he could hardly have come closer to describing it. Both Armstrong and Ellington were featured in the movie, and, as we have seen, both Dunham and Latouche had contributed to the original Broadway show.

Interestingly, Max Horkheimer and Theodor W. Adorno's *Dialectic of Enlightenment* was roughly contemporary with Agee's essay. (The book was published in 1947, but it was written during the war, largely in California, and it carries a 1944 copyright.) In making this connection, I am not suggesting an influence or equivalence. Unlike Agee, Horkheimer and Adorno came from a European Marxist tradition; they were never preoccupied by the folk (understandably so, since in Germany *volkish* theory had long been appropriated by the Fascists), and for the most part they regarded jazz as a pernicious outgrowth of the culture industry.[20] Nevertheless, like many intellectuals of the left, right, and center, they believed that industrialized capitalism and big government of the interwar years was standardizing and reifying social relations, and they shared Agee's distaste for tendentious, fake, or "inauthentic" art. In 1941, Adorno had described the "utopian" element in American life as a "desperate attempt to escape the abstract sameness of things by a kind of self-made and futile *promesse du bonheur.*"[21] For his part, Agee remained a humanist and a lover of movies; he was, however, an equally fierce critic of "sameness." In fact, when he claimed that a valuable "folk tradition" was being "thoroughly bourgeoizified" by the media,[22] he was responding to the same rationalization and commodification that had given rise to the Frankfurt school's pessimistic, somewhat Weberian analysis of "late capitalism."[23]

Arthur Freed, the producer of *Cabin*, was oblivious to such critiques; as a leading executive in America's most prosperous movie studio, however, he was sensitive to charges of racism. In an attempt to avoid controversy, he gave interviews to the black press in which he addressed "the Negro problem," committing himself to a "dignified presentation of a peace-loving and loyal people," and promising to "spare nothing" on the production.[24] The last of these pronouncements was disingenuous, since *Cabin* was the lowest-budgeted musical in the history of the Freed unit; photographed in a sepia-tinted black and white, it borrowed its most spectacular visual effect—a tornado that destroys a nightclub—from *The Wizard of Oz.* Even so, the studio made a considerable investment in the picture: it hired Elmer Rice and Joseph Shrank to assist Connelly with the adaptation (Shrank wrote the first draft and received the sole credit); it commissioned Harold Arlen and E. Y. Harburg to supplement the original John Latouche/Vernon Duke score; and it selected the popular radio personality Eddie Anderson to replace Dooley Wilson.

MGM's production resources, the cast of star performers, and Freed's efforts at public relations all helped the film to earn a modest profit at the box office. According to Donald Bogle, *Cabin* was received enthusiastically by black audiences in the south, and was widely shown at U.S. Army camps, where Lena Horne was a special favorite.[25] But tensions were evident during the shooting, and arguments over *Cabin*'s racial subject matter persisted throughout its distribution.[26] Upon its release, certain reviewers were highly critical of the results. Although *Cabin* received good notices from the *New York Times* and the *New York Daily News* (the last of which had a substantial black readership), David Lardner of the *New Yorker* scoffed at MGM for trying to produce a "lovable ol' folk fantasy,"[27] and the anonymous reviewer for *Time*—none other than James Agee—charged that the studio had treated its fine cast as "picturesque, Sambo-style entertainers."[28] *PM* magazine remarked that the film was an example of "how not to fulfill a pledge such as Hollywood made to Wendell Willkie last year, to treat the Negro as a first-class citizen in films."[29] At least one review in the African American press was even more scathing. Writing in the *New York Amsterdam News* two weeks after *Cabin* had opened its successful run at the Criterion theater on Broadway, Ramona Lewis described the film as "an insult masking behind the label of folklore. . . . It pictures Negroes, heads tied up, with crap shooting inclinations and prayer meeting propensities at a time when [they] are daily proving their heroic mettle in battle and defense plant. . . . Since box office returns convince Hollywood more than anything else that it is in the right, it's too bad the actors didn't have the courage to refuse to make the film in the first place."[30]

In different ways, each of these negative reactions was appropriate. There can be little doubt that *Cabin* was a Hollywood-ish depiction of black folklore, saturated with inferential forms of racism; nor can there be any doubt that it represented a carefully managed style of mass entertainment, designed to serve the interests of a white corporation. Nevertheless, the film has a paradoxical effect, as if it wanted to dissolve binary oppositions between the town and the country, thereby unsettling the strategy of containment that usually operated in Hollywood's folkloric narratives. Placed alongside earlier pictures in the same vein, such as King Vidor's sincere but no less racist *Hallelujah!* or the Warner Brothers adaptation of *The Green Pastures,* it seems distinctly urban in spirit, keyed to the talents of Ethel Waters, Duke Ellington, and Lena Horne. In true Hollywood fashion, the performers are treated as celebrities, so that they take on a glamorous aura and sometimes appear in cameo roles as "themselves." And because these performers have a spacious, handsomely mounted vehicle (staged on the visibly artificial, "utopian" sets that were a hallmark of the Freed unit during the 1940s), they are able to behave like something other than minstrel show caricatures.[31]

This is not to excuse MGM's racism. The studio was responding in certain ways to potential criticism from its black audience, but it was also attempting to preserve the imagery of cheerful, plantation-style darkies. My point is simply that the film's folkloric project was vitiated—partly by the black critique of Hollywood, partly by the Roosevelt administration's desire to integrate certain aspects of the wartime economy, and chiefly by the growing commodification and modernization of American life. In this last regard, I would also argue that *Cabin's* strong feeling of urbanity and sophistication derives in great measure from a fourth discourse about blackness, different from the ones I have described thus far: a chic, upscale "Africanism," redolent of cafe society, Broadway theater, and the European avant-garde.

I use the term *Africanism* in a limited and stipulated manner to suggest a cosmopolitan artistic sensibility that pointed away from the American provinces—usually toward Harlem, Paris, French colonial Africa, and the Caribbean. This sensibility was prompted indirectly by developments within black culture itself, especially by the black internationalism described in a founding document of the Harlem renaissance, Alain Locke's "The New Negro" (1925).[32] It also has something in common with *Negritude,* a word first used in print by poet Aimé Césaire in 1939. But the particular attitude I am trying to identify was chiefly a white mythology, with distant origins in the artistic and intellectual revolutions that had swept Europe during the early twentieth century. Its progenitors would include Conrad's *Heart of Darkness* (1902), Picasso's *Les Demoiselles d'Avignon* (1907), Fry's exhibition of the postimpressionist painters (1910), Freud's *Totem and Taboo* (1913), and the Dadaist experiments with "Negro poems" or *Negergedichte* (1916).[33]

Throughout the 1920s and 1930s, as European high modernism became institutionalized, African motifs found their way into "classy" forms of decoration and entertainment, operating in almost dialectical relation with narratives about the pastoral southland. (Meanwhile, in Germany, the Nazis branded both modernist art and the newer types of black entertainment as "degenerate.") This chic, highly commodified style—raised to delirious excess by Josef von Sternberg in the "Hot Voodoo" number of *Blonde Venus* (1932)—offered a "savage" urbanity in place of a "childlike" pastoralism. It was already present to some degree in the original Broadway production of *Cabin in the Sky,* where the two primitivisms seemed to combine. It could also be heard everywhere in the work of songwriters employed by the Freed unit; for instance, Cole Porter had written a series of Africanist numbers for Broadway shows like *Jubilee* (1935) and *Panama Hattie* (1940), both of which were purchased by MGM. One of the leading exponents of the style, however, was a young director Freed hired for the film: Vincente Minnelli, who had never before been placed in charge of a feature picture.

Minnelli had begun his career in the early 1920s, at the very birth of "modern times," by taking a job as a window decorator in Marshall Field's department store in Chicago; and throughout his later tenure in Hollywood, he consistently drew on post-1870s Paris—the cradle of artistic and commercial modernity—as a source of inspiration. (See *An American in Paris, Lust for Life,* and *Gigi.*) A devoted student of European painting and a great admirer of the surrealists, he was valuable to MGM precisely because, in Geoffrey Nowell-Smith's well-chosen phrase, he furthered the studio's policy of bringing "refinement to the popular."[34] He was undoubtedly offered the chance to supervise *Cabin* because during the mid-1930s he had become famous as a director-designer of sophisticated Broadway revues featuring black performers. Ethel Waters had starred in two of his most successful New York shows, including *At Home Abroad* (1935), where she was cast as the "Empress Jones," a potentate of the Belgian Congo who travels to Harlem and brings the latest styles back to her subjects. ("Cartier rings they're wearin' in their noses now," she sang.) Minnelli had also created settings for Duke Ellington's big band at Radio City, and was responsible for the extravagant and erotic costumes Josephine Baker wore in *The Ziegfeld Follies of 1936.* Robert Benchley of the *New Yorker* snidely accused him of having a "Negroid" sense of color,[35] but in his authorial signature and personal style he continued to exploit what Stephen Harvey has called "the totems of Africa *moderne.*"[36] In 1937, *Esquire* magazine praised his own dress as "a perfect marriage of Harlem and the Left Bank."[37]

An example of one of Minnelli's designs for the unproduced 1939 Broadway musical *Serena Blandish* (intended as a vehicle for Lena Horne and Ethel Waters) shows his tendency to blend surrealist motifs with an au courant Africanism. It should be emphasized that this style is no less racist than high modernism itself, and no more progressive than much of the commercial folklore of the 1930s. Like the folkloric artists, Minnelli relied on a kind of primitivism, explicitly associating blackness with sexuality, instinctiveness, and the Freudian subconscious. At the same time, however, he promoted an uptown face of jazz, tied to contemporary fashion and big-time entertainment. In this context, blackness began to signify both wildness and sophistication. The African imagery was as "stereotypical" as any other cultural code, but it seemed attractive and denatured by parody or playful quotation; moreover, because it was regarded by audiences as vanguard, it tended to problematize the distinction between the savage and the cultivated.

However one might describe the political effect of such designs, the important point about Minnelli's work is that he was far more attuned to contempo-

Minnelli's set design for the unproduced S. N. Behrman stage show *Serena Blandish* (1939) (Courtesy Mrs. Lee Minnelli).

rary New York than to the Old South, and in a picture like *Cabin* his aestheticism tended to undermine the conservative implications of the original material. This is not to suggest that he was either an auteur or an artistic subversive. On the contrary, his elegance and "exoticism" were perfectly in keeping with the institutional needs of MGM in 1943—as we can see from the studio's promotion of the picture, which tried to de-emphasize the story's rural atmosphere. Consider the lobby card from the original release showing Lena Horne, Eddie Anderson, and Ethel Waters gathered around a picket fence. The artwork and promotional copy are appropriate to a big-city nightclub, promising "entertainment galore" and "gorgeous girls," while depicting two richly costumed figures strutting off to a dance. Although the film is less brazenly "citified" than this ad, MGM's publicity department was being reasonably faithful to the values Freed and Minnelli put on the screen.

II

The historical forces and discursive categories I have been describing—the vestigial folklore of the 1930s, the NAACP's mounting criticism of Hollywood,

Lobby card from MGM's *Cabin in the Sky* (1943) (© 1943, Turner Entertainment Co., all rights reserved).

the increasing collaboration between mass entertainment and government, and the posh Africanism of high-toned Broadway musicals—have left their mark on the film, producing a kind of ideological schizophrenia. At the beginning of the credit sequence, for example, a title card announces "The Broadway Musical Play *Cabin in the Sky*," as if MGM wanted to legitimize the project by pointing to refined origins. When the credits end, however, a "crawl" moves across the screen, informing us that "Throughout the ages, powerful thoughts have been handed down through the medium of the legend, the folktale, and the fantasy. . . . This story of faith and devotion springs from that source and seeks to capture those values." Here the film seems to be claiming a different lineage, even though the word "fantasy" mingles ambiguously with appeals to patriotism, folklore, and religion, opening the possibility for a more playful reading.

Cabin continues to exhibit half-hearted concern with the religious beliefs of a "simple" couple who live outside the corrupting reach of modernity, together with a pervasive nostalgia for a lost home life. As Rick Altman has pointed out, the Hollywood "folk musical" is defined by these two qualities, especially by its preoccupation with "family groupings and the home."[38] Such films often involve both a desire for adventure and a recurrent homesickness, and they tend to be resolved by a *nostos* after a period of wandering. In *Cabin*, for example, Joe is torn between the artificial "Club Paradise" and the genuine paradise of a community church; between a sexy, brown-skinned mistress and a somewhat mammyfied wife; between a fast life of wine and easy money and a domestic life of lemonade and productive labor. He strays from home in order to find excitement and pleasure, but then he yearns for what he has left behind, and his return (or more precisely, his recovery after a fevered, guilty dream) is essential to the happy ending.

As we have seen, *Cabin* is based on a paradigmatic tension between city and country, and it gives that tension a conservative resolution, making the town lead to Hell and the country lead to Heaven. Its racist implications become especially apparent when we realize how often the two opposed realms are depicted respectively in shades of blackness and whiteness. The nightclub is situated in a noir-ish street, whereas the cabin is often flooded with light; Joe wears black tie and tails when he spends the Devil's money, and a white robe when he ascends a stairway to paradise; the Devil's henchmen (costumed as big-city elevator operators) are dressed completely in black, in contrast with the soldiers of the Lord, who wear uniforms of glowing white.

But the town is nonetheless an attractive place, and the real story is else-where—largely in the photography, the art decoration, the costuming, the performances, and the musical numbers. In fact, in order to achieve a satisfying conclusion, *Cabin* finds ways to pull its two worlds into a kind of synthesis.[39] Thus the domestic woman moves briefly into the nightclub, wearing a shiny dress, performing a spectacular and amusing dance, and beating the siren at her own game. More importantly, the cabin becomes a performing space, where tap dancing and lively pop tunes bring sexuality and entertainment under the benign influence of spirituality and married love. One of the best numbers in the picture, Ethel Waters's superb rendition of "Takin' a Chance on Love," is staged in the family kitchen, and it uses the metaphor of gambling (Joe's major vice) to speak about monogamous romance.

Here as elsewhere, *Cabin* simply borrows a few stock images from a folkloric code, putting them in the service of a new form of musical theater. In the opening credits, it makes a patriotic appeal to folklore, but then it uses jazz and jitterbug to perform the function of hymns and work songs in earlier movies of the type. As a "folk musical," it therefore differs sharply from *Hallelujah!* where, according to Rick Altman, "the tempered rhythms of the spiritual, sung in unison by the gathered community" are set off against "the syncopated rhythms of jazz and the chaotic sexual drive which they invoke."[40] Unlike King Vidor, Freed and Minnelli have utterly secular imaginations, and their film contains no Manichean musical oppositions. In fact, the only religious song heard in *Cabin* is a snippet of "Old Ship of Zion," which is immediately preceded by "Little Black Sheep," an ersatz hymn written by E. Y. "Yip" Harburg.

Cabin might be properly described as suburban rather than folkloric, because it blends MGM's middle-class values with the Freed unit's relatively elite, Broadway ethos. To see just how much it tilts toward the city, however, one needs to step far outside the studio system, viewing it alongside Spencer Williams's *Blood of Jesus* (1941), an independent film directed by a black man and aimed at an audience of southern black churchgoers. Williams's film, which has none of the production values of MGM, was designed, in Thomas Cripps's words, "to mourn the passing of the great days when Afro-Americans were embraced by a familial certitude that would later be shattered by the great black diaspora from Southern farm to Yankee city."[41] Williams portrayed the devil in the style of *aesthetique du cool,* and he made urban jitterbug seem a lurid music, appropriate to a world of crime and prostitution. In *Cabin,* Freed and Minnelli were able to use the same fundamentalist semantics, and yet their tone was completely different. For example, in one of the most exhilarating sequences of the picture, a high-stepping couple, dressed in the latest fashion and moving to the beat of Duke Ellington's "Goin' Up," enter the swinging doors of the Club Paradise; the camera dollies backward as the couple glides onto the dance floor, and then, as a crowd of neatly dressed men in zoot suits and women in bobby socks gathers around, it cranes high above the room, drifting across the scene to close in on the bandstand. Clearly, this is no smoky den of iniquity. It seems more like a showcase for a famous orchestra, and the lovely collaboration among Ellington's music, Busby Berkeley's choreography, and Minnelli's camera-crane amounts to a kind of celebration.[42]

It follows that if the nightclub is treated as relatively innocent fun, religion is depicted in perfunctory or comic ways. Unlike Williams's *Blood of Jesus,* *Cabin* imagines the afterlife whimsically, in a style similar to Lubitsch's *Heaven Can Wait* (also released in 1943). It never mentions Jesus, it never shows a crucifix, and it barely alludes to scripture; instead, it offers a nonsectarian god who behaves rather like a cosmic cost accountant, and it proffers a few simple edicts against gambling and adultery. The Devil's henchmen do their work from the "Hotel Hades," which resembles the office of an MGM producer during a story conference; and the entrance to Heaven—a vast, cloud-covered

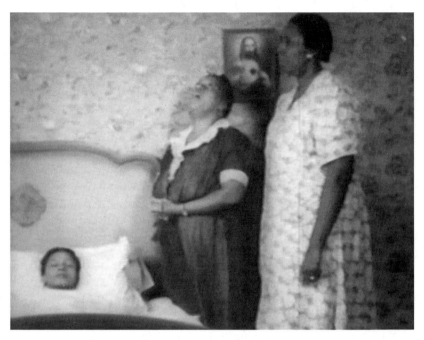

Set decoration in *Blood of Jesus,* directed by Spencer Williams, 1941.

stairway flanked by black cherubim—seems to have been derived from a Ziegfeld production number.

By the same token, the quotidian, earthbound scenes in *Cabin* resemble a pure dream world. Most Hollywood movies about the folk at least claim to represent a specific place, but here the characters inhabit a poor but utopian black universe, structured by the absence of white people and decorated with an odd mixture of artifacts. Indeed one of the major differences between the Broadway show and the film is that in the film the battle between God and the Devil turns out to be something Joe *dreams*. This change gave the picture a happy ending, and at the same time enabled Minnelli to invest the mise-en-scène with an Afro-Caribbean look that foreshadows his subsequent work on *Yolanda and the Thief* (1945) and *The Pirate* (1948). In his autobiography, he claims that he struggled with MGM's art department in order to keep the cabin from seeming "dirty" or "slovenly,"[43] but his dreamy settings also tended to aestheticize poverty, motivating some condescending jokes. At one point, for example, Joe uses earnings from a local feed mill to buy Petunia a washing machine; because there is no electricity in the cabin, he places the gleaming white appliance on his porch as a symbol of prosperity. In this context, the washer becomes a surrealistic image—a bizarre objet trouvé, both satirizing and validating the society of consumption.

Not only the settings, but also the manners and accents in the film are heterogeneous and fantastic. Hall Johnson had written to the producers advising them to use "an honest-to-goodness Negro dialect,"[44] but the script was rendered in a series of excruciatingly condescending white versions of demotic, southern-black English. Here is the way Joseph Shrank and Marc Connelly imagined Petunia praying for Joe's recovery:

> If yuh lets him die de debbil gonna git him fo' sho'. An' he aint wicked, Lawd-he jus' weak, dat's all. He ain't got no powah to resis' de debbil lest Ah watches him.[45]

And here is Joe when he discovers a pair of dice in his bedroom drawer:

> Right now I'm wrestlin' wid de devil. When I was lookin' for de necktie in de bureau drawer, I also found two clamity cubes. I aint throwed 'em away yet. If I been redeemed, why don't I pitch 'em right in de stove?[46]

Fortunately, little of this language survives in the performances—an effect that becomes especially evident in the case of a minor player, Butterfly McQueen, who never uses the spacey sing-song that audiences (even audiences of films produced by blacks) had come to expect of her.[47] Petunia's prayer has been completely revised for the completed film, and Eddie Anderson delivers the speech about "calamity cubes" in the same gravelly, urban accent he used on the radio, so that it hardly sounds like the same language. At one point, Ethel Waters sings a few lines of "Happiness Is a Thing Called Joe" in a fake dialect ("He gotta smile dat make de lilac wanna grow"), but everywhere else, she sings in crisply enunciated standard English, using the slightly elocutionary vocal technique of her best-known recordings.

Where the design of the film is concerned, Minnelli seems to have taken pleasure in making a southern locale look like the big city. In one of the most revealing comments in his autobiography, he remarks that the set he liked best was "a southern ghetto, with a warm, golden look, created from a permanent version of a New York street."[48] He also tried to glamorize the featured players: whenever Ethel Waters is seen in a bandanna, she wears fashionable earrings reminiscent of the Cartier jewelry she had sung about in *At Home Abroad;* and when Lena Horne dresses up as a temptress, she exchanges her pill-box hat for a magnolia, pinning the visibly artificial blossom to her hair like Billie Holiday.[49]

Set decoration in *Cabin in the Sky* (Rex Ingram and Lena Horne) (©1943, Turner Entertainment Co., all rights reserved).

Much the same thing could be said about the dressing of the sets. Minnelli painted his own "Africanist" murals on the walls of the Paradise nightclub, and he turned the cabin into a spacious interior, accented with reproductions of Victorian art. He gave Joe and Petunia an elaborate, wrought iron bedstead, and in each of their rooms he placed white wicker chairs designed in a lacy, rococo filigree. (The same chairs show up again in 1944, helping to furnish Judy Garland's bedroom in *Meet Me in St. Louis;* in 1950, they reappear in MGM's *Two Weeks with Love,* a Jane Powell–Debbie Reynolds musical set in a fashionable Catskills resort.) To grasp the full implications of this style, we need only glance at the stills reproduced here. The first comes from Williams's *Blood of Jesus,* where a black household has been decorated with a single picture—a dime-store image of Jesus exhibiting his bleeding heart, visible at the upper left of the frame. The second is from *Cabin* and helps to indicate the comparative opulence of MGM. Notice especially the framed picture at the upper right of the frame, showing a white cherub kissing a sleeping boy.

Largely because of this elaborate, exquisite decoration, *Cabin* seems remote from anything we commonly associate with folkloric movies. A deliberate exercise in faux-naïveté, it has more in common with what Rick Altman has called "fairy tale musicals," in the sense that it elicits identification "with fantasy, with the far away, with the imaginary."[50] Generally speaking, of course, all the classic Hollywood musicals were fairy tales; but *Cabin*'s oneiric quality has an odd relationship to its ostensible subject, making its folkloric setting seem a mere pretext. The deeper purpose of the film becomes evident when we consider two rhyming camera movements, one near the beginning of the story and one near the end: in the first, Joe stands looking at a lottery ticket he has fastened to his bedroom mirror; as he leans forward in a trance, the camera cranes up and over his shoulder, moving toward the tilted surface of the glass as if to plunge him and us into an imaginary world. In the second, Petunia looks into a mirror that has survived the devastation of the Club Paradise; she notices something reflected there, and the camera cranes downward to share her viewpoint, revealing a studio-manufactured stairway leading off through the clouds. These shots contrast Joe's dream of riches with Petunia's dream of Heaven, but they also serve as metaphors for two aspects of the Hollywood cinema. Like the movies, they appeal both to our desire for luxury and to our desire for a magical, nonmaterial existence. They invite the audience to form a subjective bond with a poor black couple, but in the process they make Joe and Petunia seem like ideal consumers of entertainment—a pair of restless American dreamers caught up in a world of music, light, and dance.

Like virtually all the Freed unit musicals, *Cabin in the Sky* involves a good deal of what Jane Feuer has termed "conservative self-reflexivity"; it banishes every social contradiction, first by appealing to its own status as entertainment, and then by presenting "a vision of human liberation which is profoundly aesthetic."[51] Notice also that the aesthetic sensibility is always expensive, dependent on signifiers of material abundance and rarified taste. Thus when Waters, Anderson, and Horne play the roles of folkloric characters, they do not look poor; and because they are treated as stars, they induce a feeling of playful masquerade. In a strange way, this transformation of blackness into a commodity-on-display has a salutary effect, even if the display has dubious purposes. We might say, echoing Richard Dyer's formulation, that the film gives us the feeling of "what utopia would feel like rather than how it would be organized."[52]

Clearly, the makers of *Cabin* were taking care to keep too much social reality from intruding on the attractive surroundings. Their strategy may seem offensive when so much of the actual experience of African Americans has been suppressed or driven into a political unconscious, but *Cabin* has a complex ideological potential. From the point of view of many social critics of the time, its Hollywood surrealism and freewheeling, commodified treatment of folklore were irredeemably decadent and false; and yet its design runs against the grain of a repressive and no more "true" set of conventions. After all, there is no such thing as an "authentic" folk movie, and *Cabin* may have been better off for its evident artificiality. Freed and Minnelli were hardly social activists, but by imbuing their film with a dreamy atmosphere and an urban Africanism, they and the performers turned it into what is arguably the most visually beautiful picture about black people ever produced at the classic studios. We might say that during the early 1940s, and within the context of a white entertainment industry, their aestheticism amounted to a modestly positive gesture.

Perhaps a better way of making the same point would be to repeat the familiar Marxist axiom that capitalism represents a progressive stage in history. Unfortunately, such progress always involves injustices and ironies. As I have already observed, *Cabin* and every other studio film about blacks simply reinforced the hypocritical, separate-but-equal policies of a segregated society. This injustice was compounded because whites were in charge of every behind-the-scenes aspect of the production, and because much of the debate over the film's merits was framed and conditioned by a white cultural establishment. It is ironic that *Cabin* can nonetheless be described as a step forward in the democratization of show business, and that a film containing so much nostalgia and synthetic folklore should have provided a showcase for some of the wittiest and most talented entertainers of the period. But the greatest irony of all is that the black performers, who were at last becoming full-fledged stars, were merely gaining membership in a conservative enterprise—a system devoted to praising the American way, and to promoting the values of glamour, charm, and illusion.

NOTES

The author would like to acknowledge several people who contributed useful suggestions for this essay: Manthia Diawara, Gloria Gibson-Hudson, Phyllis Klotman, John Hess, John Fell, Robert Stam, Susan White, and Cary Wolfe.

1. This list excludes Twentieth Century-Fox's *Tales of Manhattan* (1942), an anthology film with one episode involving black characters, and Disney's *Song of the South* (1946), which was largely animated.

2. The package-unit system began in 1955, but the end of the classic studios was in sight by 1954. See David Bordwell, Janet Staiger, and Kristin Thompson, *The Classical*

Hollywood Cinema: Film Style and Mode of Production to 1960 (New York: Columbia University Press, 1985), 330–38.

3. All six films are discussed in Thomas Cripps, *Black Film as Genre* (Bloomington: Indiana University Press, 1979) and Donald Bogle, *Toms, Coons, Mulattoes, Mammies, and Bucks: An Interpretive History of Blacks in American Films* (New York: Continuum, 1991). The only film to have received extensive critical treatment elsewhere is *Hallelujah!*; see, for example, Raymond Durgnat and Scott Simmon, *King Vidor, American* (Berkeley: University of California Press, 1989), 96–113. *Cabin in the Sky* is discussed in Stephen Harvey, *Directed by Vincente Minnelli* (New York: Museum of Modern Art and Harper and Row, 1989), 40–44; see also Rick Altman, *The Hollywood Film Musical* (Bloomington: Indiana University Press, 1987), who analyzes *Hallelujah!* and makes brief remarks on a few of the other black-cast musicals. Outside the context of director and genre studies or books on African American film, the black-cast pictures are treated as if they had only technical importance. In their monumental study of the Hollywood system, Bordwell, Staiger, and Thompson make a passing reference to *Hallelujah!* noting its camera movements; they mention *The Green Pastures* during a discussion of the focal length of camera lenses, and they provide an image from *Carmen Jones* to illustrate CinemaScope. Two standard histories, David A. Cook, *A History of Narrative Film* (New York: Norton, 1990) and Gerald Mast, *A Short History of the Movies* (Boston: Allyn and Bacon, 1992), mention only *Hallelujah!* praising its use of sound.

4. For an extensive discussion of this theme in English literature, see Raymond Williams, *The Country and the City* (New York: Oxford University Press, 1973). For an analysis of how the country/city opposition structures classic Hollywood, see Robin Wood, "Ideology, Genre, Auteur," in *Film Genre Reader,* ed. Barry Keith Grant (Austin: University of Texas Press, 1986), 59–73.

5. In-text parenthetical page number citations are to Richard Dyer, "Entertainment and Utopia," in *Genre: The Musical,* ed. Rick Altman (London: Routledge and Kegan Paul, 1981), 175–89. A similar argument can be seen in Jane Feuer, *The Hollywood Musical* (Bloomington: Indiana University Press, 1982), 67–85. Both Dyer and Feuer have something in common with Walter Benjamin, who believed that mass culture's potentially utopian, collective energy was pushed in conservative directions by capitalism. See Susan Buck-Morss, *The Dialectics of Seeing: Walter Benjamin and the Arcades Project* (Cambridge, MA: MIT Press, 1989), 525–86. More recently, Dyer has seemed more aware of the complex discursive networks in which films operate. See, for example, his discussion of Paul Robeson's star image in *Heavenly Bodies* (1988).

6. Mikhail Bakhtin, *The Dialogic Imagination,* ed. Michael Holquist (Austin: University of Texas Press, 1981), 276.

7. I use the term *discourse* heuristically, to describe several conflicting voices surrounding the production of a single film. I do not claim that my survey of these voices is comprehensive, only that it is sufficiently broad to illustrate social conflicts in the period. It should also be noted that no discursive category is monologic. Each of the categories I have attempted to isolate could be divided into others, and these could be divided again, in a process of infinite regression. For additional discussion of how

films can become the sites of conflicting discourse, see Robert Stam, "Bakhtin, Polyphony, and Ethnic/Racial Representation," in *Unspeakable Images: Ethnicity and the American Cinema,* ed. Lester D. Friedman (Urbana: University of Illinois Press, 1991), 251–76; Gina Marchetti, "Ethnicity, the Cinema, and Cultural Studies," in ibid., 277–307; and Ella Shohat, "Ethnicities-in-Relation," in ibid., 215–47. Where the response of actual historical spectators is concerned, I have much less to say. For an important analysis of spectatorship and race, see Manthia Diawara, "Black Spectatorship: Problems of Identification and Resistance," *Screen* 29, no. 4 (1988): 66–79.

8. Peter Burke, "The 'Discovery' of Popular Culture," in *People's History and Socialist Theory,* ed. Raphael Samuel (London: Routledge and Kegan Paul, 1983), 215–22, quote on 216.

9. Vincente Minnelli, with Hector Acre, *I Remember It Well* (Garden City, NY: Doubleday, 1974), 121; Harvey, *Directed by Vincente Minnelli,* 41.

10. Quoted in *The Papers of the NAACP,* December 1940.

11. *The Papers of the NAACP,* April 1942.

12. Cripps, *Black Film as Genre,* 44.

13. Quoted in Bogle, *Toms, Coons, Mulattoes, Mammies, and Bucks,* 136–37.

14. Hugh Fordin, *The Movies' Greatest Musicals* (New York: Frederick Ungar, 1984), quoted on 74.

15. James Agee, "Pseudo-Folk," in *Agee on Film,* vol. 1 (New York: McDowell, Obolensky, 1958), 404–10, quote on 407.

16. Agee, "Pseudo-Folk," 405.

17. Ibid., 404.

18. Ibid., 408.

19. Ibid., 406–8.

20. Adorno was a particularly hostile critic of show business. In "On the Fetish Character in Music and the Regression of Listening" (1938), he charges that "music for entertainment" serves only to assure that people are "confirmed in their neurotic stupidity" (in *The Essential Frankfurt School Reader,* ed. Andrew Arato and Eike Gebhardt [New York: Continuum, 1987], 270–99, quote on 286). See also his postwar essay, "Perennial Fashion-Jazz." Here Adorno describes jazz as a "slave" music, in which it is difficult "to isolate the authentic Negro elements" (in his *Prisms,* trans. Samuel and Shierry Weber [Cambridge, MA: MIT Press, 1990], 119–31, quote on 122). Needless to say, James Agee's attitude toward commercial jazz and American blacks was different. He was also a contributor to *The Quiet One* (1948), a sensitive independent film about a lonely black boy, which Bogle compares favorably with Rossellini's *Paisan* (1947) (Bogle, *Toms, Coons, Mulattoes, Mammies, and Bucks,* 141–42).

21. Quoted in Matei Calinescu, *Five Faces of Modernity* (Durham, NC: Duke University Press, 1987), 228.

22. Agee, "Pseudo-Folk," 404.

23. On the relation between the Frankfurt school and Max Weber, see Arato and Gebhardt, eds., *Essential Frankfurt School Reader,* 190–91, 207–19. Fredric Jameson (*Postmodernism, or, the Cultural Logic of Late Capitalism* [Durham, NC: Duke University Press, 1991]) believes that the term *late capitalism* originated with Horkheimer and

Adorno, whose conception of American society was "Weberian," involving two essential features: "1) a tendential web of bureaucratic control . . . and 2) the interpenetration of government and big business" (Max Horkheimer and Theodor W. Adorno, *Dialectic of Enlightenment* [1944; New York: Seabury, 1972], xvii). In what I describe as the "discourse of critical modernism," there is a strong tendency to regard the mass media as opiates or instruments of social control. Compare T. S. Eliot's conservative response to the rise of movies during the 1920s: "with the encroachment of the cheap and rapid-breeding cinema, the lower classes will drop into the same state of protoplasm as the bourgeoisie" (*Selected Prose* [Harmondsworth: Penguin, 1953], 225).

24. Quoted in Fordin, *Movies' Greatest Musicals*, 73.

25. Bogle, *Toms, Coons, Mulattoes, Mammies, and Bucks*, 132.

26. Until a studio executive ordered the MGM commissary integrated, most of the players ate lunch in L. B. Mayer's private dining room. See Ethan Mordden, *The Hollywood Studios* (New York: Simon and Schuster, 1989), 163.

27. David Lardner, "Current Cinema," *New Yorker*, May 29, 1943, 79.

28. Anonymous, "Cinema," *Time*, April 12, 1943, 112.

29. *PM*, June 1, 1943, 10.

30. Ramona Lewis, "'Cabin' Picture Called Insult," *New York Amsterdam News*, June 12, 1943, 17.

31. Bogle describes the 1940s as the "apex" of the "Negro Entertainment Syndrome," in which the nightclub was a recurrent setting for black performers (*Toms, Coons, Mulattoes, Mammies, and Bucks*, 118–19). During the period, Ethel Waters became a major star on American radio, and Duke Ellington presented a series of forty-seven weekly, hour-long broadcasts sponsored by the U.S. Treasury Department.

32. In his influential essay, Locke claimed that American blacks of the twentieth century were involved in a "deliberate flight not only from the country to the city, but from medieval America to modern" ("The New Negro," in *Black Voices*, ed. Abraham Chapman [New York: Mentor Books, 1968], 512–23, quote on 515): "The pulse of the Negro world has begun to beat in Harlem. A Negro newspaper carrying news material in English, French, and Spanish, gathered from all quarters of America, the West Indies and Africa has maintained itself in Harlem for over five years. . . . Under American auspices and backing, three pan-African congresses have been held abroad for the discussion of common interests, colonial questions and the future co-operative development of Africa. . . . As with the Jew, persecution is making the Negro international" (522). For an extensive discussion of the historical importance of the "New Negro," see Henry Louis Gates Jr., "The Trope of the New Negro and the Reconstruction of the Image of the Black," *Representations* 24 (Fall 1988): 129–55.

33. An essay of this length cannot fully document the European fascination with Africa during the modernist period. See Marianna Torgovnick, *Gone Primitive: Savage Intellects, Modern Lives* (Chicago: University of Chicago Press, 1990), 75–140, who discusses the nexus of modernist aesthetics, colonial stereotypes, and obsessions about race and gender. For a discussion of a similar phenomenon in European avant-garde culture between the wars, see Julian Stallabras, "The Idea of the Primitive: British Art and Anthropology, 1918–1930," *New Left Review* 183 (1990): 95–115.

34. Geoffrey Nowell-Smith, "On Kiri Te Kanawa, Judy Garland, and the Culture Industry," in *Modernity and Mass Culture*, ed. James Naremore and Patrick Brantlinger (Bloomington: Indiana University Press, 1991), 70–79, quote on 75.

35. Quoted in Minnelli, *I Remember It Well*, 58.

36. Harvey, *Directed by Vincente Minnelli*, 34.

37. Quoted in ibid., 30.

38. Altman, *Hollywood Film Musical*, 273.

39. For a discussion of this strategy in other Hollywood genres, see Robert Ray, *A Certain Tendency of the Hollywood Cinema, 1930–1980* (Princeton, NJ: Princeton University Press, 1985).

40. Altman, *Hollywood Film Musical*, 292.

41. Cripps, *Black Film as Genre*, 92.

42. Notice, too, *Cabin*'s portrayal of a gambler named Domino Johnson (a.k.a. John Bubbles Sublett, the original Sportin' Life in *Porgy and Bess*), whose privileged moment is a performance of Ford Dabney and Cecil Mack's "Shine." This song (also performed by Dooley Wilson in *Casablanca* and later recorded by Bing Crosby and Frankie Laine) is one of the more uncomfortably racist moments in the film, chiefly because of its references to "curly" hair, "pearly" teeth, and fancy clothes; from the point of view of the black actor, however, it functions self-reflexively, and is the only occasion when a character is allowed to acknowledge racial difference. Moreover, while Johnson is supposed to be a villain, we are never invited to think of him as truly dangerous. Sublett's dancing makes him seem charming, and Minnelli's camera movements suggest a rapport with the figure of the black dandy.

43. Minnelli, *I Remember It Well*, 121.

44. Quoted in Fordin, *Movies' Greatest Musicals*, 75.

45. Joseph Shrank and Marc Connelly, *Cabin in the Sky*. Mimeographed film script. September 21, 1942. Revisions dated October 20, 1942, p. 21.

46. Ibid., 9.

47. The black performers were working against the script, but I suspect MGM wanted to "dignify" the production. In any case, the effect of dialect humor or "local color" depends on context. Consider the following speech, from Langston Hughes's *Simply Heavenly* (1956): "Why, its getting so colored folks can't do nothing no more without some other Negro calling you a stereotype. Stereotype, hah! If you like a little gin, you're a stereotype. . . . If you wear a red dress, you're a stereotype. . . . Lord have mercy, honey, do—don't like no blackeyed peas and rice! Then you're a down-home Negro for true—which I is—and proud of it! I didn't come here to Harlem to get away from my people. I come here because there's more of 'em. I loves my race. I loves my people. Stereotype!" (Langston Hughes, *Five Plays by Langston Hughes*, ed. Webster Smalley [Bloomington: Indiana University Press, 1968], 125–26).

48. Minnelli, *I Remember It Well*, 122.

49. It should be noted that the most imposing and handsome males in *Cabin* are Kenneth Spenser and Rex Ingram, who play supernatural characters. In the earthly scenes, Lena Horne is an obviously sexualized female, playing a role similar to Nina Mae McKinney's in *Hallelujah! Cabin* is almost the only film where Horne functions

as an agent of the narrative, and where she moves provocatively around the set; even so, one of her singing numbers was cut because Minnelli staged it in a bubble bath.

50. Altman, *Hollywood Film Musical,* 15.

51. Feuer, *Hollywood Musical,* 84.

52. Dyer, "Entertainment and Utopia," 177.

Vincente Minnelli and the Film Ballet

Beth Genné

Introduction

For director Vincente Minnelli and dancer-choreographer Gene Kelly, *An American in Paris* climaxed a career-long experiment with what Kelly would call "the ciné-ballet" or more simply, a film ballet.[1] This essay looks at the development of the film ballet in Minnelli's early work on Broadway and his films *Ziegfeld Follies, Yolanda and the Thief,* and *The Pirate,* which became models not only for Minnelli's film ballets of the late 1940s and 1950s, such as *An American in Paris,* but influences on Kelly–Donen's *On the Town, Singin' in the Rain,* and others. I trace the roots of the form in dance as well as film and pay special attention to Minnelli's mutually influential relationships with three dancer-choreographers—George Balanchine, Fred Astaire, and Gene Kelly—all of whom would be important to the development of the film ballet —or as I prefer to call it, a film dance-drama.

ROOTS IN DANCE HISTORY

Both Minnelli and Kelly's conception of the "ciné-ballet" ultimately grows out the late eighteenth century *ballet d'action*. In his *Lettres sur la danse* (1758–60) French choreographer Jean-Georges Noverre championed this form, calling for a reform of ballet. Instead of a loosely related series of divertissements often interpolated into opera and designed mainly to display the techniques and talents of the performers, Noverre promoted a form of dance-drama in which movement (dance and mime) was used to express character, and along with costumes, music, and visual design, could develop a plot. Multiple act *ballets d'action* like *Giselle, Sleeping Beauty, Swan Lake,* and *The Nutcracker* became a staple of nineteenth-century repertory in the dance capitals of Paris, St. Petersburg, and Copenhagen.

Noverre's ideas were altered and expanded by the rebel Russian choreographer Mikhail Fokine and his colleagues in Serge Diaghilev's Ballets Russes (1909–29). Fokine called for an even tighter synthesis of dance, music, and design and a move away from the illusionistic nineteenth-century stage picture: Diaghilev's designers were drawn from the world of avant-garde art: fauves, cubists, futurists, constructivists, surrealists. The evening-length dance narrative was condensed into a single act that, like modernist drama, could or could not "follow logically."

Additionally, Fokine and his colleagues (Nijinsky, Nijinska, Massine, and Balanchine) began to push hard at the limits of the movement vocabulary of the traditional *danse d'école* (what we often call *classical ballet*). They largely eliminated mime and opened up traditional dance to ideas drawn from everyday movement, sports, folk, and social dance as well as the new theatrical dance forms pioneered by Isadora Duncan, the Russian constructivists and German expressionist choreographers. The new form most important for the development of the film ballet was African American jazz movement, and it was brought in by Diaghilev's last choreographer, Balanchine, who worked with the company from 1924 until the company was disbanded on Diaghilev's death in 1929.

The young Vincente Minnelli was well aware of Russian ballet and of Balanchine: he had begun his career during a time when Ballets Russes dancers and choreographers (jobless after Diaghilev's death and exiled from their native land by the Russian Revolution), began to settle in America, bringing ballet with them. The mutually influential mingling of Russian and American artists in the American melting pot would transform American dance and musical theater—and eventually dance in film. Around the time Minnelli moved East from Chicago, Balanchine immigrated to America to establish a ballet school and company. In 1935, the two young hopefuls became friends when they found themselves collaborating on three ballets for the *Ziegfeld Follies of 1936*, which opened in New York in January 1936.

Ira Gershwin, the *Follies* lyricist, brought Minnelli and Balanchine into the circle of Broadway's young innovators, including his brother George as well as Richard Rodgers, Lorenz Hart, Harold Arlen, and "Yip" Harburg. There was also Vernon Duke (a.k.a. Vladimir Dukelsky) a young Russian émigré who, like Balanchine, served both Old and New World forms. (As Vladimir Dukelsky, he composed symphonic works and a Diaghilev ballet score; as Vernon Duke he wrote songs for Broadway shows.)

Duke/Dukelsky would write the scores for the Balanchine-Minnelli *Follies* ballets. The first two, "Words without Music" and "Night Flight," clearly stemmed from Diaghilev models—using modern as well as classical movement and surrealist sets designed by Minnelli. Minnelli, Balanchine, and Duke also worked with an amalgam of jazz, modern, and ballet movement in their dance-drama for Josephine Baker, "Five A.M.," which took advantage of Baker's familiarity with jazz movement and with ballet (which she had learned in Paris, trained in part by Balanchine himself) and used a device that would become familiar to viewers of Minnelli's later film ballets as well as their Broadway counterparts: a dream ballet. Later that year Balanchine would choreograph the first ballet integrated into the plot of a Broadway musical, *On Your Toes* (1936), which he would reconceive for film in 1939—both of which Minnelli saw.

Another young dancer-choreographer, Gene Kelly, joined the dance invasion in Rodgers and Hart's *Pal Joey* (1940). Kelly, an admirer of Minnelli and Balanchine, was the product of a typically eclectic American dance education not only in jazz tap dance, Irish step dance, and "interpretative" (a kind of modern dance), but also ballet in the Diaghilev tradition. His teacher, Berenice Holmes, was a pupil of ex-Diaghilev star Adolph Bolm, and Kelly became skilled enough to be offered a place in a company of ex–Ballets Russes dancers.

After Minnelli and Kelly moved to Hollywood their ties to the New York theater remained strong. Minnelli's *Follies* collaborators Balanchine and Vernon Duke were professionally and personally related to Minnelli's first film *Cabin in the Sky*, for they had created the original 1940 Broadway hit that Balanchine had directed as well as choreographed. In the New York *Cabin in the Sky,* dance was used as a key dramatic device, and Balanchine had once again created a dream ballet in collaboration with dancer-choreographer Katherine Dunham (the original Georgia Brown character in *Cabin*). What happened to Balanchine's (and Dunham's) choreography and direction in the transition from stage to screen is a matter of speculation.

ZIEGFELD FOLLIES: MINNELLI, ASTAIRE, AND THE MOVING CAMERA

Minnelli's first ballets for film appear in another *Ziegfeld Follies*—this time an MGM version made in 1945. Minnelli worked not with Balanchine but with Fred Astaire. "This Heart of Mine" and "Limehouse Blues" are landmark moments in the integration of dance and camerawork to convey a drama in dance. Camera movement is added to the "synthesis of the arts" called for by Fokine. Astaire, a pioneer of film dance in the first decade of sound cinema, was already one of the greatest dancer-choreographers of the twentieth century—or indeed in the history of dance. (Balanchine, who saw Astaire in London in Gershwin's 1927 *Funny Face,* compared him to J. S. Bach![2])

Astaire's style drew on the Broadway dance routines of his teacher Ned Wayburn and absorbed influences from the great African American jazz dancers Buddy Bradley as well as John Bubbles (who would appear in Minnelli's *Cabin in the Sky*) and Bill "Bojangles" Robinson, who Astaire knew and admired. (Astaire's tribute to "Bojangles" can be seen in his 1936 film *Swing Time.*) In his films, Astaire performed his own distinctive form of jazz tap dance modified and transformed by influences from other dance forms like ballet and ballroom dance. Astaire was well acquainted with ballet, but had very little training in it. However, he had seen a lot. He and his sister Adele had seen Adeline Genee in *Soul Kiss* over twenty times, and when in London Astaire had consulted his colleague from the Diaghilev Ballets Russes, Anton Dolin, about the mechanics of certain ballet steps. Astaire had also danced with ballet-trained Tilly Losch in *The Bandwagon.*

In the 1930s Astaire had made the *dancer,* the human body shaping space, the focus of the viewer's experience. To this end Astaire (who had control over the filming of his dance sequences) kept camera movement, with some exceptions, to a minimum. He framed the whole of the dancer's body at all times with almost no close-ups or cutting away to break up the unified image of the dancer in space. Most of his dances were filmed in one take, so as not to break the coherency and flow of the choreography.

But Astaire's dances were not merely documents of stage performances: Astaire recognized and took advantage of the special qualities of the film medium. The camera was placed and moved along with the dancers so as to allow each audience member an ideal view of the dance. However, Astaire's *dances* (with some important exceptions) were conceptualized in terms of a proscenium stage space in their frontal orientation: the camera records the dance from a *idealized* theater seat giving each viewer "fifth row center seats" that are slightly *elevated* to place them on the same level as the dancers. From this frontal perspective, it moves with them around the stage so that the viewer's position never changes—an effect impossible to create in a real theater where the viewer's perspective is controlled by the fixed position of her seat—if the dancers move to one side of the stage, for example, the viewers must swivel their heads to see them.

Ziegfeld Follies was supposed to have been one of his last films before Astaire's retirement, but it turned out to be one of the first in a series of films he made for MGM, some of the best of which were made with Minnelli. Astaire had always retained full control over the camera work in his films of the 1930s. However, in *Ziegfeld Follies,* he loosened the reigns for the first time and trusted Minnelli to actively employ the mobile boom camera that *participates* in the dance—active in height as well as depth.

In the *Ziegfeld Follies* dance-drama Minnelli had to employ the mobile camera both for dramatic purposes and for formal effects: he tells the story by maneuvering his camera quickly and smoothly in height as well as depth, from long to medium to close shots, from high above the dancers to stage level, capturing telling facial expressions and gestures in close-ups, then gliding back to both reveal and enhance the sweep and scope of the dance as a whole. The pace of the camera blends rhythmically with the choreography and music (it seems cued to musical counts). So does the editing, which also shapes the sequence, though to a lesser extent. Impressively (and unlike much Busby Berkeley camera work of the 1930s), Minnelli moves the camera without obscuring either the line of the dancers, the shape of Astaire's overall choreographic design, or the essentially human scale on which the dance is planned. The camera movement is integrated so closely with the music and dance gesture that even in the sequence's center section, when the restless camera is given its most grand and sweeping gestures, it does not overwhelm or dominate the dancers or the dance. Rather, camera movement seems to grow inevitably and logically out of the demands of both music and choreography. A close analysis of the center section of "This Heart of Mine" demonstrates this clearly.

In the tradition of Astaire's courtship dances of the 1930s, "This Heart of Mine" can be roughly divided into four sections that trace, in general outline, a dance seduction. Here, however, the seduction is played out within the context of a dance-drama involving mime as well as dance sequences. In the tradition of Astaire and Rogers courtship dances, the entire sequence plays out a seduction in mime and dance. In his films of the 1930s, Astaire's dances were pivotal moments in the drama tracing the emotional roller coaster of courtship from initial approach-avoidance tactics to ecstatic bonding.

In "This Heart of Mine," Astaire continues this tradition, but unlike his previous films, and as in the *ballet d'action,* spoken words play no part, the entire story is danced (and sung). Astaire plays the role of a jewel thief who, at an elegant party, inadvertently falls in love with a woman (Lucille Bremer) whose diamonds he hopes to steal. He lures her into an extended ballroom dance, she falls in love with him, and, at the same time, comes to realize his intentions. At the end of the dance, she removes her necklace and hands it to him openly. Shamed, he returns the jewels, and the couple embraces.

The theme expressed through dance-drama in "This Heart of Mine" will lie at the heart of all the Minnelli and Kelly–Donen film ballets, and it stems ultimately from a popular romantic ballet theme: a man chases a female ideal who seems forever beyond his reach—a perfect subject for movement. In the nineteenth-century *ballets d'action,* he sometimes loses her. In *Giselle,* for example, like "This Heart of Mine," a man with duplicitous intentions yearns for an idealized woman and is reformed by her, but ultimately loses her to death. Astaire—and his colleagues like Kelly—is always successful, but only after a long and obstacle-ridden chase.

In the first section, the thief attempts to ingratiate himself with his "victim" by singing to her. (The first verse of the song "This Heart of Mine.") For a good portion of the song, the woman sits on a bench placed on the edge of a semicircular expanse of open floor while her would-be seducer leans over her. As he sings, she listens quietly and gravely; she seems receptive but not actively responsive to his musical advances.

During the song's second verse (played simply and straightforwardly by orchestra alone) he draws her into dance—a dance based, as will be the entire sequence, on the theme of turning and circling. Although their hands touch as she allows herself to be turned continuously under his arm and he, in turn, circles her, their bodies rarely make contact. During this first section, the camera remains fairly still, framing them, for the most part, from the front to let us absorb the song and the choreographer's initial dance statement. The second section introduces a variation for dancers, camera, and orchestra. The song is repeated in a fuller and more expansive orchestration, and a prominent countermelody is introduced by the strings as the woman, as if to rebuff her would-be seducer or, at least, to distance herself from his advances, turns away from him (and the camera) and moves to a higher level of the set—a sort of embankment that borders the floor on which they have been dancing. Undeterred, Astaire and the camera (which seems to sail through space) follow her. In an audacious visual gesture, the woman, standing motionless, glides along on a slowly moving track, while the man, in pursuit, dances after then around her—the mobile camera paralleling his movements.

The third section, in which the dancers return to the "ground" level of the set and the woman signals her willingness to respond to the thief's advances, introduces another layer of musical and visual activity. As Astaire and Bremer pose quietly at its center (his body framing hers), the floor begins revolving slowly counterclockwise while the camera, moving clockwise, glides slowly up and back. At the same time, dreamlike immobile couples enter the frame, posed on the rim of the moving floor as a chorus of voices is added to the musical accompaniment. The couples lean against stylized, bare-branched trees forming a decorative, surrealistic bracelet around the couple enclosed in their center. When the camera pauses at its highest point, the couples become active, circling the trees against which each leans.

The fourth and final section sets all forces in motion again. The dance seduction completed, the camera and dancers are given their grandest and most expansive gestures. The corps of dancers (and trees) glides magically to the second level of the set, where they form a continually moving backdrop for Astaire and Bremer, who are now alone on the still revolving circular space. The choreographed pursuit-rebuff tactics played out in the initial stages of the dance now abandoned, the couple circle this space faster and faster, their new relationship graphically illustrated by the configuration of their bodies: as they waltz, she leans back trustingly in his arms and extends her own, like wings. The camera rests quietly at the far end of the set as the constantly turning couple dance on a collision course with it. Finally, just before they meet it—and in the grandest visual gesture of all—they seem to set the camera in motion. The camera now sweeps on a diagonal up to the set's second level, riding on the nine repeated notes of the song's third line—the pedal point effect created by their repetition seeming to support the camera. The final shot of the sequence gives us a view of the entire set head-on with its several layers of movement. Then, the dance-seduction completed, the couple turn and stroll away from us toward the stylized shell of the ballroom—of course, circular—at the back of the set. This shell adds a last layer of movement as it glides slowly open, like a dollhouse, to receive them. In a brief choreographed mime sequence, Bremer openly hands him her jewels. (She's been on to him all along.) Astonished and ashamed, he runs to her arms.

"This Heart of Mine" set a new style in production numbers at MGM by turning away from the lavish, often heavy-handed spectacles of the Busby Berkeley and *Broadway Melody* films of the 1930s. Instead, Minnelli offers some of the fantastic effects expected in the film musical genre within a more intimate and dramatically coherent framework. The impact of Minnelli's "quieter" spectacles comes not from the piling up of ever more lavish sets, costumes, and visual effects but in how dance, decor, music, and camera work are coordinated to play out the stylized drama of seduction at its core. Thus while Berkeley, the major promoter of the moving camera during sound cinema's first decade, influenced Minnelli in a general way, he cannot be seen as a primary influence on the young director. As Minnelli has stated bluntly: "Berkeley's large scale spectacles never moved me."[3]

"LIMEHOUSE BLUES": CHOREOGRAPHING COLOR AND LIGHT

The "Limehouse Blues" segment of *Follies* takes the new dance-drama form even further. It introduces the fantastic, dreamlike settings and dramatic lighting and color effects that, coordinated with music, would become a major characteristic of the dance-dramas of Minnelli's subsequent films. As its title implies, the setting for the sequence is London's Limehouse district at the beginning of the century—as visualized, however, by the director in a highly personal and stylized way.

Making use of his eclectic clipping file and book collection, as well as at least one other previous film, Minnelli drew from a wide variety of visual sources to form his final vision. The song "Limehouse Blues," originally performed by Gertrude Lawrence in *Charlot's Revue* (1924), was inspired by D. W. Griffith's *Broken Blossoms* (1919). Taking his cue from that film, Minnelli evokes the melancholy mood and dreamlike atmosphere of Griffith's remarkable wharf scenes by creating around his character a fog-suffused ambiance that rivals that created by his predecessors and can be seen in part as a visual homage to Griffith.[4] (Astaire may have also been influenced by *Broken Blos-*

soms; his portrayal of the dance-drama's Chinese protagonist—his walk, stance, and facial expressions—parallel closely Richard Barthelmess's sensitive portrayal of a similar character in the Griffith film—although I know of no definite proof that he studied, or even saw, *Broken Blossoms* before this sequence was shot.)

Although Griffith may be a major influence, the "Limehouse Blues" sequence may also reflect the influence of one of Minnelli's favorite artists, James McNeill Whistler. E. R. and J. Pennell's biography of Whistler[5] was the first study of an artist that the young Minnelli ever read, and its impact on him was immediate and powerful. Minnelli especially "related to his [Whistler's] penchant for titling his paintings with musical terms," and he took special delight in Whistler's "affinity for yellow."[6] It may be, then, that the fog effects created in the first section of the "Limehouse Blues" sequence are related to those Whistler paintings with musical titles (e.g., the *Nocturnes*) in which London night and fog effects are captured on canvas. And, most certainly, the beautiful, warm yellow space of the central section of "Limehouse Blues" derives ultimately from Minnelli's interest in Whistler's use of yellow.

Another visual source for this dance-drama (the scenes set in Limehouse) is what Minnelli calls "old English mezzotints."[7] To suggest their quality, he deliberately limited the colors of the costumes and sets to black, brown, and shades of yellow, filled the stage with fog and lit it with yellow light. The idea was not only to suggest the somber ambiance of the slum area Limehouse district but also to provide a dramatic contrast between this and the second section of the ballet in which the Chinese man hallucinates an encounter with his beloved. For this section Minnelli drew on another visual source—eighteenth-century French chinoiserie.

In line with Minnelli's predilection for introducing characters enmeshed in their environment, the camera only finds Astaire, the dance-drama's central character, after first gliding down the street on which much of the action will take place. In its journey along the pale brownish yellow mist-shrouded road at the end of which the dancer stands, it gives us a look not only at the stylized, weathered architecture of the Limehouse district but also at its equally weathered inhabitants: an old woman who trundles a baby carriage in which a phonograph incongruously sits, and a group of drunks who clown and dance in front of a basement café. Through the café windows we see, surrounded by soft, smoke-suffused light, a young singer. She begins the song "Limehouse Blues." It is only then that the camera "discovers" Astaire, the "Chinese man," standing to the side of the window watching the drinkers' antics.

In the sequence that follows, Astaire plays out, in mime and dance, a fantasy romance distantly related to that played out in *Broken Blossoms*.[8] Like the Barthlemess character in the Griffith film, the Chinese man admires, from a distance, a woman with whom he is able to consummate a relationship only in dreams. We meet the woman when she pauses near Astaire to watch some costermongers ("pearlies") perform (their multiple rows of white buttons flash through the mist). After a few minutes, when she moves down the street, Astaire and the camera trail her, pausing only when she stops in front of a store window to admire a prominently displayed fan. When she passes on, Astaire, followed by the camera, enters the shop and inquires, in mime, the price of the fan. Clearly unable to afford it, he nonetheless fingers it admiringly as, through the shop window, we see a group of thugs suddenly smash the window glass and snatch some objects from the display case. Police in the street respond with gunfire and Astaire is inadvertently shot.

Amid a hail of broken glass, he tumbles to the ground dropping the golden yellow fan. The camera drops to the floor with him, gliding in to a close up of his hand as he reaches out toward the now bloodstained fan lying just beyond his reach. This image slowly dissolves and we enter the wounded man's delirious dream. The camera frames the fan from above as it floats in deep shadow among a cluster of seemingly weightless, gold and blue, lily-pad-like objects that, as the shadows gradually lighten, are revealed to be hats worn by figures that press around Astaire, who now stands erect and is dressed in deep red. The drifting boom camera continues to frame the dancer from above as he reaches again and again for the fan that floats just beyond his reach. Most of the set, at this point, is bathed in deep shadow; the hats and hands appear, for the most part, disembodied. Gradually, however, the lighting reveals that the fan is being held by Astaire's fantasy beloved.

The sudden appearance of several elaborately masked and fantastically costumed figures who emerge from the shadows to confront the dancer heralds a change in music, lighting, camera activity, and dramatic action. Astaire pushes through them and, at last, is able to grasp the hand of the woman he has followed. As if to express his joy and excitement, the set is suddenly illuminated, the music swells in volume, and the camera arcs back and up to reveal, now bathed in brilliant light, a deep, expansive yellow-orange "space" (it has no boundaries to indicate the joining of floor and wall) on which are arranged at intervals a series of silver-gray constructions around which groups of figures, costumed also in gray, are arranged. In configuration, these freestanding constructions, or sculptural forms, suggest those stylized architectural groupings (bridges, pagodas) and figures found in French chinoiserie.

We're in another world created by the delirious man's hallucinatory image of the fan where Astaire and Bremer, newly clothed in fantastic red garb, dance together at last.

The overall coloring of the first section of the Limehouse drama, while subtle and variegated has been deliberately subdued, as has been the musical accompaniment. Now, as the set is flooded with brilliant contrasting colors and light, the orchestration changes dramatically from soft, low winds and strings to a fuller orchestral palette—bringing in brass, chimes, and percussion effects—the contrast between the fantasy world of the Chinese man and his drab existence is visually and musically emphasized. The precise coordination of light, color, and the volume, texture, and timbre of sound to emphasize a dramatic moment in the dance will become a hallmark of Minnelli's dance-dramas. As Minnelli, justly proud, explains: "We accomplished this by first lighting the set. The black shields—what the industry knows as 'gobos'—were placed in front of the lights. At a synchronized count, the shields were removed to unveil the lighted set."[9]

At the dance's conclusion, gold and blue fans blot out the dancers and cover the screen space. In a slow dissolve, the variegated pattern of blue and gold resolves gradually to an image of Astaire's hand and we are returned to the Limehouse setting. The camera pulls back to reveal that the wounded man now lies stretched out on a bench in the middle ground of the screen, framed by the shattered glass storefront window immediately behind him. After first passing by this window, his fantasy-beloved, now escorted by a wealthy admirer, enters the shop. Unaware of the wounded man whose eyes follow her every move, she picks up the fan she had earlier admired, then drops it in horror when she realizes that it is dotted with blood. She quickly leaves the shop, and the camera, following the direction of the wounded man's eyes and as if fulfilling his bidding, glides suddenly up and out of the shattered window after her. On its way down the street, the camera again passes the basement cafe in which the singer who opened the sequence now completes her song as fog gradually covers the screen.

YOLANDA AND THE THIEF: MINNELLI, SURREALISM, FREUD, AND THE DREAM BALLET

The ballet in *Yolanda and the Thief* builds on the *Follies* ballet techniques, Minnelli working once again with Astaire and Bremer. It expands the theme first explored in "This Heart of Mine" into a full-length movie: a con man falls in love with his victim, a young heiress, but this time the setting is the mythical Latin American country of Patria, whose richest citizen, Yolanda Aquaviva (again Bremer), is targeted by American Johnny Riggs, and the film ballet at its core is integrated into the dramatic fabric of this story.

By the time of *Yolanda,* the trend set in motion by Minnelli and Balanchine in their *Ziegfeld Follies* ballets was in full swing on Broadway. Agnes de Mille's ballet sequence in *Oklahoma!* (1943) had arrived rather late on the scene, but like Minnelli's *American in Paris* in film—it became the most prominent example of the era—with the result that, as Stephen Sondheim has said, "you couldn't put on a show in the forties without a hallucinatory ballet."[10]

As Sondheim suggests, the ballet was often presented within the context of a dream (either day or night) imagined and expressed by a dance within a fantasy setting. Dream and "vision" sequences had been a standard part of the nineteenth-century *ballet d'action.* In the integrated musical, as in the *ballet d'action,* the device of the dream allowed the introduction of colorful, fantastic, and surreal elements, varied and elaborate dances, and, in the case of film, interesting and fantastical cinematic effects, without violating the relatively rational nature of the plot and logical behavior of the protagonists. The dream ballets in *Yolanda and the Thief* fit into this model—as did the dream section of "Limehouse Blues."

The dream dance-drama form in *Yolanda* also reflects a peak of popular interest in Freudian theory and its technique of psychoanalysis that used dream interpretation as a key analytical tool for understanding human behavior. Although Freud's *Interpretation of Dreams* was first published in Europe in 1900, it wasn't until the late 1920s that his theory was really popularized in the United States and Freudian terminology began to enter the vocabulary of American writers and artists. Minnelli, like many of his colleagues in film and musical theater, used the concept of dream interpretation as a dramatic device to show the inner conflicts of his characters. He and Balanchine used it in the dream sequence of "Five A.M." in *Ziegfeld Follies of 1936,* just as he would use it with Astaire and Eugene Loring to show Johnny Riggs's ambivalent feelings about Yolanda when his growing attraction to the young heiress conflicts with his desire to steal her money.

Minnelli's interest in the dream state was also linked to his discovery of the surrealist artists who shared Freud's fascination with dreams and dream imagery—and who showed him a new way of organizing theatrical space.[11] In 1932, during his second year in New York, works of the precursor surrealist painter Giorgio de Chirico, as well as Salvador Dalí, Max Ernst, André Masson, and

Joan Miró, were displayed at the Julien Levy Gallery in the first major surrealist group exhibition in New York. In November of 1934, Dalí made his first trip to the United States, in connection with an exhibition of his works at the Levy Gallery in November and December of that year.

Minnelli's response to surrealist imagery (to the works of de Chirico, in particular) and his attempt to translate it into theatrical terms, can first be seen in a rough, preparatory sketch for a set of the musical *At Home Abroad* that opened at the Winter Garden Theater on September 19, 1935.[12] In the sketch, a sweep of almost empty stage is bounded on the left by an arcade that, in configuration and placement, suggests similar forms in works of de Chirico, and on the right by another de Chirico–like motif—a disembodied classical head. Punctuating the stage space at wide intervals are three figures that, like many of de Chirico's figures, cast elongated shadows.[13] Surrealist imagery made another appearance in *Ziegfeld Follies of 1936* in "Words without Music," which Minnelli proudly proclaimed "the first 'Surrealist ballet' on Broadway."[14] Minnelli's brief description of this dance sequence in his autobiography does not allow us to reconstruct its look, but does suggest that the motif of the cast shadows (designed by him) may have reappeared, now animated by Balanchine: Three dancing figures in green are seen at the opening, standing at the top of a ramp that angled down toward the audience. Three black-clad figures, lying at an angle from the dancers, suggest their shadows and repeat the dancers' movements from their prone positions.[15]

Surrealist imagery also appears in the brief section titled "Beauty" in *Ziegfeld Follies*. But it is in the *Yolanda and the Thief* dream ballet that we find his most ambitious use of surrealist imagery to further plot and convey character relationships and to create a vast and seemingly limitless "dreamscape" on which his characters will dance. Boundaries between "floor" and "walls" are blurred or obscured. Punctuating the space are fantastic rock shapes, from which protrude stylized bare branches. The space itself opens up unlimited possibilities for the movement of the sweeping camera boom. It completely undermines the proscenium stage orientation of the theater, and it gives the dancers more space in which to move—room for exciting new choreographic possibilities. The expanse of seemingly limitless space created on film in the central section of *Yolanda*'s "ballet" is clearly the influence of both Dalí and de Chirico. The use of rock formations and their placement suggest the influence of Dalí and, perhaps, Yves Tanguy. The frozen figures that Minnelli places at intervals throughout the vast screen space may also be derived, in part, from the director's viewing of certain surrealist paintings: these still and sober figures, strangely withdrawn from one another and their surroundings, suggest similarly isolated figures in works of René Magritte and Paul Delvaux. To these possible visual sources, however, may also be added another—unrelated to surrealist imagery, but closely linked to *Yolanda*'s Latin American setting: Minnelli says that the undulating outline of the rock formations were meant to suggest South American baroque architecture.[16] It is important to note, though, that all of the dance takes place framed by, in opposition to, and firmly placed within the decor. This includes floor shapes as well. In the *Yolanda* "ballet," the floor is not completely flat but variegated in level—its gentle hills and valleys enter forcefully into the filming of the dance; at one point, for example, the dancers stroll up one side of a small incline, the camera starts at the other, and the two meet on the top of the "hill."

Another of Minnelli's characteristic formal devices is the use of actors as elements of the decor. Arranged in groups as *tableaux vivants,* or as solitary figures who are decoratively placed much like other elements of scenery, these frozen figures dot the surrealistic rock formations during the "horse race" sequence in *Yolanda,* and punctuate the landscape during the final pas de deux. Some, like the cigar smoking "guardian angel" figure, serve a symbolic as well as decorative function. They stand at the beginning of a long line of such images in Minnelli, culminating in the elaborate *tableaux vivants* of the *American in Paris* ballet. In a looser way, they also relate to the semi-immobile figures that dot the Bois de Boulogne in the establishing sequence of *Gigi,* and dramatically freeze to form a framework for Gigi's entrance in the climactic Maxim's sequence of that film.

THE PIRATE: MINNELLI AND KELLY

Although Kelly had worked briefly with Minnelli on a segment of *Ziegfeld Follies,* it was *The Pirate* that gave him his first chance to work extensively with the director whose *Meet Me in St. Louis* he had so admired. The relationship between Minnelli and Kelly was to be important for both men: each would profoundly influence the other's style. From the very beginning, the two worked well together. Instead of causing friction, their contrasting temperaments—Minnelli, introverted and reticent, Kelly extroverted and gregarious—seemed to complement each other. And they had more important things in common: both were committed to the concept of the integrated, cinematic musical. Both were on the lookout for new and distinctive ways to interweave dance, music, dialogue, and camera work, and both were perfectionists willing, even eager, to work painstakingly hour after hour to capture a desired effect on film. "Working with Gene was wonderful . . . wonderful," Minnelli later said with his hesitant, quiet fervor. "He understood what I wanted to say without my having to say it. He was as crazy about work as I was. We'd work at the studio all day, then go home and spend the evenings together working."[17]

As this statement indicates, Kelly—his appetite whetted by his work with Donen on the dance sequences in *Cover Girl, Anchors Aweigh,* and *Living in a Big Way*—came in *The Pirate* to take an increasing interest in the direction of the film as a whole. Although in the end it is clearly Minnelli's hand at the helm, Kelly and Minnelli were more to each other than just actor and director. As one would expect, Minnelli had Kelly participate in the planning and filming of *The Pirate*'s dance sequences, but he drew Kelly into other areas as well. His experience on *The Pirate* would thus provide for Kelly an insight into the mind and working habits of a young master director.

Director and dancer conceived of *The Pirate* as an affectionate but tongue-in-cheek tribute to both silent and sound "swashbuckler" movies, presented in the form of, as Minnelli put it, "a fantasy, . . . flamboyant, swirling, and larger than life."[18] The role of Serafin, the strolling player who disguises himself as Macoco the Pirate to impress the girl whom, during the course of the film, he courts and wins, was patterned after the great screen romantic heroes. A ham actor and braggadocio whose boyish and vulnerable nature lies just beneath the surface, Serafin was a role that took unique advantage of both Kelly's strengths and weaknesses as a performer. It allowed him to legitimately overplay and legitimately incorporate the stunt-filled, "athletic" dance gestures of which he was so fond into his dance characterizations— characterizations that translated hair-raising feats of physical daring into dance terms.

The most immediately noticeable of Minnelli's contributions to Kelly's style is the arresting visual framework that he provides for the dancer's movements. Following in the tradition of the beautifully lit and photographed dance-drama sequences for Astaire in *Yolanda and the Thief* and, especially, the "Limehouse Blues" sequence in *Ziegfeld Follies,* Minnelli in *The Pirate* surrounded Kelly with the most gorgeous, visually impressive environment within which he had yet danced. In terms of its color and imagery alone, *The Pirate* is one of the most beautiful movies of the era. Working with cinematographer Harry Stradling, whose luminous lighting he had first admired in

Jacques Feyder's *La kermesse héroïque*,[19] Minnelli discovers and coaxes from Technicolor film a palette of colors that, in addition to deep, luminous blacks and snowy whites, consists of a remarkably wide range of colors drawn from the pirate's treasure chest and the sea upon which he sails. One thinks, for example, of Manuela's soft coral dress and jewelry over which torchlight flickers in the hanging sequence, the violet lining of Serafin's cape that he cunningly manipulates like bat's wings to form a dramatic framework for his actions, the visually thrilling jumble of jewels (rubies, pearls, coral, turquoise, opals, emeralds, and sapphires) in the pirate's treasure chest over which Minnelli's camera lovingly lingers in the hanging sequence.

Just as Minnelli's color and lighting effects add a new dimension to Kelly's performance, so, too, does his camera work add another layer of interest to the dancer's street and courtship dances. In *Cover Girl*, Kelly and Stanley Donen's use of the moving camera was, in comparison to Minnelli's, restricted—especially in height. Although a gliding boom is occasionally used, as in the center and final sections of the Olivera Street sequence of *Anchors Aweigh*, it is not used continuously—nor with the ease, fluidity, and expansiveness with which Minnelli had employed it in *Meet Me in St. Louis*, *Ziegfeld Follies*, or *Yolanda*. Before *The Pirate*, Kelly and Donen had depended more on the editing together of separately angled shots filmed by a more or less static camera than on the active boom camera as ways to impart a sense of cinematic movement to their dance sequences. Minnelli and Kelly's collaboration now resulted in a new repertoire of moving boom shots and camera angles to capture Kelly's dance sequences.

Finally, in *The Pirate* Minnelli offered Kelly—really for the first time—a coherent, tightly structured musical and dramatic framework within which to integrate those dance forms that he had developed in his previous musicals. In *Cover Girl*, *Anchors Aweigh*, and *Living in a Big Way*, Kelly and Donen's imaginative and cinematically innovative dance sequences had functioned as "oases" in the midst of sprawling, loosely organized narratives in which music, dance, plot, and camera work were sometimes only tenuously related. In *The Pirate*, Kelly's street and courtship dances were planned by the director and dancer to fit seamlessly into a whole that, like *Meet Me in St. Louis*, came close to Minnelli's ideal of a movie in which all elements of the form were fully integrated. How, we need to ask, did Minnelli's camera work, decor, and lighting work to enhance the impact of Kelly's dances?

The Pirate's film and dance-drama blends ideas from both Minnelli and Kelly's previous films—the dream sequence in *Yolanda* and Kelly's "balcony dance" in *Anchors Aweigh*. Like the former, it is set within the context of a dream that provides an insight into the thoughts and hidden desires of the dreamer and, like the latter, it serves as the hero's seduction and courtship dance. There are other important influences too, like the virtuoso male dancer roles from the nineteenth-century *ballets d'action Raymonda, Le corsaire,* and countless others. Kelly, as Serafin, thrills the watching heroine Manuela (Judy Garland) with his virtuosity as a performer. Here Kelly also combines the swashbuckling athleticism of one of his idols, Douglas Fairbanks, with a Fokine dance model—a Diaghilev ballet in which one of his own teachers, Adolph Bolm, first made his reputation ("The Polovetsian Dances").

In an attempt to impress Manuela, and to prevent her arranged marriage, Serafin has lied and told Manuela that *he* is Macoco the Pirate. She watches from her balcony as he dances for her benefit in the square below. In her imagination, he is transformed into an archetypal pirate and it is *her* fantasy, her daydream, that we see enacted on the screen. The sequence burlesques her adolescent vision of Macoco: swinging his gleaming cutlass wildly, as her hero, drawing on the stunning vocabulary of the male dances with which Fokine thrilled Parisian audiences. There are huge leaps and barrel turns with ever increasing speed as Kelly wields his sword to ruthlessly cut down his enemies, scales masts seemingly hundreds of feet high, and plunges his muscular arms into piles of jewels. The expansive dance area is bathed in a dark, almost blackish, red glow—this "dreamscape" fitfully illuminated by intermittent explosions of bright white smoke and orange flames. Shadowy forms at the back of the set suggest razed buildings, and there is a tall mast for Kelly to swing up.

Lighting, decor, camera work, music, and choreography participate equally in this film dance-drama. Lighting plays a particularly interesting role. Like *The Pirate*'s dance, the lighting is "virtuosic," going well beyond even the impressive lighting effects in the *Yolanda* dance dream sequence. The great explosions of smoke and flame, varied in size and shape, are carefully choreographed into the dance. Their sound is written as well into Conrad Salinger's witty arrangement of "Mack the Black"—itself an affectionate tribute to adventure movie music and Fokine's Rimsky-Korsakov and Ippolitov-Ivanov ballets. Coordinated with the movements of the pirate and his men, these explosions make this "ballet" an almost abstract sequence of moving colored light and shadow, illuminating the screen now blindingly, with brilliant orange light, now with deeper reds and smoky whites.

Minnelli's mobile camera transports us freely through a space that—as in the *Yolanda* dream sequence—seems almost limitless. We view the action from multiple angles: from below, then high above as the pirate swings up the mast of a shadowy, phantom ship—the daring of his ride emphasized by the exaggeratedly low angle from which we view him. This camera angle is new to Technicolor film and made possible by the "Ubangi" camera device developed by the MGM camera department in conjunction with Kelly, in response to Kelly and Minnelli's needs for this particular sequence. This device was an adjustable mirrored lip that extended, only a few inches from the floor, from the bottom of the large Technicolor camera. The mirror could be adjusted to reflect the subject at the angle desired by the director, and the camera then shot "down" into the mirror.[20] The integration of all elements of form in this sequence shows how intimate was the collaboration between its director and central performer. It displays their like-minded approach both to film dance in general and to the film dance-drama in particular.

This unity of vision of director and choreographer distinguishes, in an important respect, *The Pirate*'s dream sequence from its predecessor in *Yolanda and the Thief*. In *Yolanda*, Astaire, moving away from much of his work in the 1930s, had "allowed" Minnelli's moving camera to participate in his dance. Still, *Yolanda*'s central pas de deux is a discrete unit, separable from the movement of the camera that frames it and tied to the floor on which it is performed. It could, with only minor changes, be performed framed by a proscenium arch and still retain its interest. Although, in broad outline, *Yolanda*'s dance plays out a drama of seduction, that drama is a general one—with slight modification the dance could be incorporated into any one of a number of Astaire films. Kelly's "dance" is absolutely inseparable from the camera work he and Minnelli planned, and removing it from the context of *The Pirate* and stringing it together without the camera work would make it an essentially meaningless and formally unrelated series of movements

THE DANCE-DRAMA TO END ALL DANCE-DRAMAS: *AN AMERICAN IN PARIS*

The ascendancy of the choreographer jump-started by Balanchine with Minnelli is most widely popularized in the opening credits of *An American in Paris:* "Choreography by Gene Kelly," using the term that Balanchine first insisted on in his credits for his *Ziegfeld Follies* ballets with Minnelli. By 1950, the Russian dancer émigrés had been pretty much assimilated into the American dance world: Balanchine's company had a permanent home at City Center and his School of American Ballet had produced the first generation of American ballet dancers. American choreographers Martha Graham and Doris Humphrey, building on the innovations of their compatriots Isadora Duncan, Ruth St. Denis, and Ted Shawn, had pioneered modern dance, and had become as celebrated as their counterparts from the world of Russian ballet.

Listed in the opening credit sequence as the "American in Paris Ballet," the seventeen-minute dance-drama that follows climaxes the series of dance-dramas in both Minnelli's and Kelly's films. It is the longest and most elaborate in the series.[21] Like the rest of *An American in Paris,* the "ballet" blends ideas from both director and star: Minnelli creates an elaborate and colorful framework for a dance-drama that, in choreographic style, is distinctively Kelly's.

Dramatically, this dance-drama has multiple meanings. Like its predecessors in *Yolanda,* it is a dream sequence (in this case, something closer to a daydream or fantasy projection) that serves as a dance character portrait of its male protagonist. It reveals Jerry Mulligan's emotional state by recapitulating his relationship with Lise. During the sequence, Jerry meets Lise, "courts" her, and "loses" her. The ballet is also a visual and musical homage to Paris, as inspiration for Jerry and his fellow artists. Like New York in *On the Town* and St. Louis in *Meet Me in St. Louis* it is a major character. The woman (Leslie Caron) the dancer chases through the city streets, like Ivy in *On the Town* and Yolanda in *Yolanda and the Thief,* has her origins in ballet that extend back to and before the nineteenth century. She is his ideal—his muse. This is symbolized visually in the ballet's opening moments. Jerry, dressed in black, is seen standing within the space of his black-and-white sketch. On the ground in front of him is a rose that has been associated with Lise earlier in the film—the red rose is the only spot of color in the frame. Jerry leans over, picks it up, and his sketch is suddenly flooded with color.

Visually, the ballet repeats (in a more elaborate format) ideas from Minnelli's previous film dance-drama sequences: the expansive, dreamlike space, the freewheeling mobile boom camera (more active than ever before), and the delineation and dramatization of each section by contrasted colored lighting. The color and lighting effects are subtler, varied, and more impressive than in any of the previous Minnelli "ballets," and they make this film a landmark in color cinema. The ballet's sequences that take place on the set modeled on the Place de la Concorde are a good example of these virtuoso colored lighting effects, and also of how carefully coordinated they are with the music and camera movement. As the camera swoops and sails around them, the dancers move through clouds of mist that change continually in color and light quality in response to their movements. At the peak of a musical phrase, for example, Lise is raised aloft by Jerry. In response to the movement of her upraised arms and body, the light changes from soft blue to blinding white. Soon after, an arc described by her leg throws a blanket of rose over the set.

Transitions from one set (or section) of the dance-drama to another are made by light changes coordinated with camera movement and music—some quite ingenious and without precedent (to my knowledge) in films: at the end of the section just described, for example, a shaft of light picks out Jerry and Lise in silhouette; as the music softens and slows to conclude this section, the camera, starting in a medium close shot, glides back and up at a forty-five degree angle as they slowly lift their arms. At the peak of their gesture, when the camera is at its highest point—and paralleling a musical "exclamation point"—a brilliant yellow light suddenly illuminates the set and, as if by magic, we see the dancers dressed in completely different costumes within an entirely new setting, the Place de l'Opéra.

The sets and costumes of this dance-drama are the embodiment of Minnelli's theories about the expressionistic, personality-revealing function of decor. They also give him a chance to pay his own visual homage to some of the artists he loves. Each set, representing a different section of Paris, is meant to suggest, in style and imagery, the work of an artist whom Gerry admires: the Place de la Concorde (Raoul Dufy); a flower market (Pierre-Auguste Renoir and Edouard Manet); a street in Montmartre (Maurice Utrillo); a carnival, zoo, and park (Henri Rousseau); the Place de l'Opéra (Vincent van Gogh); a cabaret interior (Henri de Toulouse-Lautrec); and overall, in its variety of beautiful color effects, Claude Monet. Works of each artist are not precisely re-created; as Minnelli makes clear, "We didn't want to copy, just evoke."[22] As in previous Minnelli dance-dramas, actors arranged in *tableaux vivants* are a crucial part of this decor, lit and costumed to suggest representative images from the oeuvre of each painter.

Choreographically, Kelly's character dancing is carefully integrated with decor and camera movement. As in *The Pirate*'s ballet, his choreographed movement functions more to create a series of dramatic, cinematic images than a dance performance, per se. Again as in *The Pirate*'s dance-drama, there are few pure dance sequences. Rather, a great deal of running and posturing takes place within the elaborate decor. In the only extended dance sequence, one of Kelly's favorite images reappears: three dancers dressed as GI's (their uniforms enlivened by clearly visible brushstrokes painted directly on their uniforms by Sharaff) join Jerry in a dance that, in feeling, recalls sequences from *On the Town* and *Anchors Aweigh*. As Kelly explained, these musical military "buddies" are used to suggest the particularly American qualities of the "American" in Paris. Their vernacular dance style (tap) and the Cohan strut (an idiosyncratic, stiff-legged walk associated with George M. Cohan) that they employ are contrasted with the pointe work of Lise and her friends to symbolize the difference between the two different worlds (old and new) from which the lovers come. When Lise and her corps adopt the "strut" in the dance's final section, it is a dance symbol for their union with the Americans.

Kelly's other dance ideas come directly from the works of artists to which the dance-drama pays tribute. The stylized profile pose (one arm upraised) of the cabaret dancer called "Chocolat" in Toulouse-Lautrec's drawing of this performer, is used as the initial gesture of a dance tribute to this artist; Lise, costumed as the dancer Jane Avril as portrayed by Toulouse-Lautrec in his poster for the *Jardin de Paris* (1893), dances Kelly's re-creation of a cancan for an audience composed of figures drawn from Toulouse-Lautrec's oeuvre and arranged in *tableaux vivants* (Oscar Wilde, Aristide Bruant, Yvette Guilbert, May Milton, and Louise Weber–La Goulue). These figures are arranged in an odd-angled composition that can be seen as derived, in general configuration, from Toulouse-Lautrec's *Au Moulin Rouge*. In the major shot of the sequence, an actress made up to resemble the face of a similar female figure in this work is illuminated dramatically from below by a green light, and is cut off laterally by the edge of the frame, paralleling the lighting effects and composition of this painting.

Following *An American in Paris,* the film ballet would become a standard element not only in MGM musicals but also in those produced by other studios resulting in self-consciously "artistic" film "ballets" in the film musicals of the 1950s. The Kelly and Donen team's last effort as such would appear in the next film in the Freed unit series, *Singin' in the Rain* in which Kelly and Donen, building on Kelly's experience in the *American in Paris* segment, employ the moving more expansively than ever before—especially in the "Broadway" ballet. Kelly would go on to make an all dance film, *Invitation to the Dance*. For Minnelli, however, the "American in Paris Ballet" marked the beginning of the end of the tradition that they had brought to fruition. After this film Minnelli would incorporate only one more film ballet into his musicals, in *The Band Wagon*. But this film, for all of its brilliance, is also clearly a satirical look at the innovations in film dance that Minnelli (and Kelly–Donen) had developed over the past two decades.

It was really the end of the dancer's musical and the ciné-ballet. Nonetheless the influences of the film ballet reverberate through film (and video) history—not only in the film musicals of Bob Fosse and more recent directors Baz Luhrmann and Rob Marshall, but also in the videos and digital imagery of the MTV generation—and its most innovative directors and dancers. One thing has been left behind, however. The "dancer centered" view espoused by Astaire, Kelly, and Donen has been abandoned. The core of the "dance" now is rhythmic editing. But that is the subject of another essay.

Notes

1. First a note about terminology: In 2006 we use the term *ballet* mostly to describe a work performed by dancers trained in the *danse d'école*—the vocabulary employed in the French and Italian courts during the fifteenth century and eventually codified under Louis the 14th by the Academie Royale de la Danse (1666) that evolved into a theatrical dance form, that, beginning in the nineteenth century added dancing "en pointe" to its already well developed repertory of steps. But ballet's original meaning was simply a dance and *ballet d'action*, a dance that told a story. All those who choreographed ballets on Broadway and in film did not *always* use the steps of the danse d'école or dancers trained in it, but it was a reasonable term for them to apply—and they used it regularly. In this essay, I will use the term *ballet* the way *they* meant it. For purposes of variety I will also use the term film *dance-drama* interchangeably, which I think is more descriptive of the actual form and may be clearer to today's readers.

2. "Balanchine: An Interview with Ivan Nabokov and Elizabeth Carmichael," *Horizon*, January 1961, 48.

3. Vincente Minnelli interviewed by John Russell Taylor on July 20, 1980, National Film Theatre of the British Film Institute, London.

4. Vincente Minnelli, with Hector Arce, *I Remember It Well* (Garden City, NY: Doubleday, 1974), 142–43, suggests the relationship to *Broken Blossoms*.

5. Joseph Pennell and Elizabeth R. Pennell, *The Life of James McNeill Whistler*, 5th. ed., rev. (Philadelphia: J. B. Lippincott, 1911).

6. Ibid.

7. This was a method of engraving popular in the seventeenth, eighteenth, and early nineteenth centuries, especially in England. Mezzotints were noted for their soft and hazy gradations of tone and their richness in the dark areas. See Howard Osborn, ed., *The Oxford Companion to Art* (Oxford: Oxford University Press, 1981), 716.

8. Minnelli, *I Remember It Well*, 143.

9. Ibid.

10. Stephen Sondheim used this phrase during the course of a program on musical theater produced by the British Broadcasting Corporation and broadcast in London on May 20, 1980.

11. Minnelli, *I Remember It Well*, 51. For Minnelli, as for many, the discovery of Freudian thought and surrealist art were linked events, part of the same general phenomenon. In Chicago, he wrote: "The world of art was already one step beyond, and even we in the provinces were taken up with the surreal. Freud was starting to penetrate the consciousness of the world. . . . Suddenly we were all interpreting dreams, and the talents of Duchamps, Ernst, and Dali burst wide open."

12. For an illustration of this sketch, see Joseph Andrew Casper, *Vincente Minnelli and the Film Musical* (New York: A. S. Barnes, 1977), 17. Lack of visual evidence and of any detailed description in reviews of this show makes it difficult to determine whether this set was actually included in the final production.

13. Minnelli's arcade relates, for example, to that found in the right foreground of de Chirico's *Melancholy and Mystery of a Street*, 1914 (private collection, illustration color plate 124, H. H. Arnason, *History of Modern Art* [New York: Harry N. Abrams, n.d.]); Minnelli's use of cast shadows in the sketch may also derive from this or similar sources. The disembodied head in Minnelli's sketch suggests that found in de Chirico's "The Song of Love," 1914 (private collection, illustration in William Rubin, *Dada, Surrealism, and Their Heritage* [New York: Museum of Modern Art, 1968], 77). By citing these paintings, I do not mean to imply that they are the direct sources for Minnelli's work, as we do not know which of de Chirico's paintings the director was able to see before 1935.

14. Program for the 1936 edition of the *Ziegfeld Follies* (Billy Rose Theater Collection, Library for the Performing Arts, Lincoln Center). Listed seventh on the program is the Balanchine-Minnelli number titled "Words without Music: A Surrealist Ballet."

15. Minnelli, *I Remember It Well*, 77.

16. Ibid., 156.

17. My interview (London, July 22, 1980). That Minnelli and Kelly's working relationship was important to Minnelli is indicated not only by these words, but also the manner in which he said them, which clearly conveyed the deep affection and respect that he held for his colleague.

18. Minnelli, *I Remember It Well*, 184.

19. Ibid., 114.

20. Called the "Ubangi" by its inventors, this device is described in Clive Hirschhorn, *Gene Kelly* (Chicago: Regnery, 1974), 163.

21. In addition to expanding the tradition of cinematic dance-drama founded by the Freed unit's own directors, an important factor in the decision to make such a long and elaborate ballet section was the striking success of the English film, *The Red Shoes* (1948), which contained at its core a lengthy "ballet" section. Interestingly enough, the "ballet" section of *The Red Shoes* may, to some extent, have been influenced by Minnelli's work on *Ziegfeld Follies* and *Yolanda,* which started the tradition that climaxed in the "American in Paris Ballet." For a further discussion of the impact of *The Red Shoes* on American audiences, see also my article on *The Red Shoes* in *The Thousand Eyes* (February 1976): 11–12.

22. Minnelli quoted in Hirschhorn, *Gene Kelly,* 201.

Queer Modernism
The Cinematic Aesthetic of Vincente Minnelli

DAVID A. GERSTNER

This essay follows through on James Naremore's important work on Vincente Minnelli and his study of the aesthetic and cultural movements in which Minnelli participated, especially in New York in the 1930s.[1] What I add here, however, is the queer inflection associated with these aesthetics that Minnelli imbibed and then carried to Hollywood. Although Minnelli married four times, had two children, and did not publicly identify himself as "gay," he certainly partook of a cultural milieu that was made up of a significant coterie of artists and critics whose aesthetic interests came to be marked as queer.

When Arthur Freed brought Minnelli to Hollywood in 1940 Minnelli's name didn't ring any bells at MGM, even though Minnelli brought with him an illustrious career as a theatrical director and costume and set designer from New York, In a memo to studio executive Eddie Mannix, Cedric Gibbons, supervisory art director at MGM, expressed his concerns over Minnelli's hiring. The letter is worth quoting in full as it sets the stage for the creative tensions that Minnelli consistently encountered with Gibbons. It frames, at the outset of Minnelli's arrival at the studio, an anxiety that cuts across not merely an individual's position in relation to the Hollywood studio but also an anxiety as it intersects with contemporaneous notions of creativity and, as we shall see, with industrial modernity within the studio system. On April 2, 1940, Gibbons writes:

> For your information we have signed Vincent Manelli [*sic*], a New York stage designer. This was done through Arthur Freed. In speaking to Arthur on Saturday he told me about this man and said he was engaged as a dance director. I said, "Nothing Else?" And he said, "for ideas on dance numbers and musical settings, etc." I am afraid Eddie, that this will probably be another Harkrider-Hobe-Irwin [*sic*]-Oliver-Messel[2] situation and if you remember you and I chatted at great length about this type of thing sometime ago—and I want to reiterate that I absolutely refuse to work under any conditions with any man designing settings unless he is brought through to me as a member of my department. The man may be the world's greatest genius. If he is, by all means give him my job. I find it tough enough as it is to work with the most sympathetic assistants I can secure. I do not feel that any of my men should take orders from anyone other than myself in the matter of set design, whether it be for musical numbers or the interiors of submarines. Do you think we need further experience in these expensive experiments? Not just the man's salary, but what he actually costs us. I, for one, had thought we had learned our lesson. Gibby[3]

Gibbons's sentiment toward Minnelli's arrival played itself out in a tension that underscored the relationship between Minnelli and the MGM Art Department for the next twenty years. At stake here was the way in which two men of modernist sensibilities struggled over the visual rendering of the burgeoning twentieth century. Minnelli's vision of modernity often worked at odds with that of Gibbons's. In fact, Minnelli has called the MGM Art Department "a medieval fiefdom, its overlord accustomed to doing things in a certain way . . . his own."[4]

Both Minnelli and Gibbons were strongly influenced by currents of the international modernist movement, and both were decidedly set in their creative ways: Minnelli was a modernist within a genealogy of Whistler, Diaghilev, and Poiret, while Gibbons was a modernist in the efficient mode of Le Corbusier, Sullivan, and Gropius. Minnelli looked to the paintings of Van Gogh, the impressionists, postimpressionists as well as the aesthetic/surrealist writings of Ronald Firbank and the fin de siècle sketches of Aubrey Beardsley.[5] He was an impeccable dandy/aesthete. He dressed, most often, in his favorite daffodil yellow blazer and black turtleneck. His home in Beverly Hills was filled with art books, novels, paintings, and sketches (his earlier New York apartment interiors were also notably absent of any "streamlined" design).[6] His bookshelves were lined with the art books of Duchamp, Dufy, Renoir, Dalí, Matisse, and the not so modern Caravaggio.[7] The writings of Flaubert, Baldwin, Bazin, and Freud lined his bedroom walls. The painting easel in his studio (overlooking his garden) always had a current work in process, just as his office desk always had the clutter of the research for his latest film project.

Gibbons's home, in contrast, sat at the edge of the California Pacific Rim in Santa Monica. Designed by Gibbons himself (with the MGM architect Douglas Honnold), it was considered the "ultimate Hollywood residence of the 1930s."[8] It embodied the cinematic in terms of the latest technology: "water sprinklers on the copper roof above . . . create the sound of rain, and a recessed light projector . . . [casts] the illusion of moonlight on a wall."[9] It was streamlined, white, and above all, "efficient." It is essential, writes Gibbons, that "the living room is as efficient as the kitchen and bathroom."[10]

Although this account of modernist creativity is simplified, it illustrates the palatable aesthetic tension Minnelli encountered upon his arrival. Gibbons's stress on the functional and efficient is clearly reinforced in his letter to Mannix. His concern with MGM's "expensive experiments" in his tightly run ship can only serve to disrupt the contained precision and functioning of his obliging (and obedient) department. His sense of ordered design and insistence on efficiency in business and creative design are hallmarks of a modernism flanked by the notion of utility and function. This efficiency shares an interesting relationship to the production and, if you will, the architecture of American masculinity in the twentieth century.[11] In effect, Minnelli's confrontation with Gibbons brought to bear the question of modernity's (not to mention Hollywood's) relationship to creativity and masculinity.

If the "efficient" architecture of the Bauhaus, Mies van der Rohe, and Le Corbusier were intended to unload the "effeminate" obstacles or "excess" that prohibited productive living, it was clearly in the service of allowing for a clean (and in keeping with the new era), functional and machinelike space, something to which Gibbons aspired. To de-historicize, for this modernist, meant to look forward because the historical carried the weight of a dead past that was found in such traditional mediums as architecture, furniture design, and the "realism" of Hollywood cinema.[12]

In fact, Gibbons, on the one hand, looked toward the day when "realism" could be abandoned from cinema so that "we may look for a setting which in itself will be as completely modern as is modern painting or sculpture."[13] As Peter Wollen remarks, "Modernism saw a teleology in the convergence of cubism with industrial techniques and materials and its development toward abstract art."[14] It is precisely the efficient modernist's aim to utilize the twentieth century's new technologies and machinations to rid the excess of everyday life so that "utility will supplant ornament."[15] Because ornament was viewed as effeminate, eliminating a decorative aesthetic reinforced a masculine, heterosexual art establishment. The virility of American creativity served to defend (male) artists from the charge of homosexuality. This rugged American cultural milieu found its apotheosis with the emergence of the American abstract artists after World War II until Andy Warhol ("the swish") challenged it in the 1960s.

Minnelli, on the other hand, arrived at MGM armed with an extravagant and flamboyant eye for excessive detail. The set designs for his films became as bright and colorful as his window displays in Chicago and his stage designs in New York.[16] While Minnelli often found himself at odds with Gibbons's art department, Minnelli emerged victorious from these creative conflicts. Living in New York for nearly ten years before coming to Hollywood provided Minnelli with the opportunity to participate within a coterie whose urbane and often chaotic demeanor was shaped in a landscape far removed from the nascent spaces of Los Angeles. Unlike Los Angeles's sprawling terrain, New York's frenetic energies, fomented in contained spaces, yielded a very different aesthetic expression. It is precisely Minnelli's immersion within the excessive place of New York that inundated and informed his later work in Hollywood cinema.

New York was also a pivotal site for the exploration of the terms for American masculinity. As many scholars have shown, men in New York during the 1920s and 1930s were confronted with complex social intersections where masculinity, "effeminacy," creativity, and homosexuality found peculiar and exciting possibilities in their cultural entanglements.[17] It is the brilliance (and tension) of this social and creative excess that Minnelli saw and experienced that informed the visual extravagance he brought to the stage and screen. This extravagance—this campy rendering of the historical world on stage and in film—might be said to be Minnelli's aestheticized laugh at efficient masculinist modernity:

> "It is a known fact that you are not a success on Broadway until legends spring up about you. Sometimes libelous, always exaggerated, these fantastic offsprings of envy and admiration are a mirror which reflects success. The Minnelli legends are legion."
>
> [Anonymous, Shubert press release, ca. 1936]

Indeed, Minnelli's creative atmosphere in New York was pressured within the conflicting historical discourses of American masculinity. It was a conflict that was long-standing and prescient for Minnelli. As Minnelli's fourth wife, Lee Minnelli, has pointed out, Vincente disliked the tough, jock sports "guy" and considered himself the Noël Coward type.[18] Minnelli's conflicted and sometimes peculiar concept of and relationship to masculinity established his ongoing creative reassessment of the contemporary scene of American gender and creativity.

MINNELLI'S MASCULINITY AND THE ARTS

Born in Chicago in 1903 but raised in the small Midwest town of Delaware, Ohio, Minnelli grew up in a Catholic French-Italian traveling theatrical family. At a young age, Chicago represented the bastion of nonprovinciality, and he soon set his sights on the urban promise of that city. While there, Minnelli worked as a window display designer at Marshall Field's department store. Known for their ornate and colorful window displays, Marshall Field's was a place where Minnelli encountered the new modernist art scene. His displays were usually of furniture, decorative accessories, and antiques. He considered his short stint as a photographer of stage celebrities dull and thought it not the medium with which he preferred to work. He attempted a brief (and failed) acting career, but most importantly he continued to sketch, draw, and paint—he would always claim painting as his first love. As his collection of work grew, he gained an entrepreneurial sense for himself and subsequently landed a job with Balaban and Katz designing costumes for their stage shows.

Minnelli first became aware of, and took great interest in, the fauves, the impressionists, and the surrealists (a movement that would have great import for his early work in Hollywood) through the Art Institute of Chicago. The works of Matisse, Duchamp, Ernst, and Dalí acted as early catalysts for Minnelli's visual imagination. Aubrey Beardsley's drawings so strongly impacted him that they resurfaced in Minnelli's own drawings (practically in a plagiarized form) for *Casanova's Memoirs,* which he illustrated when he first arrived in New York. Minnelli's absorption of the contemporary avant-garde scene was substantial; it served as an important element to his young avid mind. For Minnelli, his admiration of Cézanne, Van Gogh, Renoir, and Dufy worked concomitantly with divergent forms of painting such as cubism, surrealism, and impressionism. His intermingled aesthetics along with his childhood visions of Midwest Americana in such later works as *Meet Me in St. Louis* (1944) and *Some Came Running* (1958) reveal the diverse palette from which he worked. Inevitably, Minnelli became noted for his ability to fuse multiple genres that became the hallmark of his popular stage and film designs.

Minnelli also began to read voraciously in Chicago. He discovered E. R. and J. Pennell's biography of James McNeill Whistler that influenced his aesthetic understanding of form, composition, and color for the remainder of his career. It is instructive to consider Minnelli's relationship to his early readings of Whistler, as the artist not only embodied certain painterly principles (especially in terms of color),[19] but was also identified as a "dandy" and "gentleman." If the dandy were an enticing figure for Minnelli for its urbane and elegant ennui, Whistler would be the dandy extraordinaire because he was the dandy who, unlike the earlier dandies Byron and Baudelaire, created visually (and importantly in the medium Minnelli loved most). "I envied his childhood in the Russian court, his youth as a West Point cadet and starving artist in a Paris garret, his devotion to his distinguished wife."[20] The suffering artist routine, however, was reaffirming imagery for the youthful (and not so wealthy at the time) Minnelli. Whistler's later remarks on poverty may have assuaged any feelings of remorse that he may have had during his brief lapses of financial insecurity: "it is better to live on bread and cheese and paint beautiful things, than to live like Dives and paint pot boilers."[21] And in this version of the gentlemanly and dandified aesthetic where decorum was highly relished, both Minnelli and Whistler saw football as the demise of an elegant tradition. For Whistler, as the young cadet at West Point, he "resented each and every innovation [at this ceremonious institution], above all football."[22]

Hence, Minnelli discovered through the Pennells' book that to lack the popular American qualities of virile manhood was not necessarily a stroke of ill fate. Whistler's corporeality is described by a fellow draftsman: "I thought him about the handsomest fellow I ever met; but for some reason I did not consider him a perfect model of manly beauty—his mouth betokened more ease than firmness, his brow more reserve than acute mental activity, and his eyes more depth than penetration. Sensitiveness and animation appeared to be his predominating traits."[23] If Minnelli did not see himself measuring up to the dictates of American masculinity he certainly was able to relate to the poetic American artist abroad whose temperament eschewed those manly characteristics in order to exercise a "sensitiveness" associated with creativity. Whistler's languorous ridings in hansoms, his "cool suit of linen . . . his jaunty straw hat"[24] worn in his youth, his one white lock in his curly black hair and his "series of collars [that] sprang from the neck of the long overcoat . . . [and] extraordinary long cane,"[25] struck not only a sartorial performative image of the dandy but also a performative image of masculinity that appealed to Minnelli's concepts of creativity and gender.

In this way, Minnelli embodied the historical discourse of the dandy-flaneur (i.e., George Brummel, Charles Baudelaire, Oscar Wilde, and, of course, Whistler). It is worth noting that Minnelli's alignment with Whistler over Wilde bespeaks a curious distancing from the dandy-aesthete who would come to be associated with the homosexual. The figure of Wilde, as Alan Sinfield has shown, linked the dandy-aesthete with homosexuality.[26] Minnelli may have dismissed Wilde over his favored Whistler (this, according to Minnelli, was because he took Whistler's side in the famous Whistler/Wilde debate of the nineteenth century). But in the early part of the twentieth century the visual weight of the Wilde trial was far from lifted. The embodiment of "sexual offender" in those who were seen as "creative," "artistic," or (to this day) "effeminate" allowed the middle class the opportunity to identify a physical scapegoat who would stand in for what one ought not be. It is not surprising, then, that Minnelli defended Whistler over Wilde in his memoirs. Like Wilde's "creative" contemporaries who tried to disassociate their dandified and aestheticized physical attributes from their "behavior," Minnelli (*only twenty-five years after Wilde's death*) was in the position to account for his "feminine traits" (and thereby adhere to standardized male/female, heterosexual binaries). This is not to defend Minnelli's fear of being identified with the charge of homosexuality, but rather to provide a framework for the ideological cultural underpinnings in which Minnelli functioned and negotiated as an American twentieth-century dandy-aesthete. To be a dandy, to be a man performing within a creative cultural milieu, served to identify—and thereby warn—those guardians of manly middle-class norms, of the presence of an "Oscar Wilde."

But Minnelli did not reject the Wildean aesthetic that ushered in camp. In fact, Minnelli embraced a camp aesthetic, historically following Wilde's aesthetic import—acknowledged or not. Minnelli is somewhat ironic when he states that "[w]aste was the cardinal sin. I had learned to recycle my experience in real life and applying them to my creative endeavors. I do it to this day."[27] The process of "recycling" is, of course, the reuse of disposed waste. There is, as well, a foretelling of decadence in this notion of "waste as the cardinal sin" in that it recalls the moral lasciviousness of catholic ritual and cardinals so adored by Winckelmann and Wilde. The twentieth-century dandy, as Susan Sontag suggests, "has given rise to a certain kind of witty appreciation of the derelict, inane, *démodé* objects of modern civilization— the taste for a certain kind of passionate non-art that is known as 'camp.' "[28] This "appreciation of the derelict" is, then, an appreciation of historical debris that Minnelli highlighted in both his films and lived world. More importantly, Minnelli's eclectic turn to queer-modernist aesthetics challenged the masculinist logic of modern art that, as we saw with Cedric Gibbons, insisted on a clean, functional line.

Lela Simone, music coordinator for the Freed unit at MGM, has stated in an Academy of Motion Picture Arts and Sciences (AMPAS) interview that, "Vincente [Minnelli] was not a man who was a dictator. He tried to do it in a soft and nice way. He worked in let's say . . . I don't know whether you will understand what I say . . . he worked liked a homosexual. I don't mean that nastily. I have nothing against homosexuals."[29] Citing this interview, Matthew Tinkcom has argued that Simone's view of "working like a homosexual" reveals "labors performed by particular subjects, and not identities, can in some cases display the mark of the subject upon the product."[30] But what Tinkcom does not quote is instructive in that both the interviewer and Simone are confounded by her remarks. The interviewer clarifies Simone's response by asking her if she meant "his manner":

> *Simone:* It was soft.
> *Interviewer:* Yes.
> *Simone:* You see?
> *Interviewer:* And yet he was not?
> *Simone:* Ja.

I would add that that "mark" to which Tinkcom refers, rather than displaying an inherent (repressed?) "homosexual" set of subject knowledges that surface "upon the product," actually articulates cultural anxieties associated with masculine creativity (i.e., "effeminacy" ["soft and nice way"] and homosexuality). This quote is taken from a larger oral history project at AMPAS. As this (American) middle-class masculine anxiety persisted, Minnelli as the neodandy sought refuge from the vulgarities of this hyper masculine world by using his affinity for art in order to ironize, to situate within and against, and to "confuse" (once again) this masculine anxiety. If he was to be constantly suspect, he would seek out the conditions where he would feel comfortable exercising his creative talents. Declared or not, Minnelli participated in and visibly presented a homosexual aesthetic.

SMALL-TOWN BOYS AND DANDIFIED "HYSTERIA" IN TWENTIETH-CENTURY NEW YORK

Aside from his painterly interests in the impressionists and fauves, Minnelli's fascination with surrealism in Chicago prompted his readings, according to Minnelli, of Freud and Ronald Firbank. A subscription to New York's *World* introduced him to the city's sophisticated nightclub and party scene during the late 1920s, while *Vanity Fair* kept Minnelli current with New York's fashionable trends in literature, theater, and cinema. The *World*'s heavily produced Sunday paper offered pages of photographs and editorials giving him a peek into New York's haut couture society of stage, screen, and literature. *Vanity Fair* provided Minnelli with the forum for such eclectic figures as Carl Van Vechten, Gilbert Seldes, Colette, Vivian Shaw, Alexander Woollcott, Heywood Broun, and Cecil Beaton (who later worked with Minnelli on *Gigi* and *On a Clear Day You Can See Forever*). New York's reputation as being truly modernist spoke to Minnelli with great verve since it was a modernism that fit snugly with his aesthetic sensibility. The city offered not only a creative edge but also it was (and it was well known) a socially tolerant city.

While Chicago presented Minnelli with a powerful introduction to the arts and urban living, it had, for Minnelli, "an impudent style with little class." Its lack of an urbane sensibility smacked of a certain manliness that suggested a "sleeves rolled up" mentality.[31] This observation of a rough and tough, socially rigid Chicago was bolstered by his subscriptions to the New York *World* and *Vanity Fair*. In these pages, New York was the "swellegant" counterpoint to Chicago's version of modernist urban culture. His brief trips to New York for Balaban and Katz productions fueled Minnelli's already charged desire to move. The recent Paramount Publix merger with Balaban and Katz made his move to New York possible. Paramount Publix's New York theaters would now stage grand vaudevillian-style shows in the tradition of the Balaban and Katz Picture Palaces in Chicago. Minnelli wanted in on the venture and soon found himself with a one-way ticket to New York.

For Minnelli, New York sophistication proffered a cultural milieu immersed in Noël Coward banter and elegant decadence. Now in New York,

Minnelli was brought into the effluence of the city's unswerving energy. The roman à clef novels and essays sketched by Carl Van Vechten now came to life with an intensity that would indelibly mark Minnelli's work. Although Minnelli and Van Vechten do not, in their writings, ever mention if they directly encountered each other, their milieus overlapped as did their interests in things culturally queer.

Van Vechten (b. 1880), another dandy-aesthete from the Midwest (Cedar Rapids, Iowa) who first moved to Chicago and found it dull, was the cornerstone of the New York social world in the 1920s. For Van Vechten, there were three "essentials" to art: "vitality, glamour, and imagination."[32] He was a photographer (with quite an impressive array of portraits), journalist, novelist, "manager" for budding talent,[33] and gossip queen. As Bruce Kellner suggests, "he was [New York's] leading dilettante."[34] Van Vechten invariably knew everyone who was anyone. His novels bespoke the campy decadence of sophistication that supported the glamorous world of New York's high society. Van Vechten's decadence was the blueprint (and imprint) of an American aestheticism that did not sit comfortably in the virile tradition of American art.

The composite of Van Vechten's transcontinental social arena included Gertrude Stein, Virgil Thomson, Parker Tyler, Pavel Tchelitchev, Alfred Stieglitz, Georgia O'Keeffe, George Gershwin, and Ethel Waters. Many of these figures were key in 1920s and 1930s New York social activity—and several of them, especially Gershwin and Waters, would later intimately overlap with Minnelli's world. Interestingly, Van Vechten's friendship with Waters and Gershwin was well established during the 1920s. Van Vechten would religiously attend their concerts as well as every social gathering in New York with them. Since it would be doubtful that he would miss any of Waters's theatrical performances (it's hard to imagine Van Vechten missing *any* performance in New York) he was most likely present at Minnelli's production of *At Home Abroad* in 1935 that starred Waters and Beatrice Lillie. When, shortly thereafter in early 1936, Van Vechten photographed Waters for his own personal portfolio, one can rightly imagine that the show (considering the calamitous offstage relationship that Bea Lillie and Waters shared) was a topic of vibrant gossip between himself and Waters.

But Van Vechten's importance was not limited to his glowing coterie and extravagant personality. His writings on opera, dance, literature, cinema, and music generated an enormous current of aesthetic energy well into the 1930s. His attendance to, and his ongoing critical support of, Diaghilev's Ballet Russe in Paris paved the way for the dynamic dispersion of creative thought in New

York. Van Vechten's commingling with the dandified audience of the Ballet Russe undoubtedly resonated with his personal design of the American twentieth-century dandy.[35] Later, Minnelli's design for the sets and costumes of *Scheherazade* at Radio City received successful critical review as he utilized the "exotic" colors of Léon Bakst as they were, in one way or another, directly or indirectly interpreted and articulated by Van Vechten.[36]

Often unacknowledged or underestimated, Van Vechten's peripatetic wit and grace were in great part responsible for the impetus behind the Harlem Renaissance. His high-pitched charisma and dedication to many a budding career (especially, but not exclusively, to Langston Hughes and Countee Cullen) sparked white upper-middle-class interest in (and exoticizing of) Harlem artists and entertainment. Later, Minnelli attended the Harlem jazz clubs that were made popular by Van Vechten's prolific exposés of Harlem nightlife. Minnelli's friendships and experiences in Harlem were later brought to Hollywood when he made his first film, *Cabin in the Sky* (1943).[37]

Previously, in 1922 Van Vechten helped to spawn Firbank's literary career into American notoriety. Firbank's fantastical/surrealist fairy tales evoked the aestheticism of Wilde and Proust while liquefying his fairy tale narratives into presurrealist imagery. Firbank's literary style deconstructed the already contemporary notion of camp by further heightening the excess of camp's own strategy. At MGM, Minnelli's *Yolanda and the Thief* (1946) and *The Pirate* (1948) would unabashedly resonate with the excess of Firbank's fantastical aestheticism.

Central to Van Vechten's social and personal world was the painter Florine Stettheimer. As his close friend and social contemporary, Stettheimer had the financial wherewithal to disseminate the European art scene to Van Vechten and his New York compatriots as well as to personally introduce Van Vechten to such artists as Marcel Duchamp. Barbara Bloemink notes that as Stettheimer was "one of the few American artists privileged to have actively participated in pre–World War I European culture, she was an important carrier of that culture to a new location."[38] Like Van Vechten, one of her most important cultural deliveries was the ideas and imagery she discovered after her attendance to Ballet Russe. She was in complete admiration of Bakst's colorful costume design.[39] This impression of the colorful, the ornate, and the decorative would spill over into her paintings, albeit in a finer line. Both Stettheimer's and Minnelli's paintings and sketches share an important contemporaneous aspect in that they both represent the body as influenced by the fashionable drawings of Ralph Barton[40] and especially, I would add, Edouard

Garcia Benito in *Vanity Fair*. This modernist rendering of the body à la Benito speaks to a modernist androgyny that begins to articulate the dynamic dimension of American gender relations of the early twentieth century.

Although championed by Van Vechten, Stieglitz, and her close friend Duchamp, her paintings never achieved critical or popular recognition during her lifetime. Although already a window-display predecessor to Minnelli at Marshall Field's (Stettheimer had designed windows at Wanamaker's in New York *and* Marshall Field's in Chicago) her set and costume designs clearly informed Minnelli's sense of design. In 1934 (at the age of sixty-three), however, Stettheimer's creative path took a monumental shift and "indirectly" crossed Minnelli's path with the opening of the opera *Four Saints in Three Acts,* with a libretto by Gertrude Stein and music by Virgil Thomson and performed by an all black cast. *Four Saints* was to become a major avant-garde work of the period. As in her paintings, Stettheimer's set and costume designs for *Four Saints* were delicately ornate.

In his memoirs, Minnelli remarks on this production, calling attention to the efforts of Stein and Thomson, but not of Stettheimer. While it is not clear if Minnelli actually did see the premier of *Four Saints* in Hartford, Connecticut (February 7, 1934) or its New York opening (March 1), he most certainly had read about it in the New York press where not only Stettheimer was praised for her design work, but also photographs of her sets and costumes were reproduced. Minnelli indeed referred to *Four Saints* as a "riveting surrealistic opera,"[41] and its success (along with that of Harold Rome's revue *Pins and Needles*) would later convince Minnelli that "a surrealist revue would be viable."[42] In fact, to see the sets of his *Cabin in the Sky* is to see the echo of Stettheimer's designs for *Four Saints*. This is especially true in his use of white light placed against the white sets and costumes as worn by the all black cast.[43]

For Van Vechten, Stettheimer, and Minnelli, the cinema was the pivotal art of the twentieth century. All three were fascinated with the technical possibilities of movement with the new art. While Stettheimer leaned toward the European avant-garde movement in cinema, Van Vechten and Minnelli were unabashedly appreciative of Hollywood and the major European studio productions. For Van Vechten, his admiration of Clara Bow and Elinor Glyn pointed to his dandified embrace not only of a film such as *It* (1927), but also of his social position of having, and decadently enjoying, "it." In Minnelli's case, Jacques Feyder's *Carnival in Flanders* (1935) "embodied [his] fascination in art . . . with the artful detail and luminosity of the Flemish masters."[44] While this film clearly echoes the "Flemish masters," it is also laced with a bawdy irony that tickled Minnelli's taste for the debauch. Minnelli's unending accumulation of aesthetic possibilities from multiple mediums provided him with a vast set of knowledges that, as critics and reviewers often note, allowed him to bring together the traditional distinctions between "high" and "low" art.

Van Vechten's and Stettheimer's energetic support of *both* European and American artists sat in opposition to the America's post-Armory show sense of modernism that looked to define a new and "pure" American art form devoid of European influence. Van Vechten's and Stettheimer's import of European art set the stage for a "queer modernism" that shared an international renown for its unsettling creative and moral decadence. These creative coteries, criticized for their association with eroticism, effeminacy, decadence, and primitivism, harbored a wellspring of artists whose sense of modernism did not look toward a pure "American" art form, but rather toward a hyper-aestheticized representation, a theatricalization, of the "functional" twentieth century. Like Van Vechten, Minnelli's identification as the "queer" dandy-aesthete provided him the opportunity to "camp" and, thereby, "confuse" standard social registers of cultural meaning.

URBAN SOPHISTICATION

Van Vechten's and Stettheimer's (baroque) framing of New York's cultural and aesthetic milieu of the 1920s cannot be underestimated for Minnelli, in spite of Minnelli's apparent lack of direct personal and professional contact with them. The intellectual and creative groundwork laid during this period would be the stimuli in which the young Minnelli was soon to be immersed. Van Vechten's and Stettheimer's ardent support of trans-Atlantic "Orientalist" visions of aesthetic pleasure registered with Minnelli as a way to transgress the social demands of virile and mechanical masculinity.[45] The excess of visual aesthetic pleasure was (is) that jouissance that the functionalist modernists had lost in their rigor toward efficiency. Van Vechten and Stettheimer would leave their marks on, and yield to, Minnelli's cultural arena of the 1930s. Minnelli's leap into New York's cultural scene provided him with, at once (and these are linked) the pleasure of visual excess and the opportunity to test and challenge his multiple questions of sexual and gender identity that any "queer" midwestern boy brings with him to the big city.

The contingent and discontinuous parameters of masculinity were no-where more apparent than in New York. During the 1920s, the city was rapidly gaining a reputation (not necessarily a bad one) for its "pansy" population, drag balls in Harlem, bohemians of Greenwich Village, and its supposed tolerance of decadent behavior in both the public and private spheres that many middle-class New Yorkers and non–New Yorkers endlessly enjoyed. New York, of course, also cradled an affluent (both creatively and financially) artist population. When Minnelli was finally brought to New York in 1931 he moved immediately into the Village where the promise for creative and personal tolerance could be sought. Minnelli (bedecked as a composite of Whistler and Beardsley), according to *Esquire,* was "the incarnation of our preconceived notion of a 'Village type': flat black hat with a wide brim, loose collar and looser tie around his thin neck, a big portfolio of drawings under one arm and the cut of his long coat a triumphant marriage of Harlem and the Left Bank."[46] Minnelli certainly dressed the part, but he may very well have been somewhat disappointed with what was no longer the liberatory and bohemian Village he had once read about.

In his memoirs, Minnelli would look back at this move as his step to "greener pastures." But in the 1930s, New York was experiencing its own changes in its sociopolitical environment. While Repeal was inaugurated (December 1933), the Depression was sinking deeply into the New York economy. Jimmy Walker's graft-ridden city hall was out while La Guardia's upright moralism was in, and the tolerance that queers had once enjoyed during the 1920s was seriously on the wane. In fact, as George Chauncey argues, Repeal actually reinforced the regulation of social conditions and social order. The introduction of a diligent law to New York's cultural milieu served to oppress those already socially marginalized. It is instructive to consider Chauncey's historical analysis of New York during the period of Minnelli's arrival, because it clearly puts into perspective the New York cultural conditions of creativity, masculinity, and homosexuality in which Minnelli lived.

Chauncey argues that the 1930s ushered in New York's attempt to morally recuperate itself by eliminating the socially unwanted—especially "sexual perverts" and "social degenerates." With Repeal the New York State Liquor Authority (SLA) was instituted to regulate places of ill repute. Sweeping raids took place at bars and restaurants, especially where homosexuals were "known" to congregate. What is interesting about these raids is the way in which the SLA identified homosexuals. The SLA undercover agents searched for "their campy behavior (or, as the agents called it, their 'effeminacy'), their use of rouge or lipstick, their practice of calling each other by camp or women's names, the way they talked or the fact that they talked about the opera or other suspect topics, or other aspects of their dress or carriage."[47] The "effeminate" creatures who were busted at these "known homosexual" bars were usually part of a lower- or working-class background. The middle class, under this state reign of terror, were not only able to avoid being arrested but also were the ones who were able to wear make-up, talk about opera, and "camp it up" across town at private and select cocktail parties. The satin-padded boundaries north of the Village and Times Square were filled with financially successful artists and theater folk who could afford to be "queer" within their protective and insular neighborhood.

This uptown milieu quickly became Minnelli's new coterie. His sudden dismissal in 1933 from Paramount Publix found him momentarily penniless and with rent due on his Village studio. In what Minnelli recalls as a "deus ex machina," he was hired by Radio City Music Hall, which provided him with a move uptown from "lower class" lower Manhattan to the swank uptown location on East 52nd Street where he would work and live for the next seven years. Hence his move couldn't have been more socially apposite as just west of Minnelli Van Vechten resided at 150 West 55th Street while Stettheimer dwelled at 182 West 58th Street. According to Chauncey, the streets of the East and West Fifties, "once given over to the homes of New York's wealthiest families," one observer noted in 1932, were "now filled with smart little shops, bachelor apartments, residential studios and fashionable speakeasies."[48]

This neighborhood in the early 1930s became the site for many successful writers and artists who "fled Greenwich Village" during its "decline." Max Eastman spoke of this new chic location as the home of "the *Smart Set* and *Vanity Fair* people."[49] While the "pansies" and "fairies" caroused just south of the neighborhood in Times Square, the middle-class "invert" spent time ("covertly") in the "elegant nightclubs" such as the Rainbow Room, which sat high above in the Radio City Music Hall/Rockefeller Center complex (convenient for Minnelli's cocktail after one of those arduous and chaotic days at the Music Hall). Minnelli's social position (i.e., middle-class stage and costume designer during the Depression) allowed him to participate in the haute-couture society and, in effect, exercise his "feminine traits" in otherwise hostile conditions for men who did not act masculine.

Once Minnelli began his work at Radio City, his New York career was quickly set in motion. The year 1933 marked the moment that Minnelli became a public persona. By 1935 Minnelli's social circles were swirling with the glamour of such figures as George Balanchine, George and Ira Gershwin, Tchelitchev, Dorothy Parker, Steichen, Paul Bowles, George Platt Lynes, and Kay Swift (who, according to Minnelli, named his salon on E. 53rd Street "The Minnellium"). In 1936, the Shubert organization offered Minnelli a job as director and producer of their musical revues. The Shubert press releases described his life as "gay, sophisticated, fantastic."[50] His body and behavior were well recorded in the *World Telegram, Vanity Fair,* and *Esquire.* Minnelli was known as "twenty-nine years old [his reported age ranged often around four years younger than he actually was], with black, carefully combed hair, brown eyes and agile hands."[51] He was "versatile" and "handsome." He was also endearing, as he was known for his shyness and gentle temperament; he understood the "value of the soft spoken word."[52] His attraction to Whistler decidedly acted as one of "the dominant forces in his life," not only because of Whistler's "oils and etchings" but also, following Whistler, Minnelli "[thought] best when riding in a hansom through Central Park."[53] He is the stroller of the urban street: "Mr. Minnelli is a great walker . . . not only in Central Park, but along Fourth Avenue, where the old bookstalls are, in rummage shops and out of the way places. Why, treasures abound in these odd shops. Old prints, pictures of the theatre of fifty years ago, even strange fabrics . . ."[54] Minnelli was visibly identified as the dandy-aesthete, the flaneur—the man about town who took pleasure in the historical debris of the city.

But there must be an accounting for Minnelli's aesthetic and, thereby, unmanly preoccupations (not to mention his lack of a showgirl girlfriend, as some Shubert press releases revealed). If he takes dance lessons at Arthur Murray's ("but he keeps them a secret from his pals"), he also "plays indoor tennis because it's the best exercise he can think of. He's anxious to keep fit. He shies from any activity that might be considered effeminate."[55] As far as marriage is concerned he "hasn't the time for courtship . . . he is too busy looking at girls in the aggregate to spend much time on the one and only girl."[56] Undoubtedly, Minnelli went to great lengths to prevent being targeted as "effeminate" and, thereby, an "Oscar Wilde." These overdetermined treatises merely whitewashed Minnelli's creative sensibilities in order to sell tickets, recalling Whistler's sentiment, to the "rich, ignorant public" who loathe "effeminacy" and "softness" in a man.

While at the Shuberts (right before he left to fulfill his brief, but lucrative, contract with Paramount Pictures in Hollywood as "musical director") Minnelli designed a scene for the production of *The Show Is On* titled "Jam Session," in which he employed the use of an eight-by-ten-foot rear projection screen. This screen hung above the stage where revelers and musicians of a jazz nightclub were partying. On this screen was projected the close-up of a musician playing the trumpet. But the figure's head was not stationary. The image was a sort of hologram flashing and dissolving to the rapid rhythm of the music being played on stage. Minnelli pointed to this scene in an article he wrote for *Stage* in September 1936 where his writing style suggests the cross-current of theatrical hyperactivity during production of *The Show Is On:*

> Some radio scout should hear Hoagie [Carmichael] whistling, singing, and talking simultaneously into a telephone. He demonstrates a song with full orchestral effects including vibraphone and hot fiddle. All this to a running commentary on audience reaction, possible lyrics, and statistics on eventual sheet music sales. . . . Another composer [enters] . . . I'm looking for a certain kind of tune for this number called Jam Session. The number opens in one . . . Oh, Lord, if I have to tell this story once more I'll start eating the straw off the floor.[57]

In the bottom right-hand corner of this article is Minnelli's sketch for "Jam Session." The caption reads: " 'Jam Session': 1936! Hysteria! Harmonic interlude involving the madhouse tactics of the aggravated music of today." But this was not the only remark (and rendering) of "hysteria" that Minnelli discussed at this time. In an undated press release from the Shuberts, a portion of a speech made by Minnelli to the "Fashion Group" is given:

> The designers in the theatre today are at last on familiar ground. They are utterly in accord with their audience because their audience is part of the show. The barriers of foot-light and stage door have never been so nebulous. *The theatre and life have at last decided to meet on common ground, and that common ground—let's face it—is madness.* Never, I think, has satire in the theatre been so spirited—color so unrestrained, sophistication so genuine.[58]

It is clear at this point in his career that Minnelli saw himself ("the designer . . . on familiar ground") *within* the commingling and confusion of visual representation and the cultural world. Of course, what is striking about his surrealist vision and disposition is that "theatre and life" are fraught with "madness" and "hysteria." In his later Hollywood films (both musicals and nonmusicals) this "hysteria" and "madness" was filtered through his brand of surrealism, popular culture, and decorative art that surfaced through the filmic frame precisely through those "nebulous barriers" that allowed for this back-and-forth relationship between the historical world and its representation. I would suggest that the hysteria of which Minnelli speaks is the masculine hysteria, the excess of masculine production, of the twentieth century—of which he was so sensitive.

For Minnelli, the decor or mise-en-scène of the frame (of the stage or, later, of the film) was where the body (and most often the male body) was conditioned and manipulated by the spatial/temporal relationships that that body shared with the historical world. In other words, "theatre and life" are imbricated and immersed in historical activity while the bodies, which are situated within this madness, are forced to negotiate the unstable and hysterical parameters of the frame in which they exist. In many a Minnellian case, hypermasculinized bodies are ironically placed within his overaestheticized frame. On stage, for example, when Bert Lahr performed as a "delicate" woodsman in "Song of the Woodsman" (*The Show Is On*) the mise-en-scène literally exploded around him.[59] Later in his MGM films, Gene Kelly's virility is pressed against the soft-impressionism of Dufy in *An American in Paris* (1951), Robert Mitchum drowns in an overmasculinized house of cowboy boots, leather, and blood in *Home from the Hill* (1960), and young college studs nervously negotiate Minnelli's color patterns and dispersions in *Tea and Sympathy* (1956).

But Minnelli's frenzied vision of creativity in theater and life is unequivocally "spirited" and gives way to an aesthetics of "color so unrestrained, sophistication so genuine." Minnelli's body, placed within this social "hysteria," became a discourse generated by him and with the New York press that labeled, defined, and protected Minnelli as the quintessential aesthete–cultural producer of the musical revue. It was his years in New York that publicly and, thereby, corporeally marked the tension between masculinity and creativity that would inform Minnelli's body as it intersected with his stage and film work for the rest of his career. His dress, his demeanor, his body, his home and work place became discursive and visible sites that articulated the cultivated Minnelli within and against the efficient discourse of masculinity. His shyness, his artistic knowledge, his "agile hands," his "Chinese Red bathroom," his preference for tennis to keep fit would sit uncomfortably amid the contemporary conditions of American masculinity. This aesthetic and discursive terrain would repeat itself and identify Minnelli for the next fifty years. It is through this historical, queer modernist milieu, then, that one can begin to discern the multiple levels that served the queer-modernist architectonics Minnelli later brought to Hollywood cinema.

Notes

I'd like to thank Joe McElhaney for the opportunity to revisit and revise this essay.

1. See James Naremore, *The Films of Vincente Minnelli* (New York: Cambridge University Press, 1993), 7–50.

2. John Harkrider was a costume and stage designer on Broadway and in films between 1925 and 1942. Oliver Messel was born in England where he worked on sets and costumes for both the English and American stage and films. "Hobe-Irwin" is

Hobe Erwin who was an interior decorator in New York. He later worked in Hollywood for MGM and David O. Selznick.

3. Memo located at the Academy of Motion Picture Arts and Sciences Center for Motion Picture Study, Margaret Herrick Library (hereafter AMPAS); Special Collections Department, folder 18, MGM Art Department/E. J. Mannix File.

4. Patrick Downing and John Hambley, *The Art of Hollywood* (London: Victoria and Albert Museum, 1979), 59. Also quoted in Vincente Minnelli, with Hector Arce, *I Remember It Well* (Garden City, NY: Doubleday, 1974), 122.

5. See Naremore, *Films of Vincente Minnelli*, 7–50, and Stephen Harvey, *Directed by Vincente Minnelli* (New York: Museum of Modern Art and Harper and Row, 1989), 25–35.

6. In a Shubert press release (anon., ca. 1936) we are told that "[Minnelli] lives in a flat on E. 52nd Street which doesn't boast a single piece of chromium plated furniture . . ." (Shubert Archives, New York, see files regarding Minnelli and the programs he designed and produced).

7. I have been fortunate to see this collection firsthand through the gracious approval of Mrs. Lee Minnelli. Unless otherwise noted, all information ascribed to Lee Minnelli was recorded from personal interviews with the author during the summer of 1995.

8. Paul Goldberger, "A Hollywood House Worthy of an Oscar," *New York Times,* November 6, 1980, C10.

9. Donald Albrecht, *Designing Dreams: Modern Architecture in the Movies* (New York: Harper and Row, 1986), 91.

10. Cedric Gibbons, "Interior Decoration Vital Branch of Movie Making," *Evening World,* June 29, 1929, n.p. Other sources that discuss Gibbons's dwelling and "architectural" design include Michael Webb, "Cedric Gibbons and the MGM Style," *Architectural Digest* 47 (April 1990): 100, 104, 108, 112.

11. In *Ornament and Architecture* (1892) Louis Sullivan suggests that it "would be greatly for our aesthetic good if we should refrain entirely from the use of ornament . . . [because] we shall have learned . . . that ornament is mentally a luxury, not a necessity . . . [w]e feel intuitively that our *strong, athletic,* and simple forms will carry with the natural ease the raiment of which we dream" (quoted in Kenneth Frampton, *Modern Architecture: A Critical History,* 3rd ed., rev. [1980; London: Thames and Hudson, 1992], 51, emphasis added). Interestingly, recent renovation of Grand Central was discussed similarly: The station is said to be "getting a sex change" in that what was once "a temple to the manly cult of work" is now "[emerging] as a shrine to rituals associated with domesticity: dining, shopping and keeping up the house." See *New York Times,* February 4, 1996, 27.

12. "It is not possible to move forward and look backwards," writes Mies Van der Rohe, ". . . he who lives in the past cannot advance" (quoted in Elaine S. Hochman, *Architects of Fortune: Mies Van der Rohe and the Third Reich* [New York: Weidenfeld and Nicolson, 1989], xiv). The irony of the functional art/architecture of a modernist such as Mies was that often the living space he designed for an unburdened future became "uninhabitable," as in the case of his Farnsworth House of 1952, which was "[l]ocated on the bank of a river that was heavily infested with mosquitoes on summer

evenings, Mies would not allow a screened porch, arguing . . . that to do so would have ruined the jewel-like design" (57).

13. Quoted in *Encyclopedia Britannica* and cited in Albrecht, *Designing Dreams*, 90.

14. Peter Wollen, "Out of the Past," in his *Raiding the Icebox* (Bloomington: Indiana University Press, 1993), 1–34, quote on 17.

15. Wollen, "Out of the Past," 18. I am indebted to Wollen's essay (and ongoing dialogues) for helping me rethink the historical practices of fin de siècle decadence, creativity, and modernism.

16. Located at the Museum of the City of New York and the Metropolitan Museum of Art are several dozen sketches for Minnelli's Radio City Music Hall and Shubert productions: *At Home Abroad* (1935), *Hooray For What?!* (1937), and *Very Warm for May* (1939). Indeed, one of Minnelli's major conflicts between Gibbons and MGM's Technicolor advisor, Natalie Kalmus, was during the filming of *Meet Me in St. Louis*. Minnelli argued with Gibbons and Kalmus over the use of the colors red and green in a single shot (two colors, moreover, that Gibbons had forbidden to be used in his films). The decorative clutter of the Smith home also highlights the antithesis of the clean functional line Gibbons preferred. See Minnelli, *I Remember It Well*, 131–32.

17. See George Chauncey, *Gay New York: Gender, Urban Culture, and the Making of the Gay Male World, 1890–1940* (New York: Basic Books, 1994).

18. Minnelli's effete and urbane demeanor is quite recognizable, for example, in his interview for *The Men Who Made Movies* (produced, written, and directed by Richard Schickel, 1973).

19. Many passages in the Pennells' book (Joseph Pennell and Elizabeth R. Pennell, *The Life of James McNeill Whistler*, 2 vols. [Philadelphia: J. B. Lippincott, 1909]) recount Whistler's work that emphasized the painter's palette, undoubtedly attractive to Minnelli's penchant for color. Whistler, according to the voluminous interviews conducted by the Pennells, insisted that "colours should be arranged on the palette" (vol. 1, 50) and that precise "scientific methods . . . produce harmonious effects in line and 'colour grouping' " (222). For Whistler, "art is a science not because as some painters imagine, it is concerned with laws of light or chemistry of colours or scientific problems in the usual sense, but because it is exact in its methods and in its results as the science of chemistry"(vol. 2, 8). Yet, at the same time, color disrupts a standardized viewing: "the artist must overload everything with strong contrasts of violent colours. His success with the rich ignorant public is assured if only he succeeds in setting his colours shouting against each other" (vol. 2, 8). Clearly, Minnelli learned much from Whistler's science of art and color as well as how to sell to a "rich [if not] ignorant public."

20. Minnelli, *I Remember It Well*, 50. Minnelli highlights Whistler as "a pioneer in interior design, introducing blue and white décor and Japanese china to London. He had an affinity for yellow [Minnelli's favorite color], painting walls of his house in its most sunny shading."

21. Pennell and Pennell, *Life of James McNeill Whistler*, vol. 2, 127. Generally speaking, Minnelli rarely fell upon financial hard times. His contract with the Shuberts in 1936 (*The Show Is On*) guaranteed him: $3,500 to design "all scenery and costumes," $500 per week for staging the show's production (with a guaranteed minimum of

$2,000, 2 percent of gross weekly box-office receipts as well as 2 percent of gross weekly box-office receipts if the show traveled abroad. Besides this terrific salary, Minnelli had "complete charge of the artistic phases of the entire production." Minnelli's contract is located at the Shubert Archive.

22. Pennell and Pennell, *Life of James McNeill Whistler*, vol. 1, 38.

23. Ibid., 44.

24. Ibid., 80.

25. Ibid., 300.

26. On the dandy, see Jules Barbey d'Aurevilly, *Dandyism*, trans. Douglas Ainslie (1897; New York: PAJ Publications, 1988); Walter Benjamin, *Charles Baudelaire*, trans. Harry Zohn (1976; London: Verso, 3rd printing, 1989); Charles Baudelaire, *Selected Writings on Art and Literature*, trans. P. E. Charvet (1972; London: Penguin, 1992). On the dandy's historical association with homosexuality, see Alan Sinfield, *The Wilde Century: Effeminacy, Oscar Wilde, and the Queer Moment* (New York: Columbia, 1994); Richard Ellman, *Oscar Wilde* (New York: Vintage, 1988); Ed Cohen, *Talk on the Wilde Side* (New York: Routledge, 1993).

27. See Minnelli, *I Remember It Well*, 38; he also described *The Pirate* as "camp" in his memoir.

28. Susan Sontag, "Happenings," in her *Against Interpretation* (New York: Farrar Straus and Giroux, 1966; New York: Anchor, 1986), 263–74, quote on 271.

29. Quoted in Matthew Tinkcom, "Working like a Homosexual: Camp Visual Codes and the Labor of Gay Subjects in the MGM Freed Unit," *Cinema Journal* 35, no. 2 (1996): 24–42; quote on 24. See "Oral History with Lela Simone," interview conducted with Rudy Behlmer (October 1990–January 1991), AMPAS, Oral History Program, 1994.

30. Tinkcom, "Working like a Homosexual," 29.

31. Minnelli, *I Remember It Well*, 51.

32. Bruce Kellner, ed., *Letters of Carl Van Vechten* (New Haven, CT: Yale University Press, 1987), 49.

33. And this was not only young talent such as Langston Hughes and Zora Neale Hurston but also older and forgotten writers such as Henry Blake Fuller. Van Vechten was also capable of raising the dead as in the case of Herman Melville.

34. Bruce Kellner, *Carl Van Vechten and the Irreverent Decades* (Norman: University of Oklahoma Press, 1968), vii.

35. The historical impact of Diaghilev's *Scheherazade* cannot be underestimated in terms of the New York art scene during the 1920s and 1930s (Van Vechten even named his cat Scheherazade). For a thorough and elegant description of the "dandy-aesthete" audience who attended the Ballet Russe in London and Paris after World War I, see Lynn Garafola, *Diaghilev's Ballets Russes* (Oxford: Oxford University Press, 1989).

36. Minnelli reprimands a New York reviewer's ignorance for not recognizing his use of color and accoutrements for Earl Carroll's curtain in the 1931 *Vanities*, which were "particularly . . . inspired by Bakst and executed by Remisoff and Soudakin for the Ballets Russes." Minnelli, *I Remember It Well*, 58.

37. See my *Manly Arts: Masculinity and Nation in Early American Cinema* (Durham, NC: Duke University Press, 2006), 165–211.

38. Barbara Bloemink, "Visualizing Sight: Florine Stettheimer and Temporal Modernism," in *Florine Stettheimer: Manhattan Fantastica*, by Elisabeth Sussman, with Barbara Bloemink and Linda Nochlin (New York: Whitney Museum of American Art, 1995), 71.

39. Elisabeth Sussman, "Florine Stettheimer: A 1990s Perspective," in Sussman, *Florine Stettheimer*, 43.

40. Minnelli, *I Remember It Well*, 50, and Sussman, "Florine Stettheimer," 50.

41. Minnelli, *I Remember It Well*, 98.

42. Ibid., 102.

43. Examples of Stettheimer's set designs from the production can be seen in Kellner, *Carl Van Vechten*.

44. Minnelli, *I Remember It Well*, 90.

45. Consider, for example, Minnelli's use of "trans-Atlantic Orientalist" visions in the "Get Yourself a Geisha" number from the around-the-world stage revue *At Home Abroad* (1935), or the chinoiserie decor of "Limehouse Blues" from the film *Ziegfeld Follies*. The eroticism, exoticism, and theatricalization of "Orientalist" pleasures in Western culture points to the decadent reappropriation of an otherwise Orientalist discourse that serves to manage and subjugate the Other. As Edward Said remarks in his discussion of Flaubert's "fascination with dissection and beauty" through Oriental culture: "the Orient seems still to suggest not only fecundity but sexual promise (and threat), untiring sensuality, unlimited desire, deep generative energies, [which] is something on which one could speculate." See his *Orientalism* (New York: Vintage, 1979), 188. More concurrent with Minnelli at this time was André Breton's surrealistic favor with imagery of the "Orient" that contemporary conservatives saw as decadent and disturbing. See his "Legitimate Defense" (September 1926), in *The History of Surrealism*, by Maurice Nadeau, trans. Richard Howard (New York: Macmillan, 1965; Cambridge, MA: Belknap Press of Harvard University Press, 4th printing, 1995).

46. Hugh Troy, "Never Had a Lesson," *Esquire* (June 1937): 99, 138, 141; quote on 99.

47. Chauncey, *Gay New York*, 344.

48. Ibid., 303.

49. Cited in ibid.

50. Eleanor Lambert, "Notes on Vincente Minnelli," in an unpublished Shubert Theater press release, n.d. Lambert, a leading producer of fashion shows well into the 1970s, was a close friend of Minnelli while he worked in New York. Her influential involvement with the international fashion world had important creative resonances for Minnelli.

51. William Birnie, "A Chorine Thought and Was Wrong," *World Telegram*, November 14, 1936, 3.

52. Anonymous Shubert press release.

53. Birnie, "A Chorine Thought and Was Wrong," 3.

54. Marion Hurwood, "The Show Is On," in an unpublished Shubert Theater press release, n.d.

55. Birnie, "A Chorine Thought and Was Wrong," 3.

56. Anonymous Shubert press release, 3.

57. Minnelli, "The Show Must Go On," *Stage* (September 1936): 33–35, quote on 35.

58. Lambert, "Notes on Vincente Minnelli."

59. In the biography of his father, Bert Lahr is described in this scene as costumed with a papier-mâché ax while "posed preposterously next to a scrawny tree. . . . He wore a checkered hunter's shirt and a toupee matted on his head. He began raising both hands delicately toward his chest and then unleashing an outrageous sound." In the meantime, Bea Lillie anxiously awaited her cue when she could "throw boards, brooms, anything I could get my hands on" at the singing woodsman. John Lahr, *Notes on a Cowardly Lion* (New York: Knopf, 1969), 163–64.

The Production and Display of the Closet
Making Minnelli's *Tea and Sympathy*

DAVID A. GERSTNER

To make Robert Anderson's play *Tea and Sympathy* into a film,[1] MGM had to convince the Motion Picture Association of America (MPAA), the Production Code Administration (PCA), and even the Catholic Legion of Decency that the film would clearly punish the sexual transgression of the married woman, and that it would not overtly or covertly make any reference to homosexuality. In effect, the centerpieces of the play had to be removed. No matter how MGM attempted to rewrite the narrative to satisfy the Code, *Tea and Sympathy* would either be the play it was on Broadway or it would be morally objectionable. In his memo summarizing the making of the film, Geoffrey Shurlock (Joseph Breen's successor as the director of the PCA) pointed out to MPAA president Eric Johnston that "Any proposed treatment removing these two unacceptable basic elements of the play would make it necessary to write an entirely new story and hence would seem to make pointless the purchase of the particular play."[2]

Tea and Sympathy had already caused quite a stir when it opened on Broadway in September, 1953. Aside from the publicity surrounding Deborah

Kerr's first New York stage performance, *Tea and Sympathy* shot right for the heterosexual male jugular. The play challenged not only the social doxology surrounding masculinity, but also, worse, it waved the threat of latent homosexuality in the very faces of those whose insecurity matched the hyper-masculine figures in the drama. As one reviewer put it after seeing the film: "It may make more than one adult male squirm in his seat with unhappy memories of youth."[3] Situated within the context of 1950s America, *Tea and Sympathy* was risky business. Risky, but successful. Major studios and independents (MGM, Paramount, Warner, Twentieth Century-Fox, and Samuel Goldwyn) vied for its film rights.

According to letters and memos found in the Production Code's files for MGM, each studio's difficulty in making this film circulated around the utterance (implied or otherwise) of homosexuality. In fact, both points of Code contestation (homosexuality and the woman's sexual transgression) were imbricated with homophobia and fear of the effeminization of masculinity. Through a series of public and private discourses (which are founded upon and within a historical relationship of urban male middle-class anxiety about gender and political effeminization), the making of *Tea and Sympathy* at MGM points to what critical theorist Eve Sedgwick terms the *spectacle of the homosexual closet*. Not only is the film a marker of the spectacle of the closet, but the spectacle of the closet is generated, displayed, and reinforced precisely through the discourses of the making of the text and, more precisely, through the making of the film's structured silence.

Caught in the confines of 1950s production regulations, Vincente Minnelli was put on the job to make a film that abided by these constraints. Yet his aestheticization of the text—his color-coding of the text—effectively works within and against the enforced proscriptions of the PCA and the Legion of Decency. Minnelli's use of an aestheticized mise-en-scène makes it possible to realize the anxiety-ridden intersections that exist between the discursive practices surrounding the making of the film (what to do about the homosexual and the transgressive woman) and the social conditions in which those discursive practices were situated (in what ways do the homosexual and the transgressive women threaten American masculinity?). *Tea and Sympathy* marked the site of contestation not only in the multiple changes Hollywood faced in the 1950s but also in the wrenching changes in political gender relations in America, in which both the MGM producers and Minnelli participated.

Tea and Sympathy tells the story of Tom, a young boy at Chilton Prep School in New England. He lives in the home of the school coach, Bill Reynolds, and his wife, Laura. Laura's role is well established by her marriage to Bill—her emotional involvement with the boys is limited to serving them "tea and sympathy." All the other boys who live with them are involved in school athletics, reflecting what Bill considers a family tradition at Chilton, especially in his household. The young scions that dwell there are, on the one hand, young robust men—the regular guys. Tom, on the other hand, prefers Bach and folk songs to volleyball and football. In both the play and the film, Tom is the threatening agent of Bill's masculinity. He is not just a young boy who becomes infatuated with Bill's wife but also a male figure who threatens Bill's image of masculinity. The play and the film, however, rehearse two different versions of what this threat implies.

In the play, Tom, because of his "long-haired" proclivities, is accused of being "queer." His homosexuality is confirmed when he is reportedly seen nude on the beach with a "known" homosexual teacher from the school. In the film, he is caught by two of the school's volleyball players in a sewing circle on the beach with the faculty wives. His being caught in a "feminine" activity gains him the nickname Sister Boy, and he becomes the target of rumor and blacklisting. In fact, he is considered so far outside the parameters of the regular guys that, during the bonfire rites-of-passage scene, when the other young initiates are humiliated by having their pajamas torn off, Tom is ignored, and is thus humiliated because he is not *properly* humiliated.

Both the play and the film are about the developing relationship between Laura and Tom, which leads to a sexual liaison. In Laura he finds the one person who empathizes with him. She marks the tripartite space of mother, confidante, and lover for Tom. The oft-quoted final line ("Years from now . . . when you talk about this . . . and you will . . . be kind") will, however, carry two different conclusions. The play's ending on this note does not necessarily recommend an absolute or final (heterosexual) desire. Rather, the play potentially lends itself to the idea of choosing one's own sexual object (i.e., Tom may be with Laura at this point, but we are given no indication of what his future choices might be).[4] The film, however, through the addition of a prologue and epilogue (the framing story), will in fact turn out to be a fait accompli of heterosexual standards and regulations.

The prologue sets the body of the narrative in a flashback. Tom has returned to Chilton for a ten-year reunion, and he recalls meeting Laura and the events that followed. The epilogue immediately follows the famous final scene by introducing a letter from Laura to Tom in which she tells him that what they did was wrong and that she has realized the error of their ways. She must leave Chilton for some undisclosed place where she will never be seen or heard from again. In effect, Laura defends the production of the closet by letting Tom know that his quest and struggle for manhood, while inappropriate in the way they handled it, is good as long as he ends up married and is able to repent for the wrong they committed. Tom gets away with marriage and Laura serves time in the eternal void.

While Vito Russo is right that the "visibility [of gays] has never really been an issue in the movie," he omits the historical discourse of production of the very closet he discusses in his book. His suggestion that the film version of *Tea and Sympathy* "mutes" the homosexual text of the play is useful, however, in terms of a historical analysis.[5] Russo's contention that, "*at no time* was consideration given to making the homosexuality in *Tea and Sympathy* more explicit,"[6] elides the underpinnings of a discourse of production that actually *did* consider the possibility of including the homosexual in the film. Homosexuality is "muted" in the film insofar as that "muting" is produced through a hyperbolic cacophony of silencing that homosexuality.

The making of *Tea and Sympathy* is precisely one of the places where the Hollywood institution reveals itself making the closet. Eve Sedgwick sees the "spectacle of the homosexual closet" as the "open secret." "Closetedness [is] itself," she suggests, "a performance initiated as such by the speech act of a silence, but a silence that accrues particularity by fits and starts, in relation to the discourse that surrounds and differentially constitutes it."[7]

It is in the making of the film that the reinforcement of the "normative," or compulsory heterosexuality, is maintained. The normative supports and sees itself through its own mythic binarisms (male/female, sex/violence, normative/nonnormative, homosocial/ homosexual). This is to say that particular relationships are sanctioned within the normative. Outside the heterosexual marriage contract there lie relationships between men and between women—the homosocial—that purportedly do not participate in sexual relations. The homosocial works coterminously with the normative order's binary structures to the extent that the normative guards the homosocial against both sexuality and violence. But it is the homosocial that guards the normative binaries by defending them against degrees of difference. Variation from the established order motivates suspicion on the part of these assigned guardians. The degree of difference is decidedly valuable to the well-being of the normative because the normative maintains its mythic binaries by exposing what is outside the social order. The degree of difference is located in the homosocial through the marked outsider.[8]

The play's contextual relationship to McCarthyism is most obvious. The public postwar discourse (articulated through the speech act of smearing) facilely determined personal character by appearance and gesture. It underscored the almost maniacal fear of loss of control on the side of the Law. *Tea and Sympathy* flagged the insidiousness and the ease with which these witch-hunt campaigns could proceed. Laura, at one point, reminds Tom's roommate, Al (as well as the audience), "how easy it is to smear a person."[9]

The entanglement of moral discourses of sexuality and gender relations in America came under great stress between 1920 and 1950. Middle-class values were moving toward a more liberal stance, but conservative organizations also sprang up in response to this liberal swing. In the 1950s, *Tea and Sympathy* found itself relegated to the list of literature condemned by the National Organization for Decent Literature (alongside *From Here to Eternity, The Well of Loneliness,* and *Catcher in the Rye*). During this time, the Legion of Decency already had a stranglehold on Hollywood film censorship. Focused on FDR's New Deal and leftist policies, the Republicans denounced Communism in the late 1940s with accusations of "red" infiltration in government positions. But red is not the only color of anxiety.

John Boswell notes that, as early as AD 1215, markers of identification were utilized to locate "degrees of difference," particularly those which could not necessarily be seen. One of the rulings of the Fourth Lateran Council "ordered [Jews] to wear clothing which [would distinguish] them from Christians."[10] Boswell goes on to say that where identification of difference in homogenous areas was difficult, the wearing of the "Jewish badge" was enforced. Centuries later, the Nazis would demand the placement of an identification "badge" (Jew, gypsy, criminal, homosexual, etc.) on concentration camp prisoners in order to determine the marked prisoner's treatment and/or punishment.

It is precisely the assigning of these markers throughout history (often color coded and forced upon the body) that allowed for the easy identification of those who "needed" to be seen. During the McCarthy era, locating and marking the homosexual was necessary in order to prevent the "effeminization" of the American male. The film *Tea and Sympathy,* through Minnelli's aestheticized coloring, brings to the surface the frenetic attempt to stamp and define an identity with a predetermined color.

In the late 1930s a debate took place between the Catholic traditionalist G. K. Chesterton and the aesthete journalist Robert Lynd over the meaning behind the wearing of the color pink. Chesterton noted "the current tendency to express party politics by means of Shirts,"[11] and added that pink was "the essentially false and negative colour because it is the dilution of something that is rich and glowing or nothing."[12] This "anaem[ic]" color is a wobbly middle-of-the-road color, especially in political matters. "There is," Chesterton continued, "a merely pink humanitarianism which I dislike even more than the *real* Red Communism."[13]

Lynd refutes Chesterton in his essay "In Defence of Pink." Lynd reminds his reader that pink is chosen in most English-speaking societies as the "symbol of perfection,"[14] particularly as it is linked with high society or the leisure class. For Lynd this class position finds itself in relationship to "pink humanitarianism": "I have never blinded myself to the fact that in politics I am a wobbling sentimentalist! I have said to myself, 'If only everybody were as pink as I, all this nonsense in the world would end in a week. If only everybody wobbled like me, how well everybody would get on together.'"[15]

We recognize pink as the feminine marker of gender from birth, and such markers of identification come under careful scrutiny in a masculinist society. A careless positioning of a feminine code onto/into a masculine marker could spell the difference for the well-being of one's manly virtue. And as both Alan Sinfield and George Chauncey reveal in their historical accounts of urban middle-class masculinity in turn-of-the-century England and America (respectively), the fear of women or the potential threat of feminizing men posed a serious reconsideration of male (self) representation of virility.[16]

Sinfield points out that, historically, "effeminate" behavior has been accepted in circles of the English leisure class and intellectuals. Before his trial in 1895, Oscar Wilde's behavior was not necessarily seen as deviant or morally objectionable. As Sinfield shows, however, the upshot of Wilde's trial for sodomy was that the effeminate male would no longer merely be judged as an effete figure of an intellectual or leisure class. He would now be identified as the homosexual. While "[e]ffeminacy preceded the category of homosexual . . ." it would now "[overlap] with and [influence] the period of its development."[17]

In urban centers of America at the turn of the century, as Chauncey shows in *Gay New York*, the male middle class witnessed women entering the new industrial work force, women teaching the boys of America in schools, and (distressingly) the presence of the "invert" in public spaces. (The invert was the male figure who had a "female soul," dressed in women's clothes, wore makeup, and most often took a woman's name.) These inescapable social factors aroused an anxiety over the very "manhood" of the male heterosexual. In the era of Theodore Roosevelt, defining American manhood became the major order of business. Men consumed themselves with "muscularity, rough sports, prizefighting, and hunting as an antidote to the overcivilization of

American men, . . . the cause was taken up in newspapers, boys' clubs, and backyard lots throughout the nation."[18] All the physical rigor and construction of the homosocial was in response to this perceived effeminization of the American male. Of course, the scapegoat for this rising homosocial would be the invert, who marked what the American male must not become in terms of behavior and self-representation. The turn-of-the-century's attempt to eliminate softness, effeminization, and overcivilization from America's cultural habits would move into high gear under the auspices of the McCarthy and Eisenhower era. The cataloguing of social markers by gender played an important role in the way post–World War II America would construct its political parameters. *Tea and Sympathy* highlights this delicately balanced, stridently defensive version of 1950s male anxiety.

What becomes apparent in this evolvement of male anxiety during the first half of the twentieth century, where it intersects with politics and gender identification, is that American culture and politics were viewed by a male middle class as being threatened by women and the homosexual—both of whom, ironically, must necessarily maintain the normative condition for the homosocial precisely through their difference. To compound this half-century of male-identified anxiety, the once easily identified invert became more difficult to see. He was more difficult to see because many men who exercised any sort of homosexual desire were fearful of being read as effeminate (and thereby read as homosexual) and so acted like "regular guys."

The publication of Alfred Kinsey's *Sexual Behavior in the Human Male* in 1948 further fueled the anxiety of that which could not be seen. Kinsey's report informed the American public of the ubiquity of homosexual activity. Its most striking and threatening aspect, however, was that, as John D'Emilio summarizes, "homosexuals came from all walks of life, and . . . did not conform in appearance or mannerism to the popular stereotype."[19] Both the homosexual and the Communist were viewed as domestic and international security risks as well. On the home front, the homosexual (or the "sexual pervert") threatened not only American youth but also governmental agencies.

According to a U.S. Senate report in 1950 by the Committee on Expenditures in Executive Departments, the influx of merely "one sex pervert [*sic*] in a Government agency tends to have a corrosive influence upon his fellow employees. . . . One homosexual can pollute a Government office."[20] More terrifying, however, was the danger of blackmail for the homosexual. American secrets were in peril, ironically, because of the homosexual's fear of being discovered. It is noteworthy that in April 1953, shortly before the Broadway opening of *Tea and Sympathy*, Eisenhower issued "an executive order barring gay men and lesbians from all federal jobs."[21]

The invisible Communist and the equally invisible homosexual were frequently conflated in political discourse. Arthur Schlesinger described Communism as "something secret, sweaty and furtive, like nothing so much, in the phrase of one wise observer of modern Russia, as homosexuals in a boy's school."[22] Republican Senator Kenneth Wherry of Nebraska could not put this anxiety more succinctly: "I don't say every homosexual is a subversive, and I don't say every subversive is a homosexual. But a man of low morality is a menace in the government, whatever he is, and they are tied up together."[23]

A color is assigned to the homosexual, like the Communist, in order to talk about this sexual/juridical anxiety that threatened to seep into sacrosanct American politics. Pink and red in 1950s America marked the invisible space of fear that urgently needed to be made visible. Robert Anderson's *Tea and Sympathy* and its making into a film are seated directly at the intersection of discourse where the American masculine subject found himself nervously guarding every performance he made on a day-to-day basis. Those making the film were extremely sensitive to these current affairs of state.

In October 1953, when the major studios jumped to purchase *Tea and Sympathy* film rights, Anderson refused to sell to Samuel Goldwyn unless the company retained a "*sine qua non* that the leading lady solve the boy's problem by giving herself to him sexually" and, further, that the film "kept the boy's problem [as springing] from the *malicious* charge of homosexuality . . . homosexuality was not to be glossed over."[24] In fact, the main reason for the PCA's continuous rejection of a possible screenplay was the consistent usage of the word homosexual or its implications. After confronting the zealous denouncements by the PCA and the Legion of Decency, MGM's strategy was to erase any and all references—explicit or implicit—to homosexuality from the screenplay. With other studios competing for the scripts, Dore Schary (vice president in charge of production at MGM) announced that the character of the boy would not point to the "question of homosexuality" but rather would "center the boy's problem on the fact that he was an 'off horse.' "[25] Schary, echoing a popular and comforting sentiment of 1950s America, saw the boy's "problem" as one of "cowardice and lack of manliness." He later recalls how dumbfounded he was when the Legion insisted on the woman's punishment simply because she had "given the young student a *healthy* sex experience."[26] Schary's relationship to this film highlights the liberal attitude that straddled the extreme right and left positions of both contemporary gender relations and politics in Hollywood. His stance, and it was often an unpopular one, would distress the studio bosses at MGM, not only with this film but also with many of the projects on which he worked.

Schary pushed hard for the making of such films as *Crossfire* (1947), *Battleground* (1949), and *Tea and Sympathy*. Films like *Crossfire* were hard sells, and Schary often put himself on the line for them. Of course, *Crossfire* was based on a novel, *The Brick Foxhole*, in which homosexuality was central to its plot. Schary, in part because of the Production Code, changed the homosexual to a Jew. As with *Tea and Sympathy*, the homosexual was erased.

Tea and Sympathy (like *Crossfire*) was important for Schary not because of homosexuality but because of the speech act of smearing. Schary based his moral agenda on his ability to work with others because they were good workers, not because of their political affiliations—or their homosexuality. His middle-of-the-road liberalism maintained the homosexual as a figure of pity and invisibility. This stance would invariably inform MGM's final version of *Tea and Sympathy*.

With the bidding war in high gear for the film rights of *Tea and Sympathy*, MGM "raised the ante to the then astonishing sum of $400,000, of which $300,000 would be withheld until Anderson turned in a filmable script."[27] This filmable script would include a prologue and an epilogue that would punish the wife's wrongs. This script would also translate the question of homosexuality into a conflict of defining masculinity.

Between January and August 1955, a series of screenplay rewrites was undertaken by Anderson and MGM. To convey to Shurlock his frustration with the archaic structure of the Code and the continuous intervention of the Legion of Decency, Schary sent him a letter (dated May 16, 1955) with a copy of an article in *Look* titled "How Much Do We Know about Men?"[28] The article was flanked by a full-page vertical photograph of a small boy looking up to the statue of David (whose genitalia are covered by a fig leaf). It was written by Lawrence K. Frank, who was, according to *Look*'s biographical account of the author, the "former chairman of the International Preparatory Commission for the International Congress on Mental Health." The essay attempts to underscore changing gender relations in America in terms of society's constituted system of values; it briefly mentions homosexuality, but mainly focuses the question on what it means to be a "real man" (i.e., "modern" man, who could now share "in baby and child care, in cooking, dishwashing, housekeeping") without threatening the definitions of male and female.[29] Schary's basic contention was that if this masculinity question could be discussed in a major national magazine, ought it not be brought to the screen? Schary (and so MGM), of course, won the debate.

On September 1, 1955, Shurlock informed Schary that Anderson's revisions "now meet the requirements of the Production Code." The moral heat, however, was far from turned off. On September 25, 1955, the *New York Times* ran an article, "MGM Solves Its *Tea and Sympathy* Script Problem," in which writer Tom Pryor interviewed MGM unit producer Pandro S. Berman. Albeit skewed to shift the emphasis away from homosexuality and toward the conflict of defining masculinity, the article conveys the certainty that the audience will recognize what the script is really about. Berman states:

> The theme of the play is essentially this: what is manliness? We haven't changed that at all. The boy is regarded by fellow students and the housemaster as an "off horse" because he doesn't flex his muscles and knock himself out climbing mountains or playing basketball. To them he is soft physically and becomes suspect. They conveniently pigeon-hole their standards for manliness and anyone who doesn't conform is an oddball. *We never say in the film that the boy has homosexual tendencies—I don't believe the word homosexual was actually spoken in the play either—but any adult who has ever heard of the word and understands its meaning will clearly understand this suspicion in the film.*[30]

For the MGM producers, smearing, or the malicious scapegoating of those with a degree of difference, was what the film was about. By this point in the making of the film, the homosexual who could not be seen because of his ability to elide interpretation would now render himself on the screen and become recognizable while remaining unseen. Berman announced this invisible presence by marking his invisibility.

The *New York Times* article threw the Legion into a tailspin. How could this notion of "suspicion" still remain at this point in the production? They still, however, carried the hammer and nails for keeping the closet shut. Fearful of losing moral control over the film industry, the Very Reverend Monsignor Thomas F. Little wrote to Shurlock on September 27, 1955, expressing his wish "respectively, to advise you of our impression of the proposed story changes." From published reports that the reverend had seen, there merely seemed "an effort . . . to color and mask the essential offensiveness of the questionable material . . . hence [there is] no elkmination [*sic*] of the grounds for serious moral objection."

Shurlock's response to the reverend was to tell him of his surprise at these published reports and of his intention to bring them immediately to the attention of Berman and Schary. But his gesture was only one of perfunctory politeness. By this time the film had been approved by the PCA. Shurlock, however, offered the Legion the opportunity to write its own version of the epilogue. Their rewrite points to the discursive weight of the Legion's attempt to control social meaning.

The Legion's corrections to the epilogue reflect their need for a transparently clear reading of Laura's transgressions and her punishments. Their rewrite left no question, either, about Tom's satisfactory transition from suffering young man to well-adjusted married heterosexual.

Anderson: These are terrible things to write you, Tom, about guilt and right and wrong. But you are old enough to know that when you drop a pebble in the water there are ever widening circles of ripples. There are always consequences.

Legion: These are terrible things to write you, Tom, about sin and guilt. But you are old enough to know that when you drop a pebble in the water there are ripples that may carry afar a burden of good or of evil.

And, from Anderson: Dear Tom, have a good life, a full life, an understanding life.

The Legion, however, sought to emphasize this portion of the letter with: Dear Tom, I was so pleased to hear that you were married.

While Anderson's version survives over the Legion's more egregious (yet banal) reworking, it still needed to fall between the Legion's moral condemnation and the PCA's enforced use of the unseen but ubiquitous homosexual who acted as the marker of difference and necessarily reinforced Tom's heterosexual union. The framing story of *Tea and Sympathy* is clearly the container of the closet.

After two years of debate, *Tea and Sympathy* would begin production. Just before the film's release, Dore Schary sent a letter to Arthur Loew deriding MGM's handling of *Tea and Sympathy*. "We abandoned a principle," he wrote, "alienated a good and valuable writer, [and] . . . hurt a valuable picture." His letter points to the instability and unreliability of the moral and political ground on which Hollywood finds itself when confronted with a socially taboo subject. Schary was frustrated with "the two or three people sitting in a room [who] insisted on words that are trite and self-righteous." Even though MGM had a "good battleground on which to wage a fight . . . we have retreated and run away."[31] According to Schary, two months after he sent this letter to Loew, and one month after *Tea and Sympathy* was released, Loew handed him a letter from an anonymous "loyal studio employee" that listed an array of charges, including accusations that Schary had had sex with MGM "glamorous female stars" and that he had "encouraged male stars to lose to [him] in gin games in exchange for assigning them juicy roles."[32] Schary was out of a job. While *Tea and Sympathy* was not the deciding factor in his firing, it certainly played a pivotal role in the tense dynamics between Schary and MGM executives.

AESTHETICIZING THE TEXT

Reading the autobiographies of Dore Schary and Vincente Minnelli, one is struck by what can best be described as the cordial relationship between them. Schary mentions Minnelli as director, and Minnelli recalls Schary as the outsider who would be friendly enough to send him a kind letter when he was embarking on a new project. Schary handled the front line of production and Minnelli made sure that the product was delivered, but to see this relationship as merely one of a labor/management situation is to dismiss the ways in which they overrode the "battleground" (to use Schary's terminology) that existed because of the Code and the studio system. They both showed a certain determination, albeit directed in different ways, that challenged the constraints under which they often had to work. While Schary negotiated the politics of the studio system, Minnelli constructed a film that would hyperbolize and aestheticize the anxiety of American men over the possible effeminization of their own masculinity.

There were particular arenas during the 1940s and 1950s where the display of the male body as homoerotic was circulated. Films such as Kenneth Anger's *Fireworks* (1947), the male erotica films from Apollo and Zenith studios, and the paintings of Paul Cadmus point to this representation of homosexual male desire. To declare Minnelli's hyperbolization of the male body—consider Gene Kelly in *The Pirate* and *An American in Paris,* or the young studs in *Tea and Sympathy*—as the site of such desire is potentially (and probably) valid; the homosexual, however, is not necessarily *identifiable* as such. While Pandro Berman earlier articulated the homosexual into visibility, we still do not see a homosexual. Tom, identified as creative and gentle (rehearsing his "feminine traits"), is *not* a homosexual. We can, however, see masculine anxiety and its attendant homophobia.

It is the masculinized figure who is caught in Minnelli's aesthetically frenetic mise-en-scène.[33] Minnelli's melodrama explores an aesthetic mise-en-scène that visually heightens the cultural anxiety of masculinity in postwar America. Traditionally, melodrama has been regarded as the genre of anxiety constructed through a symptomatic mise-en-scène (heightened gesture, color, etc.) as a way of revealing the repressed middle-class angst of sexual desire (usually the woman's). But to recommend the genre as only a symptomatic rendering of the repressed is to foreclose an analysis that looks to discover the ways in which those symptoms are actually produced and represented. Following the tradition of the historical aesthete (Huysmans, Firbank, Van Vechten, etc.), Minnelli practices a process of aestheticization on the mise-en-scène in order to make visible and hyperbolize the cultural anxiety of masculinity. Indeed, melodrama and its tradition of a "melodramatic imagination" are historically constituted as a practice of heightened representation.

While Minnelli's films need to be examined individually, one can argue that they visually render the hyperactivity of men's anxiety toward the production of their own masculinity. In *Tea and Sympathy*, the hypermasculinity of the homosocial does not necessarily deliver a representation of homosexual desire, but actually works to represent American homophobia of the 1950s. In effect, homosexual desire is not met not only because of its (en)forced silence but also because of the indetermination of exactly what that homosexual desire is. What can be displayed, however, is the aggressivity of the masculine figure within the homosocial grouping.[34] The anxiety of homosocial desire between men on the screen—homophobia—becomes that which can be seen. It is, in other words, not so much a question of locating homosexual desire as it is a question of illustrating homosexual panic.[35] In much of Minnelli's work he constructs a text whereby these de-sexed and hypermasculinized figures are pressed within and against the service of an aestheticized mise-en-scène that collapses any supposed verisimilitude surrounding the social order of masculinity, as well as pushing to the surface the entrenched homophobia of that social order. Even though Minnelli could not escape the shackles of the framing story demanded for *Tea and Sympathy*, he did direct a film that elides the proscription by aestheticizing the mise-en-scène, or the place in which these men cinematically reside.

Minnelli himself continually experienced an ongoing conflict about masculinity. The use of terms such as *shy* to define himself defy a seemingly more potent personal query. "I was never told that creativity was unmanly," Minnelli recounts,

Looking at Mr. Frazier's [Minnelli's first boss at Marshall Field's where he did window displays in the early 1920s] assistant, a William Bendix type, and talking to the other display men who were all married and raising families, I saw by their example that one could function as the male animal and still give vent to his so-called feminine traits. As a result, I wasn't cowed at this impressionable age into more conventionally male avenues of expression. I am thankful for that. I'd make a miserable football coach.[36]

Minnelli's effete demeanor would clearly put him in constant conflict with the anxiety of "what it means to be a man" in 1950s America. Minnelli's placement of the male bodies in *Tea and Sympathy* against his aestheticized mise-en-scène reveal "the hystericised body [offering] a key emblem of that convergence [psychic and corporeal], since it is a body pre-eminently invested with meaning, a body become the place for the inscription of highly emotional messages that cannot be written elsewhere, and cannot be articulated verbally."[37]

Al's decision to inform Tom of his patriarchal order (as it were) is bracketed by the two boys' pathetic attempt to help each other understand the socially constructed turmoil in which they are forced to live. Tom asks his friend to show him what it is that he does "wrong." He wants to know how he can be more "manly." Al offers to show Tom how to walk—"like a man." This masculine strut is parodied until it collapses under the strain of its own laborious construction, to be finally revealed as a socially constructed joke. It is at this moment in the film that masculine anxiety, confronted with its own ridiculous construction, can no longer support itself. Al, pressed within and against the mise-en-scène of the Minnellian text and finally caught in the vestiges of masculinity, can't understand why walking a particular way is manlier than any other.

But it is color, as is often the case with Minnelli, that will motivate the intricate possibility of reading this text beyond the surface narrative and will prove to be the activating agent for revealing the dialogic relationships between *Tea and Sympathy* and the historical world. It is apposite that just as color is used in the social and historical spheres to mark what is seemingly ubiquitous but unlocatable, it is used by Minnelli to confuse the rules—he places color in the film in order to reveal the production of this silenced meaning.

If color is used on the contemporary political scene to locate the unlocatable by McCarthy and friends, Minnelli would make certain that this peculiar hyperactivity to color code would be ironically and hyperbolically rendered on

Al (Darryl Hickman) teaches Tom (John Kerr) how to "walk like a man" in *Tea and Sympathy* (1956) (Courtesy Photofest).

the screen. In 1962, Minnelli states that the "film-maker must have a point of view toward his subject."[38] This point of view will determine the way in which the filmmaker will construct the subject from which he or she is working: "In each case all [the filmmaker's] decisions which determine style are, in turn, determined by your subject. You cannot impose this style. It must come *from* the subject."[39] Making the film must be considered a "situation as real life."

Minnelli's meticulous attention to the proper selection and utilization of color within the text works in direct relation with not simply his individualized worldview but also his complex relationships within the world. In order to develop a sense of color one must "[learn] to see color. We are all surrounded by color if we will only learn to notice it."[40] The play *Tea and Sympathy* presses two colors into the service of its mise-en-scène. While Anderson assigns these colors to characters' "essence," Minnelli engulfs the characters in these color assignations, at once immersing and suffocating them within the gendered roles they are culturally forced to play. Yellow is marked as Laura's color; it indirectly suggests Laura's "essence [as] gentleness."[41] In the film Laura is framed by yellow curtains in her kitchen; at other times she will be sitting in her yellow chair in her living room or surrounded by her yellow kitchen bowls.

Anderson marks blue as the color for men who are desperately clinging to their boyhood, unable to manage the cultural conditions of manhood. He puts Tom in a blue suit before his date with Elbe (the "town whore"), where he states, "Put me in a blue suit and I look like a kid."[42] Tom will wear blue pajamas, pants, and shirts throughout the film.

Minnelli, however, disperses these colors throughout the text so that they blend into variant hues in order to associate the characters' psychological and emotional states. He weaves the yellow and blue motifs through the narrative in order to formulate intratextual references to the internal psychology of the characters. In the beginning of the film, for example, we see Laura in her garden while we hear Tom sing a love ballad from his bedroom window. As they convene in the garden, Tom comments on her "green thumb" (green, of course, being the admixture of yellow and blue), at which point she realizes with surprise that this stunning fecundity only blossomed after her arrival at Chilton.

Green also symbolizes blue's need for yellow and yellow's need for blue. This sought-after balance of blue and yellow represents, in the film, the "necessary" link between the socially constructed gender extremes. The missing blue in Laura's life is foregrounded in Laura and Bill's inadequate sex life. Laura, when she first encounters Tom in her garden, comments that her garden needs more blue. Tom, however, will compensate for Laura's lack of blue by giving her a package of blue forget-me-not flower seeds, which he places on the dashboard of her blue/green car.

Later, Laura will bring some yellow roses to Ellie, grown from her garden and wrapped in blue paper, after she overhears Tom's phone call that establishes his appointed rendezvous (in order to prove his manhood) with Ellie. When Tom is about to leave for Ellie's place, Laura is dressed in a green evening gown. Tom's blue suit still represents the "little boy" who, under the regulatory control of the social order, desperately seeks to become a "regular guy." Blue is both the little boy and the social demand of that boy's masculine behavior. Tom's acceptance of yellow fulfills the acceptance of "gentleness" into the enforced masculinity of blue. This blending of blue and yellow is Laura's urgent plea to imbue the hypermasculine structure with its deprived gentleness, as well as to inject herself with the blue that is missing in her life.

Minnelli considered film a painter's canvas upon which the admixture of colors would work in harmony, yet never achieve an exact relationship to the colors in the "real" world. His love of Whistler, Van Gogh, and Matisse points to his stylistic echoing of these painters' use of color to aestheticize fleeting moments of time and space. These painters' brushstrokes did not seek to simulate and fix an identical replica of "reality"; rather, they rendered the color of the "real world" as they saw it. When Minnelli stated that the film must be considered a "situation as real life," it is in the context of placing that situation within the filmmaker's point of view. The cinema afforded Minnelli the opportunity to explore his painterly aesthetics in "real life."

Peter Lehman, speaking in terms of normative masculinist representation, argues that cinematic representation depends upon a "realist" aesthetic to maintain ideological masculinist meaning. "Our culture asserts," Lehman suggests, "and realist representation participates in reinforcing the belief of a fixed relation between the male body and connotations of masculinity—to be a strong man is to look like a strong man, and to be a weak man is to look like a weak man."[43] If the Hollywood film depends upon "realist" representations to subtend normative practices of masculinity, Minnelli's aestheticized mise-en-scène (a transgression of the "real") serves to disrupt those normative representations. Through his process of aestheticization, Minnelli makes visible American hypermasculinity by placing his men within a textual place that does not match the anticipated Hollywood equation of "realist" mise-en-scène equals "strong and powerful" men. In effect, those "real" men are made to look ridiculous and, indeed, hyperbolic in their masculine constructions when placed within Minnelli's aestheticized text.

In *Tea and Sympathy*, Minnelli's dispersion and reassigning of color realigns the cultural dictates of marking and foreclosing identity; color in a Minnelli film refuses to stabilize meaning. His colors blend with one another, disseminate at multiple emotional levels of the text, and, thereby, ironically play with the historical and cultural assumptions ("pink for girls, blue for boys") that seek to totalize representations of meaning and identity.

NOTES

I would like to thank the following for their continuous support during the writing of this essay: Steve Mamber, Vivian Sobchack, Peter Wollen, Chon Noriega, Janet Staiger, Dana Polan, Ed O'Neill, David Pendleton, Daniel Hendrickson, Marc Siegel, Suzanne Gerstner, Charles Silver at MoMA, and Sam Gill and staff at the Academy Library of Motion Picture Arts and Sciences in Los Angeles.

1. The story of the making of *Tea and Sympathy* is well documented—especially the events involving the MPAA, the Legion of Decency, and MGM. See Jerold Simmons,

"The Production Code under New Management: Geoffrey Shurlock, *The Bad Seed*, and *Tea and Sympathy*," *Journal of Popular Film and Television* 22, no. 1 (Spring 1994): 2–10. See also Stephen Harvey, *Directed by Vincente Minnelli* (New York: Museum of Modern Art and Harper and Row, 1989), 247–51.

2. Memo dated April 26, 1955. All sources regarding the interactions among the MPAA, the PCA, the Legion of Decency, and MGM, unless otherwise stated, are taken from the MGM Production Code files held at the Academy of Motion Picture Arts and Sciences, Margaret Herrick Library.

3. Anonymous, *The Reporter*, September 25, 1956, 3, 11.

4. The play's ending proves somewhat complicated insofar as the ambiguity of its ending is not completely free of homophobic conditions. As we will see, the suggestion in any way that one was a homosexual in 1950s America—or 1990s America for that matter—was a slanderous act.

5. Vito Russo, *The Celluloid Closet*, rev. ed. (1981; New York: Harper and Row, 1987), 112.

6. Ibid., 114 (emphasis added).

7. Eve Kosofsky Sedgwick, *Epistemology of the Closet* (Berkeley: University of California Press, 1990), 3. It is especially instructive to consider Sedgwick's work in terms of the discursive practices within the making of this film and the homophobic weight that is carried by those practices as they are constituted within Hollywood. As Sedgwick later posits: "the establishment of the spectacle of the homosexual closet as a presiding guarantor of rhetorical community, of authority—someone else's authority—over world making discursive terrain . . . extends vastly beyond the question of the homosexual" (230).

8. I'd like to thank Ed O'Neill for numerous discussions on issues of homosociality and homosexuality as well as for allowing me to read his unpublished paper, "Poisonous Queers." Delivered at the Berkeley Conference on Violence and Cinema, spring 1993.

9. Robert Anderson, *Tea and Sympathy* (New York: Random House, 1953), 94.

10. John Boswell, *Christianity, Social Tolerance, and Homosexuality* (Chicago: University of Chicago Press, 1980), 274.

11. G. K. Chesterton, *As I Was Saying* (1936; Freeport, NY: Books for Libraries Press, 1966), 109.

12. Ibid., 110.

13. Ibid. (emphasis added).

14. Robert Lynd, "In Defence of Pink," in his *In Defence of Pink* (London: J. M. Dent, 1937), 2.

15. Ibid., 6–7.

16. Alan Sinfield, *The Wilde Moment: Effeminacy, Oscar Wilde, and the Queer Moment* (New York: Columbia University Press, 1994); and George Chauncey, *Gay New York* (New York: Basic Books, 1994).

17. Sinfield, *Wilde Moment*, 74.

18. Chauncey, *Gay New York*, 113.

19. John D'Emilio, *Sexual Politics, Sexual Communities: The Making of a Homosexual Minority in the United States, 1940–1970* (Chicago: University of Chicago Press, 1983), 42.

20. Quoted in ibid.

21. John D'Emilio and Estelle B. Freedman, *Intimate Matters: A History of Sexuality in America* (New York: Harper and Row, 1988), 293.

22. Quoted in Stephen J. Whitfield, *The Culture of the Cold War* (Baltimore: Johns Hopkins University Press, 1990), 43. I'd like to thank Marc Siegel for pointing out this material.

23. Quoted in ibid.

24. Anderson, according to Shurlock's memo, which recounts the transaction between Anderson and Goldwyn, originally conceived of the film version for "art house" and European markets. This transaction also highlights the centrality of the "charge of homosexuality" as "malicious." See above, note 4 (emphasis added).

25. MPAA memo, November 2, 1953. When MGM finally had won the rights to the film, Schary would define the boy's problem as a "fear of sexual impotence" (MPAA memo, April 29, 1955).

26. Dore Schary, *Heyday* (Boston: Little, Brown, 1979) (emphasis added).

27. Harvey, *Directed by Vincente Minnelli*, 249.

28. *Look,* May 17, 1955, 52–60.

29. The Kinsey report clearly had much to do with "homosexuality" finding its space of utterance in the American vernacular. The word "homosexual" in the article is mentioned only once to suggest its possible existence. But even here in the *Look* article, the utterance is lumped with the "new" social anomalies of heterosexuality: "It is believed by some that male homosexuality is increasing, and there probably is much more 'petting' and 'necking' between young men and women today." Homosexuality is "believed by some" to be on the "increase," but this "believed" is at best merely a hypothesis because it certainly remains unseen.

30. Thomas Pryor, "MGM Solves Its *Tea and Sympathy* Script Problem," *New York Times,* September 25, 1955 (emphasis added). While Berman is technically right that the word *homosexual* is not mentioned in the play, *queer* is used as well as rather blatant inferences to what the *suspicion* is all about.

31. Schary, *Heyday*, 311–12.

32. Ibid., 5. It seems that there were two camps at MGM regarding Schary. One camp was frustrated by his continuous push for the "message film" and his undermining of the import of the traditional MGM entertainment vehicles, while the other camp saw him progressively moving the studio forward.

33. Mise-en-scène is understood here as everything that the director chooses to put within the filmic frame (props, wardrobe, lighting, bodies). While this essay focuses on Minnelli's use of color as a strategy for aestheticizing the sociohistorical conditions of the narrative, my larger project considers Minnelli's use/choice of (in particular) the male body as an important variable in the aestheticization of the text. Peter Brooks's essay "Melodrama, Body, Revolution" begins to reconsider the body as the site that reveals (through its performance in melodrama) its historical and disciplined inscription. See the essay in *Melodrama: Stage, Picture, Screen,* ed. Jacky Bratton, Jim Cook, and Christine Gledhill (London: British Film Institute, 1994), 11–24.

34. A number of Hollywood films made during this period, such as Edward Dmyt-

ryk's *Crossfire* (1947) or Nicholas Ray's *Rebel without a Cause* (1955), exhibit the hypermasculinity of the homosocial. One can also turn to certain genres that depend upon a homosocial makeup (the western, the gangster or crime film, etc.).

35. Sedgwick shows how this masculine anxiety gets played out juridically. "Homosexual panic" is the popular defense whereby a perpetrator of violence against a gay person claims his "supposed uncertainty about his own sexual identity." This defense "asserts [that there is] one distinct minority of gay people, and a second minority, equally distinguishable from the population at large, of 'latent homosexuals' whose insecurity about their own masculinity is so anomalous as to permit a plea based on diminution of normal moral responsibility." Sedgwick, *Epistemology*, 20.

36. Vincente Minnelli, with Hector Arce, *I Remember It Well* (Garden City. NY: Doubleday, 1974), 45.

37. Brooks, "Melodrama, Body, Revolution," 22.

38. Charles Reynolds, "An Interview with Vincente Minnelli," *Popular Photography*, July 1962, 106–7.

39. Ibid., 116

40. Ibid., 107.

41. Anderson, *Tea and Sympathy*, 4.

42. Ibid., 18.

43. Peter Lehman, *Running Scared: Masculinity and the Representation of the Male Body* (Philadelphia: Temple University Press, 1993), 100.

IV

MINNELLI TODAY:
THE RETURN OF THE ARTIST

Brushstrokes in CinemaScope
Minnelli's Action Painting in *Lust for Life*

SCOTT BUKATMAN

MAGNIFICATION AND ACTION

In Vincente Minnelli's *Lust for Life* (1956), the intimacy of Vincent van Gogh's easel painting is enlarged to epic, CinemaScope proportions. The projected image of cinema (in its classical incarnation) is always a magnified image, or an image magnified. This magnification could be made explicit by a sudden cut to a close-up, but was always a condition of the medium.[1] Size is not the sole province of cinema, however—large-scale paintings dominate the genres of history and religious painting, to say nothing of murals—but the cinematic image speaks to the phenomenon of magnification in a way that large-scale painting does not. Where huge canvases might depict a giant battle or a storm at sea, a cinematic image stretching across forty feet may feature nothing but a pair of eyes narrowing (Leone), or trembling hands applying a smear of bright lipstick (Powell)—a fragment of a human-scaled whole becomes an entirety that fills my field of vision and consciousness. Large paintings represent epic events, while cinematic close-ups turn the mundane into the epic.

Through the amplification of Van Gogh's brushstrokes, which now stretch across the wide screen, *Lust for Life* revels in both the materiality of the paint and the physicality of the act of painting. These magnified marks, fervently testifying to the presence, if not the very soul, of the painter, align the film strikingly with the intensity of the American postwar painting grouped under the heading of abstract expressionism—the large-scale, gestural art of Jackson Pollock, Clyfford Still, Willem de Kooning, and others. Perhaps surprisingly, the Irving Stone novel on which the film was based was not contemporaneous with its MGM adaptation, but was first published in 1934. Stone's image of a primitivist, self-destructive Van Gogh seems so attuned to the romanticizing of a particular kind of artist in 1950s America. In fact, however, the novel did not become a sensation until its reissue in 1946—just as postwar American art was beginning its ascent.[2] It was not the art of Europe but that of America that was then being mythologized; abstract expressionism was a large part of how America gained prominence in modern art in the postwar era.[3]

In 1952 the art critic Harold Rosenberg had famously described contemporary American painting as "action painting," a mode that, he argued, more than anything else memorialized the gestures of the artist. "At a certain moment the canvas began to appear to one American painter after another as an arena in which to act—rather than as a space in which to reproduce, redesign, analyze or 'express' an object, actual or imagined. What was to go on the canvas was not a picture but an event." Action painting was understood as an "event" and a "performance"—a record of a kinetic event more than of pre-considered, reflective creation.[4]

The cinema, too, is a medium dedicated to the recording of action, of movement, whether the movement of the objects of the world, the movement of the camera, or even the movement of the film through camera and projector. And by the mid-1950s, with the rise of wide-screen processes like the multiprojector Cinerama and its anamorphic single-projector offshoot, CinemaScope, film had also moved toward becoming more of an "event." When postwar outdoor recreations such as camping, car touring, do-it-yourself home improvements, and trips to Disneyland began to leach off the motion picture audience, and as the rise of the domestic medium of television began to make its presence felt, Hollywood reinvented itself as an engaged form of entertainment. As John Belton argues, Cinerama, CinemaScope, 3D, and other newfangled gimmicks were all marketed as "participatory events" for the viewer, and huge road-show adaptations of Broadway hits aligned cinema with the "special event" of theater.[5] Thus American film became something more participatory, and something more of a performance, just at the moment that American painting entered the gestural, performative moment of "action."

"Anything that has to do with action—psychology, philosophy, history, mythology, hero worship," is relevant to these paintings, Rosenberg argues. "Anything but art criticism. The painter gets away from art through his act of painting; the critic can't get away from it. The critic who goes on judging . . . as if the painter were still concerned with producing a certain kind of object (the work of art), instead of living on the canvas—is bound to seem a stranger." Therefore the action painter is closer to the world of action than to the world of art. The artist's technique takes him from the ethereal realm of culture and towards an earthy, unmediated and unmeditated primitivism. The primitivism of Minnelli's Van Gogh is commensurate with Michael Leja's contextualization of abstract expressionism in terms of what he calls the Modern Man discourse, which gained considerable traction in postwar American culture.[6] The template for the new primitive could be found in what Leja terms "Modern Man" nonfiction of the postwar era, guides to the Organization Men and other bloodless configurations of the day.

Leja has argued that "Abstract Expressionism had much more in common with the mainstream culture than some of its aggressively elitist defenders would allow."[7] One did not have to look far to find other contemporaneous "cultural manifestations of fascination with the primitive and the irrational. They turn[ed] up repeatedly in Hollywood films, newspaper and magazine articles, radio programs, and books of all sorts."[8] Set against the effete Modern Man was a more brutal, self-destructive, more mythic archetype, and some abstract expressionists (a.k.a. action painters) played this role for all it was worth, setting an American brutalism against its more effete European counterparts.

Indeed, for T. J. Clark, the only abstract expressionist canvases that matter are those "truly consumed with their own empty intensity, with painting as posturing, with a ludicrous bigness and lushness and generality."[9] Abstract expressionism was characterized by a *too-muchness: too much* paint, *too much* effort, *too much* artistic persona. Clark describes the color schemes of the most popular works by Mark Rothko: "the ones where a hectoring absolute of self-presence is maintained in face of the void; with vulgarity—a vulgar fulsomeness of reds, pinks, purples, oranges, lemons, lime greens, powder-puff whites."[10] A good painting by Hans Hofmann, he writes, is "tasteless to the core—tasteless in its invocations of Europe, tasteless in its mock religiosity, tasteless in its Color-by-Technicolor, its winks and nudges toward landscape format, its Irving Stone title, and the cloying demonstrativeness of its handling."[11]

Lust for Life (an Irving Stone title, taken, it is frequently forgotten, from one of Van Gogh's letters) exhibits, not just some, but *all* of these characteristics (and many of them also apply to the rest of the extravagantly vulgar Minnellian melodramas of the 1950s). It could be said that both abstract expressionism and wide-screen melodrama sought "to devise a form of modernist visual representation that could accommodate and enrich developing models of the human individual, models that attributed new importance to irrational others within human being."[12] The "action" in both depended upon the precarious balance between control and excess; the net effect was a willful vulgarity, a rudeness that bespoke petite bourgeois aspirations and limitations.

I want to argue that Minnelli's *Lust for Life* turns Vincent van Gogh into something of an action painter, not simply in its presentation of the painter-as-hero[13]—and an American hero at that—but also in the scale and even the vulgarity of its spectacle. The new emphasis on the physicality of painting, the way the canvas becomes a record of the moment, of embodied movement, is appropriate to the ferocious physicality of *Lust for Life:* a physicality that can be found in the hunched tension of Kirk Douglas's performance, the veracity of place produced by its well-publicized location work, the sumptuous material excess of its wide-screen expansiveness, the lushness of Miklos Rozsa's score, and the vibrancy of its Ansco Color palette. The purpose of this essay is to move beyond a consideration of abstract expressionism as a significant contextual sidebar to the film, to an argument more concerned with the physicality, even the mythos of physicality, on which both *Lust for Life* and "action painting" depended.

BIOPIC, EPIC, MELODRAMA

MGM had acquired the rights to the novel in 1946, with the stipulation that their film would be produced within ten years. With their option in danger of running out, MGM gave the project to John Houseman and Vincente Minnelli. Kirk Douglas had already expressed interest in portraying Van Gogh, given the pronounced resemblance between them, and having worked with Minnelli on *The Bad and the Beautiful,* his cooperation was easy to secure. The book and film contributed enormously to the cult of Van Gogh in America.

The film is a fascinating amalgam of three Hollywood genres: biopic, melodrama, and epic. Like all Hollywood biopics about artists (or writers or musicians), it flatters the audience without shame; each time a character in *Lust for*

Life proclaims Van Gogh's paintings to be worthless, an audience member, with the benefit of hindsight, can pat him or herself smugly on the back, free to believe that he or she would surely have recognized the man's genius from the get-go. The artist's biography had been a popular literary subgenre for some two hundred years. A certain pedantry is built into the form of the biopic; it is among the most formulaic and overdetermined of Hollywood's genres. But the mythology of Vincent van Gogh, the exemplar of the tortured artist as hero, gives the film real urgency. Rosenberg wrote that in postwar American art, "The act-painting is of the same metaphysical substance as the artist's existence. The new painting has broken down every distinction between art and life."[14] One of the few major art historians to consider *Lust for Life*, Griselda Pollock, notes that its release in 1956 "coincided with the contemporary death/suicide of Jackson Pollock and the high point of Abstract Expressionism's fame as the culmination of modernism and the avant-garde." Due to this charged context, later films on Van Gogh "seem tame," she writes.[15]

Where the biopic is pedantic, the historical epic has a more pedagogic function: Vivian Sobchack has theorized the phenomenological impact of this genre, whereby *temporal* excess (the sweep of history) is encoded as a *material* excess (wide screen, thousands of extras, gargantuan sets).[16] In *Lust for Life*, the "epic" sweep encompasses approximately ten tumultuous years in Van Gogh's life; they are also the last ten years of his life, but this death has no finality since it opens onto the immortality of Van Gogh as myth. The material excess of the epic is summoned by the film's slightly excessive length, the ten-year sweep, the grandeur of CinemaScope, and the passionate score by Miklos Rozsa (like *El Cid*, which Rozsa also scored, the film chronicles a journey past death and into immortality—these are not "sad deaths," but epic deaths). The film adds to the condition of spectacle by making much of the "wantonly expansive" use of the real, historical locations. The filmmakers were allowed to do a significant amount of location shooting in the Boringe, and in Holland, Arles, and Saint-Remy. Minnelli reports being resistant to shooting the film in CinemaScope, given the prominent role that would be given to showing Van Gogh's canvases, which were more suited to Academy ratio (it would, ironically, have been perfect for filming Pollock's work), but CinemaScope was required of any MGM film of consequence.

The use of Van Gogh's actual paintings, with the intense magnification of the brushstrokes and layers of thickly applied oil paint, further speaks to the film's "epic" excess. Large-scale still photographs were made of the original artwork (in the hands of numerous collectors and museums) using brief strobic flashes that would not damage them, and these images were then rephotographed for the CinemaScope movie camera. Minnelli was also concerned about the quality of color. In the mid-1950s, MGM had shifted away from Technicolor to less expensive processes: first Ansco Color (manufactured by Agfa), then the less expensive and less vivid Eastmancolor (billed as Metrocolor). Unable to use Technicolor, Minnelli and Houseman convinced MGM to allow them to shoot with the studio's remaining reserves of Ansco Color—even opening a special laboratory to allow it to be processed—although the prints would be made with Eastmancolor.[17]

The material excess represented by the medium of oil paint has been discussed by John Berger, who emphasized "its special ability to render the tangibility, the texture, the luster, the solidity of what it depicts."[18] It was a medium well suited to the depiction of mercantile wealth. The same might be said of the lustrous product that MGM was producing in the 1950s. James Naremore argues that in *Lust for Life*, "The visual experience offered to the public by MGM, in which we see beautifully photographed montages of Van Gogh's canvases and dozens of undetectable forgeries spread across the sets in casual abandon, is in part a spectacle of *wealth*, roughly equivalent to the thrill of watching the cozily massed extras in a DeMille epic."[19] *Lust for Life* is therefore certainly steeped in what Sobchack calls the "eventfulness" of the epic.

Part biopic, part epic, *Lust for Life* is also, even primarily, a melodrama. According to Thomas Elsaesser, in his influential essay "Tales of Sound and Fury," at the center of melodrama lies an abyss of inarticulateness, an insufficiency of language that he links to the symptomology of hysteria. Melodrama presents a precarious world of individuals grappling for control in a world resistant to (their) understanding or change. That world is objectified through aesthetic and performative excess—an oppressive, stylized mise-en-scène, and exaggeratedly emotive acting. Their failure is manifested in a failure of language: a halting and painful speech that cannot say what it must, or a torrent of words that only seem to hide the impossibility of true articulation.[20]

Michael Leja rightly contends that abstract expressionism had much in common with Hollywood cinema, but he emphasizes film noir, which I think is the wrong genre. It is true that "Like Mythmaker painting, film noir attributes a complex, layered, conflicted subjectivity to its protagonists. . . . Sometimes inner compulsions are portrayed as the principal factors in [that protagonist's] destructive actions." But noir is hardly the only genre to provide such a correlate.[21] Leja seems almost to *repress* melodrama (not "tough" enough, perhaps?). While both noir and melodrama challenge a powerful, self-knowing masculinism, the former frequently displaces sexual anxiety onto the figure of a femme fatale, whereas in melodrama the feminine is internalized, yielding far more tormented, self-contradictory protagonists. James Dean in *East of Eden* and *Rebel without a Cause* comes to mind, as do Marlon Brando's more classically masculine Stanley Kowalski in *A Streetcar Named Desire* and Douglas's tormented Jonathan Shields in *The Bad and the Beautiful*.

Melodrama, with its emphasis on "the misunderstood artist," may be a somewhat clichéd approach to the telling of an artist's life. Typically, the artist articulates himself, not by language, but through an art that is misapprehended for much (if not all) of the artist's lifetime. But melodrama is also particularly appropriate to Van Gogh's life—not only because his tragic life is the very stuff of melodrama, but also because his own writings reveal something of a melodramatic imagination. The words of his cousin's rejection, the deliciously fevered "*Never, no, never!*" echo through Vincent's letters just as they do in the film (as a slightly variant "*No, never, never!*"). And he recognizes his own problems of self-expression: explaining one of his outbursts to Theo, he writes that, "what I say at such times is what I've been bottling up for a long time and then blurt out, sometimes quite bluntly."[22] Stone's novel is similarly melodramatic: "A great inarticulate surge of grief welled up in his throat."[23] Again, one thinks of Jonathan Shields's confrontation with Georgia Lorrison in *The Bad and the Beautiful,* in which a flood of words pours forth until the character breaks down into an inarticulate rage of self-loathing.

And, of course, the Hollywood melodrama has become recognized as a fundamentally antirealist genre, one that sacrifices physical accuracy and verisimilitude in favor of a distorted, intensified mise-en-scène reflective of emotional tensions and subjective states. In this context, Van Gogh's comments about his favorite painters has some resonance: they "are the true artists, because they do not paint things as they are, examined in a dry analytical manner, but as they . . . feel them to be. . . . I long most of all to produce those very inaccuracies, those very aberrations, reworkings, transformations of reality, as may turn it into, well—a lie if you like—but truer than the literal truth."[24]

THE WORLD OF THE IMAGE

It's possibly heretical to advance this claim in a book on Minnelli, but the image track of *Lust for Life* seems at first somewhat superfluous, serving the literate script and the performances of the actors. But as the film progresses and Van Gogh moves toward mastery of the image, the film's images become increasingly sumptuous and autonomous. At the height of Vincent's passion (a passion both euphoric and destructive), the film's images and Vincent's become one, and come to constitute a world of their own.

Minnelli's film effectively adapts a novel that has not aged well, and the initial restraint of the image at first seems due to the film's status as a literary adaptation. Elsaesser has written of the effect of narrative compression in Minnelli's work, a compression that results in the piling of climax upon climax, accentuating the overall tone of simmering hysteria, and this is certainly true of *Lust for Life*.[25] Vincent's disastrous, abortive love affairs, his break with both the ministry and his family (except of course, for Theo), his emotional and physical struggles and debilitations, and his fiery battles with the impressionists all take place in the film's first hour. The script was written by Norman Corwin, an important writer for radio who had produced relatively few screenplays (a good deal of the dialogue comes straight from the novel[26]). Corwin distills and largely dispenses with the interminable sections of the novel devoted to the all-star roster of Parisian artists drinking and arguing about the nature of art and is adept at providing backstory unobtrusively but effectively.

In fact, the soundtrack conveys a great deal of information: in dialogue, in Theo's voice-over readings of Vincent's letters, and in Rozsa's underscoring. There are few stretches devoid of either words or music. We are told about the horrors of the miners' life in the Boringe, and of Vincent's desire to understand and help them. Rozsa's score emphasizes the drama of life down the mines, and the exhilaration of Vincent's first encounter with the paintings of the impressionists. The palette in the early parts of the film contributes to this de-emphasis of the image. The scenes at the Boringe and at The Hague, even at the family home in Nuenen, are presented in muted earth tones: somber olives, grays, and browns. At this point, Vincent is only drawing, not painting, charcoal and chalk monochromatic studies on brown paper. The image becomes more vivid at the beach in Scheuvingen, a richer palette whipped by wind and captured in oil paint, but this is a brief interlude, and even in Vincent's studio the paintings are few and scattered, still surrounded and swallowed by the plethora of monochromatic drawings. Up to this point the image has served a primarily illustrative function, operating with restraint and with that almost Bazinian realism (long takes, deep space, and moral uncertainties) that characterizes many of Minnelli's melodramas.[27] The film seems at risk of becoming a series of *tableaux vivants,* an episode of *Masterpiece Theater,* even, perhaps, an issue of *Classics Illustrated.*

But with the image relieved of the burden of narrative, it is freed to do something else. In Paris, the palette begins to shift to lighter, brighter colors; significantly, this does not happen through depictions of sun-drenched landscapes or broad boulevards, but through Vincent's encounter with an exhibition of impressionist paintings. As Naremore notes, "In place of Parisian nightlife, *Lust for Life* offers the visual spectacle of Van Gogh's own work."[28] Work by Renoir and Monet rivets Vincent's attention, and in an epiphanic moment, the first of many, the camera holds and tracks in on a Monet, a painting of a woman in a field. Then, more words. Vincent argues with Theo, Vincent is lectured by Pissarro, but finally, finally words begin to fade, replaced now by a slow montage of Vincent's paintings, which move surely toward the liberated colors and thick dabs of paint that are recognizably "Vincent's." Yet another lecture follows, this one by Seurat, and Vincent briefly tries his hand at pointillism, painting a sun-drenched garden while closeted by night in Theo's apartment. But through Vincent's frustrations and travails, something has been added to the filmic image: a vividness, a luminosity, a bright clarity from which Vincent's paintings and the film will never return.

The image track crescendos with Vincent's arrival at Arles. He arrives at night, dumped in a creaky bed in a squalid room. Beyond the shutters, all that is visible is an inky void; there is literally *nothing there.* But, come morning, Vincent is awakened by twittering birds. Wiping the sleep from his eyes, he rises and throws open the shutters. Here, exactly one hour into the film (precisely halfway through) the image erupts in a manner not unlike Dorothy's arrival in the Technicolor Land of Oz. The intense color of the peach trees blossoms forth, not with the saturated candy colors of Oz but the subtler tones of Ansco-inflected nature. But it is more than the emergence of color— the film has already gone there—it is the addition of emphatic camera movement to vibrant color that summons a feeling of delirious, utopian plenitude. A montage sequence of moving shots takes us beneath the spreading trees, follows their upward reach to the sky, and seamlessly merges with a tilt down a painted landscape. The world experienced by Vincent has become, through montage and movement, one with the world created by his paints.

As his life in Arles continues, and Vincent works himself increasingly into a state of nervous exhaustion, the colors become feverish, hallucinatory. The close-ups become more intense, the canvases more magnified upon the CinemaScope screen. By the time he collapses in the café, Vincent has come to in-

habit his paintings. "In my picture of the Night Café," he wrote in a letter
to Theo,

> I have tried to express the idea that the café is a place where one can destroy
> oneself, go mad or commit a crime. In short, I have tried, by contrasting
> soft pink with blood-red and wine-red, soft Louis XV-green and Veronese
> green with yellow-greens and harsh blue-greens, all this in an atmosphere
> of an infernal furnace in pale sulphur, to express the powers of darkness in a
> common tavern.[29]

It is not at all surprising that this very café becomes a hallucinatory setting—
part reality, part painting, part dream—in Minnelli's film. Vincent rouses
himself from an alcoholic stupor and his bloodshot eyes absorb the unre-
lievedly flat reds, the sulfurous lamps, the slow clack of the billiard balls: a
saturated, immersive setting more truly expressionist in its saturated colors
than the black-and-white nightmare settings of *Caligari*. Subjective reality has
become the only reality, naturalism has no place here.

Vincent's awakening in the Night Café is part of a series of shots that frame
him within his own paintings. The shot begins with a striking dissolve from a
close-up of his 1888 canvas *Starlight over the Rhone* that momentarily super-
imposes Vincent's brushstrokes on the photographed figure of Vincent himself. For that instant, the artist seems a painted creation, a product of his own
fevered vision. Earlier in the film, while discussing matters with his sister in
Nuenen in a static two-shot, Vincent is framed by his first major painting, *The
Potato Eaters*, as though he were at a table with the peasant family he is
celebrating. While painting outdoors in Arles he is filmed in close-up before
one of his canvases of blossoming trees, the painting filling the background.
And, convalescing after the severing of his ear, he is awakened in his bedroom
by the sensation-seeking crowd outside. The bedroom set is a careful copy of
the room in his famous painting, which has been emphasized in an earlier
scene, in happier times, by a cut from the painting to the identically framed
set. Now, though, the room has become his prison: he is trapped in the
confines of his own aesthetic; there is no reality beyond the one he can create.

Parker Tyler wrote of Jackson Pollock's swirling brushstrokes: "If one felt
vertigo before Pollock's differentiations of space, then truly one would be lost
in the abyss of an endless definition of being. . . . But we are safely looking at it,
seeing it steadily and seeing it whole, from a point outside."[30] I wonder if this is
also true of the hysteria and excess of Minnelli's own vertiginous crescendos—

Kirk Douglas's Van Gogh in the Night Café from *Lust for Life* (1956).

if they do not edge up as closely to the abyss, then neither do they, in their wide-screen synaesthetic immersiveness, offer the viewer the same safety of "a point outside."

PERCEPTION AND PERFORMANCE

But that first morning in Arles is indisputably celebratory: the discovery of a productive vision capable of *remaking* the world. Griselda Pollock's analysis of this same scene, however, emphasizes the power of *nature* to inspire the creative vision of the artist. She argues that the film mythologizes artistic creation as grounded primarily in an act of perception. "Art is at once direct visual experience and the personal filter through which nature passes."[31] By returning to the actual locations in which the life was lived and the paintings produced, and by following his rejection of the overcultured artistic debates of Paris for the sun-drenched fields of Arles, the film proposes that Van Gogh was able to introduce "Nature back into Culture." Following Elsaesser's essays on Minnelli, Pollock writes that the only way for Van Gogh "to cut through the resistance of the world around him" is through "his gaze as an artist. Vision thus provides a moment of lyrical liberation when the artist looks at nature."[32]

Griselda Pollock links the epiphanic vision that accompanies Vincent's arrival at Arles to the Central Park sequence of *The Band Wagon* (1953) in its negotiation of "the relation of the popular and natural to the cultural and elite." In *The Band Wagon*, Fred Astaire's Tony Hunter and Cyd Charisse's Gabriel Gerard stroll past a small group of dancers to a solitary spot. There, "in the park, close to Nature, without choreography, true art is presented as something which is neither commercialized popular dance nor formalised high art, but a direct overflowing of feeling into freely expressive movement."[33] There is something to this, but I cannot accept *The Band Wagon*'s version of Central Park as nature, when it is a rather stylized MGM set. In Minnelli's films, the idea of nature is always already mediated: this remains more Tony's world than either Gaby's *or* nature's.

It is again nature that informs Pollock's understanding of Vincent's epiphany in Arles. When Vincent first looks from his bedroom window, she argues that the subsequent montage represents his point of view through a classic reverse shot, but she further suggests that the montage actually is not grounded in any precise point of view but rather with what she calls an "all-overness."[34] "The camera's movements feed a nostalgic fantasy of the total freedom of the eye," she writes, a notion of a "disembodied eye" familiar to readers of Jean-Louis Baudry. These shots of the real landscape of Arles "then dissolve into painted images while retaining the same upward and downward movement," and thus: "Pure perception slides effortlessly into art, signifying by this sleight of photographic representation that art is merely the optical register of pure individual perception." The "innocence or intensity of his artistic vision" gives us "not only his vision of nature, but Nature itself. . . . What is elided is of course [of course!] the fact of both film as a production . . . and art as a graphic and material production process."[35] Oddly, then, Pollock holds that this montage, the first vivid and stylized sequence of the film, where filmic technique is most evident, is where the work of the signifier is most transparent, most effectively hidden.

I would counter that the bleed between individual perspective and this "all-overness" rather *marks* the site of—the work of—production, not its elision. That the paintings are animated by the camera with the same pans, tilts, and dissolves used on the "natural" landscape (as natural as CinemaScope and Ansco Color could allow) suggests that Van Gogh's vision gives us a performance *unleashed,* not that "art is merely the optical register" of a pure perception.[36] What is celebrated in this sequence, what I believe the spectator identifies with, is the movement beyond an extravagant *seeing* of the world to a productive vision that *remakes* it.[37]

The bountiful region of Arles facilitates performance, a performance of creation, for Vincent. In that context, the opening of the shutters might be seen to correspond, not to liberation of vision and nature, but to the raising of

Van Gogh's opening of the shutters in the Arles section of *Lust for Life* corresponds to the "raising of a theatrical curtain," as in "The Boy Next Door" from *Meet Me in St. Louis.*

In *Lust for Life*, Gauguin (Anthony Quinn) visits Van Gogh at the cluttered yellow house in Arles.

a theatrical curtain (not unlike Judy Garland singing "The Boy Next Door" while framed by the window and curtains of her home in *Meet Me in St. Louis* [1944]). In Minnelli's hands, the arduous work of production, Vincent's frantic workings of paper and canvas, can easily be seen as analogous to the rehearsals that go on in *The Band Wagon,* while the paintings, in sumptuous color and wide screen, made kinetic by camera and editing, achieve the perfect performative synthesis of the musical numbers. I am of course invoking Elsaesser's central dictum that Minnelli's melodramas aspire to the condition of his musicals.

Lust for Life is not about the purity of perception so much as the necessity of performance. "Bring me some red," the painter Derain said on his deathbed, "some red and some green." This line is quoted by Stevie, the young artist-patient at the outset of Minnelli's 1955 melodrama *The Cobweb,* and the terror evoked is a terror of whiteness, the absence of color; the absence of color speaking to an absence of passion, of the Minnellian decor that is an extension of self, of life, of humanity. The mute (or perhaps shrieking) whiteness of the blank canvas needs to be filled, it summons performance, intervention, action (the same can be said of the blank page that terrifies the writer Jeffrey Moss in *Bells Are Ringing* [1960]). Painting becomes not the transcription of nature, but a performance of energy that brings color to the world. The array of paintings carelessly strewn about the yellow house in Arles or framed as Vincent's legacy at the film's end offers a plenitude that is testament to the obsessive work of their production.

A Painting Locomotive

Serge Guilbaut notes that during the postwar period "the United States was generally seen as a culturally dry, unsophisticated, crude, antihumanistic, and cold land. The country was young, violent, and technological, good for the movies but not fit to participate in the old traditional discourse of painting."[38] Guilbaut further identifies some of the self-identified clichés by which America and France defined themselves and each other: "America was violent, brutal, and free, while France was overcultured, suave to the point of decadence, and riddled with inner contradictions. One was rough, the other was slick. Interestingly enough, both sides agreed on the validity of these clichés for differentiating their two cultures. The catch was that each country saw its characteristics as positive compared to the negative qualities of the other."[39]

The physical work of artistic production occupied the center of Rosenberg's category of action painting, displacing other aspects of the creative process such as contemplation, reflection, sketching, and reworking. Tactically, this proved significant—painting was now a man's activity in keeping with America's image as a place that was "violent, brutal, and free."[40]—something altogether different from what was perceived as the effete, mannered, and bloodless modernism being produced over there in Europe. Jackson Pollock was the archetype of the archetype of the American abstract expressionist, his notorious drinking binges, his violence, his impropriety, and, not least, the seeming inarticulate physicality of his mode of painting, all contributing to his fame both inside and well beyond artistic circles. Rosalind Krauss captures the self-consciousness of his post when she refers to "that dissolute squat, in his James Dean dungarees and black tee-shirt,"[41] a comparison that suggested itself even before their similar deaths by car crash (a variation of what Georges Bataille has termed *automutilation*[42]). Pollock was a kind of Method actor, a performer seemingly tapped into the culture's most atavistic urges.[43] J. Hoberman writes, "The brutish Marlon Brando who galvanized Broadway in the 1947 production of *A Streetcar Named Desire* reminded more than one member of the New York art world of Pollock; two years later, *Life* introduced Pollock to America as something like the Brando of abstract art."[44]

Lust for Life Americanizes its European protagonist—Van Gogh becomes, via Kirk Douglas, an American in Paris (and Nuenen, and Arles). Theo was portrayed by the British actor James Donald, and it is Theo's voice that reads Vincent's letters on the soundtrack, as though Vincent's reflective, learned, and articulate persona had to be separated from his more primitive, intuitive, and physical self. But Guilbaut's observation that the clichéd European artist was "riddled with self-contradiction," is also figured in *Lust for Life*'s presentation of Van Gogh. While Vincent shares some of Pollock's brutal primitivism, it is Anthony Quinn's Paul Gauguin who has the swagger and hard-drinking machismo ("Two absinthes!" he shouts to a bartender).

The self-contradictions of Vincent's character are most pronounced in the film around the dialectic of *work* and *emotion*. As is often the case with postwar American melodrama, the male protagonist is feminized, primarily by a hyperemotionalism that distinguishes them from the other men in the film. This is pronounced in *Lust for Life:* Vincent doesn't work—even Theo calls him an "idler" and supports him financially. Repeatedly he is accused of shirking his responsibilities, of being unable to provide for his spouse—be it Kee or Sien—or, indeed, even feed himself. His idleness is often linked to his perceived weakness: Gauguin says that while he might have some of the same problems as Vincent, "I don't whine about it!" Kee's father accuses him of being unable to withstand pain or disappointment without "whimpering." In Arles, Vincent proves to be a very happy homemaker: when Theo takes a wife, Vincent takes Gauguin. He has decorated the room for Paul, giving him *Sunflowers.* "I painted them for you," Vincent says, to which Paul bemusedly replies, "That's very friendly of you, Vincent . . . very friendly." If Vincent can now provide a home, it is nevertheless in the guise of a wife, albeit one who can't cook. Just as he did with the women in his life, Vincent throws himself tumultuously into his relationship with Gauguin, demanding complete attention, his ardor manifesting itself in obsession, unrestrained verbiage, and "whining." Vincent is a classic hysteric. As with other male protagonists of postwar melodramas, a torrent of words cannot hide the character's inability to articulate the deepest feelings, to confront the existential despair of ultimate loneliness.

But at the same time that Vincent is presented as an unemployed idler, he is also portrayed as the most industrious of workers. He journeys down to the mines, tends the sick, and educates the young at the Boringe; in Nuenen, surrounded by his charcoal studies he resembles the unflaggingly industrious Jonathan Shields; Van Gogh's actual letters continually stress the fact of labor —hard labor—in the constructing of art. "To get to the essence of things one has to work long & hard. . . . Art demands dogged work, work in spite of everything and continuous observation."[45] In conversation with Theo, para-phrased in the film but here quoted from Van Gogh's original letter, Vincent argues:

Then there is the other kind of ne'er-do-well, the ne'er-do-well despite himself, who is inwardly consumed by a great longing for action, who does nothing because his hands are tied, because he is, so to speak, imprisoned somewhere, because he lacks what he needs to be productive, because disastrous circumstances have brought him forcibly to this end. Such a one does not always know what he can do, but he nevertheless instinctively feels, I am good for something! My existence is not without reason! I know that I could be quite a different person! How can I be of use.[46]

In Arles, he writes that he is "working like a steam engine"; in his letters he refers to himself as "a painting locomotive." Later, in the asylum at Saint-Remy, he writes that he works "like a miner who knows he is facing disaster," but, more hopefully, he describes one of the characteristic, somber silhouetted figures in a painting as "Any man, struggling in the heat to finish his work." Despite being a symbol of impending death, the sister ministering to him notes that, "It doesn't seem a bad death"; to which Vincent replies that it isn't—to "work, boldly and joyously" is the best, and the most, that a man can do.

Thus Vincent is fractured, an incoherent figure; an "idler" in a world of working men, he is also the man who works the hardest, who is never, ever not working. To live is to struggle for definition, and that struggle is work of the highest, most demanding order. Art is presented as *work, labor*—that activity of remaking the world in the terms of one's own aesthetic that is the hallmark of Minnelli's films. These paintings do not come easily to Vincent. It's difficult to imagine describing a Van Gogh painting as "effortless"; rather, the canvas manifests labor in its layers of paint, the sense of frantic haste, the pigments squeezed directly from the tube to the canvas, the quest for a visual language adequate to the intensity of the experience (as well as to the autonomy of the medium).[47] This is why Kirk Douglas is so perfectly cast: the hunched yet expansive physicality of his performance—what Naremore calls Douglas's "crouched energy and muscular, tormented gestures"—is similarly "effortful."[48] (Douglas here and in *The Bad and the Beautiful* gives us two men obsessed with *making pictures*.)

There is therefore some breakdown of the dialectic with which Vincent is constantly being upbraided: Vincent indeed suffers from an excess of emotion, but also from an excess of industry. He is a man possessed, obsessed, driven endlessly by the imperative to create. "Must you persist in the face of everything?" Theo asks, already knowing the answer. Yes, he *must*. And in persisting he both finds himself and goes mad. Jean Douchet has described "the problem of the artist" at the center of Minnelli's work, "confronted by the work of art which absorbs him, but which also menaces him in his very existence as soon as he has created it."[49] "My pictures come to me in a dream, with a terrible lucidity," he writes. At this point the film begins to resemble a canvas by Van Gogh; at this point he almost literally inhabits the frenzied intensity of his paintings. In one of Van Gogh's own letters he writes that he is "in a constant fever of work."[50] When he is finally committed to the hospice at Saint-Remy, the bureaucratic head of the facility notes in his dictated report that his patient suffers from "excesses of work and emotion." The rest of the world may distinguish between these two states, but in Vincent, principles associated with the masculine and the feminine commingle, and the clichéd constructs of "American" and "European" are not easily separated.

PERFORMING PAINTING

A hallmark of Minnelli's style is the explosion, at moments of emotional epiphany and breakdown, into a more unrestrained, hysterical stylistic realm that sweeps the spectator into a heightened sensorial emotionalism. *Lust for Life* features an abundance of such moments: the awful awakening in the Night Café and the scene of self-mutilation are but the two most dramatic. But the film is punctuated as well by epiphanic montage sequences of Van Gogh's work. In the transformation of painting to cinema that occurs in *Lust for Life*, the magnification of the brushstroke moves us beyond the *materiality of the medium* to the *physicality of production*.

At first the camera keeps a respectful distance—a zoom in or out on a complete canvas—but the montage becomes more rapid as Vincent becomes more frenzied, an array of frenetic details. Closer shots of sinuous brushwork displace the earlier emphasis on composition and location—now the *inner* landscape dominates. In the scenes at Saint-Remy the camera lingers more as the brushstrokes become more lustrous. The camera, accompanied by Rozsa's melodic theme, pulls out to reveal the glorious *Starry Night*, but two abrupt cuts, punctuated by the music, isolate the central swirl of the Milky Way and a jagged array of moon and stars. The thickness of the paint, the clashing colors, and the vertiginous brushstrokes fill the CinemaScope frame, pushing out at the edges, threatening to overwhelm everything. Now the film has pushed figural painting into the realm of abstraction—a characteristic task of modernist painting—the giant brushstrokes summoning the arabesques of Jackson Pollock's painting.[51]

In 1951, a short film of Jackson Pollock painting, produced by Paul Falkenberg and photographed by Hans Namuth, premiered at the Museum of Modern Art in New York (the film was soon followed by the publication of a portfolio of Namuth photographs of Pollock).[52] The film helps make more explicit the link between cinema and "action painting." There, onscreen, is the performing body of the artist, making the broad gestures that send his paint through space and onto its receiving surface. Pollock's body is in constant motion; the film does not depict a contemplative mode of creation. Elizabeth Frank writes that the film reveals "a sense of immediate, intuitive decision."[53] But, as she notes, the film was also instrumental in creating the sense of Pollock as a spontaneous performer, for whom acting and painting are one and the same. Rosenberg's "The Action Painters" appeared the next year.

The indexical relation between gesture and painting (what Rosalind Krauss refers to as "making an image by means of an airborne gesture through which one could see the body of the artist himself"[54]), now becomes iconic. In this transformation, Pollock becomes one with all the myriad performers whose gestures have been inscribed on celluloid. There is little difference, to paraphrase the lyric of "That's Entertainment" between the indexical trace of Fred Astaire's choreographed routines and Jackson Pollock's choreographed production of abstraction. "The painting itself is a 'moment' in the adulterated mixture of his life," Rosenberg continues, "whether 'moment' means the actual minutes taken up with spotting the canvas or the entire duration of a lucid drama conducted in sign language."[55] Again, Namuth's filming of Pollock's performance makes that connection explicit, but it was always there in the emphatic, existential relation between the artist's body and his production.

Lust for Life and the Falkenberg-Namuth film not only represent the performance of painting, they also frame painting as performance—as surely (and as sure) a performance as Fred Astaire/Tony Hunter's dancing in *The Band Wagon*. The trace of Vincent is recorded not only on the surface of his canvases, but also on the surface of the film: the grimacing, the hysteria, the abjection of Vincent's self, as well as the frantic acts of artistic production. In the 1951 film, Namuth's camera follows Pollock as he works a large canvas laid on the ground outside his studio, accompanied by his laconic commentary ("my painting is direct . . . I enjoy working on a large canvas . . ."). Then the technique of the film changes: Pollock hangs his work on the wall, turning the painting into a product, inert and complete, and the camera suddenly becomes more active:[56] close-up details and animating the work by zooming, tracking, dissolving, and panning across the surface of the broad canvas. This is precisely how the camera will treat Van Gogh's canvases in *Lust for Life,* moving from wide views to magnified details in which the concretized movement of the work's creation is revivified through an array of cinematic effects.[57]

So Rosenberg's conception of action painting does not simply posit a deep, expressive relation between the artist and the work (how could it be otherwise?), but rather emphasizes the *physical* relationship. "The act-painting is of the same metaphysical substance as the artist's existence. The new painting has broken down every distinction between art and life."[58] *Lust for Life* takes on the same task with regard to Van Gogh, not only suggesting that the paintings are expressions of Van Gogh's emotional torments and euphorias, but also that the paintings are literally extensions of Vincent. "I want to get to the point," Vincent wrote to his brother, "where people say of my work: that man feels deeply, that man feels keenly."[59] But the strategy of the film is to demonstrate the *physicality* of Vincent's emotion. The simian posture, the wheedling voice, the violent outbursts—all of these make the life of the heart legible on the surface of the body. The frenzied painting does much the same thing— Vincent rails against the world and the canvas, his self-loathing (and megalomania) directed against his work.

The performance of painting is thus part of the film's strategy of corporealizing Vincent, forging an existential bond between his excesses of emotion, the physical symptoms of that agony, and the paintings as productions of that excess. It becomes impossible to consider these brushstrokes apart from the labor or action of producing them. Naremore proposes that *Lust for Life* is "more interested in dramatizing [Van Gogh's] behavior than explaining or justifying it,"[60] and this speaks to a valuation of temporal immediacy and the moment over psychology and interpretation; this, too, is fundamental to the performance at the center of Rosenberg's conception of action painting. Rosenberg writes, "A painting that is an act is inseparable from the biography of the artist"[61]—the biography and body of the artist—and this has some relevance to the immersive biopic that is Minnelli's *Lust for Life*. In fact, in its physicality, its immediacy, and its vulgarity, and with *Lust for Life* and Namuth's film of Pollock firmly in mind, perhaps it can be said that action painting aspired to the condition of cinema.

TRANSPORTS OF JOY

Abstract expressionism was an artistic movement that, for T. J. Clark, was unafraid of emotional excess and soul-baring cacophony. "I cannot quite abandon the equation of Art with lyric. . . . By 'lyric' I mean the illusion in an artwork of a singular voice or viewpoint, uninterrupted, absolute, laying claim to a world of its own. . . . Lyric cannot be expunged by modernism, only repressed."[62] Needless to say, cinema, and melodrama in particular, often operates in a lyric mode. Naremore has praised the extravagant *Lust for Life*'s "implicit recognition that the practice of art (including the practice of movie-making) can be at once heroic, neurotic, and absurd,"[63] and Elsaesser's sense of the melodramas as musicals "turned inside out" similarly points to the dangerous proximity of self-destruction and euphoric fulfillment—*It doesn't seem a sad death*.[64] Georges Bataille has written of Van Gogh's self-mutilation in terms that evoke the aesthetic explosiveness, not only of *Lust for Life,* but also of all Minnelli's melodramas: he writes that "the movement that pushes a man in certain cases to give himself (in other words, to destroy himself) not only partially but completely, so that a bloody death ensues, can only be compared, in its irresistible and hideous nature, to the blinding flashes of lightning that transform the most withering storm into transports of joy."[65]

NOTES

Thanks to Alex Nemerov, Lela Graybill, Fabienne Delpy Adler, Richard Vinograd and Joe McElhaney for valuable feedback, and my students in The Films of Vincente Minnelli, Stanford University, Spring 2006 for allowing me to work through some of this material.

1. See Jean Epstein, "Magnification and Other Writings," trans. Stuart Liebman, *October* 3 (1976): 9–25.

2. Pollock's first solo show was in 1943, and in 1947 he developed his large-scale drip paintings. He died in a car crash in 1956—the same year that *Lust for Life* was released, and one year after James Dean's similar demise.

3. See Serge Guilbaut, "Post-War Painting Games: The Rough and the Slick," in *Reconstructing Modernism: Art in New York, Paris, and Montreal, 1945–1964,* ed. Serge Guilbaut (Cambridge, MA: MIT Press, 1990), 30–85. These ideas are elaborated in his *How New York Stole the Idea of Modern Art: Abstract Expressionism, Freedom, and the Cold War* (Chicago: University of Chicago Press, 1985).

4. Harold Rosenberg, "The American Action Painters," *Art News* 51, no. 8 (1952): 22.

5. John Belton, *Widescreen Cinema* (Cambridge, MA: Harvard University Press, 1992).

6. Rosenberg, "The American Action Painters," 22. Much has been made of the Jungian implications of Pollock's painting, but this is an aspect beyond the scope of the present essay. Angela Della Vacche has written on Minnelli, Pollock, and the Jungian aspects of AbEx in the context of Minnelli's *An American in Paris* (1951) in "Vincente Minnelli's *An American in Paris:* Painting as Psychic Upheaval," in her *Cinema and Painting: How Art Is Used in Film* (Austin: University of Texas Press, 1996), 13–42.

7. Michael Leja, *Reframing Abstract Expressionism: Subjectivity and Painting in the 1940s* (New Haven, CT: Yale University Press, 1993), 4.

8. Ibid., 8.

9. T. J. Clark, "In Defense of Abstract Expressionism," in *Farwell to an Idea: Episodes from a History of Modernism* (New Haven, CT: Yale University Press, 1999), 371–403, quote at 382. Clark revives Clement Greenberg's sense of the word *kitsch* to describe abstract expressionist production: "Kitsch is manic. Above all, it is rigid with the exaltation of art. It believes in art the way artists are supposed to—to the point of absurdity, to the point where the cult of art becomes a new philistinism" (396). *Lust for Life* gives us Van Gogh as the avatar of this cult, this exaltation. And if, in the terms of Hollywood melodrama, it goes "too far" and reaches into the realm of impassioned caricature, this, too, can be seen as analogous to the "new philistinism" of abstract expressionism.

10. Clark, "In Defense of Abstract Expressionism," 387.

11. Ibid., 397.

12. Leja, *Reframing Abstract Expressionism*, 9.

13. Leja notes of the abstract expressionists that, "The subject of the artists was the artist as subject" (ibid., 7).

14. Rosenberg, "The American Action Painters," 22.

15. Griselda Pollock, "Crows, Blossoms, and Lust for Death—Cinema and the Myth of Van Gogh the Modern Artist," in *The Mythology of Vincent Van Gogh,* ed. Kodera Tsukasa and Yvette Rosenberg (Tokyo: Asahi National Broadcasting; The Netherlands: John Benjamins, 1993), 217–39, quote on 238.

16. Vivian Sobchack, " 'Surge and Splendor': A Phenomenology of the Hollywood Historical Epic," *Representations* 29 (1990): 24–49.

17. Given the evidence of *Lust for Life* and *The Long, Long Trailer,* Ansco Color produced especially vibrant yellows and blues, which made it quite suitable for presenting Van Gogh's work.

18. John Berger, *Ways of Seeing* (New York: Penguin, 1972), 80.

19. James Naremore, "Vincente Meets Vincent: Lust for Life," in his *The Films of Vincente Minnelli* (New York: Cambridge University Press, 1993), 135–53, quote on 151.

20. Thomas Elsaesser, "Tales of Sound and Fury: Observations on the Family Melodrama," in *Film Theory and Criticism: Introductory Readings,* ed. Gerald Mast and Marshall Cohen (New York: Oxford University Press, 1992).

21. Leja links Jackson Pollock's terse language to noir, but his "spare use of adjectives, tough guy idiom ("I've knocked around some in California") and "reticence" are at least as typical of westerns—Pollock did, after all, hail from Cody, Wyoming.

22. Vincent van Gogh and Ronald de Leeuw, *The Letters of Vincent Van Gogh,* trans. Arnold Pomerans (London: Penguin, 1996), 182, 144.

23. Irving Stone, *Lust for Life* (New York: Penguin, 1984), 156.

24. Van Gogh and de Leeuw, *Letters of Vincent Van Gogh,* 418, 306–7.

25. Thomas Elsaesser, "Vincente Minnelli," *Brighton Film Review* 15 and 18 (1969). Reproduced in this volume.

26. Some examples: Vincent's earnest but inept sermon on humility, the God of the

clergy "dead as a doornail" to him, and his own analysis of one of his final paintings ("But there is no sadness in this death, this one takes place in a broad daylight with a sun flooding everything with a light of pure gold" [Stone, *Lust for Life*, 604, 452]).

27. See Joe McElhaney's essay on the long-take aesthetic of *Some Came Running* in this volume ("Medium-Shot Gestures: Vincente Minnelli and *Some Came Running*").

28. Naremore, "Vincente Meets Vincent: Lust for Life," 139.

29. Van Gogh and de Leeuw, *Letters of Vincent Van Gogh*, 534, 399.

30. Parker Tyler cited in Clark, "In Defense of Abstract Expressionism," 385.

31. Pollock, "Crows, Blossoms, and Lust for Death," 232.

32. Ibid., 230. Donald Preziosi makes similar points about the film, writing that, "The film depicts the agony and madness of the artist-hero as a measured (and measurable) distance from an objective (camera-eye) real world" ("A Crisis in, or of, Art History?" in his *Rethinking Art History: Meditations on a Coy Science* [New Haven, CT: Yale University Press, 1989], 22).

33. Pollock, "Crows, Blossoms, and Lust for Death," 231.

34. Ibid.

35. Ibid., 232.

36. I am relying on Jacques Rancière's discussion of the place of performance in the diegesis of Minnelli's films. See his essay, "*Ars gratia artis*: Notes on Minnelli's Poetics," in this volume.

37. For valuable overviews of Minnelli's career and discussions of the aesthetic mission of Minnelli's protagonists, see Thomas Elsaesser, "Vincente Minnelli," in this volume, and Joe McElhaney, "Vincente Minnelli: Images of Magic and Transformation," in the online journal *Senses of Cinema*, available at http://www.sensesofcinema .com/contents/directors/04/minnelli.html#bibl. Donald Preziosi argues that the film performs an ideological operation common to the discipline of art history by redeeming Van Gogh's careening madness through a recuperative act of hindsight, but this overlooks the resonance with both the contemporary movement of abstract expressionism and Minnelli's own body of work.

38. Guilbaut, "Post-War Painting Games," 47–48.

39. Ibid., 31.

40. Art Spiegelman later did a comic for *RAW* called "Two-Fisted Painters Action Adventure."

41. Rosalind Krauss, *The Optical Unconscious* (Cambridge, MA: MIT Press, 1993), 244.

42. Georges Bataille, "Sacrificial Mutilation and the Severed Ear of Vincent Van Gogh," in his *Visions of Excess: Selected Writings, 1927–1939*, ed. and intro. Allan Stoekl (Minneapolis: University of Minnesota Press, 1985), 61–72.

43. See Ellen G. Landau, "The Wild One," in her *Jackson Pollock* (New York: Harry N. Abrams, 1989), 11–21.

44. Hoberman adds that Ed Harris, director and star of *Pollock*, is, of course, "a product of the same Actors Studio epitomized by Brando; there are multiple Marlons in his inarticulate, tormented, highly physical, man's-man performance" (J. Hoberman, "Action Figures," available at www.villagevoice.com/film/0107,hoberman,22216 ,20.html).

45. Van Gogh and de Leeuw, *Letters of Vincent Van Gogh*, 178.

46. Ibid., 73.

47. This is another reason why I cannot accept Griselda Pollock's argument that, in the Arles montage, "Pure perception slides effortlessly into art."

48. Naremore, "Vincente Meets Vincent: Lust for Life."

49. Cited in "Specters at the Feast: French Viewpoints on Minnelli's Comedies," by Bill Krohn, in this volume.

50. Van Gogh and de Leeuw, *Letters of Vincent Van Gogh*, 474, 347.

51. As well as Roy Lichtenstein's large-scale renderings of brushstrokes produced a few years later.

52. It is no secret that the abstract expressionists were fascinated by Van Gogh: the drama of his life, his commitment to the purity of his aesthetic and ethos, the complete merging of self with art. In a lecture at Stanford University in 1996, for example, T. J. Clark pointed out that Willem de Kooning's 1958–59 canvas *Suburb in Havana*, with its dark slashes against a yellow background, is a direct quotation of Van Gogh's final painting, *Crows in a Wheatfield*. And the Falkenberg-Namuth film practically begins with an homage to Van Gogh, via a shot of Pollock's paint-spattered shoes that clearly evokes Van Gogh's *Peasant Shoes*. Frederic Jameson has traced the trajectory from modernism to postmodernism in the distance between *Peasant Shoes* and Warhol's *Diamond Dust Shoes* (1980); Pollock's shoes fit neatly between these. Van Gogh depicts worker's shoes, worn and lived, while Warhol creates abstracted, ornamental, objects—artist's shoes. But, I would argue, with Pollock's shoes, the worker's shoes and the artist's shoes are one; art and labor belong to the same realm of materiality and production. See the first chapter of Frederic Jameson, *Postmodernism: The Cultural Logic of Late Capitalism* (Durham, NC: Duke University Press, 1991).

53. Elizabeth Frank, *Jackson Pollock* (New York: Abbeville Press, 1983), 79.

54. Krauss, *Optical Unconscious*, 302.

55. Rosenberg, "The American Action Painters," 22.

56. This is preceded by a shot of Pollock's shadow looming on a wall, suggesting both Murnau's Nosferatu and Astaire's "Bojangles of Harlem" dance from *Swing Time*.

57. Clement Greenberg had noted in 1939 that the avant-garde was not immune to the blandishments of kitsch, a profitable mode: "Ambitious writers and artists will modify their work under the pressure of kitsch" ("Avant-Garde and Kitsch," in his *Art and Culture: Critical Essays* [Boston: Beacon Press, 1961], 3–21), and on some level, Namuth's film of Pollock is kitsch to the core: Pollock the iconoclast painting for the camera, and, through glass, even painting to the camera. Pollock here is perhaps kitsch in Greenberg's sense, while I'd argue that Minnelli's work stands closer to the petite-bourgeois populism of Clark's "vulgarity."

58. Rosenberg, "The American Action Painters," 22.

59. Pollock: "I want to express my feelings rather than just illustrate them."

60. Naremore, "Vincente Meets Vincent: Lust for Life," 147.

61. Rosenberg, "The American Action Painters," 22.

62. Clark, "In Defense of Abstract Expressionism," 401.

63. Naremore, "Vincente Meets Vincent: Lust for Life," 137.

64. Along these same lines, Stephen Harvey writes that, "Night Café is horror intensified by color—a bad dream unrelieved by dance" (*Directed By Vincente Minnelli* [New York: HarperCollins, 1990], 246).

65. Bataille, "Sacrificial Mutilation," 69.

Medium-Shot Gestures
Vincente Minnelli and *Some Came Running*

JOE McELHANEY

About twenty minutes into Vincente Minnelli's *Some Came Running* (1958) there is a sequence that encapsulates much of the appeal and interest of the film. This first sequence set in Smitty's Bar culminates with the initial meeting of Dave Hirsh (Frank Sinatra) and Bama Dillert (Dean Martin). There are no major dramatic fireworks here in this classic of 1950s melodrama. The sequence is deliberately underplayed, its visual style largely unobtrusive. In a frequently cited passage from his autobiography, Minnelli writes that he took his visual cue for *Some Came Running* from "the inside of a juke box . . . garishly lit in primary colors."[1] Minnelli's references to jukeboxes and garishness might lead one to expect something on the order of a CinemaScope and color version of Orson Welles's *Touch of Evil*, a film released earlier the same year. But if one comes to *Some Came Running* with the expectation of the kind of full-blown exercise in Hollywood baroque that Welles displays in his film, disappointments will inevitably arise. The only sequence that fully lives up to Minnelli's jukebox analogy is the penultimate one, the violent fairground sequence that culminates with the wounding of Dave and the murder of his new bride, Ginny (Shirley MacLaine). If one were to make a case for *Some Came Running* as a major work, that sequence would be the obvious place with which to begin.

However, I would prefer to step back from all of the lights and commotion of the fairground sequence and emphasize another aspect to the film and to Minnelli's work in general. Minnelli's reputation has often been that of a flamboyant metteur en scène, largely due to his melodramatic set pieces and for his handling of elaborate musical numbers. But I believe that an equally strong case should be made for him as a director of intimate scenes. This aspect of Minnelli's talent has not been entirely overlooked in the past. It is crucial to Barry Boys's essay on *The Courtship of Eddie's Father* (1963), published in *Movie* no. 10. James Naremore also discusses Minnelli in this regard.[2] But this type of skill is also in danger of being misunderstood or regarded as, at best, a minor talent. Case in point: In a 1998 interview, Jacques Rivette makes the astounding declaration that Minnelli neglects the actor, citing *Some Came Running* as a film in which we find "three great actors" who are "working in a void, with no one watching them or listening to them from behind the camera."[3] I must say that this runs contrary to any experience I have had in viewing the performances in a Minnelli film. Simply in relation to *Some Came Running*, I am certainly not alone in thinking that in the film Dean Martin gives what is (perhaps along with his Dude for Howard Hawks in *Rio Bravo* the following year) the best performance of his career. Rivette's attitude toward Minnelli (which is by no means an isolated one) is based on some fundamental misunderstandings.

If Minnelli's work has consistently been misunderstood it may be that certain aspects of it point toward a certain type of actor-based cinema, one that is invested in codes of psychological realism while still remaining attracted to issues of theatricality and artifice. Within the cinema of the traditional Hollywood studio system, this approach is epitomized by the work of George Cukor. Cukor's color and CinemaScope films of the 1950s, especially *A Star Is Born* (1954) and *Les Girls* (1957), suggest a connection to the chic theatricality of some of Minnelli; conversely, one can easily imagine Cukor directing some of Minnelli's films of the same period, especially *Tea and Sympathy* (1956), *Gigi* (1958), and *The Reluctant Debutante* (1958).[4] But however visually detailed and beautiful Cukor's films are, he tends to stage and frame his action in such a way that it is the actors who assume the primary focus of interest. Testimony from Cukor's actors, on the one hand, confirms his attention to the minutest details of their performances. A number of actors who worked with Minnelli, on the other hand, have claimed that he devoted more attention to the decor than he did to them. To be invested in a decor that overwhelms the actor suggests a relationship to a cinema of the baroque—that of Welles, Max Ophuls, Josef von Sternberg—in which the actor, however central, is often absorbed into an ornate and strongly authorial visual style. But while an occasional sequence in Minnelli might allow for this kind of connection, his films do not consistently give themselves over to this impulse. Whatever visual vocabulary he may share with these three filmmakers, when measured against them Minnelli's own long takes and camera movements seem modest (in comparison with the first two filmmakers), his use of costuming and decor less extreme and fetishistic (in comparison with the latter two), and his approach to matters of light, editing, and sound not nearly as audacious (in comparison with all three of them). In the same passage from his autobiography, in which Minnelli draws upon his well-known jukebox analogy, he also writes of his need to "temper" his enthusiasm when shooting *Some Came Running*, stressing the importance of "discretion" and "restraint" with material of this nature: "Part of the lore of the theater is to leave the audience wanting more, and this also holds true in films. Though you can do anything in films, you'd better not try."[5] To contemporary sensibilities, this statement suggests a carefully manicured and well-behaved classicism, one that occasionally takes a stroll into the dark alleys of forbidden cinemas but only to quickly scramble back out to more respectable spaces. But this finally does not do justice to *Some Came Running* or to Minnelli's particular talent, both of which are in need of careful attention.

Let us return to Minnelli's unhappy actors for a moment. Some of them have stated that Minnelli had enormous difficulty in communicating with them on even the most basic level. Leslie Caron:

> Vincente's style is imprinted very much on the film, but Vincente is not somebody who talks to actors very easily. In fact, I can't remember him giving me more than one piece of direction in the three films we made together. He sort of mutters and stutters and doesn't finish a sentence, which is unintelligible anyway. . . . He stutters and puckers his lips until you try exactly what he wants, but he's not going to tell you; he's incapable of it.[6]

Such claims, however, should not be taken as the final word on the matter. The written and oral history of the cinema is filled with anecdotes from actors testifying to the neglect or indifference at the hands of ostensibly uncommunicative directors, directors who nevertheless managed to extract first-rate work from these actors: Hitchcock, Naruse, Fassbinder, and such. Beyond this, however, these anecdotes about Minnelli's methods do not even follow a consistent pattern. For every actor who has spoken of their neglect at the hands of a man more obsessed with the directing of curtains and arranging of ashtrays than with their own performance is another actor who has testified to Minnelli's extremely careful direction of their every gesture and line reading.[7] This suggests that the ways in which an effective performance is captured by the camera is a highly complex process, the result of a network of elements working together at once (from the production circumstances of the film and the general atmosphere on the set to the manner in which the performances are shaped in postproduction), rather than a simple matter of the filmmaker being fully invested in continuous verbal guidance of the actor. Caron's anecdote itself bears close attention. Caron does not directly state, as Rivette would have it, that Minnelli *neglects* his actors. Rather, her anecdote implies that Minnelli is searching, however haltingly at times, for the proper ways in which to articulate the kind of performance he is expecting: "He stutters and puckers his lips *until you try exactly what he wants*" (emphasis added).

In what follows here, I wish to draw attention to Minnelli's staging, framing, and direction of actors in the first Smitty's Bar sequence. As I will argue, the actors here are not reduced to the status of mere decor. But neither are they permitted to dominate the frame, to actively determine every element of the mise-en-scène. Instead, they form part of a closely connected set of very subtle formal strategies.

Formally, the Smitty's sequence is a simple one: nine shots derived from six camera setups in a sequence running for four minutes. Camera movement here is slight from this master of camera movement, and the use of color is likewise understated from this master of color, consisting primarily of grays, blues, and browns. The "garishly lit primary colors" of the neon signs outside of Smitty's are muted by daylight. One problem that arises in writing about this sequence, though, is that traditional shot-by-shot close analysis, however much it might produce important results for such figures as Hitchcock or Fritz Lang, produces limited results for Minnelli. Indeed, for a director notorious for his fanatical attention to decor at the expense of the actor, what is often revealing about Minnelli's films is how uninteresting the individual shots are in freeze frame. What finally gives Minnelli's images their significance is how the actors are brought into these frames and how the actors move, speak, and gesture as part of a process of unfolding motion and dynamic interaction.

The opening shot of the Smitty's sequence is filmed outside of the bar in a single take lasting for just over a minute. As the camera does a slight crane down from the Smitty's sign, we see three teenage boys at the far right of the frame flipping coins. This is quickly followed by the emergence of Jane Barclay (Connie Gilchrist) from the front door of Smitty's. Jane acknowledges a man who emerges from the right and center of the frame and briefly speaks to him before she notices Dave emerging from the left front of the frame heading toward the entrance to Smitty's. She calls out to him, dismissing the other man with a friendly wave of her hand. The bulk of this shot is centered on the exchange between Jane and Dave. Their conversation here (as with so much of the dialogue throughout the rest of the sequence) revolves around childhood, adolescence, and the family, the latter a subject the film views with a great deal of ambivalence, firmly anchoring *Some Came Running* within the tradition of the small-town family melodrama. But I would like to bypass these issues of content and genre (which are certainly not irrelevant) and instead draw attention to the relationship between the camera and the actors. Even allowing for the limitations of early CinemaScope lenses for filming close-ups, Minnelli's camera is unusually distanced from his two actors. It does not move in for a closer shot of them as they converse, which would have been an entirely logical way of handling this reunion; nor is there a cut into closer shot/reverse shots for the conversation, another viable option. Instead, the camera stays in a medium long shot for the entire conversation until they each go their separate ways, Dave into the bar and Jane offscreen right and center when the camera slightly tracks back. Why does Minnelli handle the sequence in this way?

Keeping the camera at this distance allows several things to take place. First, the three boys at the far right of the frame are constantly visible in the shot while other extras walk in front of and behind Dave and Jane as they speak. Since both Dave and Jane remain in one spot in the center of the frame for most of this shot, the extras walking in front and in back of them provide a sense of movement within the shot. This attention to keeping the frame as alive as possible through careful attention to even the most minor of players (a recurring stylistic element in Minnelli's films) suggests another link with the more extreme images of Welles, Sternberg, and Ophuls. But whereas these filmmakers will use extras in a more disruptive manner to the point where

The three boys at the far right of the frame, flipping coins, form a gestural counterpoint to the movements of Dave (Frank Sinatra) and Jane (Connie Gilchrist) as they stand in front of Smitty's Bar in *Some Came Running* (1958).

they actively compete with the leading players, Minnelli uses his extras as a subtle extension of or counterpoint to the foreground action. Minnelli's refusal to more conventionally move his camera closer to Dave and Jane also allows Sinatra and Gilchrist to use most of their bodies as they speak. During this exchange, Sinatra mainly keeps his hands in his pockets (gesturing only to scratch his nose at Jane's mention of Dave's brother), while Gilchrist constantly gestures in a broad fashion, touching Sinatra, putting her hands to her face in an embarrassed gesture, shrugging her shoulders, and using both hands to hold on to her shopping bag. As this transpires, the boys flipping coins at the far right of the frame assume a type of gestural counterpoint. Near the end of the sequence, another young boy (somewhat older than the other three) stealthily moves from around the outside right corner of the bar, passing through the three boys, and then ducks into the front door. His gestures are based on the nervous smoking and eventual extinguishing of his cigarette just before entering the bar, setting up a contrast between the still somewhat juvenile behavior of the coin flipping from the younger boys with that of the smoking from the older one. Dave follows him into the bar before first turning around and glancing at his watch. Everything in this shot is centered on a subtle interplay of gesture and movement, framed within an extended medium long shot and modest camera moves.

Additional gestural counterpoint as a young male (John Brennan), smoking a cigarette, stealthily glides into Smitty's, behind Dave and Jane.

While not citing Minnelli's work, David Bordwell has drawn attention to the general decline in this type of complex ensemble staging in contemporary cinema (especially American). We are now living in a period of "intensified continuity," dominated by rapid cutting, free-ranging camera movements, and extensive use of close-ups. The nature of how performances are filmed, edited, and ultimately experienced has shifted: The face becomes the ultimate bearer of meaning, with gesture and bodily movements increasingly restricted through the alternation of "stand and deliver" scenes (in which the actors are confined to largely fixed positions) with "walk and talk" scenes (in which a moving camera rapidly follows actors as they "spit out exposition on the fly").[8] *Some Came Running*, then, may be seen as a late example of this earlier cinema of relative gestural freedom. In comparison with contemporary approaches, Minnelli's handling of the actor in *Some Came Running* feels as though it has lumbered in from another era, pointing not only to the changes that have taken place over the last forty-five years but also to how little influence this approach toward staging action has had on contemporary cinema.

Action is not only carefully staged in Minnelli but often seems to be choreographed in the most literal sense of the word, with the blocking of action conceived in terms of viewing entire bodies moving within a prescribed space, much of this undoubtedly having its basis in Minnelli's theatrical (and, specifically, musical theater) background. It is this particular way of understanding space and movement that has gradually declined over the last few decades (unless it is being cited in a self-conscious manner, as in some of the more recent theatrical adaptations of Alain Resnais: *Mèlo* (1986), *Smoking/No Smoking* (1993). Even when contemporary directors come from the stage and adapt plays, they are more likely now to create films that frantically display contemporary fashions in cinematic technique, covering up as strongly as possible any relationship the work in question might have to theater: Nicholas Hytner's film version of Arthur Miller's *The Crucible* (1995), assembled as though it were an intellectual action film, is a primary case in point. Even a device like the long take in Minnelli has a different function from the long takes of contemporary (and often American) cinema that so often seem to follow in a line of descent from the approach of figures such as Welles or Ophuls. While Welles may be a more obviously dynamic filmmaker than Minnelli, even the technically simplest of his long takes (such as the famous static camera kitchen scene in *The Magnificent Ambersons* [1942]) never gets away from the overwhelming concept of bravura. Moreover, Minnelli's use of the extended take has only a slight relationship to the modernist idea of duration, of the weight of time upon a particular shot or sequence; and in Minnelli, we find none of the record-breaking shot lengths (often accompanied by dizzyingly intricate staging) of Kenji Mizoguchi or such contemporary filmmakers as Theo Angelopoulos or Hou Hsiao-hsien. The length of a take like the one outside of Smitty's, less self-conscious than these other approaches, has more to do with allowing for a careful and nuanced observation of behavior and movement to take place within an ensemble-like cinematic playing space.

In some ways this shot also anticipates the centerpiece of the sequence, which begins with the seventh shot, as Bama steps up to the corner of the bar from his booth in the back and introduces himself to Dave, welcoming him to "Smitty's cocktail hour." Instead of standing, Sinatra now sits, his (and Martin's) performance entirely determined by expressivity from the waist up. Minnelli's lack of interest in the "purity" of the long take as a discrete unit à la Welles is obvious here since the camera setup for the shot is essentially a leftover from the third one when the underage boy who entered the bar at the beginning of the sequence unsuccessfully attempts to talk Dave into buying a pint of whiskey for him. (Minnelli repeats camera setups at the end of the sequence as well when Dave exits the bar in the same camera position from which the teenage boy exited earlier, a type of economy as old as D. W. Griffith.) The only element that marks this seventh shot off from the earlier

Bama (Dean Martin) welcomes Dave to "Smitty's cocktail hour" in a relaxed, CinemaScope two-shot.

one is that the camera slightly tracks forward and reframes as Bama sits down, the shot self-consciously composed for CinemaScope: The horizontality of the bar contrasting with the verticality of Dave and Bama, the black counter jukebox in front of and between them contrasted with the full-size jukebox in the background (a potted plant on top), a bottle of whiskey in the left foreground in front of Dave contrasted with the pasted bottles on the wall behind them, and the dark brown columns to the booths in the background—all of these show Minnelli's attention to detail. At the same time, this composition seems sufficiently loose to allow Sinatra and Martin to interact with each other and for the spectator to observe them with a minimum of distraction. Rather than following a contemporary stand-and-deliver approach, Minnelli's camera quietly settles down for the duration of this interchange. The interchange does not take up much screen time (one minute and forty-five seconds), but the pacing is relaxed, appropriate for a film set in a small town in which, as Bama says here, nothing moves quickly except for gossip.

As in the first shot of the sequence, Sinatra's playing is marked by a paucity of gesture, in contrast to Martin. But where a gifted character actress like Gilchrist works on a broad, emphatic scale, Martin's performance is one of relaxed casualness. Sinatra seems to speak the lines directly as written, but Martin repeatedly punctuates his line readings with hesitations and illustrates these readings with half-finished gestures (such as reaching for the ashtray in

The "Smitty's Cocktail Hour" camera setup illustrated on the previous page is a development out of this setup, slightly reframed through camera movement.

front of him as though to bring it forward but then only slightly adjusts it), giving an impression of spontaneity and improvisation. Sinatra's greatness as a popular singer far eclipses Martin's. But Martin is a much more inventive screen performer, a fact that Sinatra implicitly acknowledges here by essentially giving the scene to Martin and not even bothering to compete. Martin looks at Sinatra almost nonstop while Sinatra mainly attempts to avoid direct eye contact. Near the end of the scene, Martin even seems to parody Sinatra's gesture of forcefully putting his glass down on the bar by immediately copying the gesture. If this scene may be thought of as both a duet and a duel between two brilliant performers, it is Martin who ultimately wins, the final shot of the sequence belonging to him after Sinatra exits the frame. (The camera also comes closer to Martin in this scene than it does to anyone else when, in the sixth shot, he turns and responds to something that Dave says to Smitty in what might loosely be defined as a medium shot but one that also doubles as a type of close-up due to Minnelli's framing of Martin's face within the horizontal and vertical contours of the booth.) Martin's physical stature and style of dress also allow him to more fully dominate the space, his gray jacket and tie and pale pink shirt contrasted with the light brown of Dave's army uniform, which seems to shrink Sinatra and which Sinatra accentuates by slightly pulling his body inward, presumably as a defensive measure against Martin. Both

Minnelli introduces Bama by tucking him away into the left rear of the establishing shot of the bar's interior, Bama's hat just barely visible in the booth.

men are wearing hats, Dave's that of an Army uniform cap, Bama's a gray cowboy hat that far eclipses Dave's hat in stature. This icon of the western genre, slightly urbanized for the film, allows for *Some Came Running* to be seen as a kind of midwestern western, a bitter version of *My Darling Clementine* (1946) complete with town saloon, the hooker with a heart of gold who is finally shot (Ginny), the prim schoolteacher (Martha Hyer's Gwen French), and our two male protagonists meeting at a bar. Bama's hat will continue to play a central role throughout the film since he refuses to take it off, even indoors, until the moving final shot when he performs his last gesture in the film by removing his hat in memory of Ginny at her burial.

Even before Bama is directly introduced, our first glimpse of him comes in the sequence's second shot, a panning movement across the interior space of the saloon as Dave enters. This movement not only plays a role as a conventional establishing shot, it also introduces Bama as a hat, a costume rather than a body, tucked away in the rear of the frame. This idea of the body being literally engulfed by decor is one that recurs in Minnelli. Time and again we find shots in which an actor is hidden within the decor only to suddenly, surprisingly emerge out of it: the little boy suddenly waking and rising from a haystack in the opening of *Brigadoon* (1954), for example. And Bama could almost be missed on a first viewing of this shot here. But Minnelli's composition also guides the viewer's eye to this back area of the image, as the blue jeans on the boy trying to buy liquor from Smitty at the right of the frame lead the spectator's eye to a matching blue line at the top of a poster on the back wall that, along with the white light hanging from the ceiling just above, leads the eye to the gray of Bama's hat. However, Minnelli does not have Martin's Bama emerge from within the long shot but instead withholds from clearly revealing his presence until a later cut, as Bama responds to Dave's contemptuous reference to the teenage boy's failure to buy liquor: "Dumb. At his age, I never had any trouble getting fried." If actors sometimes complained that they felt as though they were little more than items of decor for Minnelli, what these two shots establishing Bama demonstrate is that these actors were not entirely wrong. Actors *are* often decor for Minnelli but only insofar as this decor will begin to move and assume a relationship to the body.

So far I repeatedly alternated between describing these two men by their character names and describing them in terms of their real-life professional names. But the sense that we are not simply watching the characters of Dave and Bama interact here but also Dean Martin and Frank Sinatra is crucial to the experience of the scene. Manny Farber has argued that the most interesting screen performances are determined not so much by the moments when an actor fully inhabits a character as when we find "suggestive material that circles the edge of a role: quirks of physiognomy, private thoughts of the actor about himself, misalliances where the body isn't delineating the role, but is running on a tangent to it."[9] Martin and Sinatra seem to be both inside and outside of their roles, and part of the pleasure in observing this interplay is in detecting what seems to be an obvious delight that these two mythological Clan/Rat Pack beings have in relation to each other. When Martin asks Sinatra, "You play any cards, Mr. Hirsh?" it is difficult to tell if the slight smile that passes across Sinatra's face as he says, "Some, why?" is supposed to be Dave's smile or Sinatra's barely suppressed amusement at Martin's inventiveness. Minnelli's direction to the two men was that they should play the scene as though they were two ex-prostitutes, now wealthy and married to film producers, who meet each other at a party in Beverly Hills and instinctively know about the other's background.[10] This gives the actors a fictional subtext to work with, but it also allows for acting to become a form of private amusement between two musical entertainers finding different ways to bend roles to fit their public personalities and of turning work into play—the latter an idea Minnelli returns to time and again.

The pleasures to be had by Minnelli's slightly distanced framing, keeping the two actors in a medium two-shot, are not those of the emphatic style of much of contemporary American cinema. Minnelli belongs to a generation of filmmakers who always thought of their images as something *projected*, larger than life, to be seen in a darkened auditorium and on a mammoth screen (and *Some Came Running* makes no allowances for the possibility that it will be viewed on something as small as a television set). A filmmaker can invest so much creative energy in so many small details in composition, performance, and staging of action because there is an inherent belief that such details will be noticed. This kind of belief, in turn, presupposes a certain subtlety on the part of the filmmaker, who rarely underlines a facial expression or gesture through a cut or camera movement, just as it presupposes a certain subtlety on the part of the film viewer, one with an attentive eye rather than an eye in need of constant and explicit guidance. If it has become increasingly difficult for American narrative filmmakers to make this kind of cinema and for spectators to respond to and understand it, it may be that it is not Minnelli but our own visual culture that is "working in a void" with no one carefully listening or watching, either behind the camera or in front of the image.

NOTES

1. Vincente Minnelli, with Hector Arce, *I Remember It Well* (Garden City, NY: Doubleday, 1974), 325.

2. Noting that Minnelli's work with actors was "consistently excellent," Naremore writes on a sequence between Dick Powell and Gloria Grahame in *The Bad and the Beautiful* in which Minnelli's actors are "relying upon a formalized, somewhat pantomimic style that resembles a dance." In James Naremore, *The Films of Vincente Minnelli* (New York: Cambridge University Press, 1993), 40.

3. Frédéric Bonnaud, "The Captive Lover—An Interview with Jacques Rivette," trans. Kent Jones, available at www.sensesofcinema.com/contents/01/16/rivette.html. Originally published in *Les Inrockuptibles*, March 25, 1998. Rivette claims in this interview that he loved *Some Came Running* when it was released but that a recent rescreening of it caused him to change his mind. Rivette's supposed one-time love for the film, however, is an exaggeration. In the July 1959 *conseil de dix* in *Cahiers du cinèma*, Rivette only gives the film two stars.

4. Minnelli claims that it was he and not Cukor who was the first choice to direct the film version of *My Fair Lady* (1964), a project Minnelli ultimately rejected due to Warner Brothers' refusal to offer the director a percentage of the profits. Instead, Minnelli opted to direct *Goodbye Charlie* (1964). See Minnelli, *I Remember It Well*, 353. Minnelli does not note that it was Cukor who was originally slated to direct *Goodbye Charlie*.

5. Ibid., 325–26.

6. Donald Knox, *The Magic Factory: How MGM Made An American in Paris* (New York: Praeger, 1973), 103–4.

7. I offer two anecdotes here: When I heard Dolores Gray speak at a screening of

Kismet (1955) in New York City in the early 1990s, she discussed Minnelli's direction of her in *Designing Woman* (1957). Gray claimed that every gesture she made, every line reading she gave in that film was carefully controlled and manipulated by Minnelli. And at a screening of *Bells Are Ringing* (1960) in New York in August of 2006, Judy Holliday's son, Jonathan Oppenheim, spoke of his mother's difficulties on that film. Holliday was, according to Oppenheim, very unhappy working with Minnelli, particularly in comparison with the relationship she had had with Cukor. While Cukor allowed for collaboration with his actors, Minnelli would insist that Holliday perform in the manner he prescribed for her.

8. David Bordwell, "Intensified Continuity: Visual Style in Contemporary American Film," *Film Quarterly* 55, no. 3 (2002): 25. Many of Bordwell's basic arguments in this essay have been extended in two books, *Figures Traced in Light: On Cinematic Staging* (Berkeley: University of California Press, 2005) and *The Way Hollywood Tells It: Story and Style in Modern Movies* (Berkeley: University of California Press, 2006).

9. Manny Farber, "Cartooned Hip Acting," in his *Negative Space: Manny Farber on the Movies* (New York: Da Capo Press, 1998), 155–59, quote on 155.

10. Minnelli, *I Remember It Well*, 1.

Minnelli in Double System

EMMANUEL BURDEAU
TRANSLATED BY BILL KROHN

The film is *Gigi*, Vincente Minnelli, 1958, MGM's last great musical comedy success. The cast: Louis Jourdan and Eva Gabor. The place: Maxim's where the scene was actually filmed. The situation: Gaston Lachaille, rich boy and ladies man, dines with his mistress Liane d'Exelmans.

The seven images reproduced here (pp. 338–39) play out a transparent scenario of boredom and worldliness. Exuberant, well-suited to her job as a brainless tart, Liane gives herself over to the situation without holding back, abandoning a hand to her lover while distributing in all directions laughter (fig. 3), curiosity (fig. 4), kisses (fig. 5). Annoyed by this performance, Gaston manages at best a composed expression (figs. 1 and 4), and at the worst doesn't bother to conceal his boredom (fig. 2), even his anger (figs. 5 to 7). Withdrawn into himself or excessively demonstrative, eye turned to heaven, he'd rather be somewhere else and already is.

On the screen, where a waltz by Fritz Loewe with words by Alan Jay Lerner is playing, it's a whole other scenario. Figs. 1 and 2: Gaston begins an inner monologue, half-spoken, half-sung. "She's a loveable one tonight, isn't she?

What is she up to . . . ?" Figs. 3 to 5: Liane's gesticulations, continuation of the recitative. "She's such fun tonight. . . . She's not thinking of me." Figs. 6 and 7: While Liane dances, the monologue becomes external, and Gaston's exasperation grows. "She's so gay tonight. . . . A gigantic romantic cliché tonight. . . . She's not thinking of me."

In short, once the sound is added (back), places are symmetrically exchanged. It's no longer Liane who is the star but Gaston, by virtue of the irritated complaint he makes inwardly, then outwardly. And now it is she, not he, who escapes, loves and thinks elsewhere, on some other track, following other desires.

This is no doubt the first aim of the exercise consisting of fixing a few seconds of a film (or several) on paper to comment on them: to be able to bring into play just such an inversion between paper and celluloid, between movement and stasis, between song and silence. But the interest of the operation would be limited if it were only to find a verification or a proof, the strictly measurable efficacy of the visible. On the contrary, it finds its raison d'être when, through a kind of irony or reversibility, the images begin to speak another language than they do on the screen.

In this case, eliminating the music from this passage from *Gigi* or putting it back allows us to isolate the mechanism of thought in Minnelli. Twice a perfect and exactly Proustian formula, "She's not thinking of me," defines it as reverie or absence. The first time, triggered by a distraction or a departure: Gaston's, as he leaves the carpet of Maxim's to speak and sing his exasperation. The second time, by the double density, real or imagined, of a presence so dazzling, so rich that it must harbor another kind of distraction: a flood of silent thoughts addressed elsewhere, to another man.

Confronted with such images, we have to imagine that a tourniquet is being twisted so that everything is first silent (as it is here), then talkative (as it is in the movie theater); so that the monologue flows now internally, now externally. Then the scene can deliver up all its power, and be reseen and reheard endlessly. Mouth open or closed, Gaston can grouse or shut up; Liane can disappear or be in fact absolutely there—we are free to interpret as we wish. All that matters is that a circulation between what is seen and what is heard has, at first in any case, diffused everywhere the possibility of thought. And that an equality has been suggested in this respect between the man who thinks and the woman of whom he thinks, to whom thoughts are only lent.

From a larger perspective, we can ask how these images help us grasp a little better what changed forever in cinema in that famous year 1958, when Minnelli,

Gaston (Louis Jourdan) and Liane (Eva Gabor) in *Gigi* (1958): Composure (fig. 1), boredom (fig. 2), laughter (fig. 3), curiosity (fig. 4), anger (figs. 5 through 7).

for example, made three brilliant films, *Gigi, The Reluctant Debutante,* and *Some Came Running,* one after the other. Look at the tired bosom and twisted arms of Liane, her eyes goggling at the off-space: She is already a mannerist body, in pieces. Listen to Gaston's monologue: It's a real-time critique, a reading of the image, and already the outline of an analysis. Does this mean that in 1958 Minnelli, like other filmmakers, sank into self-consciousness, impasto, and exaggerated strokes?

Yes and no. Yes, because what is laid out here is a gigantic cliché (as Gaston says). Yes, because the decor has never been so affected, so freighted with virtuosity. Yes, because a commentary on the film accompanies the film, adding negative accents of suspicion and jealousy. And no, because it is the film that introduces thought into the image, thereby making it a virtual image of itself, as Liane indicates by leaning dangerously forward as if she were looking into a mirror or the void. What is happening here is a fracturing of cinema. Accepting the suffocating presence of the visible, it seeks to inscribe in itself a shifter or formula that will air it out without negating it. That isn't a loss or a fall—it's the achievement of a new depth. But inevitably it leads to an ambiguity, which is one of the features of post-1958. What ambiguity? The one expressed in "She's not thinking of me," a bitter conclusion as well as a rewriting of the entire scene; a lyric of salvation as well as capitulation; the signature of a divided age of the visible, from which we still may not have completely emerged.

Style, Calculation, and Counterpoint in *The Clock*

MURRAY POMERANCE

I seemed to see, for myself, while I was there, absolutely *no* profit in scanning or attempting to sound the future—the present being so hugely fluid.
HENRY JAMES TO H. G. WELLS, November 8, 1906

Our ability to successfully move in space and our ability to know the space in which we move are distinct and in many ways disconnected, according to Yi-Fu Tuan (who of course reprises, in this thought, Heisenberg's Uncertainty Principle). First: "spatial ability develops slowly in the human young; spatial knowledge lags further behind." Then, spatial ability is converted to knowledge "when movements and changes of location can be envisaged." Finally, "people who are good at finding their way in the city may be poor in giving street directions to the lost, and hopeless in their attempts to draw maps."[1] In New York City, for example, finding one's way quickly becomes a matter of routine; it is startling to see how many people follow the same habitual routes day after day, turning at the same street corners or standing to wait at the same spot on the subway platform for the same train. Mapmaking is an entirely different endeavor, involving as it does the imagination of an outsider not wedded to a habitual pattern of movement in a space and indeed unaware of the space in those interiorized terms in which it has come to be recognized over and over by those who move regularly in it. This can be true of virtually any space, even a textual one. The author who is navigating with one particular skill through a maze of language and thought may be able to see a way forward clearly enough without at the same time having the capacity to present to a reader—who is perforce positioned outside the spatial system of the text—a map sufficiently helpful as to make progress possible. In this way it is possible to see that unintelligibility is a common enough function of prose, and that a unique skill, quite different from either thinking or speaking, is required to show someone at a distance what it is that one is intellectually grappling with here, on the inside. When such a skill is lacking, even if an author sees his philosophical way with clarity, a "difficult text" results. Aleksandr Solzhenitsyn once wondered, "How can anyone who is warm understand what it is to be cold?"

One distinct possibility is that a kind of mythical space can be opened up for outsiders, a representation of the territory so entirely different from the one that locals use on a routine basis for getting around and making sense of life that locals might not themselves attribute any meaning to it, any meaning at all, even though as myth it is sensible enough, coherent enough, logical enough, and sufficient to the needs of those whose navigation problems are of a different order. In London, for example, the bus map—a vital necessity for strangers trying to ride around the city—is virtually unintelligible to locals, who operate in routines and habits. Or, reading a fiction or watching one develop onscreen, my spatial needs are entirely inconsistent with those of the characters or, indeed, those of the actors who are playing them; they need to make their way through the fiction, while I need to comprehend the fiction through which they are moving. Watching actors stepping cautiously along a dolly track while the camera shoots a moving close-up of them (a scene showing such a procedure can be found in François Truffaut's *Day for Night* [1973]), one observes that they must lift their legs and step between the regularly placed struts of the track as the camera is smoothly pulled backward in front of them; and that in performing this activity they are conscious of a certain regularized, almost metrical space with discreet divisions and obstructions that they must rhythmically and repeatedly overcome. In the shot, the characters will seem to be negotiating a much more fluid space, one in which forward motion is not only unobstructed but also, indeed, eased and lubricated through what seems a dynamic pressure. As viewers of a film in which such a shot takes place we imagine the space in an entirely different way from those who are working to negotiate it.

A film can of course be a map. Its projection of a territory for those of us locked on the outside (constrained in our positions as viewers) need have only the most tangential relation to that territory as a space known by those who traverse it out of knowledge. Often, the character's knowledge of space is entirely isomorphic with our knowledge of him knowing; and so the gap between the character's apparent way of being in space and that of the actor is roughly the same as the gap between the actor and us. But in general, no space we see on film corresponds to itself in the act of filming. I recall spending years working in the kitchen of some friends on Long Island. The physical relationship of the stove and the refrigerator, and of both of these to the sink, the window above the sink that looked out upon a bay, and the kitchen table, was so ingrained in my practical knowledge that no thought was ever needed for negotiating between these, moving articles of food, washing up, cooking, serving, whatever. I moved naturally, more or less as an animal does, able to reach out in any direction and find a home for my impulse in a surface, a tool, a control button, a hollow, a venerated object. Later, a celebrated filmmaker shot a scene in this kitchen and I came to see it in a movie theater hundreds of miles away (as millions of moviegoers around North America did at the same time). While I could discern clearly enough that the scene I was watching had been shot in a space my body knew, the bodily knowledge I possessed and the organized perception that was being offered me by the filmmaker were virtually unrelated, this notwithstanding the strange fact that two very famous movie stars were now standing where I had always used to stand and doing roughly what I had always used to do, as they were standing there.

This brings me to Vincente Minnelli's *The Clock* (1945), a very curious film about New York. Arriving at Pennsylvania Station from some unknown location in the vast hinterlands beyond the Hudson River, and bound for military action, Joe Allen (Robert Walker) is both spellbound and confounded in this, his first confrontation with New York. The crowds in the station make him gape in astonishment; his first ride on an escalator makes him giggle boyishly; and the looming canyons of skyscrapers outside in the street—one of which, a few blocks away, is the still gleaming Empire State Building—bring chagrin to his face and a threatened squint to his eyes. He retreats back into the station, which already feels like a base of operations to him, and, sitting at the bottom of a stairway to catch his breath, or perhaps recalibrate his scales of value, he becomes an obstruction to Alice Mayberry (Judy Garland), who, scurrying along without watching the marble floor under her, stumbles on his outstretched foot and breaks the heel from her shoe. He insists on importuning a shoemaker to unlock his doors and gets the shoe fixed. She agrees to let him accompany her for a while, as she heads up Fifth Avenue.

They ride a double-decker bus, Alice acting as tour guide with Joe ravenous both to take in every possible sight and to question his attractive new friend. "There's Radio City up ahead," she suddenly points, "and Saks Fifth Avenue"; and after a brief pause, "There's Saint Patrick's Cathedral."

In many ways this is a fascinating cinematic sequence, and also, of course, a somewhat startling portrait of New York. The Empire State Building, which had just opened when Minnelli first moved to New York from Chicago in 1931, was surely still a dominating feature of midtown at the time the exteriors were shot, and was certainly close enough to Penn Station to have been visible from the street outside. But bizarrely, Radio City Music Hall, which from late in 1933 had been the site of Minnelli's working experience in New York—he became the designer of stage shows there, at first under Roxy Rothafel and soon after under W. G. Van Schmus—is on Sixth Avenue, not Fifth, and Judy Garland is very clearly *not* pointing toward it when she makes her ebullient comment to Walker.

Five possible accounts for this anomaly spring directly to mind: that Minnelli was ignorant of the location of Radio City Music Hall; that he was assuming an audience sufficiently unfamiliar with New York that the inaccuracy of the reference would not matter to them, or so unfamiliar that the accuracy of geographical references he would be providing need not have been important to him; that Alice is knowingly, and somewhat cynically, giving Joe a false direction, this being part of the director's strategy for signaling us that she wishes to be done with this freeloader as soon as possible; that although Minnelli knew where Radio City was, Alice didn't; or that Minnelli was using this device as a means of signaling an important clue as to his serious concerns.[2] The first account, I believe, can be dismissed as extremely unlikely, given the kind of movement Minnelli would have to have been making as he routinely went to work either from his East 52nd Street residence, one block uptown of Radio City and several long blocks across town; or from an earlier residence in an apartment across the street from Chumley's restaurant, in the West Village at Grove and Bedford Streets. From the Village, indeed, he might well have ridden up Fifth Avenue on the same bus that Alice and Joe take, and would have had to make his way westward over to Sixth Avenue to find the Music Hall. It seems incredible that a man of such refined graphic and spatial sensitivities as his films prove Minnelli to have been could have been confused, shooting *The Clock,* about the topography of midtown, or about the exact location of his former place of employment.

The hypothesis that he did not care much about the details of New York geography himself, or that he was making this film for viewers who would not care, makes little sense in view of the meticulous detailing he goes to extreme lengths to provide elsewhere in this film (and in others): shooting the Penn Station sequences with such care, for example—"MGM's stage 27 has been turned into a replica"[3]—or using location shots to precisely configure the seal pool at the Central Park Zoo.

That Alice might be trying to cynically detach herself from Joe through disinformation adds a note of darkness to the story that is hardly carried through; is contradicted by her quite accurate positioning of Saint Patrick's and Saks immediately afterward; and in general turns her into an ungrateful and inhospitable heroine, all this notwithstanding the curiously unsuspicious amenability she shows from the start to Joe's polite come-ons. The tone of the film is decidedly optimistic and bucolic. Character after character behaves as though frolicking through the small-town landscape of *It's a Wonderful Life*, rather than struggling to get by against the press of the masses in a colossal economic and cultural center. For example, in Central Park Alice and Joe watch the seals gallivanting, and Joe sees a boy lugging a large wooden sailboat. He reaches out to touch the boat and the boy kicks him hard in the shin, saying "Get your hands off that boat! Who do you think you are?" When the boy has disappeared, Alice says, remarkably, "What a rude little boy!" Given the omnipresence of strangers in New York, perhaps especially in the park, this boy isn't being rude at all by urban standards, he's being down to earth, practical, direct, spontaneous, and self-protective all the while continuing in his forward motion; but from a pastoral point of view, the point of view Alice is using, he's being rude.

Alice's romance with Joe, their frantic betrothal and marriage, their sincere parting at the film's conclusion as Joe goes back to boot camp (and then, presumably, off to war), are simplified and flattened into parody if indeed Alice is the sort of person truly capable of mocking Joe by treating him like a country rube to his face and announcing the presence of Radio City when she knows it's not there. Her protective guidance as he learns about New York is also flattened and diminished if we take her comment about Radio City to be stemming from ignorance on her part. The Music Hall had been open since 1932 and was a centerpiece of the city at the time that Alice was working there. As much as she knows the Metropolitan Museum, she surely knows Radio City.

But the incorrect comment about the Music Hall makes a good deal of (albeit not navigationally rational) sense if we understand it as a way of showing the difference between the space of New York as Minnelli had come to know it and that space as a more mythical terrain in which, quite apart from his knowledge, he was able to "move" in making a cinematic "map" for viewers who were not there when they were watching. What I am calling "mythical New York" was considerably different from the constraining geographical space he had had to learn, for example traveling to and from Paramount's East Coast headquarters in Astoria in the early 1930s, when "operations moved" there.[4] On his arrival in New York he worked at the Paramount Theater on Broadway—directly across Times Square from the Astor Hotel, in whose lobby Alice and Joe find a haven and a place to locate each other in the circulatory nightmare that is Manhattan—and was delighted to have the opportunity to "explore the rest of the city."[5] But the streets he walked appealed to him in ways quite beyond his aim at navigation. He writes:

> I was drawn time and again to Times Square and the color and fire of all that neon. Usually staying in a hotel on the East Side, I'd walk to the theater district, bathed in that awesome light. How well I understood G. K. Chesterton's observation when he'd seen the letters and trademarks advertising everything from pork to pianos: "What a glorious garden of wonders this would be, to any one who was lucky enough to be unable to read."[6]

What Chesterton is invoking, and Minnelli with him, is a kind of diffuse impressionism, which is not, to be sure, a denial of interpretation—reading—so much as it is a rejection of a certain *mode* of reception and decoding, that of mercantile exchange (which was, of course, what the "awesome light" of Times Square was subjugated to). The principle was to see the "color and fire of all that neon" not as a sign system for denoting the axioms of commerce, but for itself as the central component of a "glorious garden of wonders" made up of hue and incandescence punctuated by awesome darkness and possibility. In following from Chesterton, Minnelli is treating the New York streets he walked as something very far from a map that facilitates successful achievement of valuable placements in rational space. They now constitute a veritable playground. When Alice tells Joe that Radio City is up ahead, she is playing with him, and at the same time playing with New York.

Discussing the cultural meaning of play, Roger Caillois finds two distinct societal forms. In the "rational" condition, we find highlighted a combination of aleatory games that depend on subjecting one's energies to the movements of fortune; and competitive games, in which people pit their strength and status, their talent and knowledge, against one another. In "primitive" conditions, however, there is a focus on mimicry, which involves staging, masking, illusion, and revelation; and vertigo, in which the faculties of perception are suspended in dreams, trances, hallucinations, topological inversions, and the like. The treatment accorded New York in *The Clock* oscillates between these two types of play, with the carefully articulated demonstrations of rational bourgeois order delimiting a world of aleatory and agonistic action, a business scene, and the often exaggerated, even intoxicated portrayal of places and citizens—Radio City as being on Fifth Avenue; the cavorting seals; the shoemaker who opens his door to Joe merely because he is implored to; the slaphappy milkman Al who befriends Alice and Joe (and brings them home to meet his wife) for no other reason than that they are standing alone on a street at night; the drunk in the restaurant who is throwing punches indiscriminately into the air and who inadvertently smacks Al—all constituting a world of mask and trance. What is interesting about Minnelli, certainly, given that he is working in a thoroughly rationalized system of production and in the face of a city that is the apotheosis of rational capitalist bureaucracy, is his retention of affection for, and devotion to, the giddy pleasures of a "primitive" vision. Given that, as Caillois has it, members of society—read, New Yorkers—can be "ambitious, fatalistic, simulate others, or . . . enfrenzied,"[7] he can operate under wartime conditions of gravity and intensive competition to celebrate the hysterical and the mimetic. Joe and Alice let go in their New York, leaving its rational surfaces for experiences that are transcendent and meaningless. Thus, even after he has lived in New York for years, and has worked in its show business factories, and even after he has acclimated himself to MGM's factory system, he retains the ability to film a scene of pure delirium that can be interwoven with more rational material into a comprehensive whole.

Yet this is not to join Andrew Sarris in affirming "Minnelli's dreamlike style with subjects of substance,"[8] or to imagine, as Sarris does generally about this director, that with *The Clock* Minnelli took on a "luxurious [project] upon which to lavish his taste."[9] That he was capable of producing sweeping gestures of panache, then, does not merely prove Minnelli was a filmmaker who believed "implicitly in the power of his camera to transform trash into art, and corn into caviar."[10] Just as there are some moments in *The Clock* when the territory becomes oneiric, when we seem caught in an elaborately styled masquerade, there are others when we navigate the streets of New York as in a contest for momentum and success, in which we see the constantly shifting mass of people undergoing realistic chance encounters. The power Minnelli shows onscreen is not mere stylization, buoyancy, expressiveness, and flair but the ability to marshal these capacities, frame them, and place them against the background of something radically different in order to make a precise artistic statement. For example, at the instant when Alice is an entirely dreamlike cicerone, and incorrectly locating Radio City, Joe is showing deference to her kindness by rapidly—rapidly and uninterestedly—looking where she points, before returning his gaze fixedly to her enchanting face. He must rationally and wakefully compete against her "New York" in order to grasp a chance to focus on Alice herself. For Joe, although already, and very clearly, New York has been a stunning barrage of sensation and wondrous beauty, it doesn't hold a candle to Alice; and it's her he wants to know about, not Fifth Avenue. The dream space in which Alice and Joe sometimes wander in amazement is counterpoised against a rational and very serious space in which they bring themselves closer to each other through this film. Sarris's conclusion that "Minnelli believes more in beauty than in art" is, I think, facile.

A similar counterpoint between oneiric and voluptuous mimicry, what Caillois would call vertiginous play, and rational calculation is evident in a long scene at the apartment Alice shares with her co-worker, Helen (Ruth Brady). She has agreed to meet Joe at 7 p.m. under the clock in the lobby of the Astor Hotel on Times Square, and has now to freshen up and change. We come in on Helen and her friend Bill (Marshall Thompson), as Helen expresses wonder as to where Alice can be. The scene is played for comedy, with Bill being cut off by Helen every time he opens his mouth and in fact not having a chance to utter a single syllable. Eventually Alice shows up and admits she has met a soldier, which provokes Helen into drawing her into the bedroom for a private moral instruction. As in the background Helen walks through the implications of being "picked up by a uniform" for a relationship that can surely last only a few days—"And then what've you got?"—Alice turns and turns in the foreground, clearly upset and confused by what the dominating Helen is suggesting. Helen's rational lecture, however—framed as it is in the logic of sexual competition and in the play of social position and chance (one cannot know what will happen, one is gambling one's life on the possible fruit of a momentary encounter), and echoed in movement as Alice responds to her every phrase with an expression of pain or anxiety and a strained movement—is bluntly counterpoised against her own actions as she speaks. She begins by turning her back to Alice (and the camera) in order to draw off her blouse; but then, with the garment hanging down, suddenly turns for punctuation, revealing her ample breasts and striking bra. The sexual undertone of the moment, both provocative and oneiric, in effect contradicts her own lecture, thus handing Alice what amounts to a second message delivered "between the lines" of the first: that sexuality and forthrightness are natural, spontaneous, and possible. It is this second message that undergirds the action of the rest of the film: were Alice to heed only what Helen is saying to her "officially," the main plot would have to terminate at this point. Here, then, Helen's morality is juxtaposed with pleasure; her sermon on chancy competition is with a vertiginous mask.

At the Astor, meanwhile, Joe watches a sailor buy a corsage for his girl and hold her mirror so that she can fix it decoratively in her hair. As he has never seen such behavior before, Joe's social navigational skills are challenged; under what circumstances should one engage in behavior like this? What exactly can it mean? How does one finesse it? Where and how can one go dangerously wrong? Again, in his dumbfoundedness, we see a play of competition and chance. But he throws himself into mimicry and the heightening of emotion it provides, by slipping into the little flower boutique and buying the same kind of corsage. The minutes go by. Soon it is almost 7:30 and Alice still hasn't shown. Dejected, he makes for the exit and suddenly there she is, radiant, excited. Immediately thrust by her presence into the role of the lover, and, forced suddenly into the grinning mask, he offers the corsage and asks if she would like him to hold her mirror so she can fix it. She is, of course, delighted. Alice's unpredicted late entry makes their meeting seem spontaneous, unguarded, and original; while Joe's having learned the behavioral routine just a little earlier and now so carefully replicating it reveal that the hilarity and joy of the moment can be celebrated only through the dizzying pleasure of the masquerade.

Again in an Italian restaurant Minnelli uses a contrapuntal structure, again between simulation and direct, rational action. As a pianist (Roger Edens) plays soft, romantic music, Joe and Alice nestle at a corner table. A steward brings a bottle of unsolicited wine, and it turns out that an elderly gentleman at a nearby table wishes to pay compliments to the "corporal and his charming companion." The gentleman raises his glass and the young people follow, smiling. But then, before returning to their conversation about her personal life, in which Joe has been probing and she has been explaining who Helen and Bill are, Joe and Alice take a second to look at the gentleman and produce artful and sweet smiles of gratitude again. What this conscientious display of politesse produces for our protagonists is a foundation for later ritualized, conventional behavior as they constitute a "couple" together. This gentleman in the restaurant has been the first stranger to recognize in their joint performance all of its possibilities for linkage. That either Joe or Alice might have desired such intimacy, before this moment, is relatively insignificant in face of the fact that the intimacy is now openly regarded and recognized as such by a bona fide critic. Their little smiling nod, then, is something of a curtain call, in that each is committing to what has been recognized as a witting staging, is gratifying the aesthetic and social need of an audience to be verified as having witnessed something put on public view. "We are indeed appearing together in public as an actual or potential couple," this nod seems to say, "just as, in providing this lovely wine, you have applauded us for doing."

They very soon proceed to have a spat about Freddy, whom Alice has presumably been dating, and she threatens to leave, admitting aloud that Helen was right about servicemen. The gentleman at the next table, watching this in dismay, smiles a little ruefully as though the play of love is proceeding, as one might naturally expect, through all its movements of joy and torment. But then Joe notices Alice's brown eyes and she is reduced to silent surrender. Through all of this, between their bodies and in the street outside, visible through a lace curtain, a slight breeze blows and a neon light flashes on and off, on and off, on and off, on and off, as though to indicate plainly both the ups and downs of the relationship these two are having, both in general and at this table, and also the fluctuation in their engagement with their world between skillful and competitive negotiation (with each other) and commitment to role play and performance (for their audience). In love, as in other forms of meeting, one must begin by being the person one takes oneself rationally to be and then proceed to wear a mask that eventually may become a face.

Soon afterward the two are in the park by moonlight, Alice lying on the grass and Joe strolling around with a cigarette. He says that it's quiet here and she says the city's never quiet, that it's always full of sounds, "always underneath." She beckons Joe to listen and suddenly, as on cue, a train whistle sounds not far away, followed by some horns in traffic, the claxon of a barge on the river, and an ambulance siren. Given the stylization of the park, its dappling of light and shadow, the twinkling of the lamplight on the tree leaves, Alice's corsage as radiant as a little moon, the setting has in general been configured by Minnelli to be dreamlike and dizzying, the kind of place in which transcendent experience can be formed. And indeed, now upon her virtual command, the sounds of the city emerge from their closet to enunciate themselves, stirring both of the young lovers to a deeper and more pungent recognition of the living world in which they are caught. Yet, at the same time, the film operates contrapuntally here. At the restaurant, part of that personal and relatively uninteresting conversation Joe was prying from Alice—a conversation far less engaging, to be sure, than the ebb and flow of attraction between the two people—was the specific information that although at work Helen is in the Sales Department, Alice herself is in "transportation." Trains, ships, trucks: she knows all about these, and to a degree that astonishes Joe. Here now, then, it is not merely the diffuse and indistinct living city that is sounding itself for Alice and Joe in the stimulating nocturnal silence, but also, much more specifically, the practical and rational material of her working knowledge. We can hear the sounds as those of an imaginary creature, a Love God, yes; but we must also know them as emanating from agencies in a massive vehicular system that subtends American commerce (and thus national security) and interfaces on a daily basis with Alice's position and activity in a rational, calculating, and socially organized world. The same counterpoint exists between the two ways of hearing these sounds, then, as exists between Helen's voluptuous body and her stiff pronouncements about social appropriateness, rational success with men, and proper morality. At the end of the scene, as Joe and Alice embrace and kiss for the first time, there is a certain transport visible on Alice's face, and at the same time a certain indecision.

Outside the park, the two are picked up by Al, the milkman (James Gleason), a second observer who will acknowledge and legitimate the coupling they are now, with growing commitment, performing. To drive home the role of performance—which is to say, role-playing and thus masking—in the development of this relationship, Minnelli has the driver listening to his radio for a song he has requested and continuing not to hear it; but he does start singing along with a song that is being played, giving something of a little show, and we have a discreet shot of Joe and Alice sitting as his "audience." Soon another song is played that wasn't his request. "They probably didn't get my letter," says he, ruefully. Joe and Alice now suggest two ways in which chance could have interceded to block Harry from hearing his song: the letter could have been lost, or they might have played it when he wasn't listening. But now, by sudden chance, a tire blows, and Al must find a phone. A lunchroom happens to be open nearby. A drunk (Keenan Wynn) is delighted when they enter. "We get some new blood in here now. We get an entirely new consensus of opinion!" Thus the scales of competition (in argument) are reweighted by the chance entrance of Al, Alice, and Joe. Whatever the drunk's contention has been, it is difficult to ascertain since there is little continuity between his thoughts. By comparison with his "airy" vertigo, Joe and Alice now seem to be walking on hard ground, their relationship normalized and rationalized through the agency of this drunk masque. As the drunk starts to engage Al vituperatively,

the radio on the wall starts playing Al's song and he stands rapturously listening. But the drunk keeps yelling, and also gesticulating, about what's wrong
with this country, accidentally smacking Al in the eye. Alice and Joe retreat with
him to safety, while the drunk stands listening to this "beautiful" song, wishing
he could sing one just like it. Here, highly stylized performance is used to
normalize what had begun as a chance encounter between Alice and Joe,
developed as a strategic attempt on both their parts to stay together as the day
wore on, and became itself a voluptuous performance of coupling. In this
scene, once again, the "primitive" aspects and the "rational" outcomes of
stylistic play are posed against each other for structural support. Without the
drunk's excessive and vertiginous action, Joe and Alice cannot act as a team to
save Al; their rational teaming is thus a reaction to and product of vertigo, and it
is the substructure of everything that will follow.

Now, winded and with his eye injured, Al is in no shape to drive, so Joe must
take over. Joe doesn't know "whether [he] can work this thing or not," but he
pretends successfully to be the driver while Alice, going through Al's route
book, navigates them from delivery to delivery. In a series of tableaux, the two
now merge to provide at once charitable aid for Al and mimicry of stable
occupational devotion to the economy: they show what they could be as a man-
and-wife team performing a job together, making money, being economically
grounded, all the while not being these things yet; while at the same time they
allow the injured Al to rest in the truck while they save his night's work for him.
As the sun comes up, Alice sleeps near Joe as he drives into the morning light,
admitting that she likes him a little bit. "Good night, baby," says he. We then
dissolve to a scene at Al's apartment where the solidly married couple Alice and
Joe have the potential to become is embodied by Al and his wife Emily (Lucile
Gleason). At the breakfast table, Joe is concerned about asking "a girl" to marry
him, since he doesn't know where he's going to be sent, what condition he'll
come back in, or whether he'll even come back at all. "Look Joe," says the older
man, "If people thought about all the things that could happen, they'd never do
anything." And his wife chimes in, "I think if a girl and boy love each other,
want to get married, all the talk in the world isn't going to stop them." These
statements are, on the surface, direct negations of rationality: Al is acknowledging the operations of chance, and advising Joe to pay no attention to them.
Emily is acknowledging the competition that can be spelled out in planning,
arranging, and deciding whether life moves are appropriate, and suggests that
none of this has any real bearing on what people ultimately do. Action, then,
has a distinct quality of spontaneity, feelingfulness, style, transcendence, and

play in the view of these two older people, who have been together for a very long time (both on and offscreen). Yet again, the scene is not played as a stylistic flourish (as Sarris would have it) but is instead constructed carefully as a counterpoint between style, desire, and feeling on the one hand and rational calculation, concern, and fear of chance on the other.

Joe and Alice have now all but admitted that they are in love and realize, walking down the morning sidewalk in the bright sunshine, that if two people really want to be together, they don't have to have known each other for a long time and they should do what their feelings dictate. She agrees to spend this last day with him instead of going to work, but must stop off at the office for just a few moments first. At the Grand Central–42nd Street subway station, jam-packed with people on the way to work, she is pushed into a car and he is left on the platform as the train pulls out. Panic! They scoot back and forth on the subway trying to find each other but it is hopeless—Joe doesn't even know that Alice took a local train and that he took an express in chasing her, thus went careening right past her on the next platform. Outside on the street, despondent, Joe hears an advertisement blaring from a shop window that there are 7,454,995 people in New York City, the world's largest city. At a USO canteen Alice is searching for Joe. She has to admit to the administrator that she doesn't know his last name, and that in the face of their feelings for each other it doesn't make any difference. Here, then, is a meticulous and profound portrait of the agony of feeling and personal experience in the context of a massive system of social circulation, randomness, fatefulness, calculation, and competition. In the greatest city in the world, with press of business on all sides, transportation for economic gain in all directions, emotional truth might seem to have an entirely contingent existence. The names that Alice and Joe don't associate with each other are agencies of that rational system, while their appearances and thoughts, the pauses between their sentences, the qualities of their voices—the styles of their lived moments—constitute together a mutually reinforcing act of vertiginous play. What Minnelli has done is to pose that play against the backdrop of a relentless commercial, rational cityscape that is exhaustively conceived, and conceived with no penchant for style at all. The movie isn't an exercise in style; it is a statement about the importance of style.

Minnelli is using the love relationship to make a more general statement about human bonding in the modern age. The requisite negotiation of proximity, alignment, teamsmanship, behavioral coordination, and interconnected status that informs the production of a loving dyad and also that of a working crew must of necessity be accomplished in the face of numerous aleatory challenges, not least of which is the fact that in the modern crowd there are always oncomers who can display talent and drive, curiosity, devotion, and intent with some skill and aggressive focus. Joe, for example, is literally surrounded by good-looking and charming young women who are potential love mates, and Alice's sudden and horrible disappearance on the subway platform only accentuates that fact of life. At the canteen, presumably, Alice might find herself in a similar kind of surround. What binds two people together in the face of this swirling continuous randomness, where characteristics and features bob to the surface and disappear again quite swiftly, is some residue of eventfulness and experience that transcends the everyday and the superficial, in short, some element of style. One could argue that it is each other's style that Alice and Joe have fallen in love with. But this development occurs in the context of unending competition, movement, and chance. Sarris's summation of Minnelli's career is that it revolves around a "naïve belief that style can invariably transcend substance and that our way of looking at the world is more important than the world itself."[11] Minnelli does take this direction in *The Clock,* but through a carefully constructed counterbalance between style and rationality that shows the "world itself" to be a place where nothing can ultimately be redeemed except through the action of "our way of looking."

Joe returns to Penn Station, awaiting his train back to boot camp. Suddenly, standing at the top of "their" flight of stairs, he spies Alice. As they rush into each other's arms, he gasps, "Quick—what's your name?" thus now guaranteeing a future for the two of them not only in his imagination but also in the practical arrangement of labels and surfaces that we call reality. "We might never have found one another again!" he cries. When she protests, he explodes with the one statement of utter certainty we hear from anyone in this film: "I've *got* to say it!" And then, imploring, he asks her please to marry him. Minnelli thus posits marriage as the resolution of the counterpoint between style and happenstance, the one true logic that goes beyond performance, feeling, chance, and navigational skill. Now, however, rather than being a wise sentiment in the mouths of two older married people who mean to offer good advice, this is a statement of existential conviction founded in the real history of feeling and loss.

The finale that follows, elaborate and magnificent, puts Joe and Alice through a double marriage. In the first section, they are thrown into the labyrinth of the state bureaucracy. Since Joe's train will leave in a matter of hours, they must race against time, and this involves: learning at 12:22 p.m. that a blood test is required and that they must run from the licensing office to 39 Whitehall Street to get one; finding at Whitehall Street that they cannot go up for a test unless they have a pass, and that they can get a pass only on the second floor, and yet they cannot go to the second floor without a pass, and so they have to sit and wait, among other quietly fondling couples waiting for the same thing (for the same reasons); being called suddenly by the guard, who happens to have a short memory and wonders who they are, and then sent perfunctorily up for the blood test in room 318 with a special pass after all; then finding from the doctor there that the blood results cannot be available for twenty-four hours; leaving dejectedly, but telling the security guard what the problem is, which leads him suddenly to recommend that they can go to a private laboratory and get the results in a couple of hours; having their blood taken at 631 Canal Street; rushing back to the licensing office where, as "Allen and Mayberry" they are summoned to "window 5" only to be issued a permit, at seven minutes before 3 p.m., that is stamped "NOT VALID FOR 72 HOURS"; going to clerk after clerk as the clock keeps ticking, always to be told the same thing, "Not valid for three days"; and then at 3:15 being informed by a mustachioed little man that a judge of the Supreme Court may issue a waiver to permit a marriage at once; approaching Judge Forbes in room 387 only to find a man dressing to go out, who says, "It's tough luck; the judge has just gone." But chance cannot always be an adversary, by the law of chance. Joe looks down at the man's desk and sees by his nameplate that he is the cousin of the milkman, Al Henry. The man, suddenly a fountain of friendship, agrees to run out and try to catch the judge, but, "How is Al? And Emily?" Alice is panicking. "Shouldn't you hurry?" But the man says it's quite all right and goes calmly through a door at the back of the office with their license. It's six minutes to four. In a second, he's back with all the paperwork in order. The clerk's officious statement about the judge having left was clearly a performance, a kind of dark masking, to make possible his early departure for dinner and a sweet evening. Blood relations trump bureaucratic arrangements, however; and Joe and Alice's connection with the clerk's cousin undoes the performance that had been designed to obstruct them.

Now they have run back to the office of the justice, Mr. Schwartz, who is getting into the elevator to make his 4:37 train. Joe's persuasion keeps Schwartz outside the elevator, as the doors close on him. "We tried so hard!" says Joe, swept away by his own emotions to the degree that he appropriates to Alice and himself the complex of feelings and circumstances that have led to this moment. Schwartz agrees to marry them, dictating to his associate to

"Find me another train!" A cleaning woman is fixing Schwartz's potted ferns and a janitor is vacuuming his office when they reenter, but he stops them— "What do you think this is, a factory?"—and casts them in the roles of witnesses for the little ceremony that we watch from behind Alice and Joe. Behind Schwartz, through a window, we see elevated railways tracks. Obsessed with ritual and formalization, he makes them change places so that Alice is on the left. As he pronounces the legal phrases, a train goes by obscuring his voice, so that Joe can't hear. "Say 'I do,'" barks Schwartz, and Joe does. Then a train goes by in the opposite direction, so that Alice can't hear either. Finally they get the official pronouncement and the signed papers, Schwartz bustles off, the janitor turns the vacuum on again, and the cleaner goes back to her plants. "I . . . didn't have any flowers," says Alice. Nonplussed, tentative, lost in thought, the two walk out as the cleaner chirrups, "Good luck!"

This is everything, then, of ceremony without anything of joy, a perfectly rational enterprise as punctilious as a train schedule, dutifully recorded and signed, with a chain of events carried out in the proper order upon persons positioned in the proper relation to each other in a kind of cold, functional space. The delirious space that was Penn Station when Joe first discovered it, or the streets with the skyscrapers, or the happy seal pool, or the intoxicating flower shop at the Astor, or the Italian restaurant, or the park by moonlight— all this is evacuated for the brutal and harshly lit "reality" of a more functional rational-legal space, the space of bureaucratic offices, clerks' windows, subway platforms, room numbers, and ultimately confirmatory documents. At a restaurant, alone, a liminal space since it works both to organize and to celebrate the incorporation of the world by way of dining, the two lovers sit sipping soup they aren't really hungry for. An off-duty waiter places himself at the next table, smoking, watching them hungrily while he eats his pie. "Are your mother and father . . . living?" Joe asks. "Are yours?" says Alice. Awkwardly he shows her a picture of "our house, our home." Now she is beginning to cry, the waiter avidly watching, and Joe says, "I guess you're sorry you married me." She breaks into sobs and murmurs that it's just that it was so "ugly."

If the conformity of the "world itself" to our personal attitude, our "way of looking at the world," cannot always be achieved, and cannot, when it is achieved, be predictably worked through the choreographed involvement of strangers, still it can happen as a result of our relationship to place. And we are suddenly now in a position to see that every spot in which Alice and Joe have enacted any moment of feeling together has been in some way *inappropriate* as a setting for the celebration and affirmation of their experience ("inappropriate," that is, in the sense of an absence or failure of the "appropriateness" that Kenneth Burke takes as the basis of the scene-act ratio that governs commonplace understandings of social action and its relation to place[12]). The station is too enormous and too secular for a romantic encounter, its stonework utterly unhallowed; the park is too public, too much a setting where random passers-by may interrupt (this park will be transmogrified into an entirely different kind of place for *The Band Wagon* [1953]); Al and Emily's apartment is too idiosyncratic and private, another couple's personal world; and Schwartz's office is too theatrical, with its massive but entirely dramaturgical palms. But now Alice and Joe come into a cathedral immediately after a wedding party has left, the groom another man in uniform, a mirror vision of Joe, and the bride as happy as Alice wanted to seem, and in a white satin gown. Slowly they enter the space, while organ music tranquilly fills it. As the lights are turned down and the priest leaves the altar, they sit together in a shaft of light and find the marriage service in a little book. And here they perform a marriage upon themselves, once again being united yet now enriched in their union through the voluptuous transcendence that is made possible in this silent, vacant, personal, and also holy place. "Oh Joe, I love you," says Alice, "I'll love you till the day I die." An altar boy walks past and carefully puts out the candles in a large candelabrum, ending in one move the previous wedding ceremony for which these candles were lit, and the present one for which they burned. That previous ceremony, although it took place in this cathedral, was also an outgrowth of bureaucracy, but involved people with money and connections. This ceremony, by contrast, was performed through modulation of feeling and spontaneity, experienced and expressed in the moment. One has the secure sense that even if Joe will leave for the war, the marriage between these two has beautifully measured practical circumstance and passionate involvement together, has knit them, and will endure.

"Nobody asked," wrote Minnelli about this picture much later, "why a musical director was now being entrusted with a drama."[13] But the ability to bring music to drama was in fact everything. If music is the language of felt space, of bouleversement and disorientation, and drama is the language of struggle and chance, skill meeting its limit and its evacuation by circumstance, then what makes *The Clock* especially worth watching, and watching closely, is that in it Vincente Minnelli transcends his accomplishments in the pure musical by marrying an apotheosis of social organization to an epitome of the dream. Style is styled. And a way of looking at the world becomes a world itself.

Notes

1. Yi-Fu Tuan, *Space and Place: The Perspective of Experience* (Minneapolis: University of Minnesota Press, 1977), 67, 67–68, 68 respectively.

2. It must be said that there is a certain delicious ambiguity about the use of the phrase "Radio City" in this film, and the discussion that follows is one way of tracking and exploring it. In 1945, "Radio City" could have been understood in two quite different ways. The name referred to the NBC broadcasting center (originally for radio, and since the early 1930s) in the RCA Building at 30 Rockefeller Plaza, located about half a block west of Fifth Avenue; and also as an affectionate moniker for the immense Radio City Music Hall on Sixth Avenue (and not visible from Fifth Avenue at all). The music hall had opened in 1932. Even when this film was first released, there were numerous New Yorkers who thought immediately of the music hall when they heard the words "Radio City"—possibly because even by this time the hegemony of radio was in decline and the broadcasting center was not on everyone's mind. Strangers to the city, such as Joe (and even, just a few years previously, Alice), and outsiders whose view of New York was enjoyed often at a very great distance, thanks to the blandishments of advertising and publicity, would very likely have known little or nothing about the NBC facility and would have assoicated the term "Radio City" strictly with the music hall. In using this locator, then, Minnelli lays at once through both familiarity and distance to a mixed audience of New Yorkers and outsiders—people like Joe and people like Alice is now. Contemporary viewers of the film are considerably more likely to think of the music hall, indeed, even when they were born in New York.

3. James Naremore, *The Films of Vincente Minnelli* (New York: Cambridge University Press, 1993), 39.

4. Vincente Minnelli, with Hector Arce, *I Remember It Well* (Garden City, NY: Doubleday, 1974), 60.

5. Ibid., 54.

6. Ibid.

7. Roger Caillois, *Man, Play, and Games,* trans. Meyer Barash (Urbana: University of Illinois Press, 2001), 86.

8. Andrew Sarris, *The American Cinema: Directors and Directions, 1929–1968* (New York: Da Capo, 1996), 102.

9. Ibid., 102.

10. Ibid.

11. Ibid.

12. Kenneth Burke, *A Grammar of Motives* (Berkeley: University of California Press, 1969), 3–7.

13. Minnelli, *I Remember It Well,* 146.

The Immobile Journey of Helen Corbett
On *The Courtship of Eddie's Father*

CARLOS LOSILLA
TRANSLATED BY AMITY JOY PHILLIPS

For Victor, who looks and looks

The Courtship of Eddie's Father (1963) starts with a variation on a very familiar scene in American comedies of the 1950s and 1960s. A man rummages around in the kitchen, preparing coffee for breakfast. The milkman rings the doorbell. The man turns toward a bedroom to wake up a child of around ten years old, his child. It is the child's first day of school after the summer vacation. . . . This type of cinematic preamble had, in its origins and in its feminine version, a very concrete finality: it served to demonstrate a mode of living, a definitive consolidation of the economic development of the 1950s frequently symbolized by kitchen-nests where the mother organized daily family life. But at the start of *The Courtship of Eddie's Father* something is missing, a hole that Tom Corbett (Glenn Ford) intends to fill with his comings and goings, his quick steps, his movement across the halls and bedrooms. Where is this woman, this mother, this symbolic totemic figure that supports the tribe? Why is Eddie (Ron Howard) not in his bedroom? Why does he appear in his father's bed, the matrimonial bed, curled up under the sheets, completely hidden? Why is it the father who makes breakfast and wakes up the child? There is an open wound, an absence for now inexplicable, that shakes the foundations of this genre and that this film is not afraid to enunciate directly, especially given its enormity, its monstrosity. The milkman asks if he should leave fewer bottles from now on. And later in school, the father mentions to Eddie that the shirt he's wearing is one his mother ironed. . . .

His mother. Separation? Divorce? No, something much worse, irredeemable. The boy's reply follows, "Is mommy really dead?" The incredulity of the child is also that of the spectator. It brings about metafilmic connotations. In fact, something this cruel is inconceivable in a family comedy. Nevertheless, the first part of the film is dedicated to devastating the storyline along which the narrative should have moved in order to belong to this circuit of rapid consumption. And immediately it is made evident that *The Courtship of Eddie's Father*, as the title suggests, is not so much a film about a boy as a film about the father of this boy,[1] and for this reason it is not a family comedy, but rather tries to follow the conventions of the sophisticated comedies of the 1930s in order to dismantle them from the inside. The concept of remarriage, which has been justly made famous by Stanley Cavell in an indispensable book,[2] seems macabre here, since the person Tom would like to remarry is his dead wife, remarriage with a corpse. For lack of this option, he has to look for substitutes, representations. In this sense, the decor of the apartment becomes a small theater of the world for Eddie and his father, a sanctuary dedicated to the memory of the dead mother and only inhabited by ghostly replicas. The first apparition in the form of Elizabeth Marten (Shirley Jones), the neighbor, friend of the deceased and an evident substitute reference for Eddie, expands the narrative mark farther from the landing to the apartment across the hall, and is dedicated to explaining the absence that is, simultaneously, unavoidably, present. "When I opened the door and saw you, I expected to see Helen . . ." says Tom when he sees her. In other words, Helen, the absence, can appear in any space, in whatever nook or cranny of the fiction, because in reality she has never left this space of open doors, the incessant circulation of human relations, and has even never left desire, which is represented in the domestic realm. For this reason, there's a great temptation for Tom to initiate the process of remarriage: to recover Helen in the figure of Elizabeth, her double, as will occur at the end of the film. However, before this, Tom will have to travel his particular *via crucis* across the feminine universe, full of dangers and temptations. *The Courtship of Eddie's Father*, in this respect, is the story of the education of Tom, not of Eddie.

One of the key concepts Cavell uses in his book is that of conversation. Amorous relationships, the marriage, are not only a sexual interchange, and much less economic or productive, but rather a never-ending dialogue in which personalities face each other and face maturity thanks to human and emotional contact. In *The Courtship of Eddie's Father*, however, this conversation is more of an argument, a debate, even a fight. Tom and Elizabeth, like any budding couple worth boasting about, have distinct points of view on many things, including Eddie's education. The first serious confrontation comes after the boy suffers a crisis over having seen the death of one of his fish. Elizabeth puts him to bed and asks him about the relationship between this event and his feelings regarding the death of his mother. Tom, angry, goes to the living room and makes himself a drink so that when Elizabeth leaves the bedroom he is ready for battle. Similarly, in fact, this confrontation occupies the place of the key scene until the final sequence. At the same time, it is the final obstacle between the couple and the final demonstration of the film's intentions in respect to the genre or genres to which it subscribes, in particular the conventions of the sophisticated comedy and the already stretched limits that separate it, at times, from melodrama. While searching for Eddie, who has escaped from summer camp because of disagreements with his father, Tom and Elizabeth have a bitter argument in Tom's house, during which they reproach each other about their fear of compromise and of life. It is curious that Tom does not step into Elizabeth's house at any moment in the film, the sacred location where the vestal virgin whom he considers inaccessible lives, perhaps due to her resemblance to his dead wife. Paradoxically, this final argument, according to Cavell, is in opposition to the dialogue. It strengthens their ties and assures a certain understanding outside of this precarious place but does not go as far as to legitimate the entrance of the masculine into the feminine territory: in the final scene, Tom and Elizabeth talk on the phone and seem to understand each other, but each remains in his/her home, even though the doors of their respective living spaces stay open into the communal space that is the landing. The contradiction between this liberty of movement and the invisible boundaries established by the sexual and tribal conventions run parallel to the fracture that is just barely visible in the background between the sophisticated comedy and the melodrama: if in the first, primarily in the 1930s, the conversation is always ironic and biting, in the second the confrontations are usually angry and bitter. In this way, *The Courtship of Eddie's Father* progresses by means of a dialogue that is always interrupted, lacking total fluency, in which the war of the sexes is never fun, but rather more problematic and accidental.

Of course, all of this is due to Vincente Minnelli's presence on the scene, a postclassical director whose relationship to genres should necessarily end in terms of conflict, never in harmony. In fact, *The Courtship of Eddie's Father* carries the burden of being one of the last films of his career, inherited from a direct line of assumptions already established in his first works, especially in *Meet Me in St. Louis* (1944) and *The Clock* (1945). From the beginning he understands that one should film not only the body but also the psychology of the infantile mind racked by pain, more or less what will also be done by Rossellini in *Germania, anno zero* (1947) or Truffaut in *Les quatre cents coups* (1959). In filming the psychology of the infantile mind racked by pain, the goal is the formation of a couple: the difficult path toward happiness. In this way, Margaret O'Brien's character in *Meet Me in St. Louis* looks like the same character as Judy Garland's in *The Clock* or Ron Howard's in *The Courtship of Eddie's Father:* fragile and vulnerable bodies whose minutia communicate the hidden existence of a mind tortured by solitude and helplessness. And their adult reflections move perpetually in this same undefined state. Tom, in *The Courtship of Eddie's Father,* is a man marked by the possibility of tragedy; he has lost his wife and is on the verge of losing his son. It is not a coincidence that the actor charged with the task of embodying this character would be precisely Glenn Ford, as gifted in comedy as in melodramatic expression, as his severe performances in Fritz Lang's *The Big Heat* (1953) or *Human Desire* (1954) demonstrate, both being indisputable examples of Hollywood postclassicism. The final portion of *The Courtship of Eddie's Father,* the section prior to the final outcome, is as dark and somber as a film by Douglas Sirk: the news of Eddie's escape, Tom's journey in the car to the camp, his tense hope, the conversation with his son's friend in the cabin, the return in the middle of the night. . . . In the same vein, the fight between Tom and Elizabeth also takes place under shadow, with a twilight tone that is in contrast to the brightness of the first section of the film. Comedy or drama? Family film or the painful route toward the pursuit of love? Minnelli, a mannerist of contrast, combines the graceful movements of Shirley Jones between the two apartments with the hysteria of a desperate father, the musical choreography combined with the expressionism of chiaroscuro.

But there are other women in Tom and Eddie's lives, so that *The Courtship of Eddie's Father* is not limited to the conversation piece that it could have been if Elizabeth were the only woman. In his other writings on cinema, Cavell speaks of the unknown woman, it is clear, after the film by Max Ophuls, *Letter from an Unknown Woman* (1948), based on a novel by Stefan Zweig.[3] In contrast to the feminine characters from classic comedies, those who appear in many melodramas are not accepted in the social body, they remain strange to a man, their demands are outside the rules. Their destiny is solitude and, even more than this, death in life. In *The Courtship of Eddie's Father*, Tom meets Rita Behrens (Dina Merrill), a liberated woman, fashion designer, elegant and sophisticated. She is, as one would say, the foil to Elizabeth, a volunteer nurse whose attractiveness is based on her sweet and maternal manner. While Elizabeth's space is in the home, Rita's is spread between an ample spectrum of bars, restaurants, and party rooms, on top of a sophisticated apartment that includes an especially troublesome dog. This addresses the typical Hollywood confrontation between the complacent female and the worldly woman, between tradition and modernity. Nevertheless, Minnelli puts emphasis, not as much on the obstacle between these characters as in the contrast between archetypes, in the mode in which melodrama infiltrates the field of comedy. Rita is the perfect metaphor for the vanity of urban life, whose best Minnellian example would be the memorable sequence in the bar of *Brigadoon* (1954), the apotheosis of confusion and chaos. But Rita goes too far, her possessive feelings toward Tom reach the point of her asking that they live alone, without Eddie, during the first months of their future marriage, something that neither Tom nor the narrative mechanics of the film can tolerate. Rita is, for this reason, a tragic character, condemned to failure in the context of a film like *The Courtship of Eddie's Father*. And she is also a typical Minnellian character from the moment in which she puts her dreams ahead of the reality that surrounds her. She wants to change her life into a work of art in a manner that, in the end, runs into infantile pragmatism, a jealous guardian of social conventions and at the same time its transmitter, since Eddie starts to hate her when he discovers that she has small eyes, like the evil characters of his comic books. The means of communication legitimate the stereotypes that help to preserve the moral order in the same way that the Hollywood films of that era resist blurring the boundaries between genres for fear of losing their hegemony over collective thought. Minnelli speaks to all of this in *The Courtship of Eddie's Father*, in the privileged space of comedy where melodrama, and therefore Rita, does not fit.

The whole film is a type of treatise on the different tonal forms of Minnelli's work up to that point. If Rita represents the ghost of melodrama, Dollye (Stella Stevens) is the spirit of innocence, the voluptuousness that is not conscious of itself, the pure spectacle that knows nothing about its own powers of seduction. Dollye, it could be said, is an heir of the musical, although she also turns out to be indebted to Ginny (Shirley MacLaine) of *Some Came Running* (1958), one of the most powerful Minnellian melodramas. In whatever regard, it is the triumph of emotion over puritan formalism. Significantly, Dollye suffers an emotional block, she is incapable of acting in public: in fact, she missed her opportunity to be Miss Montana because she could not say a word when she rose to take the stage. Like the classical musical genre itself, Dollye has lost her attributes, but she partially recovers them in an exuberant scene, a genuinely Minnellian scene. In a jazz club where she has taken Norman Jones (Jerry Van Dyke), she suddenly stands in front of the drums and executes an impeccable version, with contagious rhythms, of "The Carnival of Venice," by J. B. Arban. The same methods of *The Band Wagon* (1953) are seen: the seamless move from the quotidian life to the world of dreams and pure form. Dollye is, then, an anachronism, in the same way that the very form of the musical started to be in the beginning of the 1970s. Minnelli will go on to direct only one more, in 1970, titled *On a Clear Day You Can See Forever*, in reality a deconstruction of the conventions of the genre. It is not a coincidence either that Tom and Eddie meet Dollye in a shopping center much like the one that Tony Hunter (Fred Astaire) passed through in *The Band Wagon*—the leisure time/space of the neocapitalist population where diversion becomes consumption, but also where social relations are established and are given free rein to spontaneity. Rita, the unknown woman, loses the game for being excessively strict, because she is incapable of being flexible enough with the concept of the artistic existence to adjust to the necessities of the quotidian life in the middle of the twentieth century. It is similar to what happens with Jeffrey Cordova (Jack Buchanan) in *The Band Wagon*, although he finally redeems himself through the conversion to popular art. Similarly, Dollye meets her ideal man in Norman, a radio talk show host who personifies all of the excesses of the masses, of the empty rhetoric of the indiscriminate sexism of his trade that he puts into practice in his relationships with women, negative characteristics compensated for by the ingenuity of Dollye. This is the future of entertainment according to Minnelli, the compromise between the people's legacy and the new rules of the market, something that neither he nor Tom—nor of course Eddie, that is to say, to the preservation of the integrity of the genres—could be less interested in, which is why the subplot featuring Dollye and Norman ends well before the end of the film. *The Courtship of Eddie's Father* is a continual struggle between the intent to give continuity to certain traditional laws of the Hollywood community and the inevitable tensions that are manifested when this effort takes place in the midst of a full crisis in classical representation.

But if Eddie is not the protagonist of this fiction, if what is really important is the inevitable generic promiscuity of the film, or rather Tom's course of action, what function does this child play who, since the beginning, is indispensably visible for the exchange of roles and feelings that are revealed in the interior of *The Courtship of Eddie's Father*? Who is, in reality, this Eddie? In order to be able to express that aloud, one must return to the beginning, to the first scene where the film opens, and also to the opening lines. In fact, the first images of the film, strictly speaking, are not those described above but rather several location shots that show the cloudy New York skies in shadow that changes the luminous photography of Milton Krasner into a subtle variation of black and white. It is an overture that reveals the antecedent, a tactic Woody Allen would put into use in *Manhattan* (1979),[4] and this detail uncovers some of the intentions of the film: it is not talking about a character, rather about a city, about a collective of bodies and sensibilities in constant friction, about a mass that is in principal homogeneous and whose voluminous appearance hides the raucous variety that teems in its interior. And so from this, the overture is scattered and deceiving. On the one hand, the voice-over is that of Norman, who is speaking through his program—"Wake up, Manhattan!"—and gets the macrocosms of the big city moving with the godlike power that is conferred upon the mass media. On the other hand, across three establishing shots of the cloudy skies, a tiny curtain is opened over a detailed shot of a kitchen, also apparently in black and white. Tom is, as noted, preparing breakfast. The voice warns of the suffering of housewives who put themselves in peril in their daily tasks, telling about harmful burns that can happen with even the simplest task. The "housewife" of *The Courtship of Eddie's Father* is Tom Corbett, and this is the first breakdown of logic from traditional comedy. The second breakdown of logic relates to Eddie and his unusual introduction in the film: in a fetal position underneath the sheets of the matrimonial bed. The scene goes from the godlike voice of Norman to the small pained voice of this child who has lost his mother, who has taken refuge in his father's bed in the middle of the night, relentlessly harassed by fear and now stammering his first words of the day while scratching his head. In the shadow of this imposing city, in the middle of the solemnity of voices and buildings, Eddie is like a tiny elf that bears the world as if it were nothing. Going further from the tradition of infantile stories that introduce boys born without feminine intervention, from *Pinocchio* to *Edward Scissor-*

hands, and whose sinister opposite would be the *Frankenstein* of Mary Shelley, *The Courtship of Eddie's Father* turns to the ambitious narrative that culminates in *Invasion of the Body Snatchers* (Don Siegel, 1956) and its two remakes, one by Philip Kaufman and one by Abel Ferrara, that is to say, it speaks of the symbolic "extraterrestrial" whose origin is completely hidden.

It could be said that the Eddie of this film is born of the heat left by his mother in the bed that she shared with Tom, a kind of beneficial "sheath" that, different from that of the body snatchers, does not arrive on Earth in order to usurp personalities, but rather to prolong them. Like Elizabeth, although from a completely different perspective, Eddie is both the double and the ghost of his mother, and his mission on Earth consists of making emotional pacts between human beings: between Tom and Elizabeth, of course, but also between Dollye and Norman, who know each other thanks to him. Just as importantly, he also is destined to preserve a certain social balance with his arbitrary decisions, and from that, the exclusion of Rita from the diegetic universe is provoked by Eddie. Like Puck in *A Midsummer's Night Dream* or Ariel in *The Tempest,* this mocking spirit from the Shakespearian tradition organizes the world as he pleases. And like the child protagonists of *The Turn of the Screw* by Henry James or *A Death in the Family* by James Agee, two classics of North American childhood literature, his fabled ability changes him into a mask that infiltrates the formal world of adults in order to unveil its secret organization. Minnelli and his screenwriter, John Gay, recycle the Anglo Saxon tradition of childhood learning in order to adapt it to daily life in America in the 1960s: in contrast to what happened in *Treasure Island,* by Robert Louis Stevenson, or in *A High Wind in Jamaica,* by Richard Hughes, or in *Moonfleet,* by John Meade Falkner, the restless Eddie of *The Courtship of Eddie's Father* is not there to learn, but rather to teach, although by laborious and frequently contradictory means. In the America of John F. Kennedy, all permutations are possible, but they can also turn out strange and perturbed. Parallel to the childhood confidence of these texts—Eddie speaks of feminine measures with his father, to his father's surprise, the result of which provoked censorship problems with the film[5]—the feminine characters are unusually strong and independent, from the sophisticated Rita to Mrs. Livingston (Roberta Sherwood), the assistant who learns Spanish in order to visit her son who is married to a Latin American woman.

However, as already stated, Eddie's point of view is not that of the film's, at least *not entirely.* From the beginning, the voice of the city dominates, conveyed in a large public space by various means of communication. And for the majority of the story, the perspectives progressively shift from one character to another, without staying with any of them. There remain, then, two possibilities. In the first, the collective point of view would appear, a polyphony of voices that would carry an incoherent and blurred narrative, very far from the unity and logic of the classics. In the second, Eddie would be something like an omnipotent thought, volatile and disembodied, that flies over the city like the voice of Norman in the beginning, demonstrating the things that cannot be seen. Both options, nevertheless, remain subsumed in the Freudian concept of the superego, in the way that Eddie would be the voice of Tom's conscience and at the same time that of the social masses that surround him—a subconscious structure that not only tries to impose its unifying perspective upon the deviations from the norm but also to restore a lost paradise held in place by the figure of the dead mother, that is to say, from the vital and affective disorder of modern life, from the orphaned contemporary society. Orphaned from family order and the classic model: this is the empty space that Eddie tries to fill. And he does it by means of his iconographic growth within the inside of the shot, from the distant fetus initially to the overflowing full-faced shot that inundates the space of the hallway in the final shot of the film.

In effect, after the argument between Tom and Elizabeth, after the enunciation of the "fear of compromise" as one of the thematic motives of the film, a portrait of the sentimental shipwreck of all of this era, a scene of inverted learning is produced. Definitively transformed into Tom's superego, the tiny Eddie forces his father to stage a possible reconciliation with Elizabeth, an enactment of their future life in common. They are in the kitchen, of course, and the boy makes him repeat amorous nicknames taken from the media and frequently distorted by his imagination, like "sugar" or "my excellent strong man." Later, he makes his father telephone Elizabeth; he goes to the landing, opens the two doors of their respective apartments and stays there, in the very center of the scene, and looks from one side to the other, from a man to a woman talking on the telephone in order to have a reconciliation that could just as well have been made face to face. Nevertheless, what is important is the transmission, the current of love that passes through Eddie and from his desire to see a reincarnated mother—from yielding his condition as ghost to sweet Elizabeth, to situate himself further from the fiction in order to contemplate this transfer of powers. Paradoxically, this marginalization is produced, as they say, in the center of the shot, thus the nucleus of the story is displaced toward the space offscreen. Making explicit the theatrical substrata of the

Eddie arranges a reconciliation between his father and Elizabeth in *The Courtship of Eddie's Father* (1963).

filmic material, distorting the natural place of the performances in the scene, Minnelli creates a memorable sequence, one of the most modern from the 1960s, and possibly, also, one of the most emotional. However, where does this emotion come from? What are the mechanisms used by Minnelli, and from what tradition does it arise that gives it form?

Without doubting the purity or the economy of the media with which he conceives of this conclusion, Eddie can then say what the protagonist of *Pickpocket* (1959), by Robert Bresson, says at the end of the film: "You don't know how difficult it has been for me to get to you!" The search for harmony, for a lost paradise of a beauty that is both humble and sublime, so typical of Minnellian ideology, is concluded in the face of this little happy elf who has seen his mission on Earth accomplished. Faced with the whirling, ungovernable contemporary universe, Eddie opts for order, for placing every character in his natural habitat, for giving everyone a role that fits: Dollye with Norman, Rita in the loneliness of an independent woman, and Tom and Elizabeth in their respective homes, but united by the umbilical cord of the telephone, the same instrument that serves to transmit the good news of Eddie's return to the house after his disappearance from camp. This narrative hiatus, this moment in which the boy looks as if he has vanished from the story, is both distressing and meaningful. His absence, assimilated with that of the mother, shows a neurotic and desperate image of what the world would look like without him.

And it is in this filmic opening where the emotion of *The Courtship of Eddie's Father* is concentrated, and where it is concentrated for a large portion of Minnelli's filmmaking career: life is an incessant circulation of individual fantasies that float through the air, in infinite encounters and partings, in order to converge in dreams that can, at times, convert into nightmares. It follows that due to all of this, one must adjust to a certain "reality principal" that changes the possible into the acceptable. The compromise between art and life is the theme of Minnelli's great musicals: *An American in Paris* (1951), *The Band Wagon, Brigadoon*. In his mind, melodramas put into play the resulting short circuit of the aspirations confronted with a ruthless reality: *The Bad and the Beautiful* (1952), *Some Came Running, Two Weeks in Another Town* (1962). And the comedies try to create a perfect world from the tensions between opposites: *Father of the Bride* (1950), *Designing Woman* (1957), and *The Courtship of Eddie's Father*, at least in the ways in which it can be considered a comedy. The fact that this "perfect world" is at times too conventional, or even conservative, has much to do with this emotional possibility, with the feeling that things could be much worse: Eddie's death could have been added to Helen's death, and because of this it makes the most sense to return to familiar territory. The emotion comes from the inevitability of this conformity, from the resignation to the convulsive beauty of things, not to the proper mechanisms of the *happy ending*.

   The Courtship of Eddie's Father then, weaves an unequivocally urban net of neurotic and sexual fantasies. Its object is to create an Apollonian atmosphere, but to present its message in Nietzchean terms. In some way, the turbulence provoked by the disappearance, by the absence, by the destabilization of the social system, is seen reflected in the mistakes in the story: absence of a fixed point of view, fragmentation, abundant ellipses, construction in episodes. . . . The classic rules of space and time are scrupulously respected, above all in the last case, as the narration covers a whole year in Eddie's life. This year is marked by a variety of celebrations: weddings, birthday parties, engagement dinners. But at the same time, the obligation to concentrate everything in this space makes a place for a scattered structure that is constructed by missteps that facilitate the restructuring of the film into an eventual television series: also along this theme, *The Courtship of Eddie's Father* reverberates with a language in crisis, trapped in full transformation.[6] However it was, this period in the history of American cinema observes while looking at itself in the same way that Eddie observes the result of his efforts in the final scene. And this succession of self-conscious observations puts into play a desire restructured into narcissism, one of the correlatives of mannerist activity.[7] In the same way that mirrors, in Douglas Sirk melodramas, superimpose visions of an anguished universe condemned to infinitely replicate itself, *The Courtship of Eddie's Father* gives body to fantasies, it represents them and confronts them in order not to be forced to exit the vicious circle that the film itself has created as a cinematic device. In the final scene, the boy's look reunites the three protagonists, but the boy also gains strength from the eternal circuit of feedback; Tom's, Elizabeth's, and his own image are reflected in the gentle waters of the reconstructed family. Traditionally, the search for perfection and beauty always refers one to his/herself; this is what puts into play the dysfunction of narcissism. In Minnelli's case, nevertheless, the struggle between desire and reality, the resulting tension, gives way to a species of aesthetic hypochondria in which the director takes morbid pleasure. *The Courtship of Eddie's Father* is as much the story of various neurotic fantasies that cross each other but never quite meet as the chronicling of an undefined, obsessive form with its own structural trajectory. Being the most classical of the postclassical directors, Minnelli could also allow himself to be the most mannerist, and in this sense *The Courtship of Eddie's Father* is one of his most explicit films: human beings isolated in their spaces-hives, the loneliness of a child-elf who wants to reformulate the world according to his own approach, the short circuit of desire in the urban labyrinth by way of a variety of normalizing rituals. In counterpoint to *Brigadoon*, this film demonstrates the disasters of daily life, but also the pacts that can be formed in order to paint over its mediocre appearance.

Only a counterpoint? There is something more that ties *Brigadoon* with *The Courtship of Eddie's Father,* and that refers to a very particular thing. The 1954 musical plays with variations on a theme of a ghostly universe, a Scottish village that returns to life once every one hundred years; it is the staging of the resurrection of the dead. *The Courtship of Eddie's Father,* for its part, describes the process by which a series of characters, hurt by the mark of an absence, try to rectify that absence by means of the complete reintegration of the universe that rules them. The deceased Helen, the little Eddie, and the virginal Elizabeth can be the same person, a reflected image in three deformed mirrors. In the same way, in the final scene, Eddie watches Tom and Elizabeth as if he were caring for the matching mirrors of his gaze. And these images reproduced so many times can do nothing else but remain captured in themselves, in love with the ghosts that create them. Narcissism is a self-referential conflict in which it is difficult to break away from oneself, and its ideals never cease to be present in its imagination at any moment. In this way, narcissism's end cannot be anything else but a melancholy longing for a lost world, a pre–Serge Daney melancholy, whose obscure object of desire is not the void left by a method of writing, or by an aesthetic option, but rather its delayed presence in the form of a specter. The proper Narcissus disappeared from this melancholy, becoming a flower, while Eddie and Tom's struggle consists of avoiding it, a struggle they are aided with by the implacable curse of the quotidian life. Eddie, after his first day of school, confesses to his father that the only thing he has not done is precisely the thing that he wants to do the most: cry. Tom sees *Mogambo* (John Ford, 1953) on television and is hypnotized by the display of affection between Clark Gable and Grace Kelly, but the appearance of Eddie in the bedroom, sick, forces him to return to his life. This constant coming and going between the pulsing stimulation of melancholy and the reality principal is also the mark of the fabric of mannerism, a style fascinated by its own condition of surviving among the ruins of classic cinema. Its obsession is, well, the proximity of death.

The films of Douglas Sirk are perhaps the best example of this landslide in Hollywood cinema.[8] Also Hitchcock, after *Rear Window* (1954), frequently uses the play of mirrors as a manifestation of a spectral reality. And do not forget *An Affair to Remember* (1957), by Leo McCarey, where those Deleuzian pleats in a white shawl serve as a rite of passage between the dead and the living. It is about a necrophilial cinema, in love with its own cadaver decomposing, like what happens to Eddie in respect to his dead mother, from whom he could have easily transmuted. In fact, Minnelli devotes all of his work in the final part of his career to re-creating this taboo, and with this he becomes the American director who best reflects the mannerist sentiment. In *Goodbye Charlie* (1964), a playboy is assassinated by a movie producer but comes back to life in the body of a woman, the invested movement of Helen-Eddie. In *On a Clear Day You Can See Forever*, a psychiatrist converts his patient into a woman who lived many years earlier and, not content with this, falls in love with her. In *A Matter of Time* (1976), a naïve woman is literally transformed into the rejuvenated version of an old countess, who at one time was one of the most beautiful women in the world. *The Sandpiper* (1965) is a necromantic exercise that attempts to resuscitate the traditional melodrama in the context of hippie America, in the same way that *On a Clear Day* tries to do the same with the musical and that the very proper *Courtship of Eddie's Father* does with the sophisticated comedy.

Fascinated not so much by beauty as by fleetingness, charged with capturing this magic moment in which it reaches its peak in order to later start to vanish,[9] Minnelli proposes with *The Courtship of Eddie's Father* a metafilmic reflection on the modes in which the brilliance of life circulates and trans-mutes, resists disappearing in the multitude. In these same years, pop art renounces the traditional canon of beauty in order to extol the ugliness of the urban context, in order to convert used objects into the *media* of art. Con-scious of its condition as a product of popular consumption, *The Courtship of Eddie's Father* also has a bit of reflection on the manner in which those cultural models affect the quotidian life, but at the same time resist allowing the harmony to escape what many consider lost. While Andy Warhol and his acolytes proposed the erasing of the author, Minnelli suggested reincarnating him in his creatures. In other words, he reincarnates himself in the center of the spectacle. And for this reason, the point of view of *The Courtship of Eddie's Father* is perhaps not Eddie's, nor of the voices of the urban chaos, but rather this absent body that at one time was called Helen and now roams among them, trying to restore an order that has disappeared. Invisible beauty, ineffa-ble, confined in another world, this absence in the form of a cadaver, or vice versa, is the unknown masterwork to which Balzac sings, that which should remain hidden so that it does not superimpose itself on its weak reflections. An idealistic director, Minnelli could have said the same thing as Flaubert, from whom he adapted *Madame Bovary,* but also with a change of a name: "Helen Corbett c'est moi."

NOTES

1. In his memoir (*I Remember It Well,* with Hector Arce [New York, Doubleday, 1974], chap. 21), Minnelli refers to the argument of this film as a film about the story of a father faced with "sacred love," "profane love," and with the "sophisticated woman."

2. Stanley Cavell, *Pursuits of Happiness: The Hollywood Comedy of Remarriage* (Cambridge, MA: Harvard University Press, 1981).

3. Stanley Cavell, *Contesting Tears: The Hollywood Melodrama of the Unknown Woman* (Chicago: University of Chicago Press, 1996).

4. To view the similarities, look at Elena Santos's analysis on the prologue of this film by Allen in *Woody Allen: Manhattan* (Barcelona: Paidos, 2003), 42–53.

5. About this and other information on this film, see Stephen Harvey, *Directed by Vincente Minnelli* (New York: Museum of Modern Art and Harper and Row, 1989), 179–83.

6. For more on the relationship between the crisis of classicism and the story of television, see José Luis Castro de Paz, *El surgimiento del telefilme: Los años cincuenta y la crisis de Hollywood: Alfred Hitchcock y la televisión* (Barcelona: Paidos, 1999).

7. Robin Wood, like Cavell, speaks of *Letter from an Unknown Woman,* and in his case, he relates it to Freudian narcissism; see his *Sexual Politics and Narrative Film*

(New York: Columbia University Press, 1998), 214–18. Also, Joe McElhaney refers to the same theme: "narcissism . . . an important step in the path towards new worlds, new identities" ("Vincente Minnelli: Images of Magic and Transformation," in *Senses of Cinema,* available at www.sensesofcinema.com/contents/directors/04/minnelli .html).

8. In respect to, and for more in general on the question of mannerism, see Jesús Gonzalez Requena, *La metáfora del espejo* (Madrid: Hiperion, 1986). It is equally curious that Slavoj Žižek uses Hitchcock to propose what he calls "the collapse of intersubjectivity," that is to say, the false circulation of a gaze that always comes back to itself, the epitome of narcissistic mannerism: the gaze of Norman Bates (Anthony Perkins) at the end of *Psycho* (1960), as Žiž himself says, but also, added by me, that of Eddie in the final scene in *The Courtship of Eddie's Father.* See the last part of the text by Žiž titled "In his insolent gaze is written my ruin" and included in his own compilation *Everything You Always Wanted to Know about Lacan (But Were Afraid to Ask Hitchcock)* (New York: Verso, 1992).

9. Roberto Campari, *Vincente Minnelli* (Florence: La Nuova Italia, 1977), 54ff.

The Impossible Musical
On a Clear Day You Can See Forever

ADRIAN MARTIN

I want to hold you
But every time I try
Something keeps you
Out of reach

I want to love you
But every time I try
Something keeps
Love away
SPAIN, "EVERY TIME I TRY"

In the quarter-century that I have been returning, off and on, to Vincente
Minnelli's penultimate film *On a Clear Day You Can See Forever* (1970), two
scenes have crystallized in my mind as standing for everything that is wonderful, and everything that is strange, in this truly *maudit* movie—a commercial
failure in its day, enshrined in a standard reference book on the musical genre
as a "confused mish-mash,"[1] and yet to find its cult-audience niche beyond the
most fervent of Barbra Streisand fans. I will begin this study of the film with
the first key scene that has stuck to me (one of its song sequences), and end
with the second (a simple, repeated editing device).

The number "What Did I Have That I Don't Have?" that occurs around
ninety minutes in (chapter 19 on the Paramount DVD)—is, in my opinion,
Minnelli at his finest, working in tandem (as he frequently did) with a great
musical star.[2] For Streisand gives a whole other axis to any mise-en-scène—
even one by Minnelli. I mean this in a quite literal way: what she brought, as a
performer, to her films of the 1960s and 1970s (and she speaks fondly of the
collaborative process with Minnelli[3]) was a certain play on *exhaustion*. Strei-

sand frequently gives the impression of being about to collapse, on the verge of implosion—and how fitting this is for the weak-willed character she plays in *Clear Day*.[4] But, just as she is crumpling up and sinking to the ground—her shoulders falling, her head drooping, her arms listless—she mimics the finding, or mining, of some indomitable energy within: she swells up, takes a step, begins to possess the frame and, indeed, the entire space of the set. And then she wilts again, and then she flowers again—so fitting, once more, for a film with so many supernaturally blooming plants—over and over. Even her character name cues us into this: Daisy. In fact, Minnelli cannily seized this aspect of Streisand's performance style and made it the veritable mise-en-scène principle of his entire film, not merely its musical sequences. Look at the marvelous, constantly varied work he does with the shell-like, *très moderne* chair into which Daisy is squashed by her less-than-friendly hypno-psycho-therapist, Marc (Yves Montand): it is the physical, bodily emblem of her discomfort, oppression, and passivity, until the dramatic moment when Daisy, transformed into her past self as Melinda, rears up in this seat (accompanied by a subtle, reframing camera movement upward) and takes over the space.

"What Did I Have" is simpler, in its range and scope of elements, than many of the anthological musical sequences for which the public at large remembers this director: "The Trolley Song" in *Meet Me in St. Louis* (1944), the "Girl Hunt" ballet in *The Band Wagon* (1953) . . . And yet its mastery of space and gesture is total, its use of significant props unflaggingly inventive, its accelerating and decelerating rhythms perfect. The scene is a soliloquy, one star "singing to herself" in Marc's expansive office space—a set upon which Minnelli is able to ring many changes of mood and aspect throughout the film.

The roughly five-and-a-half-minute song (including a "spoken word" break and Daisy's end of a telephone call) is staged across only three shots. The first, beginning with Daisy's reaction to the tape recordings of her sessions with Marc that she has accidentally discovered, runs for three-and-a-half minutes. This is the predominantly exhausted/imploded phase of the song: Daisy trudges around the set, sits defeated in her usual chair, perches on the window ledge. In a neat transition between speech and song—always the hardest transition for any musical sequence to manage—Streisand delivers the first few lines in her broad, Jewish, comic drawl before ascending into her usual vocal heaven. A cut on the very last word of the verse ("what did I have that I don't have / now") takes us into the second shot, as a quick tracking movement outward makes Daisy small in the frame. During this fifty-four-second shot, Daisy alternates between agitation and exhaustion as she talks to herself; music continues as underscore, but the song does not yet return. A visual cut on movement—a variation on the preceding cut within a sung phrase—gets us to the third shot, which lasts two minutes. Here both performer and camera become more frenzied, as the scene quickly recapitulates a number of the motifs that have been previously established in this space: Daisy spins the therapeutic chair in anger, and struggles to put on her coat. The confusion and desperation expressed in the line "where can I go?" is literally visualized in Daisy's frantic exploration of the set, which now offers no points of rest. Finally, Minnelli maneuvers Streisand into a relative close-up in the foreground of the frame—relative, because he has filmed most of the preceding action with her entire body in frame, thus giving this mid-shot special emphasis—and then the scene suddenly breaks: the music stops for a moment, the camera turns around Streisand in the silence, and then she limps away into the depth of the shot and out the door as the music comes to its melancholic, diminuendo conclusion. There are many dramatic or comic "beats" in this scene, many expert spatial modulations and mood changes—and Minnelli is nothing if not a master of stylistic modulation for emotionally expressive purposes.

Yet, for all this excellence, the scene points to a certain sense of *strain* that is evidently telling on the film, on Minnelli, and on the very genre of the American film musical at this perilous moment in its history. *Clear Day* is a transitional film—transitional not so much for Minnelli (his career was hastening to its end, a mere five years and one film away), but for the Hollywood that was taking, as it seemed, one last stab at a musical before giving up the ghost of the genre altogether (until another revival, far down the track . . .). Another kind of dramatic realism, influenced by European art cinema—the realism of Robert Altman, Sidney Lumet, and John Cassavetes—was beckoning to filmmakers in the 1970s; and eventually, a different kind of fantasy, as ushered in by George Lucas and *Star Wars* (1977). *Clear Day* is a film that is already nervous—even ashamed—to be an "old-fashioned" musical; it is part of the scramble to in some way (any way) "modernize" the genre and align it with the assumed tastes and sensibilities of an audience primed on the 1960s "youth revolution" (as signaled, for the film industry, by the stage success of *Hair* in 1967), as well as on movements in international art cinema.

It is easy to take a shot at Minnelli's film as being so evidently obsessed—cripplingly so—with its own "with it" credentials, via half-hearted inclusions of student politics and hippie mysticism (principally, ESP and reincarnation); presumably, most genuine hippies of the time gave it a wide berth, along with the mainstream audience. This is a strain we can see in many "late works" of American directors in the 1960s and beyond (in Howard Hawks or George Cukor as much as Minnelli), where the auteur suddenly finds himself slightly or wildly out of touch with the sights, sounds, and trends of contemporary popular and underground culture alike. But, equally, the strain is also endemic to much mainstream Hollywood production at the time. *Clear Day*, more clearly than most films, points in two directions. On the one hand, it places its bets on the assumed "safe prospect" of adapting a Broadway musical, as had Cukor's *My Fair Lady* (which, like *Clear Day*, had lyrics by Alan Jay Lerner and extravagant costumes by Cecil Beaton) in 1964 and Wyler's *Funny Girl* (Streisand's big screen debut) in 1968—nostalgic projects, with an airy, elongated, sometimes lumbering "stage aesthetic" that seemed to drag the musical genre back to a moment well before the innovations of Gene Kelly, Stanley Donen, Busby Berkeley, or Minnelli (let alone Jacques Demy, René Clair, or Boris Barnet).[5] It would have been easy for many viewers to casually categorize *Clear Day* as yet another "white elephant extravaganza" of the sort that stretched from the Streisand vehicle *Hello, Dolly!* (1969) to what was indeed the extremely desperate attempt to marry the artistry of émigré Miloš Forman with the once surefire hit material of *Hair* (1979).[6] Yet, on the other hand, *Clear Day* tries (however misguidedly) to look forward, to be somewhat new in its outlook and innovative in its approach: the "topical" material was precisely what the film added to the play, rather than slavishly borrowing from it; and the sole "big number" of the piece, Montand belting out "Come Back to Me" from the rooftop of a skyscraper, is an entirely modern conception of what a song sequence might be, comprised as it is of aerial telephoto shots, the Wellesian trick of "skip-framing,"[7] an array of special effects, and a vigorous montage structure. However, the fact that this montage structure is based on a flagrant *alternation*—Marc and Daisy never being in the same space at the same moment, until the exasperated ending of the song—already begins to tell us something about why *Clear Day* seems such an unlikely project for a musical: an *impossible musical* in many senses, and on many levels.

One index of the scramble in *Clear Day*, the "confused mish-mash" between classical and contemporary, is how little choreographed dancing there is to accompany the songs: we see the first signs here of the "realist" compromise that simplifies dance into everyday gestures like walking, only lightly stylized for a casual, "throwaway" effect, or eliminates dance altogether (a style that, today, we see everywhere from Alain Resnais's *Same Old Song* [1997] and the

BBC youth-musical series *I Dream* [2004] to parts of *High School Musical* [2006]). Indeed, the only number that seems to have been based upon elaborate group steps, "Wait 'Til We're Sixty-Five," was cut from the film—and, even there (from what one can gather from the surviving production stills) it was staged as a mock dance, a parody of old-style musical choreography.

As already noted, "What Did I Have" is a soliloquy. I shall return later to the very particular dexterity of Lerner's lyrics, and what they give to the deepest themes of the film. But for now, let us place the song-type of the soliloquy in a historic context. It has always been a feature of the genre; indeed, Minnelli had staged several notable examples, such as "The Boy Next Door" in *Meet Me in St. Louis*. But now, in Hollywood's frantic transitional search for a modern mode of musical, the soliloquy form suddenly became predominant, a kind of baseline option. It was an acceptable compromise between realism and artifice; people singing to themselves—and walking, swaying, not quite dancing as they did so—was deemed somehow more "believable" or acceptable to the jaded audience of 1970 than a conventional bursting-into-song-and-dance routine. It would be up to Streisand herself, as a fledgling director over a decade later, to push this woolly principle of the "realist musical" to its logical conclusion in *Yentl* (1983); there, the heroine no longer even sings to herself, she just *thinks* in song (music by Michel Legrand, arriving at the project via his prodigious collaborations with Jacques Demy in the 1960s), while Streisand stands, sits, stares into a candle . . . Minnelli gives us a preview of that mode in *Clear Day* in the scene constructed around the song "Love with All the Trimmings"—an extremely odd spectacle to which we shall return.

Clear Day is an exceptionally clear case of what the Hollywood industry gingerly calls a "troubled" production.[8] One must be careful to put the various snide, normative comments about its troubles before, during, and after shooting in a wider cinematic perspective. Many films are constructed in an ongoing, continually revised way: the script may go through many drafts and continue to be changed during shooting; shooting may depart altogether from what is on the page; editing, mixing, and reshoots may radically reconfigure the assembled material in several possible forms. This is, in many cases, a natural, unremarkable production process—and filmmakers of a more modernist persuasion, like Jacques Rivette or Terrence Malick, take this degree of perpetual openness further still. But *Clear Day* did indeed bleed and suffer all the way to its premiere. A great deal of scripted material was later cut (either before or after shooting), as the plan for the film went from a long-form musical (divided by an intermission as in *The Sound of Music* [1965]) to one that clocks in at 129 minutes. Among this cut material (which has yet to see the light of day in complete audiovisual form) is an alarming total of five songs (two entirely deleted, two trimmed, and one replaced by a less elaborate substitute)—surely a strange fate for a musical, topped only in the catastrophe stakes by the *total* evacuation of numbers from James L. Brooks's even more ill-fated *I'll Do Anything* (1994).[9]

In its eventual release version, *On a Clear Day* does not present a particularly well-constructed narrative. The film has problems spacing out and balancing diverse centers of intrigue: the sessions of hypnosis between Daisy and Marc; Marc's problems at the University; Daisy's life "on the roof" and her relationship with the dour, straight Warren (Larry Blyden); and the colorful life and death of Melinda, unfolded in flashback—itself incorporating, in fits and starts, *Tom Jones*–style silent-movie mirth, bedroom farce, high romance, and courtroom drama. And there were extra threads in the longer version of the film: the state of Marc's marriage (at first rocky and then reconciled as Marc becomes more compassionate because of his encounter with Daisy); a larger role for the laid-back Tad (Jack Nicholson), including his song to Daisy ("Who Is There among Us Who Knows?"); and quite a few more complications in the relationship between Robert Tentrees (John Richardson) and Melinda (the absence of which makes the eventual criminal trial confusing, or at least elliptical).[10] Minnelli and his collaborators seem to have had particular problems with the exposition of the film, that is, setting up enough of these threads to get the plot going; in the longer version, Tad is introduced just after the opening credits song ("Hurry, It's Lovely Up Here"), and a number performed primarily by Daisy and Warren amid the "roofies" ("Wait 'Til We're Sixty-Five") was set to appear between early sessions with Marc. One particularly striking result of the eventual reshuffle of all this material is the delay of the first song sequence after the credits, "Love with All the Trimmings"—which takes almost half an hour to reach. (It would take the experimental bent of a Jacques Rivette to double that wait before the first song in his musical *Haut bas fragile* [1995].)

All these problems are, in a sense, plainly evident from the first image and the first note of *Clear Day*. The film begins with something unusual for the musical genre in 1970: a precredit song. No previous musical had required a television-style "teaser" before the conventional statement of the theme tune —"On a Clear Day (You Can See Forever)," carried by orchestra and a swelling chorus—during the credits, which here take the mildly psychedelic shape of garishly colored, wide-screen rectangles shrinking away into the center of the screen. Moreover, this preliminary song, "Hurry! It's Lovely Up Here," is itself an odd, internally comprised spectacle, whose initial intention was "written over" during production. Lerner meant for Streisand's singing voice to be in the "off-space" throughout the entire number, with only her hands visible as she touches and carries flowers. This was to set up the gradual "reveal" of Streisand as Daisy Gamble in the first nonmusical scene, situated in Marc's classroom. However, at some point—we do not know exactly how or by whom this decision was made—material was added that shows Streisand, full body, moving among flowers in the university grounds (her magical effect on their growth is emphasized in an offscreen visual gag) and lip-syncing the track. All this, presumably, was in order to "show off the star" at the front of the film. That Minnelli shot this extra material cannot be doubted; in a superbly fluid take running for seventy seconds, the director works his customary, offhand magic with the three-way choreography of performer, character, and environment—which is, after all, just how Bernardo Bertolucci, twenty years later, would define the classical art of mise-en-scène filming: "the relationship between the camera, the bodies of the people in front of it, and the landscape."[11] But this scene, as reconceived and beefed up, makes nonsense not only of the imminent "reveal" of Daisy, but also of a key "arc" in the story, as articulated by Richard Lippe: at the beginning, the character "doesn't realize that her ability to make flowers grow is a direct expression of her creative forces."[12]

Is my commentary itself starting to sound rather too normative in its listing of *Clear Day*'s supposed faults? Placing the film in its context of industrial production and mainstream audience reception is all well and good; but is there another, radically different way to understand and redeem its strangeness, its "mistakes"? To approach such a task, a detour through critical and theoretical approaches to Minnelli (and to the genres in which he most often worked) is needed.

There is little of substance published on *Clear Day;* even Minnelli's most fervent commentators tend to downplay it, and it does not rate a single mention in James Naremore's otherwise invaluable *The Films of Vincente Minnelli.*[13] However, in the justly famous 1977 issue of *Movie* devoted to the musical genre, a short piece by Jim Cook succinctly puts the film in an illuminating and (we might say) symptomatic perspective. For him, the film can be best understood using a "roughly 'structuralist' orientation (i.e., one which attempts to demonstrate the underlying system behind surface oddities)."[14] In this patchwork production, which is indeed full of surface oddities, Cook finds an ingenious logic; the reason it seemingly "fails" to ever become a musical is because Daisy's "liberated" self—where the liberation of self is almost always the prerequisite for song and dance in the Minnelli universe—is both locked up in the past (in Melinda) and postponed to the future.

Cook's explicit aim in this piece was to unearth "evidence of the relevance of this rather conservative filmmaker to contemporary concerns of film theory and criticism."[15] Why this push? At that moment in the history of the Anglo-American appreciation of Minnelli, an intuition inherited from Jean Douchet's work of the 1960s—that every great auteur film tends to be one in which "the auteur's fundamental subject," however buried, is "his relationship to the act of creation," in a largely philosophical or existential sense[16]—met felicitously with the more "materialist" theoretical work emanating from *Screen* and, a little earlier, from the post-1968 *Cahiers du cinéma*. Jean-Louis Comolli and Jean Narboni, in their much-cited, programmatic *Cahiers* text from 1969, "Cinema/Ideology/Criticism," threw a bone to those critics unwilling to give up on their cherished auteurs by identifying a class of films

> . . . which seem at first sight to belong firmly within the ideology and to be completely under its sway, but which turn out to be so only in an ambiguous manner. For . . . they have been worked upon, and work, in such a real way that there is a noticeable gap, a dislocation, between the starting point and the finished product. . . . The films we are talking about here throw up obstacles in the way of ideology, causing it to swerve and get off course. . . . An internal criticism is taking place which cracks the film apart at the seams. If one reads the film obliquely, looking for symptoms; if one looks beyond its apparent formal coherence, one can see that it is riddled with cracks: it is splitting under an internal tension that is simply not there in an ideologically innocuous film. The ideology thus becomes subordinate to the text. It no longer has an independent existence: it is *presented* by the film.[17]

This editorial formulation by *Cahiers*—as generative and inspiring as it undoubtedly was in its day—was itself riven by methodological uncertainties and contradictions. The central idea hesitates, fatally, between an active and a passive mode: these special films in question that subvert the system from within "have been worked upon," but who is doing that work, exactly—the auteur, or the chance conjunction of warring elements in a given film, or something more amorphous like "the culture" in a specific time and place? *Cahiers* and *Screen*, while highly reluctant to stoke the engine of old-style auteurist mysticism—the idea that a great director could transcend the conformist determinations of his or her culture—still felt compelled to place *some* value upon the intervention of the filmmaker. But the exact nature of that intervention was precisely the blind spot in the argument; Comolli and Narboni note that "we must find out what makes it possible for a filmmaker to corrode the ideology by stating it in the terms of his film."[18] Yet what are the "terms" of a film, and how actively controlled can they be? The equivocation here—is a film director largely an "effect of the system" in which he or she works, just a cog in a "textual mechanism" that goes its own way, and is their "subversive" contribution a largely unconscious reflex?—was to dog commentary on Hollywood cinema, especially genres such as romantic melodramas and musicals (and particularly in relation to auteurs including Max Ophuls, Douglas Sirk, and Minnelli) for many years to come.

The widely used notion of *excess* to analyze Minnelli is perhaps the key example of this equivocation in action. According to Christine Gledhill's synoptic account of developments in theory and criticism post-1968: "Whereas the humanist-realist tradition had privileged artistic coherence as the embodiment of authorial vision, the neo-Marxist perspective looked to stylistic 'excess' and narrative disjuncture for their 'exposure' of contradictions between a mainstream film's aesthetic and ideological programmes."[19] Several influential commentators on Minnelli used excess as their Trojan horse to crack open these films: where Geoffrey Nowell-Smith metaphorized the film-text as a hysterical body that "somatizes its own unaccommodated excess, which thus appears displaced or in the wrong place,"[20] Stuart Cunningham hypothesized that Minnelli's style enacts a "going *all the way,* but *in* the representation,"[21] generating an excessive "uncathected energy" that "*is* invested, but in inadequate objects and situations," thus creating an "asymmetry or overdetermination which can be accounted for in terms of fetishisation and the cliché."[22] Most recently, Laura Mulvey has taken this line of inquiry one step further in relation to Sirk, where (as she argues) there exists an "extra-diegetic mode of address" in which "meanings are encapsulated, materialised and mapped onto the image through the signifying potential of the cinema itself."[23] Yet, in all these accounts, the *activity* of filmic style remains mysterious, and ambiguous; too much remains at the mercy of drives, impulses, and energies churning "underneath" the text that gather or explode in unforeseen ways. Nothing in this textual or sociocultural drama seems *directed,* willed, formed, or shaped. The question remains: how does excess in a film *happen* exactly, how does it come about? Putting aside the myth of the all-seeing, all-knowing, all-controlling auteur is one thing; but assuming that such a rational, practical, regulated business as filmmaking is at all moments open to the surge of unsomatized excess is quite another, finally unwarranted move.[24]

The critics associated with *Movie* and *Monogram* in the mid-1970s wanted to position Minnelli differently—to claim his relevance to contemporary theory while rescuing him from the formlessness of a melodramatic excess that simply "happens." It might be thought that, really, there is not a great distance between Cook's defense of *Clear Day*—that, like many Minnelli films, it manages to "foreground and display the very processes of transformation . . . as viewers, we can be both aware of these processes and caught up in them"[25]—and the *Cahiers* platform that states that, in special films, "the cinematic framework lets us see it [i.e., ideology], but also shows it up and denounces it."[26] But there is an important difference between these two "schools" of criticism. In opposition to what came to be known (for a time) as the *Screen* position—which prized certain films, previously regarded as bastions of classicism, as now the opportune bearers or inadvertent revealers of ideological ruptures, fissures, and contradictions—the *Movie*-style valuing of certain auteurs took the path of intuiting a species of insight (and indeed pathos) in the way that their films actively marked a gap between an ostensible project (to affirm, say, the nuclear family unit) and the emotions (for instance, emptiness or unease) that arise from the troubled attempt to carry out this project. This is what Nowell-Smith pointed to in Ophuls's *Letter from an Unknown Woman* (1948), in which "all the problems [are] laid out in all their poignancy, and none of them resolved"[27]—and it is what Richard Dyer eloquently sketched in 1981 in relation to Minnelli:

> The films address the problem of how to come to terms with the vivid urgency of the ideal against the drab necessity of living in the ordinary world. The films appear to have happy endings, in which either the ideal is realized or the character is reconciled to everyday life—yet these endings are only apparently happy. The keenness of the longing for the ideal lingers in the mind, leaving a dark undertow to even the most glittering of his musicals. It is as if the effort of imagination required to see that reconciliation between the ideal and the everyday eludes Minnelli, and more often than not he makes only a mere token gesture towards the solution.[28]

It is with this fruitful idea of the presentation of a gap in Minnelli—between the ideal and the real, between a dream and its fulfillment, between romantic fusion and frustrating separation—that I wish to start over again on *Clear Day*.

All the throwaway dismissals of *Clear Day* harp on the clash of musical textures—and hence the supposed miscasting—that is at the heart of the project: the placing of Streisand against Montand. Indeed, it is hard to imagine two more contrasting and ill-fitting vocal styles: Montand's quiet, jazz-inflected crooning versus Streisand's powerhouse, virtuosic dynamics. We are light years away, here, from the musical genre's ingenious way of blending Frank Sinatra with Bing Crosby in *High Society* (1956), or Sinatra (again) with Marlon Brando in *Guys and Dolls* (1955). No audience of university students to whom I have screened *Clear Day* since the onset of the 1980s has failed to laugh incredulously every time Montand, with his heavy French accent, begins to sing. Montand, of course, never successfully cracked Hollywood as a musical star: both this film and Cukor's *Let's Make Love* (1960) are monuments to his inadaptability to American cinema's norms—which is, of course, the pointer to a fault in Hollywood and its cultural rigidity, not in as fine a performer as Montand. For audiences now as in 1970, however, *Clear Day* is incontestably a vehicle for a still-burgeoning Streisand (it was her third film—and the theme song remains in her concert repertoire), with Montand, on the downward slope of his "international" (but not his French) career, inserted as a kind of necessary buffer, filler, or foil. Musically, she's the future while he's the past.

But surely the most telling, and peculiar, thing about this dual star casting is that Montand and Streisand *never sing together* in a duet—even if, in its final scene, Marc "passes over" the theme tune to Daisy and, in the longer version, was also given an opportunity to reprise Daisy's "He Isn't You" as "She Isn't You"—but neither of these musical connectives offer much beyond only a very attenuated, merely associative form of duet. Streisand and Montand remain as separate, as split apart, as their characters Daisy and Marc, from first scene to last—with only a fantasy flash (in Marc's mind) giving a few fleeting glimpses of the pair (as Marc/Melinda) even dancing together. Romantic comedies past and present routinely play upon a mounting sense of frustration and deferment in their target spectators, but it is rare indeed to have a supposedly feel-good movie like *On a Clear Day* in which the lovers do not manage to get together at all, and their final separation is meant to carry the requisite feel-good vibe. Once again, we are faced with the intriguing question of Minnellian interpretation: is this "discrepancy" in *Clear Day* just an unfortunate blunder, a miscalculation, or are we being confronted with the disquieting apparition of a work that lays out its problems while deliberately not resolving them, a film that is carrying out, however intuitively, its "internal criticism"?

Here it is necessary to place the film within a fairly inventive generic context—not the musical comedy, but a network of narratives that cross several genres, all dealing with "unsynchronized" lovers. From the surrealist favorite *Peter Ibbetson* (1935) and Joseph Mankiewicz's classic *The Ghost and Mrs. Muir* (1947); all the way to Rivette's modernist *Story of Marie and Julien* (2003) and the Keanu Reeves/Sandra Bullock tearjerker *The Lake House* (2006, a remake of the Korean *Il Mare* [2000]); by way of films as singular as Alain Resnais's *L'amour à mort* (1983), as sublime as Wim Wenders's *Wings of Desire* (1987), as perverse as Jonathan Glazer's *Birth* (2004), or as peculiar as Alan Rudolph's *Made in Heaven* (1987), many different story formats have been tried out to portray the dilemma of lovers fated to never be together in the same time, space, or level of reality. The relationship between a ghost (or an angel) and a human; between people stranded in two different moments in time (yet still able, magically, to communicate with each other); between a person who has survived the death of their partner, and that partner returning in a seemingly reincarnated (usually younger) body . . . the variations multiply, and it is notable how this transgeneric template of the "supernatural romance," fated to impossibility, truly crosses the line between the fluffiest comic entertainments (Minnelli had grazed this terrain once before in *Goodbye Charlie* [1964], where a tough guy reincarnates as a woman) and the most elevated art films; just the sort of mixed cultural space where, as Naremore argues, Minnelli needs (and aspired) to be placed.

Back in 1973, discussing *Bells Are Ringing* (1960), Raymond Durgnat suggested that what makes certain films, designed mainly for the purpose of entertainment, so keenly interesting is the intuitive way that, while "accepting all that is true in the conformist myth," they nonetheless "reveal at least the outlines of those parts of reality against which the myth is braced."[29] We can put this suggestive formulation another, quite concrete way: *how hard is the problem that a narrative sets itself,* in the terms of the complications (moral, ethical, sociopolitical) that it must struggle to either satisfyingly resolve, or successfully wriggle out of? The more "impossible" the central dilemma of a story, the more likely we are to feel the *gap* or discrepancy between its symbolic problem, and the standard ideological solution that will, more or less inevitably, be trotted out. One of the hallmarks of Minnelli's cinema (*Brigadoon* [1954] is exemplary in this regard) is the *difficulty of the central problem to be solved,* and the tendency (as Dyer noted) to "fudge" its solution, to end on a faintly unconvincing or diffusely melancholic note. (It is a hallmark, too, of Lerner, as Martin Sutton has pointed out; his scripts for *Brigadoon*, *Clear Day*, and *An American in Paris* [1951], like his *Camelot*, all deal with the "less happy areas of romanticism: the virtual impossibility of realising one's dreams, and the vast difficulties involved in permanent and meaningful communication between people," resulting in a "low-key wistfulness that verges at times on anguish."[30])

Clear Day stretches to the breaking point its central plot contradiction; namely, the fact that who Marc loves is not Daisy but Melinda. This is a rare convolution, even for supernatural romances. It sets the central characters at painful cross-purposes; the more that Daisy becomes confident in her "self" (a growth triggered, nominally, by the conquest of her smoking addiction), the more she entertains the fantasy that Marc is attracted to her for who she is—rather than for the *other* self that she also is, or rather was, in a previous life. And when she finally discovers the truth, she is devastated. In this sense, the film drags in a standard complication from unsupernatural romantic comedies: a love relation that is based on a misunderstanding or (in psychoanalytic parlance) "misrecognition," and then on the deceit that is necessary to maintain that misunderstanding. Of course, the misrecognition goes only one way in *Clear Day;* it is Marc, the rational "man of science" who holds all the cards of knowledge, while Daisy acquiesces as his hypnotized subject—and it is fascinating indeed to watch contemporary audiences squirm at such a flagrant, diagrammatic "exposure" of the inequality and nonreciprocity between the sexes, something that the film simultaneously avows, explores, and milks some easy, "conservative" laughs from (as in the moments where, despite Daisy's explicit protests, Marc is able to reduce her to passivity with a single hypnotic-cue gesture).

How could any film "comfortably" get out of this mess and find its way to a happy ending? One interpretation of the film aligns it with the prevalent *confusion* between the spheres of dream and reality that structures many Minnelli works. Dyer notes that the film "never reveals whether her memories are real, or products of her fertile imagination, or fantasies put to her by the hypnotist"—thus anticipating more recent cultural anxieties over repressed versus "planted" memories in psychotherapy—and this confusion continues the tradition in Minnelli whereby "always the question of illusion, of what is real and what is not real, remains unanswered, perhaps unanswerable."[31] The solution that the film does explicitly offer for its central dilemma is patently weak, a handy safety valve or exit strategy, since it results in no actual onscreen moment of communal satisfaction. Marc learns (again with his subject under hypnosis) that he and Daisy will one day get together in another, future lifetime—cueing the proto–New Age bromide that, just as Daisy is, after all, a "remarkable woman," thus we all "contain multitudes," we are all remarkable people, somewhere and somehow. Yet this resolution is hardly enough to wipe away the viewer's memory of the far more vivid scenes that gave voice to Marc's bitterness and disappointment that the woman before him on the analyst's couch is not "the dream Melinda" (to quote his song "Melinda"). The film's ostensible effort to bolster the modern ideology of "selfhood" thus ends up with the more disquieting suggestion that selves can scarcely get themselves together, let alone rendezvous successfully with their appointed Others.

Let us return, in this light, to the songs of *Clear Day*. In their various forms of oddness and ill-fittingness—and if liberated from judgment in conventionally generic terms, against some spurious classical ideal of a Golden Age "well-made musical"—they in fact play out every manifestation of split and nonalignment between, and even within, the characters.[32] "What Did I Have" is a linguistic masterpiece by Lerner, full of complications, paradoxes, and "shifters" of tense, address, and gender:[33] "Wouldn't I be the late, great me if I knew how?" sings Daisy. In the rather casually conceived and staged Streisand number "Go to Sleep"—in fact put together hastily to replace an ambitious production number named "E.S.P." that was shot but then scrapped—Daisy splits into two incarnations (her naïve, dreamy self and her rather more worldly conscience, glimpsed nowhere else in the film) and dialogues testily with herself. "Come Back to Me" turns every available man, woman, child, and animal out on the streets of the big city into vessels for Marc's sung entreaty to Daisy. And, beyond the musical sequences, a particularly psychedelic moment translates the confusion of Daisy's "repressed memories" into a wild superimposition of various, flailing Melindas in different costumes during different court trials.

The only refuge from—or compensation for—such agony of split selves is provided by a very Minnellian phantasm: the dream of romantic *fusion* with another person—something that is also the crucial motor force of many supernatural romances (as in *Peter Ibbetson*, where the nocturnal union of a brutally separated man and woman within a mutual dream space is only ever interrupted by the "thunder of the world" and the specter of death). This brings us back to "Love with All the Trimmings." To fill out the mute images that accompany this thought-song, Minnelli gives us a back-and-forth, shot/reverse shot depiction of a seduction: in a crowded, lavish dining hall,

Melinda and Tentrees have eyes only for each other, and she is going to make sure his eyes do not stray. So we are treated to an agonizingly drawn-out alternating series—eighteen shots in all—that Minnelli keeps "stepping up" in intensity in various ways: zooms, closer reframings, glamour lighting and cinematography, and especially Streisand's orgy of scintillating gestures (batting her eyes, drawing her drinking glass down over her breasts, etc).

It is hard to experience this spectacle as anything other than the highest of high camp (it has surely provided the many drag queen impersonators of Streisand worldwide with prime material). However, the scene comes with an intriguing coda or reprise that puts it in a different, richer perspective. After an intermediate discussion with Winnie Wainwhistle (Irene Handl), Melinda's seduction effort proves successful; Tentrees enters her room. As the song returns (with still no mouthing of the lyrics), Minnelli engineers a very particular kind of grand screen kiss: the bodies merge, the mouths meet, and the camera traces an almost complete circle around the new lovers. Retroactively, the principal function of that endless alternation between Melinda and Tentrees was to create a tension very specific to cinema; we long for the coming-together of these figures, at the same moment that we are reminded of the seemingly unbridgeable distance between them. (Four decades on, Wong Karwai would prove himself to be the modern master of this exquisite form of sentimental tension.) So, what is at stake in this kiss, and what makes it so quintessentially a cinematic phantasm? It is precisely a moment that aims to capture and communicate total fusion. But such fusion, in as much as it figures as an absolute, romantic ideal for cinema and popular culture generally, also presents itself as a formidable limit—an impossibility.

It has long been established in cinema theory—thanks to the work of Raymond Bellour, Virginia Wright Wexman, and Rick Altman[34]—that classical narrative cinema works by a process of *separation* in order to ensure ultimate fusion: a man and a woman (in the standard heteronormative form) are set into distinct, alternating trajectories—the man in the wilderness and the woman at home, as in a typical western (but also in a modern drama as singular as Kubrick's *Eyes Wide Shut* [1999])—in order that they can finally be brought together, happily and harmoniously, in the final scene or shot. Analyzing what he calls the *repetition-resolution effect*, Bellour gives a detailed account of how films prolong and enhance the separation phase of a story by using a technique of alternation—constantly switching between the characters in their distinct, often distant "worlds"—that builds the tension of suspense. Furthermore, cinema has other microtechniques of separation, creating the moment-to-moment texture of any scene or fragment that constantly echo and reinforce the larger, primal separation that structures the narrative. Bellour lists "the level of the various models of shot/reverse shot and of point of view, the level of camera movement, of diegetic motifs within the segment (presence or absence of a character within the frame), alternation of two settings within a given place." In relation to the specific example from which he derives many of these analytical intuitions and principles—Minnelli's *Gigi* (1958)—Bellour concludes: "we have here a film that constantly and throughout varies the principle of alternation which constructs it, through an effect of reflection and reciprocal implication between its different levels."[35] (He also notes, significantly, that a general alternating structure is "pretty much characteristic of the genre of musical comedy.") Although *Clear Day,* in the form that we have it, undoubtedly falls rather short of the classical perfection that Bellour found in *Gigi,* the film certainly multiplies its alternations and separations on the microlevels of its mise-en-scène as much as on the macrolevels of its plot; and, indeed, it invents even more fanciful multiplications of character (as we have seen), thanks to its psychoanalytic and supernatural-inflected premise.

This theory of film as repetition-resolution and separation-alternation can—as avant-garde cinema shows us—be taken right down to the smallest units of the medium: the individual film frames as much as the shots, scenes, segments, or large-scale parts. But there will always remain an aporia at the heart of this mechanism: impossible fusion, which would entail (at the logical extreme) the dissolution between one frame and the next, the disappearance of the very spatiotemporal coordinates that make cinema possible. On the level at which Minnelli works on the problem of fusion—the staging and filming of the kiss between Melinda and Tentrees—this impossibility asserts itself no less forcibly. Narrative-representational cinema has always hit this limit. How can it show a kiss, an embrace, or the sexual act, as a "oneness," as fused ecstasy; how can it show any such thing from *within* (as it were) its experience? All that cinema has recourse to, finally, is the usual bag of tricks, artifices, and conventions: the "dissecting" trope of shots and reverse-shots (alternating close-ups of each lover's face upon the shoulder of the other); accelerated montage; or (Minnelli's preference here) the totalizing movement of a camera that sweeps everything up into the figure of a self-contained, circular universe. (Brian De Palma offers us, in *Obsession* [1975], the delirious extension of such a "happy ending," so happy it might just as easily be an imagined fantasy: a loving embrace snatched from the jaws of every conceivable yawning abyss of difference and misunderstanding, filmed in a dizzying camera movement that goes around and around the actors.) The underlying "low-key wistfulness" of Minnelli's oeuvre has much to do with this: the inevitable demonstration that a dream of fusion is fated to always fall away into its component parts—the separate times, spaces, bodies, shots, and voices of baseline phenomenal reality. And *Clear Day,* across all its giddy levels and bits and pieces, offers one of his most poignant demonstrations and explorations of this profoundly philosophical truth.

We have arrived at the second moment that, for me, crystallizes this film. It involves a simple, entirely familiar editing device; in fact, another shot/reverse shot volley. Occurring quite calmly around eighty minutes in, after various plot convolutions and revelations have already surged and waned, the scene poses a conversation between Marc in his space (the study, present day) and Melinda in hers (a bedroom in the past). What a mind-boggling cinematic conjunction this is! Thanks to the standard illusion installed by reverse-field cutting, we (unconsciously) assume that these characters are looking at each other—and hence, into each other's "worlds." But, of course, no such thing is rationally possible. Marc is, in fact, gazing at a comatose Daisy in another part of his own room. So what he is "seeing" at this moment can only be his fantasy-superimposition. If so, then where is Melinda, and what is *she* seeing? What is her reality-status, exactly? "She" is actually speaking—from out of Daisy's body—so cannot entirely be simply Marc's fantasy-projection. In a sense, the phantom Melinda is projecting, and hence giving ephemeral reality to, is her world as *she* imagines (or remembers) it. And meanwhile, the dream-dialogue simply goes on, cutting back and forth, as if none of these conceptual complications really matter one jot.

It could be a scene from a Raúl Ruiz film, where divided characters often converse serenely or banally between "incompossible" worlds. But what it most reminds me of, in its melancholic, twilight hush, is not the droll, ludic humor of Ruiz, but a French film by Eugène Green called *Le Pont des Arts* (2004). In its own, unusual way, this film is also a musical, albeit of a highly classical, highbrow sort; many scenes are devoted to sublime choral singing. The story concerns a woman's suicide, and the effect it has on her remaining, living acquaintances. The film ends on a magical dialogue between a living man and the ghost (or fantasy-projection) of the dead woman; it happens in the perfectly everyday, outdoor setting of the Pont des Arts in Paris. What makes this scene so affecting is the straightforward way in which Green frames and stages it: each character stands perfectly still, within their own reality, and addresses the camera that is in the place of the Other; when the two shots are

A "dream-dialogue" between Melinda (Barbra Streisand) in the past and Dr. Chabot (Yves Montand) in the present in *On a Clear Day You Can See Forever* (1970).

cut together in the usual reverse-field way, Green creates a stark, impossible, but entirely convincing face-off of separate, incommensurable worlds, our world and a world elsewhere. This spectacle may be closer, in its inspiration, to Robert Bresson than Minnelli; but would we feel its pathos so strongly unless *On a Clear Day You Can See Forever* had not already laid out the problem for us in all its poignancy, and left it tremblingly unresolved?

NOTES

1. Clive Hirschhorn, *The Hollywood Musical* (London: Octopus, 1981), 396.

2. For a completely contrary evaluation of this scene (as "awkwardly crammed within [a] tacky space"), see Stephen Harvey, *Directed by Vincente Minnelli* (New York: Museum of Modern Art and Harper and Row, 1989), 290. My account of Harvey's book in relation to traditions of Minnelli criticism can be found in "*Directed by Vincente Minnelli,*" *Cinema Papers* (Australia) 81 (December 1990): 66–67.

3. For an example, see the Streisand episode (taped in 2003) of James Lipton's television series *Inside the Actors' Studio;* this became available in 2006 on the DVD *Inside the Actors' Studio—Icons.*

4. For brevity's sake, I shall henceforth refer to the film in this way—but it should not be confused with the UK production called *On a Clear Day* (Gabi Dellal, 2005), which bears no relation to it.

5. See Adrian Martin, "Musical Mutations: Before, Beyond, and Against Hollywood," in *Movie Mutations: The Changing Face of World Cinephilia,* ed. Jonathan Rosenbaum and Adrian Martin (London: British Film Institute, 2003), 94–108.

6. See Michael Walker, "*Hello, Dolly!*" *Movie* 24 (Spring 1977): 60.

7. This is a technique in which select individual frames are taken, here and there, out of a shot: there is a subtle "skip" in the fluidity, but not enough of a gap to create a jump-cut. See Orson Welles and Peter Bogdanovich, *This Is Orson Welles* (New York: HarperCollins, 1992), 309.

8. For accounts of the film's production, see Vincente Minnelli, with Hector Arce, *I Remember It Well* (London: Angus and Robertson, 1974), 364–67; and Harvey, *Directed by Vincente Minnelli,* 286–88.

9. Most of the information about the initial, longer version of *Clear Day* comes from the invaluable research made available on the Web site *The Barbra Archives,* devoted to Streisand's career (www.barbra-archives.com); audio clips of several cut songs can be consulted there.

10. There is a CD compilation titled *100 Years of Cinema* (Retro, 1997) that contains an archival recording of Nicholson singing "On a Clear Day You Can See Forever"; it is unclear whether this was ever slated for use in the film.

11. Bernardo Bertolucci, "Once upon a Time in Italy," *Film Comment* (July–August 1989): 78.

12. Richard Lippe, "*A Matter of Time,*" *CineAction!* 1 (Spring 1985): 13.

13. James Naremore, *The Films of Vincente Minnelli* (New York: Cambridge University Press, 1993). For an example of an excellent general piece on Minnelli that largely bypasses this film, see Jean-Pierre Coursodon's entry in Coursodon, ed., *American Directors* (New York: McGraw-Hill, 1983). I would like to acknowledge a debt here, however, to the largely unpublished lectures of Tom Ryan on Minnelli delivered at Melbourne State College in the late 1970s, which made enthusiastic use of his own 16 mm print of *Clear Day.*

14. Jim Cook, "*On a Clear Day You Can See Forever,*" *Movie* 24 (Spring 1977): 62.

15. Ibid.

16. Jean Douchet, *Hitchcock* (Paris: Cahiers du cinéma, 1999), 51. I am indebted to

Luc Lagier's *Visions fantastiques—Mission: Impossible de Brian De Palma* (Paris: Dreamland, 1999) for this understanding of Douchet's work.

17. Jean-Louis Comolli and Jean Narboni, "Cinema/Ideology/Criticism," in *Screen Reader 1: Cinema/Ideology/Politics,* trans. Susan Bennett (London: Society for Education in Film and Television, 1977), 7.

18. Ibid.

19. Christine Gledhill, "The Melodramatic Field: An Investigation," in *Home Is Where the Heart Is: Studies in Melodrama and the Woman's Film,* ed. Christine Gledhill (London: British Film Institute), 6.

20. Geoffrey Nowell-Smith, "Minnelli and Melodrama," in *Home Is Where the Heart Is,* ed. Gledhill, 73–74.

21. Stuart Cunningham, "Stock Shock and Schlock," *Enclitic* 5/6 (Fall 1981/Spring 1982): 170.

22. Ibid, 167.

23. Laura Mulvey, *Death 24x a Second* (London: Reaktion Books, 2006), 147.

24. For a fuller discussion, see my PhD dissertation, *Towards a Synthetic Analysis of Film Style,* Monash University, 2006.

25. Cook, "*On a Clear Day,*" 62.

26. Comolli and Narboni, "Cinema/Ideology/Criticism," 7.

27. Nowell-Smith, "Minnelli and Melodrama," 73.

28. Richard Dyer, "Minnelli's Web of Dreams," *Movie* 58 (1981): 1153–54.

29. Raymond Durgnat, "*Bells Are Ringing,*" in *The Film Comedy Reader,* ed. Gregg Rickman (New York: Limelight, 2001), 236.

30. Martin Sutton, "*Brigadoon,*" *Movie* 24 (Spring 1977): 57–58.

31. Dyer, "Minnelli's Web of Dreams," 1154. Mistakenly but tellingly, *Movie* labels the accompanying still from one Daisy's flashbacks as an "exotic dream sequence"!

32. The following discussion owes a debt to Jonathan Rosenbaum's magisterial nonclassical appreciation of musical sequences in "Gold Diggers of 1953: Howard Hawks's *Gentlemen Prefer Blondes,*" reprinted in his *Placing Movies: The Practice of Film Criticism* (Berkeley: University of California Press, 1995), 94–104.

33. See Lesley Stern's apposite analysis of Lerner's lyrics for a song in *My Fair Lady,* in "Acting Out of Character: The Performance of Femininity," in *Grafts: Feminist Cultural Criticism,* ed. Susan Sheridan (London: Verso, 1988), 25–34.

34. See Raymond Bellour, *The Analysis of Film* (Bloomington: Indiana University Press, 2000); Virginia Wright Wexman, *Creating the Couple: Love, Marriage, and Hollywood Performance* (Princeton, NJ: Princeton University Press, 1994); Rick Altman, *The American Film Musical* (Bloomington: Indiana University Press, 1987).

35. Janet Bergstrom, "Alternation, Segmentation, Hypnosis: Interview with Raymond Bellour," *Camera Obscura* 3/4 (1979): 83.

Ars gratia artis
Notes on Minnelli's Poetics

JACQUES RANCIÈRE
TRANSLATED BY BRIAN O'KEEFE

A STAGE OF ENTERTAINMENT

Jeffrey Cordova, the fashionable director of *The Band Wagon*, and Tony Hunter, the star of old-time musicals, would agree on one thing at least—that refrain, echoed by so many in the world of theater and film: "the world is a stage," or again, "the stage is a world of entertainment." There are two propositions here, the first of which is that artists simply represent, nothing more. It's more or less what Flaubert said, notwithstanding the moralizing tone of the prologue that was added to *Madame Bovary* to satisfy the censors. Minnelli agrees with Flaubert despite that prologue, and despite the unconvincing example of Charles Boyer in *The Four Horsemen of the Apocalypse*, urging his son to give up aestheticism for political commitment. Art has no truck with either politics or morality. Paris under the German Occupation is only different from the Paris of the belle epoque because of the colors of the German uniforms—which blend in perfectly with those high-class restaurant decors. The French Resistance makes bonfires that resemble those in *Meet Me in St. Louis*, while the choreography of its activities matches the dancer's performance in *Designing Woman* who uses his artistic skills to knock out the hired killers. And despite the technology gap, when the RAF fighters take off, the fairy-tale colors of the sky are like the painted backdrops to one of the ballets in *The Pirate*. Art has no truck with politics or morality not because of art's sublime loftiness but, on the contrary, because of its absolute identification with entertainment. Art delights in life, which is another way of changing it. Minnelli is an MGM director. And MGM is identified at the beginning of each of its films by a roaring lion surrounded by a crown bearing a Latin motto that one tends not to read because one doesn't expect to see it there. The motto says: *Ars gratia artis*, art for art's sake.

The second proposition flows naturally from the first: Art favors no particular genre. "If it moves you, if it stimulates you, it's theater," says Jeffrey Cordova, brushing aside Tony Hunter's objections. Cordova stages Sophocles, whereas Tony sings and dances in musicals. But *Oedipus Rex* is just another sort of musical, while the musical written by the Martons is a modern version of *Faust*. *Faust* is a story about damnation and therefore a fireworks display; hence, the damp squibs and choking smoke that almost suffocate Fred Astaire and Cyd Charisse.

What is the difference, really, between Jeffrey Cordova and Minnelli? Minnelli also believes that any story is a good story and that the emotions elicited by the "chap who kills his father" (Oedipus) and those stimulated by a twirling skirt are of the same order. Pyrotechnics are as much in evidence in Minnelli's films as they are on Cordova's stage. Any pretext to set them off will do: the Halloween party and the fireworks at the World's Fair (in *Meet Me in St. Louis*); the imaginary flames in the midst of which Manuela sees the actor Serafin transformed into Macoco the Pirate (in *The Pirate*); the "real" flames of a German vehicle blown up by the Resistance; the fire in the grate at old Madariaga's hacienda; or the lightning bolts of storm and apocalypse streaking down on the beaten patriarch (in *The Four Horsemen of The Apocalypse*).

The difference is that a Minnelli fire produces no smoke. Smoke is a sign of fire but it is also about the confusion of elements and genres. That's why, in the theater, it is the favorite artifice of those who want to show that they don't see any difference between Shakespeare and Bill Robinson, or even Sugar Ray Robinson. Jeffrey Cordova is one of those people. He is in the avant-garde tradition that, since Stéphane Mallarmé or Vsevolod Meyerhold, has dreamed about and actually tried to forge a new alliance between great poetry and popular pantomime, the circus spectacle and the boxing match. As for Minnelli, he represents—or wishes to represent—the wandering players whose flame Jeffrey Cordova wants to steal. These are players who don't need to be told that Shakespeare was one of their own because they've always known it. To Minnelli, the marriage of great art and popular art is a good idea—what's bad is wanting to make a show of marrying them, arranging that marriage as if it were a paradox (thereby enhancing the value of the avant-garde artist) when it has more or less always taken place in practice. It is about wanting to "elevate" entertainment to the level of art and suppressing the particularities of subject matter and genre, as the "total spectacle" pretentiously claims to do. The flames of war can indeed be associated with Halloween bonfires, and staged ballets can turn into combats, just as long as one doesn't try to reduce them, from the outset, to their common denominator. Equating subject matter and emotions is one thing; confusing them is another. Art for art's sake and entertainment are indeed the same thing. But if the aim is to *show* that they are the same thing, the result will be a caricature of that identity and one that reopens the gulf between them. To experience the equivalence of all subjects and genres, one must begin by respecting the differences between them.

Performance and Fiction

On the world's stage, as on the theatrical stage, there are performances. Performance is always a capacity for transformation, a means of galvanizing bodily movements or altering the spectacle. There's no need to flee to another world to do that. Reference is often made, and especially in regard to Minnelli, to the cinema of dreams and to the struggle of dreams against reality. But the opposition isn't as clear as it appears. Because what exactly is a dream image? Isn't it always an image signaling itself—in other words, a smoke image? Today, *dream* commonly designates a place that a travel agency might send you to. The hero's dream in *Brigadoon* is more interesting when it elicits silence amid the chatter of an urbane gathering in New York than when it materializes in the sort of images you get in the marketplace scenes and scenes of festivity, complete with Scottish kilts and shepherdesses' skirts right out of an operetta. If the dream state is a state where individuals withdraw from action then this doesn't really correspond to Minnelli's dramaturgy, where a change of rhythm always accelerates the tempo, radicalizes the action, unleashes energy. The Macoco loved by Manuela in *The Pirate* only exists by virtue of the body she gives him, which is not the fleshy body of the repentant pirate nor that of

Serafin the minstrel, but her own body, the body of her performance: a blazing declaration that instantly cancels out her rather awkward child-woman's body and gives birth to another body, one transfigured by the energy of dance and song. The flames of the ballet chase away the smoke of dreams because ballet, by doing away with the realism of setting, likewise dismisses the characters and their personalities in order to clear a space for performance alone. Once Jerry has breathed a sigh as he picks up Lise's rose (in *An American in Paris*), Gene Kelly and Leslie Caron can proceed to do the only thing that is appropriate—to dance well, in movements that are ends in themselves, within a space composed of painted backdrops that have nothing to do with any realist motivation. Strictly speaking, the shift from "reality" to "dream" is a shift away from the mixed medium of fiction to pure performance.

Of course, purity rarely exists alone. The ballet would be just one more dance routine if its suspended grace didn't first tap into the heart-stopping emotions elicited by the fiction. Minnelli's art involves cutting between these regimes. For that, the performers' bodies have to be open to metamorphosis. This is, first of all, a matter of speed. Insight into feelings and illusions, questions of belief or conscience have no place in Minnelli's work. Charles Bovary earns his wife's hatred, not for having bungled the clubfoot operation, but for not having wanted to make the attempt in the first place—what matters is one's ability to take matters in hand. In this regard, Manuela is more practical than Charles Bovary, since she doesn't lose herself in dreams. She makes her own theater: the intended victim's tearful voice-over while the beautiful girl prepares herself for the "sacrifice" by adorning her mourning garb with the most beautiful jewels. Then the solemn procession of the sacrificial victim, nobly repulsing the girl who wants to offer herself in her place by declaring: "He asked for *me*." This is the parodic equivalent of "Qu'il mourût" ["He can die!"] or the "Moi, dis-je, et c'est assez" ["Myself, and that's enough"] that summed up the sublime in Pierre Corneille's tragedies for generations of poeticians. Or consider Manuela's exalted declarations to the man she pretends to take for Macoco, or the same Manuela lashing out and breaking her fiancé's property, those "works of art," over the imposter's head—the false Don Pedro as opposed to the "true" Macoco. This grandiose theatricality simply elaborates on the dramaturgy of transformation already evident in Tootie's silent Halloween expedition, where the camera shows us the bare, ghostly face of the little girl advancing toward the house of the terrible Braukoff, and then the mask with the false nose that disguises the girl as a little devil (in *Meet Me in St. Louis*). In Minnelli's work, there is only the present. At no moment does Manuela hesitate or question herself. At no moment does she lose control of the game. In a sense, the "meeting of dream and reality" is nothing other than the pleasure of theater, that is: role changes, double meanings, and sudden reversals of fortune. The play of energy differentials resulting from that meeting generate the different levels of knowledge and ignorance that are the heart of that pleasure: some characters knowing more than others, the spectators knowing more or less than the characters, or a difference between what the spectators expect and what they see. In another sense, the meeting of dream and reality is the gap between fiction and performance. There is no doubt, of course, that fiction is ever anything but a performance. Manuela's story, for instance, ends on a stage. But as Serafin discovers, the character who isn't supposed to be playing a role always enjoys—by virtue of the cover his naïveté lends him—a certain advantage over the person who is only an actor.

In Minnelli's work, this privilege of fiction is often enjoyed by the ingenue who can redistribute the cards of comedy and seriousness to her own advantage. Halloween's special license to suspend the ordinary relationship between parents and children is stronger than the ruses of third-rate play-actors or roués. Compared to what Aunt Alicia offers, namely an initiation into the profession of a courtesan, the cinema offers something still more effective: Gigi's cinema—unabashed trickery. Gigi is more concerned with increasing the benefits she derives from an entrenched system of rewards, whether it be caramel candies, champagne, or donkey rides, than in setting herself up on the arm of an upscale man-about-town. No more for Gigi than for Gaston is the choice between dream and reality. In the negotiation of social arrangements, in play here are different degrees and possibilities of stimulation: drunkenness for Gigi, or a way out of boredom for Gaston. There is a web of conventions, relations, and attitudes, a nexus of situations you have to master, modify, or preserve, for within these systems there are new stimulations to be experienced. *Stimulation:* the word by which Coleridge and Wordsworth defined the power of poetry at the beginning of the nineteenth century. Half a century later, the word is *overstimulation:* a term deployed by obtuse commentators to denounce Emma Bovary's condition—and by extension the new malady of democratic societies as a whole. From this point of view, there is hardly any difference between the adventuress who wants to run away and become the pirate's mistress and the stay-at-home who just wants to remain in St. Louis and marry the boy next door. What counts is the theatrical possibility of a vase dropped on the floor or an extinguished chandelier. The blaze at the children's party is as good as the pirates' fire. But to preserve the possibilities of the game, it is sometimes necessary to change systems, and here too, slow deliberation isn't the way to go. Things happen all at once when Gigi has to exchange her Scottish cape and childish naughtiness for the dress of a worldly courtesan, even if having mastered the right way of behaving produces a readily foreseeable effect—a feeling of exasperation at situations and gestures that turn out to be just like the ones she already knows.

From Comedy to Melodrama

Gigi's happy ending, like *The Pirate*'s, is the utopia of musicals, the utopia of a fiction whose sole imperative is good performance. For that, the fiction has to refer back to an entirely artificial universe. That is the meaning of the great "Be a clown!" number *The Pirate* ends with. The problem begins, indeed melodrama itself begins, when one occupies a social position—in other words, a relationship to the father. The advice to be a clown, as far as I remember, is attributed to Serafin's mother. Manuela, for her part, has neither a father nor a mother, only an aunt. Likewise in *Gigi*, besides the mother who is present only as a sound, off in the wings, there are only aunts and uncles: functional characters who engender the plot by their own sheer performance, by arranging a liaison, for example, or a marriage. The melodrama begins when there are fathers, brothers, and husbands: characters who divert the plot from theatrical performance to social comedy, with its positions in society and representations thereof, its inheritances and rivalries. The Halloween party suspends all that, although we still notice that the neighbor at whose expense Tootie's heroic expedition is undertaken bears the name Braukoff—obviously no descendant of the Mayflower, and probably not a pure Aryan either. But this is entertainment's stage, where everything necessarily comes down, in true Aristotelian fashion, to the contrast between the effect we expect and the effect we actually get, like the terrible bulldog licking at the flour, as placid as his master. Braukoff isn't a clown, but he is presented to us as having neither a profession nor a lineage. Later on, Tootie's performance (the destruction of the snow men) obliges her own father to give up his promotion as well as his authority. This is the price to be paid for remaining in the universe of happy performance via the reconciliatory power of a song (although pain is still part of it, keeping the emotions of that performance from turning mawkish).

Childhood is precisely the state that can include cruelty in its games (the child kicking the soldier in *The Clock;* Tootie's terrorizing and terrorized performance to earn the glory of being "the most horrible").

So performance and fiction can join hands by closing the door on melodrama. Melodrama is mixed fiction, tied to this "real" fiction called society. There you have fathers who are always fathers, or fathers just a bit too much or too little, sometimes both at once (in *Home from the Hill*). You have a brother who is never an equal partner, like the overly charming brother of *Undercurrent,* or the bastard who makes you ashamed of your privileges (Rafe in *Home from the Hill*), or the respectable bourgeois who makes you ashamed of your marginality (Frank Hirsh in *Some Came Running*). There is the spouse who never desires you at the right time and vice versa (*The Cobweb, Some Came Running, Home from the Hill*). Finally, there are the social identities of the honest citizen or the tramp. All these positions have the effect of stopping bodies from metamorphosing or positions from being overturned, hampering the movement into pure performance. The violence of the horse's hooves crushing the bad brother (in *Undercurrent*) overwhelms the reconciliatory effect of the ballet, sidelines the dancer who is coming to the rescue. Bonfires are replaced by the gunshot that puts an end to the exploits of the bad husband (in *Home from the Hill*) or the one that puts an end to the dreams of the tramp who wants to escape her situation (in *Some Came Running*). Ginnie is the fictional sister of Tootie or Manuela, but like Emma Bovary, she is in the unfortunate situation of having been plunged into another universe—the adult universe of a "real" social world. This world also has its parties, but those festivities, unlike the clown's performance or the children's special night, do not cancel out differences. The ballet is just a society ball, a social ceremony. The ball at the Vaubyessards doesn't get Emma Bovary out of her condition so much as it more effectively confronts her with it. In this respect, the Parkman carnival is like the ball given by the Normandy nobleman. The colored bulbs that are there for decoration give off so much heat that moths come and burn themselves against them. Ginnie does the same thing though she doesn't have the same emotions as Emma Bovary, hers being a sort of bitter happiness as she comes to know both what the "beautiful things" in life are and, at the same time, how inaccessible they are to her. The pink feathers of the young bride's hairdo you'd think had been clumsily torn from Emma's "Amazon" hat are not props of a performance, nor is the embroidered cushion the dead woman is lying on, as if she had been dazzled by the light rather than killed by a jealous man's bullet. They are only store-bought items and evidence of bad taste, which is what differentiates her, even as she is dying, from all those people who have a sense, however vague, of social distinctions. Melodrama describes a situation in which performance is hindered, in which the exchange of social positions is impossible.

MADNESS, WORK, AND COUTURE

The danger isn't losing oneself in dreams. It's not the inability to play, represent, or do something. It's the whiteness Stevie talks about to the wife of Dr. McIver at the beginning of *The Cobweb,* the whiteness of the clinic where the dying painter—Derain—asks for more green and red, like Goethe asking for more light. It's the zero degree of stimulation, or stimulation turned against itself—the novel of unhappy families always returns to the madhouse. This is what the performance has to win out against, and win out again and again. *The Cobweb* is exemplary in bridging the difference between the levity of the musicals and the pathos of the melodramas. The entire drama hinges on a comic situation involving interior decorating, which is also a certain idea of mise-en-scène. Indeed, the professions often ascribed to Minnelli are "decorator," even "couturier," while the "man who is prisoner of his decor" is often presented as the summing up of any Minnelli drama. But there is another sort of complexity involving mise-en-scène—and what it represents. What we're really talking about is work and the absence of work. The clinic has three kinds of spaces: the consulting room where the patient lies on the couch and talks; the rooms where they take sleeping pills; and the workshop, where work's beneficial effect can be felt. The entire question is about knowing what work is good for one's health. The reply proposed by the patients themselves is: Good work is sick people carrying on as if they were in good health, as if it were up to them to organize their lives and decorate the house. Hence the dispute about replacing the library drapes, one that we can reasonably assume to be unprecedented as far as subjects in a melodrama are concerned. The patients want to make the drapes themselves from young Stevie's drawings—they want the drapes to represent the life of the asylum. But the performance can even be less than that. For Sue, the young agoraphobic, it's simply the decision to go to the movies. An entire modernist tradition relentlessly indicts the "passivity" of the spectacle and the spectator; Minnelli ripostes in a stupefying, almost dreamlike sequence where Stevie mimes the agility of Minnelli's camera, weaving between the characters in a crowd, threading a path to Sue through the inattentive multitude of spectators who are leaving the auditorium and brushing against her from all sides, almost prompting catastrophe. An astonishing camera movement between the room Sue returns to and the one where the strong-minded Mr. Capp vainly ingests the tranquilizers gives us the meaning of the sequence (as Minnelli prefers, wordlessly). "Passivity" works both ways. Being a spectator can also be a performance, and this performance in the film is exemplarily accomplished by a child, little Mark, silently and imperturbably playing or eating alone in his corner, watching the actors in this conjugal drama pass him by, hearing their outbursts in the upper floor of the house![1]

Flaubert had already said that the difference isn't between dreams and reality, but between two vectors of stimulation: the one that externalizes itself in work and the one that "flows inward" in the form of illness. This opposition does not define the relation between the doctors or normal people and the patients. Take McIver, the modern psychiatrist who gives power to the inmates' council. His point of view is well founded. The state of those who have "fallen into the well" represents, like a magnifying mirror, the same illness we see reflected in the normal mirror, the one we see Karen taking off her make-up in front of, so that we can witness the domestic scene between the doctor and his wife. The illness of normal people is unleashed around the issue of the drapes as violently as the illness of the inmates. Consider the extraordinary sequence where Karen takes revenge for the infidelity of the husband, not as we first expect by surprising him at his mistress's house, but by running at night to the now-deserted clinic to put up her drapes. These drapes represent both her good taste and her appeal for love; they replace the housekeeper's drapes and also the ones the inmates are making. There are no "good" drapes, and Minnelli, if he shows us Stevie's drawings at all, makes sure not to show the finished ones. He probably prefers Karen's. But above all there is no standard of health to be opposed to the illness brought on by the illusion inherent in the infinite demand for love, or by the heavy weight of social roles assigned to both parents and children. One can only "help" matters by giving power to the "patients," or by remaining, like the child, silent behind the door—or by doing an artist's work, by making "couturier" films. Subdued tones, as in a Dutch painting, or lots of mirrors as in Manet sublimate the bad effects of a demand for inexhaustible love or a fatherly bond that cannot be broken. "Can I help?" asks the watching child. "You have," replies the doctor/dramatist father.

This lesson is different from the one taught by a Proust or a Flaubert, who opposed the realization of the literary artwork to the energy expended on

In *The Cobweb* (1955), Karen McIver (Gloria Grahame) hangs her own vision of the perfect curtains for her husband's clinic, against the wishes of her husband and his patients (Courtesy Photofest/Henry Fera Collection).

creating an aesthete's life for oneself, or making one's interior decor into art. One had to choose art over and against maternal attachment or the imaginary construction of a love affair. But one also had to put that art nowhere but in the words of a book, as distinguished from those who, like Emma or Charlus, put art into the way one chooses a fabric or decorates a house. Minnelli's lesson is more ambiguous. It's not just that Hollywood relativizes both the dream of the autonomous artist and the fantasy of all-powerful dreams. For Minnelli, there is no difference between the young girl's dream, choosing fabrics, and the entertainment his oeuvre affords; there are only forms of stimulation and different possibilities of performance. The filmmaker cannot claim that he has nothing of a couturier about him, or that his art is not the same as Emma Bovary's delusion in wanting to change her life, and then put art into his drapes. The character imposes her style on the work and her law on the artist, although of course we are free to believe that this is another illusion. The best illustration of Minnelli's power as a filmmaker is not the tyrannical Jonathan Shields of *The Bad and the Beautiful*, but the honest Dr. McIver whose authority is rescinded, the better to allow chaos to sort itself out. Certainly the Demiurge whose supreme power is to disappear into the idiocy of a sentence or a particular shot is consistent with the Flaubertian norm. But Minnelli adds an extra element to Flaubert, or perhaps it's rather the case that Flaubert had to keep it to himself, in the absence of being able to recline on divans strewn with hummingbird feathers or carpets of swanskin to walk on:[2] The achievement is only possible as long as one recognizes oneself, in the end, as an entertainer and a decorator. There's definitely nothing simple about art for art's sake.

NOTES

1. The effect of this passive performance is all the more palpable because the same child actor, Tommy Rettig, was infinitely more active in *River of No Return*, where he was supposed to kill a man in order to be reconciled to his father.

2. Flaubert, in a letter to Louise Colet, dated January 29, 1854.

Panic

RAYMOND BELLOUR
TRANSLATED BY BILL KROHN

Why *Brigadoon*, among so many Minnelli films, as a point of attraction? Perhaps because it contains, in its principle and its mythical scenario, as well as in the power of the images that serve it, a *panic* of which the whole oeuvre is more or less made, undermining it even as it constructs it.

An actress, a character, and a situation can serve as the emblem of this panic: Tootie (Margaret O'Brien) in *Meet Me in St. Louis*, in the famous Halloween episode, the idea of which convinced Minnelli to accept the film. Tootie is overwrought and self-panicked from the beginning of this nocturnal scene, on which the play-acted violence of the children, veering toward the fantastic, confers a dimension between nightmare and fantasy. The strongest moment is the one where she goes to throw flour on the "horrible" Mr. Braukoff. On one side and the other of some fixed shots within this moment, two camera movements, going and coming, before and after the fateful act, are especially striking: long pull-backs, one slow, one fast, that follow the child's charge while always maintaining the same distance from the hurrying body, supporting the anticipation of the act and its effect, giving to the charac-

ter's panic its speed, its rhythm, and its volume. Afterward, that panic becomes almost part of her, when the father's decision at the end of "autumn"
(the film is divided into four seasons) to leave St. Louis for New York initiates
the film's crisis. "The scene in which she is lugged in with her cut lip, screaming half-lies and gibberish, is about the most impressive and complex job of
crying I have ever seen put on,"[1] noted James Agee. The grandiloquence with
which Agee describes Margaret O'Brien ("many of her possibilities and glints
of her achievement hypnotize me as thoroughly as anything since Garbo")
contrasts with Minnelli's recollection of the problems he had with the young
prodigy ("She was just like Sarah Bernhardt; every gesture was enormous, as
in the *Comédie française*").[2] But it is thanks to that very difficulty, worked on
and overcome, that through this magnificent film—magnificent in all respects, but all in all rather well behaved, drawing its force from its loving play
with the conventions of the past and the nostalgia for it, resulting in its perfect
success in middle America—a pure gunpowder trail of panic was able to pass.

It is the same in *Madame Bovary*, where the character's romantic agitation,
fanned into flames by the performance of Jennifer Jones, crystallizes in the
ball sequence through the sudden, almost unreal accelerations of the music,
and of the waltz that carries Emma into "an atmosphere of dazzling excitement,"[3] and of course the accelerations of the camera, until Emma's vague
malaise and the spectacular breaking of the windows that seals the panic of
her destiny.

In a very different way, one can follow the thousand and one variations of a
panic that is apparently much more realistic, concentrated throughout the
length of a film in the body of an actress: the extraordinary performance of
Deborah Kerr in *Tea and Sympathy* and the way Minnelli films it. Even though
the drama that makes the adolescent played by John Kerr want to die is, in a
sense, concentrated on him, it is Deborah Kerr, in terms of sensitivity and in
terms of mise-en-scène, who concentrates the liveliest panic. There is a very
strong moment where, twice, first finding herself in the living room, then in
the kitchen, Laura Reynolds overhears a frightening conversation between her
husband and Tom's father, both in the garden. Her body, caught in a simple
waist-level shot, or a closer shot, receives and transmits her feelings like a
photographic emulsion. Several times she is framed more or less in close-up
receiving the shock of the conflict, as if her body were ready to break out of the
limits of the frame in which she nonetheless remains, fixedly, trembling with
all her being, inducing what seems a panic of the frame.

This example seems strong because it's simple, unlike others, which are at once more slight and more complex. It is again Deborah Kerr who bears the felt weight of the event when, almost at the end of the film, after reading three letters addressed by Tom respectively to his father, his mother, and her, and fearing the worst, panicked, she jumps in her car and goes looking for the young man. The beauty of the moment that follows, when she enters the Minnellian studio forest, enchanted with fog, recalling that of *Brigadoon* and anticipating that of *Home from the Hill*—the beauty is in the sudden descent of panic, and its transformation into a second madness, a calm from beyond, a romantic madness that justifies even the forbidden kiss: the instant when Laura's hand enters alone from the left of the frame and lifts up Tom who is lying on the ground.

Jean Douchet is the one who posed first and most fully the general conditions of what we can call more specifically panic in Minnelli's cinema when he wrote, for example, on the subject of *The Four Horsemen of the Apocalypse:* "In Minnelli's vision, living means conquering the world to shape it in the image of one's dream by means of a decor. This necessarily means taking from others, through theft or destruction, the very nature of their own dream; it also means waging constant war against the conquering reality of others' dreams, which encircle and threaten our own. . . . All life is a dream that wages war with other dreams and ultimately destroys itself."[4]

That is the perspective Gilles Deleuze adopted in his own way when he wrote that "the plurality of worlds is Minnelli's first discovery, his very great position in cinema." "A strange and fascinating concept of the dream," he adds, "where the dream is all the more implied because it always refers to the dream of another."[5] He returned forcefully to this in his lecture "What Is the Act of Creation?" qualifying creation as follows: "The dream is a terrible will to power. Each of us is more or less the victim of other people's dreams. Even the loveliest young woman is a terrible devouring force, not by her soul, but by her dreams. Beware of the other person's dream, because if you're caught in the other person's dream, you're screwed."[6]

What I call panic is in a sense the difference in the charges carried by two dreams suddenly rendered more visible and more striking, or in tune with their mutual exacerbation, like the illusion of a transitory chord. Panic can be linked to the pressure that tends to build up in Hollywood films, but in Minnelli's films particularly, after the premise and exposition, which can take a long time, fixing itself in a more or less foreseeable way in the drama, so that·

dreams really do collide, determining afterward the development and the acme of suspense. But that would be too simple—we've seen this with the Halloween scene in *Meet Me in St. Louis*, which erupts suddenly in all its excess, prefiguring, in fact, the tension of the later crisis. While it can become a function of the film's progressive hold on us—as it does in *The Clock*, for example, where Time panics at being so limited as soon as the unforeseen decision to marry takes hold of the two surprised lovers—panic is far from depending on the story and its twists being programmed in this way. Ultimately, it is independent of the story, having to do with the whole film refracted in this or that moment, even in an instant when the story barely exists but as a mysterious intuition of the mise-en-scène already expressing a premonitory perturbation. The first shot of *Some Came Running* is affected by a strange acceleration of which one might not be aware at all, since the film is barely beginning: In the bus through the windows of which we see the small town of Parkman, Indiana, going by, a sudden forward movement of the camera is launched, doubling the speed of the real movement with its own energy, creating a subtle panic of the eye that could prefigure the major conflicts to come.

This is why I tend to recognize this panic, and recognize it in a manner that is no doubt irremediably subjective—because from the spectator's point of view one person's panic will never equal another's, for the simple reason that we do not all have the same body—that's why I can feel this panic in the postures of characters or script effects as well as in figures and instants of mise-en-scène, lightning flashes of shots and images.

Let's take a few more examples:

The Bad and the Beautiful, a film about the singular excessiveness of creation characteristic of cinema, filmed in black and white, transmits the madness of its dream and of the conflicts among the characters by perturbations of light. Thus one can be sensitive, among other things, to five graduated modalities of intensification of black and white that trace a line of panic through the film, from its prologue to the end of the second episode:

- In the first shot, a lively and variable contrast of light is concentrated on a telephone.
- During a screening of rushes, the insistent vibration of the luminous images that are unspooling plays over the seated bodies of the producer and director.
- The outcome of the first showdown between the producer and his future actress (Jonathan Shields/Kirk Douglas and Georgia Lorrison/Lana

Turner) is marked, in a set with vividly contrasted lighting effects, by a brutal inversion of the intensities of black and white that is not very believable in realistic terms.

- The transition between the shooting of the film and the night of the premiere is achieved by a double blinding, white on white: a vertiginous tracking shot climbs from the actress's body onto the stage and fixes on the gleaming glass of a floodlight, then dissolves to the one that violently illuminates the theater where the first screening is being held.

- Finally comes the moment of extreme panic, first between Jonathan Shields and Georgia Lorrison, then the actress alone, when she runs to her lover on the night of the premiere and discovers the presence of another woman. It's the hardest of all to suggest without images, real or reproduced. But an insistent panic of light is created on the body of Lana Turner at the wheel of her car—she is draped, as she has been from the beginning of the scene, in her twinkling fur—provoked by the succession of gusts of light from cars coming in the other direction. This continuous, modulated, and insistent effect of white light is excessive, and is filmed in relation to a body at once paralyzed and unleashed so that it seems improbable that the car can finally stop, as it does, without crashing or turning over.

But this is the surest rule of panic: passing beyond all realism, obeying no law but that of its own expansion.

We can follow similar lines, in *Undercurrent* for example, that recount, literally this time, the progressive panic of a woman threatened by the mysterious violence of her husband, who finds herself thrust into an excess of black and white. (The admirable cinematography is by Karl Freund.) Thus the moment when Katharine Hepburn, filmed in a waist-high shot on a seat in a train (on the left of the shot, under a window through which we see passing fragments of the real on the right), compulsively waves her arm as she hears the mingled voices of her husband on the phone (she has just spoken to him) and that of a woman who (in the previous scene) has accused him of being a murderer—the camera almost immediately advancing with a fatal softness to her ravaged face. And when we get to the close-up, with the whistle of the train and the dissolve it seems to provoke, the face is absorbed in the moving wheels of the machine, always reminiscent, for so long and in so many films, of the functioning of the cinema machine itself.

Finally we can recall from *Some Came Running* an instant and a moment, its famous finale. The instant is simple: When the passionate reserve of Gwen

French (Martha Hyer) is ready to cede to the amorous transports of Dave Hirsh (Frank Sinatra), it suffices to make the two bodies pull back from the light into the shadow, while the camera insistently follows them, for panic to appear, in a radiant chiaroscuro, on a woman's face.

The moment, very complex, develops in fifty-six shots and in about six minutes: Bama (Dean Martin), warned that the ex-lover of Ginny (Shirley MacLaine) has come from Chicago to kill Dave, races to tell Dave, who is just married and strolling through the dense crowd assembled to celebrate Parkman's yearly carnival. The first image sounds the first note of the various modalities that will combine to carry a panic of the mise-en-scène to its maximum intensity, here supported by the accumulated pressure of the story: violence and contrast of colors (the background of the shot is at first uniformly red; the bottom of the word "Rooms" flashes at the top of the frame in vivid yellow; the silhouette of the killer emptying a bottle detaches itself from the shadow); a choreographed dramatization of bodies, the effect of which the killer concentrates by the way he repeatedly rushes into the frame and freezes; and finally camera movements, long back-and-forth trajectories (left-right, right-left) that seem both to follow and wait for the carefree or feverish movements of bodies—as soon as the killer, in that long first shot, emerges from the red background and dives into the heart of the crowd where we almost think we've lost him among so many events of mass and color, only to reappear next to a shooting gallery and stand still facing us in a closer shot. Red is the color that, ending with Jenny's blood on the back of her dress and Dave's hand, confers a nightmare logic on the scene (but so well allied to other colors, whether by clear and cloudy surfaces, scattered or concentrated touches, fixed or mobile, as in the movement of the big carnival wheel, in a variety that only a live analysis could follow). This red is extensively treated, moving between reality and pure stylization. It returns when the killer, stopped in front of a red halo illuminating behind him part of the crowd, lifts his head and sees a window where the red word "Liquor" is flashing intermittently (to the side, the letters that we will be able to read better a bit later are aligned on the incandescent billboard of a movie theater: "Elizabeth Taylor/*Courage of Lassie*/Cartoon"). What's strange is that we at first think the halo is caused by the flashing of the neon sign, which will be intensified when the killer, appearing at the window, looks for Dave and Ginny in the festive crowd. But this isn't the case. Splashed about in space at the bottom of the stairs that lead to the red building, the halo is a pure intensification. We can count many others in this death scene orchestrated like a ballet, where the colors of the set, justified by the occasion, and numerous elements that are feverishly transported here and there, create the unmistakable impression of a movie studio.

It has perhaps been noticed that none of these examples comes from a real musical comedy. That is because in those films panic is more or less ordered, insofar as a dance can moderate its course, however mad and beautiful it might be in itself (like the famous moment—unequalled—when Cyd Charisse and Fred Astaire go from walking to dancing in the park in *The Band Wagon*). This is not the case in the straight comedies, where panic is propagated according to the modes of the genre. Because it's an example I gave many years ago (a little after the first great Minnelli retrospective at the Cinematheque in the 1960s) as a model of an art of distances inherent in the obsession of mise-en-scène, I think of the swirls and vacillations of Kay Kendall's red dress in *The Reluctant Debutante*.

But for me there is one exception among the musical comedies. It's *Brigadoon*, where the radical will to enchantment produces a special form of panic. It is largely due to the abstract power of the tale and the myth of cinema as the power of imagination that are inscribed in it as a whole.

The cards are dealt by the schoolmaster, the village sage, Mr. Lundie, to the two strangers, Tommy (Gene Kelly) and Jeff (Van Johnson), who have come by chance to this Scottish village that does not appear on any map. Mr. Lundie's long explanation begins with these words: "What I'm going to tell you, you won't believe . . . because what happened in Brigadoon is a miracle." (Could this be a Hollywood version of the "mystery" Godard invokes to describe cinema in his *Histoire(s)*?) Two hundred years earlier, the minister of Brigadoon wanted to defend his village against witches and all the evil that might come after his death. He therefore asked God to make Brigadoon disappear, to reappear for only one day every century, so that "the people wouldn't be in any century long enough to be touched by it."

Has it been noticed that the date of the day the film takes place in, when the younger daughter of the Campbell family is to marry, is 1754, the very day the film was finished two days or two centuries later, whichever you prefer, in 1954? A way to turn the past back on the present, and cinema on itself, within the dimension of inward and closed-off time to which it destines its spectator.

There are two rules in Brigadoon. The first, stated very early, even before believing Tommy and skeptical Jeff enter Brigadoon, is that no inhabitant of the village is allowed to cross the border, which would make the town disappear. The second, says Mr. Lundie, is that "a stranger can stay, if he loves someone."

We can see the richness of the two precepts when it comes to a possible panic of the story or the mise-en-scène. On the one hand, it's enough that an inhabitant wishes to flee the village for the city, and with it the magic of cinema, to be suspended forever. On the other hand, it's enough that a visitor falls in love for this world to close in on him, just as it draws the spectator in with its artifice. The film furnishes examples of both rules thanks to two sisters, one who is getting married and one who is waiting for love. The marriage of the first inflicts on the happy chosen one, Charlie, an unhappy rival, Harry, for whom Brigadoon is "a prison." The union desired with the second becomes the love-test to which Tommy will be subjected after experiencing love at first sight with the lovely Fiona (Cyd Charisse).

After the dance in the heather, which expresses all the enchantment of a studio, and during which Tommy and Fiona discover their love—something the dance often permits through the loveliest movements of bodies and camera imaginable—the problem of the territorial limit that can't be crossed is already posed by Fiona, discretely, like a tragic detail that colors the charm of the moment. But it's during the marriage of Jean Campbell and Charlie, and Harry's attempted flight, that a very special suspense, a veritable panic, shapes the collective action, half-chase, half-dance, that has to stop Harry from crossing the fatal bridge leading to the entrance of the village, until his accidental death from a rifle shot (the movement of bodies is so aerial that Jeff, walking as if in a dream—while Tommy participates excessively in the action—took Harry for a bird). In a sense, at that moment, the dramatic stakes, if we accept the rules of the game, have never been so dense with respect to all of cinema, with respect to its very survival; and rarely has the work of the camera, in conjunction with lighting and montage, been so exalted in a Minnelli film, in its fluidity, its trajectories, its velocities, its flashes of night and of sudden light.

But a second moment multiplies this panic: a sequence in New York City, to which Tommy has ended up returning, frightened by the absoluteness of the romantic gamble that draws him to Brigadoon. It begins with a vertical shot of the city in all its crazy splendor, which enters, via a dissolve, into the brouhaha of a club where the agitation and noise are almost as unbearable for the spectator as they are for Tommy and even for the skeptical Jeff. The torrent of frenzied words that Tommy's extroverted fiancée subjects him to promises, along with the purchase of a house for their upcoming marriage, a worldly, chic version of the Made in America horror that Minnelli had taken to the edge of the fantastic earlier the same year with *The Long, Long Trailer* and its titular yellow trailer.

Such is the double panic that Tommy's return to Brigadoon brings to an end, just as the film concludes on the enigma of Time without temporality. Suspended time that is intrinsic to cinema, because it has been suspended as long as the film lasts, closing on itself as soon as the miracle is accomplished. To the pure moral of the spectacle accomplished in *The Pirate* ("Be a clown, be a clown") or carried to a point of perfection that is almost too sure of itself in *The Band Wagon* ("The world is a stage, the stage is a world of entertainment"), *Brigadoon* opposes, thanks to the excellence of its myth and the transcended silliness of its Scottish kitsch, a very special romance, or an absolute romanticism. Between one bridge that is not to be crossed and another, it could be the romance version of *Nosferatu* and its phantoms.

NOTES

1. James Agee, *Agee on Film* (New York: Modern Library, 2000), 113.

2. Minnelli in an interview he gave Charles Higham and Joel Greenberg for their book *The Celluloid Muse* (Chicago: Regnery, 1969), 176.

3. Higham and Greenberg, *Celluloid Muse*, 178. Minnelli says he asked Miklos Rozsa to write "a very 'neurotic' waltz."

4. Jean Douchet, "The Red and the Green," *Cahiers du cinéma* 129 (March 1962): 48–49. Reprinted in this volume.

5. Gilles Deleuze, *L'image-temps*, Minuit (Paris, 1985), 85 and 87. Translation by Hugh Tomlinson and Robert Galeta, from *Cinema 2: The Time-Image* (Minneapolis: University of Minnesota Press, 1991).

6. Gilles Deleuze, "What Is the Act of Creation?" *Trafic* 27 (Autumn 1998): 138.

Minnelli's Messages

EMMANUEL BURDEAU
TRANSLATED BY BILL KROHN

A scene from the last minutes of *The Courtship of Eddie's Father* (1963). In the kitchen, the title character (Ron Howard, great actor at seven, lousy director at thirty-five) thinks of a stratagem for finally getting Dad (Glenn Ford, widowed, gauche, perfect) married to the next-door neighbor, Elizabeth (Shirley Jones, charming, domestic). "I've got an idea. Let's practice. Practice asking her for a date. I'll be Elizabeth; you be you." Kneeling in profile on the red banquette in the breakfast nook, Eddie begins: "I'm home, see, and I'm looking plainly out the window." "Looking how?" asks Dad, who is loading the washing machine, puzzled by the adverb "plainly." Eddie explains: "You know, not happy, not sad. Just a plain face." Playing along, Dad answers: "Well, it sounds like you're kind of anxious." Eddie ripostes: "No I'm not, my darling man." Dad winces at "darling." "Not so fast, Eddie." But Eddie redoubles his efforts, calling him "sugar man, future husband, handsome man, excellent strong man." Then, seeing that he's hit a nerve, he presses his advantage: "Call her right now, Dad. . . . She's home. . . . I made sure. . . . It's Regent 4-8599. Let's go in the living room." While Dad, still hesitant, dials the number, Eddie steps out of the apartment leaving the door open behind him, and rings at the door of the apartment across the hall. "Your phone is ringing!" Elizabeth looks bewildered—she's just going out, and the phone isn't ringing. Then it does ring: "You'd better pick it up. It could be very important. Very important!" She picks up and Eddie retreats into the hall. Shot of Dad, awkwardly opening the conversation. Shot of Elizabeth, radiant. Shot of Eddie listening, looking left (his future mom), looking right (his father). Alternating shots of each of them smiling—the camera moves closer to the boy, who continues rejoicing, until the words "The End" appear, while behind them he is still turning right, then left.

A superb ending, albeit without any visible grandeur or enchantment—in many ways the sign of an expressive retreat: a TV movie, a sitcom, or a family picture. So why start here, in the home, between kitchen and telephone? To take hold of the obscure side of the Minnelli dream, the side that hides from spectacle, from the superlative enchantment, the hallucination of MGM. To grasp it with the ear rather than the eye, listening rather than watching. Is this the obligatory tactic, the necessary slant for praising, at last, a minimal Minnelli—even a poor one—who is capable of imposing cinema below or beyond the resources of the image? Yes. We have to take advantage of the reputation the filmmaker currently enjoys thanks to the triumphal retrospective at Beaubourg to separate his oeuvre from the sole seductions of the imagination. But not really. The purpose is less to put the ear in place of the eye than to indicate how hearing actually creates the image, one woven from things other than just the visible.

Staging a scene among three characters who are in a situation that normally involves only two, Eddie's ruse proposes a kind of pedagogic demonstration. When he pretends to look "plainly" out of the window, the boy is basically repeating the pose of any Minnelli heroine at the moment when everything begins, the inception of the dream, but by subtraction: reverie, distraction, absence. That initial pallor has many gradations—each film supplies its own nuance. For example, Petunia in *Cabin in the Sky* clasping her hands at the foot of her bed, praying that the Lord will revive Li'l Joe and cure him of his passion for dice. Or Yolanda falling on her knees before a statue, imploring the help of a guardian angel. Manuela, on her balcony, becoming ethereal as she vaunts the exploits—possibly invented—of the pirate Macoco. Emma Bovary pressing her forehead to her bedroom window and gazing into the far distance from which, perhaps, a Prince Charming may appear. Kay (*Father of the Bride*) suddenly "all lit up inside," no longer hearing what her father says because she is already frolicking on some hill or cloud with her boyfriend and future husband Buckley. And Georgia, Fiona, Laura, Marilla, Sheila, Melinda, Nina, all the Minnelli heroines with an *a*.

The real beginning is not entering into the other person's dream, the man getting his feet caught in the woman's cobweb, in keeping with the schema that Jean Douchet and Gilles Deleuze have traced so well. We have to go further back, to the place where the woman formulates, to herself or out loud, the wish that someone will come and carry her off. But his arrival obeys a subtle inversion, as the ending of *Eddie* demonstrates with great lucidity: It's by taking on himself the initiative of calling that the man responds to the summons the woman was the first to utter. At the beginning of the dream, then, there is the ambivalence of a prayer that effaces itself as it advances to make room for the one who will fulfill it. To this capital combination of activity and passivity corresponds, in passing, a certain division of tasks between the man and the woman—indeed, a certain conception of sexual difference. The enigma of feminine listening comes first, expressed in the paradox, a priori inverted, of escape—of deafness to the urgencies of the present that conceals a superior quality of watchfulness and attention to what isn't there, but may arise at any moment.

How does this differ from the Douchet-Deleuze model? In one respect: What matters most in the dream is not brilliance of performance but plurivocity of address. Entering into the other's dream, even if it involves counting up to two, ends with that dream closing like a trap, whereas the inscription of two crisscrossing summons at the beginning (feminine, masculine) makes it a dialogue, a hand-off, an exchange. An opening. In other words, the essence of the dream is not to flee the world. If we consider it in terms of that binary opposition, cinema is being asked to do the impossible: to be simultaneously the measure of reality and the autonomous fulfillment of a dream. But its essence is also not to become part of the world when it has been realized. In script terms, that resolution rarely evades the sadness of convention: marriage and children (*Yolanda*), eternal love (*Brigadoon*), and such. The essence of a dream is to become a world, to obey only its own law, to feed only at its own source. Even when deployed as spectacle, it repeats the play of address(es) that initiated it.

Just one example: the ballet "Will You Marry Me?" in *Yolanda and the Thief*. One night Johnny dreams that he gets up and goes looking for Yolanda. The plot of this purple passage, with its clawed washerwomen in imitation of Salvador Dalí, its tarts and jockeys, is well known: The thief disguised as an angel is confronted with an inner conflict—having come to steal Yolanda's fortune, he is starting to fall in love with her, and suffers from not having the guts to forget her money. But the rich heiress, for her part, is not acting according to the dichotomy of love and money. After all, it was an economical angel, capable of managing her fortune, that she asked for in the first place. Then, during the ballet, Yolanda hangs a necklace from her treasure chest around Johnny's neck. She dances, taking the imposter with her but paying no attention to him. She certainly doesn't seem to want a love exempt of all interest—that is not her problem. Just as she immediately saw the lover through the straw angel, she continues to see farther, as far as a love that integrates cupidity while surpassing it.

The priority, then permanence, of a feminine summons that welcomes everything but never stops aiming beyond a masculine response that is fundamentally maladjusted is the heart of the Minnelli dream, the way it always begins. It must have two poles, female reverie and masculine hallucination, a face closed off/offered in its absence and an enchantment of a thousand colors, but the hallucination is only a step, while the reverie lasts forever. Compare Yolanda at the foot of the statue and Yolanda in "Will You Marry Me?" The same question arises about each: What exactly does she want? The Minnelli dream doesn't transform the face—it maintains it in its perpetual mystery. What we should note before moving on is how this face that barely changes is an image, as much and perhaps more than the finale of *An American in Paris,* the terminal delirium of *The Band Wagon,* or the dance in the heather in *Brigadoon.* A hypothesis: This face is an image because it encompasses other images. Because the listening that defines it reinvents the dichotomy of outside and inside, and accelerates the endless roundelay from actual to virtual and back again, from the actual visibility that a beautiful woman's face offers, to her gaze and the virtuality of the promise that it never stops making.

Such a face leads only to itself—it is the beginning and end of the dream, its impulse and its result. In this respect the ending of *Eddie* attains a kind of perfection. Starting from Eddie, it returns to him. But what are the shots of the corridor woven from? Materially, the boy's space and what he hears are strictly bounded by the location of the two apartments on either side of the corridor. Moreover, nothing is heard of what the future spouses are saying— the framing is determined by the less material circuit of the phone line. Finally, Eddie seems to rejoice in the conformity of the moment to what he had imagined earlier, as if he were reenacting the little scene in the kitchen just for himself. In any event, we can't say what music is playing in his ears. It is this uncertainty that creates the image, by linking the visible to aural overdeterminations whose multiplicity leaves it free to breathe.

Embarked on this path, we may have a chance to modify the orientation of Minnelli studies a bit. In at least four directions:

Direction #1—The voice, inside and outside the shot. Has it ever been noted that almost all Minnelli films begin with a vocal situation: announcement, apostrophe, or aside? The priority of address is a constant with Minnelli. The gospel singing in *Cabin in the Sky*. The title song of *Meet Me in St. Louis*, circulating from kitchen to stairs, from the Smith sisters' bathroom to their piano. Stanley Banks, exhausted, tying his shoe, raising his head and telling the camera about Kay's marriage, or the birth of his grandson, in *Father of the Bride*, then *Father's Little Dividend*. The characters introducing themselves in *An American in Paris*, and later in *Designing Woman*. Reading the poem in "Mademoiselle." The auctioning of the ex-star Tony Hunter's belongings, top hat, and tails in *The Band Wagon*. The prayer in the Baghdad minaret in *Kismet*. Maurice Chevalier in his boater and cream suit introducing himself as the master of ceremonies in *Gigi*.

Direction #2—Telephone calls. They are frequent, and play a double role. On the one hand, acknowledging that the story is, so to speak, "telephoned": ventriloquized, marionetted, contrived—governed by more or less foreseeable devices. (A dream is the same thing: an obviously contrived narrative.) And returning, on the other hand, to the enigma of the attentive ear, with the response muted by the receiver, so that listening is exposed in its pure state, without visible support other than itself, while mobilizing a mysterious short circuit between "on" and "off," "here" and "there." That short circuit gives Minnelli some of his most beautiful faces. Examples? The long-distance phone call in *Meet Me in St. Louis*, supposedly bringing the joy of a marriage proposal from New York to the provincial comfort of a kitchen in St. Louis, one whose arrival, long awaited, reconfigures everything, from Rose Smith's expression to the dining room where everyone holds his breath: tablecloth removed, window opened, mouth shut, and so forth. Alice, in *The Clock*, answering her date's phone call, vaguely saying yes, yes, but already planning to cancel so she can meet Joe under the clock at the Astor at seven. The phone calls that open and close *The Bad and the Beautiful*, triggering flashbacks whose only purpose is to obtain a positive answer to the question: Will you talk to Jonathan Shields? Michael lying to his wife Marilla every night in

The importance of the telephone in Minnelli. Here, Fred Amiel (Barry Sullivan), Georgia Lorrison (Lana Turner), and James Lee Bartlow (Dick Powell) share a telephone in the final shot of *The Bad and the Beautiful* (1952).

Designing Woman, assuring her that he's in Boston, Washington, Philadelphia, Detroit, when he hasn't left his New York hotel room, making his bodyguard, the punch-drunk boxer Maxie, choke each time he hears that today it's hot, cold, or mild in Boston, Washington, Philadelphia, or Detroit. The wonderful telephonic misunderstandings in *The Reluctant Debutante.* And of course the whole plot of *Bells Are Ringing,* the star of which is an operator who works for Susanswerphone. Besides making flowers grow faster, Melinda in *On a Clear Day You Can See Forever* has the gift of hearing the phone before it rings.

Direction #3—One modality of listening in Minnelli is the simple habit of smoking. Lighting a cigarette, putting it to one's lips, means giving a visible form to penetration, to disappearance into oneself, that is both simple and ever changing. Because the hand is also involved, and the ear as well if the smoker is Fred Astaire, smoking is like picking up an inner telephone. It is showing oneself, via an artifice available to everyone, to be a strategist, a thinker suddenly transported by the seductive haze of an idea. As early as *Cabin in the Sky,* Lucifer Junior's Idea Department is bathed in smoke from the cigars of the devil's employees. In *The Clock,* Arthur Freed himself offers a lighter to Joe, which he will offer to Alice (the same gift symbolizes Milo's love for Jerry in *An American in Paris*). In *Yolanda,* Johnny smokes six cigarettes at once in his dream, while the cigar belonging to the authentic angel Candle [*sic*] lights up all by itself. Serafin almost chokes on the smoke from his cigarette the first time he sees Manuela in *The Pirate*. Even better is the lesson Shields gives Georgia Lorrison on the art of smoking in *The Bad and the Beautiful*. Each gesture must conform to the injunction: "Make it mean something." In *The Four Horsemen of the Apocalypse*, the final catastrophe pops out of a cigar lighter. And in *On a Clear Day You Can See Forever*, Melinda consults the good Dr. Chabot to be cured of her habit of chain smoking.

Direction #4—There is no Minnelli film without a shot, often several, where a man, often a woman, crosses the frame, stops in the middle, stands still for a moment, changes her mind or thinks of something, turns around and leaves. No one has filmed it better: the dance of hesitation (and of course the dance as hesitation, then as certainty gradually replacing it: "Dancing in the Dark"); the supple translation of a rumination into physical form; the cursive writing in space of an inner questioning; the delicate puppeteering that makes you the marionette of your care of the day—or a marionette disarticulated by the difficulty of attuning your steps to that care. It's not easy to give examples here, because there are so many, and they happen so fast. But when you re-see *Meet Me in St. Louis,* observe the little silent dance Esther does before descending to join the party in honor of her brother Lon's departure for college. In front of the mirror, on the landing, on the stairs, she deploys the whole gamut of "I'm going," "I'm not going," "It's nothing," "It's everything."

Which Minnelli are we paying tribute to here? Certainly not the Demiurge, the tortured hero of a solitary creation doomed to disillusion. All the examples we've glanced at show the opposite, for the one who listens, telephones, smokes, hesitates is never an artist of anything but herself. Rather than sovereign master of her acts and gestures, she is a creature surrendering to a summons or a question that resonates within. Impotent but available. Thoughtless but remote-controlled.

A tribute then, to a thousand Minnellis, in no particular order: the man, the filmmaker, the characters his camera accompanied. A tribute to the compulsive smoker, to the very shy man that he was, according to all reports. A tribute to the man who, rather than giving his actors clear instructions, silently twisted his mouth, looked around him in a panic and hopped like a crab or a kid from one side of the soundstage to another. And then? A tribute to the thinker, the pensive man. And perhaps more to the late Minnelli than the early one, if it's true that listening takes a more and more central place in his work, until his last two films, *On a Clear Day You Can See Forever* and *A Matter of Time*, are literally scenarios of hypnosis and ESP. A tribute to the reader and inheritor of Proust—Proust who adored the Goddesses of the Telephone and whom the phrase "She's not thinking of me," the title of the most beautiful number in *Gigi*, suits so perfectly. To the filmmaker who, deepening that Proustian affinity, ends up substituting for the powers of dream those of memory: First fruits, the bar sequence in *Brigadoon*, then "I Remember It Well" in *Gigi*; pinnacles, *On a Clear Day You Can See Forever* and *A Matter of Time*.

When Yolanda, gently provocative and already in love, asks the fake angel Johnny if he can tell her what she's thinking, he feigns indignation at such a vulgar request: "We don't do mind reading." We're not in a circus—mind reading isn't our profession. A mere imposter's pirouette? Or an artist's discretion? For that carnival exploit and that angelic privilege were Minnelli's whole aim: the divination of listening, the supernatural power of mind reading. His grandest ambition would have been to affirm by the powers of art the intimacy of love and thought.

Bibliography

BOOKS AND ARTICLES

Alexandre, Jean-Lou. "Ars gratia artis ou Minnelli existe-t-il?" *Cinema* 9, nos. 7 and 8 (1970).

Amiel, Vincent. "Quand les corps perdent leur légèreté: Notes sur quelques melodramas de Minnelli." *Positif* 526 (December 2004).

Aprá, Adriano. "Solitùdine di Vincente Minnelli." *Filmcritica* 34 (June 1963): 343–50.

Brion, Patrick. "Un auteur à Hollywood." *Trafic* 53 (Spring 2005): 88–98.

Brion, Patrick, Dominique Rabourdin, and Thierry Navacelle. *Vincente Minnelli: De Broadway à Hollywood*. Paris: Hatier, 1985.

Bruno, Edoardo, ed. *Mr. Vincente: Omaggio a Minnelli*. Montepulciano, Italy: Editori del Grifo, 1984.

Burdeau, Emmanuel. "Minnelli en 1958." *Cahiers du cinéma* 596 (December 2004): 70–73.

Cabrera Infante, Guillermo. *Arcadia todas las noches*. Barcelona: Editorial Seix Barral, 1978.

Campari, Roberto. *Minnelli*. Florence: La Nuova Italia, 1977.

Camper, Fred, "Depth Perception." Available at www.chicagoreader.com/movies/archives/2004/0104/040102.html.

Casper, Joseph Andrew. *Vincente Minnelli and the Film Musical*. South Brunswick, NJ: A. S. Barnes, 1977.

Cerisuelo, Marc. "L'image-Minnelli: Présence du spectacle et splendeur du passé." *Positif* 526 (December 2004): 104–6.

Chaumeton, Etienne. "L'oeuvre de Vincente Minnelli." *Positif* 12 (November–December 1954): 37–46.

Chion, Michel. "Une certaine idée de la beauté." *Cahiers du cinéma* 387 (September 1986): ii.

CineAction 63 (2004). Contains Minnelli dossier. All essays are listed in this bibliography.

Coursodon, Jean-Pierre. *American Directors*. With Pierre Sauvage. Vol. 2, 232–41. New York: McGraw-Hill, 1983.

De la Roche, Catherine. *Vincente Minnelli*. Premier Plan 40. Lyon: Serdoc, 1966.

Douchet, Jean. *Connaissance de Minnelli*. Paris: Féderation française des ciné-clubs, 1964.

———. "Vincente Minnelli: La tentation du rêve. *Objectif* 69 (February–March 1964): 17–22.

Dyer, Richard. "Minnelli's Web of Dreams." In *Movies of the Fifties*, edited by Ann Lloyd, 86–89. London: Orbis, 1982.

Elsaesser, Thomas. "Tales of Sound and Fury." In *Home Is Where the Heart Is*, edited by Christine Gledhill, 43–69. London: British Film Institute, 1987.

Fieschi, Jacques. "Mémoire musicale." *Cinématographe* 34 (January 1978): 14–18.

Fordin, Hugh. *The World of Entertainment: Hollywood's Greatest Musicals*. New York: Doubleday, 1975.

Fox, Terry Curtis. "Vincente Minnelli: The Decorative Auteur." *Village Voice*, February 6, 1978, 37.

Giles, Dennis. "Show-Making." In *Genre: The Musical*, edited by Rick Altman, 85–101. London: British Film Institute, 1981.

Guérif, François. *Vincente Minnelli*. Paris: Edilig, 1984.

Harvey, Stephen. *Directed by Vincente Minnelli*. New York: Museum of Modern Art and Harper and Row, 1989.

Johnson, Albert. "The Films of Vincente Minnelli." *Film Quarterly* 12 (Winter 1958): 20–35 and (Spring 1959): 32–42.

Kaufman, Gerald. *Meet Me in St. Louis*. London: British Film Institute, 1994.

Knox, Donald. *The Magic Factory: How MGM Made An American in Paris*. New York: Praeger, 1973.

Lang, Robert. *American Film Melodrama: Griffith, Vidor, Minnelli.* Princeton, NJ: Princeton University Press, 1989.

Lebensztejn, Jean-Claude. "Une rose dans les ténèbres." *Trafic* 53 (Spring 2005): 107–10.

Levy, Emmanuel. *Vincente Minnelli: Hollywood's Dark Dreamer.* New York: St. Martin's Press, 2007.

Lowry, Ed. "Vincente Minnelli." In *The International Dictionary of Films and Filmmakers.* Vol. 2, *Directors/Filmmakers,* edited by Christopher Lyon, 373–75. New York: Perigee Books, 1984.

Masson, Alain. "Des joies fragiles: Le caméra dans les 'musicals' de Minnelli." *Positif* 526 (December 2004): 93–95.

McElhaney, Joe. *The Death of Classical Cinema: Hitchcock, Lang, Minnelli.* Albany: State University of New York Press, 2006.

——. "Vincente Minnelli: Images of Magic and Transformation." Available at www.sensesofcinema.com/contents/directors/04/minnelli.html.

Minnelli, Vincente. *Casanova's Memoirs.* Edited by Joseph Monet. Drawings by Vincente Minnelli. New York: Willey, 1944.

——. "Décors pour Broadway." *Positif* 200–202 (December 1977–January 1978): 102–5.

——. *I Remember It Well.* With Hector Arce. Garden City, NY: Doubleday, 1974.

——. "The Rise and Fall of the Musical." *Films and Filming* 7 (January 1962): 9.

——. "So We Changed It." *Films and Filming* 5 (November 1958): 7.

Morris, George. "The Melodramas." In "The Films of Vincente Minnelli." *The Thousand Eyes* 4 (1978): 8–9 and 34–36.

——. "The Minnelli Magic." *Soho Weekly News,* January 19, 1978, 19–21.

Nacache, Jacqueline. "Deux caravances: *Tous en scène* et *La roulotte du plaisir*." *Positif* 526 (December 2004): 98–100.

Naremore, James. *The Films of Vincente Minnelli.* New York: Cambridge University Press, 1993.

Positif 526 (December 2004). Contains Minnelli dossier. All essays are listed in this bibliography.

Rabourdin, Dominique. "De quelque 'parenthèses' dans l'ouvre de Minnelli." *Positif* 526 (December 2004): 107–8.

Revault d'Allonnes, Judith. "Le legs de Vincente Minnelli." *Trafic* 53 (Spring 2005): 100–106.

Sarris, Andrew. *The American Cinema: Directors and Direction, 1929–1968,* 100–102. New York: E. P. Dutton, 1968.

Shivas, Mark. "Minnelli's Method." *Movie* 1 (June 1962): 20–24.

Siegel, David, and Scott McGehee. "Hysteria." *Sight and Sound* (October 1994): 33. On *Home from the Hill* and *Tea and Sympathy*.

Siegel, Joel E. "The Musicals." In "The Films of Vincente Minnelli." *The Thousand Eyes* 4 (1978): 6–7 and 30–34.

Simsolo, Noel. "Sur quelques films de Minnelli." *Revue du cinéma* (October 1981): 97–116.

Smith, Susan. "Growing Up in Minnelli's Films: Articulating Resistance and Loss in *Father of the Bride* and *Gigi*." In *Close-Up 2*, edited by John Gibbs and Douglas Pye, 165–95. London: Wallflower Press, 2007.

Tailleur, Roger. "Bavardages emus autour d'un musical: Un numéro du tonnere de Vincente Minnelli." *Positif* 38 (March 1961).

Telotte, J. P. "Self and Society: Vincente Minnelli and the Musical Formula," *Journal of Popular Film and Television* 9, no. 3 (1982): 181–93.

Timberg, Bernard. "Minnellian Nightmare: Meaning as Color." *Film/Psychology Review* 4, no. 1 (1980): 71–93.

Tinkcom, Matthew. *Working like a Homosexual: Camp, Capital, Cinema*. Durham, NC: Duke University Press, 2002.

Tobin, Yann. "Minnelli, travailleur et artiste." *Positif* 526 (December 2004): 88–92.

Török, Jean-Paul. "Minnelli existe, j'ai vu tous ses films et je l'ai recontrè. *Positif* 80 (April 1976): 34–38.

Török, Jean-Paul, and Jacques Quincey. "Vincente Minnelli ou le peintre de la vie rêvée." *Positif* 50–52 (March 1963): 56–74.

Trafic 53 (Spring 2005). Contains Minnelli dossier. Three of the essays are reprinted and translated in this book: Jacques Rancière, "Ars gratia artis: Notes sur la poétique de Minnelli"; Emmanuel Burdeau, "Messages de Minnelli"; and Raymond Bellour, "L'affolement." All others listed in this bibliography.

Truchaud, François. *Vincente Minnelli*. Classique du cinéma. Paris: Éditions Universitaires, 1966.

Vidal, Marion. *Vincente Minnelli*. Cinéma d'aujourd'hui. Paris: Seghers, 1973.

Viviani, Christian. "Le monde menacé." *Positif* 526 (December 2004): 101–3.

Walker, Michael. "Vincente Minnelli." *Film Dope* 43 (January 1990): 39–42.

INTERVIEWS

Aprá, Adriano. "Conversazione con Vincente Minnelli." *Filmcritica* 12 (October 1961): 542–45.

Bitsch, Charles, and Jean Domarchi. "Entretien avec Vincente Minnelli." *Cahiers du cinéma* 13, no. 74 (1957): 4–18.

"A Conversation with Vincente Minnelli." *Film Notebooks,* University of California–Santa Cruz (Winter 1978): 2–10.

Diehl, Digby. "Directors Go to Their Movies: Vincente Minnelli and *Gigi.*" *Action* 7, no 5 (1972): 2–10.

Domarchi, Jean, and Jean Douchet. "Rencontre avec Vincente Minnelli." *Cahiers du cinéma* 128 (February 1962): 3–13.

Higham, Charles, and Joel Greenberg. *The Celluloid Muse: Hollywood Directors Speak,* 173–83. Chicago: Regnery, 1969.

Lehman, Peter, Marilyn Campbell, and Grant Munro. "Two Weeks in Another Town: An Interview with Vincente Minnell." *Wide Angle* 3, no. 1 (1979): 64–71.

Schickel, Richard. *The Men Who Made the Movies,* 242–68. New York: Atheneum, 1975.

Serebrinsky, Ernesto, and Oscar Garaycochea. "Vincente Minnelli Interviewed in Argentina." *Movie* 10 (June 1963): 23–28.

Sheehan, Henry. Untitled interview with Minnelli from 1977. Available at www .henrysheehan.com/interviews/mno/minnelli.html.

ESSAYS AND NOTABLE REVIEWS OF SPECIFIC FILMS

Cabin in the Sky

Gerstner, David A. "The Queer Frontier: Vincente Minnelli's *Cabin in the Sky.*" In his *Manly Arts: Masculinity and Nation in Early American Cinema,* 165–211. Durham, NC: Duke University Press, 2006.

Knee, Adam. "Doubling, Music, and Race in *Cabin in the Sky.*" In *Representing Jazz,* edited by Krin Gabbard, 193–204. Durham, NC: Duke University Press, 1995.

Meet Me in St. Louis

Agee, James. *Agee on Film.* Vol. 1, 126–28 and 356–57. New York: Perigee Books, 1958.

Bathrick, Serafina. "The Past as Future: Family and the American Home in *Meet Me in St. Louis.*" *Minnesota Review* 6 (Spring 1976): 132–39.

Genné, Beth. "Vincente Minnelli's Style in Microcosm: The Establishing Sequence of *Meet Me in St. Louis.*" *Art Journal* 43 (Fall 1983): 247–54.

Higgins, Scott. "Minnelli's Technicolor Style in *Meet Me in St. Louis.*" Available at www.findarticles.com/cf_0/m2342/3_32/55082383/.

Masson, Alain. "La douceur du foyer et le charme des soirs: *Meet Me in St. Louis*." *Positif* 374 (April 1992): 101–3.

Wood, Robin. "*Meet Me in St. Louis*." In *The International Dictionary of Films and Filmmakers*, edited by Christopher Lyon, 290–91. New York: Perigee Books, 1985.

The Clock

Agee, James, *Agee on Film*. Vol. 1, 164–66 and 357–58. New York: Perigee Books, 1958.

Bukatman, Scott. "A Day in New York: *On the Town* and *The Clock*." In *City That Never Sleeps*, edited by Murray Pomerance, 33–47. New Brunswick, NJ: Rutgers University Press, 2007.

Farber, Manny. "Dream Furlough." *New Republic*, May 21, 1945, 709.

Hands, Stuart. "Love and the City: An Analysis of Vincente Minnelli's *The Clock*." *CineAction* 63 (2004): 35–37.

Yolanda and the Thief

Jacoby, Alexander. "The Far Side of Paradise: The Style and Substance of *Yolanda and the Thief*." *CineAction* 63 (2004): 38–44.

Tobin, Yann. "*Yolande et le voleur*." *Positif* 227 (February 1980): 82.

The Pirate

Ciment, Michel. "*La Pirate*." *Positif* 64 (March 1964): 139.

Ericsson, Peter. "*The Pirate*." *Sequence* 6 (1948–49): 44–45.

McVay, Douglas. "Minnelli and *The Pirate*." *Velvet Light Trap* 18 (Spring 1978): 35–38.

Pye, Douglas. "Being a Clown: Curious Coupling in *The Pirate*." *CineAction* 63 (2004): 4–13.

Rodowick, David. "Vision, Desire, and the Film-Text." *Camera Obscura* 6 (Fall 1980): 55–89.

Madame Bovary

Amiel, Vincent. "*Madame Bovary*: L'arrière-pays." *Positif* 295 (September 1985): 67–68.

Father of the Bride

Lucas, Blake. "The Comedy Without, The Gravity Within: *Father of the Bride.*" In *The Film Comedy Reader,* edited by Gregg Rickman, 215–29. New York: Limelight Editions, 2001.

An American in Paris

Anderson, Lindsay. "Minnelli, Kelly and *An American in Paris.*" *Sequence* 14 (1952): 36–38.

Bogdanovich, Peter. "*An American in Paris.*" In *Movie of the Week: 52 Classic Films for One Full Year,* 13–17. New York: Ballantine, 1999.

Dalle Vacche, Angela. "A Painter in Hollywood: Vincente Minnelli's *An American in Paris.* In *Cinema and Painting: How Art Is Used in Film,* 13–42. Austin: University of Texas Press, 1996.

The Bad and the Beautiful

Doniol-Valcroze, Jacques. "Les clefs inutiles." *Cahiers du cinéma* 26 (August–September 1953): 52–54.

Dyer, Richard. "Four Films of Lana Turner." *Movie* 25 (Winter 1977–78): 30–52.

The Band Wagon

De Kuyper, Eric. "Step by Step." *Wide Angle* 3 (1983): 44–49.

Hogue, Peter. "*The Band Wagon.*" *Velvet Light Trap* 11 (Winter 1974): 33–34.

Klawans, Stuart. "Shined Shoes." In *O.K. You Mugs: Writers on Movie Actors,* edited by Luc Sante and Melissa Holbrook Pierson, 117–30. New York: Vintage Books, 1999.

Silva, Arturo. "Vincente Minnelli's Dream of Tony Hunter's Band Wagon's 'Girl Hunt.' " *Film Criticism* 30 (Fall 2005): 2–19.

Vitoux, Frédéric. "*Tous en scène.*" *Positif* 254 (April 1982): 50.

The Long, Long Trailer

Dorsky, Nathaniel. "*The Long, Long Trailer.*" Program notes for the Pacific Film Archive University Art Museum, Berkeley, California, July 1984. Reprinted and translated into French in *Trafic* 53 (Spring 2005): 99.

Brigadoon

Ranchal, Marcel. "*Brigadoon.*" *Positif* 19 (1956): 44.
Sutton, Martin. "*Brigadoon.*" *Movie* 24 (Spring 1977): 57–58.

The Cobweb

Bruzzi, Stella. "*The Cobweb.*" *CineAction* 63 (2004): 14–21.
Lambert, Gavin. "*The Cobweb.*" *Sight and Sound* 25 (Spring 1956): 197.

Lust for Life

Domarchi, Jean. "Monsieur Vincent." *Cahiers du cinéma* 68 (February 1957): 44–
46.
Pollock, Griselda. "Crows, Blossoms, and Lust for Death—Cinema and the Myth
of Van Gogh and the Modern Artist." In *The Mythology of Vincent Van Gogh,*
edited by Kodera Tsukasa and Yvette Rosenberg, 217–39. Philadelphia: John
Benjamins Publishing, 1993.
Seguin, Louis. "*La vie passionnée de Vincent Van Gogh.*" *Positif* 21 (1957): 27.

Tea and Sympathy

Cabrera Infante, G. "Tea for Two." In *A Twentieth Century Job,* 113–15. Translated
from the Spanish by Kenneth Hall and the author. London: Faber and Faber,
1991.
Croce, Arlene. "*Tea and Sympathy.*" *Film Culture* 2, no. 4 (1956): 25–26.
Custen, George. "Strange Brew: Hollywood and the Fabrication of Homosex-
uality in *Tea and Sympathy.*" In *Queer Representations: Readings Lives, Reading
Cultures,* edited by Martin Duberman, 116–38. New York: New York University
Press, 1997.

Designing Woman

Kyrou, Ado. "*La femme modèle. Positif* 27 (1958): 43.

Gigi

Bellour, Raymond. "To Segment/To Analyze (on *Gigi*)." Translated by Diana
Matias. In Raymond Bellour, *The Analysis of Film,* edited by Constance Penley,
193–215. Bloomington: Indiana University Press.

Some Came Running

Alferi, Pierre. "Enivrant Minnelli." *Cahiers du cinéma* 591 (June 2004): 70.

Bogdanovich, Peter. "*Some Came Running.*" In *Movie of the Week: 52 Classic Films for One Full Year,* 93–96. New York: Ballantine, 1999.

Polan, Dana. "*Some Came Running.*" Available at www.sensesofcinema.com/contents/cteq/01/19/some_came.html.

Pye, Douglas. "Tone and Interpretation: *Some Came Running.*" In *Close-Up 2,* edited by John Gibbs and Douglas Pye, 45–73. London: Wallflower Press, 2007.

Home from the Hill

Benayoun, Robert. "*Celui par qui la scandale arrive.*" *Positif* 35 (October 1961): 31.

Walker, Michael. "*Home from the Hill.*" *CineAction* 63 (2004): 22–34.

Bells Are Ringing

Durgnat, Raymond. "Film Favorites: *Bells Are Ringing.*" In *The Film Comedy Reader,* edited by Gregg Rickman, 230–36. New York: Limelight Editions, 2001.

Tailleur, Robert. "*Un numéro du tonnerre.*" *Positif* 38 (December 1961): 53.

Two Weeks in Another Town

Bogdanovich, Peter. "*Two Weeks in Another Town.*" *Film Culture* 26 (Fall 1962): 53–54.

Mayersberg, Paul. "The Testament of Vincente Minnelli." *Movie* 3 (October 1962): 10–13.

Powell, Dilys. *The Golden Screen: Fifty Years of Films,* edited by George Perry, 187. London: Headline, 1989.

The Courtship of Eddie's Father

Boys, Barry. "*The Courtship of Eddie's Father.*" *Movie* 10 (June 1963): 29–32.

Goodbye Charlie

Seguin, Louis. "*Goodbye Charlie.*" *Positif* 71 (October 1964): 74.

The Sandpiper

Hanson, Curtis Lee. "Vincente Minnelli on the Relationship of Style to Content in *The Sandpiper.*" *Cinema* 2, no. 6 (1966): 7–8.

On a Clear Day You Can See Forever

Babington, Bruce, and Peter Williams Evans. "*On a Clear Day You Can See For-ever:* Minnelli and the Introspective Musical." In *Blue Skies and Silver Linings: Aspects of the Hollywood Musical,* 205–23. Manchester: Manchester University Press, 1985.

Cook, Jim. "*On a Clear Day You Can See Forever.*" *Movie* 24 (Spring 1977): 61–62.

Vitoux, Frédéric. "*Melinda.*" *Positif* 125 (March 1971): 52.

A Matter of Time

Lippe, Richard. "*A Matter of Time.*" *Movie* 27/28 (Winter 1980/Spring 1981): 70–73.

——. "*A Matter of Time.*" *CineAction* 1 (Spring 1985): 12–14. A reworking of the above essay.

Morris, George. "One Kind of Dream: George Morris on *A Matter of Time.*" *Film Comment* 12, no. 6 (1976): 21.

Viviani, Christian. "*Nina.*" *Positif* 227 (February 1980): 82.

Filmography

Cabin in the Sky, 1943
I Dood It, 1943
Meet Me in St. Louis, 1944
The Clock, 1945
Yolanda and the Thief, 1945
Ziegfeld Follies, 1946
Minnelli directed the following sequences: "Traviata," "This Heart of Mine," "Limehouse Blues," "A Great Lady Has an Interview," "The Babbitt and the Bromide." The "Beauty" finale was originally shot by Minnelli and featured Fred Astaire and Cyd Charisse. In its final version, Charisse can be glimpsed briefly but Astaire is nowhere to be seen. Kathryn Grayson is the star of the number. However, it is not clear from either Hugh Fordin's production history of Arthur Freed's films or from Stephen Harvey's book on Minnelli if this Grayson footage is Minnelli's or not. Certainly the Daliesque middle section of the number was directed by Minnelli.
Undercurrent, 1946

The Pirate, 1948

Madame Bovary, 1949

Father of the Bride, 1950

Father's Little Dividend, 1951

An American in Paris, 1951

The Bad and the Beautiful, 1952

The Story of Three Loves 1952

Minnelli officially directed only the "Mademoiselle" episode, although portions of
the film's first episode suggest that he may have shot some of that as well.

The Band Wagon, 1953

The Long, Long Trailer, 1954

Brigadoon, 1954

Shot simultaneously in two versions: a 1.85:1 widescreen version and a 2.55:1
CinemaScope one. The differences in the two versions are minimal.

The Cobweb, 1955

Kismet, 1955

Some sequences directed by Stanley Donen after Minnelli left the project to begin
production on *Lust for Life*

Lust for Life, 1956

One sequence (a retake) directed by George Cukor

Tea and Sympathy, 1956

Designing Woman, 1957

Gigi, 1958

Charles Walters shot some retakes on the film, including portions of the songs
"The Parisians" and "She's Not Thinking of Me." Contrary to rumors, no
footage from the title song is by Walters. He did shoot a retake of it but his
footage was not used.

The Reluctant Debutante, 1958

Some Came Running, 1958

Home from the Hill, 1960

Bells Are Ringing, 1960

Four Horsemen of the Apocalypse, 1962

Two Weeks in Another Town, 1962

The Courtship of Eddie's Father, 1963

Goodbye Charlie, 1964

The Sandpiper, 1965

On a Clear Day You Can See Forever, 1970

A Matter of Time, 1976

Final version disowned by Minnelli after significant recutting by Samuel Z. Arkoff and after the dubbing and scoring were taken away from him. Footage in the prologue and epilogue as well as the stock and second-unit travelogue footage throughout the film were primarily shot by others.

MISCELLANY

As with virtually all contract directors in Hollywood, Minnelli often shot footage for films on which he received no credit. This could involve something as simple as a retake of a single sequence, finishing the work of a director who had been replaced, or being called in to bring his trademark visual flair to films otherwise felt to be lacking.

Artists and Models, 1937. Directed by Raoul Walsh. Minnelli conceived the production number, "Public Melody Number One." Minnelli: "As filmed, I found the involved production number a full scale mess."

Minnelli contributed ideas (without credit) to the production numbers of two Busby Berkeley films, *Strike Up the Band* (1940) and *Babes on Broadway* (1942).

Panama Hattie, 1942. Directed by Norman Z. McLeod. Minnelli is credited with staging the musical numbers.

Thousands Cheer, 1943. Directed by George Sidney. According to Stephen Harvey, Minnelli directed Lena Horne's "Honeysuckle Rose" number. In *The Magic Factory,* Minnelli claims that he directed all of Horne's musical numbers in films signed by other directors during this period.

Till the Clouds Roll By, 1946. Producer: Arthur Freed. Director: Richard Whorf. Minnelli directed Judy Garland's scenes only.

The Bribe, 1949. Directed by Robert Z. Leonard. Minnelli reportedly directed the final sequence. This sequence does, in fact, look like a noir-ish version of the carnival in *Yolanda and the Thief* while also anticipating the fairground sequence from *Some Came Running.*

Lovely to Look At, 1952. Directed by Mervyn LeRoy. Minnelli directed (without credit) the fashion finale.

The Seventh Sin, 1957. After Ronald Neame left the project, Minnelli finished direction of the film without credit.

All the Fine Young Cannibals, 1960. Directed by Michael Anderson. According to Gavin Lambert's biography of Natalie Wood, Minnelli directed two sequences without credit.

Contributors

Raymond Bellour is Director of Research Émérite at the Centre National de la Recherche Scientifique. He has written on literature (the Brontës, James, Dumas, Michaux, of whom he has edited the complete works in "La Pléiade"). His publications on films and images include *Le Western, The Analysis of Film, Le cinéma américain, L'entre-images, L'entre-images 2,* and (with Mary Lea Bandy) *Jean-Luc Godard: Son + image.* In 1991, with Serge Daney, he started the film journal *Trafic.*

Jean-Loup Bourget is Professor of film studies at the École Normale Supérieure in Paris, France. A regular contributor to the French film monthly *Positif,* he has written a dozen books, mostly on "classic" Hollywood and its relationship with European cinema.

Andrew Britton lectured in film studies at the University of Warwick, University of Essex, and University of Reading. The author of *Katharine Hepburn: Star as Feminist,* as well as many essays on the cinema, he was a member of the editorial board of *Framework* and *Movie* and the editorial collective of *CineAction.* Andrew Britton died in 1994.

Scott Bukatman is Associate Professor in the Film and Media Studies Program in the Department of Art and Art History at Stanford University. He is the author of three books: *Terminal Identity: The Virtual Subject in Postmodern Science Fiction,* one of the earliest book-length studies of cyberculture; a monograph on *Blade Runner;* and a collection of essays, *Matters of Gravity: Special Effects and Supermen in the 20th Century.* His latest project is a book-length study of Winsor McCay, an early innovator in both newspaper comics and animated film.

Emmanuel Burdeau has been the editor-in-chief of *Cahiers du cinéma* since 2004. The co-editor (with Charles Tesson) of *Future(s) of Film: Three Interviews with Jean-Luc Godard,* he is also editing a collection of film books for Capricci, most recently *Les Aventures de Harry Dickson, a Screenplay Written by Frédéric de Towarnicki for a Movie (Not Directed) by Alain Resnais.* They will also publish a French translation of *The Magic Hour* by Jim Hoberman. In 2007, he wrote an introduction for the new edition of *Les films de ma vie* by François Truffaut and an afterward for the French translation of *Totality as Conspiracy* by Frederic Jameson. He is also working on a book about Vincente Minnelli.

Serge Daney was an editor at *Cahiers du cinéma,* a regular contributor to *Libération,* and the co-founder of *Trafic.* His books include *La rampe, Ciné journal,* volumes 1 and 2, and *Persévérance* (POL). Serge Daney died in 1992.

Jean Douchet is a critic, teacher, filmmaker, and actor who has contributed for many years to *Arts* and *Cahiers du cinéma.* Among his books are *The French New Wave, L'art d'aimer,* and *Hitchcock.*

Thomas Elsaesser is Professor in the Department of Media and Culture and Director of Research in Film and Television at the University of Amsterdam. His books as author include *Fassbinder's Germany: History, Identity, Subject, Weimar Cinema and After, Metropolis, Studying Contemporary American Film* (with Warren Buckland), and *European Cinema: Face to Face with Hollywood* (Amsterdam: Amsterdam University Press, 2005). Among his most recent books as (co-) editor are: *Cinema Futures: Cain, Abel or Cable? The BFI Companion to German Cinema, The Last Great American Picture Show,* and *Harun Farocki—Working on the Sightlines.*

Edward Gallafent teaches in the Department of Film and Television Studies at Warwick University in England. He is the author of books on Clint Eastwood and on Fred Astaire and Ginger Rogers. His latest publication is *Quentin Tarantino* (2006).

Beth Genné is Associate Professor of Dance Studies and Art History at the University of Michigan–Ann Arbor. Author of *The Making of a Choreographer: Ninette de Valois and Bar aux Folies-Bergère*, her articles on dance and film have appeared in such journals as *Dance Research, Dancing Times, Art Journal,* and *Discourses in Dance* and in such books as *Envisioning Dance on Film and Video, Psychoanalytic Perspectives on Art, Re-Thinking Dance History,* and most recently in *Teaching Dance Studies* and *The Living Dance: Essays on Movement and Culture.* She has been recipient of fellowships from the Getty Foundation, Fulbright Foundation (French Government Fellowship), and the University of Michigan. She is currently completing a book, *Dancing in the Frame: Astaire, Balanchine, Kelly, and the Evolution of Film Dance.*

David A. Gerstner is Associate Professor of Cinema Studies at the City University of New York's College of Staten Island and at the Graduate Center where he is a member of the Doctoral Faculty in the Department of Theatre. He is author of *Manly Arts: Masculinity and Nation in Early American Cinema,* editor of *The Routledge International Encyclopedia of Queer Culture,* and co-editor with Janet Staiger of *Authorship and Film.*

Bill Krohn is the Los Angeles correspondent of *Cahiers du cinéma* and the author of *Hitchcock at Work.* He co-directed, co-wrote, and co-produced *It's All True: Based on an Unfinished Film by Orson Welles.*

Carlos Losilla is an essayist, film and literary critic, and Lecturer on Film Theories at the Universitat Pompeu Fabra in Barcelona. He is the author of *La invención de Hollywood, o cómo olvidarse de una vez por todas del cine clásico, El cine de terror, Taxi Driver/Johnny Guitar,* and the essay-novels, *En busca de Ulrich Seidl* and *El sitio de Viena.* In addition, he has edited *Paul Schrader, el tormento y el éxtasis, La mirada oblicua, El cine de Robert Aldrich, Richard Fleischer, entre el cielo y el infierno,* and *Karel Reisz o el exilio permanente* (1998), the first three with José Antonio Hurtado. He is also a member of the editorial board at *Cahiers du cinéma–España.*

Joe McElhaney is Associate Professor in the Department of Film and Media Studies at Hunter College/City University of New York. He is the author of *The Death of Classical Cinema: Hitchcock, Lang, Minnelli* and *Albert Maysles.*

Adrian Martin is Senior Research Fellow, Film and Television Studies, Monash University (Melbourne, Australia) and the author of *Raul Ruiz: Sublimes obsesiones, The Mad Max Movies, Once Upon a Time in America,* and *Phantasms;* and co-editor (with Jonathan Rosenbaum) of *Movie Mutations* and the Internet film magazine Rouge (www.rouge.com.au).

James Naremore is Emeritus Chancellors' Professor of Communications and Culture at Indiana University. Among his writings on film are *Acting in the Cinema, The Films of Vincente Minnelli,* and *More Than Night: Film Noir in Its Contexts.* His most recent book is *On Kubrick.*

Geoffrey Nowell-Smith is Senior Research Fellow in the Department of History at Queen Mary, University of London. A former head of publishing at the British Film Institute, he is the editor of *The Oxford History of Cinema.*

Dana Polan is a Professor of Cinema Studies at NYU's Tisch School of the Arts. He is the author of, most recently, *Scenes of Instruction: The Beginnings of the U.S. Study of Film* and of the forthcoming TV studies *The Sopranos* and *The French Chef.*

Murray Pomerance is Professor in the Department of Sociology at Ryerson University. He is the author of *The Horse Who Drank the Sky: Film Experience beyond Narrative and Theory, Johnny Depp Starts Here, An Eye for Hitchcock, Savage Time,* and *Magia D'amore.* He has edited or co-edited numerous volumes, including *City That Never Sleeps: New York and the Filmic Imagination, Cinema and Modernity, American Cinema of the 1950s: Themes and Variations,* and *Enfant Terrible! Jerry Lewis in American Film.*

Jacques Rancière is Emeritus Professor of Aesthetics and Politics at the University of Paris VIII. His books include *The Ignorant Schoolmaster, The Names of History, Film Fables, The Politics of Aesthetics: The Distribution of the Sensible, The Hatred of Democracy,* and *The Future of the Image.*

Robin Wood, though officially retired, teaches a graduate course every summer at York University–Toronto. He is the author of numerous books on the cinema, including *Howard Hawks, Hitchcock's Films Revisited, Sexual Politics and Narrative Film, Hollywood from Vietnam to Reagan,* and *Rio Bravo.* He is currently writing a book on the films of Michael Haneke. He is a founding editor of *CineAction.*

Index

Permissions Acknowledgments

"The Red and the Green: *The Four Horsemen of the Apocalypse*" by Jean Douchet originally appeared in *Cahiers du cinéma* 129, March 1962, 44–49. Reprinted with permission.

"*Two Weeks in Another Town*" by Jean Douchet originally appeared in *Cahiers du cinéma* 154, April 1964. Reprinted with permission.

"Specters at the Feast: French Viewpoints on Minnelli's Comedies" by Bill Krohn originally appeared in *The Thousand Eyes*, no. 4, 10–11, 37–39. Reprinted with permission of the author.

"Minnelli's American Nightmare" by Jean-Loup Bourget originally appeared in *Positif*, no. 310, 1986, 2–12. Reprinted with permission of the author.

"Vincente Minnelli" by Thomas Elsaesser originally appeared in *Brighton Film Review* no. 15, December 1969 and no. 18, March 1970. Reprinted with permission of author.

"Minnelli and Melodrama" by Geoffrey Nowell-Smith originally appeared in *Screen* 18 no. 2, 113–18. Reprinted with permission.

"It Could Be Oedipus Rex: Denial and Difference in *The Band Wagon;* or, The American Musical as American Gothic" by Dana Polan originally appeared in *Ciné-Tracts,* nos. 14–15, 15–26. Reprinted with permission.

"Minnelli's *Madame Bovary*" by Robin Wood originally appeared in *CineAction!* Winter 86–87, 74–80. Reprinted with permission.

"*The Pirate* Isn't Just Decor" and "Minnelli Caught in His Web" by Serge Daney originally appeared in appeared in *Devant la recrudescence des vols de sacs à mains,* Lyon: Aléas, 17–18 and 23–25. Reprinted with permission.

"The Adventures of Rafe Hunnicutt: The Bourgeois Family in *Home from the Hill*" by Edward Gallafent originally appeared in *Movie* 34/35, 65–81. Reprinted with permission of the author.

"Uptown Folk: Blackness and Entertainment in *Cabin in the Sky*" by James Naremore originally appeared in *Arizona Quarterly* 48, no. 4 (1992): 99–124. Reprinted with permission.

"Queer Modernism: The Cinematic Aesthetic of Vincente Minnelli" by David Gerstner originally appeared in *Modernity* 2 (2000). Reprinted with permission.

"Medium-Shot Gestures: Vincente Minnelli and *Some Came Running*" by Joe McElhaney originally appeared in *16:9,* January 2003 (www.16-9.dk/2003-06/side11_minnelli.htm) and is presented here in slightly revised and expanded form. Reprinted with permission.

"Minnelli in Double System" by Emmanuel Burdeau originally appeared in *Cahiers du cinéma,* no. 586, January 2004, 86–87. Reprinted with permission.

"*Ars gratia artis:* Notes on Minnelli's poetics" by Jacques Rancière originally appeared in *Trafic* 53, Spring 2005, 74–81. Reprinted with permission of the author.

"Panic" by Raymond Bellour originally appeared in *Trafic* 53, Spring 2005, 111–18. Reprinted with permission of author.

"Minnelli's Messages" by Emmanuel Burdeau originally appeared in *Trafic* 53, Spring 2005, 82–87. Reprinted with permission of the author.